D0105519

NELSON

ALSO BY DAVID WALDER

Bags of Swank

The Short List

The House Party

The Fair Ladies of Salamanca

The Chanak Affair
(the Anglo-Turkish crisis in 1922)

The Short Victorious War
(the Russo-Japanese War)

NELSON

A Biography By
David Walder

The Dial Press/James Wade
New York
1978

Published by
The Dial Press
1 Dag Hammarskjold Plaza
New York, New York 10017

Copyright © 1978 by David Walder

All rights reserved. No part of this book may be reproduced or transmitted
in any form or by any means, electronic or mechanical, including photocopying,
recording or by any information storage and retrieval system, without the
written permission of the Publisher, except where permitted by law.

Manufactured in the United States of America

First printing

Library of Congress Cataloging in Publication Data

Walder, David.
  Nelson.

  Bibliography: p.
  Includes index.
    1. Nelson, Horatio Nelson, Viscount, 1758—1805.
  2. Great Britain—History, Naval—18th century.
  3. Admirals—Great Britain—Biography.
  DA87.1.N4W24   1977   940.2′7′0924   [B]   78-2697
  ISBN 0-8037-6431-6

Contents

Illustrations

Nos. 1a, 1b, 2b, 3a, 3b, 4b, 6a, 6b, 6c, 6d, 7a, 7b, 7c, 7d, 11, 12a, 12b 14a and 15a are reproduced by permission of the National Maritime Museum, Greenwich Collection; no. 2a by permission of the National Portrait Gallery; nos. 4a, 5a, 5b, 9a and 10 by permission of the Radio Times Hulton Picture Library; nos. 8a, 8b, 14b and 16 by permission of the Victory Collection, Portsmouth Royal Naval Museum; nos. 9b and 13 by permission of the Mansell Collection; and no. 15b by permission of the Tate Gallery.

Acknowledgments

MY THANKS are first due to my publishers in the United Kingdom and the United States, and my literary agent Anthony Sheil, for deciding that the time had come to re-examine a national hero.

It would be virtually impossible to list every individual who has assisted me in the last three years or who has made helpful suggestions during the course of the book. However, I must record my gratitude to the Librarians and Staff, and where appropriate, the Trustees, of the National Maritime Museum, Greenwich, the Royal United Services Institute for Defence Studies, the Public Record Office, the London Library, the Ministry of Defence Library, the Admiralty Library, the Harris Library, Preston, the Libraries of the House of Lords and the House of Commons, the British Museum Reading Room, and finally, and especially, to Mr Keith Kissack of the Nelson Museum, Monmouth.

As Nelson's frigates were his 'eyes and ears', Mrs Elizabeth D. Taylor was throughout the research stages, mine. Without her enthusiastic assistance this book would not have been possible. As on two previous occasions I was also greatly helped by the expertise of Mrs Joan St George Saunders.

In May 1972 the new Victory Museum at Portsmouth was opened by Mrs J. G. McCarthy, C.B.E., and contains a vast amount of Nelson memorabilia, much of it collected and donated by herself. To her I should like to render a personal debt of gratitude.

At Portsmouth and in *Victory* herself I was grateful for the help, assistance and advice of Rear-Admiral S. L. McArdle, M.V.O., G.M., Flag Officer, Spithead, Captain A. J. Pack (R.N. retd.), Director of the Royal Naval Museum, Commander S. G. Clark (R.N. retd.), Curator of the Nelson Collection, and Lieutenant-Commander B. Twiddy, Commanding Officer of H.M.S. *Victory*.

I am particularly grateful for the kind help given to me by three Parliamentary collecgues, Antony Buck, Q.C., M.P., who when Under-Secretary of State for Defence for the Royal Navy smoothed many paths, and has continued with constructive suggestions ever since. Christopher Brocklebank-Fowler, M.P., Member for Norfolk North-West, in which constituency Nelson was born, and himself a descendant of Sir William Beechey, R.A., showed an understandable interest in my work, and has guided me on portraiture and local lore.

John Stradling Thomas, M.P., the Member for Monmouth, was instrumental in my meeting Mrs Horatia Durant, the direct descendant of Horatia Nelson. To her I am most grateful for family recollections and advice, and to her niece, Mrs William Tribe, for her hospitality and kindness and the opportunity to see portraits and relics. For guidance surgical, genealogical, and musical, I should like to thank respectively John Russell, F.R.C.S., Thomas Woodcock and Richard Baker, O.B.E.

Finally, I must thank my wife for deciphering my handwriting, and, most important of all, for a great deal of patience while this book has been in preparation.

It is perhaps almost unnecessary to conclude in the time-honoured way by saying that no one above mentioned bears any responsibility for any opinions or comments expressed, errors committed or prejudices revealed. All of those are my own.

D.W.

Prologue

'Rarely has a man been more favoured in the hour of his appearing:
never one so fortunate in the moment of his death.'
—Rear-Admiral A. T. Mahan, U.S.N.

THIRTY-EIGHT YEARS after the death of its subject the monument was
almost completed. The statue was of Grafton stone, seventeen feet tall,
and was positioned on the capital, which was embellished with a
capstan and a coiled rope, so that the vacant eyes looked towards the
distant sea.

The one hundred and five feet tall Corinthian fluted column was of
solid granite, and the four bas-reliefs on the thirty-six-feet-high pedestal
were, when completed, to represent incidents in the battles of St Vincent,
the Nile, Copenhagen and Trafalgar, each portrayed by a different artist.
The metal used on the capital was re-cast from the guns salvaged from
the wreck of the *Royal George*, which, because of her rotting timbers,
had sunk at Spithead in 1782 taking Kempenfeldt, one of Britain's most
distinguished admirals, with her. The highest point of the monument
was the stone representation of a 'chelengk' or plume of triumph. The
jewelled original, with each of its thirteen divisions representing a
French ship taken or destroyed, and its central rosette revolvable by
clockwork, had been presented by the Ottoman Sultan to the victor of
the Nile, the first Christian to receive such an honour. The recipient of
this rather vulgar decoration thereafter wore it, quite improperly, in his
admiral's cocked hat, to the annoyance of his more conventionally
minded brother officers, and to the joy of not always kindly contemporary cartoonists. From the chelengk to the pavement measured just over
one hundred and seventy feet, so that the whole monument, based on a
Roman original dedicated to Mars, the god of war, was something short
of the height from the tip of the mainmast to the waterline of a first rate
line-of-battle ship such as *Victory*.

The clearing of the site of its 'filthy and disreputable hovels' and the
erection of the column and finally the superimposing of the statue had

taken, in the view of contemporary opinion, an unduly long time. Work had commenced in 1829 and was still not completed in 1840, when the statue itself was ready. Criticism and problems had abounded. Originally there had been plans for an even taller column over two hundred feet in height, but these had been abandoned for fear of creating a potential danger to Londoners in storms and strong winds. However, the sponsors of the monument were naturally anxious that their pet project should out-top the nearby Duke of York's column, which when completed in 1834 stood at one hundred and twenty-four feet. His Royal Highness had been but an indifferent military commander involved in a scandal about selling army commissions through his mistress, and had been placed at that height, so the wits had said, only to be put out of reach of his creditors. However, in celebrating the victor of Trafalgar, by altitude as it were, might not the sponsors be setting an awkward precedent for the future, bearing in mind that the Duke of Wellington, the victor of Waterloo, and a former Prime Minister as well, was still very much alive, and might be thought after death to possess a claim to comparable, or even greater, elevation?

Then there were the problems of inflation and rising costs. Originally the Committee had been voted £30,000 by Parliament and £20,000 had been raised by public subscription. As the work progressed further appeals were found necessary, and the Committee had been very pleased to acknowledge the gracious donation of 100 guineas from Albert, the Prince Consort.

As with so many London excavations, the digging of the foundations, after the site had been cleared, had unearthed possibly interesting archaeological remains, the bones of oxen, of deer and of men, as well as what appeared to be sections of an ancient market place. Meanwhile, *The Times* of October 10, 1843, reported the presence in Exeter of a rather unusual survival from Trafalgar. Mrs Sara Frank Pitt, the widow of a marine, had been on board *Victory*, and during the battle had been employed with other sailors' wives in the customary duty of carrying powder up from the magazines to the guns. Hearing a false report of her husband's death, she had rushed on deck to be reassured by his presence, but to see Nelson fall, mortally wounded. 'She subsequently buried a boy of hers at Alexandria and another near Sicily, and now in her old age, without child or husband, she is left totally destitute, without kin or associate, with no consolation but the recollection of the glorious bloody scenes in which she spent the early portion of her married life.' Naturally enough, perhaps, Mrs Pitt was not anxious to join the procession of 200 Trafalgar veterans now being collected together for the unveiling ceremony, but she wished it to be known that if there should be 'any distribution in largesse in commemoration of the victory' she would 'be thankful to receive a portion'.

Finally, on November 3 and 4, 1843, Mr Edward Baily's statue was superimposed on Mr William Railton's column. There were a few rather undignified and anxious moments, watched by a crowd of some thousands, when sections of the stone admiral were hoisted aloft, and then lowered and hoisted again until a proper balance could be obtained. Still the whole monument was incomplete; the bas-relief panels were not finally in place until 1852, and Landseer's bronze lions, which attracted criticism both architectural and zoological, did not appear until 1867. In fact Sir Edwin had to give of his best in very trying circumstances, for the lion he used as a model sickened and died on him, and the final work of the cast had been performed with a rapidly putrefying carcass as inspiration.

Then, as now, almost anything that touched on the dead Nelson engendered controversy. At the time of the placing of the statue *The Times* had understood, mistakenly, that an actual flag from *Victory* would be flown from the column. On November 7, 1843, a correspondent detected in the use of the Union Standard an unpardonable solecism. Nelson, a Vice-Admiral of the White, had died in *Victory* under the White Ensign, appropriate to his rank. Of the monument itself, Augustus Hare said that the statue was a bad one, but that it did not matter, because it could only be seen by someone standing on the top of the Duke of York's column. Many others, more seriously, commented on what they regarded as rough, coarse workmanship.

The correspondent of the *Illustrated London News*, who, with thousands of members of the public, went to view the statue when it was exhibited on the ground at Charing Cross before being placed on the column, did not agree. He discerned a great deal in the stone countenance:

It has the sharp, angular features, and the expression of great activity of mind, but of little of mental grandeur; of quickness of perception and decision, and withal, that sad air, so perceptible in the best portraits of the warrior, of long continued pain and suffering, the consequence of his many wounds, which accompanied him throughout his brightest triumphs, though it never abated or weakened his energies. The expression is a peculiar one, it is more afflicting to the eye than the expression of deep thought; though as mournful, it is less abstracted than that of meditation.

It is the burden of the crown, and the shadow of the laurel; heavy is the first, and dark is the second, to those who obtain them, except in a few favoured instances, and one of these favoured few Nelson was not.

There are of course many memorials good, bad and indifferent to Nelson other than the until recently smoke-blackened column in Trafalgar Square. In Edinburgh, Liverpool, Birmingham, Bristol, Glasgow and Yarmouth, and, until it was destroyed by Nationalists, in Dublin; and in his native county of Norfolk, at the grammar school in Norwich which he attended; in Antigua and in Jamaica, where the visitor to his old headquarters is enjoined, while 'treading in his footsteps to remember his glory'; and on Portsdown Hill on Portsmouth Downs, erected by contributions from his former comrades, plus a deduction from their Trafalgar prize-money. Both the National Maritime Museum at Greenwich and the Naval Museum at Portsmouth are dominated by his exploits. The Nelson Museum at Monmouth is full of relics and mementoes. Lloyd's, the marine insurers, have their collection. There is a dreadful piece of statuary in St Paul's Cathedral and a monument in London's Guildhall. The wax effigy of the Admiral in Westminster Abbey was pronounced by Lady Hamilton to be very true to life, despite its dark brown hair. A handful of portraits exist, painted from life. Napoleon had a bust on his desk of the man he considered to be his principal enemy, and since Nelson's death, the representations in prints, in marble, and brass, and on plates, cups and mugs, must be almost innumerable. Canova made drawings for the design of a tomb, and there was for many years a thriving industry devoted to the manufacture of Nelson fakes, including glass eyes. Inn signs, a sure indication of popular regard in Britain, abound, especially in Norfolk and East Anglia. Sometimes the portrait is entitled 'Lord Nelson', or 'Admiral Nelson' or more simply still 'The Hero'. Quite recently there was an exhibition of paintings of Lady Hamilton at Kenwood House, Highgate. The organisers received half a dozen offers to loan the very table on which Emma Hamilton had, in her early days, danced naked. The large covered silver dish on which she was carried in for these performances can, it is said, also be vouched for.

It is hardly necessary to testify to the power of the legend. One can still be told with authority the quite baseless story that the black scarf of the British sailor mourns Nelson's death, and that the three lines of white piping on his collar commemorate the three great victories of the Nile, Copenhagen and Trafalgar (this despite the fact that French sailors also have the same number on their collars). The legend that a French family exists which can trace its descent from the man at Trafalgar who fired the fatal musket ball still persists. There is a French song which implies that 'the Provençal', the sharpshooter, who fired the musket shot from the rigging of *Redoutable*, survived the action, which is at the least improbable. However, the house in which Lady Hamilton spent her last years of exile in poverty and drunkenness was well authenticated, and could be shown to visitors until its destruction in the Battle of Calais in 1941. At Portsmouth lies *Victory*, lovingly preserved and tended, still a flagship, and in consequence with her name on the cap-bands of the ratings serving at the naval base. Over the years, the annual number of visitors from Britain and overseas has steadily increased, and at the last count numbered nearly half a million.

It is, however, entirely appropriate that the principal monument to Nelson should provide a central landmark in London, that city which, as he himself said, 'exists by victories at sea'. In its shadow every year on October 21, there gathers a mixed assembly, naval officers and dignitaries, members of the Navy League, a guard of honour of blue-jackets and buglers of the Royal Marines, and mere sightseers, to commemorate his achievements and to see his famous Trafalgar signal flown in one great mass of signal flags, not, as on the actual day of the battle, in separate hoists. On the same night at dinner in the wardrooms of ships of the Royal Navy, and in naval establishments on shore, the senior officer will rise and with unaccustomed oratory, and a little, not always accurate, history, propose the health of 'The immortal memory of Admiral Nelson', a rank which it would perhaps be a trifle pedantic to observe that he never actually held.

It is in fact not possible to be English and not know about Nelson, for Nelson is an English folk hero. Indeed much of the impedimenta of his life has been preserved and can be seen and touched: his uniform, swords, his cot, folding chair, his decorations, his cutlery and china; and the appurtenances of many of those who knew him, from the gold-braided hats of his officers to the flamboyantly embroidered dress of his mistress. In addition, the volumes of his letters and dispatches give as full a guide to the man as one is likely to obtain of anyone, anywhere, in his official capacity and in his private life. Almost all his contemporaries who were literate, and some who were not, but who crossed his path even for an instant, have put on record their recollections and impressions.

Yet for all the wealth of material the image that survives is a curious one. That he was small, scarcely five foot two inches in height and slight in stature, and did not enjoy good health, and that he lost an arm and an eye in battle and suffered from other wounds we all know. That he was a brilliant and courageous fighting admiral who struck terror into his enemies and inspired a whole Service, officers and men alike, we must accept. That he made himself a cartoonist's and gossip's butt with his infatuation for one of the most notorious women of the age, then the wife of an elderly husband, neglecting his own dull wife in the process, can easily be ascertained.

All that is enough to make a swashbuckling sort of folk hero. Yet that is not the legend that has survived. The Norfolk parson's son does not come down through history as a kind of Gascon among Englishmen, which in many ways he was. Rather, it is the personality suggested to the *Illustrated London News* reporter by the stone face of Baily's statue, suffering and sadness rather than the joy of battle and the naïve pleasure in fame and success; the over-lined face for a man of forty-seven, the never-erased pouting lip of youth, and the sad half-smile as if 'saved from the fire'. Not the man who declared that he had resolved 'to be a hero', and who asked for the knighthood of the Bath rather than a baronetcy so that he could have a red ribbon to cross his chest and show to the world, but the dying admiral, who covered his face with a handkerchief so that his men should not know he had fallen and who, in his last moments, asked his flag captain to kiss him.

It may be said that the English are a nation of hypocrites and prefer their heroes gentle rather than vainglorious, choosing to close their eyes to naval brutalities and Neapolitan adulteries. More charitably, perhaps, it may be argued that mid-Victorian England tried to turn Nelson into a very English type of hero. The difficulties of so doing did not escape the sharp eye of Gladstone and gave rise to one of his few recorded witticisms, when, at the height of arguments with the Irish party about the adultery of their leader, Charles Parnell, with Mrs Kitty O'Shea, he observed that Southey's *Life of Nelson* had been distributed by the Society for Promoting Christian Knowledge.

Horatio Nelson, whatever else he was, was not the public school, gentlemanly, modest hero beloved later on by Dr Arnold of Rugby and celebrated in a great deal of fiction and some fact. Of course the nineteenth-century hero-type only appeared when Nelson had lain at rest under the cupola of St Paul's for many years. For Nelson himself was a hero in an age of heroes and heroics. Lord David Cecil, in the biography of a politician, has described the eighteenth-century man and many a Nelson contemporary:

> Like their mode of life, their characters were essentially natural; spontaneous, unintrospective, brimming over with normal feelings, love of home and family, loyalty, conviviality, desire for fame, hero-worship, patriotism. And they showed their feelings too. Happy creatures! They lived before the days of the stiff upper lip and the inhibited public school Englishman. A manly tear stood in their eye at the story of an heroic deed; they declared their loves in a strain of flowery hyperbole.

Nevertheless, it would be wrong to think that all his contemporaries admired, or even liked, Nelson. Another hero and great commander, General Sir John Moore, who also perished in battle in his greatest hour, thought very poorly of the famous admiral he saw in Naples, 'dressed like a prince in an opera'. Others, among them naval officers, found him insubordinate, irritating or ridiculous.

Nelson does, of course, possess as a hero in any age, and as a folk hero, one great advantage. Like (as he himself put it) 'the peerless Wolfe', the painting of whose death on the heights of Abraham by Benjamin West fascinated him, he died in the hour of victory, thus stilling criticism. On hearing of Trafalgar and the loss of Nelson, no one in Britain knew whether to celebrate or mourn. West, fulfilling a half-serious promise to the living admiral, painted another death scene. Indeed Nelson's end was so perfect, it made such a dramatically suitable ending to his life that some have interpreted his recklessness in exposing himself in his much-decorated frock-coat, an obvious target, as evidence of a subconscious, or even conscious, death-wish.

Be that as it may—and he often spoke of death in battle as his likely end, and seemed to have something of a premonition of it at Trafalgar—what a falling off there would have been had he survived. The autopsy pronounced him, despite his constant bouts of ill health, capable of living into his seventies, perhaps even eighties. Admittedly, if he had not taken care, he would almost certainly have been blind by the time he was fifty, but there was no reason, despite an abnormally small heart, why he should not have lived to a considerable age, as did most of his fore-bears on his father's side of the family. The thought of a blind Nelson with nothing to do after Trafalgar, and incapable of doing what little remained, acting out his twenty or more years and sinking into his dotage, though no doubt guided and helped by his beloved Emma, hardly bears contemplation. Perhaps she, Lady Hamilton, ill-educated, vulgar, but perceptive, realised something of this when, across the foot of the last letter Nelson ever wrote to her, from *Victory*, dated October 19, 1805, unsigned, uncompleted, she scrawled, 'O miserable and wretched Emma, O glorious and happy Nelson.'

It was not only Nelson that perished at Trafalgar—it was very nearly a way of life, an era which passed away. Only twenty-two years after Trafalgar, on October 20, 1827, in Navarino Bay, one of Nelson's captains, Codrington, fought the last action performed by a battle fleet entirely under sail. And it was to be almost exactly a century after Trafalgar before another sea battle took place of comparable importance and magnitude: at Tsushima on May 27, 1905. There the British-trained Japanese admiral, Togo, flew the signal, 'The Empire's fate depends on the result of this battle. Let every man do his utmost duty.' But apart from that bat-squeak of tradition, nothing else remained. In 1815, Napoleon, on his way to exile on St Helena, asked the captain of *Northumberland* to explain to him the workings of one of the first steam vessels which they saw near at hand. When it was explained, the Emperor, whose Grand Army had been defeated by ships under sail it never saw, and who never referred to Trafalgar, save in one terse sentence, on having been vouchsafed a glimpse into the future of naval warfare, said simply, 'Mon Dieu.' Ten years later, and before Navarino, the East India Company was using a steam vessel in its Burma war.

Nowadays, the appearance of a fleet of men of war in full sail is something for the imagination. Their power, size and speed are all now difficult to comprehend. The techniques which enabled them to move and fight are now a lost art. Nelson was the last notable practitioner of naval warfare under sail, and yet in that moment he was an innovator.

From the middle of the sixteenth century to the first quarter of the nineteenth century the pattern of naval warfare changed hardly at all because the basic hardware, the sailing ship and the smooth bore muzzle-

loading gun, changed little. The size of warships increased, their shape
and appearance changed and the range and accuracy of their guns was
somewhat improved, but these were small alterations; development was
slow until the motive power changed from sail to steam. A galleon in
1588 at the time of the Great Armada was about one hundred feet long,
was capable of a speed of seven knots and carried fifty to sixty guns
which had a range of about eighteen hundred yards. They were in fact
smaller and slower than the oared galleys used at Lepanto and which
continued to be employed by Mediterranean powers into the early
nineteenth century.

A warship of the Anglo-Dutch wars was capable of eight knots, was a
little larger and her guns had an extreme range of two thousand yards.
By the middle of the eighteenth century the pattern was set which out-
lasted the age of sail. *Royal George*, Hawke's flagship at the battle of
Quiberon Bay, mounted one hundred guns with a range of two
thousand, three hundred yards and had an overall length of one hundred
and seventy-eight feet. *Victory*, Nelson's flagship, launched in 1765, and
twice refitted and modernised at considerable expense, had a speed of ten
knots, a length of one hundred and eighty-six feet and carried one
hundred guns with a maximum range of three thousand yards. As a
measure of the lack of change, Codrington's flagship at Navarino, *Asia*,
launched fifty-nine years later, was ten feet longer, one knot slower, and
carried sixteen fewer guns.

Of the three factors, speed, size and armament, speed was the most
important in producing a change in tactics, and speed did not really
change very much under sail. Indeed, it was to an extent unpredictable.
Agamemnon, for a long time Nelson's ship when he was captain, was
recognised to be the fastest ship in the fleet. More chances of design
produced this result. Hand technology could not guarantee the same
result with a precisely similar ship—each sailing ship was an individual.
In the age of transition from sail to steam there were ships like *Warrior*,
launched in 1860, powered by both, producing not very much more
speed by steam than under sail, fourteen knots against thirteen. However,
the development of the steam-powered iron ship accelerated so as to
produce in the space of less than fifty years Togo's flagship at Tsushima,
the British-built *Mikasa*, which could steam at twice the speed of
any sailing ship and destroy it from a distance of nine miles. Finally,
the battleships of World War I increased their speed to twenty knots
and the range of their guns to twenty miles, a performance that was not

greatly improved upon until the nuclear age produced another revolution in naval vessels and weaponry.

So there was a period of two hundred and fifty years during which, with minor variations, the vessels and weapons of naval warfare remained more or less constant. Those changes that did take place—and most of them, if not all, were initiated by British inventors—did not change the actual nature of sea warfare. John Harrison in 1735 invented and constructed the first chronometer, thus enabling longitude to be calculated with some exactness. His third and improved version was used by Captain Cook on his second and third voyages. In 1757 John Campbell produced the modern sextant evolved from John Hadley's reflecting quadrant of 1731. In the middle of the century Dr Gavin Knight artificially manufactured magnetised compass needles which the Royal and Merchant Navies soon adopted. By the end of the century Ralph Walker had produced an efficient, modern compass. In 1767 Dr Nevil Maskelyne's *Nautical Almanac* made its first appearance. However, these advances in the science of navigation, and in surveying and hydrography as well, did not alter the pattern of the close-fought battle.

There were, of course, some changes in the more specifically military side of naval warfare, for instance, a steady improvement in the methods of signalling which enabled the control of a fleet in action to be more of a possibility, though clouds of gun smoke inevitably made all visual signalling something of a chancy business. However, the invention of the carronade, a short gun with a large bore immensely destructive at short range—introduced into the Royal Navy in 1779—was in a sense a retrograde step as it decreased the range at which actions had to be fought, if they were to be fought—an important proviso—to destruction. The actual speed of firing was improved by the invention of the gun lock by Sir Charles Douglas, Rodney's Captain of the Fleet, who also substituted flannel for silk as a cartridge casing and used steel springs to control gun recoil. These, however, were minor changes and improvements, for strategy and tactics tended to remain constant: as in land warfare, formalism ruled the day.

It was Nelson's achievement, as will be seen, to make the break in the tactical field, and, in the comparatively short time when he was captain and admiral, to turn the naval battle into a destructive action. However, it was not simply by way of tactical dispositions that he impressed his stamp upon a navy, he did that by his personality and inspiration. These were matters not of techniques but—much more fascinating—of character and of a character which changed and developed. Here lies his attraction, for in his forty-seven years of life he appears as a number of different men, and therefore essentially unpredictable. Inevitably he invites comparison with his great contemporary, Arthur Wellesley, Duke of Wellington. No two men could have been more different, although both were indispensable, but to very different sorts of victories. They met but once and even during that brief encounter Wellesley, who was as good a judge of character as Nelson was bad, discerned two men in the admiral. It is no denigration of the stern, commonsensical, laconic soldier to say that in his long life his character changed hardly at all. Nelson, on the other hand, in a much shorter period, presented almost contradictory facets of his personality to many men and women.

In consequence, there is a very good idea of what sort of man Arthur Wellesley was; of his manner, conversation, and of his approach to his profession and to life. With the aid of his excellent biographers a very clear picture emerges, steady and constant. With Nelson, the most easily recognisable person in English history by external appearance, stature, visage, white hair, amputated arm and blind eye, who lived the last twelve years of his adult life in the fullest glare of publicity, there is no such certainty. Neither was there when he was alive, for the many who loved him, admired him, or for the few who hated, disliked or feared him. Consequently, almost any approach or reaction was, and is, both possible and excusable, save indifference.

Principal Members of the Nelson Family

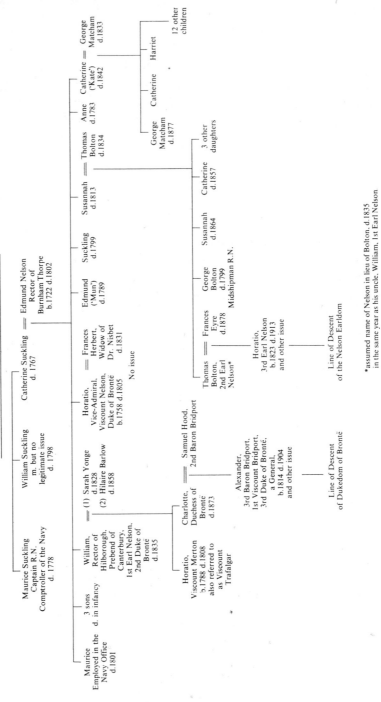

*assumed name of Nelson in lieu of Bolton. d.1835
in the same year as his uncle. William. 1st Earl Nelson.

CHAPTER ONE

Parsonage Boyhood

THE BEGINNINGS gave little hint of what was to come. On Friday, September 29, 1758, Catherine, the wife of the Rector of Burnham Thorpe, Burnham, St Albert with Alp and Burnham Norton, in the County of Norfolk, gave birth to her seventh child and third surviving son at the Parsonage House, Burnham Thorpe. The most recent addition to the Rector's family was baptised on October 9 and publicly christened Horatio on November 15. His father rather ponderously insisted on the use of Horatio, but the rest of the family called him Horace.

English history is liberally sprinkled with parsons' sons, and a few daughters, who have successfully advanced beyond the confines of the vicarage: Christopher Wren, Joshua Reynolds, Warren Hastings, Jane Austen and the Brontë sisters, whose eccentric father, curiously enough, changed his real surname Prunty to the title of Nelson's later-acquired Italian dukedom; nearer the present day, Alfred, Lord Tennyson, Cecil Rhodes and Field-Marshal Montgomery. In the eighteenth and nineteenth centuries, statistically and sociologically, clerical offspring started with an advantage and an impetus. Traditionally, clergymen had large families: Catherine Nelson bore eleven children, three sons dying in infancy. Children of the vicarage were reasonably well-educated, but were forced to make their own way in the world. Above them in the social scale the squire's son would inherit, and below them the tradesman's son would be absorbed into the family business. However, there has often been present another element: clergymen's sons, other than those who choose to follow their father into the Church, have acquired a reputation for waywardness, eccentricity or reaction against parental influence.

Therefore the traditional picture of young Horatio Nelson, born the son of a poor country clergyman, and rising to unprecedented heights as a Vice-Admiral, a Knight of the Bath and a Peer of the Realm, gives a rather inaccurate notion of the social milieu into which he was born.

Nor does it properly represent the actual circumstances of the Nelson family.

The clergy or, to be more precise, the clergymen of the Church of England, occupied in England in the latter half of the eighteenth century a curiously intermediate position in the social hierarchy. At one end of the scale there were rich and aristocratic bishops who occupied their sees by virtue of their connections, by blood or service, with noble and influential families; at the other end were a large number of very poor curates. The broad mass in between consisted of men drawn from the minor gentry and bourgeoisie, occupying a living of some financial value, their actual appointment still often due to some family connection; not great divines or scholars, not singled out for advancement in the Church, and not over-distinguished either for their evangelical zeal or enthusiasm for reform.

The steady improvement in agriculture throughout the century had increased the value both of tithes and glebe farms so that, though they were by no means rich, few occupants of country livings were made to feel that they suffered financial sacrifices for their faith. Anyhow their piety was of the mildest kind, and in an age of classicism, tolerance and 'interest', many of the clergy no doubt regarded their livings not so much as a curacy of souls but more as a piece of patronage akin to a seat in Parliament, a commission in the army or navy or a not too arduous post in Government employment.

One such, typical of his class and calling, was Horatio's father, the Reverend Edmund Nelson. His own father had also been in the Church, the Rector of nearby Hilborough, and had been educated at Eton and Emmanuel College, Cambridge. The young Edmund had apparently, because of poor health, been thought too delicate to brave the rough and tumble of public school life, but had followed his father to Cambridge. In fact both Horatio's grandfathers were clergymen, as were two of his great-uncles and eight of his cousins. Yet, though both his father's and mother's families had provided more than their quota of servants to the Church, there was a significant social difference between the two which was to prove not unimportant as far as Horatio's choice of a career was concerned. Again, both families had been firmly rooted in Norfolk and East Anglia for generations, and it was only on his father's side that there was any decline from the social norm of gentry and clerics with Horatio's paternal grandmother, whose father was John Bland, a baker in Petty Cury, Cambridge. Horatio's mother's family, the Sucklings, were considerably more distinguished than his father's, a fact which the Reverend Edmund did not resent but of which, not untypically of his own class and calling, he was naïvely proud, as evidenced in his own amateur attempts at chronicling family history.

Horatio's mother was the daughter of Dr Maurice Suckling, a former Prebendary of Westminster, and through her family could be traced a considerably more distinguished, and influential, lineage than bakers in Cambridge, or, for that matter, obscure country clergymen. The Prebendary's maternal great-grandmother was the sister of Sir Robert Walpole, principal minister to both George I and II, and known as Britain's first Prime Minister. No subsequent member of the family had attained such heights and the Walpoles themselves were now mere country grandees. However, on the Suckling side all over East Anglia there were also Durrants, Townshends, Sheltons, Bullens, Wodehouses and Permyns, relatives who had provided over the years an assortment of titles of nobility, knighthoods and armigerous bearings as well as a record of state service. In recent years there had been, for instance, two reasonably distinguished naval officers.

These distinctions of social gradation were of considerable importance to the head of the Nelson household at Burnham Thorpe, not necessarily because he was a snob, but because the England of his day was a class-ridden society. Admittedly the Rector, in his genteel way, did some-times carry things to extremes, as when in 1791 he plunged the whole family into mourning for the death of the Earl of Orford, the senior Walpole, whose grandfather had been his wife's grandmother's brother. However, class meant influence.

Yet, in contrast to the rigidity of the class systems operating in Europe, British society presented an enviable social mobility, for the younger sons of the nobility had to make their way in the world while a trades-man's son could aspire to a knighthood or even a peerage to mark the fortune which he could amass in his lifetime. Nevertheless, the advance-ment of a family or an individual usually depended on the exercise of influence, of 'interest', as it was then called, for families and individuals could rise or fall. Therefore whether a place could be obtained for a son, or a suitable match made for a daughter, was obviously an important matter for any parent, and the Rector of Burnham Thorpe, with, by 1767, five sons and three daughters to provide for out of the resources of a modest country living, would have been a very curious product of his age and class if he had been indifferent to such considerations.

In that year, 1767, the domestic situation of the Nelson family became a difficult one because of family tragedy. During the bitterly cold Christmas weather, extreme even by the standards of a very exposed part of East Anglia, when Maurice was fourteen, Susannah twelve, William ten, Horatio nine, Anne seven, Edmund five, Suckling merely a toddler and Catherine just ten months old, their mother died within a week of the death of her own mother. The effect on her husband was profound. The Reverend Edmund had the melancholy task, immediately after Christmas, of performing the double funeral service on his wife and his mother-in-law. He was apparently neither a very worldly nor a very practical man. He was not therefore, at the age of forty-six, particularly well equipped to face the task, as he put it, of being 'double parent' to eight children without any available female relative to assist him. Some men might have thought in time of remarriage as a solution, but this was not a course he considered even if the opportunity had ever presented itself. He continued to revere his late wife's memory piously, and even on his own confession can hardly have been the sort of man who was immediately attractive to women.

So, at the age of nine, Horatio was left motherless in the middle of a large family in which individual brothers and sisters would obviously have to fend for themselves. In later years the grown man was to refer to his mother in affectionate terms, but his real memory was probably somewhat hazy. The often quoted extract from a letter written when he was himself past forty—'the thought of former days brings all my mother to my heart, which shows itself in my eyes'—owes perhaps a little more to Shakespeare and a sentimentality in Nelson's own make-up than to actual recollection. Inspection of his mother's portrait, painted by an unknown artist, when she was eighteen, inevitably leads to speculation as to her contribution to the character of her famous son. The portrait shows a not unhandsome woman with a long aquiline nose, a direct almost bold glance, and firm sensual lips, a face full of character; all in all perhaps a rather surprising face for the spouse of a country clergyman, who presents in his own portrait, by Beechey, admittedly painted when he was an old man, a visage singularly lacking in individuality or strength of purpose.

It would be wrong to attach over-much importance to impressions of what are two very disparate portraits, even though everything recorded about the Reverend Edmund would seem to confirm the impression given by those melancholy indecisive features. Nelson did, however, inherit certain traits from his mother, and one was her poor health. While the Nelsons were robust and long livers, the Sucklings died young. There was Catherine herself, of course, and her naval brother Maurice who died at fifty of an unidentified cause. Of Catherine's own children three born before Nelson died in infancy and of Horatio's surviving brothers and sisters Maurice, Edmund, Suckling and Anne all pre-deceased him. This was, even by eighteenth-century standards, a poorish record. Throughout his own comparatively short life, his wounds and the rigours of service life apart, Horatio was plagued by minor complaints.

To start with, he was, despite enough experience to accustom most men, incurably seasick. His digestion was poor, he complained of pains in his chest, he was often convinced that he suffered from some heart complaint, he could not bear cold weather. It is possible to argue, even from his own words, that perhaps he was something of a hypochondriac, and that some of his ills were induced by mental strife, for certainly his aches and pains did seem to disappear miraculously or be forgotten when a decision had been made, or he had committed himself to action. Against that, though, must be considered the unduly long time he took to recover from wounds and illnesses, evidence that would argue in favour of a basically weak constitution, a handicap admittedly which he never allowed to stand between himself and considerable feats of bravery and, perhaps more important, endurance.

So much for the physical inheritance, but what of the spiritual? It would be reasonable to assume that Horatio derived his simple unswerving religious faith in a personalised Divinity which shapes our ends from his father, but his vigorous patriotism and, as an adjunct, an early regard for the navy as its instrument would seem to have come almost entirely from his mother. One thing Horatio remembered of her was that she 'hated the French', but this was perhaps to say little in an age when the French had been the traditional enemies for centuries, an enemy just across the water for anyone living in eastern England, and such a sentiment would have been almost automatically echoed in every household in Britain. No doubt Catherine Nelson had the normal feelings of any patriotic Englishwoman, reinforced by the fact that her brother, Maurice Suckling, was a serving naval officer who had achieved some distinction against his country's enemies. On October 21, 1759, the sixty-gun *Dreadnought* and two similar ships under his command had successfully engaged a numerically superior French squadron in the

West Indies, and the anniversary of that achievement was always observed as a family celebration by the Nelsons at Burnham Thorpe.

This fact lends support to the often quoted remark by Susannah, the eldest sister, also in later life remembering her mother, 'Somehow the Navy must always be interesting to me. I may say I sucked it with my mother's milk for she was quite a heroine for the sailors.' No doubt hindsight played its part in giving colour to an observation by a lady who was by then the sister of the most famous admiral of the age, but the passage makes better sense if transposed to indicate what must have surely been its meaning, that for Catherine Nelson, with her naval brother, sailors were the natural heroes. For the young Horatio too this must have been a predictable sentiment. Until he was five years old his country was still engaged in the Seven Years War with the French and what little of the outside world a youngster of that age absorbed from his parents would inevitably be conditioned by that conflict.

Horatio was, therefore, left motherless at the age of nine. A succession of local village girls was employed to help the Rector with his younger children, but the four elder ones, Maurice, Susannah, William and Horatio, were by necessity forced to become increasingly self-reliant. Perhaps in these circumstances the loss of a mother was less hardly felt than in a one-child household; in any event in the eighteenth century boys, and girls for that matter, were 'brought on' early, and expected to have acquired maturity and reached responsibility at an age when the modern child has a number of school years before it. In the eighteenth century only those young men destined by academic distinction, and luck or wealth, to go on to the Universities or the Inns of Court found their apprenticeship to adult life protracted into their late teens. When his mother died Horatio was still at school, though which of the three Norfolk schools he attended seems uncertain. From his own recollection he was sent to the high school at Norwich and afterwards moved to North Walsham. What the Parson's son was taught can only be conjectured from the later letters of the naval officer. He had a clear English style, although his punctuation was often haphazard or absent. His spelling was not always consistent, although it would be fair to say that until at least the nineteenth century there were no absolute standards in that matter, and pertinent to add that Horatio could always spell better than his father despite the latter's university education, and certainly better than many of his Service contemporaries. The rudiments of Latin were learnt and some knowledge of the classics was acquired, at least enough to produce and recognise the more familiar quotations and allusions. In common with contemporary practice no foreign living language was taught, although as an adult Horatio was, on at least two occasions, to attempt, without noticeable success, to come to grips with the French language. Not infrequently in later letters or dispatches one comes across not always perfectly recollected Shakespearean quotations (the histories would seem to have been preferred in this respect), and now and again a reference to one or another of the characters. Also, of course, natural in a parson's son, many a Biblical turn of phrase. Horatio also seems to have acquired, either at school or in their literate if not academic household, the habit of reading, a useful standby to the naval officer who by professional necessity was often confined to long solitary hours of virtual inactivity.

It was when the elder brother Maurice left home, in the same year as their mother died, at the age of forty-two, that there is the first hint of how Horatio's own career might be shaped when he came to leave school.

The Reverend Edmund had christened his son Horatio as a compliment, and perhaps a hint, to his wife's influential family. Maurice was a Suckling name too, but Horatio, or Horace, as those who bore it tended to anglicise it, was quite definitely a Walpole name. One of Nelson's two brothers who had died in infancy had first been given the name and in consequence Lord Walpole of Wolterton had been prevailed upon to stand as sponsor to the new baby. Walpole having died by the time of the second Horatio's birth, his son, the second Baron, had been asked to perform the same duty and had accepted.

Perhaps the Rector's regard for these fairly remote family connections was not misplaced, for it is pleasant to record that the prosperous and influential Sucklings did not desert the less well-off Nelsons once the living link, through Catherine, had been severed. Maurice's place as a clerk in 'the Auditor's office in the Excise' in London was found for him through the influence of Mr William Suckling, an uncle by marriage who was himself an official of the Customs and Navy office. Thus Maurice began his career at the age of fifteen. Next in age was William, but he, either through choice or parental wish, was destined to follow his father into holy orders. Susannah, the eldest daughter, doubtless through her father's contacts in Bath where, rather extravagantly, he took an annual cure, was in her turn apprenticed to a 'reputable milliner in that city'. Three years later she was to work in a shop and eventually, lucky in

two legacies, one from a family friend and the other from her uncle
Captain Suckling, she was to make a reasonable enough marriage to a
Wells merchant, Thomas Bolton, who gained a prosperous livelihood
from the corn and malt trade.

Then there was Horatio. What sort of boy he was, it is somewhat
difficult to assess. Small, slight, and not enjoying particularly robust
health, he certainly did not lack in personality. What else we know of the
boy of twelve comes from recollections of his immediate family, his
surviving brothers and sisters, passed on to the then chaplain of St
George's Chapel, Windsor. However, one cannot but feel that their
recollections were coloured by later events, by consciousness of the man
their brother had become. Three of these stories will suffice. The first is
of the young Horatio who was a keen birds'-nester, losing himself on
one such expedition when staying with his widowed grandmother at
Hilborough. When the boy did not return at his accustomed meal-time
a search was instituted. Eventually he was found sitting quite calmly by
the side of a stream he had been unable to cross. His grandmother
expressed surprise that neither hunger nor fear had sent him in search of
home, to which he replied, 'I never saw fear, what is it?' Later on we
hear of a story from his brother William over whom, without much
doubt, Horatio exercised an ascendancy throughout their lives. The two
boys were then attending the school at North Walsham. One winter's
morning the boys returned home, cheerfully enough no doubt, to report
to their father that as the road was blocked by snow they were unable to
get to school for the first day of term. Their father, always a stern
disciplinarian, put them on their honour to try again, and only to give up
if the task was absolutely impossible. The boys tried for the second time,
but it was William, the elder, who wanted to give up the struggle and
Horatio who persisted, saying, 'Remember it was left to our honour.'
Another recollection, this time contributed by an old school friend who
also entered the Royal Navy, presents a less forbidding picture of a small
boy. It is of Horatio, who apparently sported a green coat, again at
Downham Market, cajoling or forcing smaller boys to work the village
pump to produce a miniature ocean on which he could sail his paper
boats.

As a picture of a boy, who was no doubt presumed to be the father of
the man, none of it amounts to very much. The phrases are artificial and
unlikely, and even if really used and recollected verbatim indicate very
little. What parent or elder brother or sister cannot remember some

similar incident of almost any small boy? For that matter what boy, future admiral or no, has not played with boats? It would no doubt be foolish to attach too much importance to these reminiscences, but it is perhaps significant that no one remembered an anecdote of Horace—or Horatio—which showed him in anything but a serious light. No doubt the family at Burnham Thorpe was a serious one, presided over by a widowed, fairly humourless clergyman obsessed by his own predicament. Perhaps the atmosphere told, the simple unreflective religious belief imparted in a parson's household certainly lasted the man all his life, and though there were many later anecdotes of the naval officer and commander revealing his physical courage, determination and kindness, none testifies to a great sense of humour, or, perhaps unfortunately, anything approaching a sense of the ridiculous.

Therefore, from what little can be gathered, we have a picture of a small boy, perhaps over-serious for his years, embarking on a naval career, although how much personal choice a boy of twelve really exercised is difficult to tell.

Captain Maurice Suckling had previously indicated to Horatio's father that he would be prepared to take on one of his sons, if any indicated a desire for the sea service, in the normal exercise of the patronage which every post captain possessed. Thus there was a family connection and an opportunity already established. It is also important to remember that Norfolk, and indeed the whole of East Anglia, was very much sailor's country. With a long coastline open to the sea and a considerable traffic on inland waterways it was only natural that a great number of the population should gain their living from seafaring. No boy could be brought up in Norfolk in ignorance of the sea, or the large and small craft which made their way across the oceans of the world or along the local rivers and estuaries. In the eighteenth century it was from these counties and those of the West Country that there came most of the men of the Merchant Navy and the Royal Navy, in the latter case both volunteers and pressed men. These were, of course, recruits to the lower deck, but a similar geographical pattern can be observed in the case of officers as well.

In addition to the family and territorial connections there was another reason why a Nelson son might favour the career of a sea officer: relative poverty. It was fairly obvious that Horatio had shown no outstanding academic ability, so the learned professions of medicine and the law were not considered, nor presumably did he wish to follow his father into the Church. The family had no direct connections in trade and commerce, one had already become what we would today call a civil servant. The Services remained, the army or the navy. The army however tended to be the more aristocratic profession, and also the more expensive. Commissions were bought, each step up the promotion ladder had to be paid for and parental allowances were necessary to supplement the pay of young ensigns and cornets. There were poor officers of course, but their chances of promotion only really came about when vacancies occurred through casualties in action, or death by disease. Basically, to advance as a military officer, certainly in peace-time, money was necessary and influence helped. Admittedly they were no disadvantage to a young sea officer but there was no comparison between the small sum of money which could help to ease a midshipman's lot and the large amounts necessary to set a young man up in a regiment.

In addition no military officer, except perhaps the very senior and then indirectly, made a profit out of his service. In the navy with luck it was possible; prize money from captured enemy merchant ships had bought many a country house and some mansions. Freightage, a percentage of the value of precious cargoes, carried for speed or safety by warships, could provide a welcome addition to the service pay of captains. There was also 'Prize bounty' payable for ships of war destroyed or captured.

How many of these considerations operated on the mind of young Horatio or his father it is impossible to say. The Suckling offer was open. The occasion for its acceptance arose when the Nelsons were reminded of it by an item in a local newspaper.

Raisonnable, a warship of sixty-four guns, originally captured from the French but, as often happened, retaining her original name, was being put into commission again in view of the likelihood of war with Spain. Her captain was to be Captain Maurice Suckling of Woodton. The time was Christmas 1770 and the Reverend Edmund was in Bath taking his annual cure. Horatio at this stage certainly took matters into his own· hands and asked his elder brother William, properly as his senior and no doubt the more accomplished letter writer, to write to their father telling him that he wished to go to sea in his uncle's ship. The letter was written and the Rector accordingly passed on the request to his brother-in-law.

He, in his rough-humoured reply of acceptance which entirely fits Bardwell's painting of him in the National Portrait Gallery, expressed some surprise that it was Horatio who had taken up his offer, but also put the other less attractive side to the chances of a boy at sea: 'What has poor Horatio done, who is so weak, that he above all the rest should be sent to rough it out at sea? But let him come, and the first time we go into action, a cannon ball may knock off his head, and provide for him at once.'

CHAPTER TWO

Midshipman

IN 1799 when Horatio Nelson had risen to the rank of Rear-Admiral of the Red, and at the age of forty-one was acting Commander-in-Chief in the Mediterranean, he was presented with an opportunity, before his career had run its full course, of looking back and reviewing his own past life.

In that year he received a letter from John M'Arthur who had been a naval purser and in his time secretary to Admiral Lord Hood. Now, his naval career ended, he had become a naval historian, although on a rather amateurish basis by modern standards. M'Arthur with his friend and collaborator, the Reverend James Stanier Clarke, duly proceeded to write up Nelson's career. Later, in 1809, having continued their co-operation, they were to produce a two-volume *Life*, making use of many of the letters and papers then in the possession of the Nelson family and others, as well as the recollections of many of the Admiral's friends and contemporaries. Thus 'Clarke and M'Arthur' was to become the first standard and authoritiative life of Nelson. However, in 1799, the budding author was embarking on what would today be called instant history and was seeking information direct from his subject. Nelson obliged with a somewhat curious and revealing document. In the letter which accompanied it he wrote, 'I send you a sketch of my life, which I am sensible wants your pruning knife before it is fit to meet the public eye, therefore I trust you and your friend will do that, and turn it into much better language.' The 'Sketch' itself, set down in Nelson's own words, is of much greater interest than what the biographers made of the factual information contained in it. Obviously it is a mere framework of autobiography on which someone else is to work, written by a busy man, a man of action not perhaps much given to public reflection and self-analysis and possessing few literary graces but the gift of direct expression which his biographers could with advantage have emulated. To a large extent, also, it represents in outline a successful naval officer's view of what the biography of a successful officer should be and therefore, naturally enough, concentrates on later achievements rather than early struggles. Yet the 'Sketch' is by no means a factual record of service: further, Nelson was no embarrassed hero, reluctant to talk about himself, he was neither reticent nor modest. His exploits as midshipman and lieutenant are set out in a manner so favourable to himself that it would be easy to think that they had been written at the time of their performance by an over-confident and boastful teenager rather than by a certainly experienced and presumably mature commander in his forties. It is as if Admiral Nelson had never grown up. More is the pity therefore that his 'Sketch' gives us so little of his very earliest days. The period of his schooldays until his entry into the Navy is encompassed in one very short note: 'I was born in the Parsonage-house, was sent to the high school at Norwich and afterwards to North Walsham; from whence, on the disturbance with Spain relative to Falklands Islands I went to sea with my uncle, Captain Maurice Suckling, in the *Raisonnable* of 64 guns.'

As children matured early in the eighteenth century, far less attention was paid to the doings and the thoughts of adolescents than it is today, but it is regrettable that Nelson did not take the opportunity of recalling some of his feelings on his transition from the quiet family life of a country rectory to what must have been almost the other extreme of human existence, the harsh disciplined pattern of duty on board a man of war. Only much later, from the pen of another midshipman, do we gain some inkling of what the young Nelson may have felt in his early years, the actual incident occurring very near in time to Nelson's writing to M'Arthur.

On the anniversary of the battle of St Vincent the senior and most famous naval commander in the Mediterranean gave dinner, a meal then taken on board ship in the afternoon, to those officers in the fleet who, like himself, had taken part in that famous victory. The most junior officer to come aboard the flagship was Midshipman G. S. Parsons. In retirement Parsons was to entertain a Victorian public with his *Nelsonian Reminiscences, Leaves from Memory's Log* which, considering its title, was surprisingly inaccurate as to time and dates. No doubt, however, the St Vincent Dinner was an occasion which stayed in the mind. To his own consternation, but as tradition demanded, Parsons was placed on the immediate right hand of the Admiral. In awe he sat silent throughout the meal, his eyes mostly on his plate. When he did look up it was to see the thin sunshine of a Mediterranean February illuminating the ceremonial silver on the stateroom table and the lined face of his distinguished neighbour, the lock of grey white hair over the scar of the forehead wound from the Nile, the green translucent shade over the one good eye, and the empty gold braided sleeve secured to a uniform coat covered in stars and medals.

The meal over, the cloth was whisked away and the decanters began to circulate. Again in the tradition the Admiral turned to the midshipman.

'A glass of wine with you, Mr Parsons.' Parsons raised his glass. 'You entered the service at a very early age to have been in action off St Vincent.'

'Eleven years, my Lord,' replied Parsons. The smile on the prematurely aged face faded.

'Too young, too young,' murmured the Admiral as he turned to his other guests.

Young it certainly was to be exposed to a sea battle, or the tough and sometimes vicious communal life between decks, but not unusual. The novels of Captain Frederick Marryat, based as they are on his own experiences in Nelson's navy, give as good a picture as any of the midshipman's life, the squalid living quarters, the inevitable danger whether in peace or war, the harsh discipline and the rough horseplay as well as the strongly imbued sense of comradeship and duty. One at least of Marryat's autobiographically-based heroes, on seeing the midshipman's berth, 'ten foot long by six and about five foot four inches high', with little air or light, which he was to share with others, reflected, 'And this is to be my future residence?—better go back to school. There, at least, is fresh air and clean linen.'

It cannot have been an uncommon reaction among these youngsters, but this was the customary way to the quarter-deck, and was travelled by all those whose ambition it was to emerge eventually as holders of the King's Commission.

Certainly there was nothing remarkable in the age at which Nelson first joined his ship. Before him Admiral Rodney had joined at thirteen and Jervis, the victor of St Vincent, at the same age. Among Nelson's superiors Admiral Sir Peter Parker went to sea 'very young' with his own father, then a captain but destined to be an admiral, while Sir Peter's nephew George, also destined to be a future flag officer, appeared on the books of H.M.S. *Barfleur* when he was only six. This was, however, almost certainly a 'book entry', commonplace at the time, and he probably went to sea at the mature age of eleven, the legal minimum for the son of an officer. The Hon. George Elphinstone, later Admiral Viscount Keith and by no means an admirer of Nelson as a subordinate, entered the Service at the age of thirteen.

Of three of Nelson's own future subordinates, Thomas Hardy entered at twelve, but then returned to school for nearly three years, though retaining his name on the books of two ships, *Seaford* and *Carnatic*. Berry and Collingwood both became midshipmen at the age of eleven. In fact, far from being considered a hardship, early entry was sought by men of influence as an advantage for their sons. Sometimes there were 'book entries' which artificially produced the advantage of seniority in sea service, at other times the boys were really there, as the Hon. George Elliot, second son of Lord Minto, was present on board *Goliath* at the Battle of the Nile, having joined aged ten.

As some comparison, in the army, though a Service with different methods of promotion, early entry was also considered an advantage and was sought by the families of aspirant officers. John Moore, destined in his military career to cross Nelson's path more than once, was an ensign in the 51st Foot in 1776, before his fifteenth birthday. His father was a Glasgow doctor, but behind the early elevation of his son was the powerful influence of the ducal family of Hamilton to whom Moore senior was doctor, adviser, tutor and a sort of general factotum. By the age of twenty-nine by changing regiments and the purchase of steps in promotion the middle-class John Moore, having been Member of Parliament for a seat under the Hamilton influence, emerged as a lieutenant-colonel. The rise of the Hon. Edward Paget, fourth son of the Earl of Uxbridge was, commensurately with his superior social position, even more rapid. He was gazetted lieutenant-colonel to command the crack 28th Foot at the age of eighteen. Spanning both Services, Thomas Cochrane, later Earl Dundonald, through family influence was both a 'book entry' on board a number of His Majesty's ships and, notionally, an officer in the 104th Foot, though in fact still at school.

It may be thought that in an age when William Pitt, second son of the Earl of Chatham, could become Chancellor of the Exchequer at twenty-three and Prime Minister before he was twenty-five, none of this was very remarkable. But although 'a kingdom entrusted to a schoolboy's care' did arouse some adverse comment, even if only from political opponents and rivals, there were peculiar and complicated factors involved so far as the navy was concerned.

Some of course were merely reflections of the general social pattern of the age, but others were genuinely 'special', intimately bound up with the officer structure and fundamental to the whole organisation of the eighteenth-century navy. All need some explanation in an age accustomed to very different methods of officer selection and training and all, curiously enough, were present, and indeed epitomised, in the case of Horatio Nelson.

Purely by virtue of its geographical position, no nation in Europe depended so completely upon its navy and its merchant marine for its very existence as did Great Britain. The repulse of the Spanish Great Armada was still a powerful folk memory, and in the recollection of men not yet in middle age there had been two occasions when a French invasion had been a distinct possibility and a real danger. Nearly a century before, Halifax had written, 'The first article of an Englishman's political creed must be that he believeth in the sea.' Earlier and anonymously during the Hundred Years War in the *Libelle of Englyshe Polycye* the same sentiment had been put even more succinctly: 'Keep then the sea, that is the wall of England.'

Although this simple doctrine of self-preservation, of offence and defence, had originally applied to the British Isles alone, it was still equally relevant after Britain had become the centre of an overseas empire. It was demonstrated over and over again both by observance and neglect in the wars of the eighteenth century.

The principle was doubted by no one in the kingdom, yet when Midshipman Nelson first set foot on the deck of a man of war a vast gap existed between precept and practice. For the undoubted quality of the British navy lay in its men, in their skill, experience, discipline and seamanship. Even they themselves were prepared to admit that the French and, occasionally, the Spanish built better and faster ships. Yet it was not until the middle of the nineteenth century that Britain maintained a continuous service navy. In the eighteenth century the Royal Navy, proud of what Admiral Mahan called its 'combat supremacy', was in fact still a somewhat amateur affair.

In the year of Nelson's birth Britain was engaged in the Seven Years War, a conflict which though European in origin soon extended itself into the two continents where the British and the French had their rival empires. In Macaulay's graphic encapsulation in his essay on Frederick the Great, 'in order that he [Frederick] might rob a neighbour [Maria Theresa of Austria] he had promised to defend, black men fought on the coast of Coromandel, and red men scalped each other by the Great Lakes of North America'; not only black men and red men, but white English soldiers and sailors securing an empire in India, Canada and the West Indies. In that year the strength of the navy was sixty thousand men, increasing to one hundred thousand in the year following. Peace was signed in 1763 and just before the outbreak of the next war, with the revolting American colonists, later assisted by both France and Spain as allies, the numbers had sunk to a mere eighteen thousand. Between the conclusion of the American War of Independence and the outbreak of the French Revolutionary War, thousands of men were again paid off until the total remaining was sixteen thousand. Yet by 1805, the year of Trafalgar, there were one hundred and twenty thousand men serving in the Fleet manning over eight hundred ships-of-war. In consequence the link between peace-time and war-time navy, the permanent nucleus, was provided by the officers, commissioned, warrant and petty, plus a comparatively small number of men who made their life service on the lower deck.

The detail of how the rest were recruited, by the many expedients from bounties to impressment, almost literally carrot and stick, is not a subject to be dealt with here, although the products of the system, the Jolly Jack Tars of the ballad mongers, 'the people' to their officers, are present throughout, mainly silent, frequently unidentifiable, but manning every ship named. Undoubtedly, for many of them the caustic observations of Dr Johnson, writing contemporaneously, would have had force, if they had possessed the learning to read them.

'No man will be a sailor who has contrivance to get himself into a jail; for being on a ship is being in a jail with the chance of being drowned ... a man in jail has more room, better food, and commonly better company.'

That of course was the view of a landsman, a civilian and a wit, but it contained a considerable grain of truth as did Winston Churchill's later dismissal of the traditions of the Royal Navy, in argument with a pompous admiral, as 'rum, sodomy and the lash'.

Yet there is a paradox here, for Britain was proud of her navy and its sailors as she was never proud of her soldiers, yet regiments were not filled, as were ships, with men press-ganged into service. Moreover, the sailors themselves could sing the popular 'Heart of Oak', composed in 1759 to celebrate a year of victories, with its line 'for who are as free as the sons of the sea?', without, presumably, recoiling from the incongruity and inaccuracy of the rhetorical question.

In fact the methods used to supply the Navy with both officers and men reflected the limits of the power of the State and Government in the eighteenth century. As one naval officer put it, 'men of war must be manned', and if volunteers did not come forward in sufficient numbers, as they did not, then the press gang had to be used. Preferably to seize and conscript 'prime seamen', but if such could not be found then any reasonably able-bodied male between fifteen and fifty in a seaport was in danger if 'the press was out'. By law the press gang was meant to take only seamen and watermen, men experienced in the handling of ships and boats. Certain classes were specifically exempted, gentlemen and apprentices among them, but broadly speaking 'the Fleet, like the gallows, refused nothing'. Apart from the obvious injustices, which in 1755 the elder Pitt frankly and regretfully admitted in the House of Commons, the system was not even efficient. Because a large number of men were forced in time of war to man the King's ships and then allowed to return to their civilian occupation, generally seafaring of some kind, there was not that corpus of professionalism that one is accustomed to in a fighting service. There was a proportion of men who spent their whole seafaring life on board His Majesty's ships, perhaps ending their days as pensioners at Greenwich Hosptial, but a much larger proportion of a ship's complement was 'for hostilities only'. The wonder is not that such men made superb seamen, for many of them that was their profession already, but that they were made into such splendid part-time fighting sailors. For officers, however, there was a definite and ascertainable career and promotion structure. Just as the Government sought to find methods by which to fill the lower deck, so it also endeavoured to exercise some control over the choice of the officers who walked the quarter-deck. In this it also failed, for the navy itself operated a 'closed shop'.

One of the first attempts made by a Government to control the men who officered and commanded the King's ships was made by Samuel Pepys. In 1676 he was responsible for a new category of officer aspirant, the young man, nominated by the Admiralty, and given a letter from the Crown indicating that he had been so nominated. This letter was then presented to the captain of a ship who had to accept the young man as a potential officer to be trained by him in the rank of midshipman. Unfortunately however this method of entry was never popular. The young men who came to be called 'King's Letter Boys' never formed more than five per cent of the total officer intake, and the system fell into desuetude, Rodney being the last officer to achieve a place on a ship by those means. In 1733 another attempt was made at Government control by the establishment of the Naval Academy at Portsmouth where 'sons of the Nobility and Gentry' might be trained for the sea service. In 1773 this institution became the Royal Naval Academy, but, though it added to its dignity, it never succeeded in attracting many entrants.

The reason for these and other failures to formalise entry was that there always existed a much better and easier way to start a young man off on a naval career. It was open to any boy, or rather his parents, who possessed influence or 'interest'. The method was by direct approach to the captain of a ship. For apart from the established commissioned and warrant officers appointed by the Admiralty he could take anyone into his ship he liked. In some ways his powers were reminiscent of those of a colonel of a regiment, in others he had the status of a master over his apprentices, although any attempt to define a captain's power precisely only demonstrates the fact that for practical purposes he was uniquely omnipotent.

Each captain had an entitlement of four 'Captain's Servants' to every hundred men of the ship's company. His subordinate officers were also allowed servants though fewer in number, but these too were often captain's nominees or at least young men approved by the captain. Now some of these captain's servants were servants indeed, who fetched and carried, blacked boots and polished buttons, but the majority were not. However, they might be described in the ship's muster books no one on board was in any doubt as to their status and future prospects. They were there in order to become commissioned officers.

Only in 1794 by an Order in Council of April 16th was any serious attempt made to define the position of these young men. The Order talked of Class I volunteers: 'Class I. To consist of young gentlemen intended for the sea service—to be styled Volunteers and allowed wages of £6 per annum.' However, even this minor attempt at categorisation was not successful, for Volunteers Class I though they may all have been called, they were still rated on board ship by the jobs they carried out, so that one such in a short space of time could be successively described as 'able seaman', 'Captain's servant' or 'midshipman'.

At the same time, almost as if to add deliberately to the confusion, there were men on board rated in exactly the same way as those who were not aspirants for the King's Commission. Only by closer investigation into their backgrounds was it possible to tell which was which. Put crudely, John Smith, midshipman, captain's servant, or able seaman, the son of Sir Henry Smith, Baronet and Member of Parliament, and aged sixteen, or of course much younger, was destined for the quarter-deck. Whereas John Smith, midshipman, captain's servant or able seaman, the son of Henry Smith, farm labourer, and aged forty, was not.

By this method, the personal approach and the use of interest, over ninety per cent of ships' officers were found. The captains who chose the the midshipmen in effect also selected nearly all the young men who in time presented themselves for the examination for lieutenant, the first step in commissioned rank. Up until that stage the system was amateurish in the extreme and rife for abuse. As this was the age of interest the system was, needless to say, abused. Men of influence used that influence on behalf of their sons and nephews and their friends' sons and nephews and protégés without shame and hesitation. Where there were rules and regulations they were bent or avoided. Indeed those rules that there were lent themselves to abuse and invited 'fiddles'.

In the eighteenth century below the various grades of admiral there were only three commissioned ranks, lieutenant, commander and post captain. The nearest modern equivalent to the rank of Post Captain would be to call such a man a Substantive Captain, not acting or temporary, but confirmed in that rank. It was the peculiar status of the post captain which set the whole pattern of naval promotion. For once an officer had become post captain his place was set for ever in the Navy List. After that point strict seniority was the rule, no one could be passed over his head. The post captain then could confidently expect in the fullness of time, if neither death nor disgrace supervened, to reach flag rank, that is, become an admiral. Whether of course he would be employed at sea in that rank, or at what age he would reach flag rank, were other matters. The point was that until an officer had been 'made post' he was not really competing in the race for promotion to the senior ranks in the service at all. Consequently the aim of every officer was to reach post captain as soon as possible. As a consequence of that, every officer, and more important every officer's influential father, uncle or patron, used every ounce of interest he possessed to bring about that desirable result in the shortest possible space of time.

Now every armed service, today just as much as yesterday, likes to catch its recruits, whether potential officers or no, as young as possible in order to teach, indoctrinate, train and accustom. The structure of the British Navy under the four Georgian Kings made early entry vital and, the methods used to shorten the period between midshipman and post captain were dishonest to the point of absurdity. Though other families, because of their political or social position could use their interest, it was the naval families themselves, who bent the rules most outrageously, either on behalf of their own relations or those to whom they thought it wise to show favour.

Two examples will suffice. The first was Admiral Lord Rodney's son John. His father took him to sea in his own ship when he was fourteen and a half. One year and three months later he was promoted lieutenant and five weeks later became commander and post captain with only hours in between the two appointments, i.e. on the same day, October 14, 1780. Thus the Hon. John Rodney became a post captain before he was sixteen years old, which promotion was confirmed by the Admiralty, presumably out of deference to the achievements of his distinguished father. In the interests of poetic justice it is only right to record that the Honourable John's naval career did not continue at the pace of the early years, as he left the Service in captain's rank after being court martialled.

The second concerns the family of Admiral Sir Peter Parker who in his time was to favour the young Nelson. Parker achieved a reputation as a manipulator even in an age of manipulators, but the reputation did not prevent him getting his way. Due to his influence his nephew, George, became a lieutenant when he was thirteen and his son Christopher became a post captain at the age of seventeen. And the system continued. When Nelson himself was an admiral he noted 'Parker to get both steps as fast as possible'. This meant that Lieutenant Peter Parker was to be advanced to commander and captain. The reason '—his grandfather made me all I am'.

Now it may be argued that these two cases were examples of extremes, as indeed they were, but there were many more of similar quality. Of course ability and courage, especially in time of war, did receive its due reward, however, given the choice between ability or influence the budding naval officer would have been wise to choose influence, certainly in the early stages of his career. For if he had little or no 'interest' working on his behalf, he might come late, that is older than his competitors, to his examination for lieutenance. That passed he might still wait a considerable time, without a little push from the right quarters, before actually being granted his commission. Then he might languish as a lieutenant for many years, or as commander without ever reaching post rank at all. Of course at any stage some signal act of bravery or professional skill could well result in an advancement for an able officer, but generally speaking it was better for whatever reason, blood, social prestige or political influence, to be a flag officer's protégé.

After post rank influence was less important, for post captains entered a different league, where different rules applied. Perhaps the first thing to realise is that just as there never were enough men to man ships there were always too many officers. Supply always exceeded demand, especially in peacetime, but also in war as well. For here one must introduce the part-time element which also existed in the eighteenth-century naval officer's career. It arose from the fact that there was no such thing as a system of retirement. The unoccupied naval officer of whatever rank or age from midshipman to admiral went on half-pay. It was in fact slightly more than half of the entitlement of his rank, but was described by Captain Dixon writing to Nelson in 1801 as 'a sorry thing for a man with a wife and a child'. However, in many cases this did not matter for the individual had found, or possessed already, some other method of earning a living, or else was too old to consider employment, so that half pay did in these cases constitute a sort of pension. For there were both eighty-year-old half-pay lieutenants and admirals. The system of half pay emphasised the eighteenth-century differentiation between Rank and Appointment. The modern naval officer is either, say, a serving captain with a defined job and the pay of his rank or else a retired captain, no longer in the Service but with a pension. No such clear distinction was made with his predecessor of two hundred years ago. A thirty-five-year-old post captain then could be in command of a frigate and of course in receipt of full pay. The next year he could be at home doing nothing on half pay. The year after he could again be in command of one of His Majesty's ships, fully paid, and on his way again to becoming an admiral. However, common sense was applied to the system for a seventy-year-old post captain would not be in command at sea, nor would a seventy-year-old vice-admiral be in command of a squadron, although he might still be looking forward to his promotion to full Admiral. For seniority operated incxorably so far as promotion in rank was concerned, although on half pay: sensibly it did not operate so far as appointments to command were concerned.

For there existed in the navy, unofficially, what wags at the time called 'the Yellow Squadron'. The reference was to the fact that the navy was divided officially into the Red, White and Blue Squadrons. This was a relic from the seventeenth-century wars against the Dutch when the fleet had in action been so divided, the Red Squadron having the most important position in the centre, the White in the van and the Blue in the rear. Each squadron was then itself divided into Van, Centre and Rear Divisions, commanded respectively by a Vice-Admiral, an Admiral and a Rear-Admiral. Thus the most senior flag officer was Admiral of the Red and in fact Admiral of the Fleet, and the most junior of the nine was the Rear-Admiral of the Blue. By the middle of the eighteenth century the purpose of this system had disappeared, but the form remained. Though there were far more than nine flag officers, over two hundred in fact, notionally they were still promoted through the Squadrons and Divisions in order, Blue, White and Red. If they held active command at sea they flew the appropriate ensign of their rank, a red, blue or white flag with the Union Standard in the quadrant. Hence the joke about the Yellow Squadron, yellow being the quarantine flag, indicating the unwanted, or less cruelly, simply the retired.

To illustrate graphically the outward absurdity of the system the highest rank Nelson ever attained, which he held at the age of forty-seven, on the day of his death, was Vice-Admiral of the White, indicated in *Victory* by a red cross on a white ground flying at the foremast, and the White Ensign at the stern. He was exactly half-way up the promotion ladder of flag officers, though his appointment was Commander-in-Chief. To have reached the senior rank in the navy, Admiral of the Red, he would have had to live into his eighties, and outlive all his surviving seniors, competent, incompetent, and middling, none of whom, like himself, would have been at sea for thirty years or more, Yellow Admirals indeed!

These then were the career prospects of the Service that Horatio Nelson joined in 1771.

The actual beginning was inauspicious. He was noted on the books of *Raisonnable* from January 1, 1771, but he did not join the ship, which was still being refitted for sea, until the March of that year aged twelve years and three months. He travelled from school to Lynn in company with his father's servant. There he was met by the Rector who then took his son to London. In the capital the country cousin and his small son stayed in the sumptuous new house of Mr William Suckling recently built in five acres of well-laid out grounds in the then fashionable Kentish Town. It was there that father and son made their farewells and from there that the 'young gentleman' first took the stage-coach to

Chatham. *Raisonnable* was lying in the Medway and, as soon as he
alighted from the stage-coach, the young Nelson proceeded to encounter all the classic difficulties of the 'new boy'. Nobody met him,
then he had to find the ship itself. That done, he could find no boatman
to take him out to her. A passing naval officer, perhaps recognising the
dilemma, took pity on him and somehow managed to get Horatio to
his ship. The difficulties did not end there. Captain Suckling was not on
board. No subordinate, apparently, expected a new midshipman, so
Horatio walked the deck until nightfall. Not until the second day of his
naval career did someone actually notice his presence and speak to him.

CHAPTER THREE

The Arctic, India and America

THE DISPUTE between Britain and Spain over the Falkland Isles did not produce the expected conflict for which *Raisonnable* had been prepared for active service. France's foreign minister, the Duc de Choiseul, who had once planned an invasion of Britain, now used his influence to persuade the Spaniards against obduracy and the almost certain prospect of war. Accordingly, Spain agreed to cede the islands to Britain but refused to make the reparations originally demanded by Britain for 'insult to the British flag'. The compromise was accepted by George III's government headed by his new Prime Minister Lord North, and Captain Maurice Suckling found himself assigned to carrying out the unexciting duty of commanding *Triumph*, of seventy-four guns, a guardship in the Thames. Therefore, unusually for a midshipman in the eighteenth century, Nelson spent his first years of service in a navy at peace.

He had served as midshipman on *Raisonnable* for five months and a day, hardly time to gain his sea legs, and obviously to his uncle's mind there was little of use he could learn on board a guardship. Thus with a not untypical piece of management, Captain Suckling arranged a further move designed to broaden his nephew's sea education. So although Nelson stayed on the books of his uncle's new command, *Triumph*, a necessity for the time when he would present himself for his lieutenant's examination, at which he would have to produce his record of service in H.M. ships, his real service was to be elsewhere, on a ship which would give him practical experience of seamanship.

John Rathbone had been in the Navy and had served as a master's mate under Suckling's command in *Dreadnought*. Now, having left the Navy for the merchant service, he was master of a merchantman owned by the firm of Hibbert, Purrier and Norton, trading with the West Indies. It was in Rathbone's ship that Nelson now found himself mustered as 'captain's servant' (also his position on paper in *Triumph*), and it was in that capacity that he sailed to the Caribbean.

For fourteen months Nelson was away on his tropic voyage, seeing for the first time a world outside the Norfolk villages of his boyhood, which for a boy of thirteen was adventure indeed. There were however two other advantages gained from his time on a merchant ship—the second of which had probably not been in the mind of his uncle. First, as was intended, under Rathbone's eye he learnt practical seamanship, and something of the navigation necessary for one who aspired to be a sea officer. Of the second we learn from Nelson himself:

> If I did not improve in my education, I returned a practical seaman, with a horror of the Royal Navy, and with a saying then constant with the Seamen, 'Aft the most honour, forward the better man!' It was many weeks before I got in the least reconciled to a Man-of-War, so deep was the prejudice rooted; and what pains were taken to instill this erroneous principle in the young mind!

By the time Nelson wrote those words he was an admiral, so the word 'erroneous' is understandable. Rathbone was certainly an excellent tutor, and the young aspirant officer plainly had been bound to work his passage, not only to involve himself in 'officer-like' tasks. In the merchant service there was not the rigid division between officer and man which existed on a King's ship. In *Triumph* he would have walked the quarter-deck, whatever the hardships of the midshipmen's mess; under Rathbone's command he obviously carried out the duties and tasks of the ordinary seamen. In such company he would have learned their feelings about the navy and its officers—hence the reference to 'aft the most honour', where the officers had their quarters; significantly, on a man of war, separated from their men by the marine detachment, 'regular', armed and reliable, ready to put down trouble.

Curiously enough, at about the same time that Nelson joined the Navy, the divisions between officers and men were becoming even more pronounced. The rough unlearned lieutenant of the mid-century who had started life on the lower deck and 'come up through the hawse-hole', as the sailors put it, was being replaced by a less experienced, but socially and educationally superior, officer. The differences and pre-judices between Royal and merchant service were therefore increased. The contrast between the life of a seaman in a merchant ship and a naval rating—often pressed from the merchant service—were obvious. This is not to suggest that life at sea was easy, but Rathbone's seamen obviously took the opportunity to explain to the young Nelson their feelings about the iron discipline and the inequality of treatment by rank in the Navy and the resentments so often occasioned. Of course their prejudices were deep-rooted and it was to Nelson's credit that he never forgot the lesson. He was never himself a weak commander but he always remembered the feelings of the lower deck.

On his return to *Triumph*, no doubt in recognition of his increased experience, Nelson was rated midshipman and allowed in a minor capacity to put his claim to practical seamanship to the test. During the winter of 1772, again in his own words, 'as my ambition was to be a practical seaman it was always held out as a reward, that if I attended well to my navigation, I should go in the cutter and decked long boat, which was attached to the Commanding Officer's ship at Chatham. Thus by degrees I became a good pilot for vessels of that description from Chatham to the Tower of London, down the Swin and to the North Foreland, and confident of myself among rocks and sands, which has many times since been of the very greatest comfort to me.'

Later witnesses were to testify that Nelson's view of his own mastery of seamanship—and he was to allude to it on other occasions—may perhaps have been somewhat exaggerated. He was evidently proud of it but that is to say very little since he was proud of his own achievements, of his ships, of his officers and men, indeed of himself and everything connected with him. On most occasions in his life he was convinced that he knew better than others—sometimes rightly and sometimes wrongly. It is sufficient to say that when he had risen to command, he committed no glaring errors of manoeuvre or navigation, nor are there any records, as there are of other senior executive officers, of his coming into conflict with the real expert on each man of war, the sailing master.

So far Nelson's career had been shaped by his uncle's hand, the next move was obviously of his own initiative. Early in 1773 there was much talk in both scientific and naval circles of an expedition being prepared under Government auspices to explore the Arctic. As with many subsequent and similar enterprises the interests of science probably came a poor second as a motive when compared with the simple desire of men to go where no others had been before. It was not unnatural either that sea officers in time of peace should seek adventure, and perhaps official notice and preferment as well, by putting themselves forward for such a voyage of discovery as soon as rumour seemed likely to become reality.

This particular expedition had originally been the brainchild of the Hon. Daines Barrington, a lawyer by profession but a naturalist by inclination, whose brother was a captain in the Royal Navy. Barrington's hope was that another attempt could be made to find the fabled North-East Passage into the South Seas. Somehow he persuaded the Royal Society to take an interest and that body of scientifically-minded persons finally approached Lord Sandwich, then First Lord of the Admiralty. The Government was cautious and the expedition when approved was not mounted on any grand scale. It consisted of two sloops to which a number of adaptations were made to fit them for Arctic conditions. *Racehorse* was commanded by Captain Constantine Phipps, the leader of the expedition, and later to be Lord Mulgrave; the second sloop, *Carcass*, was under the command of Captain Skeffington Lutwidge. A master experienced in Northern Seas whalers was engaged for each ship, to act as pilot and render assistance to the two Royal Navy officers, and the Navy Board provided special warm woollen clothing for the two crews. There was a glut of volunteers eager to serve in *Racehorse* and *Carcass*, but it was announced that 'no boys', quarter-deck or lower deck, were to be allowed, since grown and experienced men were obviously the prime requirement for such a venture.

The prohibition did not deter Nelson, and in any event the rule against 'persons under age' was already being breached. Once again the eighteenth-century rule that the captain's choice was superior to any Navy Board instruction was being observed. Two midshipmen had already attached themselves to *Racehorse* and Nelson, who knew Lutwidge slightly, put himself forward for *Carcass*. As he said, 'Nothing could prevent my using every interest to go with Captain Lutwidge— and as I fancied I was to fill a man's place, I begged I might be coxswain; which finding my ardent desire for going with him, Captain Lutwidge complied with, and has continued the strictest friendship to this moment.'

The expedition was not a great success. Captain Phipps on his return published his account called *Voyage towards the North Pole*, which as a title observed strict accuracy, for the two ships came to within ten degrees of the Pole before being stopped and nearly hemmed in by ice. Both the midshipmen of *Racehorse*, Philip d'Auvergne and Thomas Floyd, also went into print, d'Auvergne contributing his sketches as illustrations to his captain's record, and Floyd producing a full diary.

All the descriptions follow the common form of many subsequent works. The brief Arctic summer revealed to the two ships' crews the icy landscape, the scrubby hardy plants of the region, and the usual northern fauna, many seals in packs and, glimpsed further afield, a number of whales. Sailing further north, the two sloops were soon in difficulties. The weather deteriorated, heavy cloud turned to fog, the temperature dropped considerably, and by the end of July the expedition was virtually surrounded by pack ice. No doubt to the junior members of the ships' crews it was all a great adventure, as there are records of them skating, sliding and skylarking on the solid ice and snow. However, the two captains had heavier responsibilities, advised and cautioned as they both were by the two masters, who appreciated the hidden dangers, and were well aware of the short duration of the Polar summer.

On at least two occasions, therefore, warning orders were issued to the ships' companies to prepare to take to the boats and abandon their ships to the ice. But the expedition was eventually saved by a shift in the wind which enabled the two sloops to make their way to the open sea, though not without difficulty, damage and delay. It was by his own insubordination and foolhardiness that one of the midshipmen nearly brought a promising naval career to an abrupt end. During one of the Arctic nights, of shifting and lifting fog alternating with spells of full clear visibility, Captain Lutwidge discovered that two of his junior ranks were missing in the middle watch, Nelson and another, junior to him, whose name has not survived. Where the absentees were was soon made obvious when two uniformed figures were distinguished on shore, apparently in pursuit of a polar bear which was separated from them only by a chasm in the ice. Nelson was armed with a musket which misfired, and seemed about to attack the animal using the butt as a club. The flag signal for recall had already been made but, though his companion hesitated, Nelson continued to advance upon the bear. Whereupon Lutwidge, with admirable presence of mind, gave the order for a ship's gun to be fired to scare the animal away. Luckily the polar bear, which was quite capable of disposing of one or two unarmed youths, made off, and Nelson and his companion returned crestfallen to face Lutwidge.

Years later Admiral Lutwidge, who lived until nearly ten years after Trafalgar, enjoyed telling the story and describing the demeanour of his midshipman who, his lower lip pouted in a characteristic expression, gave his excuse. 'Sir,' said Nelson, 'I wished to kill the bear that I might carry the skin home to my father.' It was not the last time that Nelson was to exhibit his reckless physical courage, nor was it the last time that he would disobey a signal.

Captain Phipps's Arctic expedition returned to Britain in September, and *Racehorse* and *Carcass* were paid off on October 15. Nelson was however not unoccupied long, for less than two weeks before he was enrolled in *Seahorse*, a frigate of twenty guns which was part of a squadron then fitting out for the East. Looking back, Nelson was to ascribe his speed of transference from an Arctic expedition to a ship bound for an equally exotic destination to his own enthusiasm: 'Nothing less than such a distant voyage could in the least satisfy my desire of maritime knowledge.' Nevertheless, a helpful word from his uncle certainly did no harm, for representations were made on the boy's behalf to Mr Surridge, the master of *Seahorse*, and a letter which Nelson himself delivered described and recommended him as 'a young lad, nephew to Captain Suckling'.

The cruise of *Seahorse*, which lasted nearly three years, was the longest time that Nelson spent on any one ship in this apprentice period of his life. While on the East Indies station the frigate visited almost every area 'from Bengal to Bussorah [Basrah]'. Curiously, Nelson himself in his 'Sketch' says little of his service under the command of Captain Farmer, perhaps because of the manner of its ending. Nevertheless, there can be no doubt that this was one of the most formative periods of his life. He was aged fifteen when *Seahorse* left Spithead in the company of *Salisbury*, flying the broad pendant of Commodore Sir Edward Hughes, and eighteen when he returned. Those three years covered his transition from boy to man.

The outward passage to India lasted, in those days, about six months, and the voyage alone must have been an education for a midshipman. *Seahorse* took the route round the Cape of Good Hope, and thence a course along the latitudes 40° to 50°, the 'roaring forties', as far south as the islands of St Paul and New Amsterdam, hundreds of miles due south of Ceylon; thence, hauling against the prevailing south-easterly winds, slowly, to Madras on India's eastern seaboard. During these months Nelson made his first acquaintance with a frigate, the fastest and most manoeuvrable warship of its day, and consequently the craft in which most young captains and subordinate officers hoped to make their mark. At the same time he saw the darker side to naval life, because Captain Farmer was what the sailors called 'a taut man', an iron disciplinarian. During the outward trip a lieutenant was court-martialled for insubordination and relieved of his duties, and countless times 'hands were summoned aft to witness punishment'—seamen were strapped to the gratings and flogged by the boatswain's mates with their cat-o'-nine-tails. Under Farmer's eye everyone on board, officers and men alike, attended to their duties or suffered the consequences, and Nelson formed a high opinion of the master, Mr Surridge, who lost no opportunity of giving the midshipmen regular instruction in navigation and accurate log-keeping.

It was January of 1775 before Nelson had his first sight of the nascent British Empire in India when *Seahorse* at last anchored in the mouth of the Hooghly. In the two previous years, while Warren Hastings had been Governor of Bengal, the East India Company, by way of the Rohilla war, had moved another inevitable step away from what Hastings had called the 'humble and undreaded character of trading adventurers', towards the position of primacy in, and eventually sovereignty over, the sub-continent. However, at the time when *Seahorse* arrived, the East India Company, though its disciplined Indian soldiers under British officers were proving themselves capable of defeating native armies, was still just one among many of the powers in India. The Mahratta Confederacy of Hindu princes, against whom Arthur Wellesley was to make his reputation, was temporarily the most important, overshadowing as it did the waning power of the Moghul Emperor. British possessions consisted of expanding enclaves round the busy commercial centres of Bombay and Madras, plus the coastline strip of the Northern Sirkars. Only perhaps at Calcutta could the pattern of things to come be discerned, for from there British territory was already stretching northwards to Cooch Behar and westwards along the Ganges towards the kingdom of Oudh.

Ships of the East Indies Station were however not confined to India. British merchants traded in the Persian Gulf and British warships were expected to visit, protect and show the flag against the influential French and Dutch and the shifting alliances of hostile native rulers throughout the area. Indeed, it was on Sunday, February 17, 1775, that, according to *Seahorse*'s log, an armed ketch in the service of Hyder Ali of Mysore was captured off the Malabar coast, thus giving Nelson at the age of sixteen his first taste of action. Judged by the standards of the time, it was in fact rather belated.

As part of the process—to reverse and inject accuracy into the old maxim—of 'the flag following trade', *Seahorse* cruised in the Persian Gulf. Basrah, where a British trading post had been abandoned because of a tribal war, was certainly visited and local tradition includes *Seahorse* in the list of the many British warships which have visited the port of

Muscat, framed in its background of jagged and forbidding mountains, and then the centre of the Gulf trade in spices. Nelson was also to see Trincomalee, then in Dutch possession, and what he described as 'the finest harbour in the world'—a sentiment which has been echoed by many generations of his successors in the Royal Navy.

It was on one of the voyages from Madras to Bombay that Nelson, now rated 'Able Seaman' from 'Midshipman', suffered a misfortune common to so many sailors, soldiers and civilians who served in the Indies in the eighteenth and nineteenth centuries. When *Seahorse* arrived in Bombay in December 1775 he was already stricken with fever. He called it a 'malignant disorder', and it was probably malaria. Treatment in those days was with alkaloids and was elementary and rarely sustained, perhaps for the very good reason that in so many cases the patient died during its course. That Nelson's case was critical and nearly fatal there can be no doubt. During his illness his hair began to change from fair to the white of the later popular prints, the normal weight he was putting on as a growing healthy young man he lost, never to regain, and the after-effects stayed with him all his life. He described his own condition as 'nearly baffling the power of medicines'. Luckily the surgeon of *Salisbury*, the squadron flagship, must have been wiser than many of his kind for he recommended a return to cooler climates as holding out the best, perhaps the only, chance of recovery.

Accordingly, the invalid was transferred to the frigate *Dolphin* under the command of Captain James Pigot, which was homeward-bound, and so on March 23, 1776, Nelson began the six months' journey back to England. The combined effect of sea air and the kindly attention of the captain, whol ooked after Nelson like a father, did have the desired effect, but the midshipman, even with youth on his side, was a long time in recovering. He suffered from recurring partial paralysis and no doubt often felt and looked more dead than alive. As so often, even while physically recovering he suffered the most severe bouts of depression, a condition also associated with the end of adolescence.

Inevitably, alone in a cot on a frigate slowly making its way at sea, he reflected gloomily on his past and future. He was not, it seems, an over-introspective boy, he had been brought up firmly in a strictly religious household, so that this sort of mental experience—at times he 'almost wished himself overboard'—was in consequence new, unusual and therefore even more alarming and intense. His reflections on his service prospects were not encouraging. Some of them were no doubt of the familiar type—Where am I going? What am I doing with my life? Others may have been occasioned by meeting with officers richer and more influential than himself, and others who had seen real action. Compared with these, his own position as an obscure midshipman did no doubt appear unpromising—'the difficulties I had to surmount and the little influence I possessed'. However, in the latter respect he did his uncle, Captain Suckling, less than justice, both on the grounds of what he had already done, and what he was to do in the future.

At some stage on the sea voyage the patient began to recover both physically and mentally and the final throwing off of the fever coincided with a rising in spirit. The mental crisis, however, was real, and was a turning-point in life. In later years Nelson no doubt often bored his captains, especially the taciturn long-suffering Hardy, with his repetition of his own private version of the light on the road to Damascus. In some state, waking, sleeping or dreaming, Nelson discerned a 'radiant orb'— the sun breaking through the clouds was a metaphor with him at a later crisis period—leading him on to glory. It is not an unfamiliar phenomenon in the lives of ambitious men: Napoleon had his star and 'the sun of Austerlitz' and even the unemotional Wellington felt the finger of Providence upon him—but only at Waterloo. For Nelson: 'A sudden glow of patriotism was kindled within me and presented my King and Country as my patron. My mind exulted in the idea. Well then, I exclaimed, "I will be a hero, and confiding in Providence I will brave every danger."' So in September 1776 the newly determined hero, thin, grey and shivery but otherwise apparently fully recovered, returned to England.

In the Indies he had changed. He had met for the first time a young sea officer called Troubridge who was to be almost a lifelong friend. He had passed through a physical and, more important, a mental climacteric. He had gained experience. He was returning to a Britain where the war with the American colonists was already a year old. Lower down the scale of importance, but undoubtedly of interest to a naval man, Captain Cook had returned from his second voyage of discovery to the Sandwich Islands and had discovered in the use of lime juice a cure for scurvy. In the year of Nelson's return Cook embarked on his third and last exploration.

A year before, George Romney, whose work as a portrait painter was to become very familiar to the lover of his most famous subject, had established his studio in London. Of the most immediate and obvious

importance, though, to a midshipman who bewailed his lack of influence,
Sir Hugh Palliser, the Comptroller of the Navy, had died, and been
succeeded in April 1775 by Captain Maurice Suckling, who in addition
was also well on his way to becoming M.P. for Portsmouth.

The post of Comptroller was technically a civil one, but these were the
days when other civil posts, including First Lord of the Admiralty, were
frequently occupied by sea officers, and of course it was also before the
time when there was any prohibition against being a serving officer and a
member of the House of Commons. Suckling's double promotion is
significant, first in showing the influence he now possessed, and second,
in giving some indication of the influence, presumably through family
connections on the Walpole side, which he had possessed before, in order
to obtain the two posts from his former position of simple post captain.

As Comptroller, Suckling was one of the four officers—the others
being the Treasurer, the Surveyor and the Clerk—of the Navy Board,
which, until abolished in 1832, was responsible to the Lords Commissioners of the Admiralty for all aspects of the Navy except the deployment of ships and the recruiting and management of personnel. The
main areas of responsibility of the Board were the building, fitting out
and repair of ships, and the administration and maintenance of dockyards
and the purchase of stores. It also controlled naval expenditure, both
paying wages and auditing accounts, and, as a rather disparate task among
all these others, supervised the Commissioners of the Sick and Wounded,
and of Victualling. Of the four officers the Comptroller was the senior
and the most important, his official orders stating his duty 'to lead his
fellow officers as well as to control their actions'. The appointment was
certainly no sinecure, but by some sea officers was regarded as a consolation prize if the chances of flag rank seemed unlikely of attainment. What
Suckling's reasons were for taking the post must remain a matter of
surmise; possibly it was his health, as subsequent events might indicate,
but what is quite plain is the increase in interest he acquired from an
obviously influential post, something which spilled over on to the
prospects of his nephew.

Nelson had now held all the possible ratings for an aspirant officer,
captain's servant, able seaman and midshipman, though none for any
very great length of time. What Suckling's elevation did procure for him
was the chance of command. Within the space of days of returning from
India, bringing to the captain a letter from his uncle, Nelson was
appointed as acting lieutenant on board a small ship of the line, H.M.S.

Worcester of sixty-four guns, then engaged on convoy duties between the Channel and Gibraltar.

It may seem strange that convoy duties were being performed at a time when Britain was not technically at war with any foreign power, only engaged in a not very successful struggle with her own rebellious subjects in America. However, it was reasonably certain that soon the French would take advantage of their rival's predicament, especially in an area as sensitive as North America. In fact in 1777 Lafayette's volunteers were already fighting the British, and in February 1778, following the signing of an alliance between France and the colonists, Britain declared war on France.

Thus the task of *Worcester* and her consorts was to play a part in those precautionary measures so familiar to members of an armed service. As often happens, too, they were not exciting duties, although for Nelson at the age of eighteen it was the first time in his career that he was to set eyes on the Mediterranean and its approaches, that theatre of war where he was eventually to exercise his qualities of supreme command. In 1777, though, Acting Lieutenant Nelson, whose appointment dates from the very day, September 24, on which *Dolphin* was paid off, could only enjoy his good fortune in attaining both promotion and a ship with a minimum of delay. The duties were routine and uneventful and the winter weather poor, but presumably the new advancement did something to dispel finally his mood of depression. Under Captain Robinson, in command of *Worcester*, Nelson was placed in charge of a watch, and in later years he recalled that 'although my age might have been a sufficient cause for not entrusting me with the charge of a Watch, yet Captain Robinson used to say "he felt as easy when I was upon deck, as any officer in the Ship"'.

It would perhaps have been odd if the Comptroller's nephew had not been a success, but no doubt the young man was pleased with the compliment, though one may wonder at the naïvety of the Admiral in bothering to recall it many years later. Also to be taken into account when judging Nelson's claim to ship management are the comments of Captain (later Admiral) Codrington who commanded *Orion* at Trafalgar, suggesting that Nelson was certainly never particularly distinguished in this respect.

It was from his service in *Worcester* that Nelson moved to his first professional hurdle, his examination for promotion to lieutenant. To pass, a successful candidate had to present his records duly authenticated

and certified, and also brave a viva voce examination by three post
captains. No doubt it was an ordeal for many, and perhaps even for
Nelson. Certainly there were midshipmen who failed to pass, and some
who passed but waited in vain for a post as a lieutenant, although, in
retrospect, Horatio, it is obvious, stood a very good chance.

His record of service was good, or at least as good as anybody else's.
It showed that he had gone to sea for more than six years in various
'Ships and Qualities', on board *Raisonnable*, *Triumph*, *Carcass*, back
again to *Triumph*, and then on board *Seahorse* and finally *Dolphin*. On his
Passing Certificate there was no mention of his service on a merchant
ship, this being covered by a 'book entry' stating that he was on board
Triumph throughout, as captain's servant and midshipman for a total
period of two years and two weeks. This however was but a minor
inaccuracy compared with the fact that Nelson 'by certificate appears to
be more than 20 years of age'. In fact he was eighteen, so that the certificate was a fraud. But so of course were most of the certificates produced
by other candidates for lieutenants' commissions, it being the common
practice to obtain a suitable document from the Admiralty hall porters
who thereby made a small profit. So common and well-known, and
indeed winked at, was this practice, that an examining captain once
observed that on one such certificate the ink had not dried in twenty
years. In fact Nelson's real record was perfectly adequate, but so little
attention was paid to the accuracy of documents that on his Passing
Certificate, though the time he spent on each ship is meticulously
recorded in years, months, weeks and days, the sum total, also set down,
is in excess by nearly three months of the true figure. The presumption
can only be that it did not really matter.

Nelson was also required to produce the journals he had kept on all the
ships he had served in, as well as 'Certificates from Captains Suckling,
Lutwidge, Farmer, Pigot and Robinson of his diligence etc'. No doubt
they were satisfactory, but of greater significance was the viva voce
examination, conducted by Captains John Campbell, Abraham North
and Maurice Suckling. Nelson's first biographers, Clarke and M'Arthur,
are responsible for an anecdote in explanation, as it were, which has been
faithfully perpetuated by subsequent biographers to the effect that
Captain Suckling kept his relationship to Horatio a secret from his fellow
captains until the young man had, apparently after a moment of confusion, produced answers which were 'prompt and satisfactory' and
'indicated the talents he so eminently possessed'. The examination con-

cluded, Suckling formally introduced his nephew. When Campbell and North expressed their surprise that he had not done this earlier, Suckling replied, 'I did not wish the younker to be favoured, I felt convinced that he would pass a good examination, and you see, gentlemen, I have not been disappointed.'

It is a nice story and perhaps had a basis of fact. Certainly there is no reason to think that Nelson, on the strength of his six years' experience, could not pass a satisfactory examination, but one wonders if Captains Campbell and North really did not notice that Nelson's first certificate was from Maurice Suckling; and even though they may not have known the family relationship, they might have surmised that their colleague, President of the Examination Board, Comptroller of the Navy and M.P. for Portsmouth, had some interest in the prospects of the young man he had taken into his own ship.

The credulity of Clarke and M'Arthur apart, the Comptroller's 'interest' was very quickly demonstrated in another way. Horatio, writing from the Navy Office, the envelope franked by his uncle, on April 14, 1777, to his brother William, who was reading Divinity at Christ's College, Cambridge, was able to tell him not only that he had passed his 'Degree', but that he had received his commission on the following day to 'a fine frigate of 32 guns'. Quite obviously the influential uncle had again been of use in ensuring that there were none of those delays in his nephew's progress which many young officers, less well favoured, were forced to suffer. The ship which Nelson entered as second lieutenant was *Lowestoffe*, commanded by Captain William Locker. Having related his good luck to William, Horatio continues, 'So I am now left in [the] world to shift for myself, which I hope I shall do, so as to bring credit to myself and my friends.' This concept of being on his own, fighting his battles unaided, was something of an obsession with Nelson all his life. Sometimes it was true, but on this occasion the expression of the sentiment was not entirely accurate.

Lowestoffe was destined for the West Indies and the Jamaica station, but was a month away from her fitting-out date. In consequence her new lieutenant had time on his hands, and it was occupied by both pleasure and duty, violently contrasted, but providing not untypical incidents in the career of many sea officers of the period.

First, the newly fledged lieutenant visited the studio at 74 Great Titchfield Street of John Francis Rigaud, to have his portrait painted in uniform. There was not enough time for the full series of sittings, so the

portrait had to await completion for four years—by which time the
uniform had to incorporate the additional gold braid of a post captain.
But, facially, we may take Rigaud's portrait as being a reasonably
accurate representation of the young man in this early stage of his career.
Although the artistic conventions of the time tended to make their
subjects a trifle more elongated than they really were, and in Nelson's
case made him appear taller than his five foot and a bit, the face is not
unhandsome. No doubt the painter gave him slightly more regular
features than he possessed in real life, and certainly a straighter nose, and
for the public's benefit the lieutenant has assumed the ghost of a smile.
However, it is not a particularly pleasing countenance, there is nothing of
humour there, but much of determination and self-will, the protuberant
lower lip, traditionally the indication of self-indulgence, is as much in
evidence as it was in all subsequent portraits when youth had faded and
the features bore the marks of hardships endured. Even discounting the
rather rigid pose, there is no lack of confidence and, less agreeably, self-
esteem. It is, however, a sensitive face and, asked to guess the occupation
of the subject, without the aids of naval uniform, it would be a long time
before one would pick seafaring.

Nelson's other task, while waiting for *Lowestoffe* to sail, provides a
reminder both of a personal problem and of the condition of the Navy.
With a base near the Tower of London he was the officer in charge of a
press gang; if volunteers did not come to *Lowestoffe* men had to be
obtained against their will. While engaged in this unpleasant business, he
suffered a malarial bout of such severity that he had to be carried back to
his post by the midshipman of the party. The lieutenant recovered to
sail with his ship, but to a destination, the West Indies, which to the
modern mind, but not to that of the eighteenth century, would have
seemed likely to provoke further recurrences of the malady.

By July the frigate had reached Carlisle Bay, Barbados, and one can
be certain that the preoccupation of her second lieutenant's mind was not
his health, which in any event had improved, but the prospect of action.
He was not to be disappointed, for American and French privateers were
playing havoc with British trading vessels in West Indian waters, and it
was the duty of His Majesty's ships both to convoy and protect British
ships and to apprehend the enemy. It was a type of warfare where the
niceties of protocol observed in fleet actions tended to go by the board.
Privateers were not greatly distinguished from pirates, and though the
captain had his 'letters of marque', authorising him to make war, any

man with a good fast ship could indulge the twin pleasures of patriotism and plunder. To counter such activities was work for a frigate. *Lowestoffe* convoyed eighteen merchant ships to Port Royal and then a month later captured an American sloop carrying rice. A little later Nelson had the opportunity of showing Locker the quality of his second lieutenant. The *Lowestoffe* had taken an American privateer, but in a heavy sea which threatened to swamp the prize. The first lieutenant failed to get a boat alongside. Locker, presumably both anxious and displeased, bellowed out, 'Have I no officer in the ship who can board the prize?' Stung into action, the master ran to the gangway, but was beaten by Nelson who said, 'It is my turn now, and if I come back it is yours.'

He did not come back, at least for some time, as his boat was thrown by the waves over the deck of the privateer and then back again, before finally the prize was boarded; but by then it too had surrendered to the elements, so that it was a day later before the second lieutenant's prize under his command was re-united with the frigate.

No doubt impressed, Locker, when *Lowestoffe* again took to sea on her third cruise, put Nelson in command of an attached schooner. It had also been taken as a prize and re-christened *Little Lucy*—in honour of his eldest child, now six years old. *Lucy* was Nelson's first real command, for she operated independently of *Lowestoffe*, and certainly the experience was much to his fancy, for as he said himself, 'Even a frigate was not sufficiently active for my mind.' It was in the schooner that, as well as taking a prize himself, he gained more valuable experience, making himself 'a complete pilot for all the passages through the islands situated on the north side of Hispaniola'. Hispaniola was the modern Haiti, and at that period a French possession.

In the late spring and early summer of 1778 two events occurred which were to have a considerable effect on Nelson's career. By then Britain had declared war on France, thus regularising a position which had been in existence in reality for some time, and Admiral Sir Peter Parker arrived from the New York station to be Commander-in-Chief in Jamaica. The Parker family was notorious even in the Navy of the day for its management and jobbing, so no doubt it was with a wry good grace that—admittedly with Locker's recommendation—Sir Peter took Lieutenant Nelson into his flagship, *Bristol*, as third lieutenant. By September, the nephew of the Comptroller of the Navy was first lieutenant. It is perhaps almost superfluous to observe that such posts in flagships under the eye of the Commander-in-Chief have always been regarded as plums by ambitious officers. By December 1778 Nelson was posted commander of a brig, *Badger*. Something of a pattern was now beginning to develop, as at the same time one Cuthbert Collingwood was appointed to *Lowestoffe*.

That pattern was preserved in June of the following year, when Collingwood got his next promotion, to be in his turn commander of *Badger*. Her commander had moved on to the position coveted above all others by eighteenth-century sea officers—post captain, of *Hinchinbrooke*, a frigate of thirty-two guns.

At the age of twenty-one Horatio Nelson had now, in the naval sense, arrived—no officer junior to him could now be promoted above his head, further advancement depended upon service, skill and survival. None of these lessons was lost on the new captain, well aware of the fate of his predecessor. 'I got my rank by a shot killing a Post Captain, and I most sincerely hope I shall, when I go, go out of the world the same way.'

CHAPTER FOUR

Nicaraguan Expedition

S O IN June 1779 Nelson was posted captain. His change of status was now marked by all those countless conventions and dignities hallowed by time and service practice. The coveted gold lace adorned the cuffs and lapels of his blue frock-coat, and his cocked hat, also with its addition of gold braid, was now worn sideways, something of a personal eccentricity, but one not permitted to lieutenants and commanders who wore theirs fore and aft. Each time he left or returned to *Hinchinbrooke* the bosun's mate and the side boys would man the side and shrill their pipes. When he walked the quarter-deck all his officers would confine themselves to the windward side so that the great man could pace undisturbed. The coxswain of his gig, approaching a man-of-war, merely extended the four fingers of his right hand to indicate the status of his passenger seated in the stern sheets. If challenged afloat after dark as to his identity the reply was not his name but the name of the ship he commanded. Subordinates addressed by the captain removed their hats as in the presence of the Almighty.

Nelson was three months short of his twenty-first birthday. By any standards it was early promotion. He had been in no significant naval action, his record of active service in the face of the enemy was, comparatively speaking, negligible. For part of his service he had been immobilised by illness.

There can be no doubt of the debt owed by Horatio Nelson to Maurice Suckling, the uncle continually placing the nephew in the right place at the right time from midshipman to commander, but there it had finished, short of the last, most important step. For in 1779 Nelson learnt that his interest was at an end. Captain Maurice Suckling had died in July of that year at the age of fifty of an unknown illness, demonstrating that familiar constitutional weakness present in the Suckling side of the family. To every one of his nephews Suckling left £500, and to each niece £1,000. His brother, Mr William Suckling, 'Clerk of Foreign Entries at the

Custom House', with whom Nelson and his father had stayed at Kentish Town, was the principal legatee, but he passed on to Horatio, as was proper, the dress sword of their kinsman, Captain Galfridus Walpole, which thus followed the naval line in the family. However, Suckling's principal service to his nephew had been rendered while he lived. In the last few months he had confided to the Rector of Burnham Thorpe the hope that he would one day see his son an admiral. That day was eighteen years off, and at the time of Suckling's death Nelson, in the rank of commander of *Badger*, was suspended, as it were, between family influence and the patronage and regard of his superiors.

On Captain William Locker, of *Lowestoffe*, he had obviously made a great impression, and they were to remain firm friends until Locker's death in 1800, exchanging letters regularly over the years. Admiral Sir Peter Parker and, perhaps more important, Lady Parker, very much the influential flag officer's wife, had also formed a favourable impression of the young man. Customarily the transition from commander to captain was fairly rapid, but there could be nothing approaching certainty in these matters in the Navy. In fact *Badger* was active against American privateers off the Mosquito shore, and in the Bay of Honduras, so busy and effective that the local settlers expressed their appreciation of her captain by a formal vote of thanks. Later, off the northern coast of Jamaica, the young commander was lucky enough to capture a small French ship, *Prudente*, and make her his prize, a proportion of the ship's value accruing to Nelson. The amount was small, but such luck, even if minimal, rarely came to Nelson again. Certainly unlike most of his contemporaries, as a senior officer no prizes came his way to make him a rich man.

So the commander of *Badger* in no way fell below the standards expected, indeed on one occasion, when the frigate *Glasgow* caught fire and burnt herself out in Montego Bay and her crew was saved largely by Nelson's prompt assumption of control over life-saving operations, he positively distinguished himself. So when Captain Hooper of *Hinchinbrooke* was killed, Nelson, no longer by influence, but on grounds of capability, was an obvious choice for her command. Curiously, perhaps because of the Admiral's fancy, perhaps because he distinguished merit in others as well as the late Comptroller's nephew, Cuthbert Collingwood followed Nelson as commander of *Badger*. 'Whenever,' wrote Collingwood later, 'Lord Nelson got a step in rank, I succeeded him, first in the *Lowestoffe*, then in the *Badger*, into which ship I was made a Commander in 1779, and afterwards the *Hinchinbrooke*, a 28 gun frigate, which made us both Post Captains.'

This pattern, whereby the older man succeeded the younger in his posts of command, and which was to persist to Trafalgar and even beyond, has often been commented upon. Certainly the two men, lifelong friends, were a splendid contrast to each other in appearance, physique and character. Nelson came from one of the traditional homes of the Navy, East Anglia; Collingwood, unusually, was a northerner, from Northumberland. Nelson was small, lean and, though mercurial, supremely self-confident. Collingwood, larger and more staid, was nevertheless a thinker and a worrier, plagued at times by melancholia and self-doubt but perhaps in consequence more dependable as a subordinate. Both men were of the middle class, but in these early years in the Navy Nelson had the edge over Collingwood with his Suckling connection. There is, however, one further sidelight on the life of a sea officer which is revealed by these somewhat rapid changes of rank, ship and command. All of these moves took place on the West Indies station, a theatre of war remarkable for its quick rotation of officers. Nelson succeeded a captain who had been shot, but that was hardly the norm. In that part of the world 'a sickly season' was something to be welcomed by the young officer anxious for promotion. Nelson's own letters are full of news of the deaths, from fever and sickness, of sea officers. Collingwood's brother died there, Locker was seriously ill, and might well have succumbed if he had not returned to England. With such a mortality rate, an enemy was hardly necessary for the Royal Navy to lose officers and men by their hundreds. As will be seen it was something of a miracle that Nelson himself, especially with his previous record and anything but a hardy constitution, was not numbered among those many forgotten officers, 'carried off', and hastily buried in the West Indies.

1779, the year in which Horatio Nelson first walked a quarter-deck in command, and Captain Cook in far-off Hawaii met his end, was hardly an auspicious one for either Britain or her Navy. The war against the colonists dragged on, and soon the Americans were to acquire another European ally, and Britain an old enemy. On June 16 Spain, having gained France's agreement to assist her in recovering Gibraltar and Florida, declared war on Britain and immediately began to lay siege to Gibraltar. Nearer to Nelson's station, two days later, a French force took the island of St Vincent and on July 4 captured Grenada. Throughout the year the principal colonial rivals, Britain and France, were to continue their world-wide tit for tat, in territories each possessed or coveted, sometimes acting directly themselves, and sometimes through their allies or each other's enemies. In January the French had beaten off an attack by the British in Senegal in West Africa, but in May were forced to cede Goree. In August the British succeeded in repulsing the American allies of the French at Penobscot, Maine, but in that same month the French fleet was dominant in the English Channel. In September John Paul Jones in *Serapis* was to defeat one of His Majesty's ships, *Countess of Scarborough*. By the end of the year the account was almost balanced when the British East India Company found itself at war with the Mahrattas, the Hindu princes of the Confederacy, who, as on past occasions, relied upon French military advice and advisers. However in Naples, pregnant for Nelson's own future, a very Italianate English baronet called Acton began to reform the Navy of the Kingdom of the Two Sicilies, and French influence was thus diminished in that particular part of the Mediterranean.

Of more immediate concern to Captain Nelson, Admiral Count d'Estaing and his squadron had now sailed from Hispaniola to Martinique, and by the middle of the year the British in Jamaica were bracing themselves to repel a French invasion. Nelson wrote to Locker, at home and convalescing, in August, telling him of d'Estaing's fleet of 'twenty sail of the line and a Flag ship with eight or nine more'. He also talked of a French force of 25,000 men, warships and transports, which was being prepared for the Jamaican invasion. Certainly he was right when he said that 'Jamaica is turned upside down since you left it', but when he talked of his fear of being made to learn to speak French as a prisoner-of-war, and of his estimate of the size of the enemy, the young captain displayed an acceptance of rumours which he was never able to eradicate completely even when he became an admiral. As part of Jamaica's preparations Nelson found himself on shore in command of the batteries of Fort Charles at Port Royal, in his view 'the most important post on this island', while in the harbour a comparatively weak force of naval vessels awaited the first sight of French sails. Nelson's estimate of the likely outcome was pessimistic, although his judgment was not put to the test. The French admiral, perhaps knowing something of the comparative ineffectiveness of ships' guns ranged against shore batteries, sailed on to Savannah on the American coast, hoping to assist the colonists from the sea, a project which failed.

The British in Jamaica could now relax and Horatio Nelson quickly

found new employment, which was very far from conventional for a
sea officer. No doubt if the plan originally devised by the Governor and
Commander-in-Chief of Jamaica, General George Dalling, and approved
by the home Government, had succeeded, the British could have inflicted
a considerable reverse on the Spaniards. Certainly it was ambitious and,
on the map, tempting. Essentially the idea was to land a military force
north-west of the Gulf of Mosquitoes on the isthmus of Panama, which
would then advance from San Juan del Norte, then called Greytown,
north-west along the San Juan river to Lake Nicaragua and capture the
Spanish forts at Grenada and Leon. These secured, it was thought the
British could sever the Spanish dominions at almost their narrowest
connecting point. How precisely this was to be done and for how long,
and what manpower was necessary to do it successfully, seems hardly to
have been considered.

The force earmarked for the original operation was woefully inadequate. As in other wars Britain, possessing considerable sea power
and mobility, and therefore an ability to land military forces on enemy
shores, tended to think little of the size of those military forces, how they
might be employed and how they might survive on arrival. The
Walcheren expedition, the Crimean War, the assault on the Dardanelles,
Suez in 1956, there have been a number of such operations. The 'Dalling
Plan' of 1780 was another, though on a small scale, and it nearly lost
Britain her most famous admiral before his time. Nelson was never
lucky on land, and this was to be his first but by no means his last
unfortunate experience. It was also his first attempt at co-operating with
soldiers, and the opinion he formed of them on this occasion, as being,
in the main, dull plodding creatures with little aggressive spirit but much
addicted to parade-ground manoeuvres, lasted him all his life.

Nelson throughout the expedition was active and energetic, if at times
impatient, and never seemed to lose his enthusiasm once the force was
committed. No doubt, though, when the expedition was being prepared
his comment in a letter to Locker—'How it will turn out, God knows'—
represented a professional assessment of its chances of success. In this
mental dichotomy he was of course merely presented with the recurring
dilemma of the serving officer who may disapprove privately of his
superior's plans but is bound in duty to try his utmost when ordered to
carry them out.

The military force which had been given the task of fighting its way
through to the Pacific consisted of under five hundred men, indifferently

selected and put together. There were detachments from the 60th and
79th Foot, about a hundred men from each regiment, and though one
day John Moore was to make the 60th one of the smartest and most
formidable of the new rifle units, that was all in the future; and the 79th
were worn out with sickness from previous service. Men of the Loyal
Irish Regiment, Jamaican European volunteers and some marines made
up the rest. The commander of this hotch-potch was a Captain Polson,
holding a brevet as major, a rank he attained a year later in the 92nd
Foot. He was therefore junior in rank to Nelson, whose only official part
in the expedition was, as he said, 'to command the Sea part of it', in other
words to get the troops to their destination and then return to Jamaica,
leaving them to fend for themselves.

As soon as he reached the aptly-named Mosquito shore, though,
Nelson realised that he could not carry out his orders. It had been
blithely assumed that natives would provide boats for transport and
themselves as guides. However, at first sight of this eighteenth-century
task force they fled into the interior. Immediately the 'light-haired boy'
in 'a very small frigate', as Polson described him, took a hand. He sailed
Hinchinbrooke up and down the coast and cajoled and forced and collected
native guides, porters and pilots. Precisely by what means Nelson
achieved his object is not known and can only be guessed, but somehow
men and boats were found. Now at least the expedition could face the
river journey. From this moment on, Nelson 'directed all the operations'
with Polson's acquiescence. The task was considerable, the course of the
river was unknown and the position and strength of the Spanish garrison
really a matter of speculation. In addition, men dressed in the inappropriate heavy, formal uniform of eighteenth-century European warfare
were facing dense tropical rain-forests. The terrain was appalling and the
time of year the most unhealthy for the dry season was about to be
succeeded by torrential rain.

With the advantage of modern equipment and medicines the officers
and men would still have faced a considerable test of endurance. Nelson
landed some of his sailors from *Hinchinbrooke* and, with their professional
assistance in the management of the boats, the expedition forged ahead.
Alternately soaked to the skin and burnt by the sun, reduced on occasions
to supplementing their rations with monkeys and reptiles, and soon
afflicted by yellow fever, somehow Polson's command, inspired by
Nelson, struggled through until they were within sight of Fort San Juan.
There a dispute arose between the two Services, army and navy. Nelson,

as was his way, favoured an immediate all-out assault, Polson and his officers insisted on the painstaking preparations for a formal siege. Presumably because he had little option, as he had only attached himself to the expedition as a volunteer, Nelson yielded, but, having done so, threw himself with all his vigour into a form of operation which must have been totally alien to his own impatient temperament. With the soldiers he 'made batteries and afterwards fought them', and in his own opinion 'was a principal cause of our success'. This was no idle boast, for Polson in his official dispatch later wrote of his naval colleague, 'He was the first on every service by night or day. I want words to express what I owe to that gentleman.' Eventually the Spanish fort surrendered, but the expedition never fulfilled the high hopes of General Dalling. As Collingwood put it, 'the Expedition to the Spanish Main was formed without a sufficient knowledge of the country—the climate too was deadly and no constitution could resist its effects'.

Long before Fort San Juan surrendered to Polson and his slow-moving soldiers Nelson was back in Jamaica. While in Nicaragua he had been informed that he now had command of the frigate *Janus*, in place of Captain Glover who, as Nelson had suspected from his sickly appearance, had died, yet another victim of the prevalent and loosely described 'fever'. But Nelson himself was also in bad health, primarily from dysentery but also because the rigours of the Nicaraguan venture had taken their toll on his weak constitution. In fact Nelson's second frigate command was never properly exercised, for though from April 1780 he was ostensibly captain of *Janus*, it was in name only, as most of the time he was sick ashore. Eventually on August 30 he was forced to write to the Commander-in-Chief, 'Having been in a very bad state of health for these several months past . . . and the faculty having informed me that I cannot recover in this climate, I am therefore to request that you will be pleased to permit me to go to England for the re-establishment of my health.' Sir Peter Parker, having seen the report of the surgeons, accepted the 'absolute necessity' and sent home his junior, of whom both he and his wife had grown fond.

The crew of *Hinchinbrooke* fared less well than their departed captain. Collingwood took over from Nelson and, during the tenure of command of the two captains, of the 200 men of the ship's company, 145 died of yellow fever, Yellow Jack as they called it, familiarly and in fear. Looking back on his old command in a later report Nelson wrote, 'I believe very few, not more than ten, survived of that ship's crew.'

Much later, Nelson was reminded of the expedition 'against the city of Grenada upon the Lake of Nicaragua'. One of his companions in the setting up and working of batteries against the Spanish forts had been a Lieutenant Edward Despard, one of two Irish brothers with the 79th. Polson in his dispatch had bracketed in his esteem Nelson and this officer, who specialised in military engineering and siege operations: 'There was scarce a gun but was pointed by him or Lieutenant Despard.' However, on February 7, 1803 Colonel Edward Despard was on trial for his life accused with thirty other conspirators of high treason. What had changed the courageous lieutenant into the ringleader of a gang of traitors planning a hare-brained scheme to assassinate George III on his way to open Parliament is not known, perhaps his Irish nationality provides something of a clue. Nevertheless Vice-Admiral Viscount Nelson, where many other men would have sought some excuse, attended court and testified before the judge, Lord Ellenborough, that 'we served together on the Spanish main. We were together in the enemies' trenches and slept in the same tent. Colonel Despard was then a loyal man and a brave officer'. But the plea was vain. The jury found Despard and six of his associates guilty and, though mercy was recommended, they were executed fourteen days later.

Nelson was back in England in time for his twenty-second birthday. Like many another serving officer returned from the tropics he complained of the cold, but perhaps with more cause for he was undoubtedly still a sick man. It was not until August 1781 that he was again actively employed.

He spent the winter at Bath, enjoying the medical care and rest which he had never experienced for long enough in Jamaica. There for a time Lady Parker had attended him in her own house, but when official duties called her away native servants had neglected him and let him lie, as he wrote miserably, 'like a log and take no notice'. Benjamin Moseley, the Surgeon-General at Kingston, who was considered an expert on tropical diseases, had done his best, but Bath provided a higher standard of medical care and of course a healthier climate. Under the ministrations of the celebrated Dr Woodward who took a lesser fee from a naval captain, whose illness, he felt, 'was brought on by serving King and country', than from his rich civilian patients, Nelson began to recover his health and strength. He stayed in the lodging house where his father put up when taking his annual cure, and there the Rector visited him and brought news of the family.

Writing to his old commander and friend, Captain Locker, who was himself still not in the best of health, Nelson recounted the course of his illness and treatment. In January 1781 he was 'much better' but 'still scarcely able to hold a pen'. His 'inside' is a 'new man', no doubt owing to a rigorous régime of being 'physicked three times a day', drinking the famous waters and giving up wine entirely. By February he had the use of all limbs save his left arm—'from the shoulder to the fingers' ends are as if half dead'—and his spirits were improving. He contemplated going to London to see John Rigaud, now a Royal Academician, with regard to his portrait, left uncompleted four years before, though he reflected that 'it will not be the least like what I am now'.

In March Nelson was, in his own view, 'never so well in health since you knew me, or that I can remember', and was out and about, staying with a brother officer, Captain Kingsmill, near Newbury, and paying visits to old friends and relations in London. By May he was turning his mind to future employment and, for Nelson, despite a slow and painful recovery from an illness which might well have proved fatal, to think of a course of action, whether in large or small matters, was to act upon it.

1781 was an unfortunate year for Britain, but it was a good year for a sea officer seeking re-employment. The other half of the cynical ward-room toast—'a bloody war and a sickly season'—was now especially relevant. Nelson had seen a great deal of 'sickly seasons' in the West Indies, and knew well their effect on the Navy List. While at Bath, he had written to Locker asking for an up-to-date copy, and now he was determined to see something of a bloody war.

Burgoyne's surrender at Saratoga four years before had changed a colonial conflict into a major war. In 1778 France had joined in and a year later both Spain and Holland. France was stronger than she had been in the Seven Years War and Britain could no longer rely on her continental ally, Prussia, to keep her enemies occupied in Europe. The British Navy was engaged and under threat in the Atlantic, in the Channel, in the West Indies and off India in the Bay of Bengal. Before the entry of France into the conflict, superiority at sea had rested entirely with Britain, but now she found her attention diverted. The West Indies sugar islands were deemed vital to British prosperity; as a consequence, Captain Nelson had found himself waiting for the appearance of d'Estaing's fleet off Jamaica. It was perhaps because of sensitivity to the threat to the Caribbean that General Sir Henry Clinton, the Commander-in-Chief in America, in accord with Lord George Germain, the Secretary of State for the

Colonies, tried to shift the land campaign to the southern states. Both general and minister were also convinced, with some reason, that Georgia, the two Carolinas and Virginia were more loyal to the British cause than Pennsylvania, New Jersey, Connecticut, Massachusetts and New Hampshire. So, 3,000 miles apart, they conceived a plan of reconquest, moving from south to north. There were initial successes, and in 1779 Savannah and Charlestown were both recaptured. Yet the same mistake was made overall as had bedevilled Nelson's Nicaraguan expedition: too much reliance was placed on sea power, and too little concern given to the strength of land forces.

It was against this background that on May 6 Captain Nelson had an interview with the First Lord of the Admiralty, Lord Sandwich, whose secondary title of Hinchinbrooke had adorned his first command. Sandwich, renowned principally for his dissolute private life and complete untrustworthiness as a political colleague, was, as always in his ministerial capacity, charming and courteous, but could offer Nelson nothing immediately. Perhaps it was not surprising; he was a comparatively junior captain with only short periods of command to his credit, and was still in poor health. Writing to his brother William at about the same time, he explained that one of his reasons for not leaving London and the comfortable Kentish Town home of their uncle William Suckling of the Navy Office, and visiting the family in Norfolk, was the fact that he had 'entirely lost the use of my left arm and very near of my left leg and thigh'. A Mr Adair, 'an eminent Surgeon', had however taken over where Dr Woodward had left off and appeared optimistic.

Nevertheless it would seem likely that some at least of these disabilities would have been apparent when Nelson had his interview at the Admiralty.

So, as soon as professional enquiries had been exhausted for the time being, and his health had somewhat improved, Nelson left for Norfolk. He was not to get a ship until August, and so it was at Burnham Thorpe, among his family and their affairs, that, no doubt a trifle unwillingly, he whiled away the next few months.

The war was going badly. In January Admiral Rodney had defeated the Spaniards at Cape St Vincent and temporarily relieved Gibraltar, and in April had fought an indecisive action against the French at Martinique, but these were localised successes. Britain was confronted by the Bourbon powers, France and Spain, and conducting a war outside Europe, without allies or even friends, since Catherine of Russia had brought Austria, Prussia, Denmark and Sweden together to counter British insistence on searching neutral shipping for contraband.

At such a time, to a young and energetic naval captain, who had packed into a short career voyages to the Arctic, the West Indies and India, who had seen some action and hoped for more, the doings of his family of prosaic brothers and sisters must inevitably have seemed very small beer, and it was certainly with pleasure that Horatio heard in August that he had been given a ship.

When Nelson assumed command of the twenty-eight-gun frigate *Albemarle*, she was having her bottom sheathed in copper, then still a comparatively new process which preserved the ship, keeping her free of wood-boring parasites and also the barnacles and other marine life collected at sea. Coppering also maintained what would now be called the streamlining of the hull and prevented any falling off in the ship's speed due to such obstructions. In *Albemarle*'s case any extra knot thus retained was welcome, for, as Nelson discovered when he took her to sea, she was a poor performer. She had been captured from the French about a year before, which occasioned Nelson's sour reflection that her previous masters must have taught her nothing except the art of running away, as she would give of her best only when going directly before the wind. In all other circumstances she was slow and unwieldy, not so surprising perhaps, bearing in mind that when captured in 1780 she had been a merchant ship and had only been converted hastily and partially into a warship. All in all, his captaincy of *Albemarle* was not the happiest period of Nelson's life.

The winter of 1781–2 was particularly vicious, with gale-force winds prevalent in the Channel and the North Sea, and storms lashing the whole coast of Britain. It was in these conditions that *Albemarle*—with *Argo* and *Enterprise* in company—was called for convoy duty in the Baltic. To a man who had grown accustomed to the West Indian climate and who had only just recovered from a serious illness, the change must have been anything but pleasant. Ruefully Nelson wondered if the Lords of the Admiralty had acted deliberately—'it would almost be supposed to try my constitution'. The convoy itself carried naval stores from Scandinavia, a source of supply which was becoming increasingly important now that North American timber and cordage was likely to be denied to Britain. The merchantmen did nothing to make the task of the escorting warships any easier. The convoy, Nelson wrote to Locker, 'behaved, as all convoys I ever saw did, shamefully ill; parting company every day'.

Returning home, *Albemarle* proved herself not only clumsy but unlucky. Early in the morning of January 26, 1782, while she tossed at anchor, one of the great East India storeships, the *Brilliant*, lost her own anchor in the storm, bore down on the frigate and crashed into her bows. *Albemarle* lost her foremast, bowsprit and mainyard, as well as having her hull holed in two places. 'All done in five minutes!' commented Nelson, 'We ought to be thankful we did not founder. Such are the blessings of a sea-life!'

Damage inflicted in five minutes took over two months to repair, and Nelson's spirits, already low, sank even further when he discovered that he was bound to winter in North America. His health undoubtedly gave him concern, and he viewed his next tour of duty with apprehension. In this he was probably wrong since his fever symptoms were more likely to recur in a warm, wet climate than a bracing, temperate one. However, a stormy crossing of the Atlantic followed by a sojourn in a notoriously cold winter climate must have presented an unattractive prospect. And, when bored or disappointed, Nelson's mental depression often reflected itself in his physical health.

Certainly, the later summer of 1782 was one of those occasions, and with Locker and other 'Navy friends' he discussed the possibility of applying for an exchange to another ship. His medical adviser, Dr Adair, was in fact the brother-in-law of the new First Lord, Admiral Keppel, the unpopular Sandwich having disappeared with the rest of Lord North's discredited ministry. Here was an obvious opportunity for exercising interest. However, it was not put to the test for Nelson, whatever his temporary disillusionment with the exigencies of Service life, was always ultimately responsive to the call of duty and it would be wrong to condemn him for trying to avoid an unpleasant posting. Throughout the American war, he held firmly to a preference for the West Indian station, not only for its climate, but because he was convinced that there lay the greatest opportunities for action and glory. It was not an unreasonable belief, and many other Englishmen of his day saw more wealth and therefore more strategic importance in the sugar islands than in the colonies of North America. It was a belief also shared by the French and the Spanish, and it was only by their own failure to cooperate and general incompetence that this theatre was not exploited as it might have been.

Accordingly, *Albemarle* sailed via Cork on what her captain stigmatised as 'this damned voyage'. Again it was convoy duty and the two frigates escorting over twenty merchantmen were *Albemarle* and *Daedalus*, commanded by Captain Pringle. In very poor weather they parted company and *Albemarle* arrived off Newfoundland without either consort or convoy.

The fault was no doubt Nelson's and it further increased his depression and irritation. Pringle was no more enamoured of the voyage than he was, but he at least had some consolation, for *Daedalus* carried bullion to the value of a hundred thousand pounds, and the captain would receive as freightage a percentage of this considerable sum. 'See what it is to be a Scotchman,' remarked Nelson. If he could have forecast his own incredible bad luck off the Canadian coast so far as prize money was concerned, Nelson would have envied Pringle even more. For of all the prizes taken by *Albemarle* not one reached port. Later in his career Nelson, in a mood of bravado, was to write to his wife, 'All money is trash,' nevertheless there were times when he could have done with money, and all his life he was short of it. Of the captains in the American theatre of war he wrote, 'Money is the greatest object here—nothing else is attended to.' It was not his way, he attended to his duty, but it was neither particularly exciting nor rewarding.

On July 14 he had an encounter which demonstrated both his own generosity of spirit and the curious half-war conditions prevalent in American waters. On that day *Albemarle* captured *Harmony*, an American fighting schooner whose master was Nathaniel Carver of Plymouth, Massachusetts. It was a small ship and its cargo meant almost everything to Carver, who was not a rich man. There were problems on both sides. The American master was nearly home, but the British warship was being buffeted by squalls and her captain was by no means familiar with the shoals of Boston Bay. Whether Nelson had any second thoughts about his own high estimate of his seamanship one does not know, but prudence prevailed. Carver was ordered on board *Albemarle* to act as pilot. The American performed his duties without protest, and with skill. Once the two ships were clear of danger, Nelson returned the captured schooner to her master and with a short ceremonial speech presented him with a signed certificate recording his good conduct. It was a chivalrous and much appreciated gesture, and later, when the signature of Horatio Nelson had become famous, the certificate was framed and exhibited on the wall of a home in Boston.

In his autobiographical sketch for M'Arthur Nelson records his only brush at this time with the real enemy, the French. Off Boston, *Albemarle*

was chased by three line-of-battle ships and a frigate. In these circumstances discretion was obviously the better part of valour. Nelson could
not rely on the speed of his converted merchantman to escape, so he 'had
no chance left, but running them among the shoals of St George's bank'.
Wisely, the large warships did not attempt to follow but left the pursuit
to *Iris*, the frigate. By sunset the two ships were within gunshot and the
three men-of-war far out of sight. The chase had lasted for 'between nine
or ten hours' and, the odds being equal, Nelson determined now to bring
it to an end, one way or the other. He ordered sail to be shortened and
Albemarle hove to in preparation for action; at this unexpected show of
defiance the captain of *Iris* lost his nerve, tacked his ship and retreated to
the safe company of his powerful consorts.

In September Nelson was forced to set sail for Quebec by one of the
current hazards of a sailor's life—scurvy. The causes of the malady which
not only affected health in the familiar ways—spongy gums, loose teeth
and muscle pains—but also induced unnatural fatigue and, with the
physical deterioration consequent upon deprivation of Vitamin C, mental
depression, were beginning to be understood by Nelson's day. Captain
Cook was a pioneer in the use of anti-scorbutics, and Nelson himself was
generally punctilious in the matter of providing his crew with fresh
food, particularly fruit and vegetables. However, *Albemarle*'s company
had eaten its last fresh meal at Portsmouth in April, and for two months
had subsisted on the standard, dreary and unhealthy diet of stale ship's
biscuit, rancid water and elderly salt beef. This was the only recorded
incident when Nelson, or those under his command, so suffered, and on
this occasion, luckily, the burden upon the men of the *Albemarle* was
lightened as a result of the reappearance of Nathaniel Carver, who drew
alongside the frigate with a gift which in wartime was technically
treasonable. The four sheep, the crates of chickens and the large quantity
of fresh green vegetables were, after decorous argument, paid for, but
honours were now even.

Albemarle finally anchored off Quebec, but with some of her company
destined for hospital ashore Nelson and his officers were given a month
in which to enjoy Canadian society. Much improved in health himself—
there are references to 'Fair Canada' and its autumn climate, and 'Health,
the greatest of blessings', in his letters—the twenty-four-year-old captain
of *Albemarle* lost no time in plunging into the social scene. It was an
opportunity, long denied, for Nelson to mix with company which was
neither that of his own family circle in Norfolk, nor exclusively naval.

It was the season of dances, entertainments and parties. One of the principal hosts, always ready to welcome visiting naval officers, was Alexander Davison, a rich bachelor of thirty-three, who derived a considerable income from his involvement in the Canadian shipping trade. But Davison was no mere money-maker, he was a man of culture, also anxious to make his way in politics. Despite nearly ten years' difference in their ages, he and Nelson almost immediately struck up a friendship, which was to last the lifetime of the younger man.

Perhaps it is not surprising that in this heady atmosphere Nelson, deprived of female company for so long, fell in love. His choice, to whom he became violently attached, was a sixteen-year-old beauty, Mary Simpson, the daughter of the Provost Marshal of the garrison, already the toast of Quebec, and perhaps rather spoilt in consequence. It was, like so many first loves, a hopeless passion, for the young lady seems not to have returned Nelson's regard. Nevertheless, with an impulsiveness in such matters which was to show itself again in later years, the young officer was prepared to sacrifice a now promising career for love, even to the extent of returning to Quebec from *Albemarle* when she was already down river preparing to escort troop transports on the way to New York. The Fleet Order which had arrived in October interrupted what, at least to Nelson, had seemed a romantic idyll. It seems very doubtful indeed whether a proposal to Miss Simpson would have been accepted by her or her father, but the matter was never put to the test. On his unofficial return Nelson met Davison by chance and the experienced, worldly-wise friend persuaded the ardent naval captain to accept the path of duty.

By November 11 *Albemarle* was anchored off Sandy Hook lighthouse south of Manhattan Island. New York, and its English society, was not much to Nelson's taste, but in the harbour lay twelve men of war which soon put Quebec and the beautiful Miss Simpson out of his mind. The squadron was under the command of Vice-Admiral Lord Hood who had most recently, on April 12 of that year, been in action as second-in-command to Lord Rodney at the Battle of the Saints off Dominica. Later Nelson was to call Hood the greatest sea officer he ever knew, and though it may have been something of a subjective compliment, as Hood in his turn was to hold Nelson in high regard, it was by no means an inappropriate one. For it was Samuel Hood who had begun a new chapter of naval history which was only to be completed by Nelson himself.

Hood was at the time fifty-eight years old, like Nelson the son of a parson, and possessed of a confusing number of naval relations. His younger brother Alexander was also an admiral, and would in time become Lord Bridport. Cousins to these two brothers were another Samuel and Alexander; the latter was killed in action as a captain while his younger brother, Samuel, became a vice-admiral and was created a baronet.

It had been the fate of the Samuel Hood whose flag now flew in *Barfleur*, within sight of *Albemarle*, to serve on two famous occasions under superiors less resolute and enterprising than himself, at the battle of Chesapeake Bay on September 5, 1781, and that of the Saints in the following April. Both battles arose out of French naval intervention in the American war, and both were fought against the same French admiral, the Comte de Grasse. Though the first presaged Cornwallis's surrender at Yorktown and the second saved the West Indies from the French, the development of naval tactics involved in both ultimately outweighed in importance the immediate results of either.

Certainly, unlike Graves and Rodney, his two superiors at Chesapeake Bay and the Saints, Hood did not lack aggressiveness, and this was a quality which appealed to Nelson. And although his tough character and rough manner made him a daunting prospect, Nelson had decided to approach him for an unusual favour. The request was to transfer *Albemarle* and its captain, at present attached to the North American station, to Hood's own command which was destined to return to the West Indies.

The reason was a simple one and stemmed from Nelson's estimate of the chances of war. After Cornwallis's surrender at Yorktown, major naval operations in the North American theatre, now commanded by Admiral Digby, had ceased altogether. It was still active service but of an essentially minor nature, whereas in the West Indies a major French offensive was expected in the next year, most probably an attempted invasion of Jamaica.

So far as his own Commander-in-Chief was concerned, doubtless he was reluctant to part with a frigate and a competent captain, but the argument Digby advanced to Nelson was even more personal. North America was still a good station for prize money, and a junior captain on his own could pick up small enemy ships without the disadvantage of having to share the proceeds with the rest of the fleet, or to give up the lion's share to a commanding admiral. Although no captain could have been more in need of money, as perhaps Digby realised, Nelson was unimpressed. 'Yes, sir,' he replied, 'but the West Indies is the station for honour.'

What arguments Nelson put to Hood are not known, but they obviously told. No doubt such an admiral was likely to be predisposed in favour of a captain who preferred the prospect of action to the hope of financial gain, for the transfer was effected.

CHAPTER FIVE

The End of the American War

NELSON HAD come too late to an unsuccessful war. The American colonists had established themselves as a nation and brought about the surrender of two British armies, at Saratoga and at Yorktown. In Britain the conflict had never been popular, the elder Pitt, among others, had openly criticised it, and a number of senior Navy and Army officers had refused to serve against the Americans. 'We are all in the dark in this part of the world whether it is Peace or War,' wrote Nelson. It was, in fact, peace. Both France and Spain were anxious for an end to hostilities; their joint hopes of a successful exploitation of Britain's difficulties had by no means been realised, and the way was open for negotiations to begin.

Hood's fleet, including *Albemarle*, sailed to the West Indies but only to play a game of hide-and-seek with the French admiral, de Vaudreuil, for no more shots were to be fired in anger. Even so, events in this final phase of a fading war were not unimportant so far as Nelson's own career was concerned.

On one of his visits to *Barfleur*, while he was negotiating his transfer, his captain's gig had been received, as was usual, by the midshipman of the watch. The midshipman remembered the incident and many years later recorded a description of Captain Nelson. Like many of his family the midshipman was a stickler for minute correctness in dress and uniform, and the appearance of 'the merest boy of a captain I ever beheld' captured his attention. 'He had on a full lace uniform, his lank unpowdered hair was tied in a stiff Hessian tail of an extraordinary length; the old fashioned flaps of his waistcoat added to the general quaintness of his figure and produced an appearance which particularly attracted my notice, for I had never seen anything like it before, nor could I imagine who he was, nor what he came about. My doubts were, however, removed when Lord Hood introduced me to him. There was something irresistibly pleasing in his address and conversation, and an

1a Horatio's parents: The Rev. Edmund and Catherine Nelson

1b The Parsonage House, Burnham Thorpe

2a Captain Suckling,
Nelson's uncle

2b Frances, Nelson's wife

3a Nelson in the West Indies, sketched by Collingwood

3b Captain Nelson by Rigaud

4a The Nile: The French flagship exploding

4b The Nile: Anonymous
portrait of Nelson
after the battle

enthusiasm, when speaking on professional subjects, that showed he was no common being.'

The midshipman, full-fleshed, bulldog-jawed and with protuberant blue eyes, was 'no common being' either, and had also been transferred from Digby's fleet to Hood's, no doubt to his own relief as his previous ship had been the fifty-gun *Warwick* commanded by Captain Elphinstone, one day to be Lord Keith, and as stern a Scots disciplinarian as could be imagined. No doubt both Rear-Admiral Digby and Captain Elphinstone were also pleased to see the back of the midshipman, though Hood welcomed him. The young man was something of a problem, but Hood stood high in the favour of his father, who was King George III.

Prince William Henry, later Duke of Clarence and, much later, at the age of sixty-five, King William IV, was the third of George's seven sons, and his profession had been chosen for him by his father. George III had consulted Admiral (then Sir Samuel) Hood, who had been enthusiastic, and though Frederick the Great of Prussia had expressed his admiration for such a choice, on the grounds of patriotic idealism, William's father had probably picked the Navy merely to keep his son within the bounds of a strict discipline. The fact that the plan went awry could no doubt to some extent be blamed on the young man's anomalous position, and also on that genius which Hanoverian kings displayed for alienating their offspring. Nevertheless, William was to prove himself something of a bully, an indefatigable if not always successful amorist, and, though rarely drunk, an energetic and persistent toper. Perhaps his two most redeeming characteristics were his excessive honesty of speech and character, and the enthusiasm he developed for the Royal Navy. If anything, on that subject, he was over-enthusiastic, for in later life in the post of Lord High Admiral, from which he was removed, he was to be described as possessing 'a morbid official activity and a general wildness'.

Certainly, when Nelson first met him, he was no better or worse in character than many an oafish brother officer, and was considerably more efficient in his professional duties. However Nelson was not exactly indifferent to the glamour of princes, and the captain commented on the midshipman when he wrote to Locker: 'He will be, I am certain, an ornament to our service. He is a seaman, which you could hardly suppose. Every other qualification you may expect from him. But he will be a disciplinarian, and a strong one, he says he is determined every person shall serve his time before they shall be provided for, as he is obliged to serve his.' On this point the Prince had an argument. A midshipman in 1779, he had to wait until 1785 for promotion to lieutenant and, as he himself said, and no doubt rightly, 'Had I been the son of an admiral instead of a king I should have been a lieutenant long ago.' However, to extricate him from an amatory entanglement, with no good grace, his father did permit him to become post captain in 1786, but with a peacetime posting to the West Indies where again he was to encounter Nelson and where their acquaintance ripened into friendship.

Nelson's meeting with Prince William Henry is also of interest in that it reveals Hood's opinion of the captain of *Albemarle*. To his distinguished midshipman the Admiral recommended Nelson as one who on 'questions relative to naval tactics, could give him as much information as any officer in the fleet'. So wrote Nelson to Locker, adding, 'My situation in Lord Hood's fleet must be in the highest degree flattering to any young man; he treats me as if I were his son, and will, I am convinced, give me anything I can ask of him.'

Realistically, it must be pointed out that Hood had no direct means of knowing what Captain Nelson knew of naval tactics, and moreover that if by familiarity with naval tactics is meant, among other things, service in a fleet in action, of that Nelson had no experience at all. Indeed, Prince William Henry, who had been engaged in action under Rodney off St Vincent, could well have argued that he knew more than the 'boy captain'. However, it has not been unknown for admirals to boost the achievements and prowess of their subordinates, especially to princes of the blood. Cynically, it can be observed that Captain Suckling and Admiral Hood had been well-known to each other and that Lady Hood's father had been the mayor of the borough which Suckling had represented in Parliament.

Whatever the reason, Hood certainly entertained a high opinion of Nelson, even to the extent of incurring some displeasure from Digby in insisting that he should have the services of *Albemarle* and her captain. The inescapable fact, which can be proved again and again, is that Nelson did possess a special quality which endeared him, despite his many faults, to superiors and subordinates alike. To call it charm would be superficial, although charm was some part of it, but there was also an evident element of courage, enthusiasm and energy which did appeal to and work its magic on adamantine old admirals as well as on simple seamen. Nelson was brimful of his own self-esteem, nevertheless his character and manner inspired confidence and trust. Captain Locker, for instance, was one senior officer who immediately liked Nelson and then became almost a confidant, treasuring the Rigaud portrait which Nelson gave him, firm in the conviction not only of friendship but that his friend would one day become a great man.

Nelson sailed with Hood on November 22, but by June 1783 *Albemarle* was in Portsmouth harbour, her captain in receipt of orders for her paying off. From the actual ship he parted with little regret—'On Monday next I hope to be rid of her'—but the men who had manned her amidst disasters and frustrations were a very different matter. July 3 was Nelson's last day of command. Having gone through the formalities necessary to divest himself of authority on the quarter-deck, he was met with what was by no means a usual request. 'The whole ship's company offered, if I could get a Ship, to enter for her immediately.'

The suggestion must have warmed his heart, but his problem was the same as his sailors', 'getting a ship'; it was now peacetime and officers and men could conveniently be tossed aside. All Nelson could do for his 'people' was to redouble his efforts to obtain their just deserts for former service. Lodged in London for three weeks he argued with unresponsive Admiralty officials. 'My time, ever since I arrived in Town, has been taken up in attempting to get the wages due to my good fellows for various Ships they have served on in the war.'

Nelson himself was to be taken to a levée at St James's Palace, and presented to George III by his former Commander-in-Chief, Lord Hood. The King was gracious and invited Captain Nelson to appear at Windsor to take leave formally of Prince William Henry who was shortly on his way to an improving European tour (disastrous, in the event, the Prince, as was his wont, seeking, and presumably finding, relief at two levels of sexual activity, in whore-houses and impossible romantic entanglements). However, Nelson's mind was still on the plight of his men, in 'The disgust of Seamen to the Navy is all owing to the infernal plan of turning them over from Ship to Ship, so that men cannot be attached to their officers or the officers care tuppence about them.'

Later the same day, still in the full-dress uniform worn for his first appearance at Court, Nelson dined with Alexander Davison, now pursuing his political and financial ambitions on the European side of the Atlantic. The discussion after dinner, though between two friends, was in essence unbalanced. Davison was rich and ambitious. Nelson was ambitious, but, despite his gold-braided uniform and the fact that he had

ended a war in his opinion without a 'speck on his character', he had
also ended it 'without a fortune', and just like the humblest member of
his late ship's company was now in effect unemployed.

With the end of the war and the paying off of *Albemarle*, Nelson, now
twenty-five, for the first time since the age of twelve found himself with
time on his hands. Throughout his service, apart from periods of sickness,
he had taken no lengthy leave of absence. Life in a peacetime Navy, as
Nelson himself admitted, was expensive, especially for the captain who
was expected to keep up some state. Admittedly he was a bachelor, so
had none of the expenses of his married colleagues, but then many of
them, as well as those unmarried, had far more private means than
Nelson, who was dependent upon his pay of £130 a year.

The need of a break from naval routine was obvious. Now that
hostilities had ceased, many Englishmen were visiting the country of
their former enemy, the well-to-do resuming the peacetime pattern of
the traditional Grand Tour. More modestly, Nelson and another naval
captain, James Macnamara (they had been lieutenants together in Sir
Peter Parker's flagship), decided to embark upon a few months' holiday
in France. Both applied to their Lordships of the Admiralty for permission to be out of the country for six months, and they arrived at Calais
on October 23, 1783.

Nelson spoke no French, though once ashore in France he bought a
French grammar and embarked impatiently on the rudiments, but
Macnamara did, and it was therefore the latter who took charge of
the arrangements. The itinerary was Calais, Marquise, Boulogne and
eventually St Omer where they were to settle in lodgings with a French
family and pursue their studies throughout the winter. None of this
worked out according to plan. Perhaps it was all too quiet and leisurely
for one of Nelson's temperament.

The France the two young men passed through provoked some
sentiments in Nelson which may indicate a somewhat advanced perception in a young sea officer. Certainly, perhaps because he was a parson's
son, he was by no means indifferent to the conditions of life of classes
below his own. Nevertheless many of his reactions were typical of the
insular and conventional Englishman abroad.

French postchaises came in for criticism, the postillions were curious
louts, the horses were poor, and the vehicles themselves unsprung. The
roads were 'generally paved, like London streets', but the speed of travel
was very slow indeed. A night's stop at a hotel, so-called, confirmed his

low opinion of the standards of the French in such matters—'a clean pigsty is far preferable'.

More generally, Nelson observed some of the contrasts of pre-Revolutionary France: well-cultivated countryside with 'stately woods, abundant game' but 'amidst such plenty they are poor indeed'. And, even more significantly, 'there are no middling class of people: sixty noblemen's families lived in the town [Montreuil], who owned the vast plain around it, and the rest very poor indeed'.

The company of English fellow travellers was neither sought nor welcome. In Abbeville a gentleman calling himself Lord Kingsland and his companion, a Mr Bullock, had recently decamped leaving a trail of debts behind them. Two fellow sea officers, Captains Alexander Ball and James Shephard, were espied, but kept at a distance. Apart from any other consideration, Nelson did not approve of their appearance, for they had decided to imitate the French officer's style of dress, and were wearing epaulettes with their uniforms, a fashion which did not come into general use in the Royal Navy until considerably later, and was only officially adopted in 1795. The feeling between Ball and Shephard and Nelson and Macnamara was apparently mutual as neither pair called upon the other; however, Ball and Nelson were to meet again in very different circumstances.

Wisely, as he wished to speak French and not English, Nelson in St Omer confined himself to visiting only two English families, the Massingberds and the Andrews, both with naval connections; nevertheless, though French 'came on but slowly', affairs of the heart moved far more rapidly. Soon, Nelson had fallen in love with the eldest Andrews daughter, whose father was a clergyman and whose brother George was a post captain. The lady was, in Nelson's view, 'the most accomplished woman my eyes ever beheld'. 'Had I a million of money,' he wrote to his brother, 'I should at this moment make her an offer of them;' but, unfortunately, 'my income at present is by far too small to think of marriage, and she has no fortune'.

Once again, as during his Canadian romance, Nelson's intentions were strictly honourable, he thought not of the love affair but of marriage, and marriage very much in the eighteenth-century mode. There was very little of passion or even its genteel reflection, romance, about the attachment. Polite accomplishments, good middle-class family and of course a little money were apparently all that he sought. Indeed it all sounds like a matrimonial blueprint for an ambitious naval officer, and in consequence rather cold-blooded for a young man of twenty-five.

Almost equally without emotion was the letter on the subject Mr William Suckling received that January from his 'affectionate and dutiful nephew' asking for help 'in a pecuniary way' to further his suit with Miss Andrews. In fact the lady is not mentioned by name but merely described—'there is a lady I have seen, of a good family and connections, but with a small fortune—£1,000 I understand'. The last fact had presumably been discovered by Nelson since his letter to his brother of three weeks before, and it had no doubt influenced his determination to propose, if his uncle could see his way to allow him £100 per year to supplement his naval pay of £130 until his income was increased by that sum, 'either by employment, or any other way'. If Suckling cannot actually give the money, he is then asked to use his interest, 'with either Lord North or Mr Jenkinson, to get a Guard ship, or some employment in a Public Office where the attendance of the principal is not necessary, and of which they must have numbers to dispose of. In the India Service I understand (if it remains under the Directors) their Marine force is to be under the command of a Captain in the Royal Navy: that is a station I should like.'

In the event, though he was prepared to agree, the uncle did not have to supplement his nephew's income, nor did Horatio Nelson's career take a new and confined course in the employ of the Honourable East India Company. Miss Andrews must have refused her naval suitor, it is quite possible that she did not regard the diminutive, shock-headed captain with his high-pitched nasal voice, Norfolk drawl and awkward manners, as much of a catch—at least, as he told his brother, 'no charming woman will return with me'.

The French excursion indeed was far from a success, even apart from the rejected proposal of marriage, and Nelson returned earlier than he had planned in spite of an unexpected invitation. In the latter days of his service in *Albemarle* in the West Indies he had captured, and released as soon as he learnt their purpose, a party of French savants exploring and charting the islands. One of their number had been more distinguished than his appearance and occupation had perhaps indicated. Describing himself at the time as the Comte de Deux Ponts he was, in fact, Maximilian Joseph, Prince of the Holy Roman Empire, and the French general who had been second-in-command at Cornwallis's surrender at Yorktown. Later, by a number of curious twists, he was to become King of Bavaria. As a return for Nelson's courtesy he now offered him hospitality and entertainment in Paris.

Nelson, however, was determined to leave for England, even without Macnamara who remained in France. He had just been informed of the death of his sister Anne at Bath, apparently as a result of exposing herself to the cold night air straight from a hot ballroom, not normally a danger to a young woman of twenty-five but perhaps another reminder of the inherent physical weakness of many of the Nelson-Sucklings, and a reinforcement of Horatio's own recurrent hypochondria. But it was neither this family tragedy, nor his own personal disappointment over Miss Andrews, nor even a failure to make great progress with the French language, originally the principal object of the whole visit, which was the real cause of Nelson's precipitate return. To two of his correspondents at the time he gave conflicting, and perhaps therefore false, excuses. To Locker, it was 'some little matters in my Accounts'; to his father it was 'to get a little good advice from some of the London Physicians'. In fact his decision was influenced by the imminent General Election. He had no intention of abandoning his naval career, but becoming a Member of Parliament would obviously for an officer add to his own influence and be of considerable advantage to his prospects.

In regarding Parliament merely as a means to his own advancement Nelson was no more cynical than any Englishman of his age, whether Service officer or civilian. The line in the contemporary song about the ambitious Sussex ploughboy who hoped to enter Parliament 'and when I've sold my "Ayes", sir, well then I'll sell my "Noes" ', epitomised the general attitude to the legislature, especially in 1784 when even the lines of demarcation between the political parties, Whig and Tory, were more than usually blurred. In addition Nelson possessed an attitude to politicians not uncommon in many successful Service officers: an outward show of rugged contempt for what is regarded as their scheming ways, allied with a total willingness to play exactly the same game themselves.

The General Election of 1784 turned out to be a landslide for the young William Pitt, but to see it in terms of a modern victory for a party or its principles would be totally inappropriate.

Back in March 1782 Lord North had resigned and with him went, at least on the surface, the party of the 'King's Friends', and George III's attempts at direct rule, although the defeat of monarchical influence was by no means complete. North was succeeded by Rockingham with Charles James Fox as Foreign Secretary. Unexpectedly in July Rockingham

died, to be succeeded by Lord Shelburne with whom Fox disagreed
and whom he mistrusted. Soon Fox resigned, just before the peace
preliminaries between Britain and France began at Versailles. A newcomer to Shelburne's administration as Chancellor of the Exchequer,
was the young William Pitt, who had only been in the House of
Commons since January 1781.

The conventional party labels seem even at this stage to have had little
or no significance as Shelburne and Fox were both Whigs and Pitt was
a Tory. However in February 1783 when Fox and North, hitherto
bitter opponents, came together to defeat Shelburne, even eighteenth-
century eyebrows were raised. By April Fox and North were both
Secretaries of State in the Ministry presided over by the Duke of Portland.
Together North, George III's confidant and toady for many years, and
Fox, the King's most bitter critic, with Portland as a mere figurehead,
concluded the definitive peace treaties, thus completing the work begun
by Shelburne.

The next shake of the political kaleidoscope began with Fox's attempt
to reform one vast section of the Government establishment, the East
India Company, both administratively and financially. Fox was sincere
in his attempt and his India Bill passed the Commons only to be defeated
in the Lords to the delight of the King, who the next day abruptly
dismissed both Fox and North. On December 19, 1783, at the age of
twenty-four, Pitt became Prime Minister and Chancellor of the
Exchequer, the only commoner in his own Cabinet.

Once in power Pitt, and the King, had at their disposal all Government
patronage, and that of the unreformed East India Company as well.
Thus armed, they were ready to face a general election, and on March 8,
1784 dissolved Parliament. This election, in which all the forces of
bribery, influence and corruption were brought to bear on the hundred
Parliamentary seats where there was a contest—in the other four-fifths
of the Commons seats, 'pocket' and 'rotten' boroughs mostly, the
members were returned unopposed—was the battleground on which
Horatio Nelson wished to engage.

Some historians have seen the 1784 election result as an expression of
public abhorrence for the cynical Fox-North coalition, but this was not
so, since the public hardly signified. Much more influence was wielded
by men such as Charles Jenkinson, later Lord Liverpool, formerly parliamentary manager of the King's Friends, but now working against Fox
and North. It was Jenkinson from whom Nelson hoped to obtain a post.

If Nelson had any preference it was for Mr Pitt against Mr Fox, the former seeming more patriotic and anti-French. This would have been the natural choice for a man of his outlook and sentiments, but it must be observed that Nelson had presumably already tried the Walpole and Whig connection, and found it ineffective. Writing to his brother William who was hoping for preferment in the Church from the same source, he said, 'As to your having enlisted under the banners of the Walpoles, you might as well have enlisted under those of my grand-mother. They are altogether the merest set of cypers that ever existed—in Public affairs I mean.'

By the date of this letter, January 31, 1784, Nelson had obviously realised that he was not to obtain, like his friend Captain Kingsmill who was soon to be the Member for Tregony, 'a Land Frigate'. 'I have done with politics; let who will get in, I shall be left out.'

It was not really Nelson's type of fight; however, his few weeks of dining and intriguing in London did produce a tangible and beneficial result. Lord Hood, who possessed considerable influence through his connections with the Grenvilles, the Lytteltons and finally the Pitt family itself, had been, not unnaturally, more successful in his search for a land frigate than his junior. It was not an easy capture, however, it had to be fought for; the Admiral was standing in Westminster, one of the few freehold franchises, and his principal opponent was the redoubtable Fox himself. Nelson expressed a hope that 'we shall unkennel Fox in Westminster', but it was no easy task. Sailors from the fleet as well as some of the King's Guardsmen were drafted in to help the Admiral and they fought pitched battles with the London sedan chairmen who sup-ported Fox. The Duchess of Devonshire traded kisses with shopkeepers for pro-Fox votes. In the end both Fox and Hood were returned, as Westminster sent two Members to Parliament, and together, though in different interests, they topped the poll.

What assistance Horatio rendered in all this is not clear; he wrote of 'canvassing but not openly' in Westminster, but he was about and presumably helpful. No doubt he obtained his reward as a result—the twenty-eight-gun frigate Boreas on March 18. His brother William wrote to him, commenting with surprise upon his good luck, and received a rather terse reply: 'You ask by what interest did I get a Ship? I answer, having served with credit was my recommendation to Lord Howe, First Lord of the Admiralty. Anything in reason that I can ask, I am sure of obtaining from his justice.'

True, there was no reason why Nelson should not have been given command of another frigate, but his over-simple reply glosses over the details of the process he had indulged in, that of putting himself in the way of men of influence. What use Nelson would have made of a seat in Parliament it is difficult to say, no doubt his vote, much more imporant than any speech he might have made, would have been at the disposal of the Hood and Pitt interest, but it is doubtful whether that extra leverage would have produced any further professional advancement at this stage. There would, however, come a time when it might have been of considerable advantage to him to be able to show himself as a loyal and useful member of a political grouping.

CHAPTER SIX

Marriage in the West Indies

THOUGH BOTH the desirable Miss Andrews and a seat in Parliament had escaped him, Nelson had every reason to be thankful for small mercies. By March 18, 1784 he knew of his appointment to *Boreas*, then lying at the Nore. There were, however, many irritations and difficulties to be suffered upon his assuming command of the frigate and he could have been forgiven for thinking that the omens were against him. If he had possessed the gift of second sight he would probably never have 'read himself in' on the quarter-deck of *Boreas* at all.

As soon as the new captain had taken over there was a minor disaster when the pilot, bringing the ship round from the Nore to Portsmouth Harbour, ran her aground, to the fury of Nelson who had nothing else to do but wait impatiently while his crew actually walked round the ship, splashing through the shallow water. High water eventually took *Boreas* off and, after a brush with the captain of a Dutch Indiaman who was trying to detain sixteen English members of his crew, the frigate sailed towards Portsmouth where she remained for some time, taking on an assorted cargo.

Nelson himself described his ship as being 'pretty well filled with lumber'. The lumber was human and consisted, in order of importance, of Lady Hughes, the wife of Sir Richard Hughes, the not very distinguished admiral who had already taken up his command in the Leeward Islands, and described by Nelson as an 'eternal clack'; her daughter Rose Mary, very marriageable though plain, and ripe for a ship-borne romance; and no less than twenty midshipmen, plus the captain's brother, William, making his first, and indeed last, essay at being a ship's chaplain.

So far as the supercargo of midshipmen was concerned Nelson only had himself to blame, for their numbers were within his discretion and choice. Perhaps his generosity had been overstrained—'everybody is asking me to take some one or another'—and he now regretted it. One was the younger brother of Miss Andrews of St Omer; Sir Richard Hughes's son Richard was also there, and a distant Suckling relative. Two of the 'young gentlemen' were destined in time to become admirals.

Perhaps in order to escape a crowded ship and as some relief from his overall depression at being assigned to the Leeward Islands when he had hoped to be attached to the East India station, Nelson, forsaking the uninspiring Miss Hughes, took another young lady out for a riding expedition. That too ended in calamity; Nelson's horse bolted on Portsmouth Common and, to save himself, he threw himself out of the saddle. The young lady's horse also ran away with her, but she was rescued by a 'gallant young man', presumably more experienced than sailors in such matters.

The West Indies, whither *Boreas* was bound, might be thought to have been a pleasant enough station in peacetime; indeed in many respects a desirable one, for the average sea officer. However, Nelson was not average, and partly by chance, partly because of his own character, nothing seemed to come his way there except trouble. Obviously West Indies society, rich and over-addicted to the easy life founded upon a colonial social system supported by black slavery, did not appeal to a young man of Nelson's temperament.

With his ship and his subordinates he was by contrast the happy man enjoying his chosen profession. Posterity is at least indebted to Lady Hughes in one respect, for she was a witness to his approach to the tasks of command. Soon after Trafalgar she sent to his brother-in-law George Macham, Kate Nelson's husband, her recollections of Captain Nelson in those days. The pen sketches are vivid and, it should be remembered, were written by an admiral's wife who in her day must have seen many varieties of sea officer and captain. Few of them, one imagines, as Nelson did, called his midshipmen, not so very many years his junior, his 'children'.

'Among the number,' wrote Lady Hughes, 'it may reasonably be supposed that there must be timid as well as bold; the timid he never rebuked, but always wished to show them he desired nothing of them that he would not instantly do himself: and I have known him say, "Well, Sir, I am going on a race to the mast-head, and beg I may meet you there." No denial could be given to such a wish, and the poor fellow instantly began his march. His Lordship never took the least notice with what alacrity it was done, but when they met at the top, began instantly speaking in the most cheerful manner, and saying how much a person was to be pitied who could fancy there was any danger, or even anything disagreeable, in the attempt.'

Lady Hughes went on to describe the way in which Nelson's example in the art of leadership was followed, as no doubt it was meant to be, down through the ship's hierarchy, the young midshipmen imitating their captain. The 'young gentlemen' aboard *Boreas* must have been flattered by the attention the captain paid to their nautical studies, but there was more to it than just pleasant relations. As Lady Hughes said, 'No one there could be behind-hand in their business when their Captain set them so good an example.'

Nelson himself was not always at ease in company, nor did he particularly relish the social round of colonial society. However, he did not in consequence forget those under his command. When Lady Hughes and Captain Nelson were landed at Barbados to dine with the Governor she was somewhat surprised to find that Nelson had brought with him one of his midshipmen, who was duly presented to the Governor with the explanation, 'Your Excellency must excuse me for bringing one of my midshipmen, as I make it a rule to introduce them to all the good company I can, as they have few to look up to besides myself during the time they are at sea.' Lady Hughes concluded by saying, 'I hope my simple narration may, in a faint degree, describe his Lordship's excellent manner of making his young men fancy that attaining nautical perfection was much more of a play than a task.'

The letter revealed considerable magnanimity on Lady Hughes' part, for she must also have remembered that there had been times when her husband must have wished most heartily to be without Captain Nelson's devotion to 'nautical perfection'.

One of these causes of friction was the application of the Navigation Acts to the lax ways of West Indian commercial life. Hardly a matter to concern a frigate captain, considered Admiral Hughes, but unfortunately Horatio Nelson thought differently. The basic purpose of the Acts was to preserve and maintain a monopoly in goods, and the carrying of them, between Britain and her overseas colonies. Both Britain and her colonies of course benefited, but a difficulty arose in the West Indies as a result of American independence. Many tradesmen, merchants, ships' captains and crews, formerly British subjects, were now United States citizens and therefore debarred from participating in trade with formerly profitable markets. Even before the war the Navigation Acts had always been difficult to enforce to the letter, strict enforcement of the law bowing to commercial advantage. When Nelson arrived in the West Indies he soon discovered that, despite the change in nationalities, trade continued much as before and breaches in the law were winked at by everyone from Governors and Council downwards, and in particular by his Commander-in-Chief, Admiral Sir Richard Hughes.

It was not Nelson's way: an Englishman was an Englishman, and an ex-enemy tended to be regarded as an enemy still. Duty was his watch-word, and commercial gain was as nothing. The lawyer's maxim, 'fiat justitia, ruat coelum', summarised his viewpoint; however, junior captains were not encouraged to be lawyers and for some time it looked as if the heavens would fall upon the head of Horatio Nelson. He recorded his attitude in his 'Sketch of My Life'. 'Our Governors and Custom house Officers pretended that by the Navigation Act they [the former American colonists] had a right to trade; and all the West Indians wished was what was so much for their interest. . . . Having given Governors, Custom house Officers and Americans notice of what I would do, I seized many of their Vessels, which brought all parties upon me; and I was persecuted from one Island to another, that I could not leave my ship.'

And so it was. It is easy to imagine the situation, the whole easy-going and profit-making colonial establishment offended and inconvenienced by the presumptious actions of one interfering young frigate captain. Among his brother officers, too, Nelson received very little support. His old friend Cuthbert Collingwood stood by him, as also did Wilfred, Collingwood's younger brother, but most of the others tended to take the line of least resistance, which was to ignore what was strictly an illegal trade.

In many ways it is easier to understand their behaviour than to agree completely with Nelson. After all, did it really matter all that much? Mercantilist theories of trade are now long since out of fashion, so it is perhaps easier still for the modern mind to think that Nelson was being pedantically officious. He said that 'conscious rectitude bore me through', and moralising too is outmoded.

However, it is impossible to deny that his virtually solitary stand, in the face of disapproval and social ostracism, did take considerable courage, or obstinacy, neither of which were ever lacking in his character. His actions were also influenced by his own very simple brand of patriotism. 'The residents of these Islands', he wrote, 'are American by connexion and interest and are inimical to Great Britain. They are as great rebels as ever were in America, had they the power to show it.'

Nelson was determined that they should not have that power, for he feared that in the event of another French war the Americans would take over the 'Loyal' islands and so deprive Britain of a further piece of her empire. His own attitude was, he maintained, the only one 'true to the interests of Great Britain'. Admiral Hughes, however, disagreed with his subordinate and promptly entered into an unholy alliance with General Shirley, Governor of the Leeward Islands, to resist what they both regarded as Nelson's unnecessary and unmannerly activity and, if possible, to get rid of the young man who showed no sort of regard for the wishes or the susceptibilities of his seniors. As General Shirley put it, 'Old respectable officers of high rank, long service and of a certain life are very jealous of being dictated to in their duty by young gentlemen whose service and experience do not entitle them to it.'

If these two elderly gentlemen thought that they could snub the captain of *Boreas* into submission they had mistaken their man. Remarking to Wallis, one of his lieutenants, that he had the honour of being as old as the Prime Minister and thought himself as capable of commanding one of H.M. ships as William Pitt was of governing the State, Nelson fought back.

Confined to his ship by social ostracism and, more seriously, by risk of arrest to answer a lawsuit, brought by the traders of Nevis claiming £40,000 in damages as a result of his seizure of four American ships, Nelson wrote long and detailed letters setting out his case to the authorities at home. True, he gained some support locally, as more officers joined the Collingwoods in considering him right to defend and obey the law, and the judge on Nevis upheld the actual seizure as legal, but his best hope lay in an appeal to higher authority. The President of the Nevis Council, John Herbert, though he had lost money himself, offered to stand bail in the sum of £10,000 for Nelson if he decided to surrender to arrest and a consequent action at law. Fair-minded and generous though this offer was, it was little consolation to a captain who distrusted local lawyers.

So, Nelson's letters home were addressed to his civil servant uncle William Suckling, to the Admiralty, to Lord Sydney, the Secretary of State, and finally, by way of a 'humble memorial', to the King himself. As they took up to three months to arrive, action on shore continued. There were difficult interviews with Governor Shirley and Admiral Hughes; protests from indignant traders and ships' captains aided and abetted by their lawyers; threats from the admiral of suspension from duty and the possibility of court martial for disobeying orders. Perhaps this danger was somewhat remote as Nelson was no doubt correct in sizing up his admiral and 'all about him' as 'great ninnies'. No doubt also the letters the senior captain had dispatched home were mentioned and had their effect. Finally Sir Richard, characteristically, stood back from the whole business; having given two sets of orders by letter, quite contrary to each other, he now neither enforced his own orders nor accepted Nelson's view of his duty. Higher authority would decide as indeed, three months later, it did. If Captain Nelson were to suffer legal action as a result of performing his duty and obeying the laws of England then the Treasury would pay for his defence. At the same time, by the same mails, presumably because governments assume that admirals do give orders to captains, or think it best to assume that they do, came tactful congratulations to Admiral Sir Richard Hughes, and the officers under his command. They were expressed by way of an extract from a letter to Mr Stephens, Secretary of the Admiralty, from Mr Rose, Secretary of the Treasury: 'I am commanded by their Lordships to desire you will acquaint the Lords Commissioners of the Admiralty that my Lords are of Opinion the Commander-in-Chief of the Leeward Islands and Officers under him have shown a very commendable zeal in endeavouring to put a stop to the illicit practices which were carrying on in the Islands, in open violation of the Law, and to the great detriment of the Navigation and Trade of His Majesty's Dominions.'

Neither Sir Richard Hughes nor Captain Horatio Nelson were of a temperament to find such a communication in the least amusing. It was at this time, in the midst of personal stress, that Nelson made a characteristic aside to one of his officers, Lieutenant Wallis, who offered sympathy. 'I hate pity,' he said, 'I shall live to be envied, and to that point I shall always direct my course.'

There was not much room for compromise of any sort in such a mind. Certainly so far as another incident was concerned, which again brought Nelson into conflict with Sir Richard Hughes, the young captain was seen in a somewhat unpleasant light.

When he first arrived in the West Indies in September 1784 and *Boreas* lay in English Harbour, Antigua, he had written to Captain Locker complaining of general boredom. The only bright spot in his life was provided by Mrs Moutray, wife of the Commissioner of the Navy on the island. Somewhat younger than her elderly husband, this lady possessed considerable charm which, within the confines of colonial society, exercised its effect upon a number of susceptible young sea officers. Even the older Collingwood, a fairly dour character even as a young man, went so far as to write romantic poetry to her. Nelson fell more heavily, and for some time nursed a romantic schoolboy passion. It is very doubtful whether it ever overstepped the bounds of eighteenth-century propriety and became overtly sexual on either side. The languors of unfulfilled love were fashionable at the time. Mrs Moutray was 'very, very good' to Horatio, who regarded her as the peak of feminine gentility and one who could very well be a model for his youngest sister Kate.

Perhaps it would have been too much to expect Nelson's affections for Mrs Moutray to extend as well to her husband, the Commissioner. Nevertheless, it was something of a breach of hospitality and kindness for Nelson, in his second brush with Admiral Hughes, to concern himself overmuch with the precise status of the elderly husband of the gracious lady he held in such high esteem. In many ways it was a trivial incident, but it underlined not only contradictory aspects of Nelson's own character, but also picked out skeins in his professional life. It concerned a flag, or to be more precise a commodore's pendant, in modern usage a pennant, in fact a small rectangular flag with two swallowtails. Flags and ensigns on ships-of-war were, and still are, like the colours of a regiment, treated with a reverence almost holy. The admirals' flags, a St George's red cross on a white ground, at the main-mast for a full admiral, at the fore for a vice-admiral, at the mizzen for a rear-admiral, were imbued with something else besides patriotic symbolism, they were the very marks of command. So in the service, a flag, and even a pendant, was no small matter. On sailing into English Harbour, Nelson, the senior captain and second-in-command on the station, espied H.M.S. *Latona* flying a broad pendant, a white swallowtail flag with the cross of St George, the insignia of a commodore. Immediately he sent for Captain Sandys of *Latona* to enquire the reason why. Aboard *Boreas* the following dialogue then took place,

Nelson: Have you any order from Sir Richard Hughes to wear a Broad Pendant?

Sandys: No.

Nelson: For what reason then do you wear it in the presence of a Senior Officer?

Sandys: I hoisted it by order of Commissioner Moutray.

Nelson: Have you seen by what authority Commissioner Moutray was
           empowered to give you orders?
Sandys: No.
Nelson: Sir, you have acted wrong, to obey any man who you do not
           know is authorised to command you.

The crestfallen Sandys then confessed that, as an officer junior to
Nelson, he felt he had been wrong, but as there were older and more
senior officers on the station he had not objected. This was natural
enough, but plainly Sandys, four years junior in rank, but six years older,
and destined to die a superannuated rear-admiral, was no Nelson.

Apparently Commissioner Moutray, by now an officer on half-pay
not on the active list, had received a 'paper' from Sir Richard Hughes
authorising him to act as commodore. When he had been on the active
list he had been more than ten years senior to Nelson, but now he
exercised only a shore appointment, in charge of the dockyard. It is
possible to feel sympathy for Sir Richard and the Commissioner. They
were both elderly men, no doubt hoping at the end of their careers for
a little peace and quiet in the Leeward Isles. The Admiral had suffered
somewhat in his last active command under the redoubtable Howe, and
the Commissioner was not in the best of health. Both, however, were in
that class of what the sailors of the day called 'old lady captains'.

Nelson was to them at first a nuisance and then a troublemaker, very
conscious of his own authority, but paying scant regard to their length
of time in the service. Even when he first arrived on the station he had
disturbed the peaceful relations established with old enemies by complaining that Boreas had not been saluted properly and promptly by the
French on entering Fort Royal Bay, Martinique. Then a visiting or, as
Nelson thought, spying French warship had been sent packing by him,
as if in such matters there was one law for the British and another for
the French.

The affair of Commissioner Moutray's pendant occasioned letters to
My Lords of the Admiralty in Whitehall, and these were closely followed
by a much more voluminous correspondence on the Navigation Acts.
In the Moutray case their Lordships took the view that might be
expected of those in authority. The twenty-six-year-old captain was
right, which fact, though not admitted at the time, was recognised by a
subsequent order regularising the position of commissioners who were
only allowed to outrank sea officers if actually themselves assigned to a

warship. However, in the particular case raised by Captain Nelson, who at least had shown sufficient tact not to order Moutray's pendant to be struck at once by Captain Sandys, the Admiralty was certainly not going to admit that Sir Richard Hughes was wrong. So Nelson was told fairly tersely that the senior captain's proper recourse in such matters was to his own Commander-in-Chief.

In a sense the Admiralty was sidestepping the issue, but by then the officials who served the Board were involved with Captain Nelson's second and more serious dispute with 'those set in authority over him'. For, by reason of the time taken by mail from the West Indies, news of the Navigation Act dispute overlapped settlement of the Moutray affair. And for that reason, too, both matters were, on the Leeward Isles station, in dispute at the same time. It is easy to see, therefore, first why the captain of *Boreas* was in a considerable state of depression, and secondly why in the small world of naval and colonial society he was regarded, in the words of the President of the legislative council of Nevis, as a 'terrible little man'.

Nelson was not really a hard man, intent only on naval duty and indifferent to the feelings of others. Ambitious he certainly was, and contemptuous of others less energetic and less enthusiastically patriotic than himself. Overall perhaps there was a sort of incredible innocence in Nelson's character. A more devious man, intent on his own advancement, would not have gone out of his way to cause trouble with his commanding admiral twice in one year, nor would such a man have taken the risk of stirring up a whole hornet's nest of wealthy, and no doubt influential, civilians on a matter of principle. And, whether right or wrong, Nelson certainly possessed courage and determination. Like a number of other Englishmen of his age who carved out careers in the sphere of arms, Wolfe and Clive among them, he did not sit easily under authority. In fact, he was right, but perhaps more important, when his character is under examination, he was absolutely convinced that he was right, and it is this second attribute that the Fates, which look kindly on heroes, seem particularly to favour. It was now, during this period of undoubted mental strain when all the world seemed against him, that Nelson found some consolation by falling in love, not for the first time, but for the second most important time in his life. When on March 11, 1785 the President of the Council of Nevis, Mr John Richardson Herbert, came down early to breakfast, to discover, to his considerable astonishment, the bête noire of all his business friends, the captain of *Boreas*,

playing with his niece's five-year-old son Josiah, a small part of the
foundation of the affair had just been laid. 'Good God,' observed Mr
Herbert, 'if I did not find that great little man of whom everybody is so
afraid, playing in the next room, under the dining table, with Mrs
Nisbet's child.' Mrs Nisbet was in fact a widow and Mr Herbert's
favourite niece. He himself was a widower and, having had some differences with his own daughter Martha, had almost replaced her in his
affections with Frances after the death of her husband.

Herbert was, according to Nelson, 'very rich and proud' and also, it
appears, something of a domestic tyrant, ruling over a large and hospit-
able household as well as his fifty square miles of prosperous tropical
island. Nelson's visit to Montpelier, the largest house on the island, a
typical eighteenth-century mansion of space, white pillars and porticoes,
was occasioned by the delivery of another niece by frigate. Miss Parry
Herbert was, no doubt, like many of her class and kind, intent, in the
most refined way, on matrimony. No doubt also some part of her
uncle's hospitality was dispensed with the same object in view.

Frances, or Fanny as she was called in the family, was something more
of a fixture. Born in early 1758, and therefore slightly older than Nelson,
her father was William Woolward, who had been Senior Judge of Nevis.
It was there that she had been born; her mother, one of John Herbert's
three sisters, died when Frances was only a small child. When she was
twenty her father fell ill and was attended by Dr Josiah Nisbet, the
second son of another well-known West Indian family also settled on
Nevis. Judge Woolward's illness proved fatal, but four months after his
death Fanny became the bride of Josiah.

Whether the marriage was in the conventional sense happy it is
impossible to tell. It was of short duration and marred by the bride-
groom's illness. Strangely, in a family which had spent three generations
settled in the tropics, and in a man who had medical knowledge,
Dr Nisbet was afflicted by sunstroke. Because of the illness—and certainly
Nelson and perhaps John Herbert, who may well have been the source
of the rumour, believed it to be not sunstroke but some form of brain
disorder—the newly-married Nisbets left the West Indies for Britain.
There, eleven months after the marriage, their son, named Josiah like
his father, was born. For nearly a year and a half after the birth of his son
Dr Josiah lingered on, attended by Fanny, until his death in Salisbury in
1781.

Fanny, a widow with an infant son, both her own parents dead, and in a virtually foreign country, had no one to turn to, save her maternal uncle. John Herbert not ungenerously invited her to return to the background with which she had been familiar throughout most of her life, and she was accordingly installed as the chatelaine of Montpelier.

Compared with other younger unmarried, and of course childless, Herbert nieces no doubt her prospects of marriage, or rather re-marriage, were not over-bright. By eighteenth-century standards she was no longer young, but she was, if no beauty, graceful and with 'an English complexion'. She possessed accomplishments much regarded at the time, music, needlework and a dress sense. No doubt also she was capable of managing a West Indian household aided by a large number of native domestics. Her portrait—and one can but hope it did her less than justice—reveals her as a thinnish woman with grey eyes and what have been called fine features. Perhaps the sad experiences of her first marriage had left their mark, for she does not look a particularly happy or vivacious woman, nor one, it must be admitted, of any obvious sexual attractions.

It would seem likely that Nelson fell for Fanny on the rebound from his hopeless passion for Mrs Moutray; indeed, by way of praise, the new love is compared to the old—'Her manners are Mrs Moutray's' his brother was told in a letter. Inevitably, too—and this is the principal difficulty in assessing Fanny's attractions or lack of them—any knowledge we have of her and any opinion we may form is overshadowed by hindsight—by the fact that subsequent events proved that the woman Nelson married in the West Indies was not to be the love of his life. If Emma Hamilton had never existed perhaps the Nelson–Nisbet marriage would have gone steadily on; yet there is still a lurking suspicion that Nelson's transition to national hero might well have proved too much for it. And that suspicion remains when one tries to answer the question, on the available evidence and as impartially as possible: why in fact did Horatio marry Fanny?

Undoubtedly eighteenth-century match-making played a considerable part. From Nelson's own accounts it was one of the chief occupations of the West Indies, and the navy and army officers who served on the station extended the field. A later generation was to call the hopeful young ladies who took long holidays in Britain's overseas possessions, particularly the Indian Empire where they were 'brought out', and of course chaperoned, by equally hopeful female relations, 'the fishing fleet'. In the West Indies in the eighteenth century a similar process already obtained, though it would have been difficult to say which sex angled and which was caught. Anyhow, Nelson's letters home, and to his fiancée when they were separated, are full of the romances and the likely engagements between Captain Such-and-Such and Miss This-or-That.

Already, before he had actually met Fanny Nisbet, Nelson must have been marked down as a likely prey. A letter from yet another Herbert niece gave Fanny a somewhat forbidding but extensive pen portrait.

> We have at last seen the Captain of the *Boreas* of whom so much has been said. . . . He came up, just before dinner, much heated, and was very silent, yet seemed according to the old adage, to think the more. He declined drinking any wine, but after dinner, when the President as usual gave the following toasts, 'the King', 'the Queen and Royal Family', and 'Lord Hood', this strange man regularly filled his glass and observed that those were always bumper toasts with him; which having drunk, he uniformly passed the bottle, and relapsed into his former taciturnity. . . . It was impossible, during this visit, for any of us to make out his real character; there was such a reserve and sterness in his behaviour, with occasional sallies, though very transient, of a superior mind. Being placed by him, I endeavoured to arouse his attention by showing him all the civilities in my power; but I drew out little more than 'Yes' and 'No' . . . If you, Fanny, had been there, we think you would have made something of him, for you have been in the habit of attending to these odd sort of people.

In one important respect, apart from her previous marriage, Fanny had a very considerable disadvantage. Not all potential bridegrooms welcome the task of taking under their wing a five-year-old stepson. To Nelson this was seemingly no sort of barrier. He was always fond of children and, when at last he had a daughter of his own, he doted ridiculously on her. In fact Josiah was to prove a disappointment to an undoubtedly affectionate stepfather, and Fanny was to mother no more children, a further disappointment for Horatio.

On the question of Nelson's marriage from its inception, there is one witness and a vital one, Nelson himself, who confided his thoughts to friends, relations and to his future bride. As on a previous occasion when matrimony seemed a possibility, Nelson's first letter was to his maternal uncle, William Suckling; and, as he was again asking for financial help, a great part of the letter was concerned with money, his own lack of it, and his future bride's prospects of either inheriting or being allowed it. Perhaps Nelson tended to exaggerate Fanny's prospects and the Herbert wealth. Equally possibly Fanny or her uncle had given both a slight gloss with an obvious motive, and the picture painted had produced the desired result in making the widow and her son just that bit more attractive.

However, Nelson must be judged by his own words. Writing to William Suckling on November 14, 1785 he begins, by way of apology, by suggesting that Suckling will say, 'This Horatio is for ever in love.' However, this time there is a difference. 'My present attachment is of pretty long standing; but I was determined to be fixed before I broke this matter to any person.'

Mrs Nisbet is then introduced, but thereafter Suckling is told that she is twenty-two and that her father and her mother both died when she was only two years old; 'and her personal accomplishments you will suppose I think equal to any person's I ever saw: but, without vanity, her mental accomplishments are superior to most people's of either sex; and we shall come together as two persons most sincerely attached to each other from friendship.' This was perhaps not the most eulogistic description of a fiancée ever written, but one also wonders who had subtracted five years from Fanny's age, and made her an orphan from the age of two— Horatio? Fanny? or was it simply that Nelson never bothered to find out? More attention is paid to the President of Nevis.

> Herbert is very rich and very proud—he has an only daughter, and this niece who he looks on in the same light, if not higher . . . I have told him I am as poor as Job, but he told me he likes me and I am descended from a good family which his pride likes; but he says, 'Nelson, I am proud and I must live like myself, therefore I can't do much in my lifetime; when I die she shall have twenty thousand pounds, and if my daughter dies before me, she shall possess the major part of my property.'

Later, still referring to Fanny's uncle, but at last coming to the real purpose of the letter: 'This is exactly my situation with him; and I know the way to get him to give me most, is not to appear to want it: thus circumstanced, who can I apply to but you?'

Then comes the application: 'I think Herbert will be brought to give her two or three hundred a year during his life; and if you will either give me, I will call it—I think you will do it—either one hundred a year, for a few years, or a thousand pounds, how happy you will make a couple who will pray for you for ever.'

The request made—which, incidentally, Suckling acceded to in part—the remainder of the letter deals with legal enquiries Suckling is making at home on Nelson's behalf relative to his dispute with authority over the interpretation of the Navigation Act. For, even while Nelson on his necessarily occasional visits to Nevis was courting Mrs Nisbet, he was still in the midst of a struggle which, if lost, could result in the termination of his naval career, and make him liable for very heavy damages if his seizure of American vessels should be held illegal.

On March 9, 1786 Nelson again wrote to his uncle, thanking him for his generosity, which was more considerable than his nephew then knew since Suckling himself was also contemplating marriage to a Miss Rumsey, a lady who had been his mistress for some time. Perhaps to reassure his uncle, Nelson also gave more details of Mr Herbert's wealth: 'Many estates in that Island are mortgaged to him. The stock of Negroes upon his estate and cattle are valued at £60,000 sterling: and he sends to England (average for seven years) 500 casks of sugar.' Among those who owed money to Herbert was a Mr Nisbet, Fanny's former brother-in-law, but apparently the Nisbet family finances were in considerable confusion, one of the contributing causes being 'Dr Nisbet dying insane, without a Will, or any Papers which were regular'. However, the letter is really remarkable for the fact that in it Nelson actually says that he loves Fanny—'for with the purest and most tender affection do I love her'. Hardly anywhere else is a similar phrase to be found.

To his clerical brother, safely home in England, but still on the books of *Boreas* as chaplain, and, not untypically, hoping to be paid for this 'book entry', Nelson gives two descriptions of his future sister-in-law. 'The dear object you must like. Her sense, polite manners, and to you I may say beauty, you will much admire, and although at present we may not be a rich couple yet I have not the last doubt but we shall be a happy pair;—the fault must be mine if we are not.' And then in a later letter: 'You will esteem her for yourself when you know her; for she possesses sense far superior to half the people of our acquaintance, and her manners are Mrs Moutray's.'

Meanwhile what of the 'dear object' herself? Whenever possible Nelson took *Boreas* into Nevis to visit her, but often she had to be content with a letter. They were not particularly loving messages, and generally contained a good deal about Nelson's own troubles, which were indeed considerable. 'I am involved in Law,' he wrote on April 17, 1786, 'and although everything will go as I wish it, yet I fear it will keep me this fortnight. I shall wish the Vessels [those seized by him] at the devil and the whole Continent of America to boot.'

It is almost as if Nelson had simply acquired another correspondent to whom he could confide his case against authority, along with his brother, Mr Suckling, Captain Locker and the rest.

Perhaps he kept his more amorous, and one would think more pleasing, sentiments out of his letters and reserved them for their private meetings. Yet he was not a reserved man, and there would come a time, when he was much older and with much greater worries and responsibilities, when he would not hesitate, indeed could not restrain himself, from putting all his love and passion, in the most exaggerated form, on paper. But those letters, written almost daily, would not be addressed to Fanny.

One passage in a letter of August 19 deserves to be quoted as containing a little imagery, reminiscent perhaps of that vouchsafed to the incomparable Mrs Moutray. 'My heart', he begins, 'yearns to you—it is with you; my mind dwells upon nought else but you. Absent from you, I feel no pleasure; it is you, my dearest Fanny, who are everything to me. Without you, I care not for this world; for I have found lately nothing in it but vexation and trouble.' This letter was certainly true, and one is bound to wonder if Fanny, and Josiah who is nearly always mentioned as well, merely represented an ideal of security and tranquillity. 'The cottage,' a metaphor Nelson used all his life, to which he would return as a refuge from the sea.

Two days later the letter is continued with sentiments from 'Your most affectionate Horatio Nelson,' which no doubt cheered Fanny's heart a little more.

'As you begin to know something about Sailors, have you not often heard, that salt water and absence always wash away love? Now, I am such a heretic as not to believe that Faith; for behold, every morning since my arrival, I have had six pails of salt water at daylight poured upon my head, and instead of finding what the Seamen say to be true, I perceive the contrary effect; and if it goes on so contrary to the prescription, you must see me before my fixed time. At first, I bore absence tolerably, but now, it is almost insupportable; and by-and-by I expect it will be quite so. But patience is a virtue; and I must exercise it upon this occasion, whatever it costs my feelings'.

And so back to duty, which one suspects Fanny was beginning to realise always came first. She was finding out something about sailors and though she was engaged to her post captain it must at times have seemed an age before the Navy would allow the time and opportunity for her to marry him.

Before that ceremony could take place it was necessary to introduce one further character on to the West Indian scene, and, as it turned out, yet another source of trial and tribulation to Nelson.

At the beginning of November 1786 an additional ship, the frigate *Pegasus*, arrived on the station under the command of Captain H.R.H. Prince William Henry. Immediately the population of all the islands was in a great flurry of patriotism and snobbery to do honour to Nelson's former midshipman acquaintance. Balls, dinners, receptions abounded, at which every colonial settler hoped to make his bow and his wife and daughters in their best dresses their deepest curtsies. The fair and fat young Prince seemed to possess unconquerable zeal and energy for such functions. Unfortunately for Nelson, who confessed it all a 'fag', it was his duty as Senior Officer to accompany him round the Leeward Islands station, Sir Richard Hughes and his lady having sailed for home on August 1. Perhaps the Admiral, castigated as a time server by Nelson, would have enjoyed the task of conducting a King's son round the islands. More perhaps than other parts of his West Indian service, plagued as he had been by, in his own view, the intractable temperament of his second-in-command. At least Sir Richard and Lady Hughes could congratulate themselves on one aspect of the tour of duty, it had enabled them to get their youngest, unlovely, daughter Mary Rose off their hands, married to Major John Browne of the 67th Regiment in September 1785. However, one almost feels sorry for the old Admiral as he departs, characteristically plagued by gout and not over-pleased to hear of trouble in his son-in-law's regiment due apparently to the latter's hot temper. Nelson's sympathy rested with Browne, and to his brother Edmund who had met the lady on the outward passage, he wrote when the engagement had been announced, 'God help the poor man; has he taken leave of his senses? Oh what a taste. The mother will be in a few years the handsomest of the two.'

Until the arrival of the new admiral, Sir Richard Bickerton, Nelson had not only the task of dancing attendance upon a royal prince, but also of holding under command the same energetic and difficult young man as captain of *Pegasus*.

With the Prince as his first lieutenant on the frigate was Lieutenant Schomberg, presumably from his name, like his captain, of Hanoverian descent. It was Schomberg's duty to act as a sort of naval nanny to his captain. Not an easy task in any event for a man of his experience and certainly not when his charge, who was also his senior officer, had the temperament of a martinet and the manners of a bully. To make matters worse Schomberg himself did not possess the most tractable of temperaments. As Nelson wrote to Fanny, 'Some are born for attendance on great men, I rather think that that is not my particular province.' Nor was it Schomberg's. However, Nelson was an ambitious man, and was therefore unlikely deliberately to run foul of the Prince, but unlike Schomberg he did not have to obey his orders, for the naval hierarchy placed him above the captain of *Pegasus*. When Nelson first went on board he had an inkling of trouble to come. Under his nose a dispute broke out between William Henry and Schomberg as to whether the ship's company should or should not be in their cloth uniform jackets. As Nelson put it in a memorandum, 'The manner in which this was spoke made a much greater impression upon me than all that happened afterwards for I plainly saw all was not right.'

So even in his last year in the West Indies, with his marriage in the offing, Nelson, having survived reasonably successfully various brushes with authority, was well on his way to taking on troubles of another sort. Certainly Fanny in whom he confided, at considerable length and detail, all his problems, was seeing early 'what it is to be married to a sailor'.

Even the timing of her forthcoming marriage became involved with the presence in the Islands of royalty, for as Nelson was very pleased to tell her, William Henry was determined to grace the ceremony with his presence and wished to give away the bride. This was a signal act of favour as up till now His Royal Highness had played his own position both ways; by not accepting invitations to private houses, but at public functions exercising the prerogative of a private individual and only dancing with ladies he found attractive. Needless to say, both ways he gave offence. As he did, this time innocently, by his promise to Nelson. For by specially favouring Nelson he gave the impression to those officers who disliked him, particularly those in *Pegasus*, that the Senior Officer was in his pocket. The two young captains were indeed constantly in each other's company, dining together almost every evening, and it is easy to see how the impression grew that complaints, and there were to be complaints, against the captain of *Pegasus* would not be well received by the captain of *Boreas*.

It is difficult to plumb Nelson's true feelings about Prince William Henry, certainly in all his letters he pays tribute to his abilities as an officer and sailor and this would seem to have been a fair assessment. It is easy to see too how the two young men, of equal rank, could enjoy each other's company. Both, for different reasons, were somewhat contemptuous of plantation society, the Prince, an over-enthusiastic amateur sailor, enjoying discussing naval warfare with the dedicated professional. Undoubtedly too there was an element of self-interest in Nelson's attention, about which he was more than frank to Fanny:

> He [H.R.H.] told me that since he has been under my command he has been happy, and has given me to understand that there is no doubt whenever he may be placed in a higher situation that I shall find him sincere in his friendship. By keeping in his esteem there is no doubt, but I shall have my right in the service if nothing more.

As it transpired, unfortunately for Nelson in the short term, the favour of Prince William Henry was no sort of advantage though there was to come a time when an elderly king would be proud to allude to a youthful friendship with a famous admiral. In this secondary capacity the Prince's views of Nelson and of the impending marriage, confided in letters to Lord Hood, his old commander, are not without interest. For instance, on March 15, 1787: 'Nelson introduced me to his bride. She is a pretty and sensible woman and may have a great deal of money if her uncle Mr Herbert thinks proper. Poor Nelson is over head and ears in love. I frequently laugh at him about it. However seriously, my Lord, he is more in need of a nurse than a wife, I do not really think he can live long.'

Perhaps the last two sentences, though of significance, should not be taken literally. On this and other occasions Nelson obviously needed not exactly nursing but mothering, and no doubt the tiny slight Nelson, with his constant complaints of ill health, appeared excessively delicate and mortal in the eyes of the stolid robust William, whose vigorous appetites were entirely unabated by a tropical climate, and who positively thrived on a daily regime of junketing and late hours without ever neglecting his naval duties.

It was to William's opinion that Nelson referred in his most revealing, and in a way most disappointing, letter to Fanny: 'His Royal Highness often tells me he believes I am married for he says he never saw a lover so easy or say so little of the subject he has regard for. When I tell him I certainly am not, he says then he is sure I must have a great esteem for you and that it is not what is (vulgarly), no, I won't make use of that word, commonly called love. He is right, my love is founded on esteem, the only foundation that can make love last—You can only marry me from a sincere affection therefore I ought to make you a good husband and I hope it will turn out that I shall.'

All very sensible, and perhaps showing a proper respect for Fanny's first marriage, but the writer was still in his twenties and but two months off his wedding day. Perhaps a little of what is even vulgarly called love might not have come amiss.

The ceremony took place on March 11, 1787 at the house of Mr Herbert, Montpelier, and the captain of *Pegasus* was as good as his word, giving the bride away and signing the register with the princely 'William'.

The day after, when the spectacle of blue, white and gold full-dress uniforms and the bride's best Limerick lace had faded, Captain Tom Pringle, with that tact so often observed in the comrades of bridegrooms, said, 'The Navy, Sir, yesterday lost one of its greatest ornaments, by Nelson's marriage. It is a national loss that such an officer should marry; had it not been for that circumstance, I foresaw Nelson would become the greatest man in the Service.' This was not an uncommon sentiment among sea officers, although Pringle, who died a vice-admiral in 1803, lived long enough to see himself proved wrong for a number of reasons.

A month or so after his marriage Nelson sailed *Boreas* eastwards and he and Fanny were to return to what, for him, was home. However, West Indian problems, naval and civil were to precede, overlap and follow his marriage date. It was as if Nelson was never to be allowed to rid himself of the problems he acquired in the Islands, both as subordinate and senior officer.

Presaged by Prince William's complaints about all his officers, the discord between the captain and the first lieutenant of *Pegasus*, already noticed by Nelson, erupted in public on the quarter-deck on January 22. The cause was trifling, as to whether Lieutenant Schomberg and Lieutenant Smollett should have informed Prince William that a boat had been allowed out of the frigate, but the result was that the Prince entered Schomberg in the ship's General Order Book as neglecting his

duty. Both men were stubborn, but William should have made allowance for Schomberg's years and experience and it is significant that none
of the other officers was happy under the Prince's efficient but over-
bearing command.

Schomberg demanded a court martial to clear his name and wrote
formally to Nelson the next day requesting one. This demand resulted in
another scene, again before witnesses, between the Captain and his First
Lieutenant. Prince or no, Nelson would in any event have been in a
dilemma, as there was not the requisite number of senior officers
available in the Leewards to hold a court martial, even if it had been
thought advisable to turn a molehill into a mountain. Nelson's action
was to place Schomberg under arrest, and make it known by General
Order to his command of six ships that other officers who demanded
courts martial for minor offences would be dealt with under the Articles
of War. At first sight this looks like a denial of justice but Nelson was
perfectly right in practice. Trifling disputes between officers could not be
dealt with in this way. If they were, as Nelson pointed out, any criticism
by a superior of a subordinate's conduct could be countered by a
demand for a court martial.

The main difficulty, as Nelson clearly recognized, was the special
position of Prince William and the adverse publicity any official action
which involved him would attract. For Nelson to recognize this did not
brand him as a pliant sycophant, indeed on his first meeting with the
Prince on the station he had made it plain that as William's new commanding officer he was bound by Admiralty orders as to the use of
Pegasus and could not bend them to conform to the Prince's desire for
a cruise round the islands, supported though it was by Commodore
Sawyer, his previous senior officer. It was fairly obvious that whatever course Nelson took he would be wrong and please nobody.
Pegasus was dispatched to Jamaica where Commodore Gardner could,
if he so decided, convene a court martial. Wisely he did not, and,
perhaps making use of his superior authority, somehow smoothed
things over. Prince William declared that he wished the whole matter
had not taken place, and Nelson prepared the way by making a broad
suggestion that the dispute was the result of a misunderstanding.
Lieutenant Schomberg went off to a new appointment, a promotion
to first Lieutenant in Lord Hood's flagship, *Barfleur*. His later career,
rising as he did to be one of the Commissioners of the Navy Board
seems to have been unaffected by his clash with royalty, although

his uncompromising temperament did get him into at least one more difficult situation. However, though the principal actors in this petty drama were now all heartily sick of it, their Lordships of the Admiralty continued to savour it and visited their displeasure on Nelson.

Before he left the Leeward Islands there was one further matter for Nelson's attention. His health was giving him concern and he was anxious to return home with Frances and Josiah so there was no question of his seeking out trouble. It sought him out, although his reputation for fearlessness in the face of authority had encouraged Mr Wilkinson and Mr Higgins on April 13, 1787 to regard him as a proper recipient of their letter, with a copy to Prince William Henry, who, however, was departing from Antigua.

Wilkinson and Higgins were merchants and had until recently been partners of a Mr Whitehead who was also Agent to the Naval Hospital. What they alleged was a far-reaching series of frauds, perpetrated by Whitehead and others, Government officials and agents, against the Customs. Probably not themselves entirely without guilt, they produced accounts, books and papers revealing frauds in the supply of stores and the victualling of the Navy in all the principal islands. Vast sums they maintained had been misappropriated, but as they themselves intended to claim fifteen per cent of all sums recovered, perhaps their calculations were optimistic. Nelson went through the documents and then dutifully wrote home to the authorities: the Prime Minister, the Comptroller of the Navy, the First Lord of the Admiralty, Lord Howe, and a number of others who might be concerned.

It was tedious work, but Nelson industriously carried out what he deemed to be his duty and it was with a considerable sense of relief that he sailed *Boreas* for Spithead in May 1787. Mrs Nelson and her son Josiah followed more comfortably in a West Indiaman, accompanied by her uncle and his daughter.

CHAPTER SEVEN

On the Beach

REACHING PORTSMOUTH in July 1787 Nelson could reasonably have expected *Boreas*, whose state he described as 'rotten', to be paid off. As to his own future, he must have been in two minds. He had just returned from a long and arduous tour of duty in a trying climate and he was but five months married, during which time he had often been separated from Fanny. Yet in Britain there was a whiff of war and therefore the possibility of action for the fleet.

'The Dutch business', he wrote, 'is becoming every day more serious, and I hardly think we can keep from a war.' Obviously the prospect was not an unwelcome one to a twenty-eight-year-old post captain who had never been involved in a fleet action and itched to prove himself in command. He was a King's officer, a professional fighting man and a pugnacious patriot. The fact that he was normally kind, considerate, and certainly not cruel and brutal, a devout practising Christian who carried an image of love in a cottage, was something different again, another aspect of his character. In the same way the man who, while *Boreas* lay at anchor, wrote to Fanny about towels and table delicacies and seemed rather more in need of motherly care than wifely love, presented an image of himself hardly consonant with that of the professional warrior lusting after war.

However, this particular opportunity of seeking his reputation was to be denied to Nelson, for Louis XVI, beset by growing internal troubles in his own kingdom, drew back from meddling in the United Provinces, the Dutch half of the Netherlands, the other part, now Belgium, being then under Austrian rule. In consequence the British need to keep the Channel Fleet in a state of war readiness disappeared. It was soon apparent that *Boreas* would not be needed, her company could be paid off and her captain moved on to the half-pay list.

Horatio Nelson was about to face five years of professional inactivity. Some of his biographers have found the fact that he was without command from 1787 to 1793, not even at sea, totally inexplicable, almost scandalous, in view of his later proven ability. It is quite possible, however, to show a number of reasons, by no means all negligible, why Nelson was not singled out for preferment. Britain was at peace and half-pay was not disgraceful or uncommon, Collingwood and Locker shared the same fate. Nelson was by no means the only sea officer, nor post captain, to go on half-pay in 1787 for it was a year in which captains' commands, men of war, line-of-battle ships and frigates, brigs and sloops, were being put into reserve, in the contemporary phrase 'into ordinary'. The supply of captains exceeded the demand.

The Government under William Pitt was intent on what a later prime minister was to summarize as peace, retrenchment and reform. Reasonably enough, as the country had only recently emerged from one unpopular war which had been lost, and which it was feared had done considerable damage to Britain's economy. That Louis XVI and his ministers had been distracted from the Netherlands by French internal affairs was naturally regarded as a blessing. That France herself seemed in the grip of economic troubles, at least as evidenced by the rather bewildering coming and going of successive Finance Ministers, caused no concern on the English side of the Channel. There were also meetings of a number of bodies with curious titles and ill-defined powers: 'The Notables', gathered together at Versailles, then the 'Parlement' of Paris met in July to be banished to Troyes by the King, only to be recalled in September. This last body demanded that Louis XVI should summon the Estates General. Even the most acute political observer in Britain could be excused for thinking that, though the French were attempting to put their own old-fashioned political house in order, this was of no concern to France's neighbours. Further afield Swedes and Russians were at loggerheads and Russians, Prussians and Austrians were involved in Poland and, also, in conflict with the Ottoman Empire. Britain for once was in a fortunate state of non-involvement.

It is easy to understand why the Lords of the Admiralty could reduce and economise with an easy conscience. Nor is it too difficult to consider how the record of Captain Nelson appeared from the point of view of officialdom.

As soon as *Boreas* had docked in Portsmouth harbour in July, official letters from Mr Philip Stephens, the Secretary to the Admiralty Board, began to descend on Nelson relative to his tenure of command in the Leewards. All contained implied rebukes of one kind or another, most of these concerned with minor matters of Service administration. The muster book of Prince William Henry's command, *Pegasus*, was not 'perfect' (i.e. complete), although, as the Admiralty pointed out, that of *Boreas* was. Appointments, which in most cases would have meant promotion and therefore higher rates of pay, by Nelson of officers within his small command of ships, were not confirmed, the Admiralty taking the view that he had not the authority to make them. Nelson's argument that Sir Richard Hughes had left him the appropriate powers was not accepted so, among others, Wallis, who had been the first lieutenant of *Boreas*, had to wait until 1784 before being properly promoted to the rank of commander, the rank Nelson had given him when he placed him in command of the sloop *Rattler* in the place of the deceased Wilfred Collingwood. In the case of William Clarke, a seaman in *Rattler*, whichever way Nelson had turned, in the eyes of the Admiralty he would have been wrong. Sentenced to death by court martial for desertion, Clarke's life was saved by the intercession of Prince William Henry who asked Nelson, who had presided at the court martial, to pardon him. Nelson, thinking he had the power to execute, also thought he could pardon and did so. Worse, thinking a pardoned man was as he put it 'a new man', Nelson released Clarke from the service to civilian life in the West Indies. In fact Nelson had neither the power of death or life; Clarke's sentence should have been suspended until the arrival of a flag officer on the station. So in releasing the seaman Nelson was wrong, if he had hanged him he would also have been wrong, in which case, 'The Law might not have supposed me guilty of murder but my feelings would nearly have been the same.'

Needless to say Mr Stephens did not take the same humanitarian view. His opinion, or rather that of his masters, the Admiralty Board, was that Nelson had on a number of occasions exceeded his authority and should before acting have awaited the approval of Commodore Parker who was on his way from Spithead in *Jupiter*. Nelson, reasonably enough, pointed out that he had no information about Parker at the time, save for an insubstantial rumour that he had left England. In this case, one's sympathy must be with a young captain with a difficult command, armed only with the old Admiralty instructions addressed to his superior which he, no doubt, in a hurry to depart, had countersigned and handed over, 'for the Service can never know what Sir Richard Hughes left me'.

However, Mr Stephens had other causes of complaint, unfortunately revolving round the necessarily catalyctic personality of William Henry. Nelson had sent *Pegasus* to Jamaica with both the Prince and Lieutenant

Schomberg, who then had been suspended from duty for 107 days, on board, in the hope, which was realised, that Commodore Gardner would sort matters out with the least fuss and publicity. However, the next destination of *Pegasus*, according to Admiralty orders, was to have been Halifax, Nova Scotia. Nevertheless, and certainly at the Prince's request, not only did *Pegasus* sail to Jamaica but she took with her *Rattler*, the object being to provide a sufficiency of captains to form a court martial on Schomberg if that could not be avoided. Further, and again to oblige William Henry, Nelson had undertaken to order *Rattler* to then sail for England with a despatch for the King informing him of the result of the trial.

As it turned out, there was no court martial, but Nelson had plainly exceeded his authority. It is easy to see how he came to do it, and once again he had been in a cleft stick: if the Prince had been involved in a court martial and the news of a West Indian scandal had slowly been borne back to his father and the Admiralty, Nelson would hardly have been commended for his obedience to orders. Nevertheless, as Mr Stephens informed the Captain, 'My Lords are not satisfied with the Reasons you have given', it was yet another black mark on the record of a man who seemed to have gone out of his way either to provoke or ignore authority.

For still in the forefront of official memory remained all the trouble over the Navigation Acts, an issue by no means closed by Nelson's sailing home. There were still individuals who wished to sue him for the damage they alleged they had suffered in consequence of his seizure and detention of their ships. Admittedly the Crown had undertaken to support Nelson's defence, but the fact that litigation was hanging over his head did not make him a more attractive candidate for further command. The defiance of his admiral in the matter of the broad pendant, though Commissioner Moutray had died recently in Bath, was again something that did not endear him to authority. Even the last problem, which Nelson called collectively 'the Frauds', probably did not help. Although eventually he was to see Mr Rose of the Treasury and impress him with his own zeal and the gravity and scope of the allegations of fraud and peculation he laid before him, Nelson was acquiring the reputation of being a troublesome officer. He had received rapid promotion, and Admiral Hood had favoured and commended him, but in time of peace when many Service careers were balanced on a knife's edge troublesome officers were likely to be passed over. Further, there was no single act of initiative or valour on active service which could be thrown into the balance in his favour.

Perhaps the most important disadvantage suffered by Nelson, who with the death of Suckling had lost his only direct lever on patronage and interest, was a fall from favour at the highest level which, for part of his five years of half-pay, kept him from preferment. It was rather imprecise, but it would seem that Lord Hood had lost his enthusiasm for the young captain he had first met off North America, and in doing this, only reflected the opinion of George III. The reason for this can undoubtedly be traced to the unfortunate crossing of careers between Nelson and William Henry.

The Prince's most recent biographer describes the relations between William Henry and his brothers—the Prince of Wales, later Prince Regent and King George IV, and the Dukes of York, Kent and Cumberland—and their father in the following way, 'They waged between themselves and with their parents a warfare savage even by the standards of the House of Hanover'. To this warfare William Henry soon proved himself an apt and enthusiastic recruit, joining the Prince of Wales's camp. Nelson was implicated since he was seen as one of William Henry's principal friends, and a senior officer who had not been very successful in maintaining his own authority within the Service. Of course the imputation was unfair, a Prince of the Blood was not somebody who could be treated like any other officer by another post captain very little his senior. Even the admirals who might criticise Nelson, would not themselves treat His Royal Highness as if he were just the captain of *Pegasus* and it is significant that when he was disciplined it was always with the authority and acquiescence of his father.

Woven into the problem of the presence in a disciplined service of this unruly young man was the fact that, because of the traditional antipathy between Hanoverian fathers and sons, politicans of different parties and factions automatically gravitated towards the rival camps of King and King-to-be.

Nelson in the Westminster election had shown his predilection for the Government party, describing himself later as a Portland Whig, which meant that he was pro-Pitt and anti-Fox, Government rather than Opposition, and therefore, King against Prince of Wales. By his friendship with William Henry, Nelson appeared to move away from his own real position in the political spectrum as that prince was seen to ally himself more and more with his eldest brother.

The manner in which William Henry set himself against his father and his authority could not, by association, have redounded to Nelson's credit. Both Lord Hood, the Commander-in-Chief at Portsmouth and Lord Howe as First Lord of the Admiralty, had occasion to cross swords with William, Hood over Schomberg and Howe over yet another incident where William had harshly treated a subordinate officer.

In the autumn of 1787 *Pegasus* abruptly sailed from Quebec and docked at Plymouth two days after Christmas. It seems that William had been recalled in disgrace, his debts being a probable cause, but in his own words 'these damned women' even more likely. In May 1789, however, Prince William was gazetted Duke of Clarence and his active naval career effectively came to an end, but however tenuously and unfairly, Nelson was now also labelled in his turn as one of William's supporters and friends, which could not have been to his advantage. Seemingly, for he made no reference to it, he himself never suspected this, and continued to correspond fairly regularly with the new Duke of Clarence, occasionally referring to his own predicament, and not very obliquely hinting that his old companion-in-arms might exercise his influence to right it. The fact that anyone favoured by the Duke of Clarence would almost automatically get very short shrift from the Admiralty seems never to have entered Nelson's head. Perhaps far away in Burnham Thorpe, where Nelson and Fanny settled down with his father making only occasional visits to London, the still rather naïve son of an unworldly country cleric failed to realise some of the facts of life of his own profession. Yet Nelson was never indifferent to, nor ignorant of, the exercise of interest nor presumably its opposite, official disfavour. Perhaps the explanation lies in one aspect of his character which he preserved to his dying day—a kind of incredible invincible innocence.

However, for whatever combination of reasons Horatio Nelson, Post Captain, remained unemployed for a period of five years and the question arises how did he spend his days? how did a man of his obvious ambition and active temperament while away the time?

The evidence is thin, inevitably. He wrote few letters and most of these were to members of his own family and relations, concerning petty domestic matters. Letters written outside the family circle were in the main seeking the posts he never received, and though they bear witness to Nelson's desire for employment they tell us nothing of how he bore each successive day, week, month and year of enforced inactivity.

His connection with his command and the sea was finally severed on November 30 when *Boreas* became a receiving ship for pressed men. Nelson's presents of wine and rum collected over three years for friends and relatives were despatched by sea from *Boreas* to various ports, and the end of 1787 and the beginning of 1788 were spent in unsettled travelling and visiting by the newly married couple. Their first Christmas was spent with Fanny's uncle, Mr Herbert, who by then had returned to England and taken up residence in Cavendish Square. Josiah was packed off to boarding school and Horatio and Fanny spent some time in Bath, Fanny not being well, perhaps adversely affected by her first real experience of English winter weather. Bristol was also visited and they took a spring holiday in the May of 1788 in South Devon, where no doubt the climate was more agreeable not only to Fanny but her husband as well, who had grown accustomed to tropical suns.

It was at this time that Nelson conceived one of his more unlikely schemes. Could not Fanny become a Lady-in-Waiting at Court? Presumably Fanny herself was not against the idea. Accordingly a letter was sent off to the Duke of Clarence in the hope that Fanny might, through his influence, be appointed to the Princess Royal's household. What, if anything, William Henry did in this respect is not known, but the thought of the quiet, ladylike Mrs Nelson as the protégée of the lecherous, drunken, disreputable Duke is one that does not linger long in the realms of practicality.

Captain and Mrs Nelson with time on their hands spent some of it visiting Fanny's new relations by marriage. Her impressions and reactions can in some cases only be surmised, but from an objective standpoint these new relations were a curious collection, and any pre-judgment she might have made on grounds of consanguinity with the man she had married would have been hopelessly wide of the mark. Nor did his brothers and sisters provide any clue to Horatio's own character.

First, and out of the Norfolk orbit, came Maurice, probably closest to Horatio. Unmarried and in London, it had always been assumed he was safe and sound in his civil service post. Yet, even while in the Leewards Horatio had heard that there were financial problems, and on returning home he was to find that Maurice was in considerable debt. Generous as always, Horatio attempted to help where he could.

Then there was William, now a rector himself like his father, married to Sarah Yonge, herself of a clerical family, and with a son and daughter. Later events were to cast William in an unfavourable light but it is doubtful if he could ever have been a particularly pleasant man, tactless, humourless and selfish, a poor advertisement for his calling. Susannah the eldest daughter had more to her: married to Thomas Bolton, the merchant, the impression given is of a noisy and numerous household, for there were eventually to be seven small Boltons. Bolton himself was also to fall into financial difficulties and eventually give up trade for farming. There seemed to have been a certain devil-may-care attitude about this couple that was not unattractive although their vulgar side did not appeal to the gentle Fanny.

In a similar way she did not react over-favourably to the Matchams, George, and Horatio's favourite sister Kate. She at least had made a favourable marriage in the financial sense, for they lived in considerable affluence and style. However, with a gathering brood of children (there were eventually to be fifteen all told) George and Kate were constantly on the move, Matcham being endlessly involved in buying and selling properties. The Nelsons were lucky to find them stationary for a time, at Barton Hall, Neatishead, although there can be no doubt that Fanny found this brother-in-law something of a puzzle and rather unsettling.

Perhaps, and it is something of a clue to her own character, she warmed more to what might be classed as the unfortunate of the family, Edmund, one of the two youngest brothers. Both Edmund and Suckling were somewhat mysterious shadowy characters. Edmund had originally been a partner with his Bolton brother-in-law, but was now merely a non-paying guest in his sister's house, having entered into some sort of depression both mental and physical. During his naval brother's period on half-pay he was to return to Burnham Thorpe, steadily declining in mind and body, and eventually dying in 1789. Fanny cared for him in his last months, perhaps not sharing her husband's tougher view that the end was something of a blessing and a relief.

Suckling, the youngest son, was even more of a disappointment, even more of a lame duck than Edmund. With his namesake's legacy he had bought a business as a grocer and draper in North Elmham. Trade was apparently not a Nelson *métier*, for the business failed and Suckling decided to enter the Church. Such a course would be another drain on the slender family finances but there were even more serious problems, such as no great intelligence and an inclination towards low life and the bottle. It was certainly a worry for the old Rector, his father. Horatio never had a great deal of patience with a brother whose problems he regarded as self-inflicted unlike those of the agreeable Maurice or even the downcast Edmund. When Suckling died in 1799, largely of drink, a fully-occupied admiral showed fewer regrets over his passing than for any other of his relations.

It was a considerable collection of human beings for Fanny to take in, almost in a matter of weeks. Some of her impressions have passed down, although unfortunately none of theirs since an opinion or two might have been illuminating, even if, as is the way in families, uncharitable. Perhaps the only substantial clue to Fanny's character is to be found in her excellent relations with Horatio's father. Certainly they were drawn together and bore their minor illnesses in companionship, perhaps a little too resignedly. For the Rector resignation was part and parcel of his calling and his age, for a still not middle-aged wife it was the very poorest equipment for the trials that were to come.

Finally Horatio and Fanny came to rest, for their second winter in England, at the Rectory at Burnham Thorpe. So at the age of thirty, Horatio and his wife made their home with his elderly, widowed father, over a hundred miles from London and a much greater distance from their mode of life when they had first met in a very different society and climate, as eligible naval captain and prosperous planter's niece.

That winter in England was particularly cold, and Norfolk with its flat terrain, swept by biting east winds, produced in Fanny and her husband a succession of aches, pains, chills and that feeling of depression common to generations of imperial Britons returned from warmer climes and superior social circumstances. It was, however, more than banks of Norfolk snow and the prospect of dull leaden skies from the Rectory windows, and the replacement of large numbers of obliging black slaves by a couple of elderly East Anglian servitors, which emphasised their changed situation.

For Fanny, at least, there were diversions, among which was making friends with her newly-met father-in-law and concerning herself with the running of the small household. She herself was a quiet unassuming woman, much to the Rector's relief, who had rather feared a grand West Indian heiress, but minor domestic tasks could hardly have obscured her mind to her husband's discontent.

That autumn and winter of 1788 the principal news at home was of King George's mental derangement and in December Parliament debated a Regency Bill to give appropriate powers to the Prince of Wales. In February of the new year the King recovered, much to the relief of his loyal subjects, especially those who had already had an opportunity of forming a poor opinion of the character of the Heir to the Throne. Across the Channel Louis XVI had agreed to summon the Estates General, to meet in May, but at this stage no British statesmen took the view that what was happening was more than a long overdue shake-up of the Bourbon monarchy. No doubt it was about time that the French had some form of representative government, but that was an internal matter for them and had nothing to do with their neighbours.

Nelson, seeing no prospect of employment at home, looked further afield for action. His old friend William Cornwallis who had commanded *Lion* when Nelson commanded *Hinchinbrooke* and whose brother had surrendered at Yorktown, was now a commodore and was taking a small fleet to India, so Nelson wrote to him in the hope of a ship. Unfortunately, Cornwallis had misunderstood Nelson's situation, thinking him recently married and content ashore. Now alerted, too late, to Nelson's real position, he replied that if more ships were sent out he would certainly be pleased to appoint him, but at the moment all subordinate commands were filled. Sadly, and as no doubt both officers realised, an opportunity had been missed.

There seemed to be no other prospects in sight and in July of 1788 there occurred a change of personalities at the Admiralty which Nelson could not possibly have viewed as being to his advantage. Lord Howe, as First Lord, had embarked on a number of naval reforms aimed principally at sound economy and good administration. One of the difficulties, often encountered in the eighteenth century, was that such aims always met stiff opposition from persons who depended for their livelihood upon poor economy and incompetent administration. Higher up the scale 'interest' could only be maintained by the preservation of sinecures and superfluous offices to which attached financial perquisites, and 'interest' was what made the whole cumbrous machinery of government and administration work. Finally Howe became convinced that the Prime Minister was not giving him his full support, although in fairness to William Pitt it must be admitted that 'Black Dick', described in a contemporary pamphlet as one 'who, upon all occasions, discovers a wonderful attachment to the dictates of his own perverse, impenetrable disposition', could not have been an easy colleague.

In July Howe resigned, to be replaced by the Prime Minister's elder brother, the second Earl of Chatham, by profession a soldier, though not a very successful one, but a great favourite with the King. For whatever reason, the new First Lord did not have a high opinion of the ambitious post captain now kicking his heels in Norfolk and pretending an interest in country pursuits. How strong Chatham's view was it is impossible to say, the most likely explanation is that Nelson's reputation as an adherent of Prince William, and as someone who interfered unnecessarily in administrative matters, had spread through government circles. Nelson somehow learnt of Chatham's opinion of him and the appointment of the new First Lord obviously struck him as a further blow to his prospects.

It was at about this time that, according to a note by Fanny, Horatio considered the possibility of offering his services to the Russian navy. Biographers of Nelson have sometimes clutched hold of this expressed intention, as if it represented an absolute nadir of his depression, and coupled with some words uttered when he gave up command of *Boreas*, that he thought of giving up his commission altogether, to suggest that his period on half-pay drove him near to desperation.

Undoubtedly this was an unhappy period in his life, but it must be stressed that some years on half-pay was a fate which overtook many other sea officers. Further, in 1789 there was no great war with his country's enemies from which Nelson was being excluded by official indifference. That he thought on returning from the Leeward Islands of giving up the service was not unnatural, there can be few naval officers, whether they have reached flag rank or not, who have not at some time thought of pursuing some less arduous and perhaps more financially · rewarding occupation. As for thoughts about the Russian service it is certainly not surprising that he entertained them, more surprising perhaps that he took no practical steps to enquire what prospects there might be in that direction. The most reasonable assumption would be that his newly acquired domestic responsibilities of a wife and stepson restrained him, for in the eighteenth and early nineteenth centuries the profession of arms, whether on land or sea, still retained a certain internationalism, something of a hangover from the days when mercenaries hired themselves out to whichever sovereign was prepared to pay their proper reward. In Nelson's day soldiers were available for hire, and Britain paid subsidies for her allies' armies. Scottish and Irish émigrés were to be found in all European armies. Hardly a warship sailed which did not contain a considerable proportion of foreign nationals, volunteers as well as conscripted former prisoners of war. John Paul Jones, before becoming the scourge of the British, had commanded warships under Catherine the Great and Nelson's contemporary, Sidney Smith, was knighted by the Swedes for service under their flag. Even a young Corsican, then with

the very Italianate name of Napoleone Buono Parte, before choosing
the French army as his profession, had considered both the French
and British navies, the latter on the ground of its generally recognised
superiority.

Therefore, for a British sea officer to consider a Russian command in
their war with the Turks, as an opportunity for experience, pay and
glory, was not so unnatural as it seemed. The only point which can be
conceded is on the grounds of Nelson's intense patriotism. 'The Swedish
Knight', as he contemptuously dubbed Sidney Smith, might take service
in a foreign navy, but it is difficult to imagine Horatio Nelson content
on the quarter-deck of any ship which did not fly the Standard of the
Union. The idea of Russian service faded, and the Nelsons continued their
life of small-scale bucolic adventures and excitements, frustrations and
boredom.

Horatio's mind was far too active and impatient for him to find much
consolation in country sports. He soon became tired of hare-coursing,
complaining of the distances he had to travel and 'a wet coat'. Nelson, a
parson's son, was not born into that social class which considered fox
hunting to be its natural prerogative, nor was Norfolk a notable hunting
county. In any event, Nelson, who in later life confessed himself scared
at the speed of William Beckford's carriage horses, was no horseman.
For one sport, however, Norfolk was, and still is, famous, shooting. Yet
Nelson recorded only one distinction in that he once shot a partridge.
Perhaps the solitary nature of his achievement is accounted for by the
fact that he carried his fowling-piece fully cocked and fired it as soon as
the target was seen, without bringing the stock to his shoulder. Military
officers who a few years later were to nickname Nelson 'the Brigadier',
because of his excessive enthusiasm for land operations, would not have
been greatly surprised by this demonstration of impetuosity. Also out of
character Nelson busied himself with the glebe farm of thirty acres, and
mastered some of the details of small-scale farming. More in character
he made model ships and read Dampier's *Voyages* which he found the
most interesting book he had ever read. Reverting to a childhood
passion he took Fanny on birds'-nesting expeditions.

Meanwhile William Pitt, who had brought about a Commercial
Treaty with France in 1787, pursued his object of restoring the nation's
prosperity after what he himself called 'the shame and affliction' of the
American War. The prime necessity was peace and accordingly British
foreign policy was shaped towards tranquillity and the acquisition of

friends and allies. The prospects when Pitt came to power were unpromising. Europe was divided up into a system of alliances between
absolute and ambitious military monarchies. Austria and Russia combined together looking for territorial gains from Poland and Turkey. A
Bourbon-Habsburg alliance, given expression by the marriage of the
Austrian princess, Marie-Antoinette, to Louis XVI, held France and
Austria together. The two Bourbon rulers of France and Spain were
joined together in the 'Family Compact'. Slightly aloof and distrusted
but feared by her neighbours, both for her unscrupulousness and the
strength of her superbly trained army, was Prussia, Britain's ally at the
time of the Seven Years War.

Pitt feared that Britain's very friendlessness might well provoke action
against her by one or other of these powerful Continental combinations.
Therefore he set out to reduce tension in the area of Anglo-French
relations, challenging the assumption that Britain and France must
always be at each other's throats. The Commercial Treaty was a step
towards Pitt's eventual aim of bringing to an end 'the state of unalterable
enmity'.

Unfortunately, however, 1789 produced a resurgence of one of those
colonial rivalries which had so often been either the cause or the effect
of European wars. In June of that year Spanish warships attacked British
merchant vessels at Nootka Sound, Vancouver, asserting the old Spanish
right to the whole of the western coastline of the Americas up to 60° N.
It was a claim out of the past, from the days of Cook and Perez, now
asserted by the Governor of Mexico, but it meant, inevitably, the consideration of two possibilities by the British Government. The first was
war with Spain and the second, war with France, her ally. Almost at the
same time, for the Estates General had assembled at Versailles, France was
becoming a very unlikely ally indeed, especially on dynastic grounds.
However, that was not a development that Pitt could necessarily have
foreseen, so the navy had to be prepared again for war. Naturally
enough 'the Spanish armament', with its bringing of ships out of
ordinary, the raising of crews and the appointment of officers, brought
hope of employment to a post captain on half-pay in Norfolk. However,
1789 was to pass as the most uneventful year of Nelson's life.

The problem of the British fur traders, they now called themselves the
'King George's Sound Company', a name that had a good patriotic ring
about it, continued off Vancouver Island. A Spanish expedition was
mounted to eject them, but Britain rejected the Spanish claim to the area

by right of prior discovery. There the British traders were, there they had settled, and there they should stay. Spain showed no signs of accepting this argument. The attitude of the other partner to the Family Compact, France, was difficult to evaluate for the pace of internal events had increased alarmingly and foreign policy was not the immediate concern of the Government, if anyone could state accurately month by month, or even week by week, who or what was the Government.

In June the Third Estate, one of the three which formed the Estates General, had declared itself a National Assembly and undertaken to devise a constitution. By the Oath of the Tennis Court the delegates swore not to depart from Versailles until they had carried out this task and a few days later the three Estates became one, the nobility and the clergy joining the bourgeoisie and thus presenting something like a united front against absolute monarchy.

In July the weak and vacillating Louis XVI, not knowing which way to turn, prepared to dismiss the Swiss banker, Necker, his Finance Minister, who even at this late hour had tried to introduce order into the nation's finances. Rumours of Necker's pending dismissal, however, sparked off more rumours, this time, of an imminent royalist coup d'état, and the Paris mob ran wild. On July 14 it stormed and took the Bastille, an ancient fortress little used, and commanded by an elderly governor with a tiny garrison, but to France and many of her neighbours the very symbol of oppressive royal tyranny. The governor and his garrison were butchered needlessly, but in Britain Charles James Fox was able to hail with genuine fervour a rather nasty little incident as 'how much the greatest event it is that ever happened in the world! And how much the best!' In August the National Assembly, which had taken unto itself the powers of an alternative government, adopted the Declaration of the Rights of Man. In October the King and his court were brought to Paris from Versailles by the so-called 'March of Women'; as a result the flow of émigré nobles out of France across her frontiers began in earnest.

As the year drew to a close it was plain that the government of France was not His Most Catholic Majesty, Louis XVI, for the National Assembly had forbidden anyone to accept office under him. In London the English Revolutionary Society congratulated the French Assembly on the falling of the Bastille, as if a peaceful revolution were over. In eastern Europe an Austro-Russian army under the Duke of Coburg had defeated the Turks and those two monarchies were now better able to turn their attention to what was happening in the west where a fellow absolutism seemed on the verge of collapse.

Meanwhile Horatio Nelson at Burnham Thorpe continued his out-wardly tranquil existence on half-pay, although the Nelsons were not actually hard up. A post captain received half-pay on the basis of seniority and the rate (i.e. number of guns and therefore size) of his last command. Accordingly, low down the list on both counts, Nelson drew half-pay as Captain of *Boreas*, of twenty-nine guns and therefore of the sixth rate. However, with that irritating lack of precision in financial affairs so curious in an otherwise orderly century, seniority also applied not only within rates, but right through the list of post captains. So the first hundred post captains in the list received more than the next 150 and only the rest drew the standard and minimum rate. A post captain of a sixth rate received £8 8s per month, plus odd allowances for servants and the like. Half-pay was therefore slightly more than £4 4s a month, with small deductions payable by all sea officers, whether on full or half-pay, towards such charities as Greenwich Hospital and the fund for naval widows and orphans. Therefore Nelson actually received something less than £50 a year, payable in two half-yearly instalments. Although a sum of not quite 3 shillings a day was hardly munificent by any standards, as a corrective and a comparison it should be remembered that an able seaman on full pay received about 10d per day, from which sum there were the usual shipboard deductions. The Norfolk farm labourers that Nelson saw every day among his father's parishioners, though probably living rent-free and with their own brand of 'perks' such as milk and eggs, would have received in actual wages 'not quite twopence a day'.

The Nelsons were however luckier than some half-pay naval families, for in addition to accommodation from the Rector, who moved to a nearby cottage to allow them full use of the Parsonage House, they received extra help from their relatives. Horatio's Suckling uncle still allowed him £100 per year, while Fanny's uncle provided a like amount for her.

Perhaps, however, the best indication of Nelson's own financial situa-tion is provided by his views on what career should be considered for his stepson Josiah. He was opposed to the idea of the Navy on the grounds that it was unsuitable in time of peace for a boy who had little or no private means, with a half-pay captain without interest as a stepfather. Perhaps, parentally, Nelson was erring slightly on the side of caution.

However, at that time, no doubt, he was right. He himself, though without private means, had possessed the valuable influence of the Comptroller of the Navy, but even though he had risen quickly in his uncle's lifetime, where was he now? 'On the beach', along with his old friends Collingwood and Locker and many others, and, though the Prime Minister had asked Parliament for an extra £1 million for the Spanish armament, he was still without any prospect of active employment.

It will be seen that as soon as hostilities began, and Josiah's own finances had improved and his stepfather's interest revived, Nelson changed his mind. Nevertheless all three barriers had to be removed before Josiah could become a midshipman. Nelson showing himself in this respect like all fond parents, a little more careful in the choice of a profession for his stepson than he had been himself. Typical of the man, though, the fact that Josiah's head might be carried off by a cannon ball in his first action did not seem to weigh very heavily as a disadvantage, even if it occurred to him at all. Fanny's feelings on seeing both her husband and her son consigned to active service were naturally somewhat different, and again it is the measure of Nelson that, seemingly, he simply could not appreciate her point of view.

Apart from her frequent aches, pains and minor illnesses, one suspects that Fanny was not unhappy, and her husband continued his correspondence with the Admiralty, with the primary object of obtaining a command but also perhaps for want of anything better to do. One reminder of his seafaring life had turned up in an unwelcome form when two bailiffs, in Nelson's absence, served a writ on Fanny for £20,000, being the estimated and, no doubt inflated, sum of damages claimed in a threatened civil action by his old enemies, the American ship owners. Here at least Nelson was able to obtain Government support and assurance, for after he had put the matter to the authorities Mr Rose of the Treasury gave his guarantee that if an action were brought Nelson's defence would be financed and taken over by his department.

His other letters to members of the Board of Admiralty and other persons thought to have influence were less successful. One of these was his old companion-in-arms, the Duke of Clarence. Undoubtedly Horatio's letters to William Henry were written out of a mixture of friendship and interest, but apparently Nelson never realised that the Prince possessed no influence at all, indeed rather the reverse. Lord Chatham was no friend to the Duke of Clarence, and by involving himself on the side of his brothers in the rather unsavoury squabbling about the Regency, William had forfeited any of his father's regard that he might have possessed. Thus from Nelson's point of view, anxious to gain favour with King and Government, his chosen and hoped-for patron was on the losing side.

In 1790 the Nootka Sound dispute showed no signs of abating and there were alarming rumours of the French being prepared to assist Spain with naval reinforcements. In these circumstances British preparations for war continued, and a number of ships were being brought out of ordinary, prepared for active service again, and commissioned. At a time when 'nearly the whole Service had been called forth', and even his first ship, *Raisonnable*, brought back into the Fleet, Nelson determined upon direct confrontation.

In May Nelson travelled to London to seek an interview with Lord Chatham, First Lord of the Admiralty. Unfortunately he was not the only half-pay officer with the same idea and on May 8 he found the waiting rooms and corridors of the Admiralty building in Whitehall crowded with sea officers of all ages, many, to judge by appearances, with far less prospect of an appointment than himself. It was obvious that there was no chance of seeing Lord Chatham, so Nelson left a note, as if explanation were necessary, stating his errand, and left to see Lord Hood at his private address in Wimpole Street.

Admiral Hood who had always had a reputation for tough economy of speech, the great corvine beak of a nose and the tight, straight line of the mouth indicated the character of the man, had shown favour to Nelson and brought him on in the service. Hood was at home and received the Post Captain but the interview was short. He could not ask the First Lord for a ship for Captain Nelson. Horatio, also a direct man, asked the reason and was told. The King was impressed with an unfavourable opinion of him. Hood was not the man to fabricate, and it is difficult not to conclude that the only reason why the King should be personally involved was the association in his mind between one of his post captains, apparently of a troublesome nature, and his own far more troublesome son. Nelson left the Admiral's house abruptly for Norfolk and resolved not to trouble Lord Hood again. He was obviously the victim of some misunderstanding beyond his fathoming.

Nelson explained it by 'some prejudice at the Admiralty evidently against me, which I can neither guess at nor in the least account for'. Curiously, even at this stage, it never seemed to occur to him that the most likely cause of the King's displeasure was his association with Prince William Henry. Indeed, in describing the incident in a letter to the Duke of Clarence Nelson, presumably out of delicacy, omitted the sentence about the King's unfavourable opinion.

So, without the benefit of Captain Nelson, various naval preparations went forward in furtherance of what might become a conflict with Spain. At the highest level the elderly veteran, Lord Howe, was brought back into service and appointed Commander-in-Chief of a fleet being assembled in the Channel and from senior Admiral of the White was moved to a dignity rare in the eighteenth century, that of Admiral of the Fleet, with the standard of the Union flying at the mainmast of his flagship.

Spain was now concerned with the attitude of France: Could she be relied on to put pressure on Britain, or by a show of solidarity with Spain force Britain to make concessions? This was difficult to tell, as the position of the French Sovereign became even more precarious. In July Louis XVI accepted a constitution and became in fact the servant of the National Assembly.

The Spanish Government finally realised that there was no one in France with the power of decision, certainly not on a major issue of peace or war. Wisely, therefore, the Spaniards backed down and in October yielded to the British demands for reparation for damage inflicted at Nootka Sound and also abandoned their claim to Vancouver Island. Nelson's chances of employment in consequence seemed to recede even further. Although it was the year in which Edmund Burke published his *Reflections on the French Revolution* his apprehension of possible dangers did not penetrate Government circles.

Nelson by now, as he moved into his fourth year of inactivity, must have almost ceased hoping for another sea command. In November there had been another General Election by which Pitt had increased the Government's majority in the House of Commons, but Nelson was unmoved, he had given up hope of acquiring a 'stone frigate' and understandably become disillusioned with politics and politicians.

Perhaps with some thought of influence which might be obtained, he had revived the connection between the Sucklings and the Walpoles and in 1790 a pattern of visits was established whereby the Nelsons annually visited their grand relations at Wolterton. Fanny no doubt enjoyed the experience but Lord and Lady Walpole were a dull couple and the family, as Nelson had previously realised, exercised little influence.

However, in writing to the Duke of Clarence Nelson could not resist mentioning his visit to 'his relative Lord Walpole'. In another letter to the Duke he wrote as much as he felt he could about his prospects, 'My not being appointed to a Ship is so very mortifying, that I cannot find words to express what I feel on the occasion.'

By the spring of 1791, when there was a minor tremor at the Admiralty and a reinforcement in the Mediterranean to counter Russian penetration into the Black Sea at the expense of the defeated Turks, Nelson must almost have given up hope. He had put his case to the First Lord, to Lord Hood and to every naval officer of his acquaintance who might have been able to help. Lord Mulgrave, with whom as a midshipman Nelson had sailed to the Arctic, now a Commissioner for the Affairs of India, had only been able to express his sympathy and even Captain Kingsmill, M.P., for whom Nelson had no great regard, had been approached. His old friend Collingwood was in a similar plight, and replying to a letter from Nelson seemed to doubt if the two of them would 'meet on the sea shore'.

The dullness of Horatio's and Fanny's life in Norfolk can only be contrasted with the pace of affairs abroad, especially in France where internal events were beginning to have their effect on her neighbours. Austria and Prussia announced themselves as being ready to intervene in French affairs. But Pitt, cautious and pacific, determined to remain aloof. It was still possible in Britain to regard events in France with tolerant interest, but certainly not dismay and alarm. After all were the French not treading now the same road as the British had done more than a hundred years before in their own Glorious Revolution?

So it was possible in February 1792 for Pitt, introducing his Budget to the House of Commons, by which, incidentally, he cut taxes and slightly reduced expenditure on the army and navy, to pat himself on the back for his restoration of the nation's finances and say, 'We must not count with certainty on a continuance of our present prosperity during such an interval but unquestionably there never was a time in the history of this country when, from the situation of Europe, we might more reasonably expect fifteen years of peace, than we may at the present moment.' Looking back it is difficult not to judge Pitt's speech as being incredibly complacent. No doubt it contained an element of wishful thinking. Britain had only recently suffered, in the American war, military defeat and the loss of a sizeable and prosperous part of her empire. Yet, against predictions and expectations, she had more than recovered her economic equilibrium. It was only human for Pitt and his colleagues to seek to avoid involvements which might imperil the new and novel peace and prosperity.

However there was another element in the outsider's view of the French Revolution in addition to governmental caution. Fox was by no means the only foreigner to welcome the Revolution. Many others, all over Europe, welcomed the events in France and hailed them as ushering in a new dawn of progress and liberty. The young Wordsworth, aged nineteen, epitomised this reaction later in *The Prelude*,

> Bliss was it in that dawn to be alive,
> And to be young was very heaven.

Coleridge and Southey shared his views and in Europe Hegel, the poets Klopstock and Alfieri, and the educationalist Pestalozzi, were some of the many whose hopes of the advent of a new society were encouraged by the collapse of the Bourbons in France. As yet none among the Revolution's intellectual admirers had any inkling of possible dangers to come. At this time a sixty-seven-year-old philosopher put their view exactly when he said that 'the French are striving for a representative régime' which he thought 'cannot be bellicose'. Immanuel Kant was to die aged eighty with the whole of Europe still at war as the result of French military ambitions.

In the last two months of 1792 the Revolution in France became an event of more than domestic importance. The fervour of the revolutionaries, as personified by Danton, had now become something which they wished to carry to other lands. Perhaps also like many other régimes before and after, the Jacobins, the party which now dominated the Assembly, chose external adventure as a method of making tyranny at home more palatable.

The effect in Britain was to bring a realisation that for all their espousal of the Rights of Man and the watchwords of Liberty, Equality and Fraternity, the new masters of France in their territorial ambitions closely resembled Louis XIV at his most acquisitive.

On November 19 the Convention in Paris, which had assumed power from the National Assembly, offered its assistance to all peoples who wished to overthrow their governments and a few days later French armies occupied Savoy and Nice. Gunboats found their way up the Scheldt, in defiance of the most solemn international treaties, and bombarded Antwerp, and British statesmen realised that France intended

to establish a Dutch as well as a Belgian satellite republic. The Dutch
envoy in London appealed for help to the British Government and Lord
Auckland, the British Ambassador at the Hagué, attempted to mediate
between all the concerned powers, France and Austria and Prussia, being
prepared to concede recognition of a French republic as part of an
agreement.

In 1793—it was the year in which Fanny's uncle John Herbert died
leaving a legacy of £4,000 to Nelson and to Josiah £500 representing,
for a young man, relative independence—few people in Britain could
have doubted that war with France was imminent.

Pitt now recognised that his hopes of peaceful prosperity were about
to be dashed to the ground. Britain could no longer remain neutral and
indifferent to the developments across the Channel. Anti-revolutionary
fervour was strong, but that alone was not enough to rally the nation;
what was lacking was however provided by the French declaration that
all lands occupied by French troops would be compelled to adopt French
institutions. This was the familiar threat, resisted by the British down the
ages, of invasion, foreign conquest, domination and forcible conversion,
and it sounded no more attractive in the mouth of Danton, champion of
the people, than that of Philip of Spain, Louis XIV or Adolf Hitler.

In December the trial of Citizen Capet, formerly Louis XVI, had
begun in Paris and on January 21 the former king went to the guillotine.
The British Ambassador in Paris, Lord Gower, had already been called
home and the French ambassador in London now requested his passport.

However, these niceties were in reality superfluous as Captain Robert
Barlow of H.M. sloop-of-war *Childers* discovered on January 2. He was
reconnoitering off the harbour of Brest on that day, for the Admiralty
wanted an estimate of the French squadron in the roads, as the French
Minister of Marine and others had been talking of an invasion of England.
The shore batteries fired on his ship, Barlow ordered the British colours
run up, whereupon the tricolour was hoisted ashore and the batteries
intensified their fire.

After some difficulty Barlow entered Fowey harbour on January 4
and hastened to London and the Admiralty, bearing with him his report
and also a French cannon ball which had hit his ship, as confirmation.

On January 31 Danton received a standing ovation in the Convention
when he declared, 'Let us fling down to the kings the head of a king as a
gage of battle'. The decree annexing the Austrian Netherlands to France
was carried unanimously and the next day France declared war upon

Britain and Holland. As Pitt said that day in the House of Commons 'unless she [France] is stopped in her career, all Europe must soon learn their ideas of justice—law of nations—models of government—and principles of liberty from the mouth of the French cannon.'

Almost in desperation, as the clouds of war had gathered, Nelson had written to Lord Chatham in October once more asking for a ship, repeating his request five weeks later. He had now waited nearly six years. If the present crisis did not produce active employment he might as well give up the sea for ever and sink into rural obscurity in the company of his tedious relations and a wife who, it must now have been obvious, would not provide him with children.

Surprisingly, Nelson's second letter received a reply. The Secretary to the Admiralty informed Captain Nelson that his letter of December 5 had been read to 'my Lords Commissioner of the Admiralty'. It can only be presumed that all the others had not been so favoured. By January 7, 1793 Nelson knew, from the mouth of Chatham himself, that he was to get a ship. It turned out to be a fourth rate line-of-battle ship.

'Post nubila Phoebus,' he wrote from London to Fanny, stung into schoolboy Latin by his relief and pleasure, 'your son will explain the motto. After clouds come sunshine. The Admiralty so smile upon me that really I am as much surprised as when they frowned. Lord Chatham yesterday made many apologies for not having given me a Ship before this time and said that if I chose to take a 64 to begin with, I should be removed into a Seventy Four.'

On January 26 Nelson knew that the 64 was *Agememnon*, only twelve years old and one of the fastest sailing ships in the fleet, and like every other sea officer he knew of Captain Barlow's taking the round shot fired from the French battery to the Admiralty. In a week's time his country would be at war, he himself was thirty-four years old. No doubt *Agamemnon* was sufficient 'to begin with'.

CHAPTER EIGHT

War with France

FROM FEBRUARY 7, 1793, when Nelson commissioned *Agamemnon*, flying mastless at Chatham, his professional life took on a new momentum, which hardly slackened until the day of his death. Writing to Fanny he achieved an almost valedictory note, 'being united to such a good woman I look back to the happiest period of my life', though he corrected that impression with his next sentence in which he told her to be in no apprehension as to his return. However, she must have fully realised her husband's present eagerness to get to sea, his sense of achievement and fulfilment in gaining a command, and his overall ambitions for the future.

Nelson's new command was a two-decked sixty-four-gun ship of the line. The term itself was an abbreviation for 'fit to stand in the line of battle', and it is necessary to realise what that meant in terms of the Navy 180 years ago. Admittedly there were bigger ships than *Agamemnon*, with more guns, in both the British and foreign navies. She was only a fourth rate; a first rate, like *Victory*, was a three-decker with 100 guns. But apart from variations within her own class, the ship of the line had no rivals. The frigate, though speedier and more manoeuvrable, was no match for her, and, indeed, when battle fleets met in conflict, accompanying frigates were normally withdrawn to the sidelines. Further, there were no hidden dangers for her at sea, no equivalent of the torpedo-firing submarine, bomb-carrying aircraft or the magnetic mine which can so easily mean crippling damage or destruction for the modern capital ship. Therefore the ship of the line was the equal of anything afloat, the superior of most, a sailing fortress which when victualled, armed and watered, was entirely independent of anything save wind and weather.

While *Agamemnon* was being fitted out for sea Nelson had also to cope with the other problem of a naval captain, the provision of a crew to man her. Accordingly, the usual recruiting notices were posted in London and the seaport towns, advertising *Agamemnon*, a fast sailer and therefore likely to pick up prizes, and her captain. Following the custom of the day, Nelson also had posters displayed in Norfolk and East Anglia. As he had expected his name and repute as a sailor and the son of the Rector of Burnham Thorpe had the desired effect in his native county, and a considerable number of men came forward, prepared to serve under him. However, though there would come a time when the name of Nelson would alone be enough to attract volunteers, that time had not yet arrived, so other means had to be employed to provide a full crew.

His old friend Locker, now also back on full pay and promoted to be the Commodore at Sheerness, was happily persuaded to do a little picking and choosing among the motley crowd of humanity that came his way, voluntarily, or scoured from the streets and the taverns, by the press gang. Among the volunteers were a number of lads provided by the Maritime Society, orphans whom the Society cared for as children and then when not much more than children sent to the navy equipped with sea kit and a Bible. Therefore while *Agamemnon* was still being fitted out at Chatham she was joined by the officers, warrant officers, petty officers and seamen who would sail and fight her.

The process of fitting out was carried out by the experienced seamen and the civilians from the dockyard, skilled in their various trades of carpentry, joinery, rigging and sailmaking. As a warship of the period was meant to be as self-sufficient as possible this process took some weeks. One of the most skilled tasks which took some time was the construction of masts and yards, rigging and sails. First the masts were stepped, that is, secured, and adjusted to the correct angle, then the shrouds, the 'standing' rigging which held masts in position, were made up and rattled down. Only then were the sails themselves, controlled by the running rigging, bent to the yards.

At the same time stores and supplies were coming aboard. On March 23 the ship moved down the river for the final stage which made her into a fighting ship. Nelson read the Articles of War, on which discipline depended, to the assembled ship's company, and in the first week of April the guns were hoisted on board and last of all, because of the ever-present danger of fire and explosion in a wooden ship, the powder hoy delivered her cargo to the magazines.

Then *Agamemnon* made her way down river, round to the Nore, and then to the Downs where on April 24 she assumed her first duty, which was convoying merchantmen to Spithead. There the final addition to the ship's company was made when a captain, a lieutenant and thirty-one men of the 69th Foot came on board to take service in lieu of marines. What these redcoats, gaitered, pipeclayed, heavily booted and clumsy, made of life on board ship at this early stage when all was professional bustle can only be surmised. However, the boys from the Maritime Society not excepted, there was another group which probably stared around themselves with equal wonderment, the newly joined 'young gentlemen', destined to be midshipmen.

Nelson had a surfeit of these youngsters, for as soon as his appointment to *Agamemnon* had become public knowledge he had been approached by parents and relations anxious to obtain a post for a son or nephew. Nelson, being kindly and also pleased to employ his newly acquired patronage, had agreed to most applications. So Messrs. Hoste, Weatherhead, Bolton and Suckling joined the ship, the first two being sons of Norfolk clergymen as was the young Bolton who was like Suckling a relation, being a son of Susannah's brother-in-law. The closest relative, though not by blood, was Josiah Nisbet, who having become financially secure under the will of his great-uncle, could now, in his stepfather's view, be allowed to pursue a naval career.

The war which Nelson and *Agamemnon* were sailing to join was to prove unprecedented. His fledgling officers, if they survived, were to be near their forties before it ended. Twenty-two years of nearly continuous warfare were ahead of them, much of it waged against the most skilled practitioner of the military arts in modern times, whose only serious mental deficiency was an inability, or refusal, to comprehend the realities of sea warfare. It was to be a war which would embrace all Europe from Madrid to Moscow, and stretch its influence across whole continents and oceans from the islands of the West Indies to the plains of central India.

Nelson was on one occasion to adjure one of his young midshipmen to 'hate a Frenchman as you do the devil', and though it was the sort of frighteningly simple advice officers are fond of giving to their juniors, he was putting his finger upon what was a verity for nearly a quarter of a century, the fact that there were only two constants in this titanic struggle, France and Great Britain. France, whether directed by a Revolutionary Committee, a Directory, a soldier Consul or a self-crowned Emperor, and Britain, controlled by an essentially civilian aristocratic oligarchy. Both nations were to acquire and lose allies so that Dutchmen, Danes, Italians, Russians, Prussians, Spaniards, Germans and all the races of the Habsburg Holy Roman Empire were to find themselves within one generation fighting now on the side of George III of Great Britain and now in support of the man the British always referred to officially as General Bonaparte.

However, whatever the cross-postings of allies, the two rivals remained separated by twenty-one miles of English Channel, the land empire dependent upon its victorious army and the sea empire dependent upon its undefeated navy. This was for the British, before 1914, 'the Great War', and not for the first or last time their country entered the struggle unprepared in a number of important respects. Most important of these, although one can hardly hold the British statesmen to blame, was for not realising until the last moment that the Revolution was overspilling the French borders, and that the French revolutionaries could positively want war. Even more difficult was it for Britain and her allies to imagine that the armies of the Revolution might be successful. There were many senior Prussian and Austrian officers who thought in those early days, as did Nelson, that the war would be a short one, the superior military power of the Allies being bound to tell very quickly against the ill-organised forces of the Revolution. Professional military opinion totally underestimated the sheer force and enthusiasm of the Revolutionary idea.

So far as Britain's own position was concerned at this early stage of the war it has become an historian's cliché to observe that William Pitt was not the equal of his father as a wartime prime minister. No doubt true, the son was much more at home with economic than strategic matters and the struggle with France failed to arouse either in himself or among members of his Cabinet any previously latent aptitudes for waging war.

Also even during the war's course the whole Cabinet continued to think more in commercial than military terms. There was for instance a tendency to pay too much attention to the protection of the sources of Britain's wealth in the plantations of the West Indies and the territories administered by the East India Company. Perhaps, however, in fairness it should be observed that Pitt's Government was neither the first nor the last to attempt to wage a present war in terms of the last. The realisation of the enemy's power and determination came slowly and was learnt painfully.

Further, Britain's military resources, on her own and discounting any contribution made by allies, were limited. During peacetime the army had been allowed to run down, but luckily for the navy there had been recent crises, 'the Spanish armament', the Nootka Sound dispute, and later the possibility of conflict with Russia in the eastern Mediterranean, occasions on which the service had been brought up to something like war readiness. For this process even Pitt had been prepared to spend money. So at the outbreak of war with Revolutionary France the Royal Navy at least was powerful, well equipped and experienced.

In August 1793 the French Convention, now controlled by the Committee of Public Safety, instituted a levée en masse, in effect conscription of all males between eighteen and twenty-five. By these means the most populous nation in Western Europe added half a million recruits to its army. Though the army had lost many of its Royalist senior officers there were still enough long service officers in the junior ranks and non-commissioned officers who could knock these *sans culottes* sufficiently into shape to carry a musket into battle and to use it and a bayonet when they got there. For lack of time in which to train, the old formal battle formations and drill were abandoned, with, to judge by later results, generally advantageous consequences. Thus in a comparatively short space of time France was able to acquire a considerable military advantage on land over any possible rivals.

Similar considerations did not, and could not, apply to the French Navy. Irrespective of political ideals, ships of war, and more important still, fleets of such ships, can only be manned and manoeuvred by hierarchies, both of the quarter and lower deck. Although an ex-trooper might be able to lead a cavalry charge as well as the noble product of a military academy, a former able seaman could not navigate and manoeuvre a squadron of men of war. The Revolutionary spirit was opposed to hierarchies and élitism, consequently many Royalist officers left the service, fled, or were guillotined. Lower down the scale, the superb corps of maritime gunners was broken up. In addition, the navy was considerably more Royalist than the army or at least less sympathetic to the Revolution, so that at a number of naval bases the fleet was divided in its obedience between its officers on the spot and the Government in Paris.

Consequently the British Navy had over its French rival the double advantage of quality and quantity, which was not, however, employed in the early years to any great purpose. There were a number of reasons, such as the unreliability of allies, why Britain did not succeed militarily in Europe. Further, the struggle between France and Britain alone was very much as Bismarck in the next century was to describe Anglo-German rivalry, a contest between an elephant and a whale. Nevertheless, the combat supremacy of the Royal Navy, which could be demonstrated by any number of its more energetic officers, was not used to the full by its political masters, largely through their ignorance of the capabilities and potentialities of sea power.

The captain of *Agamemnon* was soon to experience the frustrations of ill-conceived action. Nelson was ordered to join Lord Hood's fleet, which was on its way to the Mediterranean. Whatever personal reservations Nelson may have had about another encounter with the man who, but a short time ago, had seemed prepared to dispose of his naval career in the most summary manner, there can be no doubt that he now welcomed service under a famous and vigorous admiral in what promised to be an active theatre.

Before he met the enemy Nelson and other British captains and their officers had an opportunity of taking the measure of their new allies. Since the days of the Armada the Spaniards, or the Dons as they still called them, had never been taken very seriously by the British, either as enemies or friends. There was no doubt that on occasions they built excellent ships and individual Spanish captains were capable of demonstrating the proud courage of their race. But the long twilight of Spanish power in the eighteenth century had taken its toll; the spirit of the conquistadors, the explorers and the navigators had died, and the Spanish navy was no longer regarded by the British as a significant fighting force. Nelson found no reason to dissent from this general view.

At Cadiz the Spaniards graciously played host but Nelson, after inspecting ships and dockyards, was of the opinion that the combined captains' barge crews of the six British men of war could have boarded any of the Spanish first rates and captured them from their whole ships' complement. 'Therefore in vain may the Dons make fine ships, they cannot, however, make men.' The Spaniards also provided entertainment for their guests along time-honoured lines and the British officers were invited to what Nelson called a 'bull feast'. His reaction was typically English for his sympathy was all on the side of the bulls or the injured horses of the picadors. When the time came, he could observe a ship's deck strewn with dead, dying and wounded after an enemy broadside with something like professional indifference, but, 'the dead mangled horses with the entrails tore out, and the bulls covered with blood, were too much'. The fact that Spanish ladies actually enjoyed such spectacles, as he confided to Fanny, shocked him and was quite beyond his comprehension.

Death in the afternoon, at least of that variety, did not catch the

imagination of a Norfolk clergyman's son, and the professional sea
captain was not impressed by the alacrity with which the Spanish navy
was prepared to give up its task of watching for the French to Captain
Elphinstone and his squadron. Later on, Nelson learnt that the Spaniards
regarded sixty days at sea as excessive time in one of their frigates and
ample excuse for putting into Cartagena especially if there were many
sick on board. However, Nelson's reactions were not all prissy insularism
and professional contempt: to Fanny he confided his opinion that
Elphinstone had not responded warmly enough or even very politely, to
Spanish overtures and hospitality. A mistake in the view of *Agamemnon's*
captain, who did realise the importance of buttering-up allies especially
at a time when they were in short supply. However, it soon appeared
that allies might be found among the French themselves. In Paris the
revolutionaries moved from extreme to extreme apparently without
serious opposition, but Paris was not France and in a number of provinces
and towns resentment was building up against the acts and attitudes of
an increasingly unpopular central government. Virtually the whole
province of La Vendée had risen in a counter-revolutionary insurrection
and in Lyons, Marseilles and Toulon there were declarations against the
Paris Government and in favour of a Royalist restoration. Much of the
resistance to the Paris revolutionaries was concentrated in the south and
it was natural that Royalists there should look to the British and the
Spaniards for assistance, and Allied commanders in the Mediterranean
began to consider the possible military advantages which might be
gained from intervention. In the short term the problem for the Allies
was the maintenance of any seaborne invasion or occupation force, and
in the long term there was the much more difficult problem of assessing
the likelihood of permanent political as well as military success.

However, when Toulon, the most important French seaport and naval
arsenal in the Mediterranean, offered itself to Lord Hood it was an offer
that no belligerent could refuse. So much so that Hood committed the
fleet to the operation without even consulting his own Government,
which was informed of his decision after the event.

As soon as the news leaked out that Toulon was having dealings with
the enemy the city was proscribed by the Convention and it was obvious
that a military force would soon be on its way to put down the rebels
both there and in Marseilles. Therefore Hood's pressing need was for
troops to occupy and defend the port, in conjunction with the local
Royalist population which had, under its Commissioners, run up the

white flag of the Bourbons and declared for the young son of Louis XVI —whom they called Louis XVII—still alive and a prisoner in Paris.

Immediately British and Spanish warships entered the inner harbour and sailors and marines were landed in the town. Here was an enterprise after Nelson's own heart, certainly he was enthusiastic about it beyond what the realities of the situation justified, but he and *Agamemnon* had another part to play. More soldiers were needed so Britain approached her Mediterranean allies, the Kingdom of Sardinia and 'the Kingdom of the Two Sicilies', as Naples and Sicily under their Bourbon king were then known.

It is most probable that Hood favoured Nelson for the task of naval plenipotentiary out of regard for the young captain's abilities and character, though he may also have had in mind that his ship was one of the fastest under his command. Nelson had already written to Fanny saying that his commander-in-chief was 'very civil', not a normally noticeable characteristic, and that 'I think we may be good friends again'. Certainly Hood had offered Nelson an exchange into a more powerful ship, a 74, but, typically, Nelson had refused, saying, 'I cannot give up my officers.' So, even before the rest of the fleet had fully occupied Toulon, *Agamemnon* had set sail for Oneglia on the Genoese Riviera and thence for Naples.

On September 11 Horatio was able to write to Fanny in his cabin on board *Agamemnon*, 'now in sight of Mount Vesuvius which shows to us a fine light in Naples Bay, where we are lying to for the night, and hope to anchor early tomorrow'.

It was a fateful moment for Nelson, but so far as his destiny was concerned, there was no choice in the matter, for 'duty is the great business of a sea officer'. The next morning, awaiting him at the Court of Naples was a collection of people who were in various degrees to exercise an enormous influence over the rest of his life. They were, in order of precedence, the King, his Prime Minister, the British Ambassador, and his wife.

Ferdinand IV of the Two Sicilies was forty-two years old, and the third son of Charles III of Spain, who had taken the kingdom into the Spanish orbit. Of his two older brothers the eldest was incurably insane, and the second was now Charles IV of Spain, a simpleton under the thumb of Alvarez Godoy, his favourite and the Queen's lover, soon to be entitled 'Prince of Peace'. The Prime Minister, John Acton, was fifty-seven, and the son of a Shropshire baronet, although he had been born in France, and had served in both the French and the Tuscan navies. He had arrived in Naples, in 1778, to re-organise the navy, and soon became the Queen's favourite (scandal said her lover) and progressed from Minister of Marine to a position as First Minister, the Government in all but name.

Nelson did not on this occasion meet the Queen, Maria Carolina, because she was heavily pregnant. She was forty-one years old and the daughter of Maria Theresa, Empress of Austria, and therefore a sister to Marie Antoinette, the Queen of France. If anyone, other than Sir John Acton, that is, ruled the Kingdom of the Two Sicilies, it was Maria Carolina. Her husband, 'Old Nosey' to the Neapolitan *lazzaroni*, was ugly, vulgar, boisterous and popular. Like so many Bourbons, his overmastering passion and interest was the pursuit and death of any creature that could swim, run or fly. Maria Carolina, on the other hand, was handsome, imperious and regal, and despite a probably false reputation for marital infidelity, was intent to keep the Government of Naples and Sicily free from the dangerous influence of the Revolution, which had already claimed her sister as a victim.

Sir William Hamilton had been in Naples longer than the Queen, having first arrived as envoy when King Ferdinand was only thirteen. He was now sixty-three and was almost as much a part of the scenery as the famous volcano which he had studied and reported on to the Royal Society in London. His paternal and maternal grandfathers were respectively the Duke of Hamilton and the Earl of Abercorn, and as a child he had been the playmate of the future George III. However, he was the younger son of a younger son and had therefore virtually no money and only a little family interest. This had procured for him, after a period as an officer in the 3rd Foot Guards, his diplomatic sinecure, for until the advent of the Revolutionary war, indeed until the eve of Nelson's visit, Naples had been a backwater in which Hamilton and his first wife Catherine had managed to lead a very pleasant existence. She had been married to him for twenty-seven years and on her death had brought him something like £5,000 a year. Apart from his interest in volcanoes the Ambassador, made a Knight of the Bath for his services in 1772, had been able to indulge his interest in the arts. The pictures he had collected included works by Leonardo, Rubens, Rembrandt, Van Dyke and Franz Hals. His residence, the Palazzo Sessa, as well as being filled with vast quantities of bric-à-brac, housed a collection of Greek vases now in the British Museum, and for a time he had been the owner of what posterity was to call the Portland Vase. Sir William was, in fact, an example of that very eighteenth-century product, the informed and cultured dilettante.

Emma, Lady Hamilton, who was twenty-eight, had been married to Sir William for two years, having been his mistress for the previous three. She was the only one of the Neapolitan quintet who had had to achieve her position by any sort of effort or enterprise, though whether that had been entirely praiseworthy was open to question. Her parents had been poor, her father, Henry Lyon, being a blacksmith, and she was born at Neston in the Wirral, Cheshire. Her father died soon after her birth, and she and her mother had gone to live with her grandmother, a Mrs Kidd, near Hawarden. Mrs Kidd made her living as a carrier of goods, and Mrs Lyon cooked and sewed, and as soon as she could, Amy, as she was then called, entered domestic service to be trained as a nursemaid.

How or why mother and daughter had reached London by the time Amy was fourteen is not known, but presumably both had sought and found some sort of employment. Amy filled various posts as an under-nursemaid and lady's maid, and being both extremely attractive and, on her own confession, somewhat 'wild', was first seduced, according more to rumour than evidence, by Captain John Willet-Payne of the Royal Navy.

A combination of beauty, poverty and few moral scruples—mother and daughter sharing the latter—accounted for Amy's next three situations. Doctor James Graham was a quack and towards the end of 1780 was making a considerable amount of money at his 'Temple of Aesculapius', simplified as the Temple of Health, in Royal Terrace, Adelphi, facing the Thames. The Doctor gave lectures, advertised, and sold his cures, among which were the use of mud baths and of his 'Celestial Bed' which included magnets and glass pillars in its construction. As the ailments he specialised in were exclusively sterility, impotence and lack of virility, the presence of a number of good-looking young ladies, in appropriate but scanty costume, in statuesque poses, representing the Goddesses of Health, Beauty and Wisdom, was no doubt, therapeutically, advantageous. Amy Lyon, not quite sixteen, was among these for a short while.

At about this time both Amy and her mother changed their names, for what reasons it would be difficult to fathom. Amy became Emly, and when she learned to spell, Emily, and her surname changed from Lyon to Hart; her mother tried Doggin or Duggan but finally emerged, rather grandly, as Mrs Cadogan, without apparently bothering to marry a Mr Cadogan.

It was from Dr Graham's Temple of Health that Emily was persuaded to take up residence at Up Park in Sussex by its owner, Sir Harry Featherstonhaugh. There she was installed as mistress to Sir Harry, who was twenty-seven years old and devoting his considerable fortune to the leadership of a group of similarly privileged young men, hell-bent on the pursuit of fairly basic and boisterous pleasures. It was at Up Park that Emily was reputed to dance naked on the table for the delectation of house guests. Whether true or false such entertainment fits exactly the character of the host and the *milieu*.

Emily's stay at Up Park was brought to an abrupt end by what one might regard as an occupational hazard; she became pregnant. Either Sir Harry was particularly heartless or else, which seems quite likely, he was not the father of 'little Emma'. Anyhow, the mother-to-be returned to Hawarden from where she appealed for help to another admirer, Charles Greville, the third son of the Earl of Warwick. As a result, by 1782 Greville, who had made financial arrangements so that little Emma could be cared for by Mrs Kidd, acquired in return a young and beautiful mistress and her mother as housekeeper for his home in Edgware Row, Paddington Green.

Greville had some money, but was not rich. He was a Member of Parliament and, like his uncle Sir William Hamilton, an undiscriminating collector of objets d'art from the valuable to the nearly valueless. It was lucky, however, for posterity that Greville moved on the fringe of the world of artists and sculptors, for it was he who introduced his young mistress to George Romney. Thus Emma Hart, in her own right, earned her first footnote in history. Romney, probably half in love with her himself, painted over twenty portraits of the girl whom he called 'the divine lady', 'superior to all womankind'. The early paintings featured Emma, undoubtedly the painter's favourite model, as a number of classical characters, Ariadne, Calypso, as a Bacchante, as Cassandra and Circe, Euphrosyne and Iphigenia.

Modern taste may well prefer Emma in her more natural and better known poses at the spinning wheel, making tea and ultimately wearing the very latest piece of millinery as *The Ambassadress*, but even among the Greek helmets and the chariots and leopards of mythology, in addition to her considerable beauty, the one thing that shines out is Emma's obvious vitality, and adaptability. It is no surprise to realise, looking at these portraits, that the subject had considerable histrionic gifts, which she was to use in later life sometimes for pleasure, but sometimes in earnest, so that reality and her imaginings became inextricably mixed.

How Emma, from Greville's mistress and Romney's model, became Lady Hamilton, provides the most curious episode in the whole story.

Affection, even love, was in eighteenth-century custom and morality one thing, but interest, position and money, was another. Greville, just like his uncle in his young days, was looking round for an heiress. There were however standards in such matters and comfortably ensconced in Paddington with a teenage mistress, and her mother, he could hardly offer himself to a prospective father-in-law. In addition he had to give some evidence of 'prospects'. This was not the Victorian age, nothing so vulgar as work or a profession was ever considered. Greville's 'prospect' was his widowed uncle to whom, he hoped, he was heir. However, that gentleman on his occasional returns to England had shown disturbing signs of considering marriage again, for himself. Any offspring of such a marriage would of course displace Greville.

No doubt the plot between nephew and uncle did take some time to mature. Sir William had certainly shown more than an avuncular interest in Emma when he had met her in his nephew's house. Nevertheless, the prime mover was Greville. The eventual proposal was that Emma should be made over to Sir William and in return his uncle would stand by his declaration of Greville as his heir. The advantages to Greville were obvious, to Sir William somewhat less so. Over what lawyers call performance of this most immoral contract there was, inevitably, a very large question mark.

Two sophisticated gentlemen might agree to treat the beautiful tempestuous Emma as a chattel, whether she would be treated as such remained to be seen. Deceit had to be used to persuade Emma and her mother to travel to Naples. At first she was led to believe that Greville would join her, and that her sojourn in Italy was by way of an extended holiday. When she realised all was not as it appeared on the surface there was a period of tantrums, but eventually Emma yielded to necessity, the undoubted attraction of life in Naples, and of course to the elderly British Ambassador.

The whole of Emma's life so far, and she was only twenty-one when she arrived in Naples, can be regarded as a critical commentary on morals in the eighteenth century. As an illustration of the fate of a young, beautiful but poor girl her saga can hardly be bettered and recalls to mind the anonymous ballad, 'She was poor but she was honest', and its chorus 'it's the rich what gets the pleasure, it's the poor what takes the blame.' But there are one or two facts which do not fit very well with a theory of moral decline brought about by unjust social conditions. Plainly Emma who enjoyed life for the most part, was also capable of acting many roles, and obviously Sir William Hamilton was not a repulsive elderly satyr. If Emma and her mother had really wanted to leave Naples and return home they could have done so and it can only be assumed that they found their situation at the Palazzo Sessa not exactly intolerable. Morover, within a very short space of time Emma had succeeded in doing what the unlucky heroine of the ballad so singularly failed to do, getting herself respectably married. In 1791, signing the register as 'Amy Lyon', she married Sir William Hamilton, K.B., confidant and friend to H.M. the King of the Two Sicilies. The part of Ambassadress, in her turn confidante and friend to H.M. the Queen, and hostess to a number of distinguished English and foreign visitors, was one which Emma took to like a duck to water.

Nelson on his first visit to Naples had little time to observe its gallery of characters but a specific task to perform, with the assistance of the Ambassador, and, it was hoped, the expatriate Chief Minister as well. However, Lady Hamilton did make a favourable impression, and something of her past history must have been common knowledge, for in writing to Fanny he commented, 'Lady Hamilton has been wonderfully kind and good to Josiah. She is a young woman of amiable manners and who does honour to the station to which she is raised.'

In the same letter Fanny was informed of the success of her husband's mission, 'I am to carry the Lord [i.e. Hood] six thousand troops from hence, to help to take care of our possession, the whole of which is absolutely ours if Louis XVII is not re-established.' In which respect Nelson was ridiculously over-confident. Perhaps even his first reception at the Court of Naples had gone a little to his head. Of course, as a captain detached for special duty, Nelson had only one task. As he put it himself, 'I have only to hope I shall succeed with the King of Naples.'

Aided by Hamilton, Acton, and the natural sympathies of the King, and, even more important, the Queen, he did in fact succeed in his mission, perhaps a little to his surprise. The Kingdom of the Two Sicilies was not renowned for promptitude of action, nor military ardour. However, these were the early days of war against the French Republic, when it was possible in a number of European monarchies,

large and small, to think that the Revolution was a sort of temporary
aberration which could be dealt with by the allies without either the
need for very close co-operation or any long sustained military effort.
When the expected easy victory over the revolutionaries did not occur,
each ally went his own way.

The Kingdom of the Two Sicilies was very much a case in point.
Ferdinand, although there was a pro-British faction at his Court, was
not anti-French but merely anti-Jacobin, and in foreign policy tended to
follow Spain. His wife had the strongest of family reasons for hating the
revolutionaries who had guillotined her brother-in-law and were soon
to deal similarly with her imprisoned sister, and who opposed her
nephew, the new Austrian Emperor. There was also in the Kingdom a
considerable and natural respect for Britain as the sea power which
controlled the Mediterranean. What was not appreciated as yet was that
the allies were taking on not just a gang of revolutionaries, but nearly the
whole power of a new dynamic France.

It was in this political climate that Ferdinand received Nelson. He had
originally thought that it was the Spaniards who had invested Toulon,
but when the English captain explained that the prime mover had been
Admiral Hood, his admiration for Britain and her navy increased.
Accordingly, Nelson was wined, dined and fêted, and at a banquet
placed on the right-hand side of the monarch. Ferdinand, at Nelson's
request, wrote 'the handsomest letter that could possibly be' to Lord
Hood, and promised troops. The soldiers were seen by Nelson being put
through their parade ground paces by the King himself. What assessment Nelson made of the fighting capabilities of the men he would
receive is not set down, but certainly he realised that the King was an
eccentric, eaten up with vanities and over-confidence.

To be fair to Ferdinand, however, there was also a considerable
amount of over-confidence in Nelson's own attitude to the Toulon
operation. It is true, he was only a subordinate officer and as such had to
obey his orders, to raise as many men as possible from one of Britain's
allies. But still, Nelson thought that the war would be a short one,
although it is only fair to him to record that the Foreign Secretary,
Lord Grenville, also thought that 'the Toulon business' would be
'decisive of the whole war'.

The troops were being assembled and embarked in transports with
commendable dispatch, when Nelson and *Agamemnon* had to leave
Naples even more quickly, and cut short an agreeable and flattering

interlude. He was in the process of returning both Neapolitan and
British hospitality by inviting a number of guests aboard his ship for a
breakfast party: Sir William and Lady Hamilton and other prominent
members of the British community including Lord and Lady Plymouth,
Lord Grandison and his daughter, and the visiting Bishop of Winchester
and his family. The King himself was to come aboard at 1 o'clock, but
just before that event Nelson was informed by Sir John Acton that he
had received reports of a French warship escorting a convoy of three
merchant ships off the south of Sardinia. Sir William Hamilton said of
the Italianate cosmopolitan, 'I can perceive him to be still an Englishman
at heart'; perhaps he was right, however it is not insignificant that Acton
informed Nelson of the nearness of the enemy, not one of his own
adopted country's officers who had at their disposal in Naples harbour at
least seven of their own ships, plus a Spanish frigate. Perhaps it was just
that in four short days Acton had judged his man. If that were so he was
proved embarrassingly correct in his assessment, for the distinguished
guests were immediately bundled into boats and rowed ashore, and
King Ferdinand was left standing on the quay as *Agamemnon* was swiftly
prepared for sea. 'Unfit as my Ship was, I had nothing left for the honour
of our Country, but to sail, which I did in two hours afterwards. It was
necessary to show them what an English Man of War would do.'

So in a not untypical manner, his brisk naval efficiency contrasting
with the languid habits of his hosts, Nelson left Naples. His quest
obviously took precedence over social obligations and the effete pleasure-
loving city and its English community was not to see the energetic little
captain for another five years, and then in very different circumstances.

As Nelson and his ship, badly provisioned in the rush of departure, sail
back to action it is time to deal with a story which has grown up round
his first visit to Naples and his first meeting with Sir William and Lady
Hamilton. After Nelson's death Emma was to tell James Harrison, one
of the earliest biographers, a story which not only seemed to indicate an
immediate rapport between her then husband and her late lover, but
which also credited Sir William with a quite remarkable gift for prophecy.

Very soon after his first meeting with the naval captain Sir William
was said to have confided to his wife his first impressions of their visitor,
and to have told her that he was going to introduce her to a little man
who could not boast of being handsome, but who would become the
greatest man that England had ever produced.

History is of course littered with persons who, before the proof, discerned potential greatness in others, and almost every famous man has attracted such an anecdote. However, the tone of exaggerated hyperbole hardly fits the style of the sophisticated British Envoy and Plenipotentiary Extraordinary, who may have been a shrewd judge of character, but was no expert on the capabilities of naval officers. Nelson we know had no mean opinion of his own abilities, and may well have confided some of his ambitions to Hamilton, and certainly the two men did take to each other. Indeed Nelson found Sir William a man after his own heart, but when he said, 'You do business in my own way' he was producing something of an exaggerated compliment. Gratifyingly on this occasion the Ambassador had acted speedily in bringing his influence to bear, but he was not normally a fast-moving or decisive man. Further he had treated Nelson handsomely, putting him up in his own house in a room which had been prepared for George III's fourth son, Prince Augustus. So that there was every reason for a little mutual esteem, but the tone of adulation in Emma's story is much more her own than her husband's. At almost every opportunity she indulged her own highly developed sense of the dramatic, and had every temptation to do so after the death of both Hamilton and Nelson. That her first meeting with her hero should have been commonplace and not distinguished in any particular way would not have fitted her view of life. So no doubt she thought that, as on other occasions, reality merited a little embroidery.

Only one question is left hanging in the air and it must remain unanswered. What impression did Horatio and Emma have of each other? Obviously the thirty-five-year-old captain was not indifferent to the twenty-eight-year-old beauty and the opinion he wrote home to Fanny erred on the side of tact. To Thomas Graham, a relation who was serving at Toulon, Sir William wrote, 'I refer you to Captain Nelson . . . to give you an account of Lady Hamilton, who will never disgrace the family in which her merit has placed her. She makes me happy and is loved and esteemed by all.' Throughout his married life the elderly knight was to take a naïve pleasure in his possession of a beautiful wife who had artistic accomplishments and could perform the duties of an ambassadorial hostess. There was also present an element of self-justification for marrying a woman many years his junior and very much his social inferior. Surprise as well, no doubt, that his marriage had worked out so well. Before Emma had arrived in Naples Hamilton had had no illusions as to the realities of his own position, an elderly diplomat whom the world would laugh at for taking as a mistress, let alone marrying, a somewhat notorious, and by no means faithful, young woman. He had even ruefully anticipated the classic danger, that Emma would be seduced away from him by some younger man. Indeed, he sketched out a sort of tourist attraction for Naples which might have been advertised as 'Come to Naples and try to seduce the English Ambassador's wife.' That no one had laughed at him, at least in Naples, and that Emma still remained part of his collection, was a cause for congratulation. That other men admired her beauty and enjoyed her company was naturally to be expected and was a source of satisfaction. That Captain Nelson who, as subsequent correspondence between the two men showed, had himself made an excellent impression, was yet another visitor who had been charmed by the British Ambassador's wife was also something to be pleased about. Indeed the Captain's reaction merely helped to confirm the Ambassador's judgment and taste. At this stage, then, there was nothing more than mutual approbation by the three participants-to-be in one of the most famous, and unusual, eternal triangles, certainly no suggestion of the grand passion that was to develop later.

The six thousand Sicilian soldiers, whom the King stipulated should serve under no command other than British, sailed direct to Toulon. Originally King Ferdinand was only going to send half that number, but, as Nelson cynically observed, he was carried away by his own vanity and had insisted on sending a double complement. Perhaps, though, it was not all the King's vanity, for Nelson was in Naples to use his powers of persuasion and argument. As a result the King had expressed himself as 'very sensible of the magnitude of the Toulon operation', and had no doubt been assured of its excellent chances of success.

CHAPTER NINE

Combined Operations

NELSON in *Agamemnon* did not join the Sicilians at Toulon immediately. Having seen nothing of the French warship and its convoy, he was forced to call in at Leghorn, a neutral port, for the water and food he had missed taking on board because of his precipitate departure from Naples. While there he had a glimpse of the internal troubles which were afflicting the French Navy and which for some time made it an ineffective fighting force.

Also at anchor was an enemy forty-gun frigate which Nelson hoped to intercept if it left harbour. Not unnaturally, faced with a sixty-four-gun line-of-battle ship as an opponent, the French frigate stayed put. In any event there was enough happening on board to occupy everyone's attention. 'I have just heard', wrote Nelson to Fanny, 'that last night the crew of my neighbour deposed their Captain, made the Lieutenant of the Marines Captain of the ship, the sergeant of marines Lieutenant of Marines, and their former Captain, sergeant of marines. What a state. They are mad enough for any undertaking.'

Nelson wrote in hope and anticipation, but the former lieutenant of marines was not mad enough to risk his newly acquired command so soon and *Agamemnon* and her disappointed captain set sail for Toulon.

The situation in Toulon in October 1793 was hardly as Nelson described it to Fanny, 'wonderful', for 'the hills are occupied by the enemy who are erecting works for mortar and cannon. Whether we shall be able to maintain our most extraordinary situation time only can determine. However, one hour will burn the whole French fleet.'

In those few terse sentences Nelson summed it all up. Plainly the British and their allies were in a potentially disadvantageous and dangerous position. Yet Toulon was the most important naval arsenal in the Mediterranean, and risks were appropriate for such a prize. The French Royalists were allies, but if their Revolutionary compatriots were successful on land, then clearly the French fleet had to be destroyed or captured in the interests of Britain.

Nelson was optimistic and over-confident, but that was his normal state of mind when action was contemplated. In London Lord Grenville was also optimistic, with less excuse. However, once committed, even Hood could persuade himself that the chances were better than military reality indicated, and at all levels of direction and command there was temptation to hope that by means of a comparatively small combined operation, assisted by foreign forces and with some local assistance, the whole Revolutionary régime in France could be defeated.

The seaborne operation, the co-operative local population, the Government about to be toppled, the speedy ending to a civil war; these are factors in scenarios which have often tempted maritime powers, Britain, France, Greece and the U.S.A. among them. Other governments, and military and naval experts, at other times, have therefore committed the same mistake with not dissimilar results. In fact, Britain had invested Toulon in previous wars with the French, now that the French were divided the temptation was even stronger. Less excusably, the Toulon syndrome was to occur again in the Mediterranean war and elsewhere, for Britain seemed unable to learn from her mistakes.

The Royal Navy was, at that time, very active at Toulon, both afloat and ashore. Nelson, perhaps again because of the combination of his own abilities with the speed of his ship, was almost immediately detached for service under Commodore Robert Linzee, Hood's brother-in-law. Nevertheless a good deal of the action in and around the harbour was still observed by some of the officers and crew of *Agamemnon*. One young man wrote an illuminating letter home to his mother:

> I still like being at sea, and think I always shall. We have been at Toulon, which I think a very strong place. The Spaniards ran away every time they have engaged the French, and have behaved with the utmost barbarity to all those who laid down their arms and also the Neapolitans have behaved very cruelly in some cases.

The letter was signed by Josiah Nisbet, his stepfather customarily describing the young midshipman in his letters to Fanny as 'a good boy'.

On December 23 *Agamemnon* was back at Leghorn but by then writing to Maurice, his brother, Nelson reported that 'something very bad has taken place' at Toulon. In the meantime Linzee's squadron had been active on the southern shore of the Mediterranean, but not as active as Nelson wished. In Tunis harbour there was a French convoy escorted by an eighty-gun first rate and a corvette. Linzee and his senior officers,

Nelson among them, went ashore to negotiate with the Bey of Tunis. The Bey, who made a profitable living out of piracy, was a very smooth performer, and made polite mockery of the negotiators even enquiring of the British officers why they regarded the French with such abhorrence when they themselves, he seemed to remember, had once also executed their king and become a republic.

The Bey's attitude infuriated Nelson, who, at a council of war later on, was all for seizing the ships and negotiating afterwards, if necessary either dealing with the Bey by bribery or by knocking 'the Goletta and Porto Farino about his ears'. Linzee, however, was neither prepared to negotiate down the barrel of his ships' guns nor resort to bribery, so the Bey and the French remained unmolested.

It was at this time that Nelson, secretly worried by his own lack of involvement in actions in which contemporaries such as Captain Elphinstone of *Robust* had 'cut a very conspicuous figure', returned to his old obsession with the West Indies. The Mediterranean he still conceived of as a minor theatre of operations, where naval warfare might soon peter out, although the war on land would continue. It was an extraordinarily bad judgment both in the light of what was soon to happen in Europe and in his own subsequent career. It may have been provoked by frustration and the cautionary hand of Linzee, who was not Nelson's sort of sea officer, but it was not a view with which Nelson's naval or political superiors would have disagreed. If Captain Nelson had not yet developed into a strategist, but was more concerned with his own active employment, and his 'poor fellows' who had existed on a diet of 'honour and salt beef' without putting their feet on shore, it is only fair to say that neither the Government nor the Admiralty had given much thought to an overall naval strategy. Detachments of ships were dispatched, unfortunately after the event, where and when dangers occurred, so that the enemy always had the initiative, and in the process Nelson went where he was sent. Although the Royal Navy was the most numerous and most powerful force afloat, there was, so far, no long-term plan for its most advantageous and concentrated use.

Therefore in October, as Nelson's fellow captains, and some of his own men, landed for shore duties and gained glory at Toulon, *Agamemnon* was engaged in action off Sardinia with three French frigates and two smaller vessels. A running fight continued for four hours, but with no victory to either side, the French eventually being reinforced and *Agamemnon* suffering considerable damage to her masts and rigging and having one sailor killed and six wounded. It was not much more than a skirmish but it was Nelson's first experience of action since the American war and he sent a full report not only to Lord Hood but also to his brother Maurice in the Navy Office. It was typical of Nelson to advertise his exploits, but also of significance for the future was that when he had grave doubts whether to continue the action against very considerable odds he had called a council of war of his officers and taken their opinions. Consultation with subordinates was not part of the method of command of many sea officers, but it was a habit that Nelson was to maintain on other, and more important, occasions. What he called the 'damned Palaver' with the wily Bey of Tunis followed at the beginning of November, and in the next month all British and allied attention was re-concentrated on Toulon.

Some months before, a series of chances and coincidences had brought forward in the service of his country a very ambitious young man, ten years Nelson's junior, who had contemplated the navy as a career, but who, wisely, as it turned out, had chosen the army.

The outbreak of the French Revolution had revived in Corsica, ruled until 1769 by Genoa, the hopes and ambitions of her own native leaders including that romantic, Pasquale Paoli, who had, during his stay in Britain, aroused the admiration of Dr Johnson and Mr Boswell. Captain Napoleon Buonaparte had also toyed with Corsican nationalism, but by 1793 was reinstated in the French army and helped to organise coast defence batteries on the Mediterranean coast. By the end of July Republican forces were being concentrated against the Royalists in the south, and when Toulon in August was given over by its citizens to Admiral Hood, all available arms and men were massed against the mixed force of 2,000 British soldiers and marines, Spaniards, Sardinians and Nelson's Neapolitans, which was being landed on French soil.

The next moves in Buonaparte's career depended on chance and coincidence, but could only have happened in the French army of the time where individuals were promoted or disgraced, given responsibility or guillotined, elected to command or dismissed, almost without rhyme or reason under the shattering effect and influence of the Revolution.

Generals Carteaux and Lapoype were active in the south against the Royalists. At Ollioules, four miles west of Toulon, Carteaux became involved in a minor action with the Royalists and one of his casualties was his artillery commander, who was wounded. Buonaparte was in Ollioules at the time, occupied with coast defences, but soon to be on his way to Antibes. The road to Antibes might well have led to obscurity, but for the presence with Carteaux of Antoine Christophe Salicete, Representative of the People and political commissar, with all the power that the description implies. Salicete was a Corsican, and an old friend of the Buonaparte family, and was pleased to run into his youthful compatriot again. It needed only his suggestion and the young captain was immediately transferred to be in charge of Carteaux's artillery.

With the re-concentration of Republican forces to expel the allies from Toulon, Carteaux was replaced by General Dugommier with General du Teil in charge of artillery, who, however, was a sick man, and whose work as artillery commander fell on the willing shoulders of his young Corsican assistant. Buonaparte therefore found himself in charge of fifty-three siege guns, twenty-four 44-pounders and eight 12-inch mortars, regarding with a critical eye the allied dispositions in and around Toulon. It did not need a man of his talents to discern their essential weakness for their whole operation depended upon their retention of the peninsula of Le Caire which commanded both the inner and outer harbours. Displace them there and their fleet would be at the mercy of the land batteries.

By December the besieging army had been reinforced by as many troops as the Republic could rush to the spot, and had reached 38,000 men, outnumbering the besieging force by more than two to one. On December 17 the attack on the port began. For forty-eight hours Buonaparte's artillery bombarded the allied positions and then the infantry assault was launched. With the central column marched the second-in-command of the artillery, promoted to major since October 19. The combination of artillery bombardment followed by infantry assault proved its worth and the allies began to give way. In the final stages of the advance Major Buonaparte was wounded in the thigh by a bayonet wielded by a British soldier. Soon, vulnerable to enemy artillery on shore, the British and Spanish warships were preparing to evacuate the port, taking with them allied soldiers and marines and as many civilian refugees as could crowd aboard.

Neither Captain Nelson nor Major Buonaparte ever forgot those last few days of chaos and horror in Toulon. The exiled Emperor often recalled the scene to his entourage on St Helena—the ships burning in the harbour and the mob, now of course all fervent supporters of the Revolution, running wild in the streets.

Nelson, naturally, saw the defeat first as a failure of British arms, but the poor behaviour of foreign allies, panic-stricken Neapolitans and half-hearted Spaniards did not escape his censure. Ashore Frenchmen and their families who had supported the Royalist cause were being butchered and the state of even those lucky enough to reach safety on board a British warship was pitiful. Thus Nelson had encapsulated for him the darkest side of the Revolution and it was an impression never erased from his mind. Henceforth his hatred of France was confirmed and implacable, and this was what he was fighting against for the rest of his life, however it was dressed up, whether as Directory, Consulate or Empire.

Toulon was quite definitely the beginning for Buonaparte. Three days after the expulsion of the Allies 'this rare officer', as he was described by his superiors, was promoted 'general de brigade'. A little later an additional Representative of the People, Paul Barras, arrived in Toulon. One day in the future he was to introduce a rising young general to his mistress, Josephine de Beauharnais, widowed by the guillotine, but for the moment the favours he could dispense were purely military. By March of 1794 Brigadier Buonaparte had left the South of France to take command of the artillery of the Army of Italy.

Nelson had in the last days of the Toulon operation definitely come to the conclusion that evacuation was unavoidable. In a previous flash of pessimistic realism he had discerned that perhaps the only advantage Britain could extract from the whole operation was the destruction of the French fleet. Loyalty to, and admiration for, Hood had carried him along, brimful of confidence, in the early stages and during his mission to Naples. Now the Sicilian contingent, which had not distinguished itself, would be returning to Naples less a considerable number of dead and with many wounded. Disappointingly in the last hours of the Toulon operation the destruction of the French fleet was bungled owing to a combination of incompetence and near treachery. There were twenty-seven French ships of the line in Toulon harbour and there were two courses open to the retreating British, that they should be captured and removed, or that they should be destroyed. The removal of all of them presented obvious difficulties with the seamen at Hood's disposal, though it would not have been an insuperable task with some positive co-operation from the Spaniards. Unfortunately Hood entrusted the task of dealing with the enemy fleet to two men, Captain Sidney Smith and the Spanish admiral, de Langara. Both, for different reasons, proved unreliable.

Smith, an officer heartily disliked by Nelson, had already enjoyed a most unusual naval career. When he was twenty-nine he had served in Rodney's flagship and seen the fleet actions of 1780 but in 1790, in time of peace, had taken service with the Swedish navy against the Russians. He had distinguished himself and Gustavus III had bestowed upon him the distinction of Knight Grand Cross of the Order of the Sword with which he had been invested by his own King, George III, in 1792. Smith's next move, though still on half-pay in the Royal Navy, was to take service with the Turks, once again with Russia as the enemy. However, hearing of his own country's involvement in war, in 1793 he joined Hood before Toulon, commanding a ship he had bought out of his own pocket and sailing her with the aid of a collection of stranded British seamen he had picked up in Smyrna.

As will have been gathered there was an element of extravagance and independence in Smith's character and it made him a difficult subordinate and an unpredictable colleague. He was not therefore a good choice of officer either to carry out orders or to co-operate with others. In fact the Spanish admiral, with no strong desire to cripple the French and thus make the British masters of the Mediterranean, made very little effort to help Smith. As a result a half-hearted attempt was made to burn the dockyard, three French warships were taken out of the harbour and nine were burned, but fifteen first-class ships and a number of frigates and corvettes were left unharmed.

Five years later most of these fifteen battleships were to sail with General Buonaparte on his expedition to Egypt. Nelson was to meet them again. His path was also to cross that of the 'Swedish Knight' and their view of each other was not to be improved. Toulon was not the last occasion, either, on which Sidney Smith and Napoleon Buonaparte were to engage each other.

The British left Toulon in the worst possible circumstances. French Royalists had been delivered up to their enemy. Both Hood and the Royal Navy had lost face in the eyes of the French, and, more important, in the eyes of their Spanish and Italian allies as well, and British prestige declined in the opinion of most of Europe. The year ended with Hood's fleet at anchor in Hyères Bay, a sheltered anchorage a few miles east of Toulon. Those who directed the British Navy could now count the cost of their first Mediterranean operation, although they seemed incapable of learning its lessons. Britain's allies also counted the cost and decided that for them there were some very obvious lessons indeed.

The seventy-year-old Hood remained as the Commander-in-Chief in the Mediterranean for almost twelve more months and was in charge of other operations with which Nelson, whom he favoured, was to be closely concerned. But his days of active service were numbered after Toulon. Perhaps the old Admiral did not come up to the expectations of his reputation and previous abilities, but much of the fault rested with his political masters at home.

In essence there was no central direction of the war, nor did any machinery exist for co-ordination and planning. Further, what direction there was from the triumvirate of Pitt, Grenville, the Foreign Secretary, and Henry Dundas, the Secretary of State for War, tended to be sporadic, uneven and inadequate. However, it was something of a defence that the other powers at war with France made little attempt at co-ordination of their own military efforts and less to co-operate with Britain.

All of them had failed to appreciate that, in Lord Acton's words, 'the war begun for the salvation of monarchy became a war for the expansion of the Republic'. Yet it is possible to sympathise with their dilemma: were they fighting the old ambitious France, or the new doctrine of republicanism? The dichotomy was well demonstrated by two of Pitt's speeches to the House of Commons. In the first he found himself defending and justifying an alliance with the unpopular and absolute monarchies of Austria, Prussia and Russia; in the other explaining why the possibility, which then existed, of peace with, and therefore recognition of, the French republic would not mean the sacrifice of all the principles for which the war had been fought.

The next difficulty was the alliance itself. Spain from the start had been lukewarm. The war effort of Sardinia and the Two Sicilies could be summed up in the remark attributed to Ferdinand, king of the latter kingdom, with regard to the uniform of his own soldiers, 'dress them in red, blue or green, what does it matter, they will run away just the same'. Both the Empress Catherine of Russia and King Frederick William II of Prussia pursued totally selfish policies. At Vienna there was more constancy of purpose but none of the allies trusted each other, and none trusted Great Britain. However, her reputation as 'perfidious Albion' was due much more to incompetence and indecision than to any positive or deliberate attempts to deceive. Pitt's determination to carry on the struggle was simply not matched by an ability to translate that determination into effective military action.

Perhaps the first requirement of waging war efficiently, concentration, was most blatantly ignored. There were for Britain four theatres of war, two principal and two subsidiary. The two principal theatres were on France's northern frontiers and in the Mediterranean. The two subsidiary theatres were the West and East Indies and therefore concerned only Britain, France, Holland and Spain. What Britain did in the West Indies or in India was no concern of Austria, Prussia or Russia, the three powers which it was essential to bind together in alliance, although if Britain had been expelled from her colonial possessions by France their loss would have made a considerable effect upon her economic ability to wage war. However, at this stage there was little or no danger of that happening, certainly not enough danger to justify sending out an army. The war was going to be won or lost in Europe and there Britain's contribution was not consonant with her naval or military power, and by its paucity played a considerable part in discouraging her allies.

Nelson's sphere was the Mediterranean and under Hood he was given his first experience of independent command, remaining as captain of *Agamemnon* but frequently also being in control of a force of half-a-dozen frigates. To operate in the Mediterranean the Royal Navy needed a base and preferably one as close to the ports of France and Italy as possible. Gibraltar was too far to the west for this purpose and in the days of sail was by no means the ideal base it became for a later steam-propelled fleet. Malta, too far to the south-east, was in the possession of the Knights of Malta, a curious survival from the Crusading era. Sardinia was part of the Kingdom of Tuscany; Majorca and Minorca were Spanish possessions. Consequently when Corsica, the most convenient island in the Mediterranean, was offered to Hood he accepted with alacrity.

It was a curious irony of history that it was Buonaparte's birthplace that was made available to France's enemies. However, it was not the first time that the Corsicans had shown their independence, and Pasquale de Paoli, who made the offer on behalf of a presumed majority of the islanders, went to the lengths of proposing that Corsica should be ceded to Britain with George III as its monarch, providing that the fleet would assist in expelling the French. Neither the negotiations nor the implementation of such an undertaking were easy, and Hood, understandably, was somewhat suspicious of Paoli. In fact the 'Patriot General' was sincere, but he also found that fulfilling the bargain had its difficulties.

The negotiations had been originally carried out with Commodore Linzee but after Toulon the Commander-in-Chief gave the task to Nelson and it remained his until the British left the Mediterranean, Hood being careful to send no other captain senior to him to take part in the

operations. Although the geographical and strategic advantages of
Corsica were obvious—equidistant from Nice and Genoa and within
sixty miles of Leghorn, a principal port of British Mediterranean trade—
the military and political tenure of the island was fraught with problems.
Some were of Britain's own making and often the only person who knew
what he wanted and had any clear idea of what he was doing was the
captain of *Agamemnon*.

The occupation of the island was a combined operation. It had, however, additional complications for at no time was outright conquest of
the island thought feasible as it was large, rugged and densely wooded.
The presence of the British fleet and British soldiers depended ultimately
upon the good will of the Corsicans. From the start the army and the
navy co-operated poorly with each other, and the task of Sir Gilbert
Elliot, formerly Britain's Civil Commissioner in Toulon and now sent to
negotiate with Paoli, was hardly enviable. Elliot had problems on four
sides: his own government which moved, as usual, far too slowly; Paoli
popular, excitable and sensitive; naval officers impatient for action; and
military commanders cautious beyond belief.

French troops were in strength at three points on the island, San
Fiorenzo, where the fleet desired its base, and at Bastia and Calvi. Nelson,
with *Agamemnon* and his squadron of six frigates, began action by
blockading the whole island. The investing of the island was delayed in
January because of prolonged storms so that Hood was forced into Porto
Ferrajo on Elba and it was only by the beginning of February that
detachments of the British fleet began to appear off San Fiorenzo.

Meanwhile a party of British officers, which included Lieutenant-
Colonel John Moore, later hero of the retreat from Corunna, and
Lieutenant Andrews, brother of Miss Andrews whom Nelson had hoped
to marry in St Omer, was in touch with Paoli. Sir Gilbert Elliot
went with them as the official representatives of King George and the
designated future Viceroy of Corsica. Nelson himself was in his element
and had already commenced, in January, his own brand of seaborne
operations on the enemy's coastline, typical of his vigorous direct
approach to warfare. Britain needed Corsica and whatever one's view
of Corsican support the French had to be dispossessed. Therefore he
embarked immediately upon the task of harrying the enemy wherever
he was to be found. For instance, on January 21 he landed sixty soldiers
and sixty sailors and destroyed a flour store and a water mill and shot up
the local garrison. It was the sort of commando-type operation that

Nelson loved and his men enjoyed. And it was just the sort of action, risky and outside the proper sphere of the sea officer, which offended all the professional instincts of the soldiers.

The French soon evacuated San Fiorenzo and retreated upon their positions at Bastia and Calvi and it was then that the inter-service disagreements began in earnest. It is only fair, though, to point out that the British situation in and around the island might have been specially contrived to produce the maximum of discord. The French forces in Corsica outnumbered by more than three to one any mixed force composed of soldiers, marines and seamen which the British could deploy. The senior soldier present, entitled the Commander of the Forces, Lieutenant-General David Dundas, held the view that before he could take on the French he would need 2,000 men from Gibraltar and in this was supported by his own staff including Lieutenant-Colonel Moore. Lord Hood was determined that the matter should be settled quickly by the men available, seamen from the Fleet plus marines and the infantry, including the 69th Foot, serving with the Navy as marines. Predictably these two senior officers also clashed on the question of authority, Hood arguing that anybody in a ship was his to command, Dundas maintaining that any man in a red coat must be answerable to himself. Hood was, as he wrote to Dundas, quite willing 'to have the whole responsibility upon me', and went ahead with his intention, staying on board *Victory* in Martello Bay but using Nelson as his man on the spot.

Nelson also had no inhibitions about his task and by his reports encouraged Hood in his opinion that both Bastia and Calvi could be taken by his intrepid sailors. His opinion of soldiers was the same as that of his chief, 'Armies go so slow that seamen think they never mean to go forward'. At the same time he had no illusions about the Corsicans. Referring to some boatloads he had intercepted, he told Hood, 'Whenever we take them they are Paoli's friends; when they get away they are against him.' Six days later he wrote of another band who came to him offering help and asking for muskets and ammunition: 'They may be good friends, it is in their interest to be so; but I am rather inclined to believe they will always say, "Long live the Conqueror."'

It was a sound judgment, and not only on the Corsicans. It also fortified Nelson's optimism with regard to Bastia and Calvi for at both places a proportion of the garrison was made up of locally-enlisted irregulars who would not fight to the bitter end for the French cause. Undoubtedly the opinions and actions of one forthright and energetic subordinate confirmed and supported Hood who was in the same difficult situation within his own service as his rivals, the generals. Both services suffered from a shortage of ordinary seamen and private soldiers and an over-abundance of senior officers. Three generals and a number of colonels were engaged with the Corsican problem and Hood in a fleet of thirteen sail of the line had under him three vice-admirals and four rear-admirals. The consequent flag officers' councils were little to Hood's, or Nelson's, taste. In these circumstances, given a firm line of opinion and advice from an able subordinate, it is easy to see why Hood took Nelson's view almost exclusively and grew impatient with those who disagreed.

A clear picture emerges of Nelson at this time, March to the end of 1794, from many sources, including his reports to Lord Hood, his own 'Journals of the Campaign' and his letters to Fanny and his brothers, to William Suckling and old friends like Captain Locker. There is an outstanding impression of energy and activity, for he was commanding his own squadron and also overseeing the landing and sighting of guns. His nickname, 'the Brigadier', occurs to mind and what Sir John Jervis was often to call him—a 'Partisan'. Although fully engaged on land Nelson was not allowed to forget his responsibility for *Agamemnon*, the six frigates, and other vessels which were occasionally attached to his squadron. Even by the volume and variety of those letters which have survived it is obvious that Nelson was in his element as an organiser, attending to every detail from gun calibres to ships' stores and all the numerous other matters which affected his command on land and sea. If he had been of higher rank, these would have been taken over by a chief of staff, but as a captain he had to deal with them himself without even a secretary to write letters and give him the service that M'Arthur, the future biographer, was then rendering Admiral Hood.

It is rare to find organisational abilities combined with reckless personal courage, but a number of witnesses and events attest to the fact that 'the Brigadier' was a front-line soldier sharing all the dangers experienced by his men. Captain Thomas Fremantle of the frigate *Tartar* records how when walking with his senior officer to inspect batteries an enemy shell blew Nelson off his feet and covered them both with stones and dirt. Fremantle resolved not to take that route again, but it is doubtful if Nelson bothered.

It was at this time, as he wrote to his Suckling uncle, that he sustained 'a severe cut' in the back as a result of enemy fire. There is hardly a further mention of this wound to anyone. The adrenalin was being pumped into his system by the prospect and experience of action and Nelson was virtually indifferent to his own safety. Always ready to accept death or wounds in the course of duty, he expected, no doubt over-optimistically, the same attitude from others. Almost every report to Hood has at its foot a note of some casualties, one or two dead and a few wounded, but that was the risk and fate of those who took to the profession of arms. As he wrote to Mr Evan Davies of Swansea, the father of Seaman Thomas Davies of *Agamemnon*,

From the nature of our profession we hold life by a more precarious tenure than many others, but when we fall, we trust it is to benefit our Country. So fell your Son by a cannon-ball under my immediate command at the Siege of Bastia. I had taken him on shore with me, from his abilities and attention to his duty.

The comment of Marshal Villars, dying in bed, on hearing of the death by cannon shot of his former comrade, the Marshal Duke of Berwick, 'that man was always lucky' would have been understood by Nelson.

This sort of attitude to life involves an element of theatricality and it is easy to imagine how the stolid soldiery felt about the diminutive naval captain, all energy, bustle and heroics, who insisted on doing their own job for them. Obviously Colonel John Moore and Captain Horatio Nelson were not born to see eye to eye. Nelson wished Moore '100 leagues away' and regarded him as a malign influence upon General Dundas and when he gave up his command, because of fundamental disagreement with Hood, upon his replacement as well.

Another consideration is the effect of Nelson's enthusiasm and excessive patriotism upon his subordinates. It is difficult to tell how they felt about it for they were mostly silent and, in any event, had to obey orders. However, it is reasonable to assume that if Nelson had been merely a posturing daredevil, foolishly prepared to get himself killed to little purpose, he would soon have lost the support of the men under him and the regard of his superiors.

Neither happened, and to judge by their achievements, their com-mander's example did inspire, so that, in his words to Fanny, 'My seamen are now what British seamen ought to be, to you I may say it, almost invincible: they really mind shot no more than peas', and later, 'We are but few, but of the right sort'. This was written in April 1794 and referred to the fact that the new military commander, Brigadier-General Abraham d'Aubant, had proved no more co-operative than his predecessor Dundas, taking the view that Bastia could be starved into submission. Further, he refused to involve himself or his men in the assault, holding back his 2,000 soldiers at San Fiorenzo and leaving Nelson to his own devices with 400 sailors and the 800 soldiers, 'embarked to serve as Marines', whom he maintained under his direction.

Nelson confided all these difficulties in March to Sir William Hamilton at Naples in a letter which accompanied Lieutenant Duncan of the Artillery whom he sent there to acquire 'mortars, shells, field pieces and stores'.

Sadly, the guns and ammunition that Duncan did obtain were of little use, but Nelson voiced to Hamilton all his complaints against the Army and aired some of his sentiments. Of Lord Hood he said, 'Upwards of seventy, he possesses the mind of forty years of age. He has not a thought separated from Honour and Glory.' This was high praise coming from one whose touchstone for his own conduct was, 'What would the immortal Wolfe have done? As he did, beat the Enemy, if he perished in the attempt.'

Nelson began, on April 11, the siege of Bastia, 'a beautiful place, and the environs delightful, with the most romantic views I ever beheld', as he described it to Fanny. The French had surrendered by May 19, well over 4,000 troops having been brought to ask for a truce by Nelson's force of about a quarter of their number. Only when the truce was established did General d'Aubant at last put in an appearance with three battalions of infantry, a dragoon regiment and a hundred artillerymen, which as Nelson observed drily 'will probably terrify the Enemy'.

The British formally took possession of the town and the inner citadel on May 23. In answer to his critics Nelson was able to record in his Journal that while the enemy had lost 203 men with 540 wounded, his own losses were very small, 19 killed and 37 wounded. As he immodestly, but truthfully, observed to his brother Edmund, 'If proofs were wanting to show that perseverance, unanimity and gallantry can accomplish almost incredible things, we are an additional instance.'

The next move was the siege of Calvi after which Corsica would belong, militarily, to Britain. Before that could happen there was another change of generals, the newcomer being General the Hon. Charles Stuart, the fourth son of the Earl of Bute, an officer of ability and energy and of whom great things were expected, but which were cut short by his early death from illness in 1801. Both Hood and Nelson approved of him and regarded him as a welcome and striking improvement upon his two lacklustre predecessors. Happily Stuart turned out to be just as eager to take Calvi as Nelson, and soon showed himself the equal of his naval junior in 'front line soldiery', often sleeping within range of the enemy in the batteries with his men.

The siege operations advanced steadily until the very end of May when they were interrupted, for the naval contingent at least, by the news that the French fleet was coming out of Toulon. One of Hood's many flag officers, Vice-Admiral Hotham, was in command of the blockading squadron, but the French eluded him, whereupon Hotham hastened to join Hood, the result being the retreat of the French in face of obviously superior opposition. There were other times when Hotham would again opt for security and safety and this time, at least, the movements of the fleet did allow *Agamemnon* to refit before returning to Corsica.

Calvi was a very different proposition from Bastia. While the latter was an ordinary city, the commercial centre for the island, Calvi was more like a true fortress. It required a genuine combined operation to storm it successfully, with sailors acting from shipboard assisted by soldiers on land, rather than a mixed force, however intrepid, led by a captain-cum-brigadier.

The siege lasted until August 10 and was a much more serious affair than the capture of Bastia. Considerable numbers of guns were landed from the fleet on a remarkably inhospitable shore entailing days of hard work for the seamen in a rapidly deteriorating climate. Nelson wrote to the Duke of Clarence of what the natives called 'the Lion Sun' which was having its effect as increasing numbers of seamen and soldiers fell sick. Enemy artillery fire, which was accurate and intense, was thinning the ranks of the besieging force and Nelson had to write in haste to Fanny to assure her that if she read of a naval captain dead it was a gallant friend, Walter Serocold, and not her husband.

This must have been a period of great unhappiness for Fanny and it is not too fanciful to trace a deterioration in understanding between husband and wife from this time when, significantly, Nelson was at last involved in concentrated action. Absence may make the heart grow fonder, but for Fanny it was much more a case of 'partir, c'est mourir un peu'. During the absence of husband and son she had moved about restlessly from Burnham Thorpe to Bath, now staying in lodgings, now visiting one or other of her relations by marriage. Nelson's father, a bit of a hypochondriac himself, was the first person to notice and pass on the fact that her health, never robust, had worsened. Fanny was a worrier and her worries made her ill. Of course, with both a husband and a son serving as sea officers involved in operations against the enemy, she had cause for apprehension, but many women have survived similar situations. Certainly most wives and mothers of career officers and seamen have come to accept their lot, not perhaps gladly, but willingly, or at least have put on a convincing show. To Fanny, after a quick taste of peacetime conditions in the West Indies followed by five years of enforced domesticity, it all seemed to come as a burden too difficult to bear.

This would have led to difficulties even if Fanny had been married to an ordinary naval officer, but unfortunately for her Horatio was not in that category. Not that he was neglectful, the number of his letters written to her acquits him of that, and Josiah seldom wrote to his mother, confident that she would be receiving all the news of both of them from his stepfather. Indeed, hardly a letter from Horatio omitted a reference to Midshipman Nisbet's doings and the fact that he was a 'good boy'.

Although Horatio did his best to reassure Fanny about his welfare, their standards were very different. Restraint was never Horatio's strong point, and what was Fanny to think when almost every letter contained two or three sentences on the subject of her husband's devotion to the concept of death or glory?

Once in India Nelson had sat down at a card table and found himself playing for high stakes. That time he had been lucky and won, but he resolved never to play again in such company. He was wise, for he was no dissimulator and his cards would have shown in his face. Therefore everything went into his letters to Fanny, his hopes, his fears and his disappointments, even naval dispositions. In one he does at least realise this and apologises, 'What a military letter', but generally his wife was the recipient of all his thoughts and as he approached action each letter was written as if it might be his last. Perhaps he intended to prepare her for the worst, or leave her with a suitable written memento, but the result was that he drove her frantic with anxiety lest both Captain Nelson and Midshipman Nisbet should appear in the casualty lists.

As Fanny put it, 'My mind and poor heart are always on the rack', and as far as she was concerned 'the French could keep their fleet in Toulon'. Perhaps if Horatio had once said, even untruthfully, that he would take care of himself and avoid danger, or do the same for Josiah, she would have been reassured a little. What, though, was she to make of phrases such as 'a brave man runs no more risk than a coward' and, commenting on the early death of a civilian acquaintance, 'No age, no profession is exempt from death and the apparent dangers we go through are nothing in reality.' Fanny could be forgiven for thinking that she was married to a fatalist determined to die in battle, taking her son with him as *Agamemnon* sank beneath the waves.

In these circumstances for Horatio to ask rather irritably, 'Why you should be uneasy about me so as to make yourself ill, I know not', was to betray lack of understanding. Even the reports on Josiah, though 'he was quite a man' and 'will be a good officer I have no doubt', were not perhaps quite what a mother would wish to hear for, 'I fear he will never be troubled with the graces', whereas 'young Hoste' was 'Without exception one of the finest boys I ever met with'. Nelson's professional judgment was to prove correct, for Hoste was to become a distinguished naval officer but Josiah, despite considerable help up the promotion ladder from his stepfather, was to prove something of a disgrace. However, in 1794, all Fanny really wanted was some reassurance about the two men in her life, and this she did not receive. Perhaps she was expecting too much, though, when she asked Horatio with regard to Josiah, after a visit of her own to a dentist, 'Do make him clean his teeth not cross ways but upwards and downwards.' She thought her child should be 'good, obedient to you', although as a midshipman he had little option.

Reading Fanny's letters it seems a pity that Josiah ever chose the sea as a profession, but having done so, Fanny could never say to him, 'stay close to your stepfather, he will look after you'. For it seemed that Horatio was determined to seek action wherever it could be found, and risk himself and the whole ship's company once he had found it. Yet both Fanny and Horatio tried hard; she kept him up to date with naval and political news and gossip and with news of his family, and he reassured her about Josiah's teeth; nevertheless what Nelson's father called 'her time of widowhood' did not 'pass with as little allay as can be expected'. Though Horatio tried to keep really unpleasant news from her, she was nevertheless the recipient of the details of every disappointment and slight he suffered, imagined or real. In the circumstances, it is not difficult to see why she was always 'so sadly disappointed at your not coming home'—perhaps even for good.

CHAPTER TEN

Calvi

IT MIGHT have been thought that, with the object lesson of Bastia before them, the naval and military authorities would have co-operated better before Calvi. General Stuart was the third general officer in a short space of time to try to work with Admiral Hood and the third to fail. As Nelson and Stuart worked well together and each formed a high opinion of the other, one is driven to the conclusion that much of the fault lay with the stern, taciturn, elderly Hood. So bad did relations become between admiral and general that Nelson was forced into the difficult position of go-between, interpreting, placating, although ultimately responsible to his own service superior. Later on, when she had made his acquaintance, Fanny Nelson said of Lord Hood 'of all the silent men surely he is the most so' but there was more reason, other than his notoriously forbidding manner, for Hood's inability to hit it off with any of the army commanders on Corsica.

Toulon had not been a success and Hood's principal ambition was to redeem his reputation by a successful action against the French fleet. Perhaps at his age he was somewhat impatient. Instead of a fleet action he had been looking for an anchorage for his ships which had in turn involved him in the Corsican imbroglio, adding political and military dimensions to his existing problems. Dundas and d'Aubant had both been unsatisfactory colleagues, but now with Calvi it was the task itself which was inimical to a sea officer.

The town was well-fortified and situated on a promontory on the western shore of a gulf on the north-west point of Corsica. The coast, because of a combination of shore winds and excessive depth of water, was an extremely difficult one for the naval action required. This was unlikely to appeal to a man of Hood's temperament for naval action was definitely subordinate to military. The task of the navy was to transport and land soldiers and then assist them with landed guns and protect the whole operation from any possibility of seaborne interference from France.

The two points on which General Stuart sought Nelson's advice were first whether his force would be safe from 'the French fleet at Gourjean' (Golfe Jouan) between Toulon and Nice and, second, whether warships could help bombard fortifications. To the first he received a confident affirmative, and to the second an emphatic negative.

Because of the difficulties of the coastline a small inlet, Port Agro, about three miles from Calvi, was settled on by Nelson and Stuart as a beachhead. It was not a perfect choice but it had to do and it involved sailors, 250 at first and then 500 at the army's request, in the back-breaking task of manhandling ships' guns and ammunition up and over rocky terrain so that they could eventually be fired by soldiers. At the same time the military consumed powder and shot which might leave the fleet short in an emergency. Nelson never complained, but it is not difficult to see why his admiral's heart never appeared to be in the business.

On June 12, active as usual at the batteries, Nelson suffered his first serious wound in action. At seven o'clock in the morning an enemy shell hit the gun emplacement and ricocheted off, missing his head by inches but driving some of the contents of a sandbag filled with large pebbles into his face and eyes. He was absent from duty for only twenty-four hours, but the pain must have been intense. 'I got a little hurt this morn-ing, not much as you may judge by my writing,' he reported to Hood, but it was more than that.

There were a number of cuts and grazes to his face, and an amount of surface injury, but the serious wound was in his right eyebrow penetrat-ing through the eyelid and into the eyeball. Inevitably such a wound was extremely painful but the most important consideration was the sight of his right eye. For four days, because of the shock of the wound, he could see nothing and then there was an improvement, he was back at his duties and wrote to Hood, 'My eye is better, and I hope not entirely to lose the sight.' He could distinguish light from dark and hoped that the eye would continue to improve. It did not, the pupil became enlarged and irregular in shape, nearly covering the iris. Most likely the retina was detached. Hood was anxious that the injury should be seen to, and General Stuart wished 'he may not lose the sight of an eye', and in the next few weeks Nelson was examined on board Hood's flagship, *Victory*, by John Harness, a Physician to the Fleet, Michael Jefferson the Surgeon on shore and finally W. Chambers, Surgeon General to H.M. Forces in the Mediter-ranean. The latter's opinion was nearly as final as could be; 'the eye is so materially injured that, in my opinion he will never recover the perfect use of it again'. So it proved, and from now on Nelson had the sight of only one eye, the left. That good eye became itself considerably strained, and had to be protected by a translucent shade, a sort of sun glass, which he wore in the Mediterranean sun.

In July and August Nelson also experienced a recurrence of his 'agues', the shivering fits and feverish symptoms which are a legacy to those who have suffered from malaria. In his affliction he was not alone, Lord Hood was suffering from an unidentified illness, and General Stuart was obviously unwell. Sickness, as so often in the eighteenth century, was more of a danger than shot and shell. Nelson noticed that the army had many more sick cases than the navy, he attributed this to the sailor's greater activity, but a more likely explanation was the clothes they wore. Beaten down by 'the Lion Sun' the soldiers still wore their tight broadcloth regimentals, while the sailors were happier, and healthier, in the more free-and-easy garb of round hat, shirt and loose canvas trousers.

Nelson said little about the suffering occasioned by his wound and less about the loss of the sight of one eye. One entry in his Journal for July 12 reads: 'At 7 o'clock C.N. [Captain Nelson] was much bruised in the face and eyes by sand from the works struck by shot.' To his uncle William Suckling he wrote a little more, 'My right eye is cut entirely down: but the Surgeons flatter me I shall not entirely lose my sight of that eye. At present I can distinguish light and dark, but no object: it confined me one day, when thank God I was able to attend to my duty. I feel the want of it; but such is the chance of war, it was within a hair's breadth of taking off my head.'

It is interesting to compare the sentiments entertained by Nelson about his own wound with his father's letter on his son's misfortune: 'It is well known that the predestinarian doctrine is amongst the creeds of Military men. It may sometimes be useful: yet it must not exclude the confidence Christianity preaches of a particular Providence which directs all events. It was an unerring power, wise and good, which diminished the force of the blow by which your eye was lost; and we thank the hand that spared you, spared you for future good, for example and instruction.'

Later the Reverend Edmund wrote, 'Your lot is cast, but the whole disposing thereof is of the Lord: the very hairs of your head are numbered —a most comfortable doctrine.' Presumably the last phrase was not ironic, and plainly the country cleric found no logical difficulty in combining predestination with a doctrine of personal salvation. Nelson and his father were always very close, hardly a letter to Fanny omits the hope that she has seen or written to him, and Horatio's religious views as an experienced man were the same as those absorbed during his rectory childhood. It is also interesting to see the father echoing the beliefs of the son that he, Horatio, was being 'spared' for some further enterprise. Admittedly a not uncommon idea among ambitious men, even those of little or no deistic religious belief, and another comfortable and comforting doctrine.

Horatio first wrote to Fanny on August 1 in terms so reassuring as to be dishonest: 'I continue well as usual and, except a very slight scratch towards my right eye which has not been the smallest inconvenience, have received no hurt whatsoever.'

By August 18 he knew that it could not be disguised so Fanny was told the truth. Although assured that, 'Of 2,000 men I am the healthiest' for 'Mrs Moutray's son', 'poor little Hoste', 'Suckling that giant' and Bolton, 'are all ill', 'All the purpose of use of it [his eye] is gone. However, the blemish is nothing, not to be perceived unless told. The pupil is nearly the size of the blue part, I don't know the name. At Bastia I got a sharp cut in the back.' When this letter was written Calvi had surrendered and *Agamemnon* was at Leghorn, a neutral port and part of the kingdom of Tuscany which was heavily used by the navy for taking on stores and refitting. Other letters written about the same time reveal that Nelson was again concerned about his future, 'What may be done for me time only can show'.

In fact, released from active service through no choice of his own, Nelson was now suffering from one of his customary depressions. Physical weariness had a great deal to do with it, but elation and depression were always with him very quick transitions. 'I left Calvi on the 15th. I hope never to be in it again.'

Young Hoste had recovered but James Moutray, a lieutenant on *Victory*, son of Mrs Moutray, that perfection of womanhood Nelson had so much admired in his Antiguan days, had died of the 'Calvi fever'. His own ship's company had been sorely reduced, 150 men of *Agamemnon* being on shore sick and the rest according to the Fleet Physician 'in a very weak state'. Out of duty to the family Nelson had young Moutray's memory commemorated in stone in the church at San Fiorenzo, 'Erected by an Affectionate Friend, who well knew his worth as an Officer, and his Accomplished Manners as a Gentleman.'

Writing to Fanny he revealed his sincere sympathy for Moutray's

mother left alone in the world and yet, and it was one of the quicksilver
paradoxes of Nelson's nature, within moments he was complaining of the
lack of recognition by his superiors of his own 'worth as an Officer'.
Undoubtedly with justice, for Hood, that strange inscrutable man, in his
official account of the Bastia operation had given little credit to the very
captain he had placed in charge and whom he specially favoured.

The reason was a curious one, Hood wished to help a Captain Hunt
who had lost his ship, *Amphitrite*, some months before, and in doing so
gave the impression that the part played by Nelson was a minor and
subsidiary one. Hunt was also given the task of taking home the dispatch,
normally an indication that the officer chosen had distinguished himself.
In fact General Stuart's reports to Sir Gilbert Elliot, the Viceroy of
Corsica, left no doubt as to Nelson's activity and ability. Nor was there
any doubt in naval circles as to the part he had played. It was the outward
recognition of which Nelson felt deprived. It was the sentences of the
dispatch read by the public in the *London Gazette* which offended,
'Captain Nelson, of His Majesty's Ship *Agamemnon*, who had the command and directions of the Seamen in landing the guns, mortars and
stores, and Captain Hunt who commanded at the batteries . . . have an
equal claim to my gratitude.'

Many others received higher praise and they had done much less.
Praise for Lieutenant (now Major) Duncan particularly rankled, as that
young man had been advanced and commended by Nelson, and now
that he was a Major, and on the General's staff, had become rather
condescending.

The Calvi dispatches of both General Stuart and Admiral Hood
mention Nelson's services as 'contributing to the success' of the operation,
and spoke of his 'unremitting zeal and exertion', but along with other
officers. Although he had been wounded at Calvi it was at Bastia that
Nelson felt he had deserved special recognition. The principal recipient
of Nelson's disappointments, doubts and recriminations was of course the
unfortunate Fanny. She could have been forgiven if she had felt irritation
at her husband's complaints against Hood who on other occasions he had
regarded as a great hero and commander, and now his resentment against
Stuart. Nelson was not fond of what he called 'Scotchmen', but Stuart
had originally been welcomed as such an improvement on Dundas and
D'Aubant. In Nelson's view he must have been over-influenced by the
consistently disliked and resented John Moore, another Scot.

Obviously at the end of the Corsican campaign Nelson was a tired man who had borne many responsibilities and exertions and had in addition suffered the loss of sight of an eye as a result of a most painful injury. If he had been praised to the skies in the *London Gazette* as the moving spirit of the siege of Bastia, and among the most active at Calvi, perhaps he would have been satisfied.

As a result anyone in receipt of a letter from Captain Nelson in the autumn of 1784 was treated to a list of complaints including the fact that he had not even been listed among the wounded. As he had chosen to make light of his wound, the authorities can hardly be blamed for that. Bewilderingly, at the same time, Nelson assures Fanny, or himself, that no officer should slacken his 'zeal for his country'. Now all men complain at some time about the hardships or injustices of their chosen job or profession, yet reading Nelson's letters one is tempted to ask how his friends reacted to his complaints. What for instance of someone like Captain Hallowell, a big bluff giant of a man, Canadian-born, who accompanied Nelson when he went on board *Victory* for his session with Dr Harness and the surgeon, Mr Jefferson? Here was someone in whom no doubt Nelson confided, and who would give his own opinions in return.

It is therefore permissible to imagine what Benjamin Hallowell's reactions might have been. Might he not have sympathised with a brother officer but also reminded him that unrewarded merit, injustice, favouritism, and the unpredictable nature of senior officers were all part of naval life, as Nelson must surely know after over twenty years' service? After all to be a senior post captain at thirty-five was no bad thing, especially after five years on half-pay, and there were always others pushing up the ladder and willing to take one's place. Finally, all sea officers were in the last analysis volunteers and any officer dissatisfied with the Service could quit it. And yet while putting not unnatural words and sentiments into Captain Hallowell's mouth one wonders if anyone really did speak to Nelson in that way. No one in his family appeared to do so, for they were all in awe of their intrepid little relation and perhaps his Service equals were as well.

The final aspect of Nelson's character and behaviour which merits consideration is the question: how unusual was he at the time? His contemporaries were certainly to remark on his vanity, and his love of show, in later years when he was a known figure and a national hero. Others allowed him his eccentricities and faults because of his abilities and achievements. Is it possible though to gauge the reaction to a relatively unknown post captain, always in search of death or glory, who was elated in action, but plunged into gloom and plagued by ailments if he was kept out of things, or if his services appeared not to attract official recognition?

Unfortunately what has not come down to posterity is the view of an equal: another post captain also striving for promotion, hoping for recognition, seeking prize money and actually therefore in those respects in competition with the captain of *Agamemnon*. What is however available is a very similar case history to Nelson's, something which cccurred to another captain, and indeed a close friend, Collingwood, in another theatre of war at almost the same time as Nelson was involved in Corsica.

On July 8 Nelson wrote to Fanny 'a few lines' and mentioned that 'I am very busy, yet own I am in all my glory: except with you, I would not be anywhere but where I am, for the world.' On July 14 he sent another short note which had a slightly different tone, 'our efforts here are at such a distance, and so eclipsed by Lord Howe's great success at home, that I dare say we are not thought of'. Realistically, he was right. On June 11 news had reached England that Admiral Lord Howe had been engaged with the French fleet, no British ships had been lost, but six French warships had been taken and one sunk. The British had had little to celebrate by way of victories in a year of warfare and Howe's action was apostrophised as the 'Glorious First of June'. There were a number of features of the battle fought on 28 and 29 May and 1 June far out in the Atlantic, 430 miles west of Ushant, which impinged on the career of Captain Nelson, then engaged with his batteries before Calvi.

Howe's command was in many ways a more difficult one than Hood's, for he had a much larger sea area to operate in and consequently his task was much less well-defined. In fact when his time came for action he was forewarned of French activity but his intelligence was incomplete.

What had provoked the French Navy into activity was dire economic necessity. The harvest of the previous year had been a failure and this together with civil turmoil had meant a looming food shortage for the autumn of 1794. Lying in the Chesapeake under the control of the neutral but well-disposed United States was a vast concourse of 117 ships laden with grain and other vital supplies. The task of convoying these ships to French ports was given by Robespierre, now the most powerful man in Paris, to three admirals, Vanstabel, Villaret-Joyeuse and Neilly. Vanstabel with two ships of the line and three frigates reached America undetected, and the next move was Villaret-Joyeuses's with the main body of ships from Brest. Neilly was held in reserve to protect the convoy and assist the rest of the fleet on its return journey. The task of the French admirals was, if possible, to avoid conflict, but if that were unavoidable then their first priority was the safety of the supply ships. Howe's task was to find the French in the vast distances of the Atlantic and bring their fleet to battle.

The manoeuvres and tracks of the two fleets between May 19 and June 1 do not concern us. Sufficient to say that battle was joined for three days between almost equal forces, Howe, commanding twenty-five line-of-battle ships, four frigates and four auxiliaries, Villaret-Joyeuse commanding twenty-six line-of-battle ships, having now been joined by Neilly. The outcome was a British victory with two important provisos: the convoy reached France safely, and the initial British success was not followed up.

We are not concerned with the overall strategic failure, for it is difficult to see what else Howe could have done at the time, and it was only later fully realised what the French priorities had been. Certainly if information and strategy had been married together the French convoy would have been intercepted at its point of departure on the western side of the Atlantic. The allegation that the initial success was not followed up is more serious and relevant to Nelson's career, particularly as he once spoke of a 'Lord Howe victory' in a disparaging way, though making no criticism of the old Admiral personally. Howe's tactics when it came to battle were aimed at bringing about a mêlée, getting his own ships in among the French line, and once there, because of superior British seamanship and gunnery, destroying the enemy at close quarters. Each British ship was meant to cut through the enemy line and engage from leeward. While passing through the line the British were to deliver a broadside and then cut off the retreat of any damaged French ships which attempted to retire to leeward.

It was a good plan and it did Lord Howe, a pioneer in the improvement of signals and a precisionist, great credit. Unfortunately for a combination of reasons, including the fact that his captains did not seem to know what was expected of them and that seamanship was not up to the requirements of such a manoeuvre, only seven of Howe's twenty-six ships managed to cut through the enemy's line.

But, however imperfectly, Howe did bring about his mêlée, and in it the French crews were proved markedly inferior to British, French casualties were far heavier than British and the damage inflicted by carronades totally dismasted the enemy. At the end of the day six French ships were taken, one sunk, but many, though severely damaged, were allowed to escape. Some part of the blame falls on the shoulders of the exhausted elderly Howe who had been on deck almost continuously from the start of the action three days before, and some on the shoulders of his Captain of the Fleet, Sir Roger Curtis, a cautious fussy man. Between them they managed to miss opportunities and the bulk of the French fleet sailed on.

To the British public, who celebrated by lighting bonfires and ringing bells, these limitations were not suspected, but they swiftly became known in professional circles, hence Nelson's later remark. For ambitious potential fleet commanders there were two lessons to be derived from the First of June. First, that if an action was to be fought which broke away from the old rigid engagement in line then captains, whose initiative had to be relied on out of formation, had to be trained and briefed by their fleet commander. Secondly, though the mêlée action was more destructive of the enemy than the old-fashioned line action, nevertheless the destruction or crippling of an enemy fleet could not be encompassed simply by joining battle in a new formation. Also for those in Government and on the Admiralty Board who chose fleet commanders there was, if not a lesson, at least a hint that admirals under the age of seventy might have some advantages over their seniors however distinguished and experienced.

It will be seen how and to what extent Nelson himself absorbed the first two lessons, and how he applied them when my Lords of the Admiralty had dared to take notice of the third.

There were, in fact, a number of captains and officers in Howe's fleet known to Nelson, among them Schomberg commanding *Culloden*, Gardner now a Rear-Admiral and rewarded with a baronetcy for his services, and Cuthbert Collingwood as flag captain to Rear-Admiral Bowyer in *Barfleur*.

It is what happened to Collingwood that provides a comparison with Nelson's own situation. It is particularly interesting bearing in mind the way in which Collingwood had followed closely upon Nelson in his promotion, the manner in which the two men were to be associated in the future, and the fact that of all the officers serving under Howe on the First of June none rose subsequently to such heights of professional distinction as Nelson's friend of West Indian days.

On the day of the battle *Barfleur* did her duty splendidly, breaking through the enemy line and being involved in the thick of the fighting. Collingwood very soon acquired an additional burden as his admiral

5a Admiral Brueys

5b Admiral Villeneuve

6a Captain Saumarez

6b Captain Ball

NELSON'S SUBORDINATES

6c Captain Berry

6d Admiral Collingwood

7a Lord St. Vincent

7b Lord Howe

NELSON'S SUPERIORS

7c Lord Keith

7d Sir Hyde Parker

8 Sir William and
Lady Hamilton

received a severe wound in the leg putting him out of action, and giving over the direction of affairs to his flag captain.

Yet when Howe's dispatch appeared in the *London Gazette Extraordinary* of June 11 though Rear-Admiral Bowyer was mentioned with distinction and a number of captains also, no mention was made of Collingwood. Worse, two other captains, Nicholls of *Sovereign* and Hope of *Bellerophon*, who also had wounded flag officers aboard, were held up for 'special notice'. Then Howe went on to say that 'These selections should not be construed to the disadvantage of other commanders, who may have been equally deserving of the approbation of the Lords Commissioners of the Admiralty, although I am not enabled to make a particular statement of their merits.' That, if anything, made matters worse. Collingwood wrote, 'The appearance of that letter nearly broke my heart'. Therefore both Nelson and Collingwood, in their view, were suffering unjustly from an official slight, and not receiving the public praise they thought they deserved.

Cuthbert Collingwood was a sea officer in complete contrast, mentally and physically, to Horatio Nelson. Yet Collingwood, staid, sober and thoughtful, reacted just as fiercely as Nelson. He saw Sir Roger Curtis and wanted to see Lord Howe, he complained and he wrote letters, all to no avail. Howe, who was already a peer was made a Knight of the Garter. Two senior admirals, Alexander Hood and Thomas Graves, received Irish baronies, junior admirals were created baronets, all admirals and most captains were awarded a gold medal to commemorate their part in the action: Collingwood received nothing.

In 1797 when he had distinguished himself in the company of Nelson and under another admiral, Jervis, and was about to be awarded a gold medal for the battle of St Vincent along with every other captain, he refused it, quite properly in Jervis's view, unless he first received his medal for the First of June. 'I feel', he said, 'that I was then improperly passed over.' So eventually Captain Collingwood had two gold medals to hang round his neck. This incident puts Nelson's complaint into the perspective of the conditions of service life at that time. It is difficult to imagine the modern naval officer, passed over in some way, behaving as did Nelson and Collingwood. Private disappointment no doubt, and maybe a grouse with one or two close friends, but nothing more, largely on the basis of the unwritten law that 'it isn't done'.

Why then did Nelson and Collingwood behave differently? One reason was the difference in the whole system of awards, honours and decorations. For the successful commanding admiral a peerage and maybe a grant of money or a pension from the State. For his subordinates of flag rank either an Irish peerage, not entitling him to sit in the House of Lords, or a baronetcy. For commodores and captains either the hereditary dignity of a baronetcy, or a knighthood, generally of the Order of the Bath which was then the military and naval order. Apart from that, and the recently introduced gold medals for specific actions, there was nothing. No Victoria Crosses, Distinguished Service Orders, or Distinguished Service Crosses for degrees of gallantry. No campaign medals, with oak leaf clusters for mentions in dispatches, no general service medals for minor campaigns and no grades of the Order of the British Empire for generally meritorious service. For the officer below the rank of captain the only reward was promotion. For the warrant officer, petty officer and seaman there was no system of awards at all. Later on, it will be seen how they were given bronze medals for particular battles, and also, as they had no great financial value, how little they were regarded.

The award of gold medals to some, but not all, captains at the Glorious First of June was an innovation and an attempt to institute some sort of system of recognition. The omission of Collingwood demonstrated its imperfections.

There was, however, a discernibly different attitude to such matters as well. In the twentieth century one has become accustomed to a professional navy, lower deck as well as officers, and a service in which the status and importance of the officer as such has declined. Yet these changes have been dictated as much by sociological developments as the transition from the sailing ship to the nuclear submarine. The sea officer of Nelson's day, with very few exceptions, came from one social class and a class which in the eighteenth and early nineteenth centuries was accustomed to independence and allowed individuality. Though discipline on the lower deck was savage and brutal and at sea, between superior officer and subordinate, iron-hard, the concept of a gentleman dealing with gentleman was still present. Nelson was customarily described as Horatio Nelson Esquire, Captain of *Agamemnon*, and the Esquire was as important as the Captain. It was an age when gentlemen were accustomed to asserting their rights and opinions, even by challenging each other to a duel, when the naval or military officer was very much a private individual who happened, almost incidentally, to command a ship or a regiment.

Therefore for Collingwood to assert his private opinion and rights was by no means as outlandish as it would appear today. Equally so, Nelson's expressed disappointment, even his resolution that one day he would have 'a Gazette of his own' was very much part of the outspokenness and individualism of the age. There is plenty of evidence to show that Nelson was a complex character, a man of conflicting moods, of intense patriotism, but also of burning ambition, pious and vainglorious, and that his foibles, eccentricities and faults were noticed and commented upon by his contemporaries. It has been said that even if Horatio Nelson had been able to pass the medical examination to enter the present-day Royal Navy, it is doubtful if he would have risen very high up the ladder of promotion. No doubt true, but it is only fair to point out that many of his individualistic, eccentric, opinionated and independent-minded brother officers, not particularly remarkable in the age in which they lived, would also have come up against similar difficulties in our own conformist age.

CHAPTER ELEVEN

First Fleet Action

IN 1794 the British and their Government sorely needed the consolation of the six prizes lying at Spithead taken by Howe on the
'Glorious First', for little else in that year gave them or their allies
much encouragement in their war with France.

There had been yet another violent change of governing personalities
in France, for in July, Robespierre and his trusted lieutenant, St Just, had
been overthrown and had within days gone to the guillotine. Robespierre,
the 'sea-green incorruptible', had undoubtedly been one of the strong
men of the Revolution, and now he was gone. Yet, and this was one of
the most remarkable aspects of the Revolution, though groups and
personalities rose and fell in Paris, nothing seemed to affect the ardour
and skill of French generals and their soldiers. In the same month as
Howe's victory the Austrians had been defeated by Jourdan at Fleurus
and the Duke of Coburg had finally evacuated Belgium. Again in June
the French had crossed the frontier into Spain.

These successes had their effect on the Allies, and it was now becoming
difficult to know quite who the Allies were. In October Prussian troops,
despite a continuing British subsidy, were in effect withdrawn from
warlike operations. Though in September Britain, Russia and Austria
had, in St Petersburg, re-affirmed their co-operation against the common
enemy, the Tsarina was more concerned with her troops which had
entered Warsaw than with any activity against the French. By December
Prussia was openly negotiating for peace, as was that other lukewarm
belligerent, Spain.

By the end of the year it really did seem that the only two governments
concerned with prosecuting the war were in London and Vienna. Even
in London enthusiasm was by no means universal. In Parliament back in
July there had been a split in the Whig party over the issue of parliamentary reform and as a result the Duke of Portland and William
Wyndham had joined the Cabinet and Charles James Fox and Charles

Grey found themselves leading an opposition party of a mere forty members.

It was not, however, a silent opposition. In January Fox had moved an amendment to the King's Speech in the following terms, 'To recommend to His Majesty to treat, as speedily as possible, for a peace with France upon safe and advantageous terms, without any reference to the nature or form of the government that might exist in that country.' In March Samuel Whitbread renewed the attack but from a different point of view, concentrating on the undoubted unpopularity in Britain of her allies, more concerned with acquiring Poland than resisting France. In December another amendment was moved advising the King to negotiate for peace, this time not by a political opponent, but by an old personal friend of Pitt's, William Wilberforce. Pitt, who defended himself eloquently on all three occasions, was able to resist such criticism by comfortable majorities, 277 to 59, 138 to 26 and 246 to 73, but what Fox, Whitbread and Wilberforce, despite their different points of view, had on their side of the argument was the undoubted fact the the Coalition was breaking up. At the same time there was no doubt of French successes as they had been announced grandiloquently to the Paris Convention, 'Eight pitched battles gained, 116 towns and 230 forts taken, 90,000 prisoners and 3,800 cannons captured'.

Resolutely Pitt concluded his speech at the end of 1794 suggesting that the French would soon be moving into economic difficulties and that if necessary, Britain alone would be able to match her consequently reduced military efforts. Perhaps he really believed it would be so, it was the sort of financial argument he favoured, but, whether he believed it or not, as a prediction for the next few years it could not have been more wide of the mark.

Nelson's comment to Fanny from the Mediterranean, in the same month, presented a more accurate view, 'We don't seem to make much of this War . . .'. Lord Hood had been called home and hoped to return, though Nelson, reasonably as it turned out, had considerable doubts on this score. He himself had hoped to return with Hood and be with Fanny and his family for Christmas, but instead remained in the Mediterranean. The exigencies of the service and the prospect of some action reconciled him to his post but Fanny had no compensation for a miserable winter without the sight of the only two people who really mattered to her.

Nelson was becoming, in his own phrase, 'an old Mediterranean man'.

He was not the first nor the last Englishman to become intrigued by that sea and its shores. Dr Johnson had said that the object of all travel was to see the shores of the Mediterranean and it was a very English point of view. There have always been military necessities requiring the presence of the British, but more importantly there has always been an element of the romantic and the exotic as well. A compound of classical antiquity, of Greece and Rome, a climate not to be found in their homeland, colourful people and customs, whether Spain, the South of France, Italy, Greece, or further afield, in North Africa and Egypt. A combination of all these elements, difficult to define, but discernible nevertheless, has existed for British soldiers and sailors for centuries, the desert armies and air force in one war, the Mediterranean fleet in two, the soldiers in the Peninsula, and Nelson and his brother officers and their ships' companies.

Leaving aside the romantic elements and, in Nelson's case, a very definite preference for its climate, it is not difficult to realise the fascination of a virtually enclosed sea as a military theatre. Yet a theatre which contained in Nelson's day almost every complication, diplomatic as well as military, that could be imagined. France the enemy, Spain the lukewarm ally who was to become enemy and friend again, the Italian peninsula still as Metternich was to say much later 'a geographical expression', divided up into a number of separate states with different interests and allegiances. Then Greece, at that date part of the Ottoman Empire, guardian of the Straits, Russia's entrance to the Mediterranean, and finally Egypt, notionally in vassalage to the Sultan at Constantinople, and the independent rulers stretched along the North African coast.

There can be no doubt that service in the Mediterranean was infinitely more agreeable and interesting than in the pestilential West Indies or the storm-tossed blockading ships in the Channel, or off Ireland in the wide Atlantic. Further there can be no doubt that Nelson enjoyed it. Wherever he was, if not engaged in action, he was going to have his little complaints about his health, 'the tight band around his chest', which he experienced on waking which may have been a cardiac condition, or less seriously some digestive disorder, and of course trouble with his good and over-strained eye. He was also bound to complain about missed opportunities and the inadequacies of his superiors. These were all part of his nature and would have been present had he served in the Arctic or the Indian Ocean. Unfairly it was these matters which were confided to Fanny. She, being the sort of woman she was, no doubt worried about them unduly and became miserable. Yet in fairness to her it must be remembered that her life was fairly dull; she may not have been a very exciting woman, but the company of Nelson's elderly father and the rest of the family, from the ambitious pushing cleric William downwards, can hardly have been stimulating.

Horatio, on the other hand, was leading a very different sort of life. His last service, under his old Commander-in-Chief, had been quasi-diplomatic, rather like his mission to Naples, this time to the independent city state of Venice to request the Doge to permit facilities for rest and refitting and victualling to British ships of war. Lord Hood was informed of the success of the mission and was no doubt gratified that Britain's emissary had been treated in a friendly fashion and also accorded proper respect, the Doge advancing into the room to meet Captain Nelson, who was given 'the honours of a Senator'. Venice was also where Nelson met for the first time Mr Francis Drake, the British Minister in Genoa who also doubled with that post the representation of his country's interest in Venice. Nelson on this occasion formed a poor opinion of Drake, and passed on to Hood the fact that he was unpopular in Genoa, but this was a judgment that was to change with time. Indeed this was not an uncommon habit of Nelson's, a snap judgment on an individual which was completely reversed by him subsequently in the light of further acquaintance and experience, generally veering from a poor opinion to a better one, although there were examples of the process in reverse. This should not necessarily be thought of as a fault in Nelson's character, for it is better to be able to change one's mind than to remain opinionated, prejudiced and dogmatic. However, it does suggest that his first judgments were founded more on impulse than careful reason and he always had a tendency to jump at problems with an instant solution and react to men and women in a moment. From Venice Nelson wrote to Fanny telling her of the scenic delights, 'this City is, without exception, the most magnificent I ever beheld, superior in many respects to Naples, although it does not appear quite so fine from the sea, yet upon shore it is far beyond it. All the houses are palaces on the grandest scale. However, I trust we shall soon quit these magnificent scenes, and retire to England, where all that I admire is placed.' Retirement was extremely unlikely as it turned out; Nelson did not return that year. Poor Fanny had seen none of the magnificent scenes, neither Naples nor Venice, and her husband's letters were probably not quite enough to compensate for lodgings at 17, New King Street, Bath, a cold winter, and conversations and meetings with other naval families such as the returned Hoods, however pleasant

and encouraging they might be about her husband's prospects in the
Service.

The new Commander-in-Chief in the Mediterranean was Vice-
Admiral William Hotham, flying his flag in *Britannia*. Hotham's appointment was odd in the sense that he only exercised temporary authority
until June 1795. He had been one of Hood's large complement of admirals
until his return home and then had taken over in his chief's absence.
Nelson had been right that Hood would not return to the Mediterranean,
a guess which was probably based on his age. Curiously, though, for the
first months of 1795 Nelson went back on his guess and wrote about
Hood's return to the theatre as if that were a definite likelihood.
Obviously rumour and speculation were rife in the fleet and much of
Nelson's new conviction that Hood would return was based on personal
hopes, combined with dissatisfaction with Hotham.

Hood's fate was decided more on grounds of temperament than age,
for there was still no discernible feeling in the British services nor among
her allies, that this might be a young man's war. In December the unpopular Chatham had been replaced as First Lord of the Admiralty by the
able and interested Lord Spencer. Hood was then in England but had not
struck his flag nor surrendered his command. The Board of Admiralty
was re-constituted under the new First Lord and Hood retained his place
as one of the members. However, in March Hood was dropped from the
Board. Thereafter he was no more tactful with his political superior than
he had been with his military equals. It would also have been very strange,
bearing in mind that neither General Dundas nor General Stuart was
without political contacts, if Hood's inability to work with the Army had
not been reported back. So he stayed in Britain, still notionally a commanding admiral, recovered his health while Hotham exercised his
authority in the Mediterranean and it was only when Hotham's own
conduct of affairs provoked an outburst of Hood's domineering temper
that the old admiral was ordered to strike his flag for the last time.

Vice-Admiral William Hotham, although he was promoted full
admiral, granted a peerage and figured, at least partially, in a vote of
thanks from Parliament, was one of those men to whom history has been
somewhat unkind. Admirals may expect to be worsted in their profession
by the enemy and yet Hotham never was, his reputation suffered instead
at the hands of his own countrymen, and his brother officers. His misfortune was to find himself sandwiched between the past record of his
elderly superior and the yet to be made reputation of his subordinate. No

one impugned his courage or his amiability, but even Sir William Hamilton, who, whatever Nelson may have said out of flattery or friendship, was not exactly the shining light of his own profession, could feel free to write to Nelson, 'I can, entre nous, perceive that my old friend, Hotham, is not quite enough for such a command as that of the British Fleet in the Mediterranean, although he is the best creature imagineable.' Nelson, typically, complained of the slow pace at which the war was being conducted and almost in the same breath seemed to think that the allies might be re-admitted to Toulon or that the war would end. He was always over-credulous of rumours. 1795 was for the allies, Austria and Britain, a quiet year though it was the quiet before the uncontrollable storm of the next. In such a year it is not difficult to sense something of the atmosphere in the very confined theatre of operations that the Mediterranean proved to be, for though the whole sea was a trade route and a trading area, naval operations in the sense of fleet against fleet were limited to the western and central Mediterranean extending little beyond the longitude of Corfu in an easterly direction. 'Nelson's war' and the world in which he moved was concentrated very much in the Gulf of Genoa, the Ligurian and Tyrrhenian Seas and an arc of coastline from Toulon eastwards round to Naples taking in the French and Italian Rivieras.

The French fleet was at Toulon and the British were based on Corsica where, in name at least, George III was King. Nevertheless the island could hardly be regarded as a permanently safe base. Corsicans might be British subjects but Nelson compared them to the Irish, saying that they could not be relied on. For the moment they might be loyal, but they might well revolt at any time. In consequence he was always apprehensive of a French invasion and perhaps also overrated the importance of Corsica to France as a supplier of naval stores, such as timber, oil and rope. Collingwood, when he came to the Mediterranean, was more graphic and probably more accurate when he described the products of the island as wild hogs, assassins and generals like Napoleon Bonaparte.

However, almost equally important to Britain were the two neutral ports of Genoa and Leghorn, the latter, especially, being used very heavily by the fleet for repairs and victualling. Vado, Genoa, Spezia (Nelson called it 'Porto Especia') and Leghorn were also important in themselves as milestones in any developing land warfare. It did not need any great strategic sense to predict that if French armies were to advance further beyond their frontiers future conflict would be in Northern Italy against the Austrians and whatever local allies could be persuaded to fight alongside them.

The overall initiative on land and sea seemed to rest with the enemy, for action would occur only if the French fleet came out, or if the French armies advanced. It was not a situation to Nelson's liking, waiting upon the enemy did not suit his ardent temperament, but it does not seem to have disturbed his naval colleagues, certainly not the amiable Admiral Hotham.

Hotham, not averse to 'rollicking' in Leghorn, was forced to stir himself in March. The French fleet increased to seventeen of the line and some smaller vessels had put to sea intent on an attempt to retake Corsica. Hotham, with fourteen of the line and one Neapolitan battleship attached, sailed out to intercept. It seems likely that the sortie by the French was something of a 'try-on' to test British strength and alertness, for once the two fleets had sighted each other there was no attempt by the French admiral to provoke a general action. Nelson was forced to interrupt an already interrupted letter to Fanny as at dawn on March 8 the fleet, 'taken rather suddenly', left Leghorn. All the ships, *Agamemnon* included, were short manned, Nelson's having 150 sick, of whom fifty never recovered. Naturally enough he was concerned lest *Agamemnon*, and indeed the whole fleet, would not acquit itself well.

Nelson's first entry into a fleet action had an element of the absurd. To Fanny he had scrawled in haste—'Life with disgrace is dreadful. A glorious death is to be envied'—without thinking of the effects such a letter might have on a nervous, lonely woman who would not know for some considerable time what fate had overtaken her husband or her son. However, the grandiloquent sentiments were somewhat premature, for it was not until the 10th that Hotham signalled to form line of battle, and even then it was not until three days later that the rival ships were within gunshot. Apart from the French tactics the principal reason for delay was the weather, and Hotham was always unlucky in this respect. The Mediterranean was notoriously fickle at this season and the British fleet was bedevilled by a combination of haze, a heavy swell from the south-west, and a wind which changed suddenly both in force and direction.

The two fleets moved to the west along parallel tracks, the French line to the north, against a squally west wind, The British ships were strung out in a long uneven line, *Agamemnon* well to the westward and nearer to the enemy because of her superior sailing qualities. Her manoeuvrability and speed were often mentioned by Nelson, but she was also, as of the sixty-four gun class, the lightest and smallest of the British line and at a disadvantage compared with the French ships which were mainly of their powerful eighty-gun class. It was by an accident to one of these that Nelson was given his opportunity. It would be absurd to suggest that such an accident could not have happened in the Royal Navy but already one other French ship had returned to port having lost her topmast the night before, indicating that the French standard of seamanship and training was low.

Ça Ira, third from the rear in the French line, ran on board the ship ahead of her and in the collision lost her fore and main topmasts. Masts, sails and rigging fell overboard, carried by the force of the wind on to her leeside which was to port. *Ça Ira* rapidly fell astern, at an obvious disadvantage with some of her port gun batteries masked by the dragging ropes and canvas.

Agamemnon went about so as to place herself directly astern of the French ship, 'absolutely large enough to take *Agamemnon* in her hold', said Nelson with pardonable exaggeration, and then faced the problem of bringing her guns to bear. To gain the advantage Nelson had to present his broadside of thirty guns, otherwise he would be the unequal victim of six powerful stern chasers firing into his bows. This he managed by skilful use of helm and sails, turning into wind so as to present his starboard batteries to the French stern, then firing and then resuming course to make up distance lost and then repeating the manoeuvre. This action was continued for over two hours at a distance of about a hundred yards, and the carnage aboard *Ça Ira* was appalling, a hundred of her crew being killed, compared with seven men wounded aboard *Agamemnon*.

Nelson's speedy reaction and daring had now posed a problem for Martin, the French admiral. Should he sacrifice one damaged ship or attempt to save her, but in the process bring on a general action? Both *Ça Ira* and *Agamemnon* were similar distances from their own fleets, though the advantage of the wind was with the French. Martin decided to assist *Ça Ira* and Captain Fremantle's *Inconstant* came to help Nelson as the French took *Ça Ira* in tow. This was the situation at nightfall, but the decision not to abandon *Ça Ira* provoked the conflict of the next day.

Hotham had recalled Nelson to the main body of the fleet, as the nearest ship of either nationality was the enormous three-decker of 120 guns, *Sans Culottes*, and beyond her was the 74 *Jean Bart*, but both were, according to Nelson, within gunshot range. He rendered the second French ship's name as *Jean Barras*, now a member of the Directory which ruled France; it was not a bad guess for among other outlandish names derived from the Revolution, *Sans Culottes* was the worst example. She was to gain a more graceful name later, and as *L'Orient* Nelson was to see her again at the mouth of the Nile.

The next morning, March 14, *Ça Ira* was in tow of Censeur, a 74, about twenty miles south-west of Genoa, and it is an indication of the pace of a sail action with little wind that the two French ships were now about five miles astern of the rest of their fleet and the British were in their turn about three and a half miles from them. These were Nelson's reckonings, he was still well in advance of the main body of the fleet, but it was *Bedford* and *Captain* which were ordered to intercept the two isolated French ships.

It was at this stage that the French admiral, considerably assisted by a southerly wind, decided on a rescue attempt which consisted of wearing his ships in succession so that they were now sailing in line towards the British on roughly parallel courses. Presumably the object of this manoeuvre was to interpose his own ships between *Ça Ira* and *Censeur* and the British. Whether Martin then lost his nerve or simply miscalculated it is difficult to say, but what happened was that the French, keeping to windward, and this may well have been the deciding factor, sailed past the leading British ships, which were *Illustrious, Courageux, Princess Royal* and *Agamemnon*. The two latter, *Princess Royal* being the flagship of Vice-Admiral Goodall, Hotham's second-in-command, were parallel with *Ça Ira* and *Censeur*, masking them from their compatriots. In these circumstances as the French fleet defiled past them, firing as they went, it was *Illustrious* and *Courageux* which suffered most, losing their main and mizzen masts and having many casualties.

Curiously the action came to no decisive point for the French fleet then resumed its former course but *Ça Ira* and *Censeur* struck their flags, Lieutenant Andrews from *Agamemnon* boarding both and hoisting the Union flag.

It was now a question of what was to be done next. The French fleet consisted of eleven capital ships, two being captured, and *Sans Culottes* and another ship, which had lost her topmast, having both quitted the line. Against that *Illustrious* and *Courageux* were both disabled and *Captain* and *Bedford* had both suffered damage to sails and rigging. Thus the British had eleven effectives and two damaged, plus *Tancredi*, the Neapolitan 74. It was in this situation that Nelson embarked upon an argument with Admiral Hotham.

It could only have occurred in the days of sail, and even then in the almost windless conditions of March days in the Mediterranean. The order of ships in the British line was *Illustrious, Courageux, Princess Royal, Agamemnon, Britannia* and then *Tancredi* commanded by Commodore Caracciolo. Thus Nelson was sandwiched between the flagship of Vice-Admiral Goodall and *Britannia* in which Admiral Hotham was flying his flag. It was only because of Hotham's order for a general chase that the two flagships were so close, in any more formalised order each would have been leading a division.

First Nelson went on board *Britannia* to try and persuade Hotham to leave the two captured ships in charge of *Illustrious* and *Courageux* and some of the attendant frigates, and continue westward in pursuit of the French who were now sailing back to Toulon. He was obviously very excited and enthusiastic for he described Hotham as being 'much calmer than myself'. The admiral's reaction did nothing to cool him down. 'We must be contented. We have done very well,' he said. So Nelson was placed in the classic position, just like Hood before him, the subordinate more active than his superior. Nelson was not a good subordinate, the precepts of unquestioning obedience which he had tried to instil into his midshipmen were not for him, certainly not as a captain. So when he went on board *Princess Royal*, on Hotham's orders, with the two captured French captains, he poured out his heart to Goodall. He took Nelson's part and wrote a quick note to Hotham, but to no avail. Nelson's reaction was as might have been expected, 'Now had we taken ten sail,' he wrote to Fanny, 'and allowed the eleventh to escape when it had been possible to have got at her, I could never have called it well done. We should have had such a day as I believe the annals of England have never produced. Nothing can stop the courage of English seamen—.'

Perhaps so, if the casualty lists of *Ça Ira* and *Censeur* combined, 750 killed and wounded, against *Agamemnon*'s final thirteen wounded, were taken as the criterion. However, it must be remembered that *Ça Ira* had first been disabled by accident. No such disadvantage afflicted any of the other French ships. Admiral Goodall had also imposed a caution, if the French could be brought to action, if in fact they could be caught. The real point was not that Hotham shirked action, but should he have attempted more? With the existing wind conditions he might well have wasted his time or found that his fast sailers like *Agamemnon* were capable of catching up with the French while his four more heavily armed three-deckers lumbered behind and too late. Nelson himself, perhaps unconsciously, put the alternatives, 'Had I commanded our Fleet on the 14 then either the whole French Fleet would have graced my triumph, or I should have been in a confounded scrape.' Hotham having foiled a French plan to repossess Corsica, and taken two of their sail of the line, but having had two of his own dismasted, felt that risking 'a confounded scrape' was not his next and most immediate duty. His attitude was well summed up in his own dispatch when he spoke of the French fleet, 'their intentions are for the present frustrated'. No doubt, but it was a limited and negative objective.

Many Nelson biographers have assumed that Nelson must have been right and Hotham wrong, but the argument is as incapable of proof, after Nelson's reputation had been made, as it was on the day when Hotham made his decision. It is however justifiable to regard March 14, 1795 as an important and significant landmark in Nelson's development as a future admiral. He had not been in a fleet action before, unlike many junior officers serving under Hotham. He had therefore never experienced the old formalised warfare in which men like Hotham, captain of *Gibraltar* in 1757, had been brought up. As for the risks of continuing the general chase: the French were retreating, therefore was not the advantage of morale—'nothing can stop the courage of English seamen'—a factor to be considered?

Hotham's mind was set in the habit of the victory on points; two prizes taken, therefore a satisfactory conclusion. Nelson's mind was moving towards the knock-out victory, the action to destroy as much as possible of an enemy fleet. From the overall strategic point of view he was right, indeed his argument was supported by a misfortune which happened to one unit of Hotham's fleet not present at the March 14 action. Almost at the same time as Hotham was congratulating himself on the captured *Ça Ira* and *Censeur*, the French had captured the solitary *Berwick*, vulnerable because she had also lost a mast through negligence. Thus the 'points lead' was halved, and it can be seen that the only way for the British to assert their mastery was not by piecemeal actions but by total destruction.

As was the way in the eighteenth century, wooden ships being rarely sunk and often well-nigh indestructible, *Berwick* was to turn up again, flying the French flag and without changing her name, again the custom of the day, which must have posed as much of a pronunciation problem for the French seaman as did *Courageux* for the British. Changing a ship's name was regarded by superstitious sailors as tampering with her luck, and the eventual fate of *Sans Culottes* was later used as a telling example of the dangers. The twists of human fate were also to bring Commodore Francisco Caracciolo and, by then, Admiral Horatio Nelson briefly together again, though in very different circumstances to those of March 14, 1795.

The command of the fleet in the Mediterranean was to change on two more occasions before the year was out, as if, and it may well have been the case, the Admiralty could not make up its mind what sort of officers it wanted to use and what sort of war it wanted to wage. It was not until June that Hood's possibility of return finally disappeared. The old admiral had been convinced that he would and should return. Hotham's indecisiveness reinforced his intention and he made clear his demands in the most peremptory manner. In March his name had been omitted from the new Board of Admiralty, but he was determined to return to action and with a reinforcement of more ships of the line. However, admirals propose and my Lords of the Admiralty dispose, and Spencer, provoked by Hood's arrogance, ordered him to strike his flag for the last time. Samuel Hood's next and final appointment came in the next year, as Governor of the Greenwich Hospital for Seamen, where he spent the final twenty years of his life. 'Oh, miserable Board of Admiralty,' wrote Nelson to his brother William on hearing the news, but Hotham, the admiral who would not 'jump about', remained. However, he seemed to be reasonably well disposed towards Nelson to whom he gave independent detached commands, perhaps to their mutual satisfaction.

On July 5 *Agamemnon* with three frigates and a cutter were assigned to co-operate with the Austrian army in an attempt to recover the Genoese Riviera. In the event of the French, seventeen sail of the line and six frigates strong assumed to be in Toulon harbour, came very near to capturing Nelson. The odds were too much even for Nelson, and his tiny squadron was chased for twenty-four hours back to San Fiorenzo where Hotham and the fleet were at anchor. Only superior seamanship saved *Agamemnon* and her consorts and this time Hotham did jump about. The full fleet got under way, but unfortunately could make little progress against adverse winds. On July 12 though, the British were presented with what appeared to be another chance, the enemy were again in sight and Hotham made the signal for a general chase. Again the French retreated, but lost in the process one of their rearmost ships, *Alcide*, a 74 which, a fairly rare occurrence, blew up before she could be taken as a prize. Nelson in the van with the fast-sailing *Agamemnon* was disappointed and tended to blame Hotham, somewhat unfairly, as was proved by Nelson's own failure to engage a French ship he had marked down, for the advantage of the wind was not with the British.

Nelson was once again chosen for detached duties, but as some consolation for service under Hotham he was made a Colonel of marines. He had already hinted to Fanny, Captain Locker and William Suckling that this might happen and financially at least he seemed to prefer it to any chance of promotion to flag rank. Colonelcies of marines were sinecures and awarded normally to the six captains at the top of the post list. Notionally, as grades of admirals held the posts of generals, there was a duty to oversee the corps of marines which had no senior officers of its own, and all the lucky recipient did was to draw emoluments. Apart from the financial advantage, and without the expenses of a rear-admiral, there was another reason why Nelson may not have wanted flag rank at this moment. Quite obviously, despite all his complaining, he enjoyed the Mediterranean station, where there was already a considerable littering of admirals; as a newly promoted rear-admiral he would probably have had to return home and take his chance of a new appointment. Finally, it must be observed that Nelson was somewhat premature in expecting promotion to rear-admiral when he had not yet been a commodore, the customary intermediate appointment.

On detached service Nelson had an opportunity of renewing his acquaintance with Mr Drake, and improving his previously poor opinion of 'our man' at Genoa. They agreed that if action were to be taken against the French an obvious target was the supplies brought by sea to the south of France from Italy, Sicily and North Africa. The difficulty was to identify this small ship trade which was carried in neutral vessels by captains who, if forced to heave-to by a British man of war, would obviously fabricate any destination other than a French port.

Nelson's orders from Hotham were to 'take and obtain all vessels (to whatever nations they may belong) bound to France'. The difficulties and details of sorting out the true destinations of cargoes were not really a task for a man of Nelson's temperament. 'We have much power here at present to do great things, if we know how to apply it', he wrote to William Suckling, but obviously his methods of using Britain's sea power would have differed from Hotham's. He wrote of his superior, 'Hotham must get a new head, no man's heart is better, but that will not do without the other.'

The problem of Admiral Hotham's head was dealt with on November

1, when he struck his flag and handed over command to Vice-Admiral Sir Hyde Parker. However, he was only exercising temporary command, the day when he would command Nelson in an important engagement was yet to come, and towards the end of the year Admiral Sir John Jervis arrived at San Fiorenzo to take the Mediterranean command, 'to the great joy of some and sorrow of others in the fleet', as Nelson put it. *Agamemnon* was then being patched up and repaired at Leghorn, her sides had been secured with cables for some time, so he did not meet his new Commander-in-Chief until January 13 of the new year.

CHAPTER TWELVE

On Detached Service

THE ARRIVAL of John Jervis had a profound effect upon the Mediterranean fleet as a whole, and in particular upon one of its outstanding post captains.

Jervis, as a sea officer, was in a class of his own. There were always a number of senior naval officers who were regarded as hard, tough men, steadfast, incorruptible and inflexible disciplinarians. In all ages and in all navies it has been a 'type' of naval officer, and of admiral, and no doubt many have consciously tried to live up to it. Lord Hood came very near to filling the bill, though his action towards the end of his career fell short of his reputation. Rodney quite obviously, with his many defects of character, was not even a competitor in the contest. Howe was far too genial and gentlemanly to qualify. Nelson himself had his own very special standards, and Collingwood, though with something of a reputation as a stern commander, was in essence kindly and painstaking and rather a dull dog. Jervis, who had entered the navy with no advantage behind him, his baronetcy had been awarded for taking *Pégase* in 1782 without the loss of a man, had made his own way and was the iron disciplinarian par excellence. He never wavered from his duty and showed neither fear nor favour to any man, from some sprig of aristocracy seeking preferment to any unfortunate inhabitant of the lower deck who hoped to avoid the lash. In 1796 'old Jarvie' was sixty-two and his reputation which was known throughout the Service had preceded him to his new appointment. His arrival had aroused mixed feelings, the standards he demanded, from seamanship to dress, deportment and the punctilio of ceremonial were notorious. *Foudroyant*, his ship in the American war, had been the very model of efficiency and order. Indeed many observances now taken for granted in the navies of the world, such as the morning and evening formalities on hoisting and lowering the ensign, were originally introduced by Jervis as part of his drive to impose uniformity and smartness on the ships and men he commanded.

Sir John Barrow, in his time himself a Secretary of the Admiralty, who knew both Howe and Jervis, contrasted the two men in his biography of Howe, summing up Jervis as 'rigorous, peremptory and resolute, rigidly maintaining that the life and soul of naval discipline was obedience—his favourite word was *obedienza*'.

Looking back on the events of the previous year Nelson and his brother officers could reasonably expect some changes. For Nelson himself 1795 had been a mixed year. His duties had ranged between the two tasks of the Mediterranean Fleet, protecting the British and preying on French commerce and assisting Britain's continental allies on shore. Domestically there had been difficulties about Fanny's legacy from her uncle Herbert on which he had tried to render advice at long distance.

An additional irritant arose when allegations were made, originally by Austrian officers to their own government in Vienna, and thence, through diplomatic channels to Mr Drake and the King of Sardinia, that British officers, including Nelson, were conniving, presumably for profit, at the landing of enemy supplies on the Genoese Riviera for the French Army. It is perhaps unnecessary to add that a vigorous letter refuting the charges was dispatched from *Agamemnon* to Lord Grenville, the Foreign Secretary.

It was a false and garbled accusation and Nelson was right to challenge it, but there was something about the tone of his letter which suggests a stridency and desperation out of place in an official communication: 'and in two wars [I] have been in more than 140 skirmishes and battles at sea, and on shore; have lost an eye, and otherwise blood, in fighting the enemies of my king and country; and God knows, instead of riches, my little fortune has been diminished in the service . . .'.

Perhaps there was some truth in a letter to Sir Gilbert Elliot: 'in good truth I am almost worn out. I find my exertions have been beyond my strength. I have a complaint in my breast which will probably bear me down; but please God if I see this campaign out, if *Agamemnon* does not go to England, I must; the medical people tell me, "be on shore for a month or two, without the thoughts of service".' That letter was written towards the end of July and still in August he was writing to William Suckling telling him that he had been ill for several days, that because of trouble with his eyes he was almost blind and summarising his condition as 'alive and that's all'.

Yet 1795 was not all disappointments: the Colonelcy of the Chatham division of Marines was welcome and, having tasted a fleet action and observed the conduct of senior officers, a growing ambition had crystallised. On April 1 in the letter to Fanny describing the March 14 action he wrote—'but we are idle and lay in port when we ought to be at sea. In short I wish to be an admiral and in the command of the English fleet. I should very soon either do much or be ruined. My disposition can't bear tame and slow measures.'

It was a reasonable enough estimate of his own character. His personality was obviously cyclothymic, changing rapidly from depression to elation, but to Fanny, for once, he had managed to strike a balance and see and describe himself reasonably accurately.

Accepting that self-estimate it is easy to see how the personalities of 1795, Admiral Hotham, Admiral Man and General Baron de Vins, the elderly Austrian cavalry general with whom he was sent to co-operate with five frigates and a brig in an advance towards Nice, all provoked irritation. Hotham was happy with others, 'rollicking their time', at Leghorn, Man was a nonentity, and de Vins, like all Austrians in Nelson's view, was happy for the war to go on at a snail's pace for ever, as long as the British Treasury continued to pay out subsidies.

None of these men seemed to possess his own enthusiasm for 'the common cause', although there were times when even Nelson had succumbed to some of the pleasures and relaxations of ordinary men. The scene was Leghorn, which had acquired a seamy reputation in Hotham's time and was to become the object of scathing comment from Jervis when he took over command. The town boasted a seedy opera house among its delights, and restaurants and hotels which were adapted to the pleasures of British sea officers on leave. For a picture of the town and the habits of his contemporaries, some of whom finished up in hospital with what a later navy regarded as 'self-inflicted wounds', and an unusual glimpse of Nelson, posterity is indebted to the pen of Captain Fremantle who commanded the frigate *Inconstant*.

Fremantle's tersely worded record, a fragment of a diary, only came to light because of his subsequent marriage to Miss Betsy Wynne who was a considerable diarist; both Fremantle and his bride knew Nelson well. Some idea of Fremantle's character can be gained in the following extracts, scattered over his own service in the Mediterranean.

A few days after he and Nelson had nearly been killed at the batteries before Bastia he comments on the armaments sent from Naples:

Th. 21 [April 1794] The Neapolitan mortars not worth a farthing.

They crack. The shells don't fit them, very pretty in the nights to see the shells flying.

Later Fremantle is in Naples,

Sat. 28. May 1794. Was introduced to the King at his country house. Saw the horse race. Dine with Sir Wm. Hamilton. My lady an uncommon treat, tells stories about the King.

The next day after dinner and the opera he decides:

Lady H's maid the prettiest woman in Naples. The Queen the ugliest.

A considerable number of entries concern Captain Fremantle's 'getting mortal'—i.e. dead drunk—and his adventures with 'uncommon pretty Dollies', one of whom he describes as a 'ravenous bitch'. However, there are four entries which concern Nelson in Leghorn:

December 1794. Wed. 3.

Dined at Nelson's and his dolly—called on old Udney [the British Consul], went to the opera with him. He introduced me to a very handsome Greek woman.

August 21 [1795]

A convoy arrived from Genoa. Dined with Nelson. Dolly aboard who has a sort of abcess in her side, he makes himself ridiculous with that woman.

Sun 27th (Sept).

Dined with Nelson and Dolly. Very bad dinner indeed.

The next day he again had dinner with Nelson, or rather 'Nelsons', and the same day *Agamemnon* and her captain left Leghorn. 'Dolly' was anything from regular mistress to whore. Miss Betsy Wynne and her sister were referred to as damsels and were emphatically not dollies.

Horatio Nelson was obviously not the only unfaithful husband in the Mediterranean Fleet. Admiral Hotham for instance had an attachment to a Mrs Newnham who was referred to by his subordinate officers as 'the Commander of the Fleet'. The morality and habits implied by jokes about a 'wife in every port' and the naval toast 'Wives and Sweethearts', always followed by some wag adding, 'may they never meet', were apparently accepted by Nelson as much as anyone else. However, Fremantle's diary entries support a comment made by James Harrison, one of Nelson's first, and probably worst, biographers.

Harrison mentions only two faults as disfiguring his hero's otherwise blameless moral reputation, venery and swearing. 'The occasional use of a few thoughtlessly profane expletives in speech' though Harrison regarded it as 'that other vicious habit of British seamen' is scarcely of concern. Nelson's other 'improper indulgences' are of more significance: 'It is not to be dissembled, though by no means ever an unprincipled seducer of the wives and daughters of his friends, he was always well known to maintain rather more partiality for the fair sex than is quite consistent with the highest degree of Christian purity.' Nelson, therefore, obviously had what the Victorians called 'a reputation', sufficient for Harrison to mention it and when he did so, as he received Lady Hamilton's co-operation with his work, not to mean by 'indulgences' Nelson's passion for Emma which was obviously in a very different category indeed.

From Harrison's ponderous moralising and Fremantle's robustness it is possible to draw the conclusion that Nelson, no doubt with the excuse of war and absence, was sometimes unfaithful to Fanny, and with more than one 'dolly'. It is also reasonable to assume, looking forward, that Nelson's reputation in the small world of the Mediterranean was known to Lady Hamilton, some justification for the fact that she was often fearful that he would be unfaithful to her. However, in that respect like Tennyson's Lancelot, 'faith unfaithful kept him falsely true'.

The importance of Captain Fremantle's comments is that they destroy the portrait that Nelson painted of himself to Fanny, William Suckling, Captain Locker, and others as diverse as Sir Gilbert Elliot and the Duke of Clarence, as the stern adherent at all times to duty, suffering and striving whilst others were 'frolicking' in Leghorn.

In a way Nelson's attitude to the indulgences of others and his own was just as inconsistent as his view of obedience, it was something he expected, but did not always render. Ominous too for the future was Fremantle's opinion that Nelson, with one dolly, was managing to make himself ridiculous. Something that Fremantle, even with Hannah, Mimi, Magdalena, Nina, Miss Watson, a lady he called 'Mrs Hill', and of course Miss Wynne, the respectable damsel, always managed not to do.

1795 had been a mixed year and one in which most of the contrasting facets of Nelson's complicated character were revealed. 1796 was to prove itself an even worse year from the point of view of the conduct of the war for while Nelson cemented a relationship with his new Commander-in-Chief, a new era had begun on land, almost entirely due to the advent of one man. For if it was true, and Nelson meant it when he wrote to Fanny, 'I believe that no man has been treated so ill as myself', life had certainly offered a number of chances to General Buonaparte.

Imprisoned briefly after the fall of Robespierre, because of his close connection with the younger Robespierre brother, the young artillery general had re-emerged by October 1795 into enough favour to be in charge of artillery and second-in-command, in the Army of the Interior, to Barras. On June 10 of that year the young prince, whom all Royalists looked to as Louis XVII, had died in a Paris prison. The rightful heir to the French throne was now the Comte de Provence, serving with a foreign army and fighting against France.

Thus in a very personalised form the dilemma was posed, what form of permanent government should France have? After a long period of uncertainty, chaos, violence and bloodshed, there was obviously a groundswell of opinion in favour of some system which would give promise of security and continuity. That had been assured by the old Bourbon monarchy, but its active adherents had now thrown in their lot with foreigners. Accordingly the Convention put forward its version of a replacement, with a revised constitution. Its fault was that it erred too much on the side of permanence, so in Vendémiaire Year IV in the Revolutionary Calendar, the Paris mob, as it had done before, took to the streets. However, as an unemployed spectator Barras's new second-in-command back in August 1792 had seen the old monarchy overthrown by the mob, and it was not a prospect that had appealed to him very much. Mobs in his view should and could be dispersed with 'a whiff of grape-shot'.

So when on October 3 the Louvre and the Tuileries, where the Convention had barricaded itself in, were surrounded, the attackers were met with artillery positioned by General Buonaparte. On October 26 the Convention gave up power to a five-man Directory, and two of its members, Barras and Carnot, had both once been professional soldiers.

Early the next year in Paris Napoleon Bonaparte, in the new French spelling which he had adopted, married Josephine de Beauharnais, Barras's ex-mistress. She, like Fanny Nelson, was a colonial widow, older than her husband who brought with her a stepson whom her husband felt it his duty to advance in his own profession. These two ladies were otherwise not at all alike, the future Empress of the French showing no indication of distress in the absence of her campaigning husband.

On March 27, 1796 Bonaparte, who had been on board a French ship as part of the expedition to retake his native Corsica, and so in the action

of March 14, 1795, was back again in the same theatre as Nelson. On that
day the twenty-seven-year-old general took over in Nice the command of
the whole French army in Italy from the sixty-three-year-old Schérer.
Three of the divisional commanders he inherited were Augereau,
Masséna and Sérurier; with him to serve on his staff he brought three
officers called Berthier, Marmont and Murat. All six, and they were all
young save Sérurier, were within a decade to be Marshals of the new
French Empire and Murat, an inn-keeper's son, was to be King in
Naples, following Bonaparte's brother, Joseph, who replaced the
wretched Bourbon Ferdinand.

There is a temptation to compare the two men, Nelson and Napoleon,
who never met, but who constantly crossed each other's paths, both
supreme in their own sphere of warfare, both innovators, but using and
adapting the experience of others. But in 1796 it was too early to draw
meaningful conclusions as Nelson, unlike Napoleon, though the older
man by ten years, had not yet reached a position of independence. One
striking difference is, however, worth noting even at this stage. Both
sought command, influence, and the powers of direction, by whatever
means were available—Nelson was still dabbling with the idea of a seat
in Parliament in 1796—because both were convinced that given that
power they could use it successfully, but Napoleon already had theories
cut and dried, while Nelson, never a generaliser, was still groping
mentally towards his own formulae for battle success. It was partly for
this reason, and because Nelson's leadership was so personalised and so
much a matter of style, that he never had a successor, whereas Napoleon's
theories could be put into practice by others, though even in his case
there were probably only two out of his twenty-two Marshals, Masséna
and Davout, who were really capable of doing so.

On the same day as General Bonaparte issued a grandiloquent order of
the day to his poorly-clad, badly-fed soldiers, promising them the 'fertile
plains' of Italy and offering them riches and glory, Horatio Nelson took
another step up his promotion ladder, to Commodore 2nd Class, his
broad swallow-tailed red pendant flying at the mainmast of *Agamemnon*.
On June 11 pendant and commodore were both transferred to *Captain*, of
seventy-four guns, and the worn-out *Agamemnon* was at last sent home,
escorting a convoy. Her last service, with Nelson on the quarter-deck,
had been to capture the seaborne siege train of artillery bound for Mantua
and the use of General Bonaparte.

Under Hotham's command Nelson had coveted a broad pendant, not so much for personal reasons, but more on the grounds that it would have impressed foreign allies, such as General de Vins, when he had been on detached service. Subsequent events showed that the ensign of an Admiral of the Red displayed ten times over would not have stirred that elderly gentleman to exert himself in the common cause. Ironically now that Nelson had both a Commander-in-Chief who aroused his respect and had received from him the insignia of independent command, the allies who might have been impressed were fast fading away.

Jervis had made his personality felt even before arriving, for while coming out in the frigate *Lively* he discovered Rear-Admiral Man at Gibraltar and ordered him back to where he should have been, his station off Cadiz. The next indication that the fleet was now in different hands was the imposition of a proper blockade on Toulon. Then in the spring and early summer of 1796 Jervis proceeded to apply himself to every aspect of the Mediterranean Fleet; 'Mediterranean discipline' soon became an expression well understood throughout the Service. But Jervis was no mere martinet, he was also an organiser of an efficient battle fleet. He began with basics such as the commissariat and ships' stores and as the French grip on land increased these were to become increasingly important for a fleet with access to fewer and fewer friendly ports and anchorages. Jervis required, and achieved, well-maintained ships and healthy crews. With that foundation laid, discipline, seamanship and gunnery were improved, as were the whole manoeuvring and management of the fleet to conform speedily and efficiently to the orders issued from the flagship, *Victory*.

Not everybody welcomed the new régime; Rear-Admiral Robert Man was not the only senior officer to suffer. Admiral Mahan, one of Nelson's most skilled and professional biographers, is incorrect in saying that Jervis and Nelson had never met before 1796. Years before, Captain Locker had introduced a young Nelson whom he described as 'his élève' to a senior admiral in one of the passages of the Houses of Parliament. Whether Jervis really remembered an incident of which Nelson reminded him was however scarcely material to the favourable impression they both now made upon each other. Jervis replaced Hood in Nelson's admiration and it was obviously a great consolation to him, at a time of low ebb in Britain's fortunes, to have a Commander-in-Chief who took the same robust view as he did of the way to wage war. In addition Jervis continued the practice of his predecessors in giving Nelson independent command. The envious comment of one brother officer, which provoked 'a pretty strong answer', 'You did as you pleased in Lord Hood's time, the same in Admiral Hotham's, and now again with Sir John Jervis; it makes no difference to you who is commander-in-chief,' contained some truth, but not all of it. Hood had given Nelson some responsibility, Hotham had probably been as pleased to separate himself from an energetic and potentially difficult subordinate as Nelson had been to rid himself of the apron strings of a cautious superior. Only Jervis discerned the quality in Nelson which throve on responsibility and decision, and he had to handle a captain, now commodore, who had grown in experience even in the previous twelve months.

Jervis as Commander-in-Chief, with the main fleet, watched the French fleet in Toulon and prepared himself for the Spaniards, who, if rumour were true, were about to become enemies, while Nelson's concern was the Italian peninsula. There, as Bonaparte prepared himself for a spring campaign, only held back by a late winter, the situation, politically as well as militarily, was both complex and ominous.

Northwards and westwards of the Maritime Alps and in the valley of the Po the powers were still opposed to France and at war. To the west was Piedmont, part of the Kingdom of Sardinia with its elderly king, its capital at Turin, and to the east were the two duchies of Milan and Mantua under the control of the Habsburg Emperor. Then there was a further hotch-potch of small independent states in northern and central Italy, principally Venice, Genoa, Tuscany, and then the Papal States stretching in a broad band across the peninsula and centred upon Rome. All the other states were neutral, militarily they counted for little and existed uncomfortably poised between the two opposing sides. Venice, despite her ancient prestige, was of no great strategic importance, but Tuscany held Leghorn and Genoa's territory of the Ventimiglia, along the Riviera, contained Vado Bay and to the east the Gulf of Spezia, both excellent anchorages. In contrast to this, that is the Royal Navy's, point of view, the French saw the Italian ports and anchorages on the eastern coast as having a military as well as a naval significance, for the Riviera could provide a road into Italy. Admittedly it was a coastal road, which could be threatened from the sea, but an army along that road could be supplied from the sea by the small coastal vessels of the area which were already an irritant and a provocation to Nelson, who had unfortunately neither the small vessels nor the spare men necessary to produce an effective counter-force.

Looking at Bonaparte's whirlwind campaign in Italy from Nelson's quarter-deck, the emotions of surprise and disappointment were those most frequently experienced, for his principal duty seemed to be to report to Jervis the uninterrupted successes of the enemy.

Bonaparte, who had not wasted his time spent at the Bureau Topographique in Paris in the summer of 1795, studying the terrain of northern Italy and previous campaigns waged there, was not operating entirely on his own initiative. The Directory had ordered him to deal with France's enemies in Italy, Sardinia and the Austrians. The manner in which he did this was to give the French army its first injection of professionalism since the Revolution. A proper strategic and tactical plan, plus a new disciplined handling of the soldiers themselves. He was considerably assisted when putting his plans into practice by the conventionalism and sluggishness of his opponents.

On April 12 at Montenotte he drove a wedge between the Austrians, under the seventy-one-year-old Baron Beaulieu, and the Sardinians, commanded by a loaned, and also elderly, Austrian, von Colli. The Austrians were defeated on the 12th and the Sardinians the next day at Millesimo. There followed the battles of Dego and Mondovi and by April 28 the King of Sardinia was engaged in armistice negotiations at Cherasco. A further battle at Lodi followed Bonaparte's crossing of the Po at Piacenza, by which time the young French general had defeated Generals Argenteau, Vukassovich, Pittoni and Sebottendorf, a collection of senior military gentlemen who, if nothing else, demonstrated by their names the internationalism of an Empire which though Habsburg, and in common parlance Austrian, was still Holy Roman. On May 15 General Bonaparte entered Milan, the capital of Lombardy, at the head of his troops riding a small grey Arab horse.

Thus in a fantastically short time Bonaparte had carried out the three tasks set him by the Directory, the elimination of the Sardinians, the defeat of the Austrians and the occupying of the Duchy of Milan. The question 'what next?' was in a number of minds. Carnot in Paris, regarded by his fellow members of the Directory as 'the organiser of victory'; Bonaparte, who had a complete strategy in his own head for the whole of Italy and beyond; Austrian generals in Italy and their masters in Vienna; and finally, British sea officers in the Mediterranean. Nelson had sampled Austrian—he called them 'German'—generals, in the person of Baron de Vins who had been a great flatterer, very free with promises of action, but short on performance. What Nelson had seen of the Imperial Army after the Loano defeat had not been impressive; de Vins had resigned, in the middle of action, for reasons of ill health and 'the Austrians ran 18 miles without stopping, the Men without any arms whatsoever. Officers without soldiers.' Before the battle de Vins had complained of his Italian allies, after it he complained of a lack of British co-operation.

There was more than a grain of truth in the complaint of de Vins and others. If the British were offering naval co-operation then it should have had more substance than Nelson with a handful of frigates. If the movement of supplies by sea was to be indicted then it should have been done properly. The fact that Neapolitans and Sardinians, also allies, might have helped by providing in-shore vessels and crews to man them but did not, was no excuse for Admiral Hotham's lack of interest and failure to provide the means.

Nelson did what he could with a tiny force and could not restrain himself from passing on advice, which must have been irritating and was certainly ignored, to the Imperial high command directly, or by way of the British representatives at the various Italian capitals. There was little else that he could do and it is not too fanciful to discern, at this frustrating time, that his mind was drawn towards the formulation of his own principles of warfare. On land the pattern and tempo was changing, but that could also happen at sea in the hands of a commander with an adequate force and the liberty to pursue his own convictions.

Meanwhile, Bonaparte, having used the threat of resignation effectively, had argued the Directory into accepting his estimate of the chances in Italy and therefore his advocacy of a more forward-thrusting policy with the object of gaining even more military and political control of the peninsula. No policy could succeed against him, whatever the British navy did, unless it involved counter-measures exercised by a strong army under efficient and resolute generals. Unfortunately for the Allied cause the multi-national Habsburg Empire, though it had many hard fighting individual regiments, seemed totally incapable of providing such a combination.

Inevitably the mood of those who wished to see resolute action against the French was one of pessimism. The British diplomatic representatives, men like Mr Drake at Genoa, and the Hon. John Trevor at Turin and further afield Sir Gilbert Elliot as Viceroy of Corsica, tried hard to gather information and evaluate the situation and give some confidence to half-hearted combatants and apprehensive neutrals. However, and Nelson, who was in correspondence with all of them, knew this as well as anyone, it was impossible for the British, with only a fleet, to give much effective reassurance to Italians whose principal fear was of a French army. It was an atmosphere alive with rumours and speculation and it is interesting, especially as the Italian campaign produced the intriguing situation of Nelson and Bonaparte in confrontation for the first time, to examine a little closer one of Nelson's apprehensions, which in the event proved groundless.

The rumour which captured Nelson's imagination was of a French seaborne invasion of Italy, south of the positions already occupied by their soldiers. Writing to Trevor in Turin he told him how he had kept observation on Toulon for six days and there detected 'a visible getting forward of their Ships'. This fleet he thought was being prepared to 'cover a body of troops in Transports'. Writing to the Duke of Clarence in March from Genoa he expanded on 'the danger if the Enemy's fleet should be able to cover the landing of 20,000 men between Port Especia and Leghorn, where I have always been of the opinion they would attempt it, I know of nothing to prevent their fully possessing the rich mine of Italy'.

Nelson's estimate of the Army of Italy was 80,000 men, whereas, in fact, there were 63,000; which is indicative of his credulity in rumours. It is also interesting that Nelson attributed much of the French initiative to the presence of Saliceti, one of the two Representatives of the People with the army, although it was Bonaparte with his view of how the campaign should be fought who had prevailed over both of the Representatives and the Directory in Paris.

So by June when the Austrian Governor of Lombardy, the Archduke Ferdinand, had given up the province, Bonaparte from his headquarters in Milan sent his divisional generals pushing into the possessions of the independent states of Venice, Genoa and the Grand Duke of Tuscany. By June 21, therefore, the territories and ports which had concerned Nelson were already overrun by French soldiers. There was little or no resistance and two days later Bonaparte himself was able to sign an armistice.

On June 11, 1796 Nelson transferred his pendant to *Captain*, a seventy-four-gun two-decker classified as a third rate, one of the standard ships of the line. There were still 64's like *Agamemnon* within this category but they were being gradually phased out. The seventy-four-gun ship was in many ways the ideal ship, for above the third rate, which was a ship carrying from sixty-four to eighty guns, were the second rates, eighty to ninety-eight guns, and the first rate, 100 guns or more, such as *Victory*.

The first and second rates carried a larger armament than a 74, but both rates were three-deckers and, with their towering sides, had the disadvantage of instability in bad weather.

On August 11 Jervis assigned a separate captain to *Captain*, thus confirming Nelson in his appointment as a Commodore of the first class. It now seemed most probable that very soon Nelson would have his flag as a Rear-Admiral of the Blue, the most junior grade of Admiral. Jervis in conversation with Nelson had assumed with such matter-of-factness that this would be the next step that really there could be little room for doubt in Nelson's own mind. Promotion did not come until the next year, but in terms of pure personal advancement 1796 was a good year for Nelson. He was beginning to approach what Admiral Mahan called 'his page in history'. There was no inevitability about it nor was there anything automatic, the chances of fate in the life of a sea officer were too obvious for that and had already been demonstrated in Nelson's own life.

As 1796 drew to a close, luck and opportunities seemed to have deserted the Allied cause, and more especially the Royal Navy. One of its immediate but humiliating tasks was to evacuate British subjects from Leghorn, which was about to be captured by the twenty-nine-year-old cavalry general Joachim Murat. Nelson's convoy had to take on board, among others, the Pollard family which had looked after Midshipman Hoste when he was ill, Lady Elliot, the wife of Sir Gilbert, and the Wynnes who had escaped there from Florence. The latter were a curious family. The words 'expatriate' and 'cosmopolitan' might have been invented specifically to describe them. The head of the family, Mr Richard Wynne, after his French wife had borne him his fifth daughter, had obviously given up hope of a son and heir and had sold his property in Lincolnshire and had come to live permanently on the Continent. It was perhaps not such a wrench as it might have been for others as he himself was half-Italian, his mother coming from Venice. He was now fifty-two, still with some means, but no abilities of any sort. Incapable even of organising his own affairs or those of his family, he had collected round him about twenty dependants of various sorts and nationalities who merely added to the confusion.

Two of the daughters, Betsy and Jenny, kept diaries, and from these emerges a very good, lively picture, through the eyes of two upper-class teenage girls, of Jervis's Mediterranean Fleet and the squadron under 'old Nelson', who was then thirty. Miss Betsy Wynne was soon to lose her heart to Captain Fremantle but that did not stop her enjoying at the age

of seventeen the company of a crowd of attentive sea officers. Even old
Jervis softened towards these attractive curiosities aboard a battle fleet and
while revealing his penchant for being saluted with a chaste kiss christened
them 'the Aimables'. Some of Betsy's comments are almost too good to
be true, as for instance when she found 'the noise and crashing of the guns'
to be 'most tiring', but she was to prove herself, in the company of her
husband, and no doubt her naval hosts took care not to pass on the anxie-
ties they must have felt as to their real situation. For while to Miss Betsy
and Miss Jenny the great towering ships, spick and span, with their
agreeable officers and swift efficient crews must have appeared all powerful, the days of their presence in the Mediterranean were numbered. They
were in fact being squeezed out of the element, on which they reigned
supreme, by operations on land.

On June 2 Nelson wrote to Jervis in the course of duty and ended his
letter with a light-hearted reference to a recent capture. 'I have got the
charts of Italy sent by the Directory to Buonaparte, also Maillebois' Wars
in Italy, Vauban's Attack and Defence of Places, and Prince Eugene's
History; all sent for the General. If Buonoparte is ignorant the Directory,
it would appear, wish to instruct him: pray God he may remain
ignorant.'

Nelson's prayer was not answered and soon he and his New York-born
captain, Ralph Miller, whom Nelson had rescued from the command of
a wrecked ship off Ajaccio, found themselves actively engaged in a process
of withdrawal and retreat. This was as a result of the operations of
Bonaparte whose opponent was Field-Marshal Würmser, the successor to
Beaulieu, who had in his turn succeeded the disastrous de Vins. Each
commander appointed by Vienna was older than the last but Würmser
was a tough resolute old soldier and came very near to relieving Mantua,
where the Austrian garrison held out stubbornly, and also to defeating
Bonaparte and bringing his advance to an end.

However, the French carried the day in August at Lonato and the
closely-fought battle of Castiglione. The news of the latter had effect
outside Italy for it decided 'the Prince of the Peace', Godoy, who ruled
Spain, and on August 19 the treaty of San Ildefonso was signed between
Spain and France, an obvious diplomatic prelude, as was well realised in
London, to Spain declaring war on Britain on October 8.

In May Nelson had observed that 'Spain is certainly going to war with
somebody' and after Würmser's defeat at Castiglione he wrote to Jervis
in an even more pessimistic strain, 'Austria I suppose must make peace

and we shall, as usual, be left to fight it out'. In fact there was a few more months' fight left in the Habsburg 'white-coats'.

Pitt and his Cabinet decided on August 31 to extract Britain from the Corsican entanglement, evacuate the island and withdraw the fleet from the Mediterranean. Considering what was about to be ranged against Britain in the naval sphere, the combined fleets of France, Spain and Holland, the Dutch ships having been captured earlier by French cavalry riding across the frozen Texel, it was not an unreasonable decision. Orders were accordingly dispatched to Admiral Jervis and Sir Gilbert Elliot. There then occurred one of those developments which, it may be argued, demonstrated British indecisiveness, but much more clearly emphasised the problems Britain faced in maintaining a Continental alliance. While Würmser had finished up by being besieged in Mantua, the fortress town he had originally intended to relieve, on the German front Austrian arms were more successful. The Archduke Charles, a man of the same age as Bonaparte and his country's ablest general, defeated Bernadotte at Neumarck on August 16 just when Lord Malmesbury was on his way to Paris to begin peace preliminaries with the Directory. Thugut, the Imperial Chancellor in Vienna, was now moving in exactly the opposite direction. Britain had forced herself to consider peace, Austria was now beginning to consider it unthinkable. The Prussians were still useless, but there were rumours that Catherine of Russia might at last be persuaded to use her influence. In a rare panic the Cabinet countermanded the orders for the evacuation of Corsica, it also being thought that that island might be offered to the Russians. So Lord Malmesbury was left in Paris to engage in what must have been curiously inconclusive conversations with Delacroix, the French Foreign Minister.

CHAPTER THIRTEEN

Evacuation of the Mediterranean

THE EFFECT of the arrival of conflicting instructions from London upon the men on the spot in the Mediterranean, Sir John Jervis, Sir Gilbert Elliot and Nelson can be imagined, but the orders of August 31 to evacuate Corsica did not reach them until the last week of September. The pace of eighteenth-century communications averted chaos, for once the orders were received they were put into operation as quickly as possible and the countermanding orders arrived too late for the process to be reversed.

Although Jervis, Elliot and Nelson were all downcast at the prospect of withdrawal none of them were now under any illusions about Corsica itself. Jervis's opinion of the natives was about the same as Collingwood's, describing them as 'infernal miscreants', and no responsible officer was sanguine about the garrison's chances of repelling a resolute attempt by the French at invasion and repossession. Already, in June, Jervis and Elliot had decided that they needed a fall-back position in the Mediterranean and accordingly Nelson was dispatched to occupy Elba. On July 9 Nelson took his squadron into Porto Ferrajo and disembarked troops and marines and although Elba was part of the Kingdom of Tuscany there was no resistance to the landing.

On Corsica Sir Gilbert and Lady Elliot, who had been very Scots in the determined manner in which they had adapted the local population to their own way and view of life, realised that the time had come to bid the picturesque island farewell. The actual operation was conducted by Nelson and his mixed force in two stages. Lady Elliot and her children were spirited away by Captain Dixon and *Gorgon*, Nelson's fastest frigate, with strict orders to fly from any likelihood of action. The order was understandable for the safety of Lady Elliot, but it also indicated the inferior state of British sea power in the Mediterranean, rightly assessed as it happened, because, unknown to Nelson, a Spanish fleet was already on the prowl. The next move was to evacuate the Viceroy and his staff, the garrisons at Bastia and Calvi and a number of French royalists and Corsicans who had co-operated with the British and who would receive short shrift if left behind, reminiscent of those not easily forgotten scenes in Toulon.

Sir Gilbert's destination, as he was still a diplomat, was Naples, where he was to try and keep Ferdinand, who had already entered into an armistice with France, from becoming an active collaborator with the enemy. Sir Gilbert's tasks never seemed to be of the most promising, Toulon, then Corsica, now Naples where the situation had been described in Sir William Hamilton's succinct comment, 'as do Spain, so do Naples'.

Almost the only bright spot in the Elliots' recent history was the fact that young George, influenced by his father's regard for the Commodore, had settled for the career of a sea officer and had become a midshipman at an even earlier age than had Horatio Nelson. It was an irony of fate that Nelson, who had done so much recently to capture Corsica, should now find himself in charge of its evacuation. As soon as the Viceroy announced his imminent departure a Committee of Thirty was being formed by 'patriots', the word included a multitude of former allegiances, to take over administration and to welcome the incoming French. Paoli, the patriot supreme, had already left his homeland and was now in London complaining of the favours shown to his rival, Pozzo di Borgo.

There might well have been difficulties on Corsica if it had not been for Nelson's determination and powers of decision. Corsicans were now forming into armed bands and French troops had been landed. With the local partisans Nelson took a tough line. He was now prepared (he told them) to 'knock down Bastia' if necessary, and the threat and the attitude were effective. Jervis reported to the First Lord that 'Commodore Nelson, by the firm tone he held, soon reduced these gentlemen to order'.

Bastia presented more difficulties than either Calvi or Ajaccio and on land and sea the Corsicans attempted to frustrate the British evacuation of troops, military stores and guns. General de Burgh, the army commander, was very pessimistic, for it seemed to be Nelson's fate to have to work with either difficult or half-hearted soldiers. However, every man and vessel was got off and transported to the new base on Elba without mishap, with nothing more alarming than threatening noises and gestures from the locals.

On November 5 Nelson wrote to Locker, 'I remember when we quitted Toulon we endeavoured to reconcile ourselves to Corsica; now we are content with Elba—such things are'. The process was to continue, however, and nothing seemed to go right.

It was in *La Minerve*, a frigate captured from the French, and now standing off Bastia, that Elliot had first read the dispatch which told him if he had not already withdrawn from Corsica to countermand the orders and remain. If however Corsica was not given up, Elba was to be retained. Even Elliot, who was a resolute man, realised that Corsica could not have been held against the will of the population, but contradictory orders from home were not reassuring. Nelson asked the question, 'Do His Majesty's Ministers know their own minds?' expecting the negative response.

However, even conflicting orders from a dithering Cabinet could not provide an excuse for the next British set-back, which was brought about by the quite extraordinary conduct of Rear-Admiral Man. It was obvious to any naval or military officer that a clash with the Spaniards in the Mediterranean was imminent. On land the French Army of Italy had little to fear for on November 15, 16 and 17 Bonaparte had fought the Austrians again, at Arcole, and the Austrians were forced to retreat. On sea, however, the Spanish fleet would obviously be used, either on its own, or in conjunction with the French, to challenge the British.

The British had only contempt for the Spaniards, regarding their stately great ships of war as merely prizes for the taking. The only exception was, apparently, Admiral Man whose command was the squadron watching Cadiz and when the Spanish fleet did come out he retired discreetly, on the basis that he would be rejoining Jervis as he was expected to do, so that together they could face the Spaniards. Instead he put into Gibraltar and ignoring his orders took his squadron of six line of battle and one frigate home to Spithead. His fear was of being 'hemmed in by superiority of numbers' but the total possible Franco–Spanish combination would have been thirty-eight ships of the line; Jervis had fourteen, which, with Man's squadron, brought the British total to twenty ships of the line. Poorish odds but acceptable, for as Nelson told Fanny 'they at home do not know what this fleet is capable of performing, anything and everything'.

In less than a year Jervis had brought the Mediterranean fleet to a state of efficiency which enabled it to contemplate such a fleet action with confidence and enthusiasm. However, reduced by a third the odds were too much. Jervis talked of Man being affected by 'the Blue Devils'—of depression presumably. Nelson, reasonably, expected that some dire fate

would await him in Britain. By early November Jervis realised that Man
had left his post against orders and so he could only take his own ships to
Gibraltar; Elba was also to be abandoned, and the British were leaving
the Mediterranean to their enemies.

Incredibly, Man was not court-martialled or punished but merely
ordered to 'strike his flag and come on shore' and placed on the half-pay
list, never to go to sea again. Perhaps even more incredibly, on the half-
pay list, as his seniors died off, he continued steadily to be promoted,
reaching Admiral of the Red before he died in 1813. Apart from Man's
'incomprehensible' conduct, Jervis's description to Spencer, British conduct of the war in the Mediterranean in the last months of 1796 was in
a muddle. At the diplomatic level co-operation with the Austrians was
poor, and Russia, though her ministers had been active at Italian courts,
had not been brought into active alliance. The death of the Empress
Catherine on November 16 left a void, no one knowing what the new
Tsar, Paul, would do; the fact that he was virtually insane would emerge
later.

As far as Britain herself was concerned, the evacuation of Elba, carried
out by Nelson but complicated by the fact that General de Burgh thought
he ought to stay, was sensible. Once Corsica had gone it would have been
almost impossible to concentrate and maintain a fleet on one isolated and
inadequate island. Henceforth the fleet was to be based on Lisbon taking
advantage of the hospitality of Portugal, 'Britain's oldest ally'. However,
even an anchorage on the Tagus could not be relied on for ever, as the
Portuguese were alarmed by what was happening in Spain. The British
presence posed for the Portuguese the same question as it had posed for
the Two Sicilies: which was going to be the winning side?

Meanwhile at home Britain had weathered a financial crisis, something
which, to a man of his temperament, was bound to affect Pitt's mind
more than a strategic reverse while across the Channel the expected and
hoped-for financial collapse had not happened.

In the last half of December only the elements prevented a landing in
Bantry Bay by the French general Hoche and his army, accompanied by
Wolfe Tone, the Irish Protestant rebel. The force consisted of seventeen
ships of the line, thirteen frigates, a number of transports and 14,750
soldiers. Tone recorded his amazement that at no stage was a British man
of war sighted. The invasion force was not well organised but once
landed, given the state of Ireland, it would have encountered very little
effective opposition. That such a fleet had left Brest and reached Ireland

undetected, and then was allowed to return in the same manner, was a scandal. Only the truly appalling weather conditions off Ireland had prevented a landing on British soil. The blame rested on Vice-Admiral Sir John Colpoys, whose task it was to watch Brest, and Lord Bridport whose Channel Fleet lay throughout the invasion attempt safe and snug at anchor at Spithead.

From the point of view both of her own morale and in order to sustain doubtful and flagging allies, Britain really needed a victory at the end of 1796. As if to compensate himself for the withdrawal from the Mediterranean, which he lamented 'in sackcloth and ashes', Nelson ended the year with a little bit of action more appropriate to a young captain than a commodore. It was in *Minerve*, the thirty-eight-gun frigate to which he had transferred his pendant from *Captain*, that he sailed from Gibraltar for Elba for the last time. With him was another of his squadron of 'little ships', *Blanche* of thirty-two guns. Off Cartagena they crossed the path of two forty-gun frigates, *Sabina* and *Ceres*, flying the flag of the new enemy, Spain. Nelson immediately took *Minerve* straight for *Sabina*, the larger of the two. For three hours the two ships manoeuvred and fired at each other. This sustained action might have been expected from the response to Nelson's first formal hail to the Spaniard to surrender. With a speaking trumpet he had announced that he was a British ship and demanded surrender and back had come the sturdy response, 'This is a Spanish frigate and you may begin firing as soon as you please.'

The two frigates were very evenly matched in size, manpower and, almost exactly, as to number of guns. Nelson's ship steadily gained the advantage judging by the damage inflicted on the enemy, the very high standard of British gunnery told, but though hailed again to surrender the Spaniard continued the fight replying, 'No, Sir, not whilst I have the means of fighting left'. Finally *Sabina* did surrender, when she had no officers left alive or unwounded save her captain.

Finally on board his captor's ship he announced himself, not without pride, as being Don Jacobo Stuart, and therefore a descendant of the Marshal Duke of Berwick, the illegitimate son of King James II and Arabella Churchill. Commodore Nelson formally took his sword as the token of surrender and returned it to him in recognition of his gallantry. Hardly however had that courtly exchange taken place, and it was typical of Anglo–Spanish relations throughout the war, when a number of Spanish ships were seen in the distance. That night *Minerve*'s landing party led by Lieutenants Culverhouse and Hardy remained in control of

Sabina but the next morning Nelson was forced to fight hard against a new opponent. In the process *Sabina* had to be left behind, and in her damaged state was easily recaptured by the Spaniards. To Nelson's chagrin as he sailed away, with Don Jacobo as his prisoner, he saw the Spanish flag run aloft again. Culverhouse and Hardy and their men were now Spanish prisoners. Later they were exchanged, Nelson having sent his distinguished prisoner back to Spain under a flag of truce. He had taken to an officer, whom no doubt he regarded as something of an Englishman—'he was reputed the best officer in Spain and his men were worthy of such a commander'. Obviously the Spanish navy could not totally be disregarded. Though *Minerve* lost only seven men, damage had been considerable. *Sabina* had 164 men killed out of a crew of 250.

1797 opened as dismally for Britain as the previous year had ended and her naval and military officers, as well as their political masters, could be forgiven for asking if there was no limit to French successes. Bonaparte defeated the Imperial General Allvintzy at Rivoli on January 14, and then two days later Provera outside Mantua. Finally on February 2 Field-Marshal Würmser capitulated, giving up the fortress of Mantua to the French. While the Imperial armies had, in the Mediterranean theatre, been defeated numerous times, the British had suffered no obvious reverses at sea, but because of the deteriorating situation on land they had been forced to evacuate their bases and abandon the sea area completely. From the new base at Lisbon the priorities of naval warfare had been evaluated again, and were seen simply and starkly.

Britain's navy was reduced in 1797 to a defensive role, the protection of her own commerce, vital to an island and the repulse of an invasion force, a threat which remained a distinct possibility. Historians have tended to assume that an invasion would have had to have been one by which the whole of the British Isles was occupied and all the inhabitants subdued, but this ignores the damage which could have been inflicted by military action which fell short of this and also discounts the fact that Napoleon invaded, and retreated from, Russia and Spain and lived to raise other armies and fight another day.

Britain, then, was faced with a maritime combination in France, Spain and Holland which could, by defeating Britain's battle fleet, make an invasion possible. A fact which needed little emphasising when the French had just shown that Ireland could be invaded without a fleet action being fought. Therefore at the earliest opportunity the enemy fleet, or some considerable part of it, had to be brought to battle and defeated. If this were not done, then the threat of invasion would remain permanent.

There was a Spanish fleet at Cadiz, a French one at Toulon, and it was the task of the Royal Navy to prevent either or both of these fleets sailing north and joining up with the French fleet at Brest, thus producing a combination which could make invasion a practical proposition. Ideally, in the process, enemy ships would be taken or destroyed thus reducing the enemy force permanently.

It is perhaps strange, looking back, to find that there was a general feeling in the Mediterranean fleet at the turn of the year that the big conflict would come with the Spanish fleet. Strange because though in Madrid Manuel Godoy might delude himself into thinking he was a second Alberoni, controlling a powerful diplomatic and military alliance, Spain was very much the weaker partner. Perhaps the reason was that however active French armies might be in Italy, the Spanish fleet was much more in evidence than the French.

Nelson had already made one contact, and been forced to abandon *Sabina* and *Ceres* because of other Spanish ships in the offing. In the Bay of Gibraltar he had exchanged Don Jacobo Stuart for Culverhouse and Hardy, on board *Terrible*, one of three Spanish line-of-battle ships, and on leaving the Bay still flying his pendant in *Minerve* he was again in conflict with Spanish ships. The circumstances and the personalities involved were such that the incident deserved recording.

January and early February had been busy days for Nelson. General de Burgh had been adamant about not leaving Elba without orders and even Sir Gilbert Elliot, who was still in the Mediterranean, had been reluctant to assume authority. The General and his garrison had therefore stayed put; and with incredible luck they were all later to get to Gibraltar.

No one quite knew what was happening with regard to the few toe-holds that the British still possessed. The Wynne family had turned up on Elba for a Christmas Ball, and Captain Fremantle had also been present. Eventually the Wynnes and the Pollards found refuge at Naples where Lady Hamilton enjoyed stage-managing the wedding of Fremantle and Miss Betsy Wynne at the British Embassy. It seemed not entirely to Nelson's liking that the new Mrs Fremantle was to spend her first months of married life as a supernumerary crew member of H.M.S. *Inconstant*.

Sir Gilbert had also appeared in Naples, after a visit to Rome, and at least there had the excuse of business to transact. Encouragingly, the

Neapolitan Court still seemed pro-British. The Queen was gracious and sensible, the King less so, but the Hamiltons were obviously not greatly to the taste of a fairly dour border Scot. Sir William was also Scots, the grandson of a Scots Duke, but that in Elliot's eyes only made his position as the elderly husband of his young former mistress—who now entertained visitors with her Attitudes, a sort of one-woman charade, with Sir William in charge of lighting and effects—even more ridiculous. He wrote to his wife of the Ambassadress, 'With men her language and conversation are exaggerations of anything I have heard anywhere; and I was wonderfully struck with these inveterate remains of her origin; though the impression was very much weakened by seeing the other ladies of Naples.'

Elliot dragged in his wake two former members of his entourage on Corsica whose functions were now ill-defined. Pozzo di Borgo, Bonaparte's exact contemporary and also born in Ajaccio, had been the Viceroy's Secretary of State and been removed from Corsica for his own safety. He now assisted Elliot in a vaguely diplomatic capacity, perhaps a suitable apprenticeship for his ultimate career in the Foreign Service of Tsar Alexander of Russia. With him was Colonel Drinkwater, a former A.D.C. who had managed to attach himself even more closely by falling in love with Sir Gilbert's cousin, Miss Eleanor Congleton. The Colonel was a man of many parts, a watercolour painter of some skill and the author of *The Siege of Gibraltar*, a work which had already sold three editions. M. Pozzo di Borgo and the Colonel provided a contrast to each other, in one respect at least, for Drinkwater was fascinated by his sea trips and anything that smacked of naval warfare and his father had been a naval surgeon, while the former Secretary of State was consistently and violently seasick.

Elliot, di Borgo and Drinkwater were on board *Minerve* as she left the Bay of Gibraltar, having picked up Nelson's two lieutenants on February 11. As the frigate put out to sea, two Spanish ships of the line and a frigate weighed anchor and followed in her wake. Rather unnecessarily Drinkwater asked Nelson if he thought an action was likely and received the terse reply, 'Very possible'. For many sea officers it would have been enough but Nelson was rarely terse and the Colonel was an audience of one, so the Commodore continued with a bit of dramatics. Looking up at his pendant he declared 'before the Dons get hold of that bit of bunting I will have a struggle with them, and sooner than give up the frigate, I'll run her ashore'. If this was naval warfare the soldier obviously liked the

flavour of it, for he began to make notes of all that happened. He was not
to be disappointed.

While the Spanish ships followed behind the Commodore and his
officers and the Corsican party sat down to dinner in the long stern cabin.
The meal had hardly begun, and Drinkwater was just congratulating
Lieutenant Hardy on his release from Spanish captivity, when there was a
shout on deck, 'Man overboard.' The officers immediately hurried on
deck and Minerve's passengers became spectators of a fast developing
drama. Belying his stolid appearance and considerable bulk Hardy was
one of the first officers on deck and, getting there, must have reacted
quickly, for as the jolly boat was lowered over the side he was the officer
seated in the stern. The sea was rough and the current strong and easterly,
but there was no sign of the unfortunate seaman, and the tiny boat,
bobbing and tossing, was soon being swept astern, away from Minerve
and towards the Spanish warships. Hardy signalled by hand to his own
ship that his quest was useless, and his boat's crew bent to their oars to
regain Minerve. Despite their efforts their boat hardly seemed to move,
while the tall Spanish leading battle ship moved steadily nearer; Hardy it
seemed was about to become a Spanish prisoner again. Nelson was not
going to let that happen: 'By God', said the Commodore, 'I'll not lose
Hardy!' and then, raising his voice, taking over what was really Captain
Cockburn's task, 'Back the mizzen topsail.' The effect was as if to apply a
brake to Minerve's progress, and Hardy's boat crew, seeing Minerve's
action, immediately pulled at their oars with renewed vigour, but the
Spanish ship was now closing the gap between herself and the frigate.
Action seemed imminent, with the jolly boat bobbing about in the
middle, but then the Spanish captain presumably either suspected some
kind of trap or else simply lost his nerve. For now he too shortened sail
and fell away from Minerve, waiting for his two consorts. The respite was
enough for Hardy, and his boat's crew, and they were soon alongside
and quickly hauled inboard. Then Minerve's studding sails were spread
to give her as much wind as possible and steadily, for Cockburn was well
known as a skilful handler of a frigate, Nelson and his passengers drew
away from the Spaniards. After a few hours the pursuers were out of
sight and had given up the chase.

That Nelson had risked a fight against a Spanish ship of the line for the
sake of Hardy and his boat's crew was not perhaps so surprising, but he
was, unknowingly, putting at risk an opportunity he had determined not
to miss, of a sea action by which, as he had written to Jervis, he hoped to

make his Commander-in-Chief a viscount. That chance came a few days later off the Cape of St Vincent, the most westerly point of the European continent. Rodney and Boscawen, and before them Francis Drake, had all fought off the promontory, and Lagos its principal port. The object had always been much the same, for British ships to destroy French or Spanish formations coming out of the Mediterranean by the Straits of Gibraltar in order to concentrate on the Atlantic seaboard. The object of that concentration had generally been an invasion project, in the long or short term aimed at the British Isles.

In February 1797, however, invasion was not the immediate purpose of the Spanish fleet which had been assembled under the command of Admiral Juan de Cordoba. The object of Cordoba's sailing from Cartagena was to achieve a concentration of Spanish and French ships at Brest and, if that combined force could then wrest the command of the Atlantic seaboard and the Channel from the British, invasion could then be made possible. Throughout, the driving force for this operation had come from the Directory in Paris, and Spanish reluctance was reflected in inadequate preparation, organisation and, ultimately, conduct in battle. Cordoba's fleet was however impressive in numbers, and in the size of its ships. There were six three-decked ships armed with 112 guns, two two-deckers of eighty-four guns and eighteen two-decked 74's, making a total of twenty-seven line of battle ships with Cordoba's flagship, the giant *Santissima Trinidada*, of 136 guns, the largest warship afloat and the only four-decked ship with any fleet. There were also a dozen frigates in attendance. In addition to Cordoba himself the fleet carried no less than six other admirals of various grades.

The Spanish service did, however, lack 'prime seamen', for even aboard the flagship the majority of men were inexperienced landsmen or drafted soldiers who were expected to carry out the dual task of acting as gunners and marines. Two centuries before the Spaniards had placed the Great Armada under the command of a soldier, the Duke of Medina-Sidonia, now the fault was reversed. There was skill at the very top, though some of the captains had little battle experience, but there was not enough skill, experience or training in the lower ranks.

The most curious vessels in Cordoba's fleet, and they caused confusion at the time to the enemy, and subsequently to naval historians, were four urcas, large merchant vessels armed with twenty guns each and in appearance and size akin to the British East Indiaman, which could also, at a distance, be mistaken for men of war. Just as the function of the East

Indiaman was imperial trade so an urca was built, equipped and armed for Spain's commerce with her possessions in the Americas. The task of these four ships plus the seventy-four-gun *San Domingo* and *Principe d'Asturias*, the flagship of Vice-Admiral Moreno, was to take a cargo of mercury from Malaga via Cadiz to the mines of the New World where the element was used in the process of the amalgamation of silver ore.

Thus Cordoba, unknown to the British, had two tasks which might well impose conflicting duties upon him. He had to take his main fleet into the Atlantic and there to join the French admiral, Villeneuve, who had gathered thirty line of battle ships and a number of frigates at Brest, but at the same time he was expected to provide an escort for the mercury ships on the first stage of their journey westwards. It is difficult not to feel a certain amount of sympathy for the Spanish admiral. Originally the fleet had been assigned to Admiral de Langara, who had co-operated so badly with the British at the evacuation of Toulon. Then Langara had been promoted to the Admiralty in Madrid and the command given to de Mazaredo, but he had refused to take what he considered to be an ill-equipped and poorly-manned fleet to sea. Thus the command had fallen to Cordoba plus the extra task of escorting a valuable convoy.

It is not known precisely in what order Cordoba's twenty-seven sail of the line left Cartagena on February 1, but when first sighted by the British the fleet had been divided up, presumably under orders, in the following way: Cordoba had under his direct command seventeen ships including *San Domingo*, two ships were positioned to cover the rear, three had been sent on detached duty to Algeciras and five were assigned to escort the convoy.

In one further respect, apart from the unwieldy nature of his command, the Spanish admiral was suffering from a disadvantage, poor intelligence, and this may have had some part in his decision to go to sea, for he was under the impression that Jervis's fleet was considerably smaller than it was. The reason lay first of all in a series of disasters which had overtaken the British, duly reported by the spies and purveyors of information with which the Mediterranean abounded. In moving from Gibraltar to Lisbon the British fleet had been struck by one of those freak gales of unusual force not uncommon in the Mediterranean at that time of year. As a result *Courageux* commanded by Captain Benjamin Hallowell, Nelson's companion in Corsica, was wrecked with the loss of three-quarters of the ship's company; *Zealous* commanded by the most junior of the Hood family, Captain Samuel, ran aground and Captain Pakenham's *Gibraltar* ran on a reef. When the fleet reached Portugal, *Bombay Castle* ran aground in the mouth of the Tagus and *St George* damaged her hull on a shoal. The former proved a total loss, *Zealous* and *St George* were laid up for repairs in Lisbon, and *Gibraltar* was sent home. The Mediterranean fleet had thus been reduced from fifteen to nine line of battle ships and this was the fleet which was still suffering from the defection of Admiral Man.

Cordoba's estimate therefore was that he must outnumber any British fleet by a considerable margin, but he failed to take into account the temper of Jervis, for that intrepid old man was both impatient and pugnacious. 'Inaction in the Tagus' did not appeal to him. He had heard rumours of the French fleet being out of Brest, and he hoped for news from Nelson, among others, of the Spanish fleet. In these circumstances he conceived it his duty to get his command, however much reduced, to sea. Accordingly, Jervis left Lisbon on January 18, first to escort a Portuguese convoy on its way to Brazil and then to position his fleet off Cape St Vincent. It was courageous, but it was also a policy of simply waiting to see what turned up. Contrary winds held him back until February 6 and then, off St Vincent, he found Lord Garlies with the frigate force which kept watch on Cadiz, and at last, under Rear-Admiral Sir William Parker, the welcome addition of five sail of the line, *Prince George*, *Colossus*, *Irresistible*, *Orion* and *Namur*, and the frigate *Thalia*. Then on February 13 *Minerve*, flying the broad pendant of Commodore Nelson, hove in sight. His report to Jervis verged on the incredible, and the experience must have convinced Colonel Drinkwater that war on land was very dull compared with what could happen at sea.

After rescuing Hardy, *Minerve* sailing westwards through the Straits, had as night fell moved into banks of drifting February fog. During the early morning hours Nelson, going about his duties, told the awakened Colonel Drinkwater, but not the still sleeping Sir Gilbert, who also shared their cabin, that, judging by an occasional glimpse of a sail and sounds such as ships' bells, they were in the midst either of the Spanish fleet or a westward bound convoy. Finally Nelson did wake Sir Gilbert to explain to him that if the second supposition was true he might feel it his duty to precede the Spaniards to their destination to warn the British admiral on the West Indies station. Whatever the truth, the next morning found *Minerve* unaccompanied. In all probability, Nelson thought, he had sailed through some part of Cordoba's fleet, either of warships or urcas, but in any event Elliot, Drinkwater and the Commodore were saved an Atlantic crossing.

Having joined Jervis and reported Spanish movements of some kind Nelson shifted his pendant back into *Captain,* commanded by Miller, and with an extra captain on board in the shape of the recently promoted Edward Berry, formerly Nelson's first lieutenant. If there was an action Berry could only serve as a volunteer. In fact he was not the only officer in that position for Hallowell, without a ship, was on board *Victory* in the same capacity. Perhaps it was Hallowell's presence that prompted Sir Gilbert also to volunteer his services in any capacity, with of course Colonel Drinkwater, on board the flagship. Faced with the prospect of a quarter-deck crowded with gawping, though distinguished and enthusiastic, landlubbers Jervis firmly rejected the offer and though he gave a dinner party in Sir Gilbert's honour in the stateroom of *Victory,* he then transferred the ex-Viceroy and his party to Lord Garlies's frigate, *Lively.* It would be *Lively*'s duty to carry home the dispatches on the engagement.

There could be little doubt of the engagement itself for enemy signal guns had been heard and at Jervis's dinner party the toast had been downed enthusiastically, 'Victory over the Dons in the battle which they cannot escape tomorrow'. That night Jervis had given the order to prepare for battle, his frigates had therefore taken up their positions as scouts for the main fleet and on board the ships of the line the guns were run out, hammocks and spare canvas bolts were stowed on deck as some protection from shot, partitions were taken down and all the unnecessary gear, from water barrels to chairs and tables, was either cleared away or even thrown overboard. The last order to the fleet before nightfall was to maintain close order.

Jervis had under his command fifteen sail of the line, *Victory* and *Britannia* of 100 guns each, then two 98's, *Barfleur* and *Prince George,* two 90's, *Blenheim* and *Namur,* and the remainder were the standard 74's like Nelson's *Captain,* save for *Diadem,* the only 64. Lord Garlies's scouting force consisted of five frigates, two of them captured French vessels, *Minerve* and *Bonne Citoyenne,* and a brig and a cutter.

It was not, however, from his own 'eyes and ears' that Jervis had his final piece of intelligence, but from a Portuguese frigate with a Scottish captain which was hailed by the flagship at 2.30 a.m. The Spanish fleet was fifteen miles away to windward, sailing east-south-east with a light wind from the south-west. Obviously the recent levanter, the powerful east wind, suffered by Jervis, had taken the Spanish fleet too far out into the Atlantic, and Cordoba was now trying to make Cadiz. The frigate *Niger,* at 5.30 a.m., brought a report of the Spanish fleet even closer. An hour later sails could be seen to windward, the presumption, as entered in *Victory*'s log, being that these belonged to the Spanish fleet.

Finally, as the mist cleared, Jervis, pleased to discover the compact order of his own fleet, signalled his congratulations to his captains. During the long night he had been heard to remark, 'a victory is very essential to England at this moment'. Now the moment had arrived, for the Spaniards could be clearly discerned; in the words of the signal lieutenant of *Barfleur*, 'Thumpers, looming like Beachy Head in a fog'. Although the 'thumpers' were in no sort of order, there were a very large number of them as a classic dialogue on *Victory's* quarter-deck, between Jervis and his captain of the fleet, emphasised:

> Sir Robert Calder: 'There are eight sail of the line, Sir John.'
> Jervis: 'Very well, Sir.'
> Calder: 'There are 20 sail of the line, Sir John.'
> Jervis: 'Very well, Sir.'
> Calder: 'There are 25 sail of the line, Sir John.'
> Jervis: 'Very well, Sir.'
> Calder: 'There are 27 sail of the line, Sir John, near double our own.'
> Jervis: 'Enough of that, Sir. If there are 50 sail of the line, I will go through them. The die is cast.'

At that, Hallowell actually slapped the Commander-in-Chief on the back, exclaiming as he did so, 'That's right, Sir John, that's right! And, by God, we shall give them a damned good licking.'

Sir John's intention to 'go through' the Spanish fleet has often been hailed as marking a turning-point in naval history, and so in a sense it proved to be, yet the deployment of the Spanish fleet, when it could finally be discerned from *Victory*, was both a provocation and a problem. Cordoba's ships stretched over a wide front and were in poor order, though in fact to the British, not realising that part of the force consisted only of warlike-looking urcas, and their protectors, the order appeared even worse than it was. The wind had shifted during the night from the eastward to west-by-south, and so the Spaniards now appeared to be running for Cadiz, 150 miles to the south-east, as their course was approximately east-south-east.

It is difficult to work out what Cordoba intended to do when he sighted the British fleet. The most likely explanation is that he tried to pursue two courses of action at once, perhaps never making up his mind between them, and thus allowing the initiative to rest with his opponent.

Some of the confusion was undoubtedly due to poor ship-handling, but over the whole of Cordoba's conduct prior to action being joined, there hangs a very large question mark, posed by Nelson's experience with the Spanish ships in the fog. Undoubtedly *Minerve*, sailing westwards, had passed through some part of a Spanish fleet also sailing in the same direction. If it had been the mercury convoy why had that not gone on to the Americas with its valuable cargo? If it had been the battle fleet why was that now, apparently, returning to Cadiz? The simplest explanation is that Nelson's contact had been with another squadron or convoy which did continue westwards, in which case Cordoba now sought battle imagining that the British force would still be Jervis's original fleet less a number of ships damaged and aground.

Therefore Cordoba must have planned for both fleet and convoy to head for Cadiz and safety. However, if that were not possible then an action would have to be fought. Since the fleet and convoy were separated by about six to eight miles there was a very good chance that the convoy at least would escape the British.

As the two fleets, twenty-seven Spanish from the west and fifteen British from the north, bore steadily towards each other, their very deployment indicated a crucial difference in attitude between the two admirals, their subordinate admirals and the captains under their command. The Spanish ships, already divided into a windward group of twenty-one ships and a leeward group of six, were in considerable disorder within those two groupings. The British fleet, on the other hand, was in the double column in which it had kept order and contact during the hours of darkness. At 11 a.m. the coloured flags fluttered to *Victory's* masthead giving the order to form line of battle ahead or astern of the flagship as most convenient. The manoeuvre was performed to Jervis's satisfaction, 'with the utmost celerity'. Twenty-nine minutes later he was able to signal his intention, 'to pass through the enemy line', to divide an already divided fleet. Nelson's *Captain* was now thirteenth in a line of fifteen ships, not perhaps the most promising position in which, after twenty-six years of waiting, to sail into his first fleet action.

CHAPTER FOURTEEN

St Vincent

THE FOG had disappeared by about ten o'clock on that morning of February 14, 1797 and as the great ships moved towards each other under their top gallant sails the sea was calm. It was a perfect day for a battle.

As the British line formed with such admirable precision it must have become obvious to Cordoba that Jervis's intention was to drive a wedge between the two sections of his fleet. To counter this the Spaniards changed course from their original east-south-east, with the wind, so that their main body now stood to the northwards, bringing the two battle fleets on to approximately parallel courses, moving in opposite directions. This was in fact the classic positioning of the old type of engagement and as soon as targets offered the cannonading began. 'We gave them their Valentines in style', was the comment of one of the sailors in *Goliath*, and from the first the British showed a superiority in gunnery. The line was led by *Culloden* which by the exertions of her crew and the determination of her captain, Thomas Troubridge, had been hastily refitted for battle after a collision with *Colossus* the night after Parker's reinforcements had joined Jervis.

It is interesting to record the incidence of officers present on this St Valentine's Day who were to figure in future actions when Nelson had command. Jervis's own tenure of command had provided a nursery of future talent which was to be used to full effect by his junior. Berry and Hallowell, the supernumeraries serving as volunteers, would soon have ships of their own; Hardy, now a lieutenant, would have his first command of a brig at the Nile; and finally the established captains, Troubridge, acknowledged by all as the star of his profession; Collingwood with his insistence upon superb gunnery; Foley, courageous and skilful; and Saumarez, never a great friend of Nelson's, but a superb and gallant commander.

As the British line moved southwards Cordoba's untidy collection of ships, some abeam of each other, moved to pass astern of the British in response to Jervis's signal to his own ships to tack in succession. Troubridge in command of *Culloden*, the leading ship, had obviously been expecting such an order for his response was immediate, for *Culloden* tacked to starboard up into the wind and acknowledged the signal almost before the flagship had finished making it.

'Look at Troubridge,' exclaimed Jervis to the sailing master of his own *Victory*, fifth in line, 'he tacks his ship to battle as if the eyes of all England were upon him; and would to God they were . . .'. As they came to the point, *Blenheim*, *Prince George*, *Orion*, *Colossus*, *Irresistible* and then *Victory* turned to starboard, followed by the rest. So the British van, having passed perilously near to the Spanish ships, moving in one direction, so close that Griffiths, Troubridge's first lieutenant, had feared an actual collision, now followed them in pursuit as they turned into wind. Those British ships in rear of *Victory*, from *Barfleur* back to *Excellent*, the last in line, naturally still followed the original course towards the point at which *Culloden* had tacked. Thus while one section of the British fleet was following a course almost parallel to the Spanish ships, which were grouped untidily and clumsily in twos and threes, the other section was still sailing steadily southwards down to the turning-point.

The action was now becoming much more general and the British experienced their first casualty. *Colossus* received a chance shot and lost a foresail yard and swerved across the bows of *Irresistible* astern of her. Only quick seamanship prevented *Victory* from colliding with *Irresistible*. *Colossus* then fell out of the line out of control, and never regained her position and for all practical purposes she took no further part in the battle.

It was at this stage that the smaller division of the Spanish fleet, accompanying the urcas, made its only real contribution to the battle. It had originally been the van of the fleet but now Jervis's line had cut it off from the main body and it was considerably to the leeward of the conflict. On board *Principe d'Asturias*, the principal escort, was Vice-Admiral Moreno and he took his 112-gun ship towards the still tacking British line in an attempt to cut through. For some moments it seemed as if he was about to collide with *Victory*, a ship of comparable size and gunpower. However, at the last moment Moreno's nerve must have failed him as his ship swung round, firing her starboard guns. It was a fatal mistake, for at the moment of turning through the wind his ship was almost stationary and *Victory* raked her with a broadside, the British guns firing rapidly from bow to stern in succession in a long sustained ripple of explosions. The Spaniard's deck was reduced to a shambles of bodies, timbers, canvas and rope, her wheel was shot away and her rudder jammed. Powerless, Moreno's ship turned full circle, presenting her defenceless starboard side. Another shattering broadside of fifty guns and *Principe d'Asturias* 'in great confusion', as *Victory*'s log put it, fell away to leeward where lay the other ships of the escort and the convoy itself. No further attempt was made by this division of the fleet to join battle.

Originally the British line had been a superb example of seamanship and control, a copybook exercise on how to enter a battle. Now that the battle had commenced and both fleets had manoeuvred for position, the Spanish far less successfully than the British, the scene was confused by drifting gun-smoke and the time was fast approaching when individual captains would be thrown on their own initiative. Nevertheless, the line and the orders of the Commander-in-Chief were sacred things to be broken at one's peril. Further, Jervis had not relaxed control; his last signal, following the order to tack in succession, had been the customary 'engage the enemy more closely'. This, however, obviously applied to his van ships sailing in parallel to the Spaniards since these were the only ships that he could observe properly from his own quarter-deck. Apart from smoke and distance there were other problems close at hand. A marine near the Admiral was decapitated by a round shot and Jervis was covered from head to foot in brains and blood. The captain of marines assumed the Admiral was wounded, but on offering assistance was told there was no need, but that he wanted an orange to rinse out his mouth.

Jervis now just had to assume that ships, both towards the van and rear of his line, would be used to the best advantage while captains conformed to the pattern of action he had laid down. To one captain, Nelson, with only *Diadem* and *Excellent* astern, the Commander-in-Chief's pattern was no longer producing the results intended. The leading Spanish ships describing a course roughly in the shape of an elongated and reversed S, and with the wind now on their port quarter, were giving the appearance of escaping entirely while the van of the British line, also following the same course, simply could not catch up. From his own position, moving southwards before tacking, Nelson could see the leading Spanish ships about to out-manoeuvre the British by passing astern of *Excellent* and thence sailing clear away towards Cadiz.

Nelson then took his career in his hands and gave the order to wear ship, out of the line to port and thence astern of *Diadem* and across the bows of *Excellent* and then, almost at a right-angle, into the track of the five leading Spanish ships, the flagship *Santissima Trinidada*, and *Salvador del Mundo* and *San Josef*, 130, 112 and 112 guns respectively and *San Nicolas*, 84 and *San Isidro*, 74. Immediately all guns concentrated on the one audacious British ship, *Captain*. She lost her foremast, her sails were slashed and torn by shot, and the wheel was smashed into splinters. Nevertheless she kept up an almost continuous fire from her own broadsides whenever her guns could bear on a target. On board their frigate Sir Gilbert Elliot and Colonel Drinkwater 'with admiration mixed with anxiety' in Drinkwater's words, watched as *Captain* on her own fought the enormous Spanish flagship and the two three-deckers, her first ahead and astern. However, Nelson was not left for long to sustain 'this unequal combat'. Either in response to a signal from Jervis or more likely, on his own initiative Collingwood commanding *Excellent*, a ship which under his training could fire three broadsides in five minutes, tacked out of line and came to his friend's help. Within about thirty minutes from Nelson's decision to wear ship, the van ships of the British line, *Culloden*, *Blenheim* and *Prince George*, were overtaking the Spanish ships which had been turned from their course by *Captain*.

Nelson's manoeuvre succeeded in slowing down the Spanish fleet and thus made possible the general engagement which followed. If it had failed history might have heard little more of Commodore Nelson, for when he gave his order to the surprised but prompt and obedient Miller, he took a double risk. First, that the manoeuvre might be unsuccessful and that the mighty Spanish ships would use their overwhelming superiority in gunpower to disable, destroy or sweep aside the solitary British 74. Second, in doing what he did, Nelson deliberately disobeyed orders. The last he had received, in common with the rest of the fleet, had been to tack in succession. If he had done just that, and never fired a shot at a Spaniard, or received one, he would have been blameless. Thus when Nelson shouted at Miller he disobeyed orders in the most flagrant way possible, for the line of battle was sacred, hallowed by custom and convention, enforced by the obvious advantage of mutual protection. To break it, or leave it, for whatever reason, was to risk destroying the pattern of action as devised by the Commander-in-Chief, for what would happen to a fleet where every captain took it upon himself to go his own way?

To defend a breach of the line needed the very strongest arguments and Nelson provided them. It is significant that he gave no orders to *Excellent* and *Diadem* astern of him as a commodore he could have done. *Captain*

slowed down the Spaniards so that *Culloden* and her successors could
come up with them, and *Excellent* probably saved *Captain* for Nelson's
next move which provided his conclusive justification. The action was
now confused and at close quarters, in the art of placing one ship alongside another and then firing broadsides as quickly and accurately as
possible, the poorly trained Spaniards were no match for the British.

The Spanish fleet was now lumped in twos and threes and had lost any
semblance of order. The British almost roamed at will firing into ships
which, when they did reply, fired inaccurately and ineffectively. 'The
superiority of the British fire over that of the enemy,' observed Colonel
Drinkwater, 'and its effects on the enemy's hulls and sails, were so
evident, that we in the frigate no longer hesitated to pronounce a glorious
termination of the contest.' How glorious for his friend Nelson he could
not at that moment have predicted however, for chance played a part.

Jervis's intention was now to bring up *Victory* and the seven ships of his
own division immediately under his control, to the assistance of the
British van hotly engaged with well over twice their number of Spanish
opponents. In this he only partially succeeded, the ships astern of his
flagship failing to come up to leeward of the Spanish ships and demonstrating how vital had been Nelson's interception. However, *Victory* herself was brought into the press of Spanish ships to such good effect that
the nearest Spanish three-decker, *Salvador del Mundo*, received a broadside from the flagship and immediately struck her own flag in surrender.

Meanwhile, the intervention of *Excellent* had brought Nelson permanent assistance and temporary respite. *Captain* had suffered considerably, 'dreadfully mauled' was Collingwood's description, and Nelson
listed 'lost foretop mast and not a sail, shroud or rope left, her wheel shot
away', none of it surprising, considering that she had taken the fire of
Santissima Trinidada, *San Josef*, *Salvador del Mundo* and *San Nicolas*. As
well as *Excellent*, *Culloden* and *Blenheim* did their best to protect their
consort and inflict damage upon the closely knit group of Spanish ships.

At this stage there were no further signals from Jervis for British
captains could be relied upon to inflict maximum damage on the enemy
in their own way. There can be little doubt however that a number of
captains over-estimated the effect of their ships' broadsides and having
fired into one Spanish ship then went on to fire at another. Nelson later
praised Collingwood for resisting the temptation to join 'a parade of
taking possession of beaten enemies', but some enemies were not beaten.
In at least three cases including perhaps *Trinidada* herself, and certainly

Salvador del Mundo, Spanish colours were hauled down in surrender only to be hauled up again when the danger had passed. Further, each British captain probably had an ambition to capture *Trinidada*, a superb prize, the largest warship afloat, 'such a ship as I never saw before', wrote Collingwood to his wife. Although every British ship which came within range fired into her until she was, in Collingwood's words, 'a complete wreck', she did not sink, wooden ships rarely did save when they exploded, nor was she captured.

Damaging a Spanish ship was one thing, capturing her was another, as Nelson soon demonstrated. After Collingwood 'had gallantly pushed up, with every sail set, to save his old friend and messmate', as Nelson wrote to the Duke of Clarence, *San Josef* collided with *San Nicolas*, which, out of control, had put her head up into the wind and come to a halt. Spanish ships were now 'huddled together', said Rear-Admiral Parker on board *Prince George*, and were probably doing each other 'a great deal of injury'.

Here was an opportunity and so, as Nelson put it, 'I ordered Captain Miller to put the helm a starboard, and calling for boarders, ordered them to board'.

'The soldiers of the 60th Regiment with an alacrity which will ever do them credit, and Lieutenant Pierson of the same Regiment, were among the foremost in this service. The first man who jumped into the enemy's mizzen chains was Captain Berry, late my First Lieutenant; Captain Miller was in the very act of going also, but I directed him to remain.' Apparently, according to Miller's sister, with the words, 'No, Miller, I must have that honour'. 'He [Berry] was supported from our spritsail yard, which hooked into the mizzen rigging. A soldier having broken the upper quarter-gallery window jumped in, followed by myself and others as fast as possible. I found the cabin door fastened, and some Spanish officers fired their pistols, but having broke open the doors, the soldiers fired and the Spanish Brigadier or Commodore fell, as retreating to the quarter-deck I found Captain Berry in possession of the poop, and the Spanish ensign hauling down. I passed with my people and Lieutenant Pierson on to the larboard gangway to the forecastle, where I met two or three Spanish officers, prisoners to my seamen, and they delivered me their swords.

'At this moment a fire of pistols or muskets opened from the Admiral's stern gallery of the *San Josef*. I directed the soldiers to fire into her stern; and calling to Captain Miller ordered him to send more men into the *San Nicolas*, and directed my people to board the first rate which was done in an instant, Captain Berry assisting me into the main chains. At this moment a Spanish officer looked over from the quarter-deck rail and said they surrendered; from this most welcome intelligence it was not long before I was on the quarter-deck, where the Spanish Captain, with a bow, presented me his sword, and said the Admiral was dying of his wounds below. I asked him, on his honour, if the ship were surrendered? He declared she was; on which I gave him my hand and desired him to call his officers and ship's company to tell them of it, which he did; and so on the quarter-deck of a Spanish first rate, extravagant as the story may seem, did I receive the swords of vanquished Spaniards; which as I received, I gave to William Fearney, one of my bargemen who put them with the greatest sang-froid under his arm.'

It was a set-piece triumph, hardly anything was missing to make it truly theatrical and what was lacking was provided as *Victory* passed the stationary *Captain*, interlocked with her two prizes. Three cheers roared out from the flagship's company lining the bulwarks, to be repeated by every ship of the fleet that passed as soon as the Commodore's pendant was observed.

Nelson with the state of *Captain*, as described in the master's log, could hardly take any further part in the battle: 'our standing rigging and running rigging, with all the bending sails, was cut to pieces. Our wheel and fore topmast shot away, and the other masts severely wounded, the main mast having three shots through the heart.' In addition, out of a crew which had suffered heavy casualties, twenty-four killed and fifty-six wounded, two prize crews had to be provided for *San Josef* and *San Nicolas*. Almost immediately fire broke out in two places on board *San Nicolas* and had to be put out.

For Jervis, however, the battle was not yet over. There was still another division of the Spanish fleet, to leeward, which as the short February day faded did appear to show signs of fight. It was an appearance only, for part of the division was not composed of warships and it only hoped to give assistance to crippled ships, especially *Santissima Trinidada*, as they made their withdrawal. Caution though at this stage was obviously a virtue. Accordingly Jervis endeavoured to get his ships and his captains back into some kind of order. The signal to form line ahead was made and the British ships took up their positions heading south again in line of battle, the prizes and disabled ships such as *Captain* and *Colossus* to leeward in tow of the frigates, and with one lone frigate, Captain Foote's *Niger*, well out to windward as look-out watching the retreating Spanish fleet.

By five o'clock all firing had ceased and the two fleets moved away from each other, the British standing for Lagos and the Spanish heading for Cadiz.

That evening as dusk fell over the victorious fleet a number of officers behaved characteristically, but in that larger-than-life manner so often experienced in the aftermath of exciting and violent action. Nelson himself had the feeling of being 'in a dream'. While still on board *Captain* he carried out a little ceremony of his own with his captain, Ralph Miller. Summoning him to his cabin he addressed him formally, 'Miller, I am under the greatest obligation to you', and then handed him the surrendered sword of Don Tomaso Geraldino, the Spanish-Irish captain of *San Nicolas*, and from his own finger a ring with a topaz stone. Although the ring with its semi-precious stone was of no particular value, indeed it was the gesture which counted.

Nelson then had himself taken from *Captain* to *Minerve* where Captain Cockburn obeyed his orders to put him on board the nearest undamaged ship of the line, *Irresistible*, commanded by Captain Martin. But if Nelson was holding himself ready for more action he was to be disappointed for the Spaniards were not seen again.

At dusk Nelson obeyed a summons to go on board the flagship, which he could only do in what remained of a uniform, most of his cocked hat had been shot away, his coat and shirt were in ribbons and his face was still begrimed with smoke and gunpowder. In this state Jervis received him on the quarter-deck of *Victory* literally with open arms, and said, as Nelson put it, 'he could not sufficiently thank me, and used every expression to make me happy'. Jervis was not given to embracing his subordinates so that Robert Calder, Captain of the Fleet, must have been more than usually obtuse to hint to the Commander-in-Chief, after Nelson's departure, that the Commodore's actions had actually been against orders. Jervis's classic rejoinder has come down to us. 'It certainly was so', he replied sharply, 'and if ever you commit such a breach of your orders I will forgive you also.'

When he returned to *Irresistible* Nelson found himself in the hands of the surgeon, '. . . my bruises were looked at, and found but trifling, and a few days made me as well as ever'. This was not quite true, for he had suffered a considerable amount of bruising and appeared in the casualty list as 'bruised but not obliged to quit the deck' and suffered some form of internal contusion which caused him pain at times for the rest of his life. He described himself as 'not near as much hurt as the Doctors fancied' but he had obviously taken enough knocks to limit his note of re-assurance to Fanny: 'I am well; Josiah is well'. Two days later he wrote her a slightly longer letter, but he was obviously still weary, his letter of February 16 containing only three sentences, the middle one being hardly typical of Nelson in high spirits: 'It would not be right to attempt detailing the action, as it will come from a much better pen than mine.'

That pen belonged to Colonel Drinkwater and Nelson was to have an opportunity to brief fully the military author. One letter which was written the next morning was to Collingwood; 'My dearest Friend,' it began, a deliberate departure from the customary 'Dear Coll',

'A friend in need is a friend indeed' was never more truly verified than by your most noble and gallant conduct yesterday in sparing the *Captain* from further loss; and I beg, both as a public Officer and a friend, you will accept my most sincere thanks. I have not failed, by letter to the Admiral, to represent the eminent services of the *Excellent*. Tell me how you are, what are your disasters. I cannot tell you much of the *Captain*'s except by Note of Captain Miller's at two this morning, about sixty killed and wounded, masts bad, etc., etc., We shall meet at Lagos; but I could not come near you without assuring you how sensible I am of your assistance in nearly a critical situation. Believe me, as ever, your most affectionate, *Horatio Nelson*.

Within an hour of receiving that letter Collingwood, normally so stern and formal, replied:

My dear good friend,
First let me congratulate you on the success of yesterday—the highest rewards are due to you and *Culloden*: you formed the plan of attack, we were only accessories to the Dons' ruin, for had they got on the other tack, they would have sooner joined, and the business would have been less complete . . . .

On board Lord Garlies's frigate, *Lively*, Colonel Drinkwater continued to be an interested and involved spectator. On the day of the battle he had experienced more action than would normally be expected in a frigate for when *San Isidro* came within range the senior gunner had begged the captain to let him have a shot at her. Normally frigates did not take part in battle actions involving ships of the line, but Garlies yielded and gave his permission. The gunner laid and fired his favourite eighteen-pounder and scored a direct hit, killing, so it was learned later, five or six men.

There was therefore an element of justice in the order to *Lively* to take possession of the Spanish ship when she later struck her colours. The commander, Captain Argumosa, was brought on board to offer his sword and the ship's ensign to Lord Garlies, the latter was given to Sir Gilbert Elliot as a trophy of the day and Drinkwater chose as his memento an iron blunderbuss, a 'trabuca', which was among the spoils of victory.

On the morning of the 13th Sir Gilbert with Lord Garlies was rowed across to the flagship to congratulate Jervis. Drinkwater was to have gone with him but as he was about to go down the gangway realised that, though in uniform, he was without his sword. When he returned to the gangway he found that his place in the boat had been filled. So he stayed on board *Lively* and became the recorder of a much more interesting interview than took place between Elliot and Jervis.

Almost as soon as *Lively*'s boat had left for the flagship, Commodore Nelson came alongside from *Irresistible*. Drinkwater shook his hand on the quarter-deck,

'Where is Sir Gilbert?' asked Nelson.

'Gone with Lord Garlies to the *Victory*', replied Drinkwater. 'I hoped', said Nelson, 'to have caught him before he saw the Admiral but come below with me,' and he led the Colonel below to the captain's cabin.

There the two men sat down and Drinkwater put his interviewing technique into practice, 'How came you, Commodore, to get into that singular and perilous situation?' he began. After describing his 'prompt and extraordinary measure', Nelson went on, speaking 'with increased animation', to deal with his boarding of *San Nicolas* and *San Josef*, but 'in pencil notes on a scrap of paper', set down by Drinkwater, he had already dealt with the crux of his conduct, for the boarding of the two Spanish ships, though courageous, followed from his decision to transfer himself across the two arms of the V which represented the course of the fleet. The conclusion of Drinkwater's interview revealed the man in a slightly different light.

'The Admiral' I observed, 'of course will be made a peer and his seconds-in-command noticed accordingly.'

'As for you, Commodore,' I continued, 'they will make you a baronet.' The word was scarcely uttered, when placing his hand on my arm, and looking me most expressively in the face, he said,

'No, no, if they want to mark my services, it must not be in that manner.'

'Oh' said I, interrupting him, 'you wish to be made a Knight of the

Bath, for I could not imagine that his ambition, at that time, led him
to expect peerage.'

My supposition proved to be correct, for he instantly answered me,
'Yes, if my services have been of any value, let them be noticed in a
way that the public may know me—or them.' I cannot distinctly
remember which of these terms was used, but, from his manner, I
could have no doubt of his meaning that he wished to bear about his
person some honorary distinction, to attract the public eye, and to
mark his professional services.'

Thus Nelson, the day after a battle, confiding in the first person, with
whom he had an opportunity to relax, free from duty. Subsequently he
was to expand his views, principally in letters, but what he said added
little, and in one case only really served to confuse. Following an 'affectionate and flattering' letter from Sir Gilbert Elliot, Nelson, knowing of
course that he was going home with the dispatches, wrote to him suggesting, though not quite directly, the Order of the Bath rather than a
baronetcy as his appropriate reward. He also advanced an additional
reason, lack of funds to maintain an hereditary title. It was not a particularly powerful argument, for a baronetcy was not a peerage, but its
employment has led some biographers to adduce yet another reason for
Nelson's wish to avoid a hereditary title, the fact that he had no children
by Fanny and by now must have abandoned any reasonable hope that she
would bear again.

However, neither reason prevented his accepting a peerage after his
victory of the Nile, so it would seem more credible that Nelson's first
reason was the real one—he wanted a ribbon and a star to wear on his
uniform to show his distinction to the world. Drinkwater had already
noticed that 'the attainment of public honours, and the ambition to be
distinguished above his fellows, were his master passions', and went on
'if such pre-eminent talents as those of this most extraordinary man could
be so cheaply purchased the English nation, and indeed Europe, situated
as she then was, had only to approve and applaud his moderation'.

Nelson had his wish and he duly received from the King his broad red
ribbon to stretch across his uniform from right shoulder to left hip, and
the large star to be worn on the left breast. Jervis himself became Earl St
Vincent, one of the first examples of a peerage with a foreign territorial
title, and to help sustain the dignity was granted a pension of £3,000 a
year. Calder, his Captain of the Fleet or First Captain (both titles were

given to the Chief of Staff) was knighted. Vice-Admirals Thompson and
Parker became baronets, and Vice-Admiral Waldegrave, heir to a peerage in any event, was given an Irish peerage as well.

These rewards for the capture of four Spanish ships, and damage to a
number of others, might look excessive today, but by eighteenth-century
standards it was common form. Two promotions were already on their
way for Jervis was due a peerage, although not an earldom, and had
been so informed two weeks before St Valentine's Day and Nelson had
already been gazetted Rear-Admiral of the Blue before he leapt sword in
hand into *San Nicolas* shouting, as tradition would have it, 'Westminster
Abbey or glorious victory'.

Each captain also received a gold medal, the senior lieutenants were
promoted, and Berry became a captain. Other officers were less pleased
with the results. Saumarez because he was not the captor of the largest
ship in the world: *Trinidada* had struck to him, he maintained, and Drinkwater recollected a white flag being seen, but nothing could be done
about it, and Sir John was not best pleased when Nelson tried to be
diplomatic. 'It was true, Saumarez,' said the Commodore, 'that the
Santissima struck to you; the Spanish officers confirm it.' Saumarez
obviously detected condescension from a successful senior he did not
much like for his response was short, 'Who ever doubted it, Sir? I hope
there is no need for such evidence to establish the truth of a report of a
British officer.'

Perhaps the captain of *Orion* would have been mollified by an honourable mention in the dispatches, but that was not to be. Apparently
persuaded by Calder, though one imagines the taciturn Jervis needed
little persuasion, the Commander-in-Chief produced a model of concise
narrative. The British ships engaged are set out in the margin, likewise the
Spanish. The two frigates, *Niger* and *La Bonne Citoyenne*, which sighted
the Spaniards are mentioned by name, but apart from Captain Foote, of
Niger, and Calder, who took the dispatch home, and would 'particularly
describe' the battle to the Lords of the Admiralty, no other officer's name
appears.

Jervis, remembering the offence and disappointment Howe had caused
by the faults of both inclusion and exclusion in his Glorious First dispatch,
had solved that particular problem in the simplest way possible, by
mentioning no one. He also wrote a long letter to Lord Spencer in which
he drew attention to Nelson, Troubridge, Collingwood, Saumarez,
Hallowell and Admiral Parker among others. However, that letter was

private and Nelson was not the only officer of his day who craved public recognition. No doubt Jervis's Roman brevity and restraint was admirable and it was certainly in character, as he said of himself, 'I would much rather have an action with the enemy than detail one'. Officers such as Saumarez were disappointed, and Nelson, who had none of the reticence or modesty of his chief, had his own account published by sending it to Locker, signed by Berry and Miller as well as himself, and giving Locker permission to pass it on to the newspapers. Colonel Drinkwater also had his own first version published anonymously. A much later version, to which he was to put his name, emphasised Nelson's part to encourage contributions to the Nelson Monument.

As a result of the appearance of Nelson's account, Rear-Admiral, now Sir William, Parker was aggrieved, because he felt that the doings of his own ship, *Prince George*, had been minimised. Parker wrote to Nelson, complaining, and received a none too civil reply, but in a sense Parker was justified. Though Nelson's tactical move was vital, other captains and crews had played their part skilfully and bravely. Overall, Collingwood's comment to his wife after St Vincent, 'It is a very difficult thing for anyone, particularly one who is engaged, to relate the circumstances of a battle,' should have been posted up in the cabin of every captain and flag officer in the fleet.

In much the same sense, Parker had written to Nelson, 'I am well aware that people in action know but little of occurrences in their rear, yet when a letter is written to be exposed to public view, positive assertions should be made with circumspection.' Nelson was never circumspect, and it had been to avoid this sort of post-mortem controversy that Jervis had written his impersonal dispatch. However, Nelson and Parker fell out, and Saumarez wrote of 'our desperate Commodore', despite Jervis's handsome letter written on the morning of the 16th to every captain, 'No language I am possessed of can convey the high sense I entertain of the exemplary conduct of the flag-officers, captains, officers, seamen, marines and soldiers, embarked on board every ship of the squadron . . .', and concluding, 'and give my thanks and approbation to those composing the crew of the ship under your command.' Reading those words it is right to remember that though Nelson carried out two separate feats, the first tactical and the second of personal bravery, the whole fleet had been trained and fashioned by Jervis.

The Spanish navy, in contrast, had been revealed as well below standard. Discounting the urcas Cordoba had been defeated and put to flight by a force little over half his own—Drinkwater's calculation was 1232 British guns against 2308 Spanish—and had lost four ships to the enemy. Throughout the French wars there was always present somewhere, whether in the minds of the Directory, or of Napoleon and his admirals and marshals, an idea that British sea power could be broken and Britain invaded, if a suitable collection of ships could be brought together, French and Spanish, French and Dutch, or French and Danish. St Vincent knocked out the Spanish navy as a significant partner for some time. The Spanish naval historian Duro called the battle 'combate ignominioso', Cordoba and his admirals on their arrival at Cadiz were arrested arraigned before courts martial, and dismissed the service.

It is questionable whether the fault lay with the admirals. Drinkwater reported what he heard after the battle from captured officers, and what had been seen by British prize crews who had come to close quarters with Spanish so-called seamen. He heard of refusal by inexperienced landsmen to go aloft in the rigging though threatened by punishment, even death; of gun crews firing one broadside and then lying flat or deserting their posts, of guns on the *San Josef* still with their tompions in the muzzles though on the side engaged by the British.

It has been seen how British sea officers, Nelson among them, customarily despised the Spanish navy. However, to accept that estimate of their opponents diminishes their own achievement. It was this paradox which Mahan, in his *Influence of Sea Power upon the French Revolution and Empire*, was attempting to describe when he produced one of his most inelegant sentences, 'The Spanish Navy had been but a bugbear but as a bugbear it was great.'

Jervis had said that Britain needed a victory and his intuition was confirmed by the reception accorded to Sir Gilbert Elliot and Colonel Drinkwater when they arrived at Plymouth on March 5 with their news of the battle. Calder had previously been disembarked at St Ives but had kept his information to himself. Elliot and Drinkwater found they were at first disbelieved, the locals were much more concerned with the news that the Bank of England had suspended cash payments, and it was with difficulty that they borrowed fifteen guineas for travelling expenses. British morale needed a boost and it was provided in particular by Horatio Nelson. He was now a Hero. His method of taking two Spanish ships became known, as he told Fanny, as 'Nelson's Patent Bridge for taking Spanish First Rates'. He had his red riband and his star, and in consequence the pleasure of a minor engagement with the College of

Heralds. A new Knight of the Bath had to have a coat of arms and a pedigree, and Nelson himself provided much of the information. It shows the origins of the Nelson family in Lancashire in the sixteenth century, though with no connection with the town of that name which was a nineteenth-century 'new town' named after a public house, the Lord Nelson, situated on a central crossroads. However the northern connection is not surprising as Nelson was originally a Norse name and there had been many Scandinavian settlements in Yorkshire and Lancashire. More pertinent perhaps is the fact that the detailed pedigree of Horatio Nelson re-emphasises the difference between his father's and his mother's sides of the family. Sucklings, as well as being related to Walpoles, had married aristocratic Cavendishes and Cholmondeleys while Nelsons had found their spouses among local lower-middle-class families.

However, with Horatio the Nelsons achieved a coat of arms, entirely appropriate to their most distinguished son. The supporters were a British seaman, dressed more neatly than on board ship, and a British lion, the figure head of *Captain*, the sailor holding a spear with a commodore's broad pendant, the lion chewing and trampling on Spanish colours. The motto 'Faith and Works', not inappropriate to a clergyman's son, was a phrase Nelson had already used in correspondence with his brother. The crest was heraldically curious since it was a stern view of *San Josef*. For their services of design and registration the Heralds requested payment of 400 guineas which Nelson refused, arguing that it should be a public expense. In fact he never paid, and the precedent was followed by, among others, Field-Marshal Lord Roberts.

It is not difficult to imagine Nelson's pleasure in his achievement and its recognition. Only Fanny struck a characteristically careful note, 'What can I say to you about Boarding? You have been wonderfully Protected; you have done desperate actions enough. Now may I—indeed I do—beg you never Board again! leave it for Captains.'

CHAPTER FIFTEEN

Mutiny in the Fleet

NINE MONTHS after Nelson's conversation in the captain's cabin of *Irresistible* with Drinkwater, the two men were to meet and talk again in London. On this occasion Drinkwater was again impressed by the thirty-nine-year-old Rear-Admiral's 'peculiar energetic manner' though he was now recuperating from a severe wound. Both officers were anxiously waiting to hear news from the Admiralty as to how Admiral Duncan had fared against the Dutch. Though Lady Nelson tried to restrain her husband, 'so intense was his eagerness' that he stood, and stretching out his left arm towards Drinkwater exclaimed, 'I would give this other arm to be with Duncan at this moment.'

The news when it came could not have been better. The battle of Camperdown, fought close in to the Dutch shore on October 11 and 12, had been a signal success. A British fleet of sixteen of the line under the command of the gigantic sixty-six-year-old Scot, Adam Duncan, had fought a tough, hard-slogging battle against a Dutch fleet of eighteen almost equally matched ships, and at the end of the day eleven had been captured though damage to many from gunfire had rendered them virtually useless. Indeed three prizes sank or were wrecked before reaching England. Casualties and damage on both sides had been high, the Dutch being in a very different class from the Spaniards, as the British, their reluctantly admiring opponents, were always ready to admit.

By beating the Dutch at Camperdown Duncan had knocked out another of France's naval allies and, even more effectively than at St Vincent, had disabled an enemy fleet. Two victories at sea within one year, but St Vincent and Camperdown by no means represented the whole story. A great deal had happened in those nine months, since Nelson had last talked to Drinkwater of his career, the fleet in which he served, and of the progress of the war.

On the Continent the situation had gone from bad to worse. Wherever the British looked among their old friends and allies who had once formed a coalition, however loose and unsatisfactory, there could now only be counted nations which had either succumbed or relapsed into neutrality and inaction.

In November of the previous year Catherine of Russia had died. And with her there perished any possibility of active military co-operation. The new Tsar, Paul, was no longer an unknown quantity. The fact that he was actually insane was already coming to be appreciated, and with this new ruler there had been a shift in policy so that Russia was now benevolently neutral towards Revolutionary France despite the presence in northern waters of a fleet of twelve of the line and six frigates under a trio of admirals, Mackaroff, Honickoff and Tate, the latter of Scots descent. This fleet had for the last two years maintained a desultory presence on the Dutch coast with Duncan, alternating some sort of co-operation in the business of blockade with returns to the Baltic in the winter. In fact the Russian ships were really more of a hindrance than a help and by Camperdown had deserted the British completely.

Prussia, in the last year of the reign of the dissolute Frederick William II, was a broken reed, and fully deserved the strictures expressed by Nelson against 'Germans' generally, willing to accept British subsidies, but unwilling to render military assistance. Elsewhere in Europe the growth of satellite republics evidenced the growth of French military power. Holland had become the Batavian Republic, Switzerland the Helvetian, and the states of Italy were rapidly following in the wake of a steady succession of Bonaparte's military triumphs.

The only active member of the original coalition, apart from Britain, was the Habsburg Empire, and it was her army which had provided the last resistance to the French in the Italian peninsula. Five days after St Vincent Pope Pius VI had ceded the Romagna, Bologna and Ferrara to France, and Bonaparte was one step nearer to his project of advancing French armies through the Tyrol to Vienna. Faced with that danger, and after exactly ten years of unsuccessful warfare, the Empire succumbed, and on April 18 a preliminary peace settlement was agreed, at Leoben, between Austrian and French delegates. A final treaty was not signed until October at Campo Formio, but meanwhile Ligurian, Cispadane and Cisalpine republics absorbed what remained of Italy's northern and central states.

Britain had certainly needed a victory in February but now, two months later, she was on her own. Admittedly, there had been successes in the West Indies: Demerara, Essequibo, Berbice, St Lucia, Grenada and later Trinidad had been captured, but these were nothing when the whole of western Europe was dominated by French arms. The sole evidence of alliance and friendship left was the Portuguese provision of an anchorage for the British fleet in the Tagus. There was talk in Britain that spring of invasion, Ireland had been tried once and was now in a state of rebellion which was an obvious encouragement to an enemy. The attempt in February, which had put ashore a collection of ex-criminals and ruffians at Fishguard, had been farcical, the invaders being fooled by the stratagem of local women, in traditional red cloaks and steeple hats, masquerading at a distance as infantry until the yeomanry rounded them up. However, the fact that men could be landed in Wales and, save for the elements, could have been landed in Ireland, demonstrated that even the Royal Navy could not provide an absolute guarantee of impregnability.

With Government and people in this state of apprehension, something of the shock can be imagined when the news reached London, on April 17, that the fleet had mutinied at Spithead. On April 16 when Admiral Lord Bridport had ordered the Channel Fleet to put to sea from Portsmouth the crews had swarmed to the yards, given three cheers and refused to move.

Neither at the time, and the Government was anxious enough to find it, nor since, has any convincing evidence been produced to show a political or revolutionary motive behind a movement which spread from Spithead to the Nore and to Plymouth and Yarmouth and touched St Vincent's Mediterranean fleet. Nor, apart from the curious and pathetic Richard Parker, who acted as spokesman at the Nore, has anyone ever been identified as the ringleader of a mutiny which in its early stages was marked by restraint, unanimity and efficiency.

At the time, in the mood of surprise and fear engendered by the news of the immobilisation of the fleet in home waters, there were many in Government and naval circles who immediately discerned the malign effect of revolutionary doctrines from across the Channel, the influence of Jacobins and the Corresponding Societies. If that suspicion had been proved correct it would have meant a tremendous coup for the revolutionaries and the agents of France. In fact Britain's enemies could not take the credit. They were not even sufficiently well-informed to take advantage of the crippling predicament which now faced an island vulnerable to invasion and deprived, at a stroke, of its principal method of defence. The search for extraordinary reasons as to why the men of the fleet should refuse duty was a waste of time. Both Collingwood and Jervis naïvely settled upon the pernicious growth of literacy in the fleet plus the introduction of a free postal service for seamen. It is true that by such means potential mutineers had communicated with each other, but it was scarcely the cause of the outbreak.

Nelson, who in 1785, when captain of *Boreas*, had written to the Postmaster General advocating a free postal service, for the 'poor seamen' and had paid out of his own pocket for sailors' letters, would hardly have agreed. He saw deeper than that and often criticised his brother officers who 'forget and are negligent of Poor Jack'. Conditions on the lower deck were appalling and seemingly unknown, perhaps understandably, to the public at large, but also, inexcusably, to the Government and the Admiralty. If an immediate cause be sought for the outbreak of mutiny in 1797 it is to be found in the fact that bad conditions had become worse.

Seamen's pay, twenty-four shillings a lunar month for able seamen and nineteen for ordinary seamen, was one grievance. In fact, after deductions, the seamen were fortunate to get their hands upon ten shillings a month. That was bad enough but the sums a sailor was entitled to were often two to three years in arrears. Pay was only issued in full when a ship was finally paid off, and always in tickets only convertible into cash at the commissioning port. The sick on board, whether by wounds, injury or illness, received no pay at all. In the merchant service, on the other hand, the same man could get three times his rate of pay and an even closer comparison was soldiers' pay which had recently been substantially increased to take account of rises in the cost of living and as an incentive to recruiting.

The standard of food was usually very low, sailors receiving inedible bone and gristle or fat, biscuits full of weevils, cheese was inhabited by long red worms, and water stored overlong in unclean barrels was rancid. The only clean and generous ration was rum, half a pint a day served diluted in two portions a day. Even these unsavoury rations were served short, two ounces in every pound being pursers' 'savings' under a system which seemed deliberately designed to turn even an honest purser into a cheat and a thief. Leave was in fact virtually non-existent as once men got ashore they would not return to their ships, but that could hardly be counted surprising. Medical attention was another grievance for often the wounded or sick seaman had to steel himself to the attentions of some drunken, incompetent and brutal student of medicine whose character or lack of skill had unfitted him for practice on shore.

Finally, discipline, and here the complaints were surprisingly moderate. There was no suggestion of abolition of hanging at the yard arm, or flogging at the gratings, or the boatswain's mate's habit of 'starting' with a cane or a rope's end. All that was asked was that punishment should be within the 'Regulations and Instructions relating to His Majesty's Service at Sea', which, for instance, limited the number of lashes a captain could order without court martial. What the two sailor delegates from each ship at Spithead demanded was an end to arbitrary and excessive punishment by tyrannical officers, and that there should be some system whereby complaints could be considered.

There can be no doubt that the delegates' complaints were justified, and indeed it is surprising that there had been no previous general refusal of duty. Before Spithead it was only on individual ships, where men had been ill-treated beyond endurance, that mutinies had broken out, which had then been put down with the customary severity.

Before the men of the Channel Fleet acted in unison there had been petitions to Lord Howe and letters to the Admiralty from individual officers concerned both with conditions and an observable state of unrest among the men, but they had all been ignored.

Nevertheless, unless some general action had been taken the general run of conditions would have continued. Revealing at Spithead was the fact that the delegates were not malcontents, but in a majority of cases, 'prime seamen', often senior petty officers, gunners' mates, yeomen of signals and quartermasters, men with skills and trades and responsibilities. Equally significant was that the marines, the epitome and guarantee of discipline, threw in their lot with their shipmates.

After some initial false moves Spencer and his colleagues, conscious of the power of the seamen, their reasonable conduct and their patriotism, were persuaded to remedial action. By no means all the mutineers' demands were met, but by an Act, hurried through Parliament, pay was improved and the Royal Pardon was granted to those who had mutinied. Spencer and the seventy-one-year-old Howe visited every ship at Spithead and St Helens and persuaded the men back to their duty.

The mutiny was settled a month after its outbreak, and the Channel Fleet was ready again for sea, when red flags, the signal for 'Prepare for Action', were hoisted at the Nore and Yarmouth. These two mutinies, and especially the one at the Nore, were of a very different nature from the successfully concluded events at Spithead. The Nore mutiny seems to have been a sort of sympathy strike, but while the Spithead sailors had accepted the Government's terms and the Royal Pardon and returned to duty, at the Nore the delegates were more violent and less well-organised.

There was talk of a 'Floating Republic' and eventually Richard Parker, one-time schoolmaster, former midshipman, a heady orator but possibly mentally unstable, was pushed into being its President. At Spithead the seamen made specific demands and never over-reached themselves but at the Nore it was never clear what any body of men really wanted and in consequence the Government, even if it had wanted to grant further concessions, never knew what was expected from it and reacted in panic with suppressive measures.

The incidents at Sheerness provided a sad postscript to those at Portsmouth. Later, Aaron Graham, the magistrate who, with his colleague David Williams, investigated the whole matter for the Government, could report, 'Nothing like want of loyalty to the King or attachment to the government can be traced in the business'. Nevertheless, because of the incompetence or unreasonableness of the men at the Nore coupled with the fact that just across the North Sea, in the Texel, the Dutch fleet was ready to sail and would have found the Thames estuary undefended, both mutineers and authorities reacted against each other. There were threats of blockading the Thames and of starving the mutineers into submission. One after the other the disaffected ships did surrender until only *Sandwich*, Parker's ship, remained. Finally, he was given up by his former comrades and answered for his conduct at the end of a yard arm. So, too, did twenty-nine of his fellow conspirators, out of fifty-nine actually sentenced. Though 408 men were tried apart from these fifty-nine, only nine were flogged and twenty-nine imprisoned. As a postscript it may be mentioned that a tradition in the Spencer family has it that the First Lord provided financially for Parker's widow. In fact she died in poverty, but did receive money from the London magistrates and Nelson's friend the Duke of Clarence, by then King William IV.

The formerly mutinous ships and their crews were re-distributed within the Navy, some coming Nelson's way but the majority going to *Ardent, Belliqueux, Director, Montagne, Isis, Monmouth* and *Lancaster* which were all part of Duncan's fleet at Camperdown. What Pitt called 'the manly and generous character of British seamen' had been restored, but the mutinies had also revealed something of the material with which Nelson had to deal. Simple, often illiterate, suspicious of politicians but loyal to the King, patriotic in a manner almost incomprehensible today, tough and uncomplaining, only seeking consideration, fairness and leadership to prove themselves the best sailors afloat. On the mutinies Nelson expressed his opinion:

I am entirely with the Seamen in their first complaint.
We are a neglected set.

This comment referred to Spithead, but of the Nore mutineers he took
the conventional view, stronger perhaps than Pitt's 'deluded persons who
have persisted in disobedience', for he declared himself prepared to
command a ship against such scoundrels.

Much of the new flag officer's time since the battle of St Vincent had
been taken up with the pleasures of the aftermath. A letter from a
gratified elderly father had recalled a prophecy from his relation by
marriage and began with simple archness, 'My dear Rear-Admiral'.
Three sets of letters had arrived from friends, first on the news of the part
he had played in the battle, secondly on his promotion to flag rank, and
finally on his elevation to be a Knight of the Bath.

The sword of the Spanish admiral with a Dutch surname, Don Xavier
Francisco Winthuysen, given up on board his flagship *San Josef*, was sent
to the Mayor of Norwich. The Cities of London, Bath, Bristol, and of
course Norwich itself, wished to give the admiral their freedom. There
was the matter of his coat of arms and heraldic motto and questions of
prize money to be sorted out. There were, however, also duties for the
new admiral which, with St Vincent as Commander-in-Chief, had soon
to be attended to.

Nelson's first task was as a commander of the inshore squadron,
blockading Cadiz, with his flag in *Captain* and then, after May, in *Theseus*
with Miller still as his flag captain. The ship itself provided an object
lesson and commentary upon the mutinies which were still in progress,
the Nore disturbances not coming to an end until June. Contrary to
what has been assumed by a number of Nelson's biographers she had
played no part at Spithead because she was on the Mediterranean station
by May. However, she had been unlucky in her previous captain and first
lieutenant and the ship's company had in consequence become surly and
unco-operative, and had sent a letter of complaint to Lord Howe. The
captain had then become worried lest his men would mutiny and his
suspicions and precautions had made his men even worse. Mrs Fremantle,
no doubt taking the cue from her husband, commented, 'the *Theseus* men
the most tiresome noisy mutinous people in the world'.

It was St Vincent's opinion that this situation could only be remedied
by a twofold cure, good officers and a taste of action and adventure, but
there was one other consideration, often overlooked, the physical

condition of the ship itself. *Agamemnon* was held together by cables, on her return journey, *Sandwich*, the centre of rebellion at the Nore, was a foetid hulk broken up after the mutiny, and even in Duncan's flagship, *Venerable*, the admiral's cabin was almost uninhabitable when at sea in bad weather.

When *Theseus* came to Nelson it was in a similar category; though sound structurally she was without stores of any kind. In March she had been provisioned for foreign service and two months later there was nothing. Nelson and Miller found themselves concerned with every type of stores from nails for the carpenter to green vegetables for the crew. The fault lay with a dishonest purser or his assistants, and some scheming dockyard contractors. The burden, under indifferent officers, fell on the lower deck.

St Vincent's judgment was seen to be correct when, only a couple of weeks later, Nelson was shown a piece of crumpled paper, which had mysteriously found its way at night on to the quarter-deck. On it in an illiterate hand, was written:

> Success attend Admiral Nelson! God bless Captain Miller! We thank them for the Officers they have placed over us. We are happy and comfortable, and will shed every drop of blood in our veins, and the name of the *Theseus* shall be immortalized as high as the *Captain's*.

The signatory in large block capitals was simply, 'SHIP'S COMPANY.' The second part of the cure, a taste of action, was soon to come the way of the seamen and marines in the Mediterranean Fleet under Nelson's control.

The whole of St Vincent's command was now concerned with the close blockade of Cadiz, 'Spain shall have no trade,' as Nelson put it. He had command of the inshore squadron which cruised continously just outside gunshot of the harbour; so close were Nelson's ships that elegant Spanish ladies could be spied taking their promenade along the mole.

St Vincent still had to concern himself with former or potential mutineers, for the disaffection had spread widely and in some of his ships the problem could not be solved as easily as on board *Theseus*, although malcontents transferred to the Mediterranean soon learned the sort of man they were now serving under. Wise advice was contained in one overheard dialogue. When *London*, one of the principal mutinous ships at Spithead, arrived in the Tagus one of her company shouted derisively at a sailor watching her from one of the flagship's ports, asking him what he had been doing while others had been 'fighting for his beef and pork'. The response was not shouted, 'If you'll take my advice, you'll say nothing at all about all that here, for by God if old Jarvie hears ye he'll have you dingle-dangle at the yard-arm at eight o'clock tomorrow morning.' While St Vincent made representations to the Admiralty about deficiencies in food and clothing and delays in pay and prize money, on board *Alcmene*, *Emerald*, *Marlborough* and *St George* men were hanged, at St Vincent's order, by their own ship's company. Nelson concurred with promptitude and severity, but his was not the burden of principal command, and he could concern himself with other projects, and, being Nelson, they were always projects for harrying the enemy. It is difficult not to feel a sympathy for old St Vincent, faced with the prospect of the Spanish coming out again, having to deal with mutinous crews and weak-kneed admirals and captains, while also receiving a barrage of letters from his impetuous junior.

In Italy, as Nelson wrote, referring to the French, 'there seems no prospect of stopping these extraordinary people' but with their allies, the Spaniards, surely something could be done. His first thoughts were for the garrison of 3700 men left on Elba under General de Burgh who had pompously refused to move them, save on direct orders from London. Now they were to be convoyed to Gibraltar. St Vincent had already arranged an escort, but Nelson picked up the convoy in April with ships from his own command, and as soon as he was reassured of their safety wondered if such a body of troops might not be used more usefully than by swelling the garrison of Gibraltar.

It is difficult to pinpoint precisely when Nelson settled on the idea of an assault upon the Spanish island of Teneriffe in the Canaries, and its port, Santa Cruz. Passivity always made him restless, perhaps the idea of those unoccupied 3700 soldiers provoked him, or perhaps it was the rumours about the Viceroy of Mexico's arrival with a treasure fleet. Certainly in April, while still flying his flag in *Captain*, he had tentatively unfolded a plan to his old friend Thomas Troubridge. St Vincent had been apprised of the idea and had not been averse to hearing more detailed proposals from two of his most highly regarded officers.

It was not as if there were no other prospects of action against the Spaniards, for the blockade of Cadiz, with Nelson in charge, was not just some tiresome chore of endless cruising and waiting, with the interception of small merchant vessels as its only diversion. Nelson's letters at the time also show that he had to deal with his quota of administrative tasks as well. There was still the complicated matter of prize and head money from the Corsican operation to be sorted out with M'Arthur, Hood's secretary, who had written telling Nelson that the matter was not yet before the Admiralty Prize Courts. At the same time Nelson was preparing a case for the opinion of counsel on conflicts which had arisen on the same subject between captains on his present station.

The blockade had three purposes. First, to prevent trade in and out of Cadiz, a crippling blow to Spain in an age when the transport of any large cargo had to be by sea. The effect on a maritime power was of course cumulative, if ships were destroyed there was a need to repair or replace them. To do that, timber, masts, canvas and cordage had to be brought in by sea. If such commerce were prevented then the merchant marine declined and the navy was paralysed. Secondly the hope in the Royal Navy that if the screws were tightened sufficiently on Spain's principal sea ports then the Spanish fleet would in desperation have to come out and fight. Finally, in Spain's particular case, as she was dependent upon the gold and silver mines of the New World for her own economy, the British blockade either held back the Lima and Havana convoys from Cadiz, or else put them at risk of capture. In either case the merchant community faced ruin and it was not only the fashionable ladies who watched the British fleet and wondered what might happen next.

The answer was provided by Nelson with his ten sail of the line, reinforced by bomb and mortar vessels. Cadiz was subjected to two nights of bombardment which, far from bringing the Spanish fleet out, only forced it to withdraw further into the inner harbour to escape damage. This was in June and it was during this period that Nelson revealed that, though nearing forty, he had lost none of his boyish enthusiasm for a fight. His conduct was more that of a bloodthirsty midshipman than a senior officer entrusted with an important command. No doubt to the junior officers and the seamen he led he was an inspiration, and obviously he had no regrets himself, his own complacent observation being 'It was during this period that perhaps my personal courage was more conspicuous than at any other part of my life.'

It is questionable whether Nelson was performing his proper duties when he became involved in a night-time clash between his squadron's boats and a number of Spanish gunboats and armed launches. Nevertheless, there he was, not in his flagship, but engaged in boat work that would normally have occupied a lieutenant, and in his own words, 'I was boarded in my barge with its common crew of ten men, coxswain, Captain Fremantle, and myself, by the commander of the gunboats; the Spanish barge rowed twenty-six oars, besides officers—thirty men in the whole. This was a service hand to hand with swords, in which my coxswain, John Sykes, now no more, twice saved my life. Eighteen of the Spaniards being killed and several wounded, we succeeded in taking their commander.'

So much for Fanny's advice about leaving boarding to captains! Of course if Admiral Nelson should not have been there, neither should Captain Fremantle, now in command of *Seahorse*. John Sykes, who was rewarded by St Vincent for his gallantry with a gunner's warrant, but was killed soon after by the explosion of a cannon, parried blows aimed at the Admiral with his cutlass, and on the last occasion, as the only way of saving him, took a blow on his own head. Nelson lifted up the wounded man, saying, 'I will never forget this' to which Sykes gasped out, 'Thank God you're safe, Sir.' It is difficult to think of another admiral behaving in this way, and no doubt for just that reason no other senior officer inspired the same sort of devotion. However, Nelson had not been promoted Rear-Admiral to fight in boats with a drawn sword. The fact that he did has more than passing significance, for it was his pugnacity and impetuousness which led him to his next adventure, which was disastrous.

An attack on Teneriffe had become an *idée fixe* since his first talks with Troubridge. Some of the purpose had disappeared; the rumours about treasure fleets, with or without the Viceroy of Mexico, which would assist Britain's economy or pay her subsidy bill to foreign powers, had evaporated. Nor were the means immediately at hand for a combined operation. General de Burgh's troops from Elba were destined for Portugal, Gibraltar and home posting, and the old general would not have them diverted elsewhere. General Charles O'Hara, who possessed more aggressive spirit—he was known as 'the Cock of the Rock'—was however not prepared to lend troops from his own Gibraltar garrison.

Nevertheless Nelson continued to pester St Vincent with his scheme. He was in the same mood as when he had attacked, and failed to capture, Turks Island in the Bahamas in 1783, and was as prepared to ignore the opposition as on Corsica. There, on one occasion, he had suppressed information about the enemy's strength lest Hood be deterred. Now, having started with the idea of a conjoint attack, he was prepared to go ahead with a purely naval force.

On May 29 boats from the frigates *Lively* and *Minerve*, commanded by Lieutenant Hardy, had cut out and captured the French frigate *Mutine* but surprise and luck had been on the side of the attackers. Now there was yet another rumour of a treasure ship, but it was not a reward adequate for the risks involved. For Nelson, asking for 200 extra marines, to say, 'With "General Troubridge" ashore and myself afloat, I am confident of success', was much more bravado than calculation.

Eventually, however, St Vincent yielded as a pestered parent might yield, to the persistent importunities of a favoured child. On July 15 *Theseus* with *Culloden* (Captain Troubridge), *Zealous* (Captain Samuel Hood), *Leander* (Captain T. Thompson), the *Seahorse* frigate (Captain Fremantle) and two more frigates, *Emerald* and *Terpsichore* (Captains Waller and Bowen) and the cutter *Fox* were detached from the main fleet. St Vincent's orders were to capture Santa Cruz, seize the rumoured treasure ship, capture or destroy all other enemy vessels, 'and having performed your mission you are to make the best of your way back to me'.

Nelson's response contained more truth than perhaps he realised. 'Ten hours shall either make me a conqueror or defeat me.'

CHAPTER SIXTEEN

Failure at Teneriffe

ST VINCENT addressed Nelson rather sententiously, at two stages of
the Teneriffe operation, using almost the same phrase, and it was one
with a classical ring to it, 'I am sure you will deserve success, to
mortals is not given the power of commanding it', and 'Mortals cannot
command success'. The first was a warning delivered before the detached
squadron left, the second was the old Admiral's consolation to the younger
when the expedition returned. It was now to be a naval attack upon a
port with fortifications and a considerable garrison. Though Nelson had
a poor opinion of soldiers, 'Soldiers, excepting General O'Hara, have not
the same boldness in undertaking a political measure that we have; the
soldier obeys his orders, and no more'; still soldiering would have to be
done, and by a small force of marines and seamen from the crews of his
own squadron.

What was Nelson hoping to throw into the balance to counteract his
shortage of numbers? Apparently, the element of surprise and some
attempts at subterfuge. He was also taking the risks of wind and weather
to get his ships in and out of Santa Cruz. The north-east Trade wind,
prevalent all through the summer, would bring his ships into the
harbour, but even Blake's ships had to be warped out after action,
though Nelson seems not to have discovered that. In the final analysis the
counter arguments were disregarded, for what Nelson believed in were
his own inspiration and leadership. 'I do not reckon myself equal to
Blake, fortune favoured the gallant attempt and may do so again.' While
plans were going forward he wrote to Fanny on July 12 and corrected the
address on one of her letters and gave her the proper one, but went on to
say that it hardly mattered, 'any direction will find N.—you will recollect
the Italian compliment I told you of, "There is but one H.N. in the
world". I have had flattery enough to make me vain, and success enough
to make me confident.'

It was a dangerous mood in which to embark upon a hazardous enterprise. Yet he did not mount his attack upon Teneriffe carelessly for

however confident he may have been of success he neglected no element of small-scale military planning. There were discussions with the captains and the senior officers of marines. Nelson circulated at least one paper with a number of questions set down for their opinions. Then there followed, on July 17, his own instructions for the six divisions of boats containing sailors and marines, detailing how they were to be equipped and what their actions were to be once they had gained the shore. The basic plan was that the boats from the squadron should be put ashore by the frigates at night between a fort to the north-east of Santa Cruz Bay and the actual town. Then landing parties under Troubridge with the assistance of Captain Oldfield, the senior officer of marines, were to attack and overcome the two batteries which commanded the bay, and to aid them in this task they were to take special scaling ladders Nelson had designed which were being made by the ships' carpenters. The line of battle ships was to bombard the town once the landing-parties were ashore. When the batteries were neutralised and the fort captured, the town was to be called on to surrender. As a final, perhaps over-hopeful, detail Nelson drafted his summons to the Governor to give up the treasure ship from Manila, 'property of the Philippine Company', and surrender his men within half an hour of receiving the proclamation which would be delivered as soon as Troubridge was in control.

Nelson's armada had the snow-topped Mount Teide in sight before sundown on July 20 and the island of Teneriffe was some fifty miles distant. The next morning about a thousand seamen and marines with their officers were transferred to the frigates, ships of the line being kept out of the way so as not to alarm the Spaniards. The first assault was to be made upon the heights behind the fort under the cover of darkness. By midnight the frigates were in position within three miles of the landing place. It was then that those forces which had originally worried Nelson took control, wind and weather. A strong wind blew up from the land which, combined with a powerfully running current, kept the frigates off-shore. They were still a mile away when day broke and with first light all attempts at surprise had now failed. Early that morning Troubridge went on board *Theseus* to consult Nelson. He was prepared to go on and Nelson agreed, so at 9 a.m. the boats shoved off for the shore.

However, the Spaniards were at least the equal of 'General' Troubridge as tacticians, and the heights had been manned by a considerable number of troops. Troubridge's force could make little headway against heavy and concentrated musket-fire. Nelson endeavoured to bring up his 74's and his 50 to provide support with their broadsides but they were less manoeuvrable than the frigates, and could get no nearer than three miles off-shore, well outside the range of their guns. Throughout the day the wind freshened, so that eventually they were forced to stand off to sea. That night a downcast Troubridge re-embarked his men on board the frigates. The next morning Nelson recalled them, the seamen and marines returned to their own ships, and the whole squadron put out to sea under sail.

It should all have ended there for the time being. The garrison had been alerted, and had seen the whole British force deployed and could make a very fair estimate of its strength and capabilities. It was obvious that the Spaniards were both sensibly commanded and in considerable strength. The Teneriffe wind and current had been sampled and shown to be very much on the side of the defence. Yet Nelson's pride was hurt. Somehow he could not just sail away to fight again another day and so at 8 p.m. on July 24 he wrote to St Vincent:

> I shall not enter on the subject while we are not in possession of Santa Cruz; your partiality will give credit that all has hitherto been done which was possible, but without effect: this night I, humble as I am, command the whole, destined to land under the batteries of the Town, and tomorrow my head will probably be crowned with either laurel or cypress. I have only to recommend Josiah Nisbet to you and my Country. With every affectionate wish for your health, and every blessing in this world, believe me your most faithful, *Horatio Nelson.* The Duke of Clarence, should I fall in the service of my King and Country, will, I am confident, take a lively interest for my Son-in-law [i.e. his stepson] on his name being mentioned.

This letter is typical of Nelson and is the last he wrote in the fine legible copperplate of his right hand, excelling himself and also revealing a great deal of his character.

St Vincent is told next to nothing of the new plan save that Nelson will command on shore in person. It is hardly necessary to say that it is not a humble letter, but only mock humble. Naturally St Vincent would hope to hear how Santa Cruz was to be taken, but all the letter tells him is that his subordinate is about to risk his life, and most probably, in his own view, lose it. It is almost as if he is now trying to expiate previous failure by seeking death.

The 'laurel' and 'cypress' alternative was often in Nelson's mind; it is the same as 'Westminster Abbey or glorious victory' at St Vincent and the sentiment was to be echoed again before the Battle of the Nile. Those were, indeed, the alternatives, but by their repetition, Nelson did mis-represent himself as a sort of vainglorious fire-eater, afflicted with a death-wish. St Vincent is left in 'this world', a familiar phrase to a clergy-man's son, Nelson is destined for the next. A dead rear-admiral will have no 'interest', therefore Josiah will have to depend for advancement, it is hoped, upon St Vincent and the Duke of Clarence.

The same evening Nelson made his will, leaving £500 to his stepson and £200 to his favourite brother Maurice, and the remainder of his estate to Fanny and then to Josiah in the event of his mother pre-deceasing him.

Nelson was not the only officer to make his will, as any experienced man could form a good idea of the risks that the landing force would now run. Josiah, on board *Theseus* with his stepfather, was given an even clearer indication of the possibilities, for Nelson told him he would destroy all his letters from Fanny, though seemingly could not have done so. It was probably at this time that Josiah made his request to take part in the landing. At first Nelson refused, 'Should we both fall, what would become of your poor mother?' In any event Josiah's place was on board his ship, at which the boy insisted, 'I will go with you tonight if I never go again'. It was a courageous response and Nelson, letting his heart rule his head, allowed him to take a place with the landing party.

The final glimpse of them all, Nelson, Troubridge, Bowen and the other captains, is through the eyes of Mrs Betsy Fremantle, who, though pregnant, was on board her husband's frigate, *Seahorse*. That night she acted as hostess of a dinner party. Whether out of consideration for her, or, to keep their own spirits up, they must have put on a brave show of confidence, for she wrote in her diary, 'As the taking of this place seemed an easy and almost sure thing I went to bed after they had gone, appre-hending no danger for Fremantle.' Nelson, with more knowledge, felt otherwise, yet persisted:

> Although I felt the second attack a forlorn hope, yet the honour of our country called for the attack and that I should command it. I never expected to return.

At 11 o'clock the boats shoved off into the night and the Atlantic swell, each one filled with marines and seamen led by an officer or midshipman. Their equipment was sword and pistol for the officers, muskets and cutlasses for the men, and many seamen, on Nelson's orders, wore spare marines' red tunics and equipment, presumably so as to be better recognised by their comrades in the dark. The scaling ladders for use on shore were stowed in the boats which also carried stocks of spare ammunition. This time there was very little finesse in the attack, darkness might provide some element of concealment and surprise, but otherwise it was a straight frontal attack on the mole by a thousand men to take the two batteries and then to reform into one body which would battle itself to the town square.

It was not much of a plan and it lost even the advantage of surprise as soon as the Spaniards, though the night was dark, detected the fleet of boats making its way through a strong running sea. Immediately the church bells sounded the alarm, and when the British were within range a heavy fire opened up. The result was near chaos. About half the force, with Troubridge as the senior officer, never made the mole at all, but found themselves attempting to land through heavy surf. Boats were wrecked on the rocky beach, scaling ladders were lost, ammunition ruined and men thrown into the water. The cutter *Fox* was struck by a shot under water and began to sink.

Nelson's party did succeed in making the mole and attacking and spiking some guns, but was then pinned down by concentrated musket and grapeshot fire from the citadel and nearby houses. The Spaniards had not wasted their time since the first attack and had prepared advance defensive positions. Somehow, Troubridge with about three to four hundred men forced his way to the main square, there to make his rendezvous with Nelson's party. However, Troubridge waited in vain, for as he was landing from his boat, sword in hand, Nelson had been struck by a musket shot which shattered his right elbow. He transferred his sword to his left hand, but then exclaiming 'I am a dead man,' staggered and fell backwards into the arms of Josiah, close behind him.

Willing hands placed the admiral in the bottom of the boat and Josiah, seeing that Nelson's faintness and nausea was increased by the sight of blood pumping from the wound, covered his arm with his hat. Then taking his cravat from his neck he tied it as a tourniquet above the wound. Lovel, one of the admiral's bargemen, tore his shirt up as a make-shift sling, and then he and Josiah got the boat away from the shore. All this time they were under heavy fire from the guns on shore.

The safest course seemed to be to keep the boat close to the mole so that the cannon fired over them and this Josiah ordered, Lovel steering a course parallel to the shore. In the confusion they then came upon *Fox*, rapidly sinking, with its complement of nearly a hundred men swimming, floundering and drowning in the water.

Nelson, conscious but in considerable pain, insisted that they pick up as many survivors as they could. Then the overloaded boat was rowed out of the fleet. *Seahorse*, one of the inner line of frigates, was first seen, but Josiah's relief must have been dashed when Nelson categorically refused to go on board, but insisted on being rowed the greater distance to *Theseus*. Josiah told him he was risking his life, 'Then I will die,' said his stepfather, 'for I would rather suffer death than alarm Mrs Fremantle by her seeing me in this state, and when I can give her no tidings of he husband.'

So they rowed on to *Theseus* as, behind them, whatever battle could be fought was sustained by Troubridge and those who had been lucky enough to get on shore unscathed. Reaching the flagship Nelson brushed aside all offers to help him on board, 'Let me alone, I have yet my legs left and one arm,' he said, and winding his left arm through a rope he made his way up the ship's side.

On board *Theseus* Hoste, who had been a midshipman on *Agamemnon* and hero-worshipped Nelson, watched the return of his hero, 'his right arm dangling by his side, while with the other he helped himself to jump up the ship's side'.

On deck, the Rear-Admiral, his shattered arm in his blood-soaked sling was received in the usual way with saluting marines and his officers with doffed cocked hats. Nelson returned their salutes with his left hand and with a no-nonsense manner told 'the surgeon to get his instruments ready for he knew he must lose his arm, and that the sooner it was off the better'. Hoste watched in admiration and felt jealous of Josiah who had been presented with the opportunity to save the great man's life, someone who had been a 'second father' to him.

The operation was performed in the early hours of the morning by Thomas Eshelby and his assistant Louis Remonier, the two surgeons on board *Theseus* who had also served in *Captain*. Nelson's right arm was taken off high up, towards the shoulder, and the appropriate entry was made in the surgeon's journal:

1797 July 25. Admiral Nelson. Compound fracture of the right arm by a musket ball passing through a little above the elbow, an artery divided: the arm immediately amputated and opium afterwards given.

The wound had been caused by one musket ball but whether from a lucky shot from a musket or as part of a discharge of grape shot, which was a collection of musket balls fired from a cannon, it is impossible to say, though the latter seems more likely, considering Nelson's range from the enemy when wounded.

While Nelson recovered from his operation, which Hoste recorded he had borne with 'firmness and courage', his only complaint being the first shock of the surgeon's cold knife, his expedition to capture Santa Cruz foundered on shore. Troubridge and about half of the effectives waited in the main square for an hour. Then he sent a sergeant of marines with two local men to summon the citadel to surrender. Considering his own position it was a brave attempt to overawe the Spaniards, but it didn't work; the sergeant was never seen again and Troubridge could only assume that he had become a casualty on the way.

When day broke he examined his own position and made a roll call of his remaining men. 'About eighty Marines, eighty Pike men, and one hundred and eighty small arm Seamen', that is eighty with muskets, eighty pikes and the rest armed with cutlass and pistol. Ammunition was short, most of it either having been lost or ruined by sea water. It was hardly the force or the weaponry with which to capture a town and a citadel even if it had not been hopelessly outnumbered and deprived of any means of returning to the fleet. In fact the party was surrounded, and likely at any moment to be destroyed or captured. It says a great deal for Troubridge in the circumstances that he sent a flag of truce to the Spanish Governor with the message that he did not want to burn the town, but might be forced to! Either the bluff worked or the Spaniard decided to outdo his nation's reputation for the courteous gesture. The truce was accepted and the sailors and marines were sent bread and wine and transported back to their ships in local boats which Troubridge described as being treated 'in the handsomest manner'. The conditions were that the British could depart with their arms and equipment, the prisoners on both sides to be exchanged, but only if Nelson's squadron would not make any further attempt on the town.

This being agreed, the British wounded were taken into hospital, and the remainder of the invasion force marched in good order to the mole and then embarked. Troubridge found out during his negotiations that after the first assault preparations on shore had included the siting of forty guns, and the deployment of a garrison of 8,000 men.

Until July 27 the repulsed squadron stayed off Teneriffe, fresh provisions being supplied by the Governor to his former enemies. Nelson's wound seemed to be recovering well, The morning after the operation the surgeon recorded, 'rested pretty well and quite easy. Tea, soup and sago. Lemonade and tamarind drink.' By the 29th when the squadron was on its way to Cadiz, the stump 'looked well'. No bad symptoms whatever occurred. 'The sore reduced to the size of a shilling. In perfect health. One of the ligatures not come away.' The medical report revealed a source of considerable future trouble, and the lightning recovery was something of an illusion.

However, Nelson, not to be outdone in courtesy, wrote to the Commandant General of the Canary Islands, Don Antonio Gutierrez, in the grand style:

Sir,
I cannot take my departure from this Island, without returning your Excellency my sincerest thanks for your attention towards me, by your humanity in favour of our wounded men in your power, or under your care, and for your generosity towards all our people who were disembarked, which I shall not fail to represent to my Sovereign, hoping also, at a proper time, to assure your Excellency in person how truly I am Sir,

your most obedient humble servant,
Horatio Nelson.

No doubt His Excellency was gratified, and perhaps also by the gift of 'a cask of English beer and a cheese'.

Nelson had now to teach himself to manage without a right arm and carry out unaccustomed tasks with his left. One of the most difficult was writing, and immediately he had to start preparing his report of the action in the squarish uncertain hand of a man pushing a quill up and down, rather than across, a sheet of paper.

It made melancholy reading. Seven officers, including Captain Richard Bowen of *Terpsichore*, had lost their lives and 171 seamen and marines had been killed, shot or drowned. Four officers, including Nelson himself and Fremantle, also hit in the right arm, had been wounded and one hundred and seven seamen and marines. Five seamen and marines were missing. On the material side the *Fox* cutter was lost and so were a number of boats and of course the expedition itself had achieved nothing.

The shore where Nelson was wounded and where Troubridge and his sailors and marines landed is now a pleasure beach backed by hotels and villas but in the Church of Nuestra Senora de la Concepcion at Santa Cruz there are still preserved two faded boat ensigns, the old Standard of the Union, without the red St Patrick's cross superimposed over the white cross of St Andrew, patched and sewn by sailors' hands, and one still has the rough lettering indicating that it came from the frigate *Emerald*. They are placed well out of reach, for there was a time when midshipmen from visiting British warships used to attempt to recapture these symbols of Nelson's defeat.

As his squadron, joined by the frigate *Leander* which had arrived to take part in the second assault, made its way back to the main fleet Nelson wrote one of his first letters with his left hand to St Vincent, and it was sent ahead in *Emerald*. It was a short letter and well revealed his sense of depression and failure:

My dear Sir,
I am become a burden to my friends, and useless to my Country; but by my letter wrote the 24th, you will perceive my anxiety for the promotion of my son-in-law Josiah Nisbet. When I leave your command, I become dead to the World; I go hence and am no more seen. If from poor Bowen's loss, you think it proper to oblige me, I rest content you will do it; the Boy is under obligations to me, but he repaid me by bringing me from the Mole of Santa Cruz.
I hope you will be able to give me a frigate, to convey the remains of my carcase to England. God bless you, my dear Sir, and believe me, your most obliged and faithful,
Horatio Nelson.
You will excuse my scrawl, considering it is my first attempt.

A great deal can be forgiven a man who has just seen an enterprise he planned collapse ignominiously in disaster and who has just had his arm amputated without benefit of anaesthetic, but it was just when Nelson was at his lowest level of depression that he revealed the more curious aspects of his character. Certainly he owed Josiah a debt, perhaps by his prompt action his stepson had saved his life, but though the death of Captain Bowen of *Terpsichore* had caused a vacancy, he had died because of Nelson's insistence upon the second foolhardy attempt. A man with a little more tact, less impatience and more real humility might have waited for some other occasion to advance his stepson's career.

Finally, one suspects that no man would have been more taken aback than himself if St Vincent, or the Admiralty, had taken him at his word in his second letter to the Commander-in-Chief on August 16 when he was in sight of his flag:

> A left-handed Admiral will never again be considered as useful, therefore the sooner I get to a very humble cottage the better, and make room for a better man to serve the State.

Perhaps when he wrote that he really did believe it; at the same time he was writing in much the same vein to Fanny though to her he used more realistic phrases, 'But I shall not be surprised to be neglected and forgot, as probably I shall no longer be considered as useful'. However, there can hardly be anyone who would believe that if he had been told to strike his flag, and go home to half-pay, that Horatio Nelson would really have resignedly taken himself off to his cottage.

Presumably the thought did not occur to St Vincent either for he welcomed Nelson back with his classical consolation about mortals and success, promoted Josiah to master and commander of the hospital ship *Dolphin*—'pretty quick promotion', observed Hoste, who was promoted lieutenant himself in another dead man's place—and ordered that Nelson should transfer his flag from *Theseus* to *Seahorse*. She was ordered to Spithead and thus carried home two wounded officers, Nelson and Fremantle, her captain.

Neither was in the best of health. Fremantle's arm gave trouble, despite his wife's care, and though Nelson's prognostication to Jervis, 'Fremantle I think very bad, and a month hence he may lose his arm' was over-pessimistic, the captain of *Seahorse*, after reaching England, was unable to undertake active duty for more than a year. Nelson's condition was certainly as painful and uncomfortable, Mrs Fremantle described him as a 'very bad patient'. It must have been an extremely unpleasant journey. She was in the first queasy stages of pregnancy, her husband's flesh wound, instead of drying out and healing, became more wet and inflamed and he showed signs of fever. Dr Weir, Physician to the Fleet, had treated Nelson's stump while he had been with St Vincent's command, Dr Eshelby from *Theseus* was now on board *Seahorse*, but had in his charge not only the two wounded senior officers, and of course the pregnant Mrs Fremantle, but a number of others wounded at Santa Cruz. To make things worse *Seahorse* ran into weather conditions extremely uncomfortable for invalids. First, strong westerly winds which made the frigate rise like a horse to a fence at the waves, then a period of rough buffeting winds which did not improve Nelson's temper. His arm gave him pain, he was never a good sailor, and fairly obviously this was a period of regret, after the initial brave front immediately after his wound, for the loss of Bowen and 'a great many gallant officers and men'—the elderly lieutenant of *Fox*, Gibson, who had drowned with many of his men, had been a poor man and a widower, who left behind 'an only daughter, the darling of his heart'.

The Admiral's sailor-servant Tom Allen, a Norfolk man who had succeeded Frank Lepée, discharged for drunkenness, now mothered his charge, and exercised the patience of his kind in getting Nelson into his uniform coat which now had a slit right sleeve secured by ribbons to facilitate daily dressing of the wound.

Nelson had written to Fanny in February after the battle of St Vincent, 'I shall come one day or other laughing back, when we will retire from the busy scenes of life'. In neither respect was that prophecy to be fulfilled, but he had also written to say that the first she would hear of him would be when he was at the door, and that proved to be true.

After docking at Spithead and having received formal permission from the Lords Commissioners 'to strike his Flag and come on shore', as he had requested, 'for the recovery of my wounds', Nelson immediately set out for Bath where both Fanny and his father were living in a rented furnished house. It was there in the late evening of September 3 that Fanny heard her husband's voice, raised as on the quarter-deck, giving orders to a coachman to stop and put him and his servant down with baggage accumulated during many years' absence.

Later that night a doctor had to be summoned as Nelson's arm had not been attended to all day while travelling, and Fanny had her first experience as a conscripted sick-berth attendant helping with an extremely unpleasant wound which was not healing as quickly as might have been expected.

The next day the newspapers published the first news the public had heard of the failure of the expedition against Teneriffe. The British had experienced a poor year save for St Vincent, which had raised their spirits, but these had sunk again during the Spithead and Nore mutinies. Nevertheless, they were not accustomed to naval reverses. Consequently editors made much of what was, however significant a view it provided of Nelson, only a minor disaster. Blame was attached to the Prime Minister, and to Dundas who, though merely Secretary for War, had acquired an overall interest in, if no particular knowledge of, strategy, and to St Vincent, the Commander-in-Chief. The one person who escaped unscathed was Horatio Nelson, almost universally described as 'the heroic' or 'the gallant'. The implication was that this unfortunate, and now badly wounded, officer had been forced to undertake a hopeless task on the orders of either incompetent or reckless superiors. Perhaps this reaction might have been predicted, for Nelson had been recognised by the crowd and received with acclamation during his brief sojourn in Portsmouth, staying on shore at the George Hotel. Now the Press agreed with, or followed, the public. Nelson, and he was now sufficiently well-known to be referred to in that manner, without other name, rank or title, had become a hero.

Nelson's activities, while on shore for the rest of that year and into the spring of the next, were essentially those which, even in the most romantic view, should occupy a returning hero.

CHAPTER SEVENTEEN

Convalescence

SEVENTEEN-NINETY-SEVEN WAS Nelson's thirty-ninth
year. After an absence of some years he was at last re-united with his
devoted wife and, seemingly almost as important to him, his elderly
and proud father. His manner, despite a painful wound, was still active
and vigorous, but his appearance as he approached his thirty-ninth year
was of a man much older. Perhaps owing to physical inactivity induced
by his wound he had put on a little weight, and there is actually a description of him as being 'stout', although the term must have been comparative for he was always slight.

As so often happens in a time of war and political and social turmoil
fashions in dress and coiffure, masculine as well as feminine, were
changing. As the new century approached, younger men, perhaps in
imitation of the revolutionaries in France, were wearing their hair shorter
and abandoning the old habit of powder and pigtail, which made all men
look white-haired yet ageless. On board a British man of war, however,
the marines still had their hair dressed and powdered as white as their
crossbelts and secured at the back in a pigtail, with a black bow, while the
sailors, although they often retained a pigtail had their hair in its natural
colour. Far away in India a young infantry colonel, ten years Nelson's
junior, called Arthur Wellesley, had abandoned powder and had his hair
cut short.

Nelson had always been conservative, if not positively old-fashioned,
in his dress and appearance. Prince William Henry had remarked on his
outmoded hair style and waistcoat when they first met, and he himself
had disapproved of Alexander Ball and his friend whom he had seen
wearing epaulettes on their uniforms before that fashion became regularised. His own hair therefore stayed long and rather untidy, for it was that
sort of hair, but the 'light-haired boy' of former days had no need of
powder. The abundant white hair contrasted with a ruddy complexion
roughened by exposure to wind and weather. Although for a man still
short of forty it was an over-lined face, caused perhaps by pain, illness and

wounds, it still possessed an almost feminine quality, small with a high forehead and delicate features and a full sensual mouth and high-arched eyebrows over penetrating blue eyes, the right with its enlarged iris, being sightless and staring.

Nelson's latest and most serious wound, while it inflicted pain, and inconvenience, also imposed the burden of acquiring new skills in such tasks as eating and writing. Although, as Mrs Fremantle remarked, 'it looks shocking to be without an arm', amputations were far more common then than now, providing the only chance of preventing blood poisoning and death. Broadly speaking internal wounds were sown up in the hope, sometimes surprisingly justified, that all would be well while serious injuries and wounds to a limb meant amputation. One of the captains that St Vincent rebuked for lenience to mutineers had 'lost an arm in the Service'. Nelson lost his, and Fremantle very nearly followed suit. Samuel Hood was to lose an arm later. The one-armed officer, still serving, was not therefore uncommon and the prints of the period depicting pensioners at Greenwich rarely omitted an old sailor with an empty sleeve or a peg leg. Despite Nelson's first reaction there was still employment for a one-armed admiral.

The first problem for Horatio and Fanny was the actual healing of the wounded arm. Eshelby had done his best and perhaps something may be excused a surgeon who had to operate speedily in poor light in the cockpit of a man of war rocked by rough weather close to an enemy shore. By now the ligatures should have come away and the wound closed cleanly, but this had not happened. There was pain and irritation, the wound had to be dressed daily and Nelson, who refused to accept that he was ill as well as wounded, was forced to take regular doses of opium in order to gain a reasonable night's sleep. The actual site of the amputation was high up in the arm, just below the insertion of the deltoid at the level where the median nerve crosses the brachial artery. The civilian doctors in Bath were not the most experienced in amputations and the end results of gunshot wounds, prescriptions for gout and indigestion in the elderly were much more in their line. They had theories about nerves being constrained by ligatures, and there was talk of further amputation and cutting down on the nerve bulb by way of another operation.

The explanation of Nelson's pain and discomfort was the fact that Eshelby had left the silk ligatures long and hanging out of the wound. The patient in consequence had to bear each day an experimental tugging, something that did not come easily to the tender-hearted and sensitive

Fanny, until within two to four weeks of the operation suppuration having ceased, the silk could be broken. In fact Eshelby had used an old fashioned technique.

In 1786 Lancelot Haire, then the Assistant Surgeon at the naval hospital at Haslar, writing in the *London Medical Journal*, had recommended for such operations the 'short ligature' which left in, and left to itself, 'commonly made its way out by a short opening in a short time, without any trouble or the patient being sensible of pain'. To be fair to Eshelby and his French assistant, identical operations can produce very different results in different patients, but the latter two conditions did not apply to Nelson. Therefore it was decided by the family, and finally by an impatient admiral, that, on a principle still familiar in the medical profession, a second opinion should be sought and the advice of 'a London man' taken.

Accordingly, Sir Horatio, accompanied by his sailor servant, Lady Nelson and her maid, took the stage for London. Nelson's brother, the Reverend William, also accompanied them on their journey to the rooms they had booked at Mr Jones's lodging house at 141 Bond Street.

Nelson, in reply to well-wishers who included the Duke of Clarence, Lord Spencer and Lord Hood, put on a brave face, talking about his arm being in 'the fairest way of healing' and assuring the Royal Duke that 'not a scrap of that ardour with which I have hitherto served our King had been shot away'. That was no doubt true, but the purely physical report erred on the side of optimism. If Nelson really believed that, and was not merely putting his correspondents' minds at rest, he was due for disillusionment when the bows on his slit sleeve were undone for inspection of his stump by Mr William Cruikshank and his son-in-law Mr Thomas who had acquired a great deal of experience under the famous William Hunter at St George's Hospital. Two old acquaintances also carried out examinations, Mr Jefferson who had been surgeon in *Theseus*, and Dr Moseley who had attended Nelson in the West Indies. Finally, the famous Mr Thomas Keate, the Surgeon-in-Chief of Chelsea Hospital, was called in.

None of these gentlemen was speedy in his diagnosis and prognosis, and the general conclusion was disappointing to a patient whose temperament favoured instant, clear-cut decisions. All the medical men invoked the Great Healer, time alone was their cure. Typically, Nelson's reaction was to perform the only professional duty he could perform, attending at the Admiralty nearly every morning. The first duty imposed upon him was the preparation of a formal 'Memorial to His Majesty', which was the customary way in which a sea officer sought, or rather justified, as the grant had already been made, a service pension for wounds received. Fremantle was doing the same as officialdom had decided that his injury should also be compensated. Nelson was awarded £1,000 a year, a considerable amount, but then his record and services, when set down in black and white, were not insignificant. The document delved back into past history and ranged over his whole naval career, from twelve to twenty-one in junior rank, then nearly eighteen years in the same rank, post-captain, and finally as commodore and rear-admiral. It was a career which had increased in momentum and, contrary to the normal pattern one in which action and wounds had come thick and fast with age and seniority. The 'Memorial' 'humbly shewed' that the Memorialist had been in 'four Actions with the Fleets of the Enemy, in three Actions with Frigates, in six Engagements against Batteries, in ten Actions in Boats employed in cutting out of Harbours, in destroying Vessels and in taking three Towns—also served on shore with the Army four months, and commanded the Batteries at the Sieges of Bastia and Calvi'. During the present war he had 'assisted at the Capture of seven Sail of the line, six Frigates, four Corvettes, and eleven Privateers of different sizes, and taken or destroyed near Fifty Sail of Merchant Vessels' and had 'actually been engaged against the Enemy upwards of one hundred and twenty times'. In which service the Memorialist had 'lost his right eye and arm, and had been severely wounded and bruised in his body'.

There are a number of points which are of particular interest: the totals, whether of ships taken or actions fought, are in excess of any figure ascertainable by examination of Nelson's letters or dispatches or what remains of the records and logs of ships in which he served. Obviously there must have been a number of minor engagements, serious and dangerous enough at the time, which escaped any other record. It is in many ways a more accurate picture of the sea officer's life, spent almost entirely at war with the French and the Spaniards and their allies, than the impression, given by some of the old biographers, of a career which con-sisted of a few grand set-piece battles in which Nelson, either as com-modore or admiral, invariably played a principal part.

The 'Memorial' is also, although by its nature shorn of particular detail, more informative about Nelson's other wounds and injuries apart from his eye and arm. The wounds and bruises include the 'severe cut in the back' in Corsica and another injury which Nelson made light of at the time, the severe bruising suffered when he boarded one of the Spanish ships at St Vincent. It is likely that he sustained a bowel hernia, certainly he had an 'internal lump' thereafter, which at times increased in size and caused discomfort and to which he later attributed recurrent internal spasms, and, with less justification, a persistent cough.

As far as active service was concerned the 'Memorial' spanned a period from February 19, 1775 when *Seahorse*, with a sixteen-year-old Nelson on board, had intercepted an armed ketch off the Malabar Coast belonging to Hyder Ali, to the most recent actions in a year in which Tippoo Sahib of Mysore, Hyder's son, succumbed to French influence to the extent of planting a Tree of Liberty in his capital, Seringapatam, and allowing himself to be addressed by his French friends as 'Citoyen Tipou'.

It also referred to two failures of a very similar nature, separated by fourteen years, against Turks Island in 1783 and against Santa Cruz in 1797. In 1783 as the American war drew to a close Nelson, seemingly on his own initiative, had taken a detachment of small ships against the recently-installed French garrison, and been soundly repulsed with considerable losses. His own force was inadequate and the French had been waiting for him, well prepared. Hood, his Commander-in-Chief, had said little, but one officer, James Trevenen, who had taken part called it 'a ridiculous expedition', 'undertaken by a young man merely from the hope of seeing his name in the papers—ill-depicted at first, carried on without a plan afterwards, attempted to be carried into execution rashly . . .'.

That criticism could equally well have been applied to Santa Cruz, except that with the passage of time Nelson had learned the advantages of preparation and planning, while still retaining his youthful rashness. On both occasions, in his report to his superiors, the 'Letter of Proceedings' as it was called, he had drawn attention to the gallantry of his subordinate officers and men. The extent to which his essential nature did not change was demonstrated by his comment after Santa Cruz, hardly fair to Troubridge, 'Had I been with the first party I have reason to believe complete success would have crowned our efforts. My pride suffered.' Mahan called that particular sentence self-accusatory, but it can also be interpreted as a complete inability to admit mistakes.

The application concluded on a farcical note with a clash between Admiralty officialdom and clerks and a short-tempered and still-suffering admiral. Nelson had to prove by medical certificate the loss of an arm and an eye. The 'Memorial' and a covering letter had been dispatched to the First Lord but Rear-Admiral Sir Horatio was required to attend at 6 p.m. on the first or third Thursday of the month at Surgeons' Hall to have his losses authenticated and duly certified. Nelson issued an ultimatum to the Admiralty that, he would attend on a day between the hours of ten and four and did so, accompanied by Thomas Bolton, his brother-in-law. Even then bureaucracy did not immediately strike its flag for in answer to some official, still unwilling to yield, Nelson had to explain his purpose, 'this is only for an eye: in a few days I shall come for an arm: and in a little time longer, God knows, most probably for a leg'.

Nelson was wise to occupy mind and body with routine tasks while he waited for the fulfilment of the surgeons' prophecy with regard to his arm. There was never any harm in keeping in touch with those who decided the careers of sea officers and in any event someone of his temperament needed activity. It was not until December 1797 that he was finally released from pain by the falling away of the ligature and with it the poisonous matter which had collected around it, but in the latter part of the year he had enough activity, and of a pleasant sort, to take his mind away from his throbbing arm, and that feeling, not uncommon in amputation cases, of still possessing a 'phantom limb'.

Perhaps one of the principal consolations of being an invalid in London was the opportunity it provided of seeing friends. Among them was Captain Locker, older and less robust, but still cheerful, who journeyed up from his post as Lieutenant-Governor to Lord Hood's Governorship of Greenwich Hospital, which provided a last home for a small proportion of seamen who had been worn out by age or disabled by wounds in their country's service. Another visitor was Alexander Davison, who still acted as Nelson's prize agent. He, however, had risen a long way in the world since their last meeting five years previously. His wealth came from large-scale Government contracting and for him wartime was an opportunity to make profits out of supplies to an expanding army. He had his factories in Millbank, a country estate in Northumberland and a smart town house in St James's Square. Davison was eventually to experience disgrace and see the inside of a debtor's prison, but none of that could then have been predicted for the rising successful man who exchanged confidences with an old friend whose star also seemed to be in the ascendant.

Another old friend who was doing well, though quietly and respectably, was the handsome ex-Viceroy of Corsica. The withdrawal from that island might well, on the familiar governmental principle of failure by association, have spelt the end of Gilbert Elliot's diplomatic career, but fortunately it was not to be so. His talents were still appreciated, his opinion was still sought, and he was to be raised to the peerage as Lord Minto. The future peer thought that his old friend, with whom he had seen so much Mediterranean experience in a climate very different from that of a dank London autumn, was 'better and fresher than I ever remember him'. Sir Gilbert's opinion was to be found of some importance in the not too distant future. Also in London was Pozzo di Borgo whose success in public service was in the future.

Nelson was now also a public figure. Naturally the public wanted to know what a public figure, indeed a hero, looked like and Nelson was not the man to deprive them of the opportunity. He was never indifferent to public opinion and regard and, unlike the future Duke of Wellington, was prepared to be very patient, for a normally impatient man, with the only means available in a pre-photographic age with which to satisfy the public's curiosity as to his appearance.

There can be no doubt that the demand existed, for Captain Locker had already received an enquiry from a printseller and engraver to see if he could use the Rigaud portrait in his possession to convert into a likeness of the Admiral. Fanny had also been approached by another engraver, a Mr Laurie who had more skill than Locker's man, Mr Shipster, and she had lent him a small portrait by an anonymous Italian artist which her husband had sent her two years before. Both artists had considerable difficulty in altering a captain's uniform and insignia to that of an admiral, adding the ribbon and star of the Order of the Bath, and replacing a right arm with an empty uniform sleeve.

Old St Vincent described the whole business in one caustic phrase, 'the foolish little fellow has sat to every artist in London'. It was an exaggeration, though Edridge, the miniaturist, and Lawrence Gahagan, the sculptor, also tried to capture the new hero's features and character. Lemuel Abbott, Locker's discovery, was neither famous nor successful, and certainly made very little money out of painting, and perhaps because of that, was willing to paint the Admiral on his visits to his old captain at Greenwich. The result was pleasing, certainly to the subject, his wife and father, and is one of the best-known portraits of Nelson and the basis of many reproductions. It was a trifle flattering as there is little suggestion of the irregularity of his features nor any indication of the workings of pain and age. Certainly while still recovering from his wound, though his manner was still animated, Nelson's appearance was a comment upon his tough mode of life.

The remarks of Jane Austen's Sir Walter Elliot Bt., in *Persuasion* come to mind. Sir Walter took a poor view of the Navy for two reasons, 'First as being the means of bringing persons of obscure birth into undue distinction, and raising men to honours which their fathers and grandfathers never dreamt of; and secondly, as it cuts up a man's youth and vigour most horribly; a sailor grows old sooner than any other man. I have observed it all my life. A man is in greater danger in the navy of being insulted by the rise of one whose father his father might have disdained to speak to, and of becoming prematurely an object of disgust himself, than in any other line.'

Strong words from an arch snob who never 'took up any book but the Baronetage' which he always contrived to leave open at the entry devoted to his own family, but the authoress, through her three sailor brothers, was not unfamiliar with the Navy. Both considerations applied to Nelson; he had been raised to honours which his father, and certainly his grandfather, would not have dreamt of, and his youth and vigour had been cut up most horribly. Whether anyone felt insulted by his rise it is difficult to say, there were officers who were professionally jealous of him, perhaps the aristocratic Saumarez might have felt that he had risen above his social station and that may have given an edge to his disdain, but that would not have been the view of Berry whose own father was a tradesman, nor of Hoste, whose father, like Nelson's, was a Norfolk clergyman. Social considerations are difficult to evaluate precisely. Waldegrave, more aristocratic than Saumarez, had the warmest admiration for his comrade at St Vincent, and on the other hand it is possible that Nelson owed some of his appeal as a popular hero to his relatively humble origins.

Technically, Sir Horatio was still not Sir Horatio until he had been invested with his Order of Chivalry. This was, however, remedied on September 25 at St James's Palace after Nelson's presentation at a levée, the first of the autumn season. According to custom he was allowed to make two presentations to the King and the two gentlemen he took with him for that honour were an interesting choice. First his brother, the Reverend William, and second, Captain Berry. William is not difficult to explain since he was the senior although not the favourite brother, and was a pushing man who had already started to pester his distinguished brother to see if he could use his influence to gain him ecclesiastical preferment. Berry was perhaps an odd choice, for he would not have been presented before and was newly promoted to captain. Nelson had a high regard for him, he referred to him early on in their friendship as 'an officer and a gentleman' not then the trite expression it has become. Perhaps Miller or Troubridge had already been to a levée and Nelson felt that Berry should be favoured. In fact, he was inexperienced and somewhat careless, but emphatically he was Nelson's type of man, for despite his fair and delicate, almost diffident, appearance, he was courageous and dashing and, as he had shown at St Vincent, always anxious to throw himself into the fray.

Nelson made his bow, with these two well-contrasted companions, to the red-faced blue-eyed old gentleman whose mental processes and conversational mannerisms were alike equally eccentric. 'You have lost your right arm,' exclaimed the King.

'But not my right hand' replied Nelson, 'as I have the honour of presenting Captain Berry.'

In case it may be thought that the reply sounds too neat and pat, it can only be said that the witness for its veracity was Berry himself who passed on his report of the occasion to his fiancée.

Among the press of courtiers, ministers, generals, and admirals around the King, was Lord Eldon who in later life was fond of recalling that George III, rather surprisingly, had the last word, though of course it was his right, saying, 'But your Country has a claim for a bit more of you'.

After the levée the King had an opportunity of expressing perhaps more felicitously his regard for his admiral's services when he conferred on him the insignia of knighthood. In this respect Nelson was lucky. Even among his contemporaries he had a very personalised view of the monarchy and saw George III much more as a man than an institution. He had written to the King in the midst of his troubles with the Navigation Acts, he had served with one of his sons whom he counted among his friends, and when on half-pay the rumoured stigma of Royal disapproval had bitten deep. If Nelson had not been wounded at Teneriffe and therefore returned home early, he would have been knighted in the normal course of events by Lord St Vincent deputising for the Sovereign. The circumstances were therefore of the happiest, in that Nelson was invested with the honour by the King himself which to other men might have been of little consequence, but to Nelson it obviously mattered.

These few months, though occupied with official and social occasions, provide one of the few opportunities of observing Nelson, as it were, standing still. It is no wonder that painters and sculptors have provided so many differing versions of his features for it would have needed the movie camera to do him justice. His character was revealed in action and speech, in his mobility and energy. It is significant that only a wound could slow him down sufficiently for his contemporaries, and posterity, to take a long look at him. Previously he had not been sufficiently well-known outside his own professional circle for his personality and manner to be much noticed. Now he was a public man and contemporaries recorded their impressions.

He was still impatient to throw off his disability and, naturally enough in time of war, interested in further employment. However, he had very recent achievements to his credit and could therefore, for the first and also the last time, bask a little in his glory among old friends and his family before increasing fame, coupled with domestic strife, rendered that pleasure impossible. And pleasure it was, for though Fanny may not have been a very stimulating woman, to suggest some sort of crucial incompatability between the two at this stage is to allow one's judgment of facts, as they then were, to be over-influenced by one's knowledge of later events.

Overcoming her sensitivity, Fanny proved herself as a nurse, and in a domestic capacity the equivalent of the lost right hand, writing letters on her husband's behalf, and completing many others when the initial effort of a sentence or two with his left hand had exhausted him. Apart from answering letters and the management of domestic and social matters, she also had a great deal to do with the choice and purchase of the first permanent Nelson family home. While he had been at sea the question had been mentioned in letters, and Horatio had given Fanny a free hand, for the obvious reason that he was not on the spot. Now the choice was neither the humble cottage, Nelson's idealised escape from life at sea, nor one of the large and expensive properties that William was always coming across and suggesting as a suitable country seat for his distinguished brother. No doubt William thought less of the Nelsons' convenience as occupiers, but more of his own future pleasure and self-importance as a guest.

Roundwood was a small country house near Ipswich suitable for a married couple of modest means, with only a growing stepson by way of family. It cost £2,000 and Nelson had found it through the good offices of Samuel Bolton, his sister Susannah's brother-in-law. It was over ninety years old and had been built to last. 'All looks like a gentleman's house' in Nelson's view, and he and Fanny had been wise to rely on the commercial Boltons. Susannah had been paying her sister-in-law a visit when her brother had arrived in Bath. She and her husband and his relations moved in the property world, and Samuel himself lived near Ipswich. They were unlikely to recommend anything other than a good bargain, and it was a particular sadness therefore that Nelson was destined never to live in just the sort of house in the part of England he preferred, which had formed the stuff of his daydreams which he had shared with Fanny in their letters. At the present though, there were no clouds on the horizon and during these brief months every aspect of Nelson's behaviour harked back to his family origins and a return to domestic felicity.

When at last the ligature came away from his wound one of his first actions revealed his relief and the reaction and obligations of a son of the vicarage. The nearest church to the lodgings in Bond Street was St George's, Hanover Square, and the Vicar received a note:

> An Officer desires to return thanks to Almighty God for his perfect recovery from a severe wound, and also for many mercies bestowed upon him, December 8th 1797 (for next Sunday).

Early in the next year the Society for Promoting Christian Knowledge, that one day was to distribute copies of Southey's *Life of Nelson*, received a request from the Rear-Admiral for Bibles and Prayer Books for the men of his future command; apparently, as far back as his *Agamemnon* days, sailors on Nelson's ships had experienced their commanding officer's concern for their spiritual as well as their corporeal well-being.

Nelson had nothing but praise for Fanny. When they returned to Bath in the new year Lord Lansdowne lent them his private box in the theatre and it was an opportunity, Nelson confessed, to see and meet 'some of the handsomest ladies' but 'as I am possessed of everything which is valuable in a wife, I have no occasion to think beyond a pretty face'. However, to read the fullest account of Horatio's relationship with Fanny at this time it is necessary to jump to March 1798. The words are Lady Spencer's, the wife of the First Lord, a lady with a direct style and an uncomfortable regard for accuracy as was shown in her first description of Nelson himself: 'The first time I saw him', she wrote, 'was in the drawing room of the Admiralty, and a most uncouth creature I thought him. He was just returned from Teneriffe, after having lost his arm. He looked so sickly, it was painful to see him, and his general appearance was that of an idiot; so much so, that when he spoke, and his wonderful mind broke forth, it was a sort of surprise that rivetted my whole attention.' The impression must have been considerable to produce the second incident Lady Spencer remembered, which deserves to be quoted in full.

> The day before he was to sail Admiral Nelson called upon me as usual, but on leaving, he took a most solemn farewell, saying that if he fell, he depended upon my kindness to his wife—an angel who had saved his life! I should explain that, although during Lord Spencer's administration no sea-captain ever returned [to sea] without being asked to dinner by us, I made it a rule not to receive their wives. Nelson said, that out of deference to my known determination, he had not begged to introduce Lady Nelson to me; yet, if I would take notice of her, it would make him the happiest man alive. He said he felt convinced I must like her. That she was beautiful, accomplished; but above all, that her angelic tenderness to him was beyond imagination. He told me that his wife had dressed his wounds, and that her care alone had saved his life. In short, he pressed me to see her, with an earnestness of which Nelson alone was capable. In these circumstances I begged that he would bring her with him that day to dinner. He did so, and his attentions to her were those of a lover. He handed her to dinner and sat by her; apologizing to me, by saying he was so little with her, that he would not voluntarily lose an instant of her society.

From the pen of a very sharp observer this is by no means the conventionally accepted view of the Nelson marriage as a dull tolerated affair which needed but a flicker of Emma Hamilton's eyelashes to put it in danger.

There were two official engagements for Nelson to perform before that last day on shore, one pleasant, the other somewhat daunting. The first engagement was to be present in St Paul's Cathedral when the King performed his ceremonial thanksgiving for the naval victories of the war. It was a mixture of a parade and a pageant and Nelson had the close company of Captains Berry and Noble.

It must have come as a relief after a worrying solo performance, the receipt of the Freedom of the City of London in the Guildhall. Custom required a speech on the occasion but Nelson was wise to keep his short, for he was speaking in the presence of one at least of the most skilful and effective orators of the age.

The Chamberlain presented the scroll in a gold box 'valued at a hundred guineas' and the holder of that office was Alderman John Wilkes, the bête noire of the Establishment, who had defied the House of Commons, the Government, and even the august personage who had recently knighted the hero of St Vincent. On this occasion Wilkes was at his most mellifluous but did reveal that he had made some study of the career of the City's guest,

> Many of our Naval Commanders have merited highly of their country by their exertions, but in your case there is a rare heroic modesty which cannot be sufficiently admired. You have given the warmest applause to your Brother Officers and the Seamen under your command, but your own merit you have not mentioned even in the slightest manner.

It may be argued that on such an occasion Wilkes could say no other, and though modesty does not occur to mind as one of Nelson's attributes, Wilkes was no fool, and with his second point had seized on a characteristic of Nelson's, observable throughout his service, that of giving praise and, more important, help and consideration, to subordinates, however lowly, a trait not always found in all successful men.

CHAPTER EIGHTEEN

Special Mission

NELSON'S NAME and appearance were now known to his fellow countrymen. His appearance, a slight one-armed admiral frequently, and inaccurately, given a black patch, generally over the right eye, but sometimes the left, was familiar from the printseller's shop. With a little more fame that appearance, the immediate picture in the mind's eye of Nelson to this day, was to become a gift to the cartoonist.

His reputation, though in general terms, had become public knowledge. He was now a hero, just as he had wanted to be, and the fact pleased him. His 'reception by John Bull' was 'all that he could expect', but he was still only one of a number of successful and courageous naval commanders.

One of his few full nights of rest, while his arm still gave him trouble, had been interrupted by a boisterous crowd surging down Bond Street on October 13 and some of their number beating on the door of his lodging house to demand why the windows were not illuminated, like the others in the street, in honour of Duncan's victory at Camperdown. On being told who slept within, and of his need for rest, the crowd moved on, less noisily, one of the leaders saying apologetically, 'You will hear no more of us tonight'. Curiously, it was the first confirmation the Nelsons, very much a worried wife caring for a sick husband, had received of the rumours they had previously discussed with Colonel Drinkwater. The incident, normally advanced by biographers to demonstrate Nelson's fame, was also evidence of the fact that there were other victories than St Vincent and of course other admirals. It was in the next year, 1798, that Nelson advanced on to the world stage so that his name became exalted over that of any competitors within his own service. It was the year which began what Mahan called 'Nelson's page in history'. There were, however, a number of chances and imponderables in the train of events which placed one junior rear-admiral in a position where success, if he achieved it, could not only immeasurably increase his own renown, but also significantly influence the whole course of the war.

The Treaty of Campo Formio in October 1797 gave formal recognition to the end of hostilities and to the military domination of a vast tract
of western Europe by one power. The creation of puppet republics
signalised that Holland, Belgium, Switzerland and Northern Italy were
all ruled from Paris. The Empire had ceded Belgium and Lombardy to
France and had obtained Istria, Dalmatia and Venice and by a secret agreement the left bank of the Rhine from Basle to Andermach was also to be
French. Spain was a French ally, Prussia under a new King, Frederick
William III, was still cravenly neutral and Russia, because Tsar Paul
reversed all the policies of his predecessor, veered towards France. Only
Portugal remained, officially at least, an ally. In October of the old year
General Bonaparte, fresh from his triumphs in Italy, had been given
command of the invasion operations against Britain.

In this situation the decision of Pitt's Government to return to the
Mediterranean with a naval force was equivalent to Winston Churchill's
courageous resolution to send tanks and aircraft to reinforce the Middle
East while at home, immediately after Dunkirk, the obvious danger
seemed to be that of imminent German invasion. So Lord Spencer began
to think of 'some discreet flag-officer' to command a squadron. 'Discreet'
referred to the nature of the operations which would have to be conducted rather than to any personal qualities the chosen officer might
possess.

When only an ambitious commodore, Nelson had made approaches to
the First Lord and the Admiralty for his flag; now that he was a flag
officer and recovered from his wound, he was an obvious candidate for a
command in the theatre of operations where he had notably distinguished
himself. He had once described himself as an 'old Mediterranean man',
now more than ever was that description true. Lord Minto, a firm friend
and a persuasive advocate, put that argument forcibly and succinctly
when he told Spencer that Nelson was as familiar with the Middle Sea
and its shores as the First Lord was with his own room in the Admiralty,
and was therefore 'the fittest man in the world for the command'.

The strongest argument against Nelson was his lack of seniority. In the
Navy List he was one of the most recent Rear-Admirals of the Blue,
itself the most junior grade of flag officer. Fortunately the process of
choice and appointment went in stages. The first was a decision to put
Nelson into *Foudroyant* with Berry as his flag captain, and return him, as
a subordinate admiral, to St Vincent's fleet blockading the Spanish ports
from its base in the Tagus. Nelson had warned the newly-married Berry

that his honeymoon might be shortened, but in fact *Foudroyant* was not as ready for service as the Admiral desired or the Admiralty expected. It was not until March 1798 that Nelson hoisted his flag, the blue ensign at the mizzen, in *Vanguard*, *Foudroyant*'s replacement, and sailed from Portsmouth to rejoin St Vincent, at the same time as the Commander-in-Chief received a letter from the First Lord, 'I am very happy to send you Sir Horatio Nelson again, not only because I believe I cannot send you a more zealous, active and approved officer, but because I have reason to believe that his being under your command will be agreeable to your wishes'.

This was a broad hint from Spencer that Nelson was to be used and St Vincent was quick to reply, 'I do assure your Lordship that the arrival of Admiral Nelson has given me new life. You could not have gratified me more than in sending him', and went on to explain that a flag officer the Admiralty regarded with favour was to be detached from the main fleet 'to endeavour to ascertain the real object of the preparations in the making by the French'.

News, rumours and tantalising snippets of information on those French preparations were already being examined at the Admiralty. The realisation that some enemy operation was being planned on a large scale almost exactly coincided with Nelson's return. He stayed with St Vincent for only forty-eight hours and then departed for reconnaissance off Toulon in command of *Vanguard*, *Orion* and *Alexander* plus attendant frigates. The two captains of the other 74's which he joined at Gibraltar, were not without interest themselves, and their lives were to become intertwined with Nelson's own. Sir James Saumarez of *Orion* has been noticed before as somewhat critical of Nelson. This was not surprising for they were close rivals: both were outstanding officers, and after Nelson's death Saumarez gained considerable distinction in the Baltic both as admiral and diplomat. In 1798, however, they were closely matched, a baronetcy against a knighthood of the Bath, a scion of a distinguished naval family against the son of an unknown Norfolk clergyman, but one was a rear-admiral while the other was still a captain. It was no wonder that Saumarez, a proud handsome man as his portraits reveal, watched his superior with something akin to envy. Nevertheless it was no more than that for the interests of the fleet came first. No better evidence of that could be advanced than the case of the captain of the other 74 Alexander Ball. A thin-faced, bald, intellectual-looking man, he was to become Governor of Malta and earn praise not only as an administrator but as a man of sense and humanity, from his secretary, Samuel Taylor Coleridge.

Nelson had met Ball during his French holiday when they had both been lieutenants, and had been reinforced in his poor opinion of him by the fact that Ball was aping French fashions and wearing epaulettes on his uniform. Now they were both senior officers and wore epaulettes proper to their rank. Nevertheless, and surprisingly, as he was not a 'good hater', Nelson seemed to preserve the youthful aversion, for his first greeting to *Alexander*'s captain was surly and off-putting, 'What,' he said, when Ball reported to him, 'are you come to have your bones broken?' Ball's reply has not survived, it is more than likely that he made none, but it says something for both men that in adversity their relationship improved dramatically.

On the evening of Sunday, May 20, Nelson, with his force of three 74's, four frigates and a sloop, left Gibraltar with discretion enough to please the First Lord, at dusk so that spying eyes would not report a British squadron sailing eastwards. Since Mr Pitt had 'begun to think of the Mediterranean' the wheels had turned. Minto had used what influence he had, Spencer had exercised his judgment, St Vincent had happily concurred. If the Duke of Clarence was not exaggerating when he later confided in Berry even Majesty itself had expressed active approval.

As Nelson sailed out of Rosia Bay on his special mission he knew that the eyes of the Service would be upon him and his 'small but very choice' squadron. What he could not know was that wheels were still turning and that as *Vanguard* sailed into the Mediterranean, he was himself moving into a totally different phase of existence, personal as well as professional.

If there could be any doubt as to the preferment which had been shown him it is only necessary to consider the reactions of two of his brother officers also serving under St Vincent, Sir William Parker who had quarrelled with Nelson after the battle of St Vincent, and Sir John Orde. Sir William was a Rear-Admiral of the Red, Sir John was a Rear-Admiral of the White, the former was fifty-five and the latter was forty-six.

Neither of them knew that after *Vanguard*'s detachment from the fleet St Vincent had received another letter from the First Lord which revealed a decision to escalate the naval force in the Mediterranean and as clear an instruction as was likely as to the identity of its commander, 'The appearance of a British squadron in the Mediterranean is a condition on which the fate of Europe may at this moment depend', wrote Spencer.

Therefore St Vincent was not to 'be surprised that we are disposed to strain every nerve and incur considerable hazard in effecting it'. The only real choice left to St Vincent was whether to take the whole fleet himself or send a detachment under another officer. If the choice was for a detachment then, 'I think it almost unnecessary to suggest the propriety of putting it under the command of Sir Horatio Nelson whose acquaintance with that part of the world, as well as his activity and disposition . . . qualify him in a peculiar manner for that service.'

Whatever reservations St Vincent had about Nelson, and he had some and had expressed them, there was little choice left. 'An excellent partisan but does not sufficiently weigh consequences' Nelson might be, and 'his zeal does now and then (not often) outrun his discretion' but the Commander-in-Chief would have had to find some weightier arguments to have chosen any other man. This, however, was unknown to Parker and Orde and, typically, St Vincent never informed them. The Commander-in-Chief had given the order therefore he took the responsibility. So far as Parker and Orde were concerned it was not responsibility but blame, for both thought they should have had Nelson's post, and felt slighted that they had been passed over for a younger man junior in rank.

Both protested and wrote 'strong remonstrances', as St Vincent called them. To Nelson he admitted that 'a faction fraught with all manner of ill will to you' had sympathised with, and perhaps encouraged, 'the two Baronets'. As soon as St Vincent had received the two letters of protest for onward transmission to Lord Spencer, he ordered both officers to strike their flags, leave the fleet, and return home. Parker accepted, though hardly with good grace. Orde, on the other hand, continued to protest officially and unofficially and transferred his resentment into a vendetta against St Vincent and finally when both were in England challenged his former Commander-in-Chief to a duel. It gives the flavour of the times to record that the gallant old man accepted and the two admirals were only prevented from firing pistols at each other by the temporary arrest of Orde and the King's command to St Vincent to stay at home.

Finally it should be said that though both Parker and Orde made fools of themselves, neither were stupid men nor incompetent officers and that certainly in Orde's case his previous excellent record gave him some grounds for his grievance. Meanwhile, as more information flowed in about the French armament, and orders were prepared to increase the British counter-force, the object of Parker's and Orde's resentment

suffered a considerable and salutary blow to Nelson's pride. As he wrote
on May 24:

My dearest Fanny, I ought not to call what has happened to *Vanguard*
[on May 20] by the cold name of accident: I believe firmly, that it was
the Almighty's goodness, to check my consummate vanity. I hope it
has made me a better officer, as I feel confident it has made me a better
man. I kiss with all humility the rod.

Figure to yourself a vain man, on Sunday evening at sunset, walking
in his cabin with a Squadron about him, who looked up to their Chief
to lead them to glory, and in whom this Chief placed the firmest
reliance, that the proudest Ships, in equal numbers, belonging to
France, would have bowed their Flags. . . . Figure to yourself this
proud, conceited man when the sun rose on the Monday morning, his
Ship dismasted, his Fleet dispersed and himself in such distress, that the
meanest Frigate out of France would have been a very unwelcome
guest.

The calamity had come upon *Vanguard* towards midnight off Cape
Sicie off Toulon. The day had been calm, the evening only slightly less so,
but a very rapid change to gale conditions had caught the flagship unawares. Perhaps it would be more accurate to say the flagship's captain,
for Berry blamed himself, and no similar disaster overtook the far more
experienced Saumarez and Ball. *Vanguard* was dismasted, the main and
mizzen topmasts going over the side and the whole of the foremast
crashing in two pieces over the focs'le. Helpless and encumbered by
dragging masts and rigging she rolled and floundered until the afternoon
of the next day when, the storm easing a little, Ball in *Alexander* managed
to take her in tow. The danger was still great and at one stage Nelson
ordered Ball to leave *Vanguard* to her fate. However, he, with one act,
drove all previous petty dislikes between himself and the admiral firmly
into the past. He refused point-blank to leave the flagship in the lurch
even at the risk of his own ship, saying 'I feel confident I can bring her in
safe. I therefore must not, and by the help of Almighty God, will not,
leave you.' His stubbornness, skill and courage paid off, and when both
ships were safely anchored in San Pietro Bay on the coast of Sardinia,
Nelson went on board *Alexander* and used the same expression he had
written to Collingwood after St Vincent, 'a friend in need is a friend
indeed'. Henceforth Ball was Nelson's man.

Almost miraculously, the Governor of Sardinia, allied to France,
having been overawed, *Vanguard*'s crew assisted by craftsmen from

Alexander and *Orion*, managed to rig jury masts and in four days produce again a serviceable ship. As it turned out, the most serious loss suffered by Nelson was not damage to his flagship, but the disappearance of his frigates. They lost touch with him in the gale, and knowing of *Vanguard*'s disablement assumed Nelson would put into Gibraltar for repair; accordingly, as Nelson learned from Captain Hardy's brig *Mutine*, under their senior officer, Captain Hope, they were now on course for Gibraltar.

It was an example of Nelson's constant restraint in dealing with subordinates, though not superiors, that Berry was not blamed for *Vanguard*'s accident and the only comment of a sorely tried admiral on his vanished frigates was 'I thought Hope would have known me better'. The need for frigates was soon to become even more important for Hardy also brought news of increased French activity and of new British counter-measures.

The confusing mass of intelligence and information was fast becoming crystallised into certainty. Activity at Toulon, Marseilles, Genoa and Civita Vecchia indicated the fitting-out of an expedition with a fleet as escort. General Bonaparte, last heard of on the Channel coast, was now at Toulon but whether to be in command or not was not known. Cavalry and artillery horses had now been embarked on the transports, a sure indication that departure was imminent. A curious snippet of information from Sidney Smith, lately a French prisoner, that mathematicians and other unwarlike men of learning were also part of the cargo, was for the moment disregarded.

What the Cabinet, the Admiralty, St Vincent and Nelson wanted to know was not so much what, as where? Over 30,000 troops, in nearly 300 transports with fifteen battleships and a number of frigates were ready to be loosed into the Mediterranean. Ministers and Admiralty officials could only assemble a list of likely guesses of their destination. The English mainland itself, or more probably Ireland, Portugal, Malta or southern Italy, Greece, the Adriatic, even the Black Sea. Only Henry Dundas, that mine of strategic concepts, favoured Egypt with the consequent threat to India. One suspects that the fact that Sidney Smith had also mentioned Egypt as the destination of his mathematicians and scientists did little to recommend Dundas's guess to his Government colleagues.

Bonaparte's expedition, with more troops and fewer sail of the line than rumour had reported, had left Toulon on May 19 moving along the coast towards Genoa to escape detection, on the first stage of its journey to Egypt.

Nelson had to rely on the necessarily doubtful and suspect information he could pick up from any vessels of passage, mostly French or Italian, intercepted by his slow-moving squadron and it was not until the 28th that he knew that Bonaparte had left Toulon. Now the question was, in which direction? Frigates, about half the burden of battleships and capable of much more than their average speed of five knots, might have been able to tell him but, as he observed later, 'lack of frigates' when he died would be discovered written on his heart. His captains and the other officers could already observe the strain the uncertainty imposed on his impatient temperament.

His meeting with Hardy, a poor substitute for his frigates, was on June 4 and it was then, as he carried St Vincent's dispatch, that Nelson learnt of reinforcements on the way, ten ships of the line and the fifty-gun *Leander*, commanded by Troubridge. Also orders for his new increased command, 'to use his utmost endeavours to take, sink, burn or destroy the Armament preparing by the Enemy at Toulon'. The 'Armament' was now at large and it was now Nelson's task to find it. If it was sailing westwards it would have to be intercepted and fought, preferably before it was through the Straits, as in that case its destination was most likely Ireland or some other part of Britain. If sailing eastwards its landfall could not be conjectured and the possibilities were almost endless.

Two days later, on June 7, Nelson saw the heartening sight of the towering sails of ten of the line, *Culloden, Swiftsure, Majestic, Bellerophon, Defence, Minotaur, Theseus, Audacious, Zealous* and *Goliath*. St Vincent had dispatched 'some choice fellows of the in-shore squadron' and in fact the intrepid Troubridge leading in *Culloden* was nearly out of sight by the time Curtis, in command of the reliefs, had taken station. The captains were the pick of St Vincent's fleet and many were well-known to Nelson: Hallowell, Westcott, Darby, Peyton, Louis, Miller, Gould, Samuel Hood, cousin of the old admiral, and Foley.

Nelson would have liked to have made Troubridge his second-in-command but Saumarez, marginally the senior of the two, had to have the post. However, with typical address to the essentials of his task, Nelson set sail almost immediately. By the 14th he knew that the French fleet had been sighted off the western end of Sicily, but ten days previously. To Lord Spencer he wrote the next day:

if they pass Sicily . . . they are going on their scheme of possessing

Alexandria, and getting troops to India—a plan concerted with Tippoo
Saib, by no means so difficult as might at first view be imagined.

To posterity, of course, Bonaparte's Egyptian-Indian ambitions are
well-known and his desire to emulate Alexander the Great a commonplace. By, at the lowest a hunch, at the highest some kind of insight, one
British rear-admiral at the time guessed his objective. What happened
subsequent to Nelson's putting his signature on his letter to the First
Lord, from June 15 to August 1, provides an object lesson in the chances
of history.

Afloat in the Mediterranean was a French fleet of men of war, another
fleet of transports and in supreme command, resigned to sea-sickness, but
with a considerable library, including unidentified 'English novels' and
the *Voyages of Captain Cook* as a distraction, was the man who was soon
to found a Consulate and then an Empire which would continue to fight
Britain and her allies for ten years after Nelson's death.

Seeking that fleet with a superb force of warships and skilled captains
was Britain's most vigorous admiral, delayed by poor winds and inaccurate information, but the one commander of whom it can be said
with absolute certainty that he would not be deterred by the odds against
him. The fact that the thirteen French battleships had a considerable gun
superiority to Nelson's thirteen 74's was a matter of indifference, for he
knew his captains, his men and his ships, and he had fought and beaten
bigger ships than his own at St Vincent. If he had fallen upon the French
at sea the chances of Bonaparte's death by gunfire or drowning or his
capture would inevitably have been very high. Nelson realised at the
time some of the flavour of an encounter which never materialised for
throughout the hunt he itched 'to try Bonaparte on a wind; for he
commands the Fleet as well as the Army'. There were a number of
chances and quirks of fate as the two fleets made their way steadily
eastwards, although not by the most direct routes.

The journey was a leisurely process and Nelson had ample time to
gather information and help nearby, as his Commander-in-Chief sug-
gested, to 'open a correspondence with His Majesty's Ministers at every
Court in Italy, at Vienna and Constantinople, and the different Consuls on
the Coasts of the seas you are to operate in'. Hardy in *Mutine*, Thomas
Thompson in *Leander*, the only 'small ships' in the fleet, were kept active.
Among Nelson's correspondents was of course his old friend the British
Minister and Envoy at Naples. Meanwhile Bonaparte and four French

admirals, Brueys, the Vice-Admiral, and Rear-Admirals Blanquet du Chayla, Villeneuve and Decrés, their ships, and the slow-moving transports which held them back, progressed at an average speed of sixty miles per twenty-four hours.

Nelson learnt on June 17 that the French fleet was off Malta and about to attack the island which was ruled by the Knights of St John, under their Grand Master, de Hompesch. Properly, as a neutral, de Hompesch refused entry of a belligerent fleet into Valetta harbour, save for two vessels. Bonaparte, who had had some experience of dealing with crumbling powers in Italy, declared he would enter by force. The Knights made a token resistance, the native Maltese took the opportunity to revolt against the unpopular Order, and the island was swiftly occupied by the French.

Meanwhile Nelson had turned south towards the island and by June 22 was off Cape Passero in the south-eastern tip of Sicily. It was here that *Mutine* intercepted a Genoese brig which had actually left Malta a day before. Whether the information the master of the brig gave to Hardy was deliberately false, accidentally inaccurate, or merely became garbled in the telling or translation, is not known, but Nelson certainly understood that after capturing Malta on June 15, on June 16 the main French fleet had then, almost immediately, sailed in the direction of Sicily, leaving behind a garrison to hold the island. In fact the French fleet did not leave Malta until three days later, on the 19th, allowing Bonaparte time to give lightning instructions for the reorganisation of the government and administration, and also to indulge in some concentrated and selective looting.

However, the harm from Nelson's point of view was done. Correctly, taking into account likely objectives and the prevailing westerly wind in the Mediterranean, he reasoned that the French were heading east, which meant Corfu, Turkey or Egypt with the latter as the most likely destination. Because of the information from the Genoese brig master he assumed that the French must be well on their way. Accordingly, and it was not by any means a usual practice, he sent a questionnaire to his senior captains, Saumarez, Troubridge, Ball, Darby and Berry which read as follows:

June 22 1798.

The vessel spoke with this morning is from Malta one day, he says the two frigates in sight are French, that the French colours and garrison are in Malta, that the Fleet and transports left it six days today, but they did not know where they were going, some said to Sicily. With this information, what is your opinion? Do you believe under all circumstances which we know that Sicily is their destination? Do you think we had better stand for Malta, or steer for Sicily?

Should the armament be gone to Alexandria and get safe there our possessions in India are probably lost. Do you think we had better push for that place?

The replies came back on the same day. Darby was cautious and confined himself to saying that the French had obviously sailed 'eastwards', the remaining four all said that in their opinion the French fleet was now on its way to Egypt, and must therefore be followed immediately. All sail was set and the British squadron steered its course for Alexandria. The assumption was that the French were ahead, therefore the need for haste, but in fact the two fleets were very close. Two French frigates were actually sighted some way off, and possibly one ship of the line, but Nelson ignored them. His orders to his captains enjoined concentration and in any event he had nothing fast enough to catch frigates which would only attempt to lead pursuers away from their own fleet. If he had had the enemy timings right he could have estimated the French position as being very near to his own, in which case he would have spread his squadron to sweep and search as large an area as possible.

By the most incredible chance on the night of the 22nd to the 23rd of June the paths of the two fleets crossed. Officers and crews of Brueys's squadron, moving in silence, heard in the dark the boom of British signal guns being fired close at hand, to keep Nelson's ships concentrated on station. Bonaparte, perhaps because he had seen the British navy worsted at Toulon, was unconcerned, but Brueys ordered a change of course to the north and, aided by a persisting early morning haze, his ships escaped detection. If only some British look-out or keen-eyed midshipman had espied a French sail, though the world would have heard something of Bonaparte it might have known nothing of Napoleon.

The British fleet sailed on unawares, with every stitch of canvas spread aloft, and reached Alexandria on June 28. The French, moving more slowly, had headed north towards Candia and then south-eastwards so the view of the main anchorage presented to Nelson when he took his first sight on the 29th was of an ancient Turkish man of war, some frigates, and the usual collection of native craft.

With no real information to work on, Nelson had to resolve a dilemma. Saumarez, his second-in-command, and also the closest in nervous temperament to his superior, had noticed the strain of the last weeks showing in Nelson's manner and congratulated himself on the fact that the decision was not his. There were three courses open: the first depended on Nelson's estimate of the correctness of his own judgment. Certain that the destination of the French fleet was Egypt he could just have stayed put and waited for it. Even for someone, at least outwardly, as confident as Nelson it would have been an almost intolerable decision to carry out in practice, laying in wait off Alexandria when each day, each hour, might bring news of a French landing somewhere else. The second course was to resume the search at sea endeavouring to pick up and sift information from friend, foe and neutral. The third, was to wait a bit, rest his ships and crews in Egyptian waters, and then search. Three years later, in answer to a question from Mr George Baldwin, the British Consul, who had been absent at the time, Nelson wrote that he would have 'remained a few days to get some water and refreshments' if Mr Baldwin, and not a stupid deputy, had been there to exercise his good offices with the shore authorities, but it seems likely that he was only being polite or else deluding himself. Nelson, of course, could never wait and so he took up his sea search again. 'His active and anxious mind,' wrote Captain Berry, 'would not permit him to rest a moment in the same place.' Watched by apathetic Egyptians on shore, the British fleet, on June 28, made sail and headed north-east on the first leg of a search of the eastern Mediterranean and the coasts of Asia Minor.

A day later the same Egyptians could see the topsails of the French fleet approaching from the north-west. Two days later, Bonaparte, with Brueys's fleet, and the transports carrying soldiers, horses and guns, entered the harbour. By twenty-four, or, at the most, forty-eight, hours, Nelson had missed his second, and last, chance of taking on Bonaparte at sea.

Speedily, for the French general too was an impatient man, troops and their impedimenta were disembarked. Five thousand men put off into the water and with this force Bonaparte took Alexandria from its small garrison. By July 2 the French were in complete possession of the port and the rest of the army came ashore in safety. Almost immediately, with no time to accustom themselves to their strange surroundings, the blue-clad veterans of Italy and the Rhine were marching into the desert, assailed by thirst, flies and marauding Bedouins, on their way south to Cairo.

Their enemies, when they were encountered, turned out to be, like the

Maltese Knights of St John, a survival from a vanished age, but considerably more warlike. The Mamelukes, under their two Beys, Murad and Ibrahim, though originally an order of military slaves, were by 1798 a ruling warrior caste battening on the pacific native fellaheen, although Egypt was still officially part of the Turkish Empire. Contemptuous of the French, for the last invader from that country, Louis IX, had been defeated and captured at Mansourah, Murad impetuously led his Mameluke cavalry and Sudanese infantry against the disciplined squares of French infantry at Shubrabbit. The result there was but a foretaste of what was to happen on July 21, outside Cairo, within sight of the Pyramids.

Bonaparte told his staff and the soldiers of his escort on that occasion that forty centuries of history looked down on them and the pattern of the battle was one which was to be repeated from Assaye to Omdurman and from Algeria to Turkestan. Picturesque charging tribal warriors, armed with sword and lance and outdated firearms, were mown down by disciplined volleys of modern musketry. At the battle of the Pyramids the Mamelukes lost over 2000 men and many horses, camels and guns, while the French lost thirty dead, suffered about 300 wounded and took Cairo.

Meanwhile Nelson back-tracked in his search for French ships still at sea. 'Be they bound to the Antipodes,' he had written to Lord Spencer, 'your Lordship may rely that I will not lose a moment in bringing them to action.' Brave words, but the frustrations must have been immense. On a personal, professional level, as a junior rear-admiral preferred above his seniors, and also because the whole fate of Europe might depend on his success or failure. At home, Nelson's old supporter, Admiral Goodall, was already being asked, 'What is your favourite hero about?' And Nelson anticipated in his mind such complaints.

For a month the British squadron cruised in Greek and Italian waters and almost every difficulty came Nelson's way. It is surprising that he allowed only a mild note of acerbity to creep into his correspondence with Sir William Hamilton, not, of course, directed against that friendly and obliging gentleman, but over his own lack of frigates and what he called the 'shivering' of the Neapolitan government. On their way to Alexandria, Troubridge had been sent into Naples to seek assistance from a nation still assumed to be friendly and now, anxious for the fate of Sicily, Nelson's squadron had returned. On both occasions it was apparent that the Kingdom of the Two Sicilies was anxious not to antagonise France too much by overt co-operation with Britain. Mahan in a classic understatement said, 'But Nelson could not expect his own spirit in the King of the Two Sicilies.' The trouble was that he did, and thus increased his frustrations. Sailing eastwards he had tried to get home the warning, 'Malta is the direct road to Sicily' and now sailing westwards, further irritated by the fact that dispatches from Hamilton sent to await him at Cape Passaro had been sent back to Naples, he found the attitude of the Governor of Syracuse yet another Sicilian thorn in his flesh. Sir John Acton had assured Troubridge that supplies would be obtainable at the ports of any of King Ferdinand's dominions. This was not so at Syracuse for the authorities were friendly but neutral and only three or four British ships were allowed into the harbour. Lady Hamilton always claimed that through her influence over the Queen of Naples the Governor was secretly empowered to give Nelson the assistance he required. The evidence is slight and includes a 'secret epistle', a letter of thanks from Nelson which may never have been written by him.

Lady Hamilton by then was arguing for a Government pension on the basis that without her intervention the battle of the Nile would never have been fought, which was an extension of the 'for want of a nail the battle was lost' type of reasoning. A later enraptured Nelson was not of course the man to deny her claim.

Whatever the reason the Governor of Syracuse did eventually co-operate, because all Nelson's ships did take on water, fruit and vegetables of which they were in dire need, and the French Minister at Naples protested when he heard about it. The fleet was at Syracuse for three days and then left, as Nelson prepared a letter to inform 'the Commanders of any of his Majesty's Ships', 'I shall steer direct for the Island of Cyprus, and hope in Syria to find the French fleet'. It was in fact in Greek waters on July 28 that Nelson at last obtained reliable information. Troubridge and Ball intercepted two separate vessels, the first of French nationality, and obtained virtually the same intelligence, which was immediately communicated to Nelson, then off Cape Matapan. The French fleet had been seen steering south-eastwards from Crete, but four weeks ago. This could only mean that the original deduction of Nelson and his senior captains had been correct, and the French were now in Egypt and must have been there for some time. As quickly as possible outlying ships were brought in to concentrate the squadron which then bore up yet again under full sail for Alexandria.

The final confirmation to an excited fleet and an impatient admiral came on August 1. By noon the Pharos at Alexandria could be seen, but on closer investigation there proved to be no warships in the harbour. Saumarez, and no doubt many others, felt 'hopeless' as the fleet turned north-eastwards along the coast. Later Nelson confessed that the search had nearly 'broken his heart', and gave an account of symptoms which suggested either an actual heart 'flutter' or severe dyspepsia. At half-past one hands were piped to dinner. That meal, the main one of the day for officers and men alike, was still being eaten when the masthead lookout of *Goliath* saw thirteen enemy line-of-battle ships and some frigates at anchor fifteen miles from Alexandria in a bay, unknown to him, but known locally as Al-Bekir. Midshipman Elliot, Lord Minto's second son, on watch, ran to Captain Foley but did not hail him, hoping to anticipate Captain Hood's nearby *Zealous* with the news, but he was not quick enough, the flags were already fluttering up the rival's signal halyards, 'Enemy in sight'.

On board the British ships cheers broke out as the news spread along the line. In *Vanguard* Nelson, who had been uncustomarily fussy and irritable with his officers in the last few days, and had eaten and drunk little, ordered the general signal, 'Prepare for Battle' to be hoisted and then asked for his own dinner to be served. Having finished his meal he announced to Captain Berry and his officers 'Before this time tomorrow, I shall have gained a Peerage or Westminster Abbey'.

CHAPTER NINETEEN

The Nile

ONE OF the simplest signals in the signal book, the plain red flag signifying 'prepare for battle', fluttered up *Vanguard*'s halyards and broke at the mainmast. Nelson at last could sit down to his dinner in his day cabin in the stern, but around him all was disciplined activity as the ship's company moved to action stations, activity which was being repeated in all the other ships of his squadron within visual distance of his signal. From the captain's order 'send the hands to quarters', addressed to the first lieutenant, and repeated by him to the bosun and marine drummer—'drummer, beat to quarters'—to the moment when ship and crew were ready to face an enemy, took only six minutes in a well-drilled ship, and all Nelson's ships were well-drilled.

As soon as the marine drummers, mere lads still, in white-piped red regimentals and white crossbelts, brought their sticks down and began to pace the quarter-deck, rolling out the staccato of the traditional 'Heart of Oak', the ship's companies, urged on by hoarse shouts from the bosun's mates, began to double to their stations and duties.

On each gun-deck, two on a 74, over a hundred men ran to their guns while others hurried to the other positions, poop, quarter-deck, bow and stern, to prepare weapons ranging from the heavy carronades to light swivel guns firing grapeshot. For the main armament the wooden tompions were extracted from the muzzles, the port lids in the ship's side were lifted, the small lead sheets, the aprons, removed from the touch holes, and the guns run back on their thick rope tackles.

Behind each gun the loader, his assistant, and the sponger checked the tools of their trade. The copper ladle on its wooden handle for inserting the cartridge bag, the rammer to force home cartridge, wads and shot; the 'worm', like an enormous corkscrew, and the sponge, both on stiffened rope handles, to clean the barrel after each discharge.

Meanwhile the captains of each gun would have hurried to the gunners' storeroom to draw their leather cartouche boxes, containing the tin or quill priming tubes for insertion in the touch holes and their supply of

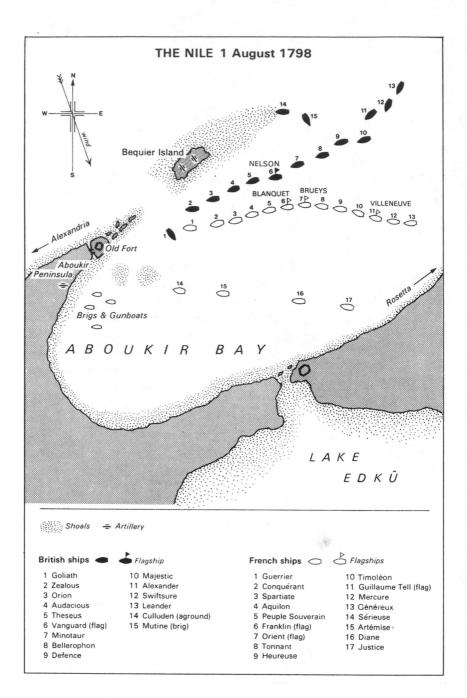

THE NILE 1 August 1798

N
W — E
S
Wind

Bequier Island

NELSON

BLANQUET   BRUEYS

VILLENEUVE

Alexandria

Old Fort

Aboukir
Peninsula

Brigs & Gunboats

A B O U K I R   B A Y

Rosetta

L A K E
E D K Û

Shoals   ≡ Artillery

British ships ● 🚩 *Flagship*

1 Goliath
2 Zealous
3 Orion
4 Audacious
5 Theseus
6 Vanguard (flag)
7 Minotaur
8 Bellerophon
9 Defence

10 Majestic
11 Alexander
12 Swiftsure
13 Leander
14 Culloden (aground)
15 Mutine (brig)

French ships ○ 🏴 *Flagships*

1 Guerrier
2 Conquérant
3 Spartiate
4 Aquilon
5 Peuple Souverain
6 Franklin (flag)
7 Orient (flag)
8 Tonnant
9 Heureuse

10 Timoléon
11 Guillaume Tell (flag)
12 Mercure
13 Généreux
14 Sérieuse
15 Artémise
16 Diane
17 Justice

finely ground priming powder. In some ships off Aboukir Bay the gun captains also equipped themselves with the newly-introduced flinted gun-locks, but most still relied on the old system of ignition, by 'matches', thick lengths of slow burning twisted cotton wicks soaked in lye. These were placed ready by each gun, in metal tubs, rather like outsize ash trays, the matches fitting into notches round the rim so that the smouldering ends overhung either sand or water. Gun wads, known as 'cheeses', and round shot in rope 'garlands', were also laid out by each gun and the gun captain was now ready to take up his position behind the gun. In his belt, his priming iron to force through the touch hole and the cloth case of the cartridge, and the powder horn of fine powder for the priming pan. His experienced eye would survey his mates and crew, crowbars and hand-spikes ready in their hands to move the gun on its heavy wooden-wheeled carriage at the next command.

'Load', shouted the two lieutenants, one fore and the other aft on each gun deck. By each gun the powder monkey, not always a young boy, sometimes a quick-moving grown man, handed a cartridge, a flannel bag of black gunpowder, painted different colours for varying strengths of charge, to the assistant loader. He deftly transferred it to the loader who slid it down the muzzle with his ladle; in quick succession wad and shot were then rammed home on top of it. The guns' crews then stood back to indicate that their task was completed.

'Run out', the lieutenants shouted through their speaking trumpets. The gun crew, except for the captain and the powder monkey, then seized the rope tackle or pushed and shoved at the crows and spikes until the front face of the gun carriage fitted flush against the ship's side and the muzzle pointed through the open port. 'Prime': In went the gun captain's priming iron, through the touch hole and into the cartridge, then the priming tube into the vent and finally a sprinkling of fine powder into the pan. 'Gun deck ready', reported each lieutenant to the first lieutenant who then reported with a salute and a flourish to the captain.

While the armament of each ship, its seventy-four guns, was made ready, other men carried out their tasks. The carpenter and his mates unshipped the light wooden bulkheads, many of them in the captain's and officers' cabins, and stowed them and any loose furniture in the hold. Even Nelson, his dinner over, lost his household comforts as guns were positioned to fire aft through cabin ports. The preparation for battle at Aboukir was comparatively leisurely as the fleet sailed slowly towards the bay and the stationary enemy. In a more pressing emergency bulkheads and furniture simply went over the side along with any other loose wooden objects including the pens and coops, with their live contents, from the manger below decks. Also below decks, men from each mess cleared or secured their messmates' simple possessions, kit-bags, sea-chests and the like. The object was not to save anyone's belongings, but to remove obstacles to movement and a potential source of wooden splinters from gunfire—more to be feared than round shot or musket balls because of the jagged, automatically gangrenous, wounds inflicted. On deck sand was strewn to give a firmer footing to men, often bare-footed, on planks which could well soon be soaked with sea-water and blood. Below decks much of the woodwork was painted dull red so that if and when blood was spattered over it, the squeamish should not be distracted or scared by the sight of it. Water tubs were placed by the guns to prevent fire, to swab out the guns or to wash powder-begrimed eyes and faces. Rolled hammocks were stowed along the bulwarks and in the lower rigging as protection from ball and shot, while aloft the heavy yards were secured by chains and extra rigging so that in the event of damage they would not fall free to the deck below, inflicting death and injury.

Strong rope nets were spread from mast to mast to provide a sort of canopy as protection from falling objects. Now the carpenter and his mates were below at the stations they would keep during action, checking their various devices, large conical wooden bungs for plugging leaks and pieces of lead sheeting, ready nailed, to place over holes. It was also their task to look to the steering mechanism of the ship transmission—from wheel to rudder being by wood and rope—maintaining and repairing it if necessary. Many of the preparations for battle emphasised the principal danger to a ship made largely of wood and canvas, fire. Round the powder magazine below the water-line canvas screens soaked with water were rigged and inside it men wore felt slippers, for nailed shoes or boots might well strike a spark. The cook's first task on hearing the drumming to quarters was to douse the galley fire. On deck every available bucket was filled with water and handpumps were set ready on the poop while the lower courses of the sails, the booms, and the ships' boats were liberally drenched with water. By now nearly all the men were stripped to the waist with their black silk kerchiefs round their heads for use as ear plugs or sweat rags. The only exceptions to this general piratical rig were provided by the appearance of the officers and warrant officers in blue and white and the striking contrast made by the scarlet-coated marines formed up on the poop and quarter-deck, their muskets ready and the boys of their drum and fife band in attendance with spare ammunition. The task of the 'bullocks', whose noisy clumping ways amused the sailors, was to engage sharp-shooters in the enemy's fighting tops and rigging and to provide the nucleus of boarding parties if required. Other marines were told off to guard the small fore and aft hatches, empowered to shoot anyone, other than an officer, a powder monkey or a midshipman acting as a messenger, who attempted to go below. On the same principle of preventing the cowardly or panic-stricken from deserting their posts, the main hatches were closed.

Finally, in grim preparation for the result of most actions, tourniquets and swabs were distributed along the decks and below in the cockpit the surgeon and his assistants got ready with the 'loblolly boys' whose task was to carry the wounded, dispose of the dead, and hold their shipmates under the knife. Tables were cleared for amputations, the only form of operation performed, and tubs were placed in convenient positions for the reception of what the sailors gruesomely called 'wings and limbs'. In the cable tier on the same deck the thick anchor cables were coiled flat and covered with spare canvas to provide a crude resting place for the wounded awaiting the surgeon's attention.

The sound of the marines' drum meant the imminence of death, wounds and destruction, about to be inflicted in the most savage manner possible. Death was bound to come, quickly or slowly, to a number aloft, on deck or in the bowels of the ship, and officers and men made wills, wrote last letters to loved ones, if they were literate, and made compacts with each other as to the disposal of their personal kit and possessions if they fell. The crews of all of Nelson's ships had cheered at the sight of the enemy, but though to some the prospect of action, and perhaps prize money, produced elation, for others it must have meant apprehension and fear, only to be controlled, when battle was joined, by discipline and suppressed by pride or the shame of letting down one's shipmates.

Nelson's own immediate reaction was obviously a compound of relief and the elation that he certainly felt at the prospect of battle. After his failure to find the French fleet he had been so obsessed and frustrated that he had written a long letter to St Vincent of explanation and self-justification. It was another example of his own complicated character at work. The simplistic view of Nelson is that he was self-confident to the point of egotism and brimful of personal vanity. Yet such a man would have stayed put in Alexandria *knowing* that he was right and that the

French *must* come. Such a man would never have written a letter to his Commander-in-Chief in expiation and nor would a more careful, reticent man. Nelson had written his letter on June 29, the day that Hardy in *Mutine* rejoined the fleet off the Pharos Tower to bring the news that he could find no sign of the French. Obviously it was a black moment, but there were phrases unlikely to be found in the correspondence of any other commander. For instance, 'Although, I rest confident, that my intentions will always with you have the most favourable interpretations, yet where success does not crown an Officer's plan, it is absolutely necessary that he should explain the motives which activate his conduct, and therefore I shall state them as briefly as possible.'

At first sight the sentiments appear eminently reasonable, but in a disciplined Service they are not. All Service tradition and practice enjoined, and still enjoins, 'no explanations' in case of failure. 'Nothing to say, sir', the standard response in case of fault, in the eighteenth century was put even more forcibly, 'no croaking' (i.e. no complaints, no excuses, one had done what one had done and it would be judged). Excuses smacked of being attempts to evade responsibility and were therefore unmanly and unworthy of an officer.

St Vincent knew his Nelson, but after reading the dispatch which set out the movements of the fleet and Nelson's reasons for his actions, and after noting the problem produced by the lack of frigates and the fact that the admiral had consulted his senior captains, he was no wiser. Nelson still had no frigates and still had to find the French and since St Vincent could give him neither help nor news, the task was Nelson's. The letter ended in much the same style as it had begun:

> I am before your Lordship's judgement (which in the present case I feel is the Tribunal of my Country) and if, under all circumstances, it is decided that I am wrong, I ought, for the sake of our Country, to be superseded, for at this moment, when I know the French are not in Alexandria, I hold the same opinion as off Cape Passaro—viz, that under all circumstances, I was right to steer for Alexandria, and by that opinion I must stand or fall. However erroneous my judgement may be, I feel conscious of my honest intentions, which I hope will be ar me up under the greatest misfortune that could happen to me as an Officer—that of your Lordship's thinking me wrong.

It is hardly surprising that Ball, to whom Nelson showed the dispatch, another example of his own insecurity, advised against sending it at all, writing, 'I should recommend a friend never to begin a defence of his conduct before he is accused of error'. Even given that sensible advice, and perhaps more, for if Nelson showed his dispatch to Ball in sufficiently formal circumstances to provoke a letter, it was probably also shown to his other senior captains and Saumarez, his second-in-command, he still sent it off.

Yet this man, racked by self-doubt and led by it into absurd posturing —he cannot really have thought he would be superseded in command— was the same one who wrote to Hamilton on June 18, before the dispatch, saying 'present my best respects to Lady Hamilton. Tell her I hope to be presented to her crowned with laurel or cypress', and meaning it, and to his wife on July 20, after the dispatch, 'Glory is my object, and that alone', and meaning that.

Nelson, however, had acquired one great advantage during his long search and that was a well-trained fleet. From the testimony of his captains and in particular that of Berry it is obvious that, whatever private stress and strain he endured, Nelson did not waste his weeks at sea. The ships' crews improved in efficiency simply from time at sea, gaining experience in their manifold duties, becoming thoroughly familiar with their ship and more speedy and proficient with daily practice and gun drill. At the same time the instruction of the captains was not neglected. It was a regular occurrence for them to be summoned aboard the flagship to be entertained to a meal, and then to be required to take their part in a tactical discussion. Not so much strategy—where was the French fleet?— but what should be done when it was discovered. What formation should be used against a fleet at sea? and against a fleet at anchor? How best to attack an enemy fleet and destroy it?

This was the first manifestation of 'the Nelson touch', and it is interesting to note that on this occasion, as on the others, Nelson did not decide on his battle formation and tactics in isolation, but hammered them out in discussion with his captains, the men who would be required to put them into practice. His was, of course, the deciding voice, but because his captains were there, plans were devised which took into account what they would be expected to do when, in the confusion of battle, they would have to act on their own initiative. Not all admirals encouraged this degree of independence, but Nelson wanted the maximum results from a battle and having exercised his own judgment and disobeyed orders at St Vincent, was prepared to give his own subordinates the same sort of latitude. This germ of independence, which meant a breakaway from the old formalism, owed something to Captain Locker's advice about 'laying your ship alongside a Frenchman' and it caught Nelson's professional imagination. That phrase, or something very like it, was used by him a number of times and finally in its best-known form, 'that no captain could do much wrong who laid his ship alongside one of the enemy's'.

After Aboukir Bay Berry was to describe Nelson's 'tutorial periods afloat' as follows:

> It had been his practice during the whole of the cruise, whenever the weather and circumstances would permit, to have his captains on board the *Vanguard*, where he would fully develop to them his own ideas of the different and best modes of attack, and such plans as he proposed to execute when falling in with the Enemy, whatever their position might be, by day or by night. There was no possible position in which they could be found, that he did not take into his calculation, and for the most advantageous attack of which he had not digested and arranged the best possible disposition of the force which he commanded.

Nevertheless, the position taken up by the French fleet was a formidable one, and though Nelson, searching the Mediterranean, complained to Hamilton that 'the devil's children have the devil's luck' it must be admitted that, finally, he did have a little luck himself.

Aboukir Bay can best be visualised as a crescent moon lying on its back, Aboukir Point at its western tip, and Rosetta Point at its eastern. Alexandria is to the west and the mouth of the Nile to the east, but the east-west axis of the 'moon', drawn across the two horns of the crescent, is tilted so as to be roughly east-north-east/west-south-west. The bay is sixteen miles across and six miles deep, but these distances give a deceptively spacious impression of it as an anchorage, for from the shore the depth of water increases only very gradually, so that only three miles from the shore is there sufficient water to take a capital ship. In addition two miles off Aboukir Point lies Aboukir Island, linked with the mainland by a line of half-submerged rocks which continues to the north-east with shoals, thus creating a reef which is both a barrier and a protection from seas from the north-west.

It was therefore the western end of the bay which was used as a summer roadstead for shipping and it was there that Brueys's fleet lay at anchor in a diagonal line curving out slightly from the shore. The French line also conformed to the generally prevailing wind direction, north-west to south-east, but in the Mediterranean there was no certainty in this matter, either of force or direction. However, on August 1 the wind was, as Nelson noted, 'nearly along the line'.

There were therefore natural features which Brueys could have turned to his fleet's advantage, but this he had failed to do. Sensibly he had concentrated his most powerful ships, including his own flagship *Orient*, in the centre of the line, but seems to have taken few other precautions against attack. Ideally he should have shifted his fleet with any lasting changes in the wind to deny an opponent a free run along his own line with the wind steadily astern. The danger of any line formation was at the van and in the rear and in Brueys's case, considering the wind, more especially in the van. His dispositions must have been made to prevent an enemy doubling on him, and therefore his van ships should have been as close to shore as possible, but *Guerrier*, though close to the shoal to port, was still in thirty feet of water, which was enough to allow the passage of an enemy between her and the shore. The ships which succeeded *Guerrier* in line neither hugged the shore nor were closed up sufficiently to prevent an enemy passing between them, there being up to five hundred feet between each ship.

A line of anchored ships should have been turned into an impregnable line of floating fortresses, but the French ships were far from that. Cables could have been strung between them to prevent penetration of the line and if springs had been attached to their anchor cables they could have been manoeuvred to present their broadsides and avoid being raked from stem to stern. Neither of these precautions had been taken and the fleet swung at anchor, a fact which revealed to Nelson's quick eye that there must be sufficient depth of water available to allow him to risk close action without running his own ships aground in the process.

Since he was so close to shore another form of protection was available to Brueys, land batteries, but he availed himself little of the advantage. There were French guns below the old fort which occupied the tip of Aboukir Point, but their range and positioning was such that they provided no assistance to a fleet three miles distant from them.

If it is possible to read the mind of Vice-Admiral de Brueys before August 1, 1798, it can only be assumed that he knew that his position was unsatisfactory. According to Bonaparte at a later date, Brueys had sketched out to him on their way to Alexandria the disadvantages of a fleet at anchor. They were, however, remediable, and well within living memory two opponents of the French, Admirals Barrington and Hood, had both repulsed superior fleets while themselves at anchor. Brueys though had been satisfied with a number of half-measures, the appearance of the first ships of Nelson's fleet must have brought home to him some realisation of his own danger. He may have thought that a British fleet would not find him, or thought that the Royal Navy would no longer be concerned with the fleet which had provided an escort.

At the moment of sighting the British ships he was concerned with planning a celebration of the victory over the Mamelukes near the Pyramids. Recalled to present problems by the sight of British 74's, he realised that he was short-handed, a number of men from each ship's company being ashore digging wells, with a larger number of guards to protect them from unfriendly Bedouin tribesmen. It was perhaps this which produced a moment of indecision, as to whether to meet Nelson at anchor or at sea. Certainly some French ships prepared to put to sea, presumably on orders, but then they stayed put. The explanation of this and other indecisive activity—seamen, for instance, being transferred from the frigates to the battleships, and on some ships the guns not being run out on the landward side—must lie with the French admiral's last and most crucial mistake. His assumption that the enemy would not attack that day.

This was not an unreasonable assumption. His own position, despite its defects, was by no means contemptible for his ships were large and powerful and only a few hours of daylight remained. Rocks and shoals presented an obvious hazard for an attacking force and surely a prudent admiral would reconnoitre first, or perhaps attempt a preliminary sortie, but attack tomorrow. This took everything into account save the personality of Horatio Nelson. 'His idea', according to Berry, 'was first to secure the victory, and then to make the most of it according to future circumstances.' He was not a prudent admiral, made few signals and never hesitated.

Alexander and *Swiftsure* were still some way off towards Alexandria, *Culloden* with a French prize, a brig carrying wine, was lagging behind to windward but all three were telegraphed to join the main body. The next signal, to the whole fleet, indicated that, in Berry's words, 'his intention was to attack the van and centre as they lay at anchor, according to the plan before developed'. The ten 74's nearest to *Vanguard* had already formed line of battle, 'in the order of sailing', with the maximum speed and the minimum fuss. It gives some idea of the leisurely pace at which battle fleets came into action in the days of sail, and some justification for Brueys's assumption that the British would not attack that day, to realise that Nelson's fleet had sighted the Pharos at Alexandria at noon and the enemy fleet in Aboukir Bay at about 2 p.m. Almost immediately *Vanguard* had hauled to the wind, followed by the rest of the fleet. Then the ten 74's formed line of battle, and with the advantage of a steady but strong wind from the north-north-west, moved into the bay. Yet according to Berry's precise account, action did not commence until 'sun set, which was at thirty-one minutes past six p.m.'.

The British approach must have seemed dauntingly confident and relentless to the French for the hazards presented by nature were by no means negligible. Rear-Admiral Blanquet du Chayla was therefore convinced that the British must have experienced pilots on board their ships, but in fact the information they had about the coastline and bay was horrifyingly meagre. Nelson and his captains had to rely almost entirely on their own skills and seamanship. Foley in *Goliath* had a modern French atlas; Hallowell, in *Swiftsure*, had possessed a rough sketch of the coast, taken from a French prize, but he had given it to Nelson; Hood had an English map which he discarded in favour of the surer, safer, but slower method of the leadsman in the bows, taking his soundings as *Zealous* moved slowly into the shallows.

As both *Vanguard* and *Zealous* came abreast of the shoals at the entrance to the bay Nelson hailed Hood to ask if they were far enough eastwards to clear. Hood reported that he was in eleven fathoms, 'If you will allow me the honour of leading you into battle, I will keep the lead going'. Nelson gave his leave and doffed his cocked hat. Hood returned the compliment, but his hat blew out of his hand, 'Never mind, Webley', he said to his first lieutenant, 'there it goes for luck. Put the helm up and make sail.' The French brig *Alerte* attempted diversionary tactics to lure the British 74's on to the shoals but the ruse failed. As Blanquet remarked in reluctant admiration, 'he [Nelson] hauled well round all the dangers'.

At 6.28 as the sun was setting both fleets hoisted their battle ensigns, and the watching Bedouin on shore as well as sundry Frenchmen, began to hear and see the thunder and flash of ships' broadsides. Another hazard was approaching darkness, especially for the moving fleet in manoeuvring and firing, because of the danger of shooting at one's own ships as each British 74 sought its place on either side of the French line. It was for this reason that Nelson, though a Rear-Admiral of the Blue, ordered the hoisting of the White Ensign, as being more easily seen and identified, and three lanterns horizontally at the mizzen mastheads. This was almost certainly the beginning of a custom which was to become universal throughout the Royal Navy.

The first British ship inside the French line was Foley's *Goliath* which crossed the bows of the leading French ship *Guerrier*, firing a broadside as she did so, and then swung round to take up position opposite her. However, a hung sheet anchor prevented the full manouevre being executed, and it was the rival *Zealous* which Hood brought up to *Goliath*'s intended position opposite *Guerrier* while she proceeded further down the line to a position abaft the stern of *Conquerant*, the second in the French line. *Orion*, *Theseus* and *Audacious* under Captains Saumarez, Miller and Gould, followed and passed the two leaders, penetrating further down the French line.

By the time the red Egyptian sun finally disappeared, there were five British 74's within the French line firing their broadsides as close and as quickly as possible into the leading French ships. It was only now that the British captains realised how poorly prepared the French had been for from a distance, protected by shoals and shore guns, which had proved ineffective, the French line had appeared formidable. Close to, it could be seen what unprotected stretches of water yawned between each ship, and soon it was realised that on their port side the French had not even bothered to run out their guns, but had left them loose and encumbered with baggage and furniture cleared in a panic from starboard.

The next ship in the British line was the flagship herself, *Vanguard*, and Berry brought her round to anchor outside the French line abreast of *Spartiate*, the third in the French line, and already engaged to port with *Theseus*. *Minotaur* and *Defence* then passed beyond the flagship so that by 7 o'clock, and true darkness, the five leading French ships, *Peuple Souverain*, *Aquilon*, *Spartiate*, *Conquerant* and *Guerrier*, were effectively sandwiched between eight British. It would be wrong to think that the French put up no resistance, for as Berry said, 'the Enemy received us with great firmness and deliberation', but the pace and concentration of British fire on the least powerful ships in the French van was maintained at a terrific level. After less than twelve minutes of this bombardment *Guerrier* was dismasted, to a great cheer from the British ships nearby. Ten minutes later *Conquerant* and almost simultaneously *Spartiate* went the same way, a considerable part of their masts, sails and rigging falling over the side. At half-past eight the fourth and fifth ships in the French

line, *Aquilon* and *Peuple Souverain*, had both been taken by boarding
parties of British marines.

Astern of the first five ships lay the heavier-armed vessels: *Franklin*, the
flagship *Orient*, *Tonnant*, *Heureux*, *Timoleon*, *Guillaume Tell*, and finally
Mercure and *Genereux*.

Foley had obviously used his own initiative in taking *Goliath* inside the
French line, for it was not a manoeuvre that could have been precon-
ceived, although it may well have been the sort of move that Nelson and
his captains had discussed when they rehearsed situations. Nelson com-
plemented Foley's action by taking *Vanguard* along the outside of the
French line and thus doubling on the enemy. In any event five 74's were
now inside the French line, having had the advantage of some lingering
light. As the battle inevitably became more confused with drifting gun-
smoke and darkness, the increased risk of taking more ships between the
shoals and the French was obvious to any experienced captain, and
Nelson's captains were both experienced and intrepid. Controversy
which existed and is recorded, as to whether the attack inside the French
line was a totally preconcerted action between Foley and Nelson or not,
was in a sense so much spilt ink, for each captain acted in a situation as it
was presented to him at the time. Whether Foley ever received precise
orders to go inside the line, or outside the line, which he contravened
when he saw a better opportunity, would only be relevant if either
Nelson or Foley had subsequently criticised each other's conduct. They
did not. The rest of the British fleet took up positions past *Vanguard* and
close to an opponent, in order, *Minotaur*, *Defence*, *Bellerophon* and
Majestic. It was now the turn of the British to suffer casualties and damage:
Bellerophon missed *Franklin*, which was the first French ship of eighty
guns, and which was being engaged by the little *Leander* with her fifty
lighter guns. As a result Captain Darby found himself taking the broadsides of the largest ship in action in Aboukir Bay, *Orient*, which, with 120
guns mounted on three decks, had almost twice her own armament. All
three of *Bellerophon's* masts went over the side and, out of control, she fell
out of the line towards the lee and away from the enemy. Captain
Westcott acted with an excess of zeal which cost him his life, *Majestic's*
jib boom actually crashing through the main mast rigging of *Heureux*.
Temporarily fixed in a position in which her own guns could not be
brought to bear, she suffered considerable damage from French gunfire.
After Westcott had died with a musket ball in his neck, Cuthbert, the
first lieutenant, extracted the ship and had her anchored on the bows of

the next ship in line, *Mercure*, and began to exchange fire at the near point-blank range at which most of the battle was fought.

Nelson sustained another wound in battle at about 7 o'clock. When, standing on *Vanguard*'s quarter-deck in conversation with Berry, he was struck on the forehead by a piece of langridge, chain or scrap shot used against sails or rigging. Most likely the shot, from *Spartiate*, was spent, or had already found a target aloft and then fallen or ricocheted, otherwise the Nile would have been Nelson's last battle. As it was it sliced out an oblong of skin and flesh which, falling over his good eye and filling it with blood, both stunned and blinded him. Understandably for a time he believed he had been mortally wounded. Berry caught the admiral as he fell and heard him mutter, 'I am killed, remember me to my wife'. He was taken down to the cockpit amidst many other wounded, insisting, though he must have been semi-conscious, that he should not receive preference but 'take his turn with his brave fellows', and there examined by Mr Jefferson. The surgeon was reassuring but Nelson still felt that his last hour had come. It was almost a rehearsal for the scene seven years later though the dramatis personae were changed. *Vanguard*'s chaplain was sent for, as Nelson waited for the bloody wound to be stitched and bandaged. Mr Comyn was entrusted with a message for Lady Nelson, Captain Louis of *Minotaur* was to be thanked for his help to *Vanguard* when she had been under fire from both *Aquilon* and *Spartiate*. Berry came to report that *Spartiate*, dismasted, had ceased firing, *Aquilon* and *Peuple Souverain* had both surrendered, *Orient*, *Tonnant* and *Heureux* were considered as completely subdued.

Someone persuaded Nelson, who had lost a lot of blood, to settle down in the bread room in the hold, but he was incapable of settling down. His secretary was sent for to write a dispatch to the First Lord of the Admiralty, but Mr Campbell, who had suffered some minor injury himself, was too disturbed and agitated, either by his own condition or the sight of the Admiral's, to do his job properly. He did not stay long on *Vanguard* after giving such a poor account of himself, for he was not Nelson's type of man. So Mr Comyn was sent for, but he apparently was no better and perforce the Admiral began himself, prematurely, for all was by no means over, in the grand manner, 'Almighty God has blessed His Majesty's arms in the late Battle . . .'.

Berry interrupted him to report that *Orient* was on fire and Nelson insisted that he should be taken on deck. More French ships were surrendering, though the night was still intermittently lit up by the flash

9 Ferdinand and Maria Carolina
of the Two Sicilies

10 Nelson in Naples, by Grignon

The HERO of the NILE.

11 The Hero of the Nile as seen by Gillray

'Ah, where, & ah where, is my gallant Sailor gone? *DIDO, in Despair!* {He's gone to fight y Frenchmen, t'loose t'other Arm & Eye.}

12a The Baltic Expedition: Emma as Dido

12b The Baltic Expedition: The British Fleet enters the Sound

of gunfire. On board the French flagship a steady glow near the mizzen chains was not gunfire. *Orient* with her superior gunpower had knocked *Bellerophon* out of the battle but now, weakened by her smaller adversary, it was her turn to learn the same harsh lesson. Her place was at the centre of the French line with six of her consorts ahead and six astern, the line bending from her position at a slight angle towards the shore. Two ahead of her *Peuple Souverain* was assailed to port by *Orion* and to starboard by *Defence*, then her anchor cable was parted by a chance shot from *Orion* and she drifted, damaged, out of the battle to be captured soon. *Franklin* still held out, raked by *Leander* anchored at right-angles across her bows but *Tonnant* was dismasted.

Now *Orient* had anchored on each side of her the two late-comers to the battle, *Swiftsure* and *Alexander*, whose appearance had lowered French morale even further as, unwelcome in itself, it also suggested that the British might have still more untouched warships in reserve. The appearance of fire on the flagship's deck caused both Hallowell and Ball to order their gunners to concentrate their aim on the site of the flames and their marines to keep up steady musket fire to kill, wound or deter potential fire fighters. It was instinctive action on the part of the two captains but it may perhaps have been an example of overkill, for the situation on board *Orient* was already parlous. The fire which might well have been started, as Ball maintained, by the 'combustible preparation' he had for use in close action, thrown on board the French ship by one of his lieutenants, spread over the poop and the after-deck where, oil and paint in use before the battle had not been removed before action. Fire was, however, not the only problem on board for casualties had already been heavy and among them were two of the principal officers of the fleet. When the flames began to penetrate below and lick along the newly-painted sides of his flagship Admiral de Brueys was already dead. Despite wounds in the legs and one in the head he had insisted on remaining on the quarter-deck with tourniquets on his wounded limbs, propped up on a chair against an arms chest. It was there that a cannon ball literally cut him in two. His flag captain, Commodore Casabianca, accompanied by his son, was already wounded as was the ten-year-old boy and both were either lost in the mounting conflagration or subsequently. There could be no doubt that the French flagship was doomed, and officers and men could be seen, as in Mrs Hemans's poem, fleeing the burning deck though some brave souls continued to fire lower-deck guns almost to the end.

Many officers and men in the British fleet, and no doubt the French as well, who were not actually engaged in some pressing duty, watched, fascinated, and a number of eye-witness accounts survive of what was the centre-piece of one of the most dramatic night-time actions ever fought at sea. Captains of nearby ships gave orders to move their ships from the vicinity of *Orient*, except for Hallowell who had decided that he was so close that the explosion, when it came, would leave *Swiftsure* untouched. Marine sentries were placed on the cable, to prevent some panic-stricken man trying to cut it, ports and hatchways were closed, the sails and rigging was soaked, and officers and crew took cover and waited.

There were already Frenchmen in the water, and Nelson, surveying the scene from under a bandage and with an only recently cleaned eye, ordered *Vanguard*'s one undamaged boat to be launched to pick up enemy survivors. At about ten o'clock the magazine of *Orient* exploded with a shattering roar. Those nearby were momentarily deafened, and the noise was heard fifteen miles away by French soldiers in Alexandria, and at Rosetta, five miles nearer, it was recorded by M. Poussielgue, the civilian Controller General of Finance to General Bonaparte's army, as 'the most dreadful explosion'.

All witnesses agree on what followed next. A most profound silence, lasting for minutes, to be followed by the sound of wood from masts, yards and spars, metal from guns, ammunition and fittings, and all the debris of a ship blown apart, including the dead bodies of her crew, falling into the dark waters of the bay.

A fiery glow disappeared under the surface and with it *Orient*, formerly *Sans Culottes*, took with her something like £600,000 worth of gold and treasure, forced out of the Swiss and the Romans and intended to finance Bonaparte's Egyptian venture, as well as loot picked up on the way, three tons of gold and silver plate, twelve life-size silver statues of the Apostles and the decorative gates of Valetta Cathedral, once the property of the Knights of Malta.

After what Berry called 'an awful pause and death-like silence' battle was resumed. *Franklin*, the flagship of Rear-Admiral Blanquet who like Nelson was wounded in the head, was one of the first ships to recover and recommence firing. Her position was ahead of *Orient* and, astern of the site of the sunken flagship. *Tonnant* also put up a spirited resistance. Further astern, however, the captains of *Heureux* and *Mercure*, taking discretion as the better part of valour, both slipped their cables to avoid what seemed inevitable destruction when the two lines of British 74's left their first positions to transfer their attentions to the rear of the French line. But the British failed in their second objective and for this Nelson took the blame. Certainly his view, which he passed on to St Vincent, was that more could have been done, had he not been incapacitated temporarily, 'wounded and stone blind'. Perhaps this is true but in fact all the British ships were involved to their maximum capacity under universally resolute commanders except *Culloden*, under the command of Troubridge, which had gone aground on a shoal and was forced to serve simply as a guide, and, when darkness fell, a lightship, for her consorts who passed her into action.

Ball afterwards told Coleridge, his secretary, of the weariness which came over his own men after more than four hours of intense physical activity and danger. After the explosion of the French flagship men sank down on the deck beside their guns and literally fell asleep where they lay. Ball's first lieutenant reported to him, as set down by Coleridge, 'the hearts of his men were as good as ever, but that they were so completely exhausted that they were scarcely capable of lifting an arm'. *Alexander*'s crew was allowed to rest and then rose again to continue the fight, Ball later discovering that French crews had been similarly overcome by sheer fatigue. The general conclusion must be that both sides had in effect fought each other to a standstill.

After what was merely the outcome of chance, the arrival of two fresh ships, *Alexander* and *Swiftsure*, there could hardly have been any new developments in the conflict; *Culloden* despite strenuous efforts remained where she was, out of the battle. *Heureux* and *Mercure* were not saved, both were taken by the enemy and burnt, as was *Timoleon*, astern of *Heureux*, which was deliberately run on shore by her captain. Firing continued intermittently between the two fleets until about 3 a.m. by which time Miller described his 'people' in *Theseus* as dropping under the capstan bars asleep, 'in every sort of posture, having been working, or fighting, for near twelve hours'. By this time the moon was up, but Aboukir Bay was shrouded in a great pall of black smoke from guns and burning wreckage which made accurate observation difficult. A wounded and somewhat fretful Nelson was persuaded to go below though still issuing orders, some of which could not be conveyed and were not obeyed. Although it is always remembered that Nelson was wounded, it is frequently forgotten that of his captains Westcott of *Majestic* was dead, Troubridge was out of action, and Darby in the disabled *Bellerophon*, Ball in *Alexander* and Saumarez in *Orion* were all wounded, and their ships by no means unscathed. All made light of their wounds and Hallowell suffered from what he called 'a graze', but few of them could have been at peak performance, and there were many casualties among their officers and crews. The ever active Hood did suggest at one stage to Miller, who had been snatching half-an-hour's sleep, that *Theseus*, his own *Zealous* and *Goliath* should go down towards the rear of the French line, but nothing seems to have come of it.

With the light of dawn, firing did break out again, but the battle was effectively over. The bay presented an incredible spectacle of wrecked, dismasted and burnt ships. Of thirteen French battleships only two remained, *Guillaume Tell*, the flagship of Rear-Admiral Villeneuve, and *Genereux* at the rear of the line; of the rest one had been destroyed, seven captured and three burnt. Of four frigates only two, *Diane* and *Justice*, remained, and of the others the first was sunk, while the second was set alight by her own crew. Before noon these survivors, the two battleships and the two frigates under Villeneuve's command, weighed anchor and put out to sea. Again it was only Hood who showed the final spark of resolution and *Zealous* prepared to pursue, but no other British warship made sail. The odds and the chances were too great, and *Vanguard* signalled for the recall of *Zealous*.

Nelson, 'weak but in good spirits', as Miller described him, could now send his 'Letter of Proceedings' to the Commander-in-Chief, the Earl of St Vincent. He retained his grandiloquent beginning which he had penned the night before, but for the rest it was, rather surprisingly, short. Of his subordinates he said simply 'Could anything from my pen add to the character of the Captains, I would write it with pleasure, but that is impossible.'

With his dispatch Nelson forwarded the customary calculation of enemy ships taken and destroyed, an estimate of enemy casualties and the losses suffered by his own side. In addition to the principal ships of war the French had lost a bomb vessel and a number of smaller vessels, some of which had been beached by their commanders near Aboukir Fort and some, like *Salamine*, with Rear-Admiral Ganteaume on board, had made their escape. British casualties were 218 killed and 677 wounded, but Nelson could only roughly estimate the French casualties and it is probable that he over-estimated as he credited each French ship with its full complement, not knowing that men were on shore from each ship. Nevertheless, even with minor inaccuracies measured in tens and dozens, the total was appalling: 5235 officers and men were killed or were missing; seven French captains had been wounded and three killed; 3105 men, many wounded, who had been picked up or otherwise captured by British ships, were put ashore; 200, mainly captains and officers and warrant officers, were still prisoners; 400 men had escaped before their ships were beached, burnt or surrendered.

Nelson was right when he said 'Victory is not a name strong enough for such a scene,' for he had done two things: set a new standard of achievement in engagements at sea by bringing about a battle to destruction, and had trained and prepared a fleet in which each unit could be relied upon to contribute its utmost to the fight. It was not until January 8, 1799, in reply to what must have been one of his most welcome letters of congratulation, from Earl Howe, that Nelson summed up what had been the second essential of his success, 'I had the happiness to command a Band of Brothers'.

CHAPTER TWENTY

Naples and the Hamiltons

ON AUGUST 2, 1798 the Rear-Admiral of the Blue revealed that he was still the son of the Vicar of Burnham Thorpe. By his order all the ships' companies of the battered British men of war mustered on deck in clean and tidy uniforms and faced aft to take part in a Service of Thanksgiving for their victory.

Interested spectators of the ceremony were the French prisoners of war, mostly officers and senior men, who still remained on board. Their reactions were mixed, some were contemptuous or indifferent, for atheism was the official creed of the French Republic, but others expressed admiration, not for a parade of piety, but for a demonstration of discipline and *esprit de corps*. These prisoners in their turn were objects of interest to their captors, for their attitude was very different to that of the Frenchmen of the old easy-going days of former wars. John Nicol, serving in *Goliath*, had assisted at the powder magazine in the battle because he was then over forty. He had volunteered for the Navy when he was twenty-one and had an infinity of experience on the lower deck all over the oceans of the world. Twenty-four years after the Battle of the Nile when Blackwoods, the publishers, found him penniless in Edinburgh and persuaded him to write his memoirs he still recalled those captured sailors of Revolutionary France. 'In the American War, when we took a French ship . . . the prisoners were as merry as if they had taken us, only saying "Fortune de guerre"—you take me today, I take you tomorrow. Those we had on board [after the Nile] were thankful for our kindness, but were sullen, and as downcast as if each had lost a ship of his own.'

This observation from an intelligent and literate seaman is worth remembering as some counterbalance to the implied criticism of those who are puzzled by Nelson's own naïve and apparently unthinking hatred of Frenchmen. Spaniards he tolerated, for they were incompetent but they showed courage and pride, accepted a God and had a King. Frenchmen, however, atheistic and republican, seemed to him to be the works of the devil. It was, of course, an over-simplified judgment, utterly typical of Nelson's loves and hates, but Nelson was not the only one to take that view. Even Collingwood, always more moderate than his friend, had written in January 1798, 'The question is not merely who shall be conqueror—but whether we shall be any longer a people— whether Britain is still to be enrolled in the list of European nations.' The Frenchmen produced by the Revolution were a new sort of enemy; courageous, resolute and enterprising certainly, but imbued with a conviction and an enthusiasm for the establishment of a new order in Europe which, though it had the watchwords, 'Liberty, Equality and Fraternity', seemed, to many more than Nelson, to be in practice just a new military despotism.

Nelson had now struck a blow against their ambitions and those of their most able general, having thwarted their project of a new colony in Egypt and the complementary object of threatening British supremacy in India. These were the short-term results of the battle of the Nile, the British had returned with their navy to the Mediterranean and a French army, perhaps their best, had been locked up in Egypt.

Accordingly, while his captains and crews set to work to repair their own damaged ships and to inspect and, if possible, repair the six French ships, which had not been burnt or rendered almost total wrecks by raking gunfire, Nelson sat down to spread the news of the dramatic change in the balance of power which had just taken place under his direction. All his captains had called on him or else written their congratulations, and as a body they had announced their intention of forming an 'Egyptian Club' and having his portrait painted and presenting him with a sword. He in his turn had complimented them, and their officers and men, but now had to turn his attention to a wider audience.

The honour of bearing the dispatch to the Commander-in-Chief went to Berry and he took passage in Captain Thompson's *Leander*. However, there was always the danger of dispatches being intercepted by the enemy, and therefore a copy was prepared for Lieutenant Capel, who had been signal lieutenant in *Vanguard*, to take to the nearest British diplomat, Sir William Hamilton in Naples. Capel sailed in *Mutine* which had been Thomas Hardy's command and he went to *Vanguard* as flag captain, in Berry's place. It was the beginning of a close relationship with Hardy, who though a year younger, was a much steadier and more reliable officer than Berry, a relationship which only ended with Nelson's

death. The other officer who left Aboukir Bay with an account of the
action was Lieutenant Duval of *Goliath* who was recommended because
of his knowledge of languages, necessary, no doubt, for an officer whose
route was to be to India, by way of Alexandretta, Aleppo, Basra and
the Persian Gulf. Apparently he was 'a very clever young man' with
diplomatic connections, a combination which fitted him for the task of
informing British Consuls on the way and eventually the Governor of
Bombay and the Honourable East India Company that their enemies, of
whom Tippoo Sahib was the principal, were now without the likely
support of their French ally.

Letters were also prepared for the British Minister at 'the Porte'
(Constantinople) so that he could inform 'the Grand Signior' (the
Ottoman Sultan) of the disaster which had overtaken those who had
violated what was technically still an Imperial domain. There was also
a letter for Lord Spencer and a packet of captured correspondence,
including letters to and from General Bonaparte, and the sword of Rear-
Admiral Blanquet du Chayla, destined for the Lord Mayor of London.
All this, however, had to wait some days until British ships could be
rendered seaworthy and serviceable enough to make the various journeys,
an indication that the Nile had been no one-sided affair and an easy
victory for Nelson.

As the means were prepared for communicating with the outside
world, communication in the opposite direction was re-established.
Dispatches of a rather complaining kind from St Vincent off Cadiz
arrived by way of three small ships, *Emerald*, *Alcmene* and a sloop,
commanded by Josiah Nisbet, which fired their saluting guns to the
Rear-Admiral's flag on August 12. St Vincent complained that he and
the Admiralty had received no news of any activity on the part of
Nelson's squadron. In fact it was nearly two months before he did hear,
and the passage of Nelson's dispatches provides an excellent example of
the pace of communication at the time.

Nelson had been wise to provide duplicates and send them by different
routes for *Leander* fell in with *Genereux*, which had escaped with
Villeneuve from Aboukir Bay, off Candia and a 50 was no match for
a 74. After a six-hour battle Captain Thompson, wounded, as was Berry,
struck his flag. Both officers were treated roughly by the French, despite
their wounds, and they did not arrive in London, by way of an exchange
of prisoners, until the last week in November, the first opportunity
Lord Spencer had of hearing an official eye-witness account.

The dispatches sent via Naples took two months and a day to reach London. These, the first written account, were preceded by numerous rumours which filtered through Europe, but which, naturally, tended to get blocked or corrupted when they reached France. The most accurate report that the Admiralty did receive, five days before receipt of the official dispatches, had come in a report from a French brig, conveyed to the Governor of Rhodes, and by him to the British Minister at Constantinople, and thence to his opposite number in Vienna, and had finally reached London by a ship out of Hamburg.

The midget squadron with Josiah Nisbet in command of a sloop only found Nelson in Aboukir Bay by chance. The dispatches it carried ordered him to sail west to Minorca, on the basis, of course, that the French fleet had continued to elude him. Nisbet's presence however was not chance, for St Vincent had a number of complaints to make of his conduct to his stepfather and hoped that the two of them would eventually meet up.

Assuming, rightly, that the recently fought battle wiped out orders made in ignorance of it, Nelson now made his own dispositions of his patched-up fleet and its prizes. Saumarez, his second-in-command, in *Orion*, took command of *Bellerophon*, *Defence*, *Theseus*, *Majestic*, *Audacious*, *Minotaur*, and the six French prizes for their westward passage to Gibraltar. Hood was left in command of a blockade of the Egyptian coast with the remainder while *Audacious* and *Minotaur* were to rejoin Nelson who set sail with *Culloden* and *Alexander* for Naples. The flagship was still sailing with jury masts and the first object of Nelson's call was urgent repairs, now more necessary than ever; his second purpose was to persuade the King of the Two Sicilies into co-operation with news of the defeat of the French. This double decision, as far as his private life was concerned, was the most momentous that Horatio Nelson ever made. Nothing thereafter was ever the same again.

It took Nelson with his flagship *Vanguard* (Captain Hardy), *Culloden* (Captain Troubridge), *Alexander* (Captain Ball), and the sloop *Bonne Citoyenne*, commanded by Josiah Nisbet, who was not yet a post captain, from August 19 to September 22 to sail against contrary winds to the Bay of Naples. Considering the involvements that Nelson found in Naples it appears as if he had deliberately sailed away after his victory, wounded and exhausted, into a convenient hedonistic backwater. It was not so for his intention was to stay in Naples only so long as it took to repair and refurbish *Vanguard* and the other two damaged battleships.

Moreover, once in Naples he became entangled not only with the amorous wife of the elderly British ambassador, but also with the political and
military problems of Britain's most curious ally, the Kingdom of the
Two Sicilies. No doubt if he had not been attracted to Emma Hamilton
he would not have become so closely involved, or for so long, with
the Neapolitan Bourbons, their ministers, Sir William Hamilton and
all the rest of that extraordinary comic opera court. Nevertheless,
it must be remembered that although Ferdinand's kingdom, when
last visited, was a lukewarm ally and fearful of the French, it was
the only toehold the British had, apart from Gibraltar, in the Mediterranean. If the victory of the Nile was to be capitalized upon, if
the British were to re-establish a presence in the Mediterranean, then the
friendly state which occupied the foot of Italy and the island of Sicily
deserved attention. Any British officer commanding in the Mediterranean
was in duty bound to involve himself with the Two Sicilies. The degree
of involvement was a question of judgment, character and temperament.
In this respect the fact that Nelson was the man he was, proved to be
almost totally disastrous.

Meanwhile as Nelson's small squadron beat its way north-westwards
the news of the disaster to the French expedition to Egypt spread rapidly
throughout Europe and the Near East, like the ripples from a stone cast
into a millpond. The French themselves were primarily concerned and
perhaps understandably their first reaction erred on the side of pessimism.
M. Poussielgue, Bonaparte's Comptroller-General of Finance, who had
observed the battle from a tower near Rosetta and meticulously recorded
the periods of gunfire and the times of explosions, had this to say in a
letter, intercepted by a British warship:

> The fatal engagement ruined all our hopes; it prevented us from
> receiving the remainder of the forces which were destined for us; it
> left the field free for the English to persuade the Porte to declare war
> against us, it rekindled that which was barely extinguished in the
> heart of the Austrian Emperor, it opened the Mediterranean to the
> Russians and planted them on our frontiers; it occasioned the loss of
> Italy and the invaluable possessions in the Adriatic which we owed to
> the successful campaigns of Bonaparte, and finally it at once rendered
> abortive all our projects, since it was no longer possible for us to
> dream of giving the English any uneasiness in India. Added to this,
> was the effect on the people of Egypt whom we wished to consider as

friends and allies. They became our enemies, and, entirely surrounded
as we were by the Turks, we found ourselves engaged in a most
difficult defensive war, without a glimpse of the slightest advantage
to be obtained from it.

All French commentators at the time, and of course Nelson himself,
placed great emphasis on the thwarting of Bonaparte's Indian ambitions
without considering in any detail how a French army, even if aided by a
still extant French fleet, and augmented by reinforcements from France,
would have wrested supremacy from the British in India—and overcome
any native opposition. Blocking Bonaparte's plans was, however, a
negative achievement and the positive side of the Nile victory was, as
Poussielgue saw, the revival of a European coalition against France.
What Nelson had demonstrated to hesitant Austrians, doubting Russians
and reluctant Turks was that the French were not invincible. The news
of a French defeat spread rapidly through Europe. To St Petersburg
where a demented Tsar was already being turned away temporarily
from his settled determination to favour the French, by the news from
Malta, an island in which he had a personal interest as protector of the
Knights of St John. To Vienna, where Thugut, the Austrian Chancellor,
was most cautious in public, although how he and his Imperial master
felt in private was a different matter. Joseph Haydn expressed more
enthusiastically his countrymen's pleasure than the careful statesman. In
1798 he was composing his *Missa in Angustiis*, a mass in time of need and
while so doing heard of the Nile victory, and in consequence wrote the
triumphant trumpet calls at the end of the *Benedictus* as his own tribute
to Nelson. The Mass itself has always been known since as the *Nelson
Mass*.

Although Nelson may have never realised that this tribute had been
paid to him, others more tangible began to appear almost as soon as he
reached Naples. *Vanguard* dropped anchor in the Bay of Naples on
September 22, and thus began an interlude in Nelson's career which
historians have either revelled in, tried to ignore, or condemned,
according to taste. Nelson's own contemporaries, ranging from observers
in Naples to gossip writers in English newspapers, were divided in their
view. What there could be no doubt about was that Nelson's doings in
Naples were news, eagerly related to politicians, reporters and naval and
military officers at home. Nelson was news, so was any development in
the fight against the French, so was the notorious Emma Hamilton, so

was the dissolute Court of Naples. Consequently the involvement of a famous war hero with a sexual scandal was meat and drink to the gossips, so one can hardly imagine that Fanny at home remained in ignorance for very long.

Perhaps the most remarkable aspect of Nelson in the Naples episode is that it covered only a little over two years of his life, from September 22, 1798 to November 6, 1800, when he, and the Hamiltons, disembarked at Yarmouth. Two years in the career of an admiral on the active list in time of war. Later, when she was expecting his child, Nelson wrote to Emma Hamilton specially recalling February 12, 1799, with pleasure, and no regrets for later consequences. It would seem to be almost beyond doubt therefore that it took five months of constant propinquity, often under the same roof, before Horatio and Emma actually finished up in bed together. Once they were lovers a great deal of Nelson's attention was devoted to Emma Hamilton and her attraction for him was a magnet which kept him close to the Kingdom of the Two Sicilies. Nevertheless, there was much more happening in and around Naples than a love affair between a British admiral and the wife of the British Ambassador. Though that relationship was to become, and remain, central to the whole of Nelson's private life, it should be remembered that from the moment *Vanguard*'s anchor splashed into the blue water of the Bay of Naples Nelson found himself embroiled in circumstances which would still have demanded his attention, even if Sir William Hamilton's wife had been elderly, plain and chaste, or if he himself had remained faithful to Fanny.

The reception accorded to the victor of the Nile was typically Neapolitan, it was lavish, colourful and theatrical, and contained a large element of self-interest and insincerity. While a French fleet and expedition had been at large in the Mediterranean the attitude of the Kingdom of the Two Sicilies had been cool and cautious towards its British ally. Now that that fleet was destroyed, and the expedition marooned in Egypt, Naples went wild in an excess of gratitude, puffed-up patriotism and bogus belligerence.

The spectacle would have gladdened the heart of the producer of some Hollywood epic and its star was Emma Hamilton. Her patriotic sentiments, like those of her husband, were impeccably sincere but it would have been too much to expect a woman of her essentially theatrical character to resist playing such an attractive role. Apparently she didn't even try.

The effect on a susceptible, vainglorious and still concussed admiral can be imagined. In his own words, writing to Fanny,

> I must endeavour to convey to you something of what passed; but if it were so affecting to those who were only united to me by bonds of friendship, what must it be to my dearest wife, my friend, my everything, which is most dear to me in this world?—Sir William and Lady Hamilton came out to sea, attended by numerous Boats with emblems &c.

Lady Hamilton had already fainted away and bruised herself on first hearing the news, not such remarkable behaviour then as now. The actual sight of the wounded victor produced a further reaction: 'the scene in the boat was terribly affecting, up flew her Ladyship, and exclaiming "O God is it possible?" she fell into my arm, more dead than alive. Tears, however, soon set matters to rights; when alongside came the King. The scene was, in its way, affecting. He took me by the hand, calling me his "Deliverer and Preserver", with every other expression of kindness. In short, all Naples calls me "Nostro Liberatore"; for the scene with the lower Classes was truly affecting. I hope some day to have the pleasure of introducing you to Lady Hamilton, she is one of the very best women in the world. How few could have made the turn she has. She is an honour to her sex and a proof that even reputation may be regained, but I own it requires a great soul.'

A little later in the same letter, Nelson wrote what can hardly have been the most tactful thing to say to a fond mother, 'Her Ladyship if Josiah was to stay, would make something of him, and with all his bluntness I am sure he likes Lady Hamilton more than any female. She would fashion him in 6 months in spite of himself. I believe Lady Hamilton intends writing you.' The letter ended with a typical Nelson flourish: 'Should the King give me a peerage I believe I scarcely need state the propriety of your going to court. Don't mind the expense. Money is trash. Again God Almighty bless you.'

That letter was begun at sea on September 16 and completed on the 25 when *Vanguard* had anchored. Three days later Nelson was able to keep Fanny further posted as to his triumphal progress ashore: 'The preparations of Lady Hamilton for celebrating my birthday tomorrow are enough to fill me with vanity. Every ribbon, every button has "Nelson etcetera", the whole service are "H.N. Glorious 1st August". Songs, sonnets, are numerous beyond what I ever could deserve. I send the additional verse to "God Save the King" as I know you will sing it with pleasure.'

Josiah was well, but Lady Hamilton's tutelage was again recommended and the extra verse to the national anthem followed:

Join we great Nelson's name
First on the roll of fame
    Him let us sing.
Spread we his praise around
Honour of British ground
Who made Nile's shores resound
    God save the King.

With this letter Josiah 'inserted a paper' which included a twenty-six-line poem printed in Naples, probably of his own composition, which among many excruciating sentiments contained an observation which was laughably inaccurate. The hero is described as being, 'deaf awhile to every vain applause', for Nelson enjoyed the acclaim of the Royal Family and the populace, the adulation of the Hamiltons and enjoyed being recognised and fêted as a conquering hero.

At this early stage, however, he still saw realistically. He could still write to St Vincent, on September 30, despite being, as he wrote to Saumarez, 'killed with kindness', 'I trust, my Lord, in a week we shall all be at sea. I am very unwell, and the miserable conduct of this Court is not likely to cool my irritable temper. It is a country of fiddlers and poets, whores and scoundrels.'

If Nelson had been allowed to sail for home or to rejoin the main fleet his personal life, and perhaps his service career, would have followed a different course. His letters to Fanny were full, frank and still full of affection, and his view of the Kingdom of the Two Sicilies was detached and objective. Unfortunately the Government, the Admiralty and his superior officers, emboldened by the Nile victory, thought that more could now be done in the Mediterranean, and who better to do it than their most successful admiral? When, in consequence, he attempted tasks beyond him and also became involved in a scandal, the blame was entirely his. Perhaps the only person who sympathised was St Vincent who knew Nelson better than most, appreciating his limitations as well as his virtues.

While news of honours and letters of congratulations poured into

Naples the Government at home was busy formulating new objectives of naval policy in the light of one spectacular victory. The Admiralty's enlarged intentions, communicated in the first instance to the Commander-in-Chief, were 'the protection of the coasts of Sicily, Naples and the Adriatic and, in the event of war being renewed in Italy, an active co-operation with the Austrian and Neapolitan armies'. Next in order of importance came the isolation of the French army in Egypt and the French garrison holding Malta and finally, co-operation with the Russian and Turkish naval squadrons expected soon to appear in the Mediterranean. Already, as he had learnt on his way to Naples, Nelson had acquired a new ally, and an addition to his strength of four Portuguese ships of the line under the command of Admiral the Marquis de Niza.

Before considering how Nelson tried to discharge the tasks entrusted him one must look more closely at the means provided. The most important point is that the entire burden fell upon Nelson with his small squadron of ships, many of which such as his own *Vanguard*, with jury masts, and *Culloden* with a sail wrapped under her keel to help plug the leaking bottom, were in very poor sailing and fighting condition. The Admiralty's orders were directed to St Vincent but he, and his second-in-command, Lord Keith, stayed firmly in the western end of the Mediterranean watching the French and Spanish fleets to prevent a conjunction of the two. Therefore it fell to Nelson from Naples, though he would have preferred Syracuse on the eastern coast of Sicily as a base, to look to the blockade of Alexandria, and the possible investment of Malta, as well as hold himself in readiness to assist any resumption of hostilities in Italy.

A more careful man, a more reflective and patient commander, perhaps even a senior officer in better health would have confined himself to two of these tasks. A reasonable approach would have been to apply himself to those within his own competence and push to one side, or play down, the land operation in Italy, which required qualities and resources which he did not possess. However, there was everything in Naples which could be thrown into the scales to unbalance Nelson's normally sound tactical judgment. These elements were of situation and personality, and they reacted upon each other.

To try to list them in order, endeavouring thereby to seek out a primal cause, is almost impossible. Victorian biographers naturally assigned pride of place to Emma Hamilton, but to do that is to oversimplify, and also to give insufficient credit to other characters almost as incredible as herself.

Impossible also to avoid theatrical metaphors as colourful characters, actors and actresses, did appear and disappear on the Neapolitan stage with the bewildering frequency of poor tragedy or bad farce. For a couple of years Naples and Palermo provided an exotic backdrop for a great deal of drama and even furnished choruses and extras ranging from *lazzeroni, banditti*, revolutionaries, English sailors and French soldiers and at the centre of the stage there was always Nelson, in the words of John Moore who came in at the end of a piece which he did not enjoy, 'He is covered with stars, ribbons and medals, more like a Prince of an Opera than the Conqueror of the Nile'. The Scots general, not much taken by Neapolitan extravagances, went on to say, 'It is really melancholy to see a brave and good man, who has deserved well of his country, cutting so pitiful a figure.'

So it is better to start with the central character himself. It might be thought that his reception by the Court, the Hamiltons, and the omnipresent crowd, carriage and gondola processions, coloured pigeons released from baskets, fireworks, illuminations, tableaux, parties and banquets, was exaggerated if a look was not also taken at what was happening in his native country, in his absence.

The First Lord of the Admiralty fell to the floor in a faint on hearing the news, and the garrulous old King was struck silent. The Countess Spencer, wife of the First Lord, and very much the sophisticated aristocrat, wrote, 'Joy, joy, joy to you brave, gallant immortalized Nelson! May that great God, whose cause you so valiantly support, protect and bless you to the end of your brilliant career! Such a race surely never was run. My heart is absolutely bursting with different sensations of joy, of gratitude, of pride, of every emotion that ever warmed the bosom of a British woman, on hearing of her Country's glory—and all produced by you, my dear, good friend ——. This moment the guns are firing, illuminations are preparing, your gallant name is echoed from street to street, and every Briton feels his obligations to you weighing him down.'

The description of public rejoicing was no exaggeration. London and, as the news spread, other cities, went wild. Villages throughout the land had their bonfires and their toasts to 'the Hero of the Nile'. Stage coaches were daubed with slogans, 'Nelson' and 'Victory', so that the news should be carried far and wide. Those with a taste for such things could appreciate the discovery by a clergyman that an anagram of the admiral's name was 'Honor est a Nilo': The staid *Times* newspaper took to unlikely verse:

Nelson! thy name from shore to shore shall ring
Joy to the Nation! Joy to England's King
Such prowess every tribute justly craves,
E'en Arabs shout, 'Britannia rules the waves'!

The night that the capital heard the news the audience at the Drury Lane Theatre yelled so often for the orchestra to play 'Britons Strike Home' that one irritated playgoer shouted above the din, 'Why dammit, they have, haven't they?'

Official appreciation followed more slowly and notifications, honours and gifts made their way to Naples. Lord Hood's prediction to Fanny, following a conversation with Mr Pitt, that she would find herself Viscountess Alexandria, proved to be an over-estimate. Duncan had been made a Viscount for Camperdown, Jervis had been created an Earl after St Vincent, but both had been commanders-in-chief which Nelson at the Nile was not. On October 6 he became, according to the *London Gazette*, 'Baron Nelson of the Nile and Burnham Thorpe in the County of Norfolk' which many people thought niggardly, not least his brothers Maurice and William for different reasons, and Fanny, because her hopes had been raised.

Perhaps therefore Emma Hamilton's observation to Nelson, 'If I was King of England I would make you the most noble puissant Duke Nelson, Marquis Nile, Earl Alexandria, Viscount Pyramid, Baron Crocodile and Prince Victory, that posterity might have you in all forms,' was not so outlandish as it sounds today. Persons and bodies other than George III were anxious to honour a hero. The City of London voted to one of its most recent freemen, almost by exchange for the sword of Rear-Admiral Blanquet, a sword worth 200 guineas. There was a gold medal from the King and following the new custom, for all captains in the action, and Nelson's old friend Davison, appointed prize agent for the fleet, gave medals, ranging through gold, silver and copper, to every officer and man engaged. With his barony Nelson received a pension of £2000 a year, and the East India Company's recognition of his service to its interests was £10,000.

From the Sultan of Turkey there came an emissary by frigate bearing a rich red pelisse lined with sable, a diamond-studded box from the

Dowager Sultana and a richly decorated sword, scimitar and musket. The most notable gift though from the 'Grand Signior' was the chelengk, the diamond-studded representation of a plume of triumph. This was, according to Nelson, taken from the Imperial turban; according to others, specially designed, presumably speedily, so that each separate strand of the plume represented a French ship taken.

Paul, Tsar of all the Russias, sent another diamond-studded box which contained his portrait in miniature. The Island of Zante sent a gold-hilted sword and a gold-headed walking stick. Captain Hallowell of *Swiftsure* sent his admiral a coffin made entirely from material taken from *Orient* 'that when you are tired of Life, you may be buried in one of your own Trophies'. This present fitted so well with Nelson's view of mortality that he was quite content to have this memento mori stowed upright in his cabin, behind the chair he sat in for his meals. Only the entreaties of his servant, Tom Allen, a superstitious old sailor, persuaded him eventually to have it put away in the hold. Nelson's renown gave him an extra push, at the age of forty, up the ladder of admirals and, by association, saved his stepson Josiah from disgrace. In February 1799, on a general promotion, Nelson jumped the White Squadron altogether and emerged as a Rear-Admiral of the Red. Meanwhile a request that Nisbet should become Post Captain was granted by an indulgent Admiralty, when in strict justice that young man should have been broken. As St Vincent reported, among his vices were a fondness for low company, drunkenness and insubordination. His record of justly alienated subordinates made Prince William Henry appear a model of benevolent authority by comparison. Only the name of his stepfather had saved him on numerous occasions, but even Nelson was beginning to lose patience with someone he realised he had spoiled, and he could not help conveying some of his feelings to Fanny, who was still the fond, undisillusioned mother.

The Hamiltons were bound to bolster up Nelson's invincibility and omniscience in all matters warlike even if Emma had not been sexually attracted to him, and they had a ready audience for their persuasions in a simple-minded and cowardly king, who was dominated by a queen, who was ruled by the twin passions of hatred and fear for the French and their Revolution. Unfortunately both she and Nelson saw a Jacobin revolutionary under every bed and the result was the creation of a mutual admiration society consisting of the Queen, Emma Hamilton and Nelson, the King, Sir William Hamilton and Sir John Acton.

Sometimes Nelson seemed to see clearly, as at a later stage when he referred to his conscience being 'Sicilified', but in all important respects his judgment was overcome and one of the most important influences must have been his developing passion for Emma. Attracted by her, he was dragged deeper into the Neapolitan *imbroglio*, and she thus became a corrupting influence. It did not matter to anyone except Fanny, Josiah, and possibly Sir William, that Horatio went to bed with Emma but what did matter as a result of this was that because Nelson fell madly in love with her, she came to exercise a strong influence over him.

Emma's own origins, character and physique, have all been examined and re-examined by both critics and admirers to an extent that suggests she possessed some hidden mysterious qualities, whereas Nelson was the only person who thought and believed that. We know from portraits what she looked like, although in 1798, at the age of thirty-two she was beginning to put on weight, no doubt because of her own self-confessed enjoyment of 'guttling', her version of guzzling. She was a big, handsome, bosomy woman, with magnificent dark auburn hair. She had a slight fault in one eye, and large feet. She wrote exuberant, misspelt, unpunctuated English, spoke good Italian, but still retained her own strong Merseyside accent, and was very definitely 'non-U'. Most men were attracted to her, sexually if not socially. Old St Vincent wrote endearments to her, Captain Ball flirted with her. Troubridge, saddened by news of the death of his own wife in England, disapproved of her from the start, as did Nelson's old friend Lord Minto; Lord Keith when he did meet her, accompanied by his aristocratic Scots wife, positively recoiled, but her influence over Nelson offended them more.

Emma had the virtues of courage and patriotism, and was the close and faithful friend of the Queen of Naples and the rest of the Royal Family, although she may have been influenced by snobbery. Her famous 'attitudes', her dramatic poses in the guise of heroines of classical antiquity, undoubtedly possessed artistic merit, but she made the mistake of carrying her theatricality into her ordinary life. More than most she regarded life as a drama in which she had a permanent role as heroine. Perhaps she never forgot her first love, Greville, Sir William's nephew, but once enamoured of Nelson she remained faithful to him until his death, and to his memory afterwards. If jealousy without cause is one of the standards by which the intensity of love affairs can be measured then, as both Horatio and Emma were intensely, ridiculously jealous, this was indeed a grand passion.

It is difficult to argue that Nelson should have used more judgment in choosing a mistress, or that he should have conducted his extra-marital affair with discretion. In fact the word 'discretion' dies on the lips when one thinks of Emma Hamilton, and neither was it Horatio Nelson's most notable characteristic. He was not a sophisticated eighteenth-century gentleman, the sort of man William Hamilton had been at his age, but the son of a clergyman, and very much a passionate nineteenth-century romantic.

It would have been too much to expect of ladies socially superior to Emma to be fair to her, and they were not. Those who visited Naples were not slow in getting their opinions down on paper. Thus Lady Holland in 1794, 'The Hamiltons were as tiresome as ever; he as amorous, she as vulgar . . .', and two years later she describes the 'attitudes'. 'She [Lady Hamilton] had worked one's imagination up to a pitch of enthusiasm in her successive imitations of Niobe, Magdalen and Cleopatra. Just as she was lying down, and her head reclined upon an Etruscan vase to represent a water-nymph, she exclaimed in her provincial dialect, "Doun't be afeard, Sir William, I'll not crack your joug". I turned away disgusted, and I believe all present shared the sentiment.' A Mrs St George, later Mrs Trench, listed all Emma's physical attributes many years later but her summary of her manner was terse, 'bold, forward, coarse, assuming and vain'.

Perhaps a masculine pen, that of Lord Minto, was fairer. He admired and enjoyed the attitudes, and her dancing of the *tarantella*, he commented upon her size, but it was his estimate of her character that is of the greater interest. 'She is all Nature, and yet all Art', he said in 1796, 'that is to say, her manners are perfectly unpolished, of course very easy, though not with the ease of good breeding, but of a barmaid; excessively good humoured, and wishing to please and be admired by all ages and sorts of persons that come in her way; but besides considerable natural understanding, she has acquired, since her marriage, some knowledge of history and of the arts, and one wonders at the application and pains she has taken to make herself what she is.' Minto was to become very anti-Emma when she became the cause of the break-up of the Nelson marriage, but this description was written two years before his friend Nelson had anything but a passing friendship with the Hamiltons.

It was ironic that it was to Lady Hamilton, when he knew she was Nelson's hostess, that St Vincent wrote:

Pray do not let your fascinating Neapolitan dames approach too near him; for he is made of flesh and blood and cannot resist their temptations.

What he, in his turn, made of a letter from Nelson can only be conjectured:

I am writing opposite Lady Hamilton, therefore you will not be surprised at the glorious jumble of this letter. Were your Lordship in my place, I much doubt if you could write as well; our hearts and our hands must be all in a flutter. Naples is a dangerous place, and we must keep clear of it.

Unfortunately Nelson could not, and soon discovered that there were further complications for emboldened by his presence, the Government of the Two Sicilies was contemplating war against the French. Nelson's orders had mentioned a possible resumption of hostilities in Italy, but such a development postulated the assistance of the Habsburg Empire. It was Nelson's mistake that, bamboozled and flattered, he allowed himself to be drawn into a position where he became chief military adviser to the Neapolitan kingdom and in that capacity encouraged an isolated land operation which proved to be a complete disaster.

At sea all was well although his resources were overstrained, Ball was off Malta and Hood was blockading Alexandria and the four Portuguese ships under de Niza, their courteous but not highly competent commander, could at least help to relieve British warships. Further down the scale were units of the Sicilian navy under Commodore Prince Caracciolo, who was unfortunately jealous of Nelson, bearing him some grudge harking back to their service together three years ago.

It was not at sea that Nelson was to take the initiative but on land, apparently undeterred by his experience on Teneriffe.

Nelson first met General Baron Karl Mack von Leiberich on October 11 at Caserta, a few miles north of Naples. They were introduced by Queen Maria Carolina who had said to the elderly soldier, 'General, be to us by land, what my hero, Nelson, has been by sea!' It must however have been a difficult interview for the Queen spoke French, Mack could speak no Italian so used less fluent French, Nelson spoke only English so the Hamiltons translated. Nelson's first impression that 'he is active and has an intelligent eye, and will do well, I have no doubt' was to fade rapidly.

Immediately however he himself had to sail off to Malta where Admiral the Marquis de Niza was worried about serving under English captains, leaving the general to come to grips with the Neapolitan army. In fact Mack's appearance in Naples gave something of a false impression, for Thugut, the Imperial Chancellor, was being very cautious and the only help forthcoming was embodied in the person of the Austrian general. Nelson presumably appreciated this and it is the burden of the accusation against him, and the measure of his seduction by the Neapolitan Court, that he nevertheless continued to be a persistent and energetic advocate of military operations to be commenced as soon as possible against the French army to the north.

British operations at sea continued reasonably successfully. The French garrison on the island of Gozo, threatened with bombardment, surrendered, but on nearby Malta the French in the fortress of Valetta continued to hold out resolutely despite a fearsome shortage of food. Returning to Naples Nelson handed over the French colours taken on Gozo to King Ferdinand, technically the sovereign of that island, and looked again at Neapolitan preparations for war.

They were not, and could not have appeared to be, impressive. Mack at a review of 30,000 soldiers, assured the admiral that he was looking at 'la plus belle Armée d'Europe', but Nelson's view was that the army was 'with some few exceptions wretchedly officered' and his opinion of their commanding general was rapidly going downhill, especially when even showpiece manoeuvres ended in confusion.

Still, at a council at which it was obvious that no help was to be obtained from Vienna, nor any money from London, Nelson's advice to their Sicilian majesties was, 'Either to advance (trusting to God for His blessing on a just Cause), to die with "l'épee à la main", or remain quiet and be kicked out of your Kingdoms'. It was the worst advice that Nelson ever gave anyone and unfortunately for themselves, a naturally craven King and an unnaturally pessimistic Queen, it was taken.

CHAPTER TWENTY-ONE

Palermo

AFTER THE Treaty of Campo Formio which removed the influence of the Habsburgs from the Italian peninsula, relations
between the surviving Italian kingdoms and principalities and the
French Republic were both curious and individual, not least those of the
kingdom of Ferdinand IV of the Two Sicilies.

To the north the four Papal States were occupied by a French army,
Rome was garrisoned by French troops and the Pope, after General
Berthier had entered the Holy City, had been spirited off to exile in
France. There now existed a Roman Republic supported by French
soldiers and from this base a number of threats were made against the
Two Sicilies, but there was no overt military action, and the two states
were at peace. Ferdinand had resisted republican pressure both from
outside and inside his dominions and at this stage, at the end of 1798, the
French were content to let matters be. On the larger European stage,
following the stimulus of the Nile victory, there was the possibility of a
new coalition of Britain, Austria and Russia so that France had enough to
cope with without concerning herself with Naples and Sicily.

This of course was not Nelson's view of the situation; he favoured
bold measures, but bold measures need bold men to translate them into
action, and there were not many of them about in Naples. Somehow he
deluded himself into thinking that he alone could put backbone into
a country which was quite content invertebrate. As he wrote, 'this
Country with its system of procrastination will ruin itself; the Queen
sees it and thinks as we do. The Ministry, except Acton, are for putting
off the evil day, when it will come with destruction. War at this moment
can alone save these Kingdoms.' That letter was written to St Vincent,
who should have realised that Nelson was going beyond, if not the
letter, at least the spirit of his orders from the Admiralty. Assistance
and co-operation are very different things from encouragement and
instigation.

On November 23, however, five columns of the Neapolitan army, led by General Mack with its King somewhere in the background, began to advance over the frontier into French-occupied territory without the formality of a declaration of war. Meanwhile Nelson, who was, for the Neapolitan Court and populace, a sort of talisman of victory, occupied himself in his proper element and used his squadron to transport 5000 Neapolitan soldiers, under General Noselli, to Leghorn. The operation was a success, the intention being to occupy Leghorn and thus threaten French communications, and this was done, but it was success which contained a strong element of farce. Leghorn was in Tuscany, whose Grand Duke was a son-in-law of Ferdinand, but who saw that as an insufficient reason for Neapolitans taking his territory. Noselli and Nelson did not get on, the admiral's complaint being that the general sought to treat him as 'a nothing, as a Master of Transport'. The Tuscan Grand Duke protested to Mr William Wyndham, the British Minister, who travelled from Florence in an attempt to sort things out. Was he being 'protected' by Admiral Nelson or Ferdinand of the Two Sicilies? Mr Wyndham, embarrassed by the question, indicated the Neapolitan general; the Grand Duke, forced to choose, preferred a British admiral.

In the background as another irritant for Nelson was Lady Hamilton, already writing more like a lover than a friend and urging him, in her haphazard spelling, not to go ashore at Leghorn, as 'their is no comfort their for you'. What she meant by comfort she did not define, but perhaps she had heard, through the Fremantles, of Nelson's former 'dolly'. If that is correct, this was the first sign of her incredible possessiveness which Nelson, not normally a patient man, bore with humiliating submissiveness.

In the end the Governor of Leghorn came aboard Nelson's flagship and on the quarter-deck surrendered the town. General Noselli was much put out, but found some consolation in the fact that his soldiers were able to capture a sizeable and important port without having to fire a shot. The main Sicilian army under Mack was also meeting with similar bloodless success. Championnet, the French general in Rome, reacted to the approach of a Neapolitan army rather as a surprised stoat might if suddenly bitten by a rabbit. He retreated, and as a result Ferdinand IV was allowed a brief moment of glory as, at the head of his soldiers, he made a triumphal entry into Rome on November 29. However, the French had not given up quite as easily as that, a small garrison remained in the Castle of St Angelo and the main body had only withdrawn as far as Civita Castellana. Mack decided to attack, marching his men northwards out of Rome to do so. The stoat was however now prepared for the rabbit and in the space of about twenty-four hours a small French army routed and put to flight a much larger Neapolitan one. 'The most beautiful army in Europe' simply disintegrated under musket fire. Officers deserted their men, men deserted their officers, all ranks divested themselves of their uniforms and their arms. Mack did what he could to block the road to Naples at Capua with a few loyal troops but it was a hopeless task. Championnet re-occupied Rome and passed on southwards. King Ferdinand had already bolted for home in his coach. On December 6 the Directory in Paris, almost as an afterthought, declared war on the Kingdom of the Two Sicilies.

Nelson, having left Troubridge to deal with Leghorn and General Noselli, arrived back in Naples in time to welcome a retreating king, now in civilian clothes, and a returning mob which had once been dressed as an army. He was also delivered an epitaph on a venture, for which he bore, at least, some of the responsibility. 'The Neapolitan officers have not lost much honour, for God knows they had but little to lose, but they lost all they had'.

It gives some idea of the perpetual movement and confusion in Naples, to realise that on about the day that Ferdinand returned to his capital and was forced to appear on the palace balcony to reassure his supporters, a number of other significant events were taking place in and around that crowded city.

The Portuguese admiral, de Niza, arrived on board his flagship, *Principe Real*, which generally meant that he either wanted Nelson's help or advice, or else had come to complain that British officers, junior in rank, were treating him with scant respect. This was not surprising considering that on a previous visit to Naples *Principe Real*, instead of firing the customary ceremonial salute, had loaded shot and fired a salvo of cannon balls into the town. At the same time H.M.S. *Alcmene* was in the harbour with dispatches from Hood in command of the Egyptian blockade. Ferdinand and Maria Carolina, discerning ominous parallels between events in Naples and those in Paris nine years before, now decided to desert Naples for their other capital, Palermo in Sicily. Nelson was about to be used again as a transport master, though more willingly this time as Emma Hamilton had taken on the task of travel agent and removal specialist. Then Kelim Effendi, the Turkish Ambassador, turned up on board a frigate, with a large company of picturesquely robed attendants, to present Nelson with gifts from his Imperial master.

A dispatch arrived on December 18 from Mack rather unnecessarily detailing and confirming a full retreat, and predicting the imminent French occupation of Naples.

There followed a few days of chaos, unrest, subterfuge and a lot of cloak and dagger work which, one suspects, Lady Hamilton secretly enjoyed, and then the Sicilian Royal Family was transported to Palermo by the Royal Navy, sundry transports hired or commandeered for the occasion, ships of the Portuguese navy, and two corvettes of the Sicilian navy.

Once again, it was a typical Neapolitan incident, midway between tragedy and farce. The secret passage from the royal palace to the departure quay was guarded by British seamen armed with cutlasses. There were secret messages, passwords and countersigns. An estimated £2½ million worth of Royal jewellery and property was put on board British ships labelled 'Stores for Nelson'. Somehow or other a number of the distinguished refugees, just before departing, managed to attend a reception given by Kelim Effendi who, unfortunately, did not leave his impressions for posterity. One lady did, Miss Cornelia Knight, in her pen portraits of this confusing cast of personalities. Nelson applying his power of command and organisational talents to what must have been his most extraordinary naval assignment. The cowardly yet indifferent King, the frantic Queen, whom Nelson held in high regard, and to whom he promised aid. Emma in her element, Sir William feeling rather ill. Count Thürn, a commodore in the Sicilian navy and regarded as a man of the highest loyalty and devotion. Commodore Prince Carraciolo, plunged into silent gloom because his monarch preferred the services of the British navy to his own. Mrs Cadogan, Emma's mother, who had been the chatelaine of the Palazzo Sessa and was now busy as a sort of female quartermaster. General Mack appeared with more tales of woe, preparatory to his own departure, eventually to surrender himself to the French. Lady Knight, mother of Miss Cornelia and widow of a British admiral, plus sundry princes, dukes and countesses of the international set, including a Count Esterhazy who was so frightened of the sea that he threw a snuff box decorated with a picture of his naked mistress to the waves, to signify his repentance and hopes for salvation. It was somewhat bizarre jetsam, but the Count's apprehension was justified.

Nelson himself, caught in a storm with a wind which suddenly changed from east to west, confessed that 'it blew harder than I have ever experienced since I have been at sea'. Topsails in *Vanguard* were split by the blast and the only civilians on board who kept their heads were Lady Hamilton and her sturdy old mother, who spent their time ministering to the sick and scared. Sailors are adaptable creatures, adept at do-it-yourself techniques, and preparations had been made in Naples for taking on board a large number of civilians and their wives and families. However, so many turned up that Miss Knight and her mother had to be directed by an embarrassed Captain Hardy away from the overcrowded *Vanguard* to the *Rainha de Portugal*. Miss Knight described her confusing and frightening experiences on board that ship, but they differed little from conditions in the British flagship for both were ill-adapted to supercargoes of refugees.

The behaviour of Sir William Hamilton, the very essence of the phlegmatic English gentleman, can be taken as some indication of the intensity of the whole experience. He was discovered by his wife in his cabin in *Vanguard* with a loaded pistol in his hand, determined not to die with the 'guggle-guggle-guggle' of sea water in his throat. He had therefore made up his mind to shoot himself as soon as the ship began to sink.

The second day of passage was somewhat calmer; it was also Christmas Day but there were no celebrations. That evening the six-year-old Prince Alberto, the youngest of Maria Carolina's many children, who had had convulsions during the storm but had appeared to recover, died in Lady Hamilton's arms. The motley convoy sailed into Palermo harbour before dawn the next day. At the main mast of the British flagship flew the royal standard of the Kingdom of the Two Sicilies, and a welcoming crowd soon assembled ashore to greet Ferdinand IV, but the whole operation had hardly been either dignified or inspiring.

The Court and Government of the dual kingdom had now been transferred to Sicily proper, and also the flag officer commanding the British squadron. With 1799 almost upon him it was time that Nelson returned to his naval duties. In fact he stayed at Palermo until May 19. This was the period when his love affair with Emma became a physical relationship and the fact that they were lovers must have been obvious to many people, not least among them Emma's husband. At a later stage Cornelia Knight was to deny that anything of this was apparent to her, but, as will be seen, she had a special reason for so doing and seems to have been deliberately blind to a situation that was perfectly clear to others who saw much less of Nelson and the Hamiltons than she did.

No one now believes that Emma and Horatio's relationship was platonic, but when there were people who did, or said they did, their principal argument rested upon Sir William's behaviour. Crudely put, if Horatio and Emma were lovers, why didn't Sir William notice, and if he noticed, object?

The answer is very simple. Not only did he notice, but he knew, but chose not to object. He was fond of his wife, he was also fond of Nelson. Years before he had predicted that some younger man might take Emma from him. Now it had happened, but the forty-year-old admiral was a hero and a friend. When Sir William had married Emma, Casanova, who died in 1798, had delivered a judgment upon the couple: 'A clever man, marrying a young woman clever enough to bewitch him', and then later, 'Such a fate often overtakes a man of intelligence when he grows old. It is always a mistake to marry, but when a man's physical and mental forces are declining, it is a calamity.' In fact Sir William Hamilton was just as wise as Casanova, but deliberately chose not to make his declining years a calamity. There was an element of fatalism in his character and he was not the man, by temperament or upbringing, to make unseemly scenes. Like Lord Chesterfield his view was 'manners before morals', for so long as Emma and Horatio did not openly declare their relationship, Sir William was not going to reveal what he thought was none of the public's business.

It was a different matter for Nelson. Although deeply in love, it would have been very odd if he had not been plagued by conscience. Fanny may have been dull and unexciting but she was blameless, as he was later to admit. But he was a stubborn man, and throughout 1799 he was determined to stay in 'the Sicilian world', which meant with Emma, as long as possible. It was an escape from the real world and it is a wonder that his professional career did not suffer more than it did. Compared with the usual Nelson, he was inactive reacting sluggishly to people and events rather than seeking to mould and master them. It would be pleasing to think that though he was not as active and energetic an admiral as he could have been, at least he had the consolation, in his private and emotional life, of being a happy man. It would be pleasing, but most probably untrue. For the first time in his life he was truly in love, and had attained a sexually satisfying and stimulating relationship with Emma. Unfortunately she was married to, and lived with, Sir William Hamilton and back in England Fanny was still impatiently waiting.

The obvious solution to the modern mind would have been divorce,

Sir William divorcing Emma on the grounds of her adultery with Nelson, and Lady Nelson divorcing her husband on the grounds of his adultery with Emma. However, that remedy was not then available at English law. Divorce was a rare, complicated and costly process. Only a year before, in 1798, the House of Lords had regularised a curious blend of judicial proceeding and legislative process.

In practice a divorce could be obtained by an innocent husband against an adulterous wife firstly by obtaining a divorce 'a mensa et thoro', from bed and board, from the Ecclesiastical Court, this being equivalent to a modern judicial separation. Then, if the husband wished to be free to marry again, he had to apply to the House of Lords for a Divorce Bill. This application had to be supported by a verdict obtained in the Crown Law Courts against his wife's seducer for damages 'for criminal conversation'.

If Emma and Horatio had set up house together and lived openly in adultery, Sir William could have divorced Emma without great difficulty and if he had chosen to create a scandal and claim damages from Nelson he could have obtained his Bill of Divorce. But Nelson would not have been free to marry Emma, because Fanny, even if she had chosen to try, would not have succeeded in divorcing Horatio.

All this postulates a willingness on the part of Sir William and Lady Nelson to institute proceedings. There is no evidence that either even considered doing so most likely because such a course did not occur to either although they looked at the problem from very different personal standpoints.

Nelson could enjoy his lover and mistress relation with Emma, but married bliss, with the pleasure of legitimate children, was not to be his lot. Even if he had survived Trafalgar marriage would have been impossible during Lady Nelson's life so that his frequent talk of marriage when Emma's 'uncle', the lovers' method of referring to Sir William, died, was mere wishful thinking.

To a man of Nelson's deep religious convictions his love affair with Emma must have been distressing and the necessary subterfuges and deceptions a constant irritant. In addition although he had acquired, in his own phrase, 'a loving friend' the circumstances were temporary and artificial. The situation in Sicily could not last for both Nelson and the Hamiltons would have to return to England, which was no doubt one of the main reasons why Nelson allowed himself to become embroiled in the very localised affairs of the Sicilian kingdom.

His old friend Alexander Davison wrote to him, 'Your object now ought to be that of contributing to the Tranquility and Comfort of your Inestimable Wife'. Nothing could have been further from Nelson's purpose, and when Fanny wrote to him suggesting that she should 'join the Standard' or come out to Lisbon for her health, he either produced silly reasons why she should not, 'Lisbon was the most dirty place in Europe, covered with fog', or else curtly rejected her offer by saying that if she came out he would have to strike his flag and bring her home again.

Few men have pursued honours and glory more assiduously than Nelson, and none have ever admitted so frankly their ambitions. 'If it be a sin to covet glory', he confessed to Lady Hamilton, 'I am the most offending soul alive'. In 1799, aged forty, he was a Rear-Admiral of the Red, a peer of the realm, with the star and riband of the Order of the Bath and two gold medals to wear on his full-dress frock coat. He was a Freeman of the City of London, had a pension of £2000 a year, a gift of £10,000 from the East India Company, the chelengk from the Sultan, ceremonial swords, canes and numerous ornamental boxes, and, at home, a decent sized country house.

However, Nelson was not happy. The simplest solution would have been for him to leave the Mediterranean and come home, but this was the one decision that Nelson, prisoner of his attraction to Lady Hamilton, could not take. Therefore he stayed in Naples or Palermo where there was not quite enough military activity to justify his presence, but a sufficiency of incidents and crises to bring trouble, tarnish his reputation, and collect critics and criticism. Troubles of course never come singly and Nelson, writing home to Fanny, though enamoured of Emma Hamilton, still made her his confidante so far as many personal problems were concerned. He told her that his letters were short because of the pressure of work and official letters which had to be written. This apology and excuse contained a considerable element of truth, but Fanny, as a result, received letters almost entirely made up of complaints, sometimes on a rather peevish note, about her husband's health or his allies, his superiors or his subordinates.

One subordinate of considerable interest to her was Captain Josiah Nisbet, but the news of him was not of the type which a loving mother would wish to hear. Josiah obviously resented Nelson's affair with Emma Hamilton and at a reception given in Naples by the Hamiltons he got drunk, made a scene and had to be escorted away by Troubridge.

Whether the cause of his bad behaviour was his stepfather's attentions to
the Ambassador's wife, as was suggested, is uncertain but certainly, at a
later stage, observing his one-armed stepfather, boarding his flagship
with difficulty, he was heard to express the hope that he would fall and
break his neck. It is easy to sympathise with Josiah's taking up the
cudgels on behalf of his absent mother, though Captain Nisbet was very
far from faultless himself, particularly in his capacity as a sea officer.
Josiah was boorish and uncouth, with a hot temper and a pronounced
liking for strong drink. This was a vice with which Nelson, very abstemious himself, had little sympathy, but the most serious complaint was
that Josiah was unable to exercise the restraint and self-control necessary
for the proper performance of his duties. He was self-willed, and
so insubordinate and disobedient that the suspicion must be that he
had grown to expect that his stepfather would always come to his
rescue.

Josiah had, of course, been over-promoted for, despite a poor record,
he was made a post captain at Nelson's insistence after the Nile. Nelson,
though regretting that he had been over-indulgent, continued to be so.
There had already been complaints from St Vincent and now they came
from Troubridge. Josiah had been given command of a first-class frigate,
Thalia, with two lieutenants hand-picked by Nelson and easy tasks such
as escorting the Turkish Ambassador back to Constantinople. But he
still seemed to be incapable of obeying any order without introducing
variations of his own, or, the other requirement of an officer, managing
those who had to obey him.

On January 17 Nelson wrote from Palermo to his 'dearest Fanny', 'I
wish I could say much to your and my satisfaction about Josiah, but
I am sorry to say and with real grief, that he has nothing good about him,
he must sooner or later be broke, but I am sure neither you or I can help
it, I have done with the subject it is an ungrateful one'. But by April he
had resolved to give his stepson another chance for he wrote to Fanny,
'Josiah is now in full possession of a noble frigate. He has sent to say
that he is sensible of his youthful follies, and that he shall alter his whole
conduct. I sincerely wish he may, both for his and your sake.' In June
when *Thalia* was look-out frigate and therefore very much under
Nelson's eye, 'Josiah is here and promises to do everything in his power
to make us happy I hope to God he will.' Josiah, however, never made a
good officer, and after Nelson's return home and estrangement from
Fanny his 'interest' in his stepson slowly ceased to be exercised. After

1801 Josiah was no longer employed on the active list and eventually he left the service to discover a talent for making money on land.

Nelson was writing to Admiral Duckworth as late as October 1799, 'I wish I could say something in his praise. Perhaps you may be able to make something of Captain Nisbet, he has by his conduct almost broke my heart.'

Nelson was a kind-hearted man, fond of children and one who did his utmost with his money and influence to help a set of fairly worthless relatives. The East India Company's gift was distributed in a large part to relations, including his old father, and a number of nephews, and more distant relations, were placed in the Navy. No doubt he never really forgot 'the good boy' he had first met and played with on Antigua. Lest it should be thought he was unduly harsh in his judgment of Fanny's son it is instructive to read a letter from her as late as April 15, 1800:

My dear Josiah,—I received a letter from Lord Nelson dated January 25th where he mentions your improvements with tenderness and kindness. His love for you is very great. He flatters himself he shall see you a good and great man. It is in your power to be both—You are more conspicuous than you imagine. Be assured you are much envied for having such a father to bring you forward, who has every desire to do it. To convince you I have very good reason to write to you on this subject, I will in confidence repeat to you a conversation a captain of the Navy had with an intimate acquaintance of mine, not knowing I was in the least acquainted.

I am trying all I can to remove Mr ——, first lieutenant of the *Thalia*, for her captain is not great things. Then [he] vented his ill-natured disposition, never once allowing himself to think he had been young. This acquaintance of mine is rather what is called passionate. He immediately said, 'Do you know you are speaking of the son of a friend of my wife's, and the son-in-law of Lord Nelson?' 'Yes' was the answer, and immediately this captain turned and left this gentleman, but in a minute returned saying, 'For God sake don't mention what I have said'. . . . All this happened a year and a half back.

My dear Josiah, take yourself to account every day. Don't excuse any foibles. I do assure you your first lieutenant has always wrote of you in a handsome manner, I have seen his letters to his mother. Silence on this subject. There is an admiral who has got himself much laughed at in wishing to defame my Lord's understanding. He wishes to be acquainted with me of all things. I suppose to speak well of my husband.

God bless you and believe me your affectionate mother,
Frances H. Nelson.

This letter also provides an interesting sidelight on his mother's character, both as a woman of considerable sense, and so far as her husband was concerned, forbearance.

There were also, apart from Josiah, others who seemed to have been deliberately created to plague him; principally, and ironically, his own naval superior, Admiral Lord Keith, second-in-command in the Mediterranean. St Vincent, elderly and with poor health, was tending to spend more and more time on shore at Gibraltar, so that executive command devolved upon Keith, who was to take over as Commander-in-Chief when St Vincent went home in August 1799. Between St Vincent and Nelson, by no means uncritical of each other, and later involved as opponents in a lawsuit over prize money, there always existed a relationship of familiarity, if not close friendship. Perhaps the older man remembered with gratitude that a young commodore had once promised him an earldom and had fulfilled that promise, in battle.

There was no such bond between Keith and Nelson. The senior admiral was a distinguished, if not brilliant officer, sober and persistent rather than inspired, an orthodox commander and a stern disciplinarian. Unfortunately he had also the keen eye of a dour, canny Scot for the absurd, pretentious and the ridiculous, and Nelson in 1799 erred in all those directions.

Keith, as he was bound to do, took the Government line, which went back to the official instructions to Sir William Hamilton as Ambassador, not to encourage the Sicilians beyond their means. Opinion in London was that this was just what Hamilton, aided and abetted, and perhaps overborne, by Nelson had done. Ferdinand and his Queen, whom Nelson described as 'a Great King', had taken up arms and attempted to capture Rome. They had failed ignominiously and been forced to retreat to Sicily while the French now occupied Naples and were setting up a puppet administration, the Parthenopean Republic, named, with that penchant the Directory had for classical mythology, after a Greek sea nymph. London had never regarded the Sicilian Kingdom as particularly important, especially without Austrian support and now it was even less so.

Nelson, however, stressing his promise to the Queen not to desert her, and to keep British warships in the area, committed two mistakes, in supporting an unimportant and not particularly worthy cause, and also by making promises which he, as a subordinate commander, was not entitled to make. His loyalty was to George III of England, not Ferdinand IV of the Two Sicilies. Finally, gossip and rumour had already suggested quite plainly that the real reason for the Admiral's devotion to Queen Maria Carolina lay in his relationship with the notorious wife of the British Ambassador who was the Queen's closest confidante and adviser.

The difficulty for the Government, St Vincent and Keith was that Nelson was the principal hero of the war. A public rupture with the Hero of the Nile had to be avoided at all costs. As will be seen, Nelson under criticism and rebuke became more obstinate and immersed himself even more closely in Neapolitan affairs. Ultimately there was a limit to official forbearance but St Vincent, Keith, and Spencer did their utmost to avoid provocation. The process of coaxing, cajoling and, finally, directly ordering Nelson to conform did not of course make Nelson's own life any easier.

Given his viewpoint, blinkered though it was, it must have seemed, as he suggested in his letters to Fanny, that he had no friends at all in the Mediterranean save the Hamiltons and the King and Queen of Naples, upon whom he lavished the most fulsome praise. In 1799 Nelson was getting very near to the state where he believed that only those few people who agreed with him, or who flattered him, and sought his opinion and advice, could be right. Contrary opinions tended to be dismissed and disregarded as actuated by malice. In short, success had gone to his head.

However, it must be admitted that events did crowd in upon him to an extent which would have tried a very different man. In the professional sphere alone there were a number of problems. The success of the Nile, demonstrating that the French could be beaten, had given a boost to William Pitt's attempts to form a new coalition. Assisted by British subsidies, old and new allies were beginning to emerge, among which were two empires traditionally the enemies of each other, Turkey and Russia. As a result Nelson was promised the assistance of a Turkish and a Russian squadron both of which finally did appear under the commands of Abdul Cadir Bey and Vice-Admiral Theodore Ouschakoff. It would be an exaggeration to suggest that they co-operated with him, even to the extent that the Portuguese and Sicilians obeyed his general directions. What they did together was to blockade the island of Corfu though principally to keep an eye on each other's activities. Nelson preferred 'the old Turk', distrusting the Russians although they sent troops and marines to help in the reconquest of Naples. In this he was right, for though the Turks were incompetent they were sincere in their opposition to French activities in the Mediterranean, whereas the Russian squadron conformed to the unpredictable moods of its Imperial master, alternating between friendship, neutrality and obstruction. Turkish participation had been stimulated by the isolation of a French army in Egypt, but Nelson was soon to learn something of the qualities of resilience possessed by Bonaparte.

The effect of a purely naval victory could not last for ever, and almost at the same time as the Parthenopean Republic was being formed, and Turks, Russians, Austrians and Englishmen were beginning to combine against Republican France, Bonaparte was on the move again. In January he began to advance his army into Syria. Nelson's opinion, that the Sultan had but to 'trot his army into Syria' to mop up the French, was over-optimistic, although they were brought to a halt by the actions of Sir Sidney Smith. He was brave, unorthodox and enterprising, and like Nelson had a taste for land operations, and though he offended his superiors he possessed a gift for leadership, and, less agreeably, for self-advertisement. His presence in the Mediterranean became known to Nelson by chance for he suddenly discovered that another naval officer, a mere captain despite his English knighthood and his foreign decoration, was apparently in command of the 'forces in the Levant'.

The explanation was partly muddle and partly thoughtlessness in the Admiralty. Nelson's squadron, augmented by de Niza's ships, was stretched from Malta to Alexandria in addition to its commitment to Sicily and Naples. Bonaparte and his army were again active and the Ottoman Empire had to be encouraged and kept within the new alliance. It is easy to see therefore why Lord Spencer, or perhaps one of his officials, thought it would be no bad idea to have another sub-command in Turkish waters, co-operating more closely than Nelson could with both Ottoman sea and land forces. What better choice for the post than the energetic Captain Sir Sidney, especially as his brother Spencer Smith was the new British Minister at Constantinople? To Lord Grenville, the Foreign Secretary, and Lord Spencer at the Admiralty, it sounded an admirable arrangement, although the latter had realised that 'there might be some prejudices' against Sir Sidney, but suggested that he and his brother could exercise a sort of dual control.

It was not such a bad idea except that Nelson learnt from Sir Sidney Smith that he was taking over command of Captain Hood and *Zealous*, *Swiftsure*, *Lion* and *Seahorse* off Alexandria. Typically, Smith had also written to Sir William Hamilton, announcing, not without a touch of grandiloquence, his new naval and diplomatic responsibilities. Nelson wrote in protest to Mr Nepean, the Secretary of the Admiralty Board, Lord Spencer, and St Vincent. Nelson began his letter to St Vincent: 'I do feel, for I am a man, that it is impossible for me to serve in these seas, with the Squadron under a junior Officer:—could I have thought it!—and from Earl Spencer!' It was from St Vincent that Nelson received the most tactful reply for plainly he did not much like Smith: 'I am not surprised at your feelings being outraged, at the bold attempt Sir Sidney Smith is making to wrest a part of your Squadron from you.' However, Nelson was adjured to 'moderate your feelings and continue in command'. 'Employ Sir Sidney Smith in any manner you think proper; knowing your magnanimity I am sure you will mortify him as little as possible, consistently with what is due to the great characters senior to him on the List, and his superiors in every sense of the word.' Needless to say Nelson was in no doubt as to who one of those 'great characters' might be. It was, of course, the grossest flattery from a Commander-in-Chief who superscribed himself, 'God bless you, my dear Lord, be assured no man loves and esteems you more truly than your very affectionate, St Vincent.'

The tactless manner of Sir Sidney Smith's appointment can be criticised, but now it seemed as if Nelson had to be treated much more like a temperamental prima donna than an admiral on service. As chance turned out, Smith was to acquit himself admirably in the rest of the year, while Nelson's own career fell into the doldrums.

CHAPTER TWENTY-TWO

Sicilian Counter-revolution

NELSON COMPLAINED in almost every letter that he wrote during 1799. There was something wrong with his situation or his allies, his health or the burdens of his task. He complained to his brother William and to Fanny that letters from home were not reaching him and to the latter he wrote that he was 'tired of war', while to others, such as his old admirer Lady Parker who had written to congratulate him, he almost suggested that he was tired of life.

Only in his letters to his allies, the Russian Ouschakoff, the Turk Cadir Bey and the Portuguese de Niza, do we get a glimpse of the other Nelson, the man who never really forgot 'the common cause', and who tried by a mixture of flattery and persuasion to keep his lukewarm or uncooperative partners up to the mark. One of the root causes of his depression was that they, and even more so the Sicilian officers who came under his command, did not behave in their professional duties like officers and men of the Royal Navy. There was not the drive or the discipline, perhaps not even the will, certainly not the capability. There was too much of what an exasperated Troubridge called 'the Neapolitan shuffle'. The wonder is that Nelson maintained his patience and his regard for the Sicilian Royal House as firmly as he did, and one can only conclude that Emma Hamilton's preferences and prejudices must have influenced him. Admittedly the Neapolitan Bourbons, though possessed of little courage, were firmly anti-French and Nelson was extremely opposed to the French and any Jacobin of other nationality who sided with them. Yet still one wonders that Nelson did not, like many senior naval officers and statesmen, equally patriotic and anti-French, dismiss the Kingdom of the Two Sicilies as an ally both tiresome and incompetent and therefore, despite the strategic significance of southern Italy, hardly worth maintaining within the alliance.

Personally, Nelson was in poor health, and probably also suffering from a guilt complex. As his correspondence with Spencer, St Vincent and Keith shows, he hovered perpetually between a wish to come home to England, and a desire to remain in Naples and Sicily. However, to stay in close proximity to Emma Hamilton meant to be enmeshed in the toils of Neapolitan intrigue, politics and petty diplomacy, and so like a mouse on a treadmill, Nelson remained, getting nowhere.

To Fanny he said that he was 'tired of war', and to one who had now been almost thirty years a sea officer it was not a surprising sentiment, but unfortunately for his peace of mind conflict was very soon to escalate.

In the December of the previous year the alliance between Britain and Russia, the foundation of the Second Coalition against France, had been signed. On March 12, 1799 the Austrians declared war on France and in April, as an indication of the new state of affairs, the Conference at Rastadt, which had been assembled to settle affairs between France and the Empire as far back as December 1797, now broke up in a confusion of mutual recrimination. By then hostilities had already commenced in Europe between Austrian and French troops, and the Habsburg dynasty had produced a new, young and successful general in the Archduke Charles. A Russian army under an incredible old man, Marshal Alexander Suvorov, 'hero, buffoon, half clown and half dirt', Byron called him, was also on the move.

Amidst this renewal of hostilities Bonaparte was again active. Nelson received on May 12 dispatches informing him that, taking advantage of a heavy fog to avoid Admiral Bridport's blockade of Brest, a French fleet under Admiral Bruix had escaped into the Mediterranean and was now at large. Its purpose could only be surmised but there were a number of possibilities: the relief of Malta, an attack upon Alexandria or an attack upon Sicily or Naples where the Parthenopean Republic was in considerable difficulties with a counter-revolution on its hands. Actually the last course was the least likely, and St Vincent and Keith were much more concerned lest the French fleet should combine with the Spaniards and thus oppose the British with numerical superiority.

Bruix's fleet had been sighted off Oporto and was being tailed by the British. The French admiral had intended a junction with a Spanish fleet, but was prevented by the presence of Keith off Cadiz. Accordingly Bruix passed the Straits heading for Toulon, reached there on May 14, and sailed on eastwards twelve days later. St Vincent with sixteen of the line was in pursuit, taking over from Keith, but the admiral's own eastward movement had allowed a Spanish fleet of seventeen battleships to break out of Cadiz, and make Cartagena though suffering considerable damage in stormy seas.

Not all this information was available to Nelson; he merely knew that a French fleet was at sea and sailing eastwards. He could also judge the dangers and imagine the problems of his two seniors. He kept his squadron at Palermo with lookout ships off the north of Corsica and the west of Sardinia. He explained to St Vincent that he saw his task as 'preserving Sicily', but it was an unusually passive role for Nelson to play, though ships under his command were still off Malta and Alexandria. Nelson's command was reinforced on June 5 by the arrival at Palermo of four ships of the line under Rear-Admiral Duckworth. Three were 74's plus a new two-decked 80-gun battleship, *Foudroyant*, and it must have been with a sense of relief that Nelson transferred his flag to her from the patched up *Vanguard*. The additional ships were intended to enable him to cover with more ease his three responsibilities, Malta, Alexandria and Sicily, plus the overall task of interception of the French fleet.

The arrival of reinforcements persuaded Nelson to a task which was probably not contemplated by St Vincent, the restoration of Ferdinand IV and his Queen to the other half of their kingdom on the mainland. It may have been a misuse of the ships or a poor estimate of priorities for a British admiral, but it must be admitted that in Naples the time was ripe, for quite an unusual counter-revolution was taking place. Revolutionary ideals and the prospect of change and reform had received no sort of welcome, very much the reverse, from the mass of the people. In other parts of Europe disillusionment followed actual experience of exported Libery, Equality, and Fraternity, backed up by bayonets, but in Naples initial enthusiasm had only been shown by a very small class of intellectuals and lawyers. To the *lazzaroni* the Parthenopean, sometimes called by Nelson the Vesuvian, Republic made no appeal whatsoever.

Neapolitans were quite satisfied with their oafish king with his terse ideals of government, 'festa, forca e farina' ('feasts, the gallows and flour'). As H. C. Gutteridge put it in his *Nelson and the Neapolitan Jacobins*, 'It is not altogether surprising, therefore, that the lazzaroni should in spite of their misery, have been warmly attached to a government which left them to practise their superstitions in peace, relieved them from the burden of taxation, and refrained from harassing them with unwelcome reforms.'

The Kingdom consisted of the crown, the church and the mob, and each was opposed to secular republicanism. So the few pro-French, and rather ineffective, middle-class intellectuals were isolated, and irregular bands of partisans in the countryside and assassins in Naples proved themselves to be much more dangerous to the French army than the Neapolitan regular forces had ever been.

Ferdinand chose as his lieutenant on the mainland another Neapolitan character who might have stepped from the pages of Dumas or been found in an early Verdi libretto. The sixty-year-old Cardinal Fabrizzio Ruffo was a most worldly cleric. He had only ever taken minor orders and had gained his cardinal's hat as Papal Secretary. He was still a large landowner in Calabria, and his written works were not theological but ranged over natural history and scientific matters to infantry drill and the equipment of cavalry. He seemed therefore to be an ideal man to stir up a revolt among the peasantry of the Neapolitan provinces. He was given authority as the King's Vicar-General, and his 'Army of the Holy Faith' was soon a large and powerful, if ill-disciplined, force. This Prince of the Church obviously began to see himself as a latter-day Italianate Richelieu and the King, in his proclamation to his subjects, made reference to the Sicilian Vespers.

In Naples the French army was in difficulties. Queen Maria Carolina noted with glee the large numbers of soldiers who were being murdered, and no doubt robbed, in the brothels. General Championnet was replaced by General Macdonald so the Jacobins could now rely for support upon a Jacobite's son, for his father had fled from the Highlands to the service of the French King after the failure of the 1745 Rebellion. He became a Napoleonic Marshal in 1809 and was a much tougher soldier than Championnet. Macdonald proceeded to send as much loot back to Paris as his soldiers could collect from Neapolitan palaces and galleries, and then started to think of withdrawing his army, thus leaving the Neapolitan Republicans, his friends and allies, to the mercies of the counter-revolution.

The French began to withdraw in May, and the counter-revolutionary war to reclaim Naples became systematised. Ruffo's army advanced from the south on the capital, aided by a force of nearly a thousand Russian marines from Ouschakoff's fleet and a smaller body of Turkish soldiers To the north partisans, irregulars and bandits paid some attention to the orders of all sorts of picturesque and villainous leaders including the self-styled Fra Diavolo. At sea Nelson sent off Troubridge with a small squadron to blockade Naples and mop up the islands of Ischia, Procida and Capri with the result that he soon had a collection of rebel prisoners on his hands who in his view, and Nelson's, should be tried and hanged as soon as possible.

These operations and the British fleet's participation were interrupted by the news of Bruix's fleet which meant that Nelson and his two subordinate commanders, Troubridge and Ball, had to take up positions with their squadrons to intercept the French admiral should he seek to penetrate eastwards.

Consequently Nelson and his main command did not become directly involved again in the task of putting down the remnants of the Parthenopean republic until late in June. One of the most curious features of this last operation was the comparatively large part played by Nelson and the small part played by Neapolitan forces. This was a domestic internal matter, yet it was managed almost entirely by the British fleet. When Nelson had been preparing his first venture, interrupted by news of the French fleet, he had taken the Sicilian heir to the throne on board *Foudroyant* to give authority to his actions, for the cowardly King had made it clear that he had no intention of returning to his dominions until they had been made safe for him by British warships. In June Nelson took the Hamiltons with him, but not the Hereditary Prince, and by then any resistance likely to be encountered was even less than it had been earlier. The French had departed long before, leaving behind only an isolated garrison of 500 men in the Castle of St Elmo. Ruffo's men, dignified by the title of an army, had already penetrated the outskirts of Naples and in answer to Nelson's entreaty General Stuart had placed two battalions of British infantry at Messina.

It might have been thought that Nelson could now have left Ferdinand IV to recover the part of his dominions which was still in rebellion. It is surprising that Nelson bothered to help and even more surprising that he could still maintain his regard for Ferdinand who had demonstrated himself incapable of leadership. Ferdinand, orally, gave Nelson complete authority to act in his name, over-riding Ruffo, his Vicar-General, whom he was beginning to distrust, and superior to that possessed by any of his own naval or military officers. In addition he gave Nelson a warrant to arrest Ruffo if necessary. Thus armed Nelson set sail for the Bay of Naples where there were pockets of resistance on land and a naval force under the command of Commodore Carraciolo, who had returned from Sicily to Naples to see to his estates, and had then gone over to the republicans.

Nelson's fleet of eighteen ships of the line, flanked by bomb and mortar vessels, arrived in the Bay on June 24 bringing home to the republicans, holding out in the forts of Uovo and Nuovo at the mouth of the harbour, that their cause was lost. They had been hoping for a French fleet to appear and the sight of the Red Ensign at the mizzen of the *Foudroyant* signalised the end of their expectations; it was said that they tore their handkerchiefs with their teeth in rage and disappointment. *Seahorse*, under the command of Captain Foote, was already there but she, very much to Nelson's surprise, was flying a white flag, indicating a truce, the same colour being repeated on the flagstaffs of the two forts. Prompt enquiries revealed that hostilities had been suspended and that Cardinal Ruffo was negotiating with the rebels for the evacuation of the forts, while Captain Foote, in agreement with him, waited upon events. Nelson's reaction was simple and immediate, his authority superseded that of Ruffo and the arrival of his ships, in overwhelming force, put an end to the truce. His message to the rebels was accordingly short and not to be misunderstood:

> Rear Admiral Lord Nelson, K.B., Commander of His Brittanic Majesty's Fleet in the Bay of Naples, acquaints the Rebellious Subjects of His Sicilian Majesty in the Castles of Uovo and Nuovo, that he will not permit them to embark or quit those places. They must surrender themselves to His Majesty's royal mercy. Nelson.

Cardinal Ruffo, however, refused to have Nelson's letter delivered to the forts and came on board *Foudroyant* to argue his point of view, with Sir William Hamilton interpreting. Both men were adamant and angry, and Hamilton had the task of peacemaker as well as translator. The events which followed this confrontation have been a matter of controversy ever since. Southey regarded them as a stain on Nelson's character and memory; Charles James Fox, though never mentioning Nelson by name, spoke in the House of Commons condemning British assistance to a cruel and corrupt régime. Almost every biographer of Nelson has been forced to condemn or excuse and it is interesting therefore to follow the events as recorded in *Foudroyant*'s log, remembering that nautical time ran from noon to noon, so that incidents after noon on, say, June 11 are recorded as taking place on June 12:

> Tuesday 25th: at 4 Naples Town. N.E. 3 or 4 leagues. Answered a salute from the shore, of 13 guns, At 9, anchored abreast of Naples. a.m. at daylight, weighed and stood further in. Moored ship. Fleet

moored in a line S.S.E. and N.N.W., consisting of 18 Sail of the Line, 1 Frigate and 2 Fireships.

Wednesday 26th. Saluted a Cardinal who came on board with 13 Guns. a.m. employed occasionally.

Thursday 27th. At 4p.m. landed 500 Marines from different Ships. Captain Troubridge went on shore to take command. Arrived, a King's Messenger from England.

Friday 28th. A.M. A Boat, manned and armed from each Ship, went into the Mole, and attended some Vessels coming out, having Prisoners on board.

Saturday 29th: Several of the principal Officers of the Rebels were put in confinement in different Ships. A.M. at 9, a Court Martial assembled on board, to try for rebellion Cavaliere Francisco Caracciolo.

Sunday 30th. At 5p.m. landed the remainder of the Marines from each Ship. The sentence of the Court Martial of yesterday was put in execution, on board a Neapolitan Frigate on Cavaliere Francisco Caracciolo, and he was hanged accordingly. A.M. Mustered Ship's company to quarters.

Monday 1st July. A.M. Several of the Rebel party were brought on board. Saw several shot and shell fired at and from Castle St Elmo.

On Sunday July 7th John Jolly, Marine, was court martialled and sentenced to death but sent on shore the next day as a prisoner.

Thursday 11th. At 4p.m. his Sicilian Majesty and suite came on board the Ship [from *Seahorse*]. Each Ship in the Fleet saluted with 21 guns. A.M. Sailed *Seahorse* and *Thalia*.

Friday 12th. The French hoisted a Flag of Truce on the Castle of St Elmo. At 9a.m. the Neapolitan Colours were hoisted at the Castle of St Elmo; each Ship saluted with 21 guns. Sent a Launch to assist to embark the French prisoners. At Meridian, Captain Troubridge brought on board the keys of the Castle St Elmo, also the French colours, which were delivered to his Sicilian Majesty.

The two accusations which have dogged Nelson's memory are that first, he broke Ruffo's, and Foote's, truce with the rebels and deceived them into giving up their forts so that they surrendered not to freedom, as they expected, but to imprisonment or death, and secondly that he connived at the improper execution of Commodore Caracciolo. After Nelson's death Captain Foote published a *Vindication* of his own conduct but much of the comment upon these incidents, both by British and

Italian writers, has been inspired, not unnaturally, by disapproval of the
Neapolitan Bourbons. Some, of course, has been simply untrue, alleging
that Lady Hamilton and the Queen were gloating witnesses of
Caracciolo's hanging, while one 'explanation' of Nelson's conduct has it
that he was jealous of Caracciolo's superiority as a sailor. General
Macdonald, safely away in the north, regretted that he had persuaded
Caracciolo to take the republican side, and criticised Nelson's severity,
though he had a short way with rebels himself.

Nelson's view of the truce was that it should not have been entered
into, he called it 'infamous', although it is easy to see why Ruffo, the
Russian and Turkish commanders, and Captain Foote, had come to some
agreement with the French and the rebel Neapolitans. They did not
know that Nelson would turn up and they feared the arrival of Bruix.
Therefore some arrangement was preferable to a long drawn-out siege.
The terms agreed were that the rebels should surrender the forts and in
exchange, along with the French garrison at St Elmo, would be carried
to Toulon in Sicilian ships. Foote was obviously a bit doubtful about
this as he entered a caveat to his signature saying that in signing he could
not commit himself to anything which prejudiced the interests of his
own sovereign George III. Rumours of the truce had reached Ferdinand
IV in Palermo who predictably disapproved of this lenient treatment of
traitors as did Nelson who took the view that any agreement entered
into by Ruffo was outside his power, and any temporary armistice
was brought to an end by his own arrival, with superior powers and
force. Ruffo was adamant that his honour was involved and said that he
would not assist Nelson with either arms or men in a course which he
regarded as a breach of faith. Nelson confessed that an admiral was no
match for a cardinal in argument, but persisted in his determination that
either the rebels surrendered unconditionally or else the fight went on.

A great deal hinges on how far the arrangement for the surrender had
gone, in fact the transports for the rebels had not yet arrived, although
Sir William Hamilton, elderly, confused and tired, was later to persuade
himself that they had. As the surrender was to take place when they did
Nelson took the view that as that had not happened everything reverted
to the original position, the temporary armistice was at an end.

Cardinal Ruffo must have realised that a cardinal was no match for a
determined admiral with eighteen sail of the line who was prepared to
bombard any number of rebellious forts. Nelson gave Ruffo his written
'opinion', because it was easier than oral argument, and demanded the

surrender of the rebels on his terms. In so doing he became the whole-hearted champion of legitimacy. even his own powers in his view not being sufficient to grant any variations in the terms of surrender. That could only be done by Ferdinand IV. As he wrote to Keith, 'Under this opinion the Rebels came out of the Castles' and as he put it brutally to his old friend Davison, 'as they ought, and I hope all those who are false to their King and Country will, to be hanged, or otherwise disposed of as their sovereign thought proper.'

The rebels were accommodated in transports, guarded by the guns of the fleet. They had surrendered, in Nelson's phrase, 'to His Majesty's royal mercy', and as that was not a quality much exercised, they languished in appalling Neapolitan prisons and most of them later died on the gallows.

In Nelson's own ship, just before sailing into the Bay of Naples, two seamen had received sentences of fifty and 250 lashes for looting the quarters of one of Ruffo's officers. Marine Jolly's offence had been to strike an officer, but his death sentence was not carried out because he managed to get Lady Hamilton to intercede on his behalf. Troubridge talked happily of hanging rebels and reported to Nelson that to demonstrate his loyalty some 'jolly fellow', a Neapolitan, had sent him the severed head of another Neapolitan, less loyal.

The Neapolitans, and the Neapolitan Bourbons, were cruel and vindictive, but these attributes were mitigated by their incompetence and corruption. Nelson was uncompromising but not cruel, although unfortunately on the question of loyalty to the Crown of the Two Sicilies he had closed his mind like the gun port on one of his own battleships. He wrote, unsuccessfully, to Ferdinand IV pleading for the life of one elderly republican who seemed to have done little active in the way of rebellion, but to Acton he wrote, 'degrade this HOG', of a cowardly Neapolitan military officer who in fact escaped all punishment. Nelson never seemed to realise with what material he was dealing, 'I cannot bear such gracious monarchs should be so ill served', he wrote to Acton without realising that in treachery, deceit and cowardice sovereign and subject in the Two Sicilies were very well-matched. 'Il Re Lazzaroni' was not 'Farmer' George, Neapolitans were not Englishmen unless one includes Englishmen in Ireland, as Maria Carolina realised when she wrote to Emma at the time of the surrender of Uovo and Nuovo, 'I recommend Lord Nelson to treat Naples as if it were an Irish town in rebellion similarly placed'. This Nelson did, issuing a proclamation to rebels who had occupied offices under the Republic, giving them twenty-four hours to surrender unconditionally and those outside the city were given a further day.

Given these general conditions it is perhaps a little surprising that the case of Caracciolo has attracted so much attention, and it is perhaps only because Nelson was directly concerned. The Prince had been in one of the forts in command of the Republic's fleet until shortly before Nelson's arrival. He fled inland, but was captured and brought on board *Foudroyant* where Hardy, recognising him, had him treated in a manner more becoming to his rank and former position. There was little doubt of the offences he had committed, for as a naval officer he had entered into rebellion, ships under his command had fired on both *Seahorse* and the Sicilian frigate *Minerva* which had suffered two men killed and four wounded. Nelson accordingly issued the warrant for his court martial, the court to consist of seven Neapolitan officers presided over by Commodore Count Thürn.

The court sat on board *Foudroyant* and no proper record of proceedings has survived. What evidence there was for the prosecution, or how it was produced, is not known, but that is hardly important as Caracciolo, who defended himself, admitted the offence, but pleaded that he had been coerced.

The trial lasted two hours and at the end the prisoner was found guilty, five officers voting for the death penalty, by hanging, two against. The trial was 'open', and British officers wandered in to hear the proceedings, commenting on Caracciolo's distinguished appearance although one also recorded that he was 'about seventy', in fact only forty-seven. The condemned man asked for some more dignified form of execution, more becoming to a nobleman, and Sir William Hamilton and Count Thürn asked Nelson for twenty-four hours grace for the prisoner. Both requests were refused and Caracciolo was duly hanged at the fore-yard arm of *Minerve* at 5 o'clock that afternoon. Queen Maria Carolina called it 'the sad and merited end of the unfortunate and mad-brained Caracciolo'.

Nelson was the supreme authority in convening the court martial, in confirming its findings, and ordering the execution. Criticism must be on the grounds of unseemly haste for, as Mahan put it, 'It was not decent, for it was not necessary, that capture should be followed so rapidly by trial, and condemnation by execution'. There were no pressing circumstances, the rebellion was over and there was no need for an example to quell further violence and insurrection. Both the judges of the court martial and Nelson, with authority to review or confirm, could have been allowed time to consider.

Ultimately, Nelson forgot that he was not the agent of the avenging Bourbons but a flag officer, and a famous one at that, in the Royal Navy of King George III. Later in November he wrote to Acton:

> Could it ever happen that any English minister wanted to make me an instrument of hurting the feelings of His Sicilian Majesty, I would give up my commission sooner than do it—I am placed in such a situation—a subject of one King by birth, and as far as is consistent with my allegiance to that King, a voluntary subject of His Sicilian Majesty—that if any man attempted to separate my two Kings, by all that is sacred, I should consider even putting that man to death as a meritorious act.

Accepting that Naples brought out the worst in Nelson and that in letters to Russians, Turks, Portuguese as well as Sicilians, he tended to flatter outrageously for his own ends, this still ranks as the most absurd letter he ever wrote. One can only wonder at the submersion of the proud, patriotic, insular Englishman, and regret that Nelson, a parson's son, had not recalled the Biblical adage about the inability of one man to serve two masters.

The arrival of Ferdinand IV in the Bay of Naples—with due regard for his own safety he remained on board *Foudroyant*—finally put responsibility where it properly belonged, on the shoulders of the supreme power in the State. Perhaps something of the atmosphere can be gauged by a macabre aftermath of Caracciolo's execution. After his death the Commodore's body was cut down and, weighted with shot, sunk in the sea. Some time later the corpse came bobbing to the surface of the bay and drifted towards *Foudroyant*, its head above the water. Before the body was secured by Nelson's orders and taken ashore for burial, Sir William Hamilton suggested to Ferdinand, to quieten his superstitious fears, that doubtless the corpse had come to seek his forgiveness.

It was now time on shore for the royalists to take their revenge on the republicans and soon the *lazzaroni* were being entertained by the popular spectacle of daily executions of rebels, men and women, before the Convent of Santa Maria del Carmine. Some of the hundreds of victims may have been guilty of active rebellion, but many were mere emotional or intellectual sympathisers with the ideals of freedom and republicanism.

Their deaths were by hanging and less dignified than Caracciolo's; the crowd jeered and laughed, the executioners and their assistants, some of whom were dwarfs, clowned as their victims strangled slowly.

Thus Ferdinand IV came back to his kingdom under the protection of the British fleet although unfortunately for Nelson's reputation he did not attempt to use his influence with his adopted monarch to prevent the excesses and abominations being practised on shore, which were eventually to scandalise Europe. In answer to a correspondent, Mr Alexander Stephens, a historian who wrote to him in 1803 enquiring of events in 1799, Nelson replied, 'I can assure you that nearly all relative to Naples is destitute of foundation or falsely represented'. There may have been some truth in that, but it was by no means a complete excuse or explanation. Nelson had exactly twelve months more of service in and around the Two Sicilies, but the year only continued to demonstrate the melancholy truth that he should have taken the opportunity, which was still open, of flinging off what the recent editor of his letters to his wife rightly calls his 'Neapolitan chains'.

King Ferdinand, though welcomed back by a vociferous populace, many of whom Nelson was shrewd enough to realise might well have been republicans a few weeks previously, showed a curious reluctance to set foot on his own territory. The Queen confided in Lady Hamilton that her husband regarded his Neapolitan subjects as 'Hottentots', and so majesty kept state and did business on board *Foudroyant*. Ferdinand had once said 'ma femme sait tout' but now he embarked on an independent line of his own, at least so far as the suppression of republicanism was concerned. 'Revenge is a dish preferably eaten cold' says an old Sicilian proverb, and Ferdinand was savouring the flavour. More and more his wife was looking to her Imperial relations in Vienna for advice and guidance.

Nelson, complaining, but bound by duty as he saw it, regard for the Queen, affection for Sir William and love for Lady Hamilton, and a stubbornness which increased with criticism, stayed put; a central star in this minor tawdry galaxy. August brought a celebration of the anniversary of the Nile, but by then events in the outside world were beginning to obtrude.

The war of the Second Coalition against France was escalating. The incursion into the Mediterranean had been only one aspect of it, the Archduke Charles had defeated a French army commanded by Moreau at Stockach in March, and in June Maria Carolina's relative had driven

Masséna, perhaps the cleverest of future Napoleonic marshals, back into Zurich where reports said the besieged were starving. The British had not been inactive at sea and soon were to become more active on land, and though St Vincent and Keith had not met up with Bruix, at the other end of the Mediterranean the laurels had gone to Nelson's bête noire Sidney Smith. In February the impatient Bonaparte had captured El Arish and invaded Palestine, and far from waiting for the Sultan of Turkey to bestir himself, as Nelson had hoped he would, had gone on to capture Jaffa, massacring 2,500 Turks of the garrison who had surrendered. By March 17 he had reached Mount Carmel and to the north, across the bay, was the old Crusader fortress of Acre held by Ahmed Pasha Jezzar, the Governor of Syria. It was under its walls that Bonaparte, who had recently learned that in Paris Joséphine was being unfaithful to him, had another disappointment.

Sidney Smith, from his flagship *Tigre*, took charge of the defences, helped by an emigré French artillery colonel, Louis-Edmond de Phélipaux. Smith's task was made easier by capturing the transports carrying Bonaparte's siege artillery and by an outbreak of bubonic plague among the besiegers, but nevertheless his conduct was exemplary during the following two months while his vastly out-numbered force of Turkish soldiers and British soldiers and marines held the French army at bay. Nelson might not like the Swedish Knight, particularly in his guise of diplomat at large, but he was generous enough to congratulate him in due course on this purely military exploit.

Bonaparte, having prepared a totally false explanation for the Directory at home, broke the siege of Acre on May 20 and began his retreat across the Sinai back to Cairo which was reached by a decimated and demoralised army on June 14. Bonaparte was almost immediately involved in repelling a Turkish force which, escorted Smith's warships, had landed in Aboukir Bay. It was after this battle, a complete victory for the French, that Sidney Smith, overdoing the courtesies of war, probably changed the course of history. French prisoners were returned and with them a supply of newspapers, the first information Bonaparte had of Austrian and Russian successes in Europe and the consequentially parlous state of France under the Directory. Here was an excuse to abandon the Army of the Orient which had now twice been worsted by the British Navy. Bonaparte, with only a few chosen friends, nearly all of whom were future Imperial Marshals, began to lay his plan. He left Alexandria on August 22 with Admiral Ganteaume on board the frigate

Muiron, and landed at St Raphael on October 9. His view was that in France 'the pear was ripe'.

Nelson's natural enthusiasm for Sidney Smith's victory, expressed in a letter to Troubridge, 'Adieu Mr Bonaparte', was unfortunately premature. Smith, however, was still with him and was subsequently to cause more friction by entering into a truce, which allowed surrendered French prisoners in Egypt to return home to fight another day.

Meanwhile, St Vincent, on grounds of ill-health, had gone on shore and applied to the Admiralty to come home. Nelson, on hearing the rumour, wrote an impassioned, flattering letter to his chief:

> If, my dear lord, I have any weight in your friendship let me entreat you to rouse the sleeping lion.

However, the lion was elderly as well as ailing, and by July Lord Keith had formally taken over as Commander-in-Chief. It was from him therefore that Nelson received an order on July 13 to send as many of his ships as possible to Port Mahon as he feared a French attempt to reconquer Minorca. Nelson did not obey. He had two reasons, that a large part of his ships' companies were on shore and that he did not think a French attack likely. Both reasons were unacceptable, his sailors on shore were inland engaged against Neapolitan rebels, not their primary duty, and Nelson had no means of judging Keith's need. Nelson wrote a frank letter to Lord Spencer, but its contents were not relevant to a refusal to obey, 'sensible of my loyal intentions, I am prepred for any fate which may await my disobedience'. He promised to send, 'eight or more ships when the French and the republicans had been overcome'.

In fact there was no danger to Minorca, but that is not the point, and one wonders what would have been Nelson's reaction if any of his subordinates had refused to obey an order of his and then written to the First Lord of the Admiralty explaining why. Spencer, though well disposed to Nelson, was not convinced, and Keith's order was reinforced; Admiral Duckworth with three line of battle and a corvette were dispatched. These were too few for Keith's purpose and by then the French fleet had escaped into the Atlantic. If Minorca had been attacked and lost it is hard to see how Nelson could have escaped court-martialling. To the Duke of Clarence he wrote another explanation, making out his private distinction between 'great orders' and 'little ones' but this is obviously nonsense in a disciplined service.

Nelson had chosen to support the interests of his friends in Naples as against a clear order from his Commander-in-Chief. It should therefore have been no surprise to him that he was building up criticism and gossip about himself. As a consolation, he learnt on August 13 that he had been created a duke of Brontë in Sicily. The Sultan had already added to his previous gifts by making him a member of a newly-instituted order which could be awarded to Christians, the Order of the Crescent, accompanied by a handsome star which with the Star of the Bath, and the gold medals for St Vincent and the Nile, looked well on his gold-braided admiral's uniform. Although reluctant to accept the honour he was finally persuaded by Maria Carolina, and thus became lord of a domain said to yield £3000 a year. Typically of Sicily, this figure was quite false, and typically of Nelson, he immediately pledged the first £500 of the unrealised revenue as a gift to his old father.

The Dukedom of Brontë was a poverty-stricken piece of rough country with a few peasant holdings, and some dilapidated dwellings. It was not even, as represented, Crown property but really belonged to the Church from whom it had been stolen by the Bourbons a century before. Nelson appointed one of Sir William's dependants, Graeffer by name, a landscape gardener, as his agent to re-organise his estate on progressive British lines. Perhaps Graeffer made a profit, certainly Nelson never did. The only unalloyed pleasure he derived from his dukedom was that of deciding whether 'Brontë Nelson', 'Brontë Nelson of the Nile' or the final and more restrained 'Nelson and Brontë' was the most agreeable form for his new signature. 'Brontë' was, in the view of the Sicilian Court, an appropriate name as it meant thunder, suitable for an admiral who with the threat of broadsides had restored the monarchy.

Nelson described the celebrations to Fanny in a longer letter than usual: 'The King dined with me; and when His Majesty drank my health, a Royal Salute of 21 guns was fired from all his Sicilian Majesty's Ships of War, and from all the Castles. In the evening there was a general illumination. Amongst other representations, a large Vessel was fitted out like a Roman galley, on its oars were fixed lamps, and in the centre was erected a nostral column with my name; at the stern were elevated two angels supporting my picture. In short, my dear Fanny, the beauty of the whole is beyond my powers of description. More than 2000 variegated lamps were suspended round the Vessel. An orchestra was fitted up, and filled with the very best musicians and singers. The piece of music was in a great measure to celebrate my praise, describing their previous distress. *But Nelson came, the invincible Nelson, and they were preserved and again made happy.* This must not make you think me vain; no far, very far from it. I relate it more from gratitude than vanity. I return to Palermo with the King. May God bless you all. Pray say, what is true, that I really steal time to write this letter, and my hand is ready to drop.'

At another event, organised this time by Maria Carolina, on September 3, there were fireworks, a Temple of Fame, waxworks of Nelson, Sir William and Emma, and bands playing 'See the conquering hero comes'. It was of course much enjoyed by the 'tria juncta in uno', Emma's collective for the subjects of the waxworks, the reference being to the motto of the Order of the Bath worn by two of them. All the officers of the fleet were invited and as were all the midshipmen, who in their number one dress coats, enjoyed it too. Towards the end of these festivities 'the young gentlemen', perhaps not so abstemious as their admiral, decided on a bit of amusement and drew their ceremonial dirks and charged Ferdinand's Footguards. A shaken guardsman shot one of them through the leg, but happily the wound was not serious. Nelson cancelled their shore-leave for six months.

CHAPTER TWENTY-THREE

Mediterranean Activity

ON AUGUST 20, 1799 Evan Nepean, the Secretary to the Admiralty Board, wrote to Nelson:

My Lord,
I am commanded by my Lords Commissioners of the Admiralty to inform your Lordship that, from the circumstances of Lord St Vincent's having returned to England for the recovery of his health, and Lord Keith, with other flag officers, having quitted the Mediterranean in pursuit of the combined fleets of the enemy, which are arrived at Brest, your Lordship is become senior officer of His Majesty's ships in the Mediterranean; and that, till the return of Lord Keith, or some other superior officer, you will have all the important duties of that station to attend to.

Keith was commanded by the Admiralty to resume his command on November 30, and this news Nelson received on January 6, 1800. Nelson, therefore, held the position of Commander-in-Chief for nearly six months but without, as he complained, the actual dignity, or any of the perquisites, and none of the extra resources attached to the post. This was not just hurt pride, for one of the most sorely missed attributes of supreme command, especially to a one-armed, one-eyed admiral, was a secretary with perhaps a few assistant scribes. Even in those days the paper work of command was considerable, especially remembering that save by word of mouth and visual signals there was no other method of communication. Those letters therefore which had to emanate from 'the senior officer of His Majesty's ships' had to be written and signed by that officer who described himself to Commissioner Singlefield at Gibraltar as 'a worn out, blind, left-handed man'. Eventually Nelson did have the services of a Mr Tyson who sometimes initiated letters himself, but who was mainly employed taking copies, by hand, of Nelson's communications for the official Letter Book.

Nelson put some of his grievances to the Admiralty in November 1799, stung by a rebuke that he had permitted a convoy to return home without dispatches. On the 26th of that month he wrote, 'As a junior Flag Officer, of course, without those about me, as secretaries, interpreters etcetera, I have been thrown into a more extensive correspondence than ever, perhaps, fell to the lot of any Admiral, and into a political situation, I own, out of my sphere'. This was certainly not the boastful self-confident Nelson, nor the obverse, a man tired of life and plagued by physical ailments, but simply an over-worked man making a reasonable statement of his actual condition. To put his complaint into perspective it is instructive to look at what, in terms of ships and the distances involved, Nelson did command on September 21, 1799, the date he sent his 'Disposition of the Squadron' to the Admiralty.

There were on the coast of Egypt, described as in 'bad state', two 74s, *Tigre* and *Theseus* and the 18, *Cameleon*. Blockading Malta under Alexander Ball's command were two 74s, *Alexander* and *Audacious* and a 64, *Lion*, all in 'very bad state'; with them were two frigates and two bomb vessels.

'Off Civita Vecchia, and if they do not succeed to return to Palermo' were two 74's, *Culloden* and *Minotaur*, under the command of Troubridge, now a commodore. There were at Port Mahon, Minorca, two 74's, *Bellerophon* and *Northumberland*, two frigates in poor condition, and a couple of smaller vessels. There were also three frigates either off Genoa or on convoy escort and the *Santa Dorotea*, at the time of Nelson's report described as 'not known, very bad'. At Gibraltar and off Cadiz there were seven 74's, four frigates and some small craft with Rear-Admiral Duckworth as the senior officer. 'Off Malta, blockading that island—all very bad state' was the Portuguese squadron of a 92, two 74's, a 64 and two minor vessels. Nelson's flagship, *Foudroyant*, was 'Gone to Sardinia to convey his Sardinian Majesty and family to Leghorn, or some part of the Continent'. The disposition ended, 'Any other ships on the station not known'.

It was with these ships and their captains, officers and men that Nelson had to perform the duties which Nepean had set out in the remainder of his letter of August 20. Among these were 'the speedy reduction of the town of Malta' meaning Valetta, 'the protection of the island of Minorca', and 'the watching and blockade of Cadiz'. It was hoped that soon it would be possible 'to call the ships away from Egypt', in which respect the Admiralty was over-optimistic, but a permanent duty throughout the Mediterranean was to be 'attentive to the trade of His Majesty's subjects and that of his allies'. Significantly there was no specific reference to operations on land or sea in connection with the Kingdom of the Two Sicilies, but Nelson was adjured 'on all occasions, to cultivate, to the utmost of your power, the most perfect harmony and good understanding with all his Majesty's allies: co-operating cordially with, and assisting, as far as circumstances will admit, their fleets and armies, and protecting their subjects'.

This was obviously a terrific task and so far as allies were concerned those of George III were both various and curious. There were the Turks, for whom Nelson had an affection, yet it needed his presence on their flagship at Naples to defuse an internal mutiny, sparked off by a murderous brawl with Neapolitan sailors aided by the local populace. Then there were the Russians who apparently had no more intention of being at sea during winter in the unfrozen Mediterranean than at home in the frozen Baltic. Nelson's most reliable friends at sea were the Portuguese, although the Marquis de Niza needed constant letters of advice, encouragement and downright flattery to keep him active and obedient.

On land in the north of Italy there were Austrians and Russians, and further south the native princes and their peoples, and finally Nelson's friends in Naples. The actions of Habsburg and Romanoff generals however were dictated by a remote, unresponsive Imperial bureaucracy in Vienna, and an even more remote, and mentally unstable, Imperial autocrat in St Petersburg, over whom Nelson could exercise no sort of influence. It is therefore understandable that he continued to concentrate upon those allies he could have some hope of controlling.

The period when Nelson was in command in the Mediterranean in Keith's absence was not active in any major sense, although Nelson was kept busy. The siege of the fortress of Valetta dragged on and Ball, now referred to as 'Governor' or 'Chief of the Maltese', having taken on the status of an uncrowned king, and Troubridge, who was the link-man between Malta and Sicily, both complained bitterly of the indifference of Ferdinand and his court to what was also part of his kingdom. The main problem was food, but despite many requests, none was sent from Sicily to the starving Maltese. Eventually Troubridge, always impetuous, seized Sicilian grain ships by force, and thus remedied the deficiency. He noted scathingly at the time the reaction of the Sicilian Government to this piece of high-handedness. It was again indifference.

Troubridge had his problems no less than Nelson, and though the latter was in a position which, according to Sir Nicholas Harris Nicolas, the editor of his Letters and Dispatches, 'mortified his feelings' the Commodore was a tougher, more robust, character than his admiral. Weighed down with problems, many of them petty, Nelson tended to become depressed and physically ill, while Troubridge was inclined to lose his temper and seek relief in violent action.

It was he who at the end of 1799 became, rather to his surprise, the instrument of fulfilling an unlikely prophecy. An Irish priest in Naples had predicted that Nelson with his ships would take Rome. Troubridge found that the French commander in 'the Roman states' in negotiation with a British commodore, operating a small force of seamen and marines on shore, was in fact prepared to surrender the whole city. Once again Neapolitans, also under Troubridge's command, entered Rome, and British boats' crews appeared rowing on the Tiber. Troubridge's pleasure expressed in a letter to his wife, reflecting on the decline of the former Imperial City taken with such ease, was moderated when he heard from Nelson that Ferdinand IV was sending General Noselli as the Sicilian governor, his old acquaintance of Leghorn days. Nelson's view of that unco-operative and indecisive individual was the same as his own, 'The Court had nobody better—you may think they can have nobody worse'.

Nelson became more and more impatient with the slow progress of the siege of Valetta. General Sir James St Clair Erskine, yet another Scot, became a target for sarcasm. Nelson's original requirement was for 1200 soldiers, either for Malta or the Roman States, but Troubridge had shown what a man of determination could do there, so it was for Malta that the admiral finally wanted redcoats. Unfortunately Erskine, who commanded all British soldiers in the Mediterranean from Port Mahon on Minorca, 'enters upon the difficulty of the undertaking in a true soldier way' and his subordinate and compatriot, Brigadier-General Graham, at Messina, was no more helpful. Erskine, not unreasonably, was resentful of Nelson's attempts to persuade Graham to do something which he had no power to do. Finally, with the replacement of Erskine by Major-General Fox, Lord Holland's fourth son, Nelson got his way and on December 10 British infantry joined the Maltese irregulars and his own sailors, laying siege to General Vaubois's stubborn garrison.

Elsewhere Britain and her allies of the Second Coalition, in a year which had opened promisingly, were not being noticeably successful.

In September the Duke of York, George III's second son, had taken an army to Holland, but a few days after it had landed the Austrians and Russians were defeated by the French at Bergen ap Zoom. In the latter part of September General Masséna, holed-up near Zurich, sprang on an over-stretched Russian army under Korsakov and defeated it; the main Russian army under Suvorov tried to come to the rescue, but too late, and was in its turn forced to retreat over the Alps. The Archduke Charles began to fall back towards the Danube.

The Tsar Paul who only cared for one section of his subjects, his soldiers, was affected by their sufferings in retreat and put the blame on the Austrians and began to show signs of disillusionment with the whole alliance. The Duke of York's invasion attempt came to an inglorious end on October 18, his army surrendered and British troops left the Continent. Russia had left the Coalition by October 22 and as Nelson observed, 'the Marshal [Suvorov] was on his way to Poland'. Much the most significant event, however, happened in France itself. When Bonaparte returned to France he found Paris in civil disorder and seizing his opportunity, the 'Brumaire' coup d'état overthrew the Directory, on November 9, and the 'Constitution of Year VIII' established the Consulate with Napoleon Bonaparte as First Consul for a period of ten years from December 24. Bonaparte was now, in fact if not quite in name, the ruler of France.

The dilemma this posed for Britain and Austria, the two remaining active members of the Coalition, was acute. Nelson had shown that the French could be beaten at sea, but on land the story was very different. The First Consul, assisted by his new foreign minister, Talleyrand, put out peace feelers. France within its 'natural frontiers', would have been acceptable to the two allies, but Bonaparte wanted the conquests of the Revolution with no compensating advantages to the other powers. Britain and Austria rejected such terms and the war continued into the new century.

Nelson had only a few months of the new year in the Mediterranean and he was again under the command of Lord Keith. This time, however, whether by accident or design, it is almost impossible to tell, Keith exercised a more direct control over an officer he regarded as a difficult subordinate. On Nelson's personal affairs he had already expressed a view. To his sister he had written, 'the Queen, Lady Hamilton and General Acton and Lord N—n cutting the most absurd figure possible for folly and vanity'. Perhaps, because of that view, he never gave sufficient credit to Nelson's real difficulties, which had to be dealt with, or smoothed over, by an admiral trying to keep together a mixed crew of allies. At no stage in his own command did he have to deal with such a situation. Nelson, talking of his allies putting to sea in poor weather said, 'the Russians will not, and the Turks cannot' but at the same time he had to write to the Sultan, with a letter to Spencer Smith explaining why he was doing so, saying that 'Cadir Bey is with me every day, and a better man does not live in the world, or a better officer: he is my brother'. Such problems did not come Keith's way and he resumed his command with a brisk approach to his junior who was ordered to sail in *Foudroyant* and join the main fleet in the Leghorn Roads, Nelson's eventual task being the continuation of the blockade and siege of Malta. But, for his last months in the Mediterranean, Nelson could not stay still on one station. Keith, twelve years older, was more active in actual opposition to the French detachments still at large and his flag flew in his flagship at sea, while Nelson's tended too often to be transferred to a lowly transport in harbour at either Naples or Palermo.

In January Nelson was hoist with his own petard, disobedience to a superior officer. The junior was not surprisingly again Sir Sidney Smith. Ever since the Battle of the Nile, the problem of the French army in Egypt had been a headache for two allies, the British and the Turks. Though their viewpoint differed, Britain did not want a considerable body of French veterans released into Europe, Turkey simply wanted them off her own territory. The result of the difference was a muddle. Nelson was adamant that not a single French soldier should be released by any sort of agreement, armistice or truce. Britain's diplomatic representatives in Constantinople, including Spencer, Sir Sidney's brother, were obliged to show more sympathy with the opinion of the Turks. As far back as March 18, 1799 Nelson had given a positive order to Sidney Smith which embodied his hope, expressed later, 'I wish them to *perish* in Egypt.' The Earl of Elgin who became ambassador in Constantinople, Spencer Smith reverting to Secretary, endeavoured to play an innocently double game.

The result came on January 24, 1800 when the Convention of El Arish was signed on board Smith's flagship, *Tigre*. The signatories, as Smith was quick to point out, were only Turks and Frenchmen, one of whom was that M. Poussielgue, who had witnessed the battle of the Nile. Nelson, nevertheless, took the view that Smith had a responsibility for the terms, by which 16,000 French soldiers were allowed to return to

France. The existing confusion was further compounded by the fact that Elgin thought that Nelson was still in command in the Mediterranean and so wrote to him instead of to Keith. When the matter finally came to Keith's attention he also disapproved, as did the Government in London, but by then the damage had been done. Nelson felt that Smith had disobeyed him and he wrote to Elgin expressing disapproval of 'permitting a vanquished army to be placed by one Ally in a position to attack another Ally'.

Whatever Smith's degree of culpability, his excuse was as good, or as bad, as Nelson's own in flatly disobeying Keith in the previous year: 'It is better to save the Kingdom of Naples and risk Minorca than to risk the Kingdom of Naples to save Minorca'. Yet it is not for subordinate officers to maintain localised opinion against their superior's wider view, although it is doubtful if it occurred to Nelson that what applied to Captain Sir Sidney Smith should also apply to Rear-Admiral Lord Nelson of the Nile, Duke of Brontë.

It was a sad commentary on Nelson's condition that it was during Keith's period of resumed command, and increased activity, that the balance of profit and loss remaining from the battle of the Nile was finally adjusted in Britain's favour. *Leander*, lost to *Genereux* after the battle, had been finally recovered, not without difficulty and delay, from the Russians who had captured her at the surrender of Corfu. Now it was the turn of *Genereux* herself, and *Guillaume Tell*, the only ships of the line which had escaped from Aboukir Bay. The fleet, with Nelson in *Foudroyant* as second-in-command, had just sailed from Leghorn to Palermo where, after what the Commander-in-Chief called 'nine long days', it was quite obvious to both parties that the Neapolitan Royal Family and Admiral Lord Keith would fray each other's nerves for ever. It was with relief that Keith set sail for Malta and off Cape Passaro *Foudroyant* with *Northumberland*, *Audacious* and *Success* had the good luck to sight a small French squadron under Rear-Admiral Perrée flying his flag in *Genereux*. Because of a heavy sea and intermittent fog the progress of the British fleet had been slow and it was *Success*, a mere frigate, which first joined battle, swiftly followed by *Northumberland*.

The ubiquitous Midshipman Parsons on board *Foudroyant* has left a lively record of Nelson's impatience, 'working his fin', agitating the stump of his right arm, when he realised he was about to come to grips again with his old opponent. Sir Edward Berry, the flag captain, was overwhelmed with superfluous orders to 'make the *Foudroyant* fly'.

But Nelson in action was still Nelson, and Parsons was lucky to observe a typical incident, involving another midshipman, as the French flagship replied to *Foudroyant*'s first broadside. 'As a shot passed through the mizzen stay sail, Lord Nelson, patting one of the youngsters on the head, asked him jocularly how he relished the music; and observing something like alarm depicted on his countenance, consoled him with the information that Charles XII ran away from the first shot he heard, though afterwards he was called "The Great" and deservedly, from his bravery.' 'I therefore', said Nelson, 'hope much from you in the future.' It is easy to see why, though senior officers as different as Troubridge and Keith disapproved of Nelson's private life, his vanities and his faults, lieutenants, midshipmen and ordinary sailors cared not a damn.

Fired on both by *Foudroyant* and *Northumberland*, *Genereux*, much damaged, struck her tricoloured ensign. Berry boarded her and brought back the sword of Rear-Admiral Perrée, left dying of wounds on his quarter-deck. Keith in his dispatch wrote appropriately, though hardly glowingly, of Nelson's success, however when his second-in-command told him that he had sworn to strike his flag if he captured *Genereux*, he received that observation with a non-committal silence. Alexander Ball, delighted with his hero's success wrote to Lady Hamilton, 'We may truly call him a heaven-born Admiral, upon whom fortune smiles where-ever he goes. We have been carrying on the blockade of Malta sixteen months, during which time the enemy never attempted to throw in succours until this month. His Lordship arrived here the day they were within a few leagues of the island, captured the principal ships and dispersed the rest, so that not one has reached the port.'

Ball was one of the few senior officers who admired Nelson and liked Lady Hamilton. Keith, if he had read those sentences could only have reflected wryly that Nelson was only in *Foudroyant* and not on shore with the letter's recipient, his flag flying in the transport *Samuel and Jane*, not because of some divine concern, but only in reluctant obedience to the orders of Lord Keith.

Genereux surrendered on February 18, and a month later *Guillaume Tell* was taken, again by *Foudroyant*, but this time in Nelson's absence, Berry having the command, and being greatly assisted by an intrepid frigate specialist, Captain the Hon. Henry Blackwood, commanding *Penelope*. Significantly, on hearing of the capture of the last of Brueys' command, which had been endeavouring to slip past the Malta blockade, Nelson wrote to the captain of *Penelope* a congratulatory letter which had an almost psychic undertone, 'Is there a sympathy which ties men together in the bonds of friendship without having a personal knowledge of each other? If so, I was your friend and acquaintance before I saw you. Your conduct and character in the late glorious occasion stamps your fame beyond the reach of envy . . .'

By the time of *Guillaume Tell*'s capture Keith had sailed eastward, leaving Nelson in charge of the Malta blockade, but with the broad hint to him that Syracuse, Augusta and Messina were all admirably placed as bases for that operation. Nelson nevertheless chose Palermo from where he wrote to Blackwood and where he received Berry's report of *Foudroyant*'s second success. The flag of a Rear-Admiral of the Red still flapped at the mast head of a transport.

The remaining months in southern Italy, from March to July, were very much a decline of Emma's 'tria juncta in uno'. The Royal Family exhibited its worst characteristics to an extent which must have made even Nelson wonder whether that exercise had been worthwhile. He still retained a chivalrous regard for the Queen but the King was now impossible, unpopular, obstinate and cowardly. Maria Carolina was anxious to return to her Imperial relations in Vienna, and Ferdinand afraid to set foot in Naples obviously wanted to see the back of her. Sir John Acton consoled himself at the age of sixty-four by marrying his niece for which ecclesiastical dispensation was necessary as, apart from the problem of consanguity, she was not yet quite fourteen.

Nelson himself would obviously have liked to see the end of the siege of Malta, but the state of his health, real or imagined, deprived him of the determination and the patience. To Minto he had written 'Greenwich Hospital seems a fit retreat for me, after being *evidently* thought unfit to command in the Mediterranean', and one wonders if the responsibility of the overall command would not have pumped adrenalin into his system. Perhaps so, but he now complained of positive ailments rather than his customary headaches and trouble with his eye. He talked of a 'swelling of the heart', and he may have suffered some minor heart attack or temporary collapse. Ball and Troubridge were both worried about his condition and attributed it to overwork.

In Palermo he was constantly in the company of the Hamiltons; the town did not enjoy the healthiest of climates and the habits of Lady Hamilton were tiresomely nocturnal. Many witnesses testify to the undignified picture of an elderly ambassador and a tired admiral dragged in the wake of an ebullient Emma who insisted on being the life and soul of every party. Their days of prominence in the heady and shoddy atmosphere of the Court were definitely numbered. As far back as 1798 Sir William had asked the Foreign Secretary about a possible replacement after more than thirty years abroad, but on the basis that he would receive a substantial pension. The nearest Grenville came to accepting Hamilton's offer was to talk about 'long and faithful service' entitling Sir William to 'His Majesty's favour on your retreat', but when the news reached him in February that the Hon. Arthur Paget, a young son of the Earl of Uxbridge, was on his way to become the new Envoy Extraordinary and Plenipotentiary, the old man was surprised and bitter.

To Nelson he wrote, 'I suppose it is a Cabinet job wishing to provide for Paget and they could do it no other way than by satisfying me. I see it gives much uneasiness at this Court, and poor Emma is in great distress, but let me get hence and settle my affairs and she and the Queen may dispose of my old Carcass as they please.' Hamilton had already received news of one major disappointment, the sinking of *Colossus* in the Scilly Roads, which contained his 'Second Collection' of ancient ceramics and Etruscan pottery, and his hopes of being 'satisfied' by a grateful Government were to prove illusory. The Neapolitan Court was more than uneasy, since the Hamiltons had been regarded as fixtures; the Queen talked of 'the inevitable fatal Paget' assuring him of anything but a warm welcome.

The only benefit Sir William could salvage was 'the extreme satisfaction of returning home with our dearest friend Lord Nelson'. Emma complained to the Queen of the ingratitude of governments and of the iniquities of an, as yet, unknown Paget. Perhaps it was some consolation to her that one government at least had recognised her diplomatic activities though in a rather roundabout way. Nelson had written to the Tsar, in his new capacity as Sovereign of the Order of Jerusalem, the military knights who had surrendered Malta, seeking some recognition for Commodore Troubridge and Lady Hamilton for their services in connection with the island. Paul was graciously pleased to accede, and Nelson received a holograph letter in French, and Troubridge became a Commander of the Order and Lady Hamilton Dame Petite Croix. Later that year Johann Schmidt of Dresden painted a portrait of Emma with the small cross and ribbon resting on her ample bosom and a companion piece of her lover with the blue of his uniform coat scarcely discernible for the gold, silver and enamel of his own collection of stars and medals.

This portrait was Nelson's favourite and it was hung in his cabin, although the Tsar's cross soon became rather inappropriate.

It was Nelson's turn in June to receive a decoration, the clumsily entitled Order of St Ferdinand of Sicily and of Merit. It was created by Ferdinand IV to honour Nelson, the Tsar and Marshal Suvorov, while Troubridge, Hood and Hallowell all became Commanders.

Nelson, the Hamiltons and the Sicilian Royal Family can have been nothing more than a nuisance, in these last few months, to those who were busy preparing for war against the French who had recently arrived in Italy. For a month *Foudroyant* disappeared from Lord Keith's control or knowledge with, on board, Nelson, the Hamiltons and Cornelia Knight, whose mother, the admiral's widow, had died leaving her alone in the world, but not incapable of looking after herself. *Foudroyant* was being used as a pleasure cruiser, taking Nelson to see his estates at Brontë, then to Syracuse and Malta, not returning to duty at Palermo until June 1. Keith was off Genoa blockading the harbour, an Austrian army surrounded the city and inside was General Masséna with an intrepid garrison resisting bombardment, starvation and typhoid while the First Consul was active with other armies somewhere in the Alpine passes. 'It was no time for a Queen to be making visits' Lord Keith complained, and he was right. Mr Paget had arrived at his post and was trying to get down to some work in a confusing situation. By July General Sir Ralph Abercromby had arrived at Leghorn with part of an expeditionary force to deal with the French troops under General Kléber in Egypt. The General's second-in-command was Brigadier-General John Moore who disapproved of Sir William and Lady Hamilton 'attending the Queen of Naples' and Nelson 'attending upon Lady Hamilton'. If Nelson did think of anyone apart from Emma, it was Josiah who was in conflict with nearly all his officers in *Thalia*, including the surgeon who was under arrest and the master who had been told to jump overboard.

It was about two years since Nelson had sailed into the Bay of Naples and since then gossip had had time to find its way back to Britain. Many people had written home to record their impressions for friends or relations. The background political situation was unsavoury, but the centre-piece affair between the Admiral and the Ambassadress was very savoury indeed. The combination was irresistible. All the letters were critical of either Nelson, Lady Hamilton or both. Some were written vindictively and contained inaccuracies or exaggerations, but many were written by friends, who were genuinely concerned by the harmful effect that the liaison was having upon his life and career. Principal among those who were not friends, was Charles Lock, the British Consul-General at Naples and assistant to Sir William, a young man of means with a diplomatic task which hardly overstrained him. The real importance of Mr Lock though was that he was married to Cecilia, daughter of the Duchess of Leinster, and a cousin of Charles James Fox.

Lock did not take to the Hamiltons and liked Lord Nelson even less, and as Mr Lock was short-tempered there were scenes in public, the most extraordinary taking place when the Consul-General accused the Admiral, on his own quarter-deck, of peculation with supplies of meat to the fleet. This provoked an ill-advised but understandable letter from Nelson to the Navy Board which contained a puffed-up silly sentence, 'I defy any insinuation against my honor. Nelson is as far from doing a scandalous or mean action as the Heavens are above the Earth.' More serious was the fact that Lock was fairly obviously Fox's informant with regard to the broken truce and the treatment of the Neapolitan republicans which resulted in Fox's speech in the House of Commons and provoked further rumours. These accusations should have been replied to seriously and it is regrettable that Nelson never really bothered. When Arthur Paget arrived in Naples he and Lock gravitated towards each other out of dislike for the departing Hamiltons. Naturally they corresponded with other British diplomats, such as Mr Wyndham at Leghorn, and their letters contained no compliments to Nelson and his friends.

No doubt it takes one woman to describe another, and Lady Elgin was admirably suited by nature and position to be critical of Lady Hamilton. When her husband was on his way to take up the post of ambassador at Constantinople the two of them broke their journey, as guests of the Hamiltons at Palermo in 1799. She had obviously heard rumours before she arrived, because she had already written 'they say there never was a man turned so vainglorious in the world as Lord Nelson. He is now completely managed by Lady Hamilton.'

That impression was confirmed and reinforced when the Elgins were entertained to dinner, 'She [Lady Hamilton] looked very handsome at dinner, quite in an undress; my Father would say, "There's a fine Woman for you, good flesh and blood." She is indeed a Whapper! and I think her manner very vulgar. It is really humiliating to see Lord Nelson, he seems quite dying and yet as if he had no other thought than her. He told

Elgin privately that he had lived a year in the house with her and that her beauty was nothing in comparison to the goodness of her heart.'

Later she wrote, 'We dined at Sir William's yesterday and only think of Elgin being so scandalous as to drink "Lord Nelson" upon which my Lady actually GREETED. For she loves him better than a brother.' Lord Elgin left a description of the subject of his toast: 'He looks very old, has lost his upper teeth, sees ill of one eye, and has a film coming over both of them. He has pains pretty constantly from his late wound in the head. His figure is mean, and in general his countenance is without animation.'

Two friends who wrote to Nelson offering good advice were Commodore Troubridge and 'Governor' Ball. Both were concerned about his health and his reputation, but were, perhaps because they were writing to their superior officer, either excruciatingly tactful or incredibly naïve, for their criticism was levelled at late hours and card-playing, in the company of Lady Hamilton. Thus Troubridge, 'I know you can have no pleasure sitting up all night at Cards why then sacrifice your health, comfort, purse, ease, everything, to the Customs of a Country where your stay cannot be long.' Then Ball, 'I feel infinite concern that your Grace has a complaint in your Eye—I am afraid Sir William's hours do not agree with it. I shall lay the fault to her ladyship, because if she were to go to bed early, Sir William would soon follow.'

Troubridge continued in the same vein: 'if you knew what your Friends feel for you I am sure you would cut all Nocturnal partys, the gambling of the people at Palermo is publicly talked of everywhere. I beseech your Lordship leave off, I wish my pen could tell you my feelings. I am sure you would oblige me. Lady H—— character will suffer, nothing can prevent people from talking, a gambling Woman in the Eye of an Englishman is lost, to say they can leave it off when they please, might amuse a School Boy, but people who has seen the World know better, you will be surprised when I tell you I hear in all Companys the sums won and lost on a Card in Sir Wm's house, it furnishes matter for a letter constantly, both to Minorca, Naples, Messina and C and C and Finally in England. I trust your Lordship will pardon me!'

Perhaps because of Troubridge's representations, the late-night card parties were discontinued, but Nelson showed no intention of reading between the lines. There were fewer inhibitions in Minto's letters, but then he was not writing to Nelson. 'He does not seem at all conscious of the sort of discredit he has fallen into, or the cause of it, for he writes still, not wisely, about Lady Hamilton and all that. But it is hard to condemn and use ill a hero, as he is in his own element, for being foolish about a woman who has art enough to make fools of many wiser than an admiral. He tells me of having got the Cross of Malta for *her*, and Sir William sends home to Lord Grenville the Emperor of Russia's letter to Lady Hamilton on the occasion. All this is against them all, but they do not seem conscious.'

Perhaps the bluntest to Nelson was Admiral Goodall, writing from England, 'They say here you are Rinaldo in the arms of Armida'.

Naturally enough, as Nelson at last prepared to leave Naples, his most scathing critic was Lord Keith, and as all the trials and tribulations of the departure of 'the Nelson party' came his way, that busy man had every excuse.

The departure of an admiral and the return of an ambassador and his wife from his post plus a visit of a Queen to her relations was got up like some immense combined pleasure trip, no doubt due partly at least to Emma Hamilton and Maria Carolina.

There were rumours even at Palermo that Bonaparte was crossing the Great St Bernard Pass to reconquer Italy, and that another French army had won a victory at Biberach. It was part of the grand strategy that Masséna held out in Genoa for so long, but in the second week of June there was a round of farewell parties before *Foudroyant* could leave for Leghorn.

By the time that Lord Keith arrived at Leghorn from Genoa on June 24, Bonaparte had completely defeated the principal Austrian army under General Melas at Marengo on June 14. Maria Carolina now wanted, she thought, to return to Palermo. Nelson was quite adamant that he had a special responsibility for the Queen's safety—'nothing shall separate me from her'. Keith described his own part 'to be bored by Lord Nelson for permission to take the Queen to Palermo, and princes and princesses to all parts of the globe'. His concern was with the possibility of a French fleet coming out of Brest, something that Nelson would not consider seriously.

Finally, on July 13 Nelson struck his flag and gave up the idea of returning home by sea. Keith was adamant that, at this time, he should not use *Foudroyant*, he and the Hamiltons could go home in the *Seahorse* frigate, or a troopship, which could be picked up at Malta, then Lady Hamilton announced that she would not go by sea and, according to Miss Knight, that she wished 'to visit the different Courts of Germany'.

On July 17 Nelson, the Hamiltons, Mrs Cadogan and Miss Knight and sundry attendants began the overland journey to Vienna by way of Florence, Ancona and Trieste. The Queen with her family and a suite of retainers had left two days earlier.

To one body of men the land journey came as a disappointment. The barge crew of *Foudroyant* wrote Nelson a letter offering to go with him 'in any Ship or Vessel'. No doubt they would have liked to go to England too, but the letter shows that their admiral still had the capacity to retain the loyalty and affection of simple men. Lord Keith, less simple, was plainly pleased to see the back of the whole ménage and be able to order *Foudroyant* to Minorca for repairs, refitting and future active service.

During his last days at Leghorn Nelson had received two letters, both from the First Lord of the Admiralty. They were masterpieces of polite rebuke and a suitable commentary on the whole Neapolitan episode. In the first Lord Spencer said how concerned he would be if a French fleet came into the Mediterranean and that Nelson might hear of its arrival 'either on shore or in a transport at Palermo'.

The second was more peremptory:

It is by no means my wish or intention to call you away from Service, but having observed that you have been under the necessity of quitting your station off Malta on account of the state of your health, which I am persuaded you could not have thought of doing without such necessity, it appeared to me much more advisable for you to come home at once than to be obliged to remain inactive at Palermo while active Service was going on in other parts of the Station.

You will be more likely to recover your health and strength in England than in an inactive situation at a foreign Court, however pleasing the Respect and gratitude shewn to you for your Services may be.

CHAPTER TWENTY-FOUR

Homecoming: the End of a Marriage

T HE QUEEN of the Two Sicilies had to travel overland in order to return home to Vienna. However, for an easily identifiable British admiral, and a retired ambassador and his wife to attempt a much longer journey was not only highly inconvenient, but somewhat dangerous. But Lady Hamilton had decided on this course and it was Nelson who became responsible for the party which included an elderly gentleman not in good health, Mrs Cadogan who, though robust, was not young, Miss Knight and a collection of servants, as well as Emma herself. On his own account Nelson risked the ignominy of capture.

The battle of Marengo had established French domination over a sizeable part of the Continent, there remaining only one state in Italy hostile, the kingdom of Naples and Sicily. Elsewhere on land the French had little opposition. A formal peace with the Austrians was not signed until February of the next year, but it was not only that one army had been beaten by Bonaparte, for France had other successful generals. In May, Moreau had defeated the Austrians at Biberach. Five days after Marengo he was the victor again at Hochstadt, and these two successes were confirmed in December at Hohenlinden from whence he could advance on Vienna. Thus when Nelson began his journey home the Habsburg Empire was almost out of the war, only Britain remaining as an active belligerent. In these circumstances a progress from Florence to Ancona, across the Adriatic to Trieste, and thence to Vienna, Prague, Dresden and Hamburg was something of a curiosity. After reaching Vienna, where Maria Carolina bade emotional farewells to her best friends, the British party was in little danger of not completing the rest of its itinerary. Nevertheless before Vienna, when there was danger from nearby French troops, it was decided that Mrs Cadogan and Miss Knight should be left behind, for as Miss Knight put it 'it was of less consequence we should be left behind, or taken, than they'.

Lord Minto was Ambassador in the Imperial City and neither he nor his wife, having digested news and rumours from the Sicilies in the last two years, looked forward to renewing their acquaintance with what they heard their old friend Horatio Nelson had become. They were much relieved therefore to find that the Admiral's manner was just as simple and charming as it had been in the old days. 'He is just the same with us as ever, I don't think him altered in the least', was Lady Minto's comment. Her husband was equally pleased, in his official capacity, to discover that he had a star attraction at the Embassy for Viennese of all classes. The capital of the Empire was downcast after the French victories, in consequence the British and their admiral might well have been unpopular. In fact the situation was the reverse. Almost alone among protagonists on the allied side, here was a man who had won a spectacular victory over the French and looked like a hero, though Lady Minto, with that horror of ostentation so typical of her race, described him, dressed for his presentation at Court, as 'a gig, from ribands, orders and stars'. Furthermore, as Nelson demonstrated with almost every word he uttered, here was a warrior who had not given in to defeatism, but was prepared to continue fighting. A typically pugnacious view was expressed to his hostess when she suggested, partly in jest, that she wished he commanded the Imperial army, 'If I had,' replied Nelson, 'I would use only one word—advance.'

The Nelson-Hamilton trio lingered in Vienna for some weeks and were entertained by a kaleidoscopic slice of the old Empire. At the theatre the audiences rose to applaud a foreign naval hero and Lady Hamilton was pleased to show off her prize at dinners and dances to a society notoriously formal, but passionately addicted to scandal. Sir William was not well for most of the time but was allowed a little fishing, one of his favourite diversions, on the banks of the Danube. Lord Nelson sat to the painter Füger who produced the only likeness in civilian dress, which presents the admiral handsome, fine-drawn, intense, and thoughtful, looking anything but an admiral. By removing the gold braid and glitter the pictures emphasised how much the martial metal and enamel contrasted oddly with Nelson's slight figure and small, sensitive features.

Wherever Nelson stayed a crowd collected at the door and a number of simple people travelled many miles just so that their children might see him, or better still, be touched by him for good luck. The Admiral was happy to oblige and hoist up youngsters with his remaining left arm, as he had always been fond of children. At Eisenstadt, the domain of one of the grandest of the Imperial nobility, Prince Esterhazy, pleasures were of a more sophisticated kind. Among suppers and balls, at which cannons were fired when Nelson's health was drunk, four concerts were arranged to which the Prince's retired Oberkapellmeister, Joseph Haydn, returned in the role of accompanist. That elderly gentleman, now sixty-eight, had introduced a flourish of trumpets into a previous work, so it is to be hoped that he found the task of putting music to grandiloquent words written by Miss Knight and sung by Lady Hamilton, not too uncongenial. Lord Fitzharris, who was present, found Lady Hamilton coarse, ill-mannered and disagreeable, and seemed to think she slighted 'the famous Haydn' by deserting him for the card table, but Nelson was more considerate, presenting the eminent musician with a watch and, in turn, receiving a pen as a memento of the occasion.

The Austrian populace obviously took to Nelson. What the fashionable world made of him is not known. His compatriots, however, as usual, were not reluctant to make their comments. Especially of course upon Nelson and Lady Hamilton. Lady Minto in her description foreshadowed many similar ones which would be made once the lovers reached Britain,

> He has the same shock head and the same honest, simple manners; but he is devoted to Emma and he thinks her quite an angel and talks of her as such to her face and behind her back, and she leads him about like a keeper with a bear. She must sit by him at dinner to cut his meat and he carries her pocket handkerchief.

This was not a moral or priggish judgment and Lady Minto, in comparison with others, was quite restrained, and she and her husband were both genuinely fond of Nelson. Of course there was an element of snobbery in it all, everyone knew of Emma's origins and reputation— she was thus an easy target. Nevertheless whatever Emma's background had been, the present lady, though undeniably handsome and sexually attractive, was a fairly preposterous and not always pleasant creature. Even if Nelson had fallen in love with a duchess with impeccable manners he would still have looked rather silly with his parade of dog-like devotion—as it was, he could not help but make himself ridiculous.

The next port of call was Prague, and the party of seventeen reached the Bohemian capital just before Nelson's forty-first birthday on September 29. From Vienna he had written to both Fanny and Alexander Davison using almost the same words to each, his health had improved but he warned them to expect the return of an old man. However, the birthday celebrations should have dispelled some of his gloom, for his host was the Archduke Charles and Sir William remarked upon his pleasure at being seated at table between the greatest general and the greatest admiral of the age.

At Dresden, the capital of Saxony, reached after a leisurely and attractive journey on the Elbe, the tria juncta in uno delivered themselves over to a perfect nest of gossips. The British Ambassador who had to take charge of the distinguished guests was Lord Minto's brother, Hugh Elliot; younger, more clever and with no old friendship with Nelson to inspire charity. At Dresden also there was a taste of things to come for, despite protests from Nelson, though the Elector of Saxony received him, the Electress was not prepared to meet Lady Hamilton. 'On account of her former dissolute life', according to Mrs St George who was the very epitome of the travelling, letter-writing, upper-class Englishwoman of her time, if an Irish widow may be so described. At the Elliots she noted that Lady Hamilton was 'bold, daring, vain even to folly and stamped with the manners of her first situation much more strongly than one would suppose, after having represented Majesty, and lived in good company fifteen years'. 'Her ruling passions seem to me vanity, avarice, and love for the pleasures of the table—' Mr Elliot was more restrained, but within his family circle talked of 'Anthony and Moll-Cleopatra'.

Mrs St George, who like everyone else realised that Lord Nelson and Lady Hamilton were totally infatuated with each other, recorded a minute description of 'Moll-Cleopatra' from her head to her toes. A well shaped figure but 'colossal', 'hideous' feet, a very attractive face seriously marred by a coarse complexion, and a brown spot in one of a pair of blue eyes. A loud voice, 'yet not disagreeable', and dark hair which was 'never clean'. Unexpectedly however, Mrs St George was an admirer of the famous attitudes and drew a contrast, as did others, between Emma acting her many silent parts and Lady Hamilton in real life. Poor old Sir William, presumably under the influence of the large quantities of champaign, duly noticed by Mr Elliot, was also described as skipping about and playing the clown. Nelson was 'without any dignity', Miss Knight was 'a decided flatterer' and Mrs Cadogan was 'what one might expect'. Mrs St George did not however have the last word on the company which had invaded Mr Elliot's world so boisterously and over-poweringly. The evening they left, he had that privilege when he enjoined his family not to laugh or speak out of turn but, for a welcome change, to be 'very, very quiet'.

Mrs Melasina St George may be dismissed as a very skilled backbiter indeed, but her comments are valuable not only on appearance and manners but behaviour. Soon Nelson was to rejoin his wife, and Emma and Fanny were to meet for the first time. Any doubt Fanny might have had about the relationship between her husband and Lady Hamilton 'exceedingly embonpoint' because she was pregnant, must have been dispelled when she saw them together. In Mrs St George's words 'Lady Hamilton takes possession of him, and he is a willing captive, the most submissive and devoted I have seen'—'she puffs the incense full in his face; but he receives it with pleasure, and snuffs it up very cordially'. In Dresden, Magdeburg and finally Hamburg there were receptions, guards of honour, parties and dinners. On occasions there was music and Lady Hamilton sang Miss Knight's words to the tune of 'Heart of Oak', written on Emma's birthday on April 26 on board *Foudroyant*:

Come cheer up, fair Emma, forget all thy grief,
For thy shipmates are brave, and a hero's their Chief,
Look around on these trophies, the pride of the main,
They are snatched by their valour from Gallia and Spain,
Heart of Oak are our ships, jolly tars are our men
                              etcetera.

Perhaps the British residents in Hamburg, who gave a dinner, and heard a rousing performance from the large lady with the powerful, but not quite true, voice, enjoyed it. Perhaps the Germans thought it was some old English custom. In Vienna Nelson had met Haydn, in Hamburg he visited the poet Klopstock who had once welcomed the French Revolution; and was in turn visited by the French general Dumouriez, the victor of Jemappes, like Moreau a convinced republican, but now an exile having refused service under a First Consul.

Foreign observers were almost all overwhelmed by the personality of Lady Hamilton, but taken aback by the puny physique of the great Admiral. All agreed that his face, especially about the nose and eyes, bore the look they expected of a conqueror, but his lack of inches and emaciated, slight frame did not impress them. His stars and medals (he had written from Vienna to the College of Heralds for advice about wearing them in England) made his small figure already emphasised by the presence of the buxom beauty at his side appear even more insignificant. To a number he appeared sad, certainly he hardly ever smiled, perhaps he was conscious of his lost teeth to which some referred. He spoke no language save his own, though he endured a number of speeches and theatrical performances in German with something like good grace. He signed Bibles and prayer books and managed to ward off those who wanted money or favours. It would not have been surprising if he had been tired and weary of it all. Perhaps he was sad. If he had forethoughts about his return to England, it would not have been strange if he was at times reserved and quiet and appeared pre-occupied, and so gave to one German observer the appearance of 'a typical Englishman'.

In Dresden the poet and cleric, Thomas Kosegarten, thought Nelson 'one of the most insignificant figures', in the physical sense, he had ever seen, and was shocked when Lady Hamilton put on his admiral's hat, 'she led him, often took hold of his hand, whispered something into his ear and he twisted his mouth into a faint resemblance of a smile'. At Magdeburg the Freiherr von Dalwich who described 'Die Hamilton' as 'a woman full of fire' saw a more robust Nelson, 'Among the many spectators there were some from the commercial school, including many Englishmen, he busied himself a good deal with them, assuring them that he was nothing less than a great man, they must be loyal and industrious, then they would do equally well; but above all he urged on them an eternal hatred of the French'. The last the Freiherr saw of the Admiral was as he left by a gondola, standing alone on deck, doffing his hat to the crowds that lined the banks of the Elbe.

At Hamburg there had been promise of a frigate, at least Mr Elliot in Dresden had thought it would be so, but perhaps he had seized upon a rumour to speed his guests on their way. However, the frigate did not materialize, although Nelson had requested one from the Admiralty. The consequent delay in Hamburg allowed Nelson to go shopping with Miss Knight and 'buy a magnificent lace trimming for a Court dress for Lady Nelson, and a black lace cloak for another lady, who, he said, had been very attentive to his wife during his absence'.

On October 21 the whole party, it being clear that a naval vessel was not being provided, embarked from Cuxhaven for Yarmouth in *King George*—a civilian packet. At noon on Thursday November 6 after an extremely rough crossing indeed, Nelson disembarked, by boat, from the mail vessel at Yarmouth. He was home at last after an absence of three and a half years.

Nelson faced three receptions in England. From the populace at large, from the Establishment—the Government, the Admiralty, the First Lord, senior naval officers and society—and from his wife.

John Bull, and his wife, as usual took the little admiral to their hearts. At Yarmouth, Ipswich and Colchester the pattern was almost identical. Similar to his visits to Continental towns and cities, but less formal and more enthusiastic, for this was a British hero returning to his own country and at Yarmouth, to his own county of Norfolk.

The visit to Colchester was unscheduled and the townsfolk had to act quickly, so they removed the horses from Sir William's 'German travelling carriage' and did the job themselves. At Yarmouth and Ipswich, given more notice, there was the gift of the towns' freedoms, short speeches by Nelson and simple humour. The landlady of the Wrestlers' Arms at Yarmouth, whose name was Suckling, and who was therefore a kinswoman, asked his lordship's permission to rename her inn the *Nelson Arms* to be reminded that he only had one. The same day the town clerk made himself an unenviable local reputation for when Nelson was about to take the oath by placing his only hand on the Bible he requested loudly, 'Your right hand, my Lord'. The yeomanry turned out, the bands played 'See the Conquering Hero Comes' and 'Rule Britannia', and there was a church service for the parson's son at Ipswich. The locals cheered and if there was a grey-haired distinguished-looking elderly gentleman and a large bosomy lady constantly with the Admiral no one cared very much. The people had come to see the diminutive flag officer with his medals and stars, the second most visually interesting person in the party was the buxom lady's black female attendant, 'a Copt', called Fatima, acquired by the Admiral after Aboukir and given to Emma in Naples. The British people had had little to celebrate since the news of the fall of Seringapatam and the death of Tippoo Sahib and that had been only a minor victory, and no one in East Anglia yet knew anything of General the Hon. Arthur Wellesley.

The unheralded visit to Colchester was caused by a misunderstanding which at the outset did not improve Horatio's feelings towards Fanny. Forgetting that while in Naples he had requested her to meet him in London he expected her to be at Roundwood. But that house was unoccupied so the party, Nelson, the Hamiltons, Miss Knight, Mrs Cadogan, Fatima, two Italian maids Julia and Marianne, and Sir William's valet Gaetano, as well as a newly acquired factotum called Oliver and other minor servants, spent the night in Colchester before taking the London road the next morning.

There, obedient, like a good sea officer's wife, to her last instructions, waited Fanny with 'our father', the asthmatic, elderly Reverend Edmund.

The old man was in a state of mixed anticipation and apprehension as he awaited the sight of his famous son who had now moved into spheres beyond his father's experience. His own portrait had recently been painted by Sir William Beechey as a present for his son's return. Beechey also painted Horatio, the beginning of a friendship which put a Beechey son, under the patronage of Nelson, his godfather, into the Royal Navy to become in time an admiral. The portrait shows the elderly cleric in the last years of life. Not robust, even in youth, diffident and unworldly. He had once been apprehensive at the thought of welcoming his newly-acquired daughter-in-law, visualising some grand West Indian heiress, but they were now great friends and almost constant companions.

For the last twelve months Fanny's husband had become a more and more infrequent and indifferent correspondent, at the same time rumours cannot have failed to come to her notice. London society, titillated already by snippets of Neapolitan and Sicilian innuendo and gossip, awaited Nelson and the Hamiltons in a state of the liveliest salacious expectancy. So Fanny must have waited at Nerot's Hotel, 17 King Street, St James's, in the most miserable mental state imaginable, and although it may have showed a little in her manner, it did not show in her face.

Lady Hamilton later remembered that she felt 'an antipathy not to be described' when at last she met face to face with Lady Nelson. It was three o'clock in the afternoon of Sunday November 9, a day of a violent freak storm, dark clouds and thunder. It was, dramatically, an appropriate background for the confrontation between the two rivals.

There could have been little doubt in Fanny's mind that she was fighting a losing battle. Here after all was Lady Hamilton still in the company of her husband, who obviously doted on her. No private reunion between husband and wife, with the Hamiltons tactfully sent off about their own affairs, not even for twenty-four hours. In Italy there had been cheerful talk, by both Nelson and Lady Hamilton, of the two couples making one happy family a sort of extension of Emma's 'tria juncta in uno'. It may have sounded all right in Naples, even as pictured by the Admiral to Miss Knight, with the Hamiltons revelling into the early hours, but the Nelsons, the quieter couple, going off to bed. Such dreams faded on a dark English afternoon in a small London hotel, a fitting contrast to sun-drenched southern villas and palazzos.

Nelson had already written to the Admiralty offering himself for active service, and, incidentally, asking for full pay and allowances for his journey from Palermo to Yarmouth on the basis that he was but returning from one post to another. Needless to say that request was turned down flat. Keith had sent him home specifically on the grounds of ill health while the siege of Valetta still continued, and the idea that the Admiralty should help pay for a tour of European capitals was preposterous. Presumably Nelson's health had now improved, but whether it had or not, perhaps he hoped to escape from the Fanny and Emma entanglement by a speedy return to sea. This was, of course, moral cowardice for he could not give up Emma now for she was well advanced in pregnancy. Nor could he bring himself to announce to Fanny that their marriage was at an end.

Thus Nelson, the dynamic, impatient leader of men who often talked of the boldest actions being the wisest was in his private affairs incapable of decisive action. He let things drift between his wife and his mistress, hoping that it would be decided for him. It is obvious, from later letters that Nelson wrote to Emma, that she was pressing for a decision. Apart from her pregnancy it was in her own interests so to do. The waiting game, with no reproaches and no dramatic scenes, which Fanny tried her best to play, was to the advantage of the wife, not the mistress. The contrasting strategies typified two very different protagonists, Emma big, noisy and emotional, with little restraint or patience, versus Fanny, controlled, lady-like and long-suffering. While fashionable London watched, aided by the gossip columnists, unrestrained by any libel laws worth mentioning, the Hamiltons and the Nelsons met, dined together and visited the theatre where they provided a spectacle much more interesting than that performed on the stage.

Their comings and goings, separately and in company, were closely watched and chronicled, and the dresses and physical appearance of Lady Nelson and Lady Hamilton were faithfully described. There was even a highly social sub-plot to keep the public guessing whether Lady Hamilton would be received at Court. She might be, as one or two journals emphasised heavily, and inaccurately, 'a Lady of the Bed Chamber' to the Queen of Naples, but would that give her entrée to the drawing-room of the highly respectable couple who were King and Queen of England? The answer was emphatically no. Even if her affair with Nelson had never taken place, or become public knowledge, she would probably not have been received. Sir William Hamilton yes, but his notorious wife, late of the Temple of Health, formerly the mistress of Featherstonhaugh, then Greville, then Hamilton himself, no. Add her affair with

Nelson to all that and it is easy to see why the doors of St James's Palace stayed closed.

This was obvious to Lord St Vincent when he wrote to the Secretary of the Admiralty. 'It is evident from Lord Nelson's letter to you on his landing, seeking an active appointment, that he is doubtful of the propriety of his conduct. I have no doubt that he is pledged to getting Lady H. received at St James's, and everywhere, and that he will get into much brouillerie about it.' Another aspect was equally obvious to Sir Thomas Troubridge, now a member of the Admiralty Board, who called upon Miss Knight to explain to her the impropriety of an unmarried lady continuing to live with the Hamilton household. She took the hint very quickly, and decamped to the respectable house of Mr and Mrs Evan Nepean, a much more suitable abode for an admiral's daughter.

Soon after the meeting at Nerot's Hotel both the Nelsons and the Hamiltons took up separate, but temporary, accommodation. Thus the conventions of the time were observed as they would have been flouted if all four had continued to stay in the same hotel. Horatio and Fanny and the seventy-six-year-old Reverend Edmund moved to 17 Dover Street, a house obtained by Alexander Davison, who now managed Nelson's business affairs. Sir William and Emma and their Neapolitan entourage transferred themselves to 22, Grosvenor Square, a house which though its free provision was no doubt of considerable advantage to Sir William's pocket, did nothing for anyone's reputation. It belonged to the forty-one-year-old William Beckford, millionaire, eccentric, and author of *Vathek*, who maintained Fonthill, one of the most famous Gothic follies of the age. He was also a great collector of rather worthless works of art, and, though married, a notorious homosexual with 'a knowledge of Italian manners to which that Charming Lady [Emma] must ever remain a stranger'. His one unfulfilled desire in life was to have a peerage and he had formed the extraordinary idea that the Hamiltons, and maybe Nelson, could help him to attain his object. He was very much of the demi-monde and for Lady Hamilton to be beholden to him was what many people might have expected, but for Sir William dependence on Beckford was very much a step down in the world.

The conventions were observed and Lord Nelson and Lady Hamilton were no longer under the same roof, although there can hardly have been a knowledgeable contemporary who had any doubts about the nature of their relationship. Lord St Vincent, perhaps hopefully, contributed the observation that Horatio and Emma were 'a couple of sentimental fools', but it was not really very convincing. No doubt there were others of Nelson's brothers-in-arms who hoped that the 'Admiral' and his 'Famous Woman' would, now that they had left Naples behind, revert to their previous marital states with their own spouses. It was possible to maintain a ménage à trois on the Continent, but not in England.

Sir William's complaisance and Lady Nelson's self-control helped to present, for a time, an outward appearance of decorum and respectability which cloaked a developing domestic crisis. Sir William maintained his sangfroid with only minor lapses of irritability towards Emma; it was, not surprisingly, Fanny's self-control which broke down in what was obviously for her an intolerable situation. Nelson himself right up until the birth of his child was never quite capable of making the break with his wife, partly because she did not allow any obvious public rift in the marriage to appear as a provocation and no doubt also, as he was to admit, because of her complete blamelessness.

The re-induction of a distinguished naval officer returning from foreign service had properly to begin with a levée. Accordingly Nelson in full dress repaired to St James's to make his bow to his Sovereign. Collingwood was one of the sea officers also present and a witness of a chilling scene. The King asked briefly after Nelson's health and without waiting for an answer turned aside to engage in a lengthy and cheerful conversation with an undistinguished army officer, 'it could not be', wrote the loyal and angry Collingwood, 'about *his* successes'. A number of reasons have been advanced for George III's rudeness. The fact that Nelson had attended the Lord Mayor of London's Banquet at the Guildhall, at which he had been presented with his 200 guinea sword, before attending the Royal drawing-room was technically a breach of etiquette. So was the fact that he wore his foreign decorations, not yet gazetted, and therefore not yet permitted to be worn in England, a curious lapse as Nelson had written from Naples enquiring about them. It might have been either of these social solecisms, but the most likely reason for the royal snub was that the King disapproved of his admiral's liaison with Lady Hamilton and of all that had followed in consequence, including the effect on the performance of his naval duties. George III must also have heard of Nelson's attempts to get Lady Hamilton received at Court. Nelson's unconsciously ironic comment on the fact that Sir William was received but not Emma, 'and such a wife!' was no doubt echoed, but in a very different sense, by a king who, whatever the failings of his sons, was himself a moral man and a faithful husband.

The same evening Nelson and Fanny were invited to dinner by the wife of the First Lord, and he arrived, still not recovered from a public humiliation, with a face like thunder. His mood provoked a scene which could not have taken place in more unfortunate surroundings and company. Lady Spencer, who was neither discreet nor restrained, described it all with relish, harking back to the previous time when the Nelsons had been her guests and a loving husband had then asked to sit next to his wife. 'Such a contrast I never beheld.'

During dinner Fanny, no doubt as always with the best intentions, had peeled some walnuts and putting them in a wine glass pushed them across to her husband. Irritably he shoved it away so violently that it hit a dish and broke some table china. Fanny burst into tears and later, when the ladies retired from the dining-room, told Lady Spencer, in explanation, 'how she was situated'.

It may well have been at the end of that calamitous day that Nelson 'in a state of absolute despair and distraction' wandered about the London streets finishing up at the Hamiltons' house at four in the morning where the elderly ex-diplomat advised his friend, and his wife's lover, to concentrate upon his professional career as the only way to happiness. The authority for the incident is Harrison, who gained most of his information from Lady Hamilton. It is not an unlikely incident, even the picture of Sir William giving advice is not inconsistent with what was a most unusual triangular relationship.

There remained one more occasion when Fanny's self-control snapped, before the final break-up, and it took place in the most artificially dramatic circumstances possible, in a playhouse. The theatre was much more a social meeting place than now and performances could easily be interrupted or changed to mark the presence in the audience of a famous personality. The anticipated presence of Nelson and the Hamiltons ensured a full house and a reference to the hero could easily be interwoven into the performance. There could even be a full-blown rendering by the cast, with the audience joining in, of one of the popular sea shanties of the day. Thus Kemble, performing the part of Rolla in Kotzebue's *Pizzaro*, was ensured of a good house at the Drury Lane Theatre on November 24. Nelson was in the stage box, with Fanny, the Reverend Edmund, Sir William and Emma and their friend from

Neapolitan days, the Princess Castelcicala. Switching roles, Fanny was dressed in purple satin with a turban surmounted by ostrich plumes, Emma was entirely in white. Cheers and 'Rule Britannia', sung by the audience, greeted their appearance almost as a matter of course.

It was at the end of Act Three that Mrs Powell, standing in for Mrs Siddons, had her opportunity to show her mettle as Elvira, entreating the relentless Pizzaro to spare the life of Alonzo of whom he was unreasonably jealous. Her last line was delivered with full force, 'Come fearless man! Now meet the last and fullest peril of thy life; meet and survive— an injured woman's fury, if thou cans't'.

A shriek turned all eyes in the audience to the Nelsons' box. Fanny had fainted. The curtain came down and Lady Nelson, back on her feet, was helped out by Lady Hamilton and her father-in-law. None of the three returned, but Nelson sat out the rest of the play. He and his wife only appeared together in public again on one more occasion when, a few days afterwards, they dined with the Hamiltons at Lord Abercorn's. When William Beckford, through his friends the Hamiltons, invited Nelson to stay at Fonthill for Christmas, he tactfully did not invite Lady Nelson.

It is not known what transpired between Fanny and Horatio during the very last days of their marriage. They never lived under the same roof after January 13, 1801. Neither seemed quite to accept or realise that it was a final parting. Like many another estranged couple they found it difficult to break entirely with old habits. Letters were exchanged, and when the time came Fanny sent her husband what he wanted to make the cabin of his new command habitable, though not to his satisfaction. He still tried, though unsuccessfully, to gain promotion for Josiah, now in England, beyond his command of *Thalia*. It was the solicitor William Hazlewood, employed to act in a dispute over prize money, who recalled, forty-five years later, an exchange which may well have been final. It took place at Dover Street at breakfast time. 'A cheerful conversation was passing on indifferent subjects when Lord Nelson spoke of something which had been done or said by "dear Lady Hamilton". Lady Nelson rose from her chair and exclaimed with much vehemence, "I am sick of hearing of dear Lady Hamilton, and am resolved that you shall give up either her or me". Lord Nelson, with perfect coolness said, "Take care, Fanny, what you say. I love you sincerely, but I cannot forget my obligations to Lady Hamilton, or speak of her otherwise than with affection and admiration". Without saying one soothing word, but muttering something about her mind being made up, Lady Nelson left the room, and shortly after drove from the house. They never lived together again. I believe that Lord Nelson took a formal leave of her ladyship before joining the Fleet under Sir Hyde Parker.'

It is possible that a more formal conversation took place on that later occasion for which one authority was Sir William Hamond, Comptroller of the Navy. According to Sir William, Lady Nelson asked her husband if he had any reason to doubt her faithfulness to him, to which he replied, 'Never'. Fanny's own recollection was that Horatio's last words to her were, 'I call God to witness, there is nothing in you, or your conduct, I wish otherwise'. Whatever the exact words, the sense was the same. Although an unpleasant element of bitterness and vindictiveness later crept into Nelson's attitude to his wife, obviously he could not blame her in any way, only excuse himself. The formality of their final words was not false, they were symptomatic of what had become only a formal relationship.

CHAPTER TWENTY-FIVE

Armed Neutrality

IN THE month or so that it took for Nelson's marriage to dissolve irretrievably he still performed a number of duties, attended public dinners and functions and carried out private and family obligations.

Although he was having trouble with his good eye, Nelson no longer complained of ill health, but was anxious to be employed again as quickly as possible upon some active service. It was typical of him that although the shadow which had fallen over his career was entirely his own fault, he was much hurt by the rebukes of Spencer and Keith and now sought opportunities to redeem himself.

A few days before the incident in the theatre, on November 20, he took his seat in the House of Lords, introduced by Lord Romney and Lord Grenville. On St Andrew's day, November 30 both he and Sir William were the guests at dinner of the Scottish Corporation and the next day they were both entertained by the Court and Directors of the Honourable East India Company. There was also a magnificent private dinner given by Alexander Davison in his palatial mansion in St James's Square, where the guest list was headed by the Prince of Wales, who, true to Hugh Elliot's prediction, was lecherously anxious to meet Emma. Also included were the Prime Minister, Lords Spencer and Chatham, two admirals, one of whom, John Willet-Payne, was reputed to be Emma's first seducer, and Sir William Hamilton.

Indeed there was so much entertainment, though Nelson was known for his abstemiousness, that Lord St Vincent, despite their pending law suit, was anxious about the health of his former protégé and advised him against 'going out of smoking hot rooms into the damp putrid air of London streets'. Less strenuously, Nelson sat to an artist called de Koster who produced a sketch which soon became a popular print, and to Lemuel Abbott who touched up his 1798 portrait and painted in the new decorations; Mrs Damer, the fashionable sculptress, also had the Admiral's time for a bust destined for the Guildhall though she complained that he couldn't keep his head still for one moment.

Death and its effects also claimed Nelson's attention at this time. He was one of the executors of the estate of his uncle William Suckling, the news of the death of his former benefactor had reached him when in Italy. 'I loved my dear uncle for his own worth', Nelson said at the time. Now there was a legacy of £100 and the minor chores of executorship. His own brother Suckling, named after that side of the family, had also died a few months later but his death was neither unexpected nor regretted. 'If he has now taken to drink', Nelson had written some time before, 'the more he drinks the better, it will the sooner finish his disgrace and the part we must all bear in it.' Much more deeply felt was the death on December 26 of an old brother-in-arms, Captain Locker, who had earlier advised his junior 'always lay a Frenchman close, and you will beat him'. Nelson attended the funeral in Addington, Kent, on the first Saturday of 1801, dressed in his new uniform having been promoted on New Year's Day to Vice-Admiral of the Blue.

Nelson's promotion, and the confirmation he had received in mid-November that he was still required in his professional capacity, was part of a chain of events which went back as far as the surrender of Malta. 'Mine will not, I hope', he had written to Berry, 'be an inactive service', an obvious reference to Lord Spencer's previous criticism of his Sicilian lethargy. When the King opened Parliament on December 31 he was conducted to the throne in the House of Lords by two of his most distinguished admirals, representing the old tradition and the new achievement, Lords Hood and Nelson. For the junior of the two it was an obvious mark of rehabilitation and on January 7 Nelson kissed hands at a levée on his promotion. Two days later he was at the Admiralty receiving his orders.

The contents of the Gracious Speech indicated fairly obviously why the services of Vice-Admiral Lord Nelson were still in demand, for Britain had acquired a new enemy, the donor of the 'little cross' of the Order of the Knights of Malta to Lady Hamilton, Paul, Tsar of all the Russias. One of the least predictable results of the collapse of the Second Coalition had been, in the latter part of 1800, the marked improvement of relations between Russia and France. The Tsar had withdrawn his troops from Italy out of disgust with the performance of his Austrian allies, and then the return of 5000 Russian prisoners of war in French hands, for whom Britain had refused to pay ransom, had produced an effect in St Petersburg which had been calculated, and hoped for, in Paris.

An insane monarch, hyper-sensitive both to fancied slights and gross flattery, was delighted to welcome back his soldiers re-equipped at French expense, and with their regimental colours intact. An amicable correspondence began between the 'Citizen Chief Consul' and the Tsar, dictated on one side by obvious self-interest in separating Britain from her friends and allies, and on the other by a genuine admiration, for, in Paul's words, he was 'a man who knows how to rule and how to fight'. Much of the correspondence dealt with the iniquities of the British and soon a Russian envoy was being received at the Tuileries, where the First Consul had now, reverting to Royalist tradition, transferred the seat of government.

The fate of Malta provided the next stepping-stone towards a Franco-Russian rapprochement. Bonaparte, realising that its fall was inevitable, affected to return the island to its proper suzerain The Grand Master of the Order of St John who was, though quite improperly, the Tsar. It is doubtful if anyone, save Paul himself, believed in his entitlement to an office which required from its occupant, chastity and adherence to the Catholic religion. Nevertheless Britain had acceded to the claim, for as Nelson himself had put it, 'It [the Order of Malta] is the hobby horse of the Emperor of Russia and England wishes of all things to please him'. Thus the Mastership, and a large cash subsidy, became the price for the Tsar's co-operation. It had been Nelson and Ball on the spot who had faced the tricky task of reconciling Britain's ambiguous policy with the claims of both the Tsar and the King of the Two Sicilies. When Russia receded from the Coalition, Pitt's Government tried to backpedal furiously as it saw the possibility of having to hand over the island to a disaffected ally who was quickly becoming a potential enemy. Hence Bonaparte's pre-surrender move, nicely calculated to demonstrate British perfidy, and at the same time to bring the Tsar more closely to his side.

British governments on other occasions have made promises during wars, which have been regretted later, but it is difficult to feel sympathy for Tsar Paul with his bogus claim, for bogus it was, because even if he had properly been Grand Master of the Order of St John that did not mean that Malta thereby became Russian. There was however another, and more justified, reason for what he called his 'dissatisfaction' with Britain. It was a matter of longer standing and concerned nations other than Russia and was therefore an even better issue for Bonaparte to encourage so as to forge a weapon against Britain.

The genesis was the position of neutral ships carrying what belligerents might regard as 'contraband of war'. The neutrals were Sweden, Denmark (which then included Norway), Prussia and, much less concerned than the other three, Russia. The belligerents were of course Britain and France but Britain, reliant upon the power of her navy, was a much more interested party than her enemy. In 1780 Russia, Sweden and Denmark had formed the 'Armed Neutrality' to protect their carrying trade. Naturally enough what Britain regarded as contraband made up a far more comprehensive list than that put forward by the neutrals who confined themselves to firearms, powder, fuses, cannon and musket balls, swords, and pikes and bridles and saddles for cavalry. The British Government thought much more in terms of flax for sail-making, timber for masts and spars, hemp, canvas, pitch and tar, made-up ropes and indeed nearly all the articles which made and sustained ships of war. None of these, save copper and iron for ships' fittings, were easily obtainable save from the Baltic countries, especially now that American supplies were no longer controlled by Britain.

These commodities were the major exports from the Scandinavian and Baltic countries. Britain had two objects, to obtain warlike supplies for herself and prevent similar supplies reaching her enemy. She could not on her own win a land war with France, but she could win a sea war, and Baltic supplies were the sinews of that war. Therefore Britain had to insist on the right of search, and the stopping and searching of their merchantmen was just as galling to neutrals as the refusal of the British to accept their narrow definition of contraband.

So there had been, in the last few years a number of times when Britain had asserted 'the incontestable right of a belligerent power'. In January 1798 a convoy of Swedish merchant ships were all captured by Commodore Lawford. In December 1799 a Danish frigate captain fired on the boats of a British warship attempting to search off Gibraltar. In the following July when the previous incident was still the subject of angry diplomatic notes, another convoy of six ships escorted by the frigate *Freya* was captured, but not until a minor naval action had taken place. The Danes demanded restitution; the British sent Admiral Dixon with ten ships of the line to Copenhagen to assist the diplomacy of Lord Whitworth on land. Eventually *Freya* was restored and a compromise was effected by a convention signed on August 29, 1800. As Hamburg, a 'free port', was one of the outlets of the Baltic trade, Nelson, when he was there, may well have heard talk among the English merchants of a dispute with which he was soon to be closely involved.

Poor relations between Britain, Denmark and Sweden provided the Tsar with his opportunity. On August 27 he had issued an invitation to the kings of Denmark, Sweden and Prussia to join in a reconstituted Armed Neutrality designed to prevent the recurrence of British high-handedness as in the *Freya* incident which was specifically referred to in his declaration. When he learnt of Admiral Dixon's arrival in the Baltic, which Paul regarded as a Russian lake, all British property within his Empire was ordered to be sequestrated. The realisation in November, after General Vaubois and Rear-Admiral Villeneuve had surrendered Malta a month before, that the island was not now to be his, pushed the Tsar's uncertain temper up to boiling point and he imposed an embargo on all British vessels in Russian ports. There were more than 300 such ships and their crews were forcibly removed and marched, in vile weather, to prison camps. At Narva two crews resisted and escaped with their ships; this so enraged Paul that all the British ships remaining were, on his orders, burnt and destroyed.

By December the London Government was forced to realise that it now had a new enemy who was cajoling three hitherto neutral states into breaking the blockade, the only weapon left with which to combat Bonaparte's continental supremacy. There followed a declaration by 'The Convention of Northern Powers' of its limited view of contraband and what it regarded as the right of neutrals, plus a definition of blockade. Both were totally unacceptable to Britain.

Neutral ships could move from any harbour to any other, provided it was not blockaded, and could carry, free of let or hindrance, any cargo not regarded by the Convention as contraband. The definition of blockade was legalistic and unrealistic. 'When the disposition and number of belligerent ships' was such as to 'render it apparently hazardous to enter'. This meant a close and obvious blockade, such as the British navy only operated to prevent a fleet of enemy warships leaving harbour, as it did at Brest, and later at Cadiz. Even then, the blockading squadron was often held some distance off while frigates kept observation closer inshore. All a blockade had to be was effective; it was not necessary, in order to intercept merchant ships, to have British ships permanently on a maritime sentry-go at the mouth of every French and Spanish harbour.

With the turn of the year the British Government, not noticeably enterprising in such matters, was driven to the conclusion that action was required, and speedily. Since November Nelson had known that he would receive a new command, on New Year's Day he was promoted, and in the following weeks it became increasingly obvious that his next employment would be in the Baltic. In the middle of January, leaving his married life with Fanny behind him forever, he travelled to Plymouth to join St Vincent's Channel Fleet. There was to be an independent command but first he had to have a flagship. Pleasingly she was the formerly Spanish *San Josef*, which he had himself captured. She was a large ship of 112 guns, with a company of nearly 900, and a good sailer. Her captain was Thomas Masterman Hardy, and when his flag, as Vice-Admiral of the Blue, broke at her foremast on January 18, a cheer went up from all the nearby ships.

On the jackstay above the bowsprit beyond the prow flew another new flag, but in a different sense from the Vice-Admiral's blue ensign. In the old century the Union Standard had been the red cross of St George superimposed upon the white saltire cross on a blue ground of St Andrew; now the red saltire cross of St Patrick was added, to make up the red and white diagonals on blue of the so-called 'Union Jack'. The change marked the coming into being of the United Kingdom of Britain and Ireland on January 1, 1801. On that day the Act of Union came into force which had passed the two parliaments in London and Dublin in the previous year. As a result there was soon to be a change of government, for already Nelson's hero, Mr Pitt, had advocated Catholic Emancipation in the new Kingdom, which George III regarded as being contrary to his Coronation oath to maintain the Established (i.e. Protestant) religion. This conflict between King and Pitt would produce a vacillating and unsure Ministry under a nonentity as Prime Minister, a poor combination, as Nelson was soon to discover, for the prosecution of a war.

On his way to join his new command Nelson visited Mrs Westcott, widow of his only captain who had been killed in Aboukir Bay. The Westcotts had never been wealthy and now she was living in straitened circumstances. Nelson discovered that she had never received the Davison commemorative gold medal for the action, and, characteristically, gave her his own. It was a little hard therefore that when he reported for instructions to St Vincent, his superior's comment was, 'Poor man! he is devoured with vanity, weakness and folly; was stuck with ribbons, medals etcetera and yet pretended that he wished to avoid the honour and ceremony he everywhere met with upon the road.' Admittedly Nelson enjoyed wearing his decorations, but it is well to remember how they were earned. His friend Captain Ralph Miller had been killed by a gun blowing up aboard *Theseus* after leaving Nelson's command for Acre, and his gold medal had arrived too late, and Nelson had the melancholy task of forwarding it on from the Mediterranean to his family.

Perhaps the prize money case being pursued in the courts between them did not exactly help Nelson and St Vincent to fall into each other's arms on being re-united, but St Vincent was no doubt right in his description of his subordinate, 'Nelson was low when he first came here'. There was quite a lot to be low about. He was still having trouble with his good eye, for which hourly bathing and rest in a dark room had been prescribed. More important, though Fanny had taken herself to Brighton, and Emma was in London, the two women in his life must still have been a cause of concern. Of the discarded wife he could write, 'Let her go to Briton [sic] or where she pleases. I care not'. Yet Nelson was still, just for a little more, curiously dependent upon her. She wrote thanking him for the fairness and generosity of his financial settlement upon her, he told her of his safe arrival and also complained, rather peevishly, of the jumbled and damaged state of his cabin furniture, and what lares and penates a sea officer could assemble. Fanny was no doubt incompetent, but also distraught. A more spirited woman like Emma would never have sent them, but thrown the lot, from pickle jars to silver cups, out of the window.

Emma was at the moment officially indisposed and being looked after by her mother and Francis Oliver, who had been employed in the past by Sir William and picked up again in Vienna, acting now as 'confidential steward' to Nelson. Such care was necessary as Emma was in the last stages of pregnancy, sustained by daily letters from her lover, and discreetly sheltered under her husband's roof. It was at this time that Nelson invented the transparently fictional figure of Thompson or Thomson, rank undefined, on board his own ship, with his pregnant mistress on shore, whom he would marry when her 'uncle' (Sir William) had passed on. The idea was that if a letter should fall into the wrong hands Horatio's and Emma's secret would be safe. Only one side of the Thomson correspondence survives, that from Nelson to Lady Hamilton, as he, sensibly, destroyed her letters, but she, contrary to his instructions, kept his. Just as Nelson could never decide whether the love-lorn tar was Thomson or Thompson, so he wrote sometimes in the first person and sometimes in the second, often in the same letter. Despite the fact that they were not married, Thomson's mistress was 'Mrs Thomson' and was being cared for, out of the goodness of her heart, by Lady Hamilton. In fact the subterfuge would not have deceived a child of ten. All lovers are boring or a trifle ridiculous to everyone else save themselves, however the world is indulgent to young, preferably first, lovers, but neither Horatio nor Emma were in that category. Their passion was genuine, their jealousy was real, their brief happiness was intense, which does not prevent Thomson's letters sounding pathetically mawkish. In addition the reader knows more about Lady Hamilton than Nelson did, so perfection and innocence are difficult to attribute, especially as Emma never revealed to Horatio that she was already the mother of 'little Emma', now Miss Carew aged nineteen.

On January 29, or possibly 30th, Emma gave birth to a girl, almost certainly the survivor of twins, according to a Thomson letter, unless this was yet another subterfuge to mislead the inquisitive. No father could have been as delighted as 'Thomson', though the baby Horatia, as she became, was removed swiftly in the best melodramatic tradition. A reliable nurse, a Mrs Gibson who was a widow with a young daughter of her own, was suitably recompensed. She was prepared to look after the very young baby, brought to her at night by Lady Hamilton travelling in a hackney coach, if accompanied, then only by the confidential Oliver. Thus secrecy was preserved, but not anonymity, for the baby was soon visited by an officer who, even from his appearance alone, can hardly have been unknown to Mrs Gibson of 9, Little Titchfield Street, Marylebone. Before however Nelson could travel up to London to pretend more than usual concern with Thomson's child, political, diplomatic and naval affairs had advanced considerably.

A not uncommon thing had happened. The newspapers had got hold of the story of the planned naval expedition before the Government had really made up its mind that there was going to be an expedition at all. The press had also designated a commander and talked of the imminent departure of the Hero of the Nile for the Baltic. There was in fact some excuse for governmental dilatoriness. On February 9 the Treaty of Lunéville had been ratified between the Habsburg Empire and France. It gave the coup de grâce to the old Holy Roman Empire and considerable territorial acquisitions to the new France. Bonaparte gained the left bank of the Rhine, and recognition of his satellite republics. Might this not be an appropriate time for Britain, after eight years of war, to agree to a peaceful settlement even if it meant the acceptance of French primacy in Europe? The temptation was there, especially strong for the new Government.

William Pitt had tendered his resignation, ostensibly on the grounds of Catholic Emancipation. 'I am sorry Mr Pitt is out,' wrote Nelson to Emma, 'I think him the greatest Minister this country ever had, and the honestest man.' Even those less favourably disposed were forced to admit that Mr Addington, previous Speaker of the House of Commons, was a poor replacement. Practically all that is remembered about Henry Addington, today, is George Canning's damning couplet,

Pitt is to Addington
As London is to Paddington,

but even he could not be blamed for the next confusion which was introduced by the illness of the King. Officially George III had caught a chill at a church service on February 13, but most people, including Nelson, seemed to be aware that it was what he called 'the old complaint', that is, one of the monarch's recurring bouts of insanity.

Thus each of the three nations, Britain, Denmark and Russia, moving steadily towards armed conflict was ruled by a monarch whose reason could not be relied upon. George III's condition was the least harmful, because it was periodic, and because his Ministers made nearly all decisions of state. Christian VII of Denmark, who had once been married to George III's sister Caroline Mathilda, was a sadistic debauchee with homosexual tendencies. His marriage to the English princess had come to an end in a welter of intrigue and brutality. The Court physician, Dr Struensee, an accused but probably innocent lover, was tortured and executed, while the divorced Queen, with her infant son, was imprisoned in Elsinore Castle. Only the threat of war had released her to a British warship but without her son, as promised. It was that son, the thirty-two-year-old Crown Prince Frederick, and his advisers, who now exercised power while Christian VII, though still King in name, was virtually confined under palace arrest. Only the Tsar exercised real power, and his was absolute, and he was the only one of the monarchs who could be classified as totally insane. The British Government concentrated its diplomatic offensive upon Denmark, traditionally a friendly nation and because of her geographic position, the guardian of the Baltic and the furthest away from direct Russian influence.

Thus during January and February while Nelson was waiting for *San Josef* to be prepared for sea he lived on two planes of existence.

Privately, with no one in whom he could confide, as the lover pleased beyond measure that he was now a father and yet plagued by separation from his mistress and Horatia. His only method of communication by letters which had either to be couched in 'Thomson' terms, or else entrusted to the hand of the occasional reliable visitor such as Alexander Davison. At the same time in his professional capacity he knew that a naval expedition was most likely to sail for the Baltic if diplomatic pressure failed, and that again it was most likely that he would be in command of such a force.

Nothing, irritatingly, was definite, though Nelson's professional zeal was already aroused. Harrison is the authority for the story, related to him by Davison, of Nelson's saying, 'If I had the chief command I know well enough what I would do,' and, realising that his knowledge of Danish waters was elementary, sending Davison to Mr Faden's shop at Charing Cross for the most up-to-date chart. Thus equipped he began to mark the positions of the twelve battleships he surmised would be allotted, the pencilled marks corresponding almost exactly to the situation of his own squadron on the actual day of battle. This preparation and enthusiasm on Nelson's part contrasted strikingly with the attitude of the admiral who was in fact given the chief command, Sir Hyde Parker, Admiral of the Blue.

Very little in Sir Hyde's history singled him out as a man to be in charge of what would obviously be a considerable undertaking. If the worst came to the worst the British fleet would have to take on three foreign navies, the Danish at Copenhagen, the Swedish operating from Carlskrona, and the Russian, in small numbers at Reval, and greater strength at Cronstadt. Even taking into account that until the end of March the Russian fleets would be immobilised by ice the potential opposition in the Baltic was daunting. The Danish navy had to be the first to be engaged, for though the smallest, it could cut off any returning, or damaged, British ships from the United Kingdom; but to deal with the Danish navy meant facing the peril of shore fortifications and batteries in the naval sphere, leaving aside any consideration of diplomatic activity which might come his way, the qualities required of the British commander would be decisiveness, superabundant tactical sense and initiative.

Just to list those requirements is enough to make Sir Hyde Parker appear sadly inadequate for the task before him. At thirty-seven, under Lord Howe, he had distinguished himself in the American War of

Independence, in command of the frigate *Phoenix*. He was rewarded with a knighthood and later did excellent service on an expedition to Savannah and off Cuba, but by the age of forty-one Parker's active career was over. He was at the minor battle of the Dogger Bank and then at the siege of Gibraltar, but when peace came in 1783 he went on half-pay. When he was forty-eight and again when he was fifty-one he was given command of a line-of-battle ship, but on neither occasion did he put to sea. Only with the French declaration of war in 1793 did Parker become a flag officer—after ten years on shore. As a rear-admiral he was Hood's Captain of the Fleet in the Mediterranean, and Nelson had first come across him when he was a vice-admiral, and third-in-command to the over cautious Hotham.

Parker was sent from the Mediterranean to the congenial West Indies station with his base on Jamaica. There as Commander-in-Chief he stayed until in his sixty-first year he returned to England in September 1800, having amassed a fortune, from prizes taken by his frigate captains, estimated to be at least £200,000. French and Spanish merchantmen failing to break the Caribbean blockade had ensured him his third of the share of the proceeds, without his ever commanding a force of ships in action. Many years before Nelson had been asked by the Austrian general Beaulieu if he did not risk *Agamemnon* too close to shore and had replied, 'Of course, for a ship of war is built to be risked in proper circumstances, and if destroyed will no doubt be replaced by another.' It was not an answer that would have occurred to Parker, who was fussy and devoted to cautious routine, a cast of mind confirmed by the passage of years and his last command.

In one respect only did Parker and Nelson have a concern in common, and that was in their sex lives. Though it would be difficult to imagine a relationship more removed from Nelson's tempestuous illicit affair than the romance upon which Sir Hyde had embarked on returning home. A widower with three sons, almost as soon as he stepped on shore he had celebrated his marriage to the eighteen-year-old daughter, compared by St Vincent to batter pudding, of his brother flag officer, Admiral Sir Richard Onslow, who though senior to his son-in-law, was eleven years younger. Just as the Press, aided by the cartoonists, could not resist speculation, broad innuendo and sly gossip at the expense of Nelson and the Hamiltons, so Sir Hyde and his youthful bride were most suitable subjects for comment. The *Morning Post* was typical, 'Should the gallant Admiral who late entered the Temple of Hymen be sent to sea

again, he will leave his sheet anchor behind him.' Nelson soon discovered that was indeed the case.

Nelson was able to snatch a few days' leave in London, on February 24
to see Lady Hamilton and his daughter Horatia. He had been prepared
to call his daughter Emma after her mother, but presumably the existence
of the other, previous, Emma had persuaded Lady Hamilton to name her
second daughter after her father.

Nelson tried to conduct as much business as he could from Lothian's
Hotel in Albemarle Street, including arranging for Davison to bid for
the Romney portrait of Lady Hamilton as St Cecilia, which Sir William
had put out to auction. Lady Hamilton had also sold her diamonds so
plainly the ex-ambassadorial couple were feeling the pinch of trying to
live in London. Sir William was still angling for his pension and in the
process, Nelson knew, hoping to invite the Prince of Wales to dinner.
The Prince, who might well soon be Prince Regent, because of his
father's incapacity, had let fall a remark as to 'how Lady Hamilton had
hit his fancy'. This had released the most incredible outbursts of jealousy
from Nelson. Letters had been written almost daily from *San Josef*,
one from 'Thomson' included the incredible proposal that Horatia should
be christened as the daughter of Ioham and Morata Etnorb, which did
not need a very keen brain to decipher as anagrams of Horatio and Emma
plus Brontë spelt backwards. Others blithely proposed marriage at some
future date, presumably after Sir William had died, but as if Fanny did
not exist. Emma is assured that she is regarded as the perfection of
womanhood, though apparently unable to resist the Prince once he is
allowed to step into her house.

'Good God he will be next you, and telling you soft things. If he does,
tell it out at table, and turn him out of the house. Do not sit long. If you
sing a song, I know you cannot help it, do not let him sit next you, but
at dinner he will hob glasses with you. . . . O, God, that I was dead!'
The next day the letter was added to, in the same vein. 'God strike him
blind if he looks at you—that is high treason and you may get me
hanged by revealing it . . .'.

The whole business got so out of hand that Sir William, revealing his
awareness of the relationship between his wife and his friend, wrote a
letter to Nelson explaining very gently the thoroughly decorous entertainment, culinary and musical, planned for His Royal Highness.
However, Nelson was now positively hysterical and unconvinced; the
Prince was a 'villain', Sir William's conduct was 'dishonourable' and the

love of his life about to yield to royal advances to obtain a pension for her husband. Emma had not missed the implication and must have been stung into some form of retaliation for Nelson was forced to assure her, pathetically, that his knowledge that women in the West Country wore black stockings was founded on nothing more than mere observation, 'You cannot help your eyes, and God knows I cannot see much'.

Sir Thomas Troubridge had to go to London to take up his new position as a member of the Board of Admiralty and so Nelson managed, by giving him a letter for Emma, to get him invited to 23 Piccadilly on the fateful night.

He himself promised to dine nowhere without Emma's consent though, 'with my present feelings, I might be trusted with fifty virgins naked in a dark room ...' Presumably Nelson was confident that Troubridge's presence would prevent Emma's violation by the Heir to the Throne during a musical soirée, for within a few hours 'Poor Thompson seems to have forgot all his ill health, and all his mortifications and sorrows.' Two days later the writer was able to reassure himself of his mistress's continued love, and to see Horatia, who he thought would probably have twin brothers or sisters as a result.

Nelson had arrived in London on a Tuesday, by the Friday of the same week he was back at Spithead, and up to his neck in professional duties. There was now quite plainly to be a naval expedition to deal with Denmark and, if necessary, Sweden and Russia. Sir Hyde Parker was to command, with Nelson as his second and Rear-Admiral Graves as the next senior officer. It now seems incredible that Parker should have been given command over Nelson, and it appeared hardly less so at the time. Nevertheless it was not a mistake or an oversight. Lord Spencer approved, and St Vincent, who, with the change of Government, had moved from Commander-in-Chief of the Channel Fleet to take up Spencer's post, approved the appointment twice over, in both his capacities. There could be no doubt that both Spencer and St Vincent knew what sort of officer Parker was, and therefore there could be only two reasons why he was appointed. The first was seniority, as the fleet was a sizeable one, and it was a poor reason. The second was perhaps a feeling that Parker, an older steadier man, might be of service in restraining the impetuous Nelson when it came to the diplomatic rather than the naval side of their task. As it turned out this was almost as poor a reason as the first.

The fleet was due to sail, but a last-minute attempt to settle the dispute with the Danes was not neglected. The Government was in limbo, with

Ministers half in and half out of office, Pitt, though he had resigned, still had to present his Army and Navy Estimates to Parliament, but somehow or other Addington and Lord Hawkesbury, the new Foreign Secretary, had managed to assemble a last-minute diplomatic mission to assist Mr William Drummond, the British Minister in Copenhagen. Admittedly it was not a very impressive mission, as it consisted only of Mr Nicholas Vansittart and Dr Beeke, his clerk. Vansittart was a thirty-four-year-old barrister who had been called to the Bar ten years previously; five years later he had been elected as M.P. for Hastings and literally a few days before had been appointed by Addington as one of the two new joint Secretaries to the Treasury.

Vansittart then was not a Foreign Office Minister, nor of course a professional diplomat, and as ministers ranked he was about as low as it was possible to be in the hierarchy. Originally it had been thought that he should travel to Copenhagen in a frigate, but it was finally decided that he would go in the civilian packet boat from Harwich to Cuxhaven and thence on to Hamburg. The lowly status of his mission was perhaps explained by the fact that he was being sent in response to a vague peace-feeler which had been conveyed in a roundabout fashion to the British Government by Prince Charles of Hesse, the Danish Crown Prince's father-in-law.

The official negotiations were still being conducted by the British Minister in Copenhagen, and the Danish Minister in London, Count de Wedel Jarlsburg. On February 23 the Count delivered a note to Lord Hawkesbury which was couched in such adamant terms that Addington and his Cabinet must have realised that the recently-departed Vansittart was off on a wasted journey. Accordingly orders were given, in the King's name, 'to the Fleet destined for the Baltic to sail without delay'. The final offer to the Danes was to be sent by way of a dispatch in the hands of Sir Hyde Parker.

The ships of the fleet had been assembling and fitting out since January. At the end of March Denmark had placed an embargo on all British ships in her ports, Danish troops had entered Hamburg, and the Elbe had been declared closed to British merchant ships. A few days later Lubeck had also been occupied, to bring British seaborne trade to a halt. Diplomacy might continue, but it was about to give way to what Louis XIV had inscribed on his guns, *ultima ratio regis*, in George III's case the broadsides of twenty ships of the line.

In fact there were a number of changes to the ships earmarked for the

Baltic, dependent on their state of readiness, but the final choice was of two 98's, *St George* and *London*, the flagships of Nelson and Hyde Parker, respectively, eleven 74's, *Edgar, Warrior, Elephant, Saturn, Ganges, Defence, Bellona, Monarch, Defiance, Ramillies* and *Russell*. There were five 64's, *Raisonnable, Polyphemus, Ardent, Veteran* and *Agamemnon*, plus one 54, *Glatton*, and one 50, *Isis*. In addition there were six frigates, two sloops, seven bomb ketches and two fire ships. This was a bigger and more powerful force than Nelson had commanded at the Nile where he had thirteen well matched 74's, one 50 and a brig. In the process Nelson lost *San Josef* which had too deep a draught for work off the Scandinavian shores but had acquired the first ship he served in, *Raisonnable*, and the first first rate he had commanded, *Agamemnon*.

Some idea of the durability of wooden ships may be gained by looking at the ages of these components of a picked force. Only *Ardent* was a new ship, built in 1796, for the rest the average age was about twenty years, while some were thirty years old and *Bellona*, only a trifle older than *Monarch* and *Raisonnable*, had been built in 1760, more than forty years previously. *Glatton* was the most curious ship in the fleet, but her presence indicated the sort of action which might have to be fought. She was a converted East Indiaman, and was being tried out as a floating gun platform with a new armament of twenty-eight 68 pound short-range carronades and twenty-eight 48 pounders of the same type. *Glatton*'s role would be close bombardment of positions on shore, a curious task perhaps for her captain, William Bligh, who had survived a 3000-mile voyage across the Timor Sea, after being set adrift by the mutinous crew of *Bounty*. Of the other captains, Thomas Foley of *Elephant*, had commanded *Goliath* at the Nile and Sir Thomas Thompson now of *Bellona* had commanded *Leander*. As well as Hardy there were other officers like Atkinson, *Elephant*'s Master, who had been at Teneriffe and the Nile, and Bertie, *Ardent*'s captain, a fromer messmate with Troubridge and Nelson on board *Seahorse*. Commanding *Ganges* was Betsy's husband, Thomas Fremantle.

Nevertheless there was not the 'band of brothers' atmosphere of the Nile, and though many officers were destined to serve at Trafalgar, for most of them the coming operation was to be their first experience in action with an admiral hitherto known only to them by reputation. In their private lives both Nelson and Parker had reasons for not relishing an immediate departure to cold Northern waters. Yet it was Nelson the clandestine, passionate and jealous lover who was far more impatient for battle than the respectably wedded husband of a teenage bride. Some of the difference was due to age, some to temperament, but a great deal was due to the fact that Nelson had grasped the essence of the Baltic operation while Parker had not.

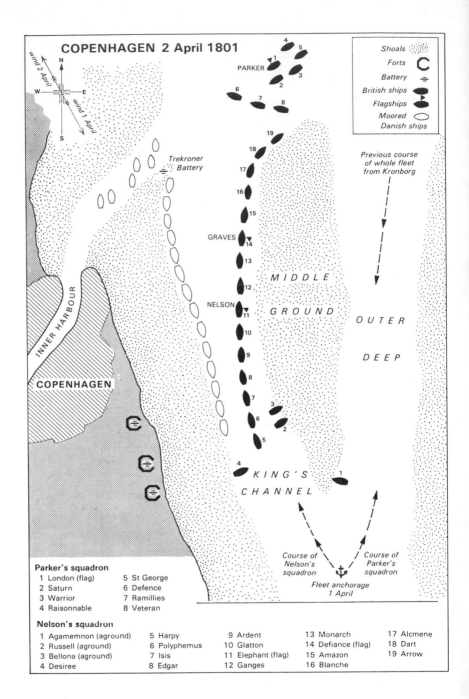

COPENHAGEN 2 April 1801

N
W E
S

wind 2 April

wind 1 April

PARKER

Trekroner Battery

INNER HARBOUR

COPENHAGEN

Previous course of whole fleet from Kronborg

MIDDLE

GROUND

OUTER

DEEP

GRAVES

NELSON

KING'S

CHANNEL

Course of Nelson's squadron

Course of Parker's squadron

Fleet anchorage 1 April

Shoals	
Forts	C
Battery	⚓
British ships	
Flagships	▼
Moored Danish ships	◯

Parker's squadron

1 London (flag)	5 St George
2 Saturn	6 Defence
3 Warrior	7 Ramillies
4 Raisonnable	8 Veteran

Nelson's squadron

1 Agamemnon (aground)	5 Harpy	9 Ardent	13 Monarch	17 Alcmene
2 Russell (aground)	6 Polyphemus	10 Glatton	14 Defiance (flag)	18 Dart
3 Bellona (aground)	7 Isis	11 Elephant (flag)	15 Amazon	19 Arrow
4 Desiree	8 Edgar	12 Ganges	16 Blanche	

CHAPTER TWENTY-SIX

Copenhagen

HORATIO NELSON had never possessed a great deal of patience, nor tolerance of the faults of others, though he expected more than Christian charity to be extended to his own. However, the attitude of Sir Hyde Parker to the Baltic expedition which he commanded gave every excuse for impatience, even to one of a far more docile disposition than his second-in-command. The ships were ready, and 860 soldiers of the 49th and 95th Foot under the command of an efficient young colonel, the Hon. William Stewart, were waiting to act as a landing force, but Sir Hyde dallied on shore, looking forward to a ball planned by his bride.

Fortunately for posterity Lieutenant-Colonel Stewart, whom Nelson, as soon as he returned from London, ordered to get his troops on board in double quick time, followed in the steps of his predecessor Drinkwater at St Vincent, and turned out to be another military diarist. His 'Journal of the Baltic Expedition' gives a characteristic glimpse of Nelson on board *St George*: 'His Lordship was rather too apt to interfere in the working of the ship and not always with the best success or judgement.' On such occasions Hardy, the flag captain, apparently disappeared tactfully into the background. So off Dungeness in a poor wind Nelson gave the order to put the ship about, as a result she missed stays, that is failed to tack. Whereupon after a terse exchange with the sailing master the Admiral stalked off to his cabin leaving the captain, the master and the ship's officers to sort the matter out. Perhaps it was just another manifestation of Nelson's impatience, though there were other more weighty reasons why the Baltic Expedition should get under way, than what Southey called Nelson's 'ardent temperament'.

If the operation were to be successful speed was of the essence. Delay only favoured the potential enemy. The Danes were proving intransigent, not only through fear of Russia but on their own account; the Swedes were an unknown quantity, and the Russians actively hostile. Time was being thrown away during which the Danes could, and did, prepare Copenhagen against attack and the Baltic weather became warmer, thus unfreezing the Russian fleet. Something could be done, what Nelson was later to call 'a home stroke', by a fleet off Copenhagen or elsewhere in the Baltic, but nothing was being achieved by a fleet of warships swinging round their anchors in an English port.

This was the situation Nelson found on joining Sir Hyde in the Yarmouth Roads on March 6. In an attempt to shake his Commander-in-Chief out of his lethargy Nelson reported his arrival, and announced that he would wait upon his superior the next morning for orders after breakfast which to Nelson, always an early riser, meant 8 o'clock in the morning. Nelson knew that Sir Hyde had already received his general orders hoped by arriving at the door of the Wrestlers' Arms, where Sir Hyde and Lady Parker were comfortably quartered, as Stewart put it, 'amusingly exact to that hour' to shame his superior into action. However, Sir Hyde, was not to be hurried into anything precipitate by an impatient junior. To Nelson's, and Stewart's, disgust, his mind was still concerned with festivities on shore. Parker, not a foolish man, even if an idle one, must have been wary of his famous second-in-command, but if he hoped to keep him at bay with social chit-chat he severely underestimated him.

Nelson sent off a letter post-haste to Troubridge, now, under St Vincent, at the Admiralty. Relations between Troubridge and Nelson had recently deteriorated, probably because of Troubridge's attitude to Lady Hamilton coupled with the fact that Sir Thomas was now, in his present post, superior to his former chief. Nevertheless Nelson wanted action, and was prepared to use any means to get his way. He wrote:

> I know my dear Troubridge, how angry the Earl [St Vincent] would be if he knew I, as second in command, was to venture to give an opinion, because I know of his opinion of officers writing to the Admiralty. But what I say is in the mouth of all the old market women at Yarmouth—Consider how nice it must be laying in bed with a young wife, compared to a damned cold raw wind. But my dear Troubridge, pack us off . . .

The express order from the Lords of the Admiralty arrived within days and so, despite filthy weather, Nelson could write triumphantly to Troubridge on March 11:

> Now we can have no desire for staying for her Ladyship [Lady Parker]

is gone, and the ball for Friday night knocked up by you and the Earl's unpoliteness to send gentlemen to sea instead of dancing with nice white gloves.

So the fleet at last went to sea, with its second-in-command still writing daily letters to his mistress assuring her of a 'heart susceptible and true', in the midst of more pressing professional problems. As a fleet it was still much more a collection of warships travelling in the same direction at a rather slower pace, rather than a close-knit, organised, and co-ordinated, fighting force.

Some preparations had been made for action in the Baltic, but they were by individual officers provided, sensibly, by the Admiralty. In particular Captains Frederick Thesiger and Nicholas Tomlinson both of whom had served with distinction in the Imperial Russian Navy. Naturally enough, they spoke Russian, and Thesiger spoke Danish as well. Neither captain commanded a ship but were present as volunteers, Tomlinson on board Sir Hyde's flagship, *London*, and Thesiger on board *Elephant* which was eventually to wear Nelson's flag. Also on board *London*, though not due to any Admiralty wisdom, was the Reverend Alexander John Scott, a favourite of Sir Hyde's and destined to be Nelson's chaplain at Trafalgar. Scott had one outstanding talent, a gift for languages. He already spoke French, German, Italian and Spanish, in addition to the classicist's knowledge of Latin and Greek. As soon as a Baltic action had been mooted he set to work to familiarise himself with Russian and Danish.

All very useful if diplomacy and negotiation was in prospect, but unfortunately, Sir Hyde made no use of the professional knowledge of the Baltic possessed by the two officers. Not surprising, perhaps, in a fleet commander who only on the day of sailing managed to issue through Domett, his Captain of the Fleet, his Order of Sailing and Order of Battle, both in a confused and unsatisfactory form which had to be changed when action was in the offing. Admiral Graves, the junior admiral, had not yet joined the fleet, and Nelson fretted in the wake of a commanding admiral who had not yet bothered to communicate with him save in the most perfunctory fashion.

It is true that Sir Hyde's orders from the Admiralty, so far as they applied to Denmark, counselled alternative courses for making the will of the British Government felt, 'amicable arrangement' or 'actual hostilities', whereas so far as Russia was concerned 'an immediate and vigorous attack' on Reval was enjoined. Yet Sir Hyde was not a diplomat, but an admiral in command of a battle fleet and there was no excuse for delay in actually getting to Denmark and Copenhagen where, as Nelson wrote to Davison, the visible presence of the British fleet 'would give weight to our negotiations'. 'The Dane should see our Flag waving every moment he lifted his head'. Nevertheless it was not until March 19 that the fleet reached the Skaw, the northernmost point of Denmark, and in the evening of the 20th Parker anchored in the Kattegat, still some distance from Copenhagen. There was a favourable wind to take the fleet to the Danish capital, but Parker acted as if determined not to make a show of force, which was, as Nelson felt, surely the whole point of having diplomats on shore and sailors afloat.

Fortunately there had been some breakdown of the barrier previously existing between Parker and Nelson. Whether the improvement in relations really occurred because, as Lieutenant Layman of *St George* afterwards maintained, Nelson sent a turbot, caught by Layman on the Dogger Bank, to Sir Hyde as a sort of peace offering, is rather doubtful. However, there was at last some communication, but Nelson still only knew from Sir Hyde 'a little of his intentions'. In fact, it is doubtful if Parker himself knew what he intended to do. Only when the fleet was at anchor and the problem of what the next move was to be had to be resolved, did Parker, by calling a council of his flag officers and captains, at last take the opinion of his experienced second-in-command. As Nelson wrote to Emma, with considerable truth, 'Now we are sure of fighting, I am sent for. When it was a joke I was kept in the background.'

Parker had learnt on the 23rd from Vansittart, when he came out to the fleet, that his last-minute mission had failed and that Copenhagen was being prepared to resist. Now that the issue was to be put to the arbitrament of arms Nelson had to be consulted.

Nelson found the council of war on board *London* both pessimistic and undecided. The pessimism was occasioned by the fact that an attack by ships on shore batteries, plus whatever the Danes had prepared in the way of moored warships and floating batteries, was bound to be a risky business. The indecision stemmed from the geographical position of Copenhagen. There were two approaches, and they were also the two entrances to the Baltic. From its anchorage in the Kattegat the British fleet could make its way directly through the Sound past the eastern shore of the island of Zealand (Saeland) on which the capital stands, or else enter the Baltic by the much wider Great Belt and thence round the whole western and southern shore of Zealand and thereafter northwards up the eastern coast to Copenhagen. The Sound route was obviously the quicker, with difficult winds perhaps by as much as two weeks, but it was considerably more dangerous because of the narrowness of the channel which could be covered by shore batteries from both the Danish and Swedish shores.

This was the real problem which faced the sea officers assembled in the Admiral's great cabin on board *London*. Also present were Vansittart and Colonel Stewart and though no notes or formal minutes of the meeting were taken it is possible to chart the ebb and flow of the argument by way of subsequent letters written by the civilian and the soldier as well as by Parker and Nelson themselves.

Vansittart's role was to give a report on the negotiations, but he also gave an alarming picture of Danish preparations. Nelson brushed these aside as the inexpert opinion of a mere civilian, he had no high opinion of what he called 'pen and ink men'. Instead Nelson put forward the proposal, novel and alarming to Sir Hyde, that Copenhagen could be by-passed. Russia was the enemy, it was the Russian fleet which should be destroyed. If the trunk of the Northern Coalition could be cut through, the branches would wither away. In essence he was right, but Sir Hyde's counter-argument had considerable force. If the British engaged the Russians and perhaps the Swedes, and suffered loss and damage, what chances would their crippled fleet, endeavouring to make its exit from the Baltic, have against an untouched Danish navy? Nelson conceded the point, but unwillingly. What separated him from the attitude of his superior was that he never thought save in terms of victory.

The argument was now between the Belt and the Sound. Having heard from Vansittart that the Danish strength was at the head of their line, Nelson first argued that their fleet should therefore be taken from the rear, and so the long and difficult passage of the Belt should be attempted. Perhaps it was not a very good argument, but Nelson's mind was not so much on alternative approaches as the necessity of making some approach, and quickly.

'Let it be by the Sound or the Belt or anyhow', he said, 'only lose not an hour.' Lieutenant Layman who had caught the turbot and steered Nelson's gig to *London*, noticed, on first seeing so much gold braid assembled on board the flagship, 'all the heads were very gloomy'. It was this atmosphere that Nelson was so desperately anxious to dispel and it is not difficult to imagine his sense of frustration, not being in complete control, but forced to defer to naval seniority in the shape of Sir Hyde Parker. Not that Parker roused in him the same feeling of positive dislike he had for Lord Keith, it was perhaps for this reason that there was never anything like open disagreement between the two admirals. Undoubtedly the younger man used all his powers of persuasion not only on his senior but on his junior, Graves, and the assembled captains as well. As a result, when he left *London* the collective opinion appeared to be, but only appeared to be, that an attempt would be made by the Belt.

Returning to his own ship, fearful that there might be second thoughts, that perhaps the cautious Captain of the Fleet might influence Parker in the wrong direction, or that Sir Hyde might find his resolution evaporating, Nelson drafted a long, able and tactful letter:

My dear Sir Hyde,

The conversation we had yesterday has naturally, from its importance, been the subject of my thoughts; and the more I have reflected, the more I am confirmed in opinion, that not a moment should be lost in attacking the Enemy. They will every day and hour be stronger; we shall never be so good a match for them as at this moment.

The only consideration in my mind is how to get at them with the least risk to our Ships. By Mr Vansittart's account, the Danes have taken every means in their power to prevent our getting to attack Copenhagen by the Passage of Sound. Cronenburg has been strengthened, the Crown Islands fortified, on the outermost of which there are twenty guns pointing mostly downwards, and only eight hundred yards from very formidable batteries placed under the Citadel, supported by five Sail-of-the-Line, seven Floating batteries of fifty guns each, besides Small-craft, Gun-boats etcetera, etcetera. And that the Revel Squadron of twelve or fourteen Sail-of-the-Line are soon expected as also five Sail of Swedes.

It would appear by what you have told me of your instructions, that Government took for granted you would find no difficulty in getting off Copenhagen, and in the event of a failure of negotiation, you might instantly attack; and that there would be scarcely a doubt but the Danish fleet would be destroyed, and the Capital made so hot that Denmark would listen to reason and its true interest. By Mr Vansittart's account, their state of preparation exceeds what he conceives our Government thought possible, and that the Danish Government is hostile to us in the greatest possible degree.

Therefore here you are, with almost the safety, certainly with the honour of England more entrusted to you than ever yet fell to any British Officer. On your decision depends, whether our country shall be degraded in the eyes of Europe, or whether she shall rear her head higher than ever; again do I repeat, never did our Country depend so much on the success of any Fleet as on this. How best to honour our Country and abate the pride of her Enemies, by defeating their schemes, must be the subject of your deepest consideration as Commander-in-Chief; and if what I have to offer can be the least useful in forming your decision, you are most heartily welcome.

I shall begin with supposing you are determined to enter by the Passage of the Sound, as there are those who think, if you leave that Passage open, that the Danish Fleet may sail from Copenhagen, and join the Dutch or French. I own I have no fears on that subject; for it is not likely that whilst their Capital is menaced with an attack, 9000 of her best men should be sent out of the Kingdom. I suppose that some damage may arise amongst our masts and yards; yet, perhaps there will not be one of them but could be made serviceable again. You are now about Cronenburg; if the wind be fair, and you determine to attack the Ships and Crown Islands, you must expect the natural issue of such a battle—Ships crippled, and perhaps one or two lost; for the wind which carries you in, will most probably not bring out a crippled Ship. This mode I call taking the bull by the horns. It, however, will not prevent the Revel Ships, or Swedes, from joining the Danes; and to prevent this from taking effect, is in my humble opinion, a measure absolutely necessary—and still to attack Copenhagen.

Two modes are in my view; one to pass Cronenburg, taking the risk of damage, and to pass up the deepest and straightest Channel above the Middle Grounds; and coming down the Garbar or King's Channel, to attack their Floating batteries etcetera, etcetera, as we find it convenient. It must have the effect of preventing a junction between the Russians, Swedes and Danes, and may give us an opportunity of bombarding Copenhagen. I am also pretty certain that a passage could be found to the northward of Southolm for all our Ships; perhaps it might be necessary to warp a short distance in the very narrow part.

Should this mode of attack be ineligible, the passage of the Belt, I have no doubt, would be accomplished in four or five days, and then the attack by Draco could be carried into effect, and the junction of the Russians prevented, with every probability of success against the Danish Floating batteries. What effect a bombardment might have, I am not called upon to give an opinion; but think the way should be cleared for the trial.

Supposing us through the Belt, with the wind first westerly, would it not be possible to either go with the Fleet, or detach ten Ships of three and two decks, with one Bomb and two Fire-ships, to Revel, to destroy the Russian Squadron at that place? I do not see the great risk of such a detachment, and with the remainder to attempt the business at Copenhagen. The measure may be thought bold, but I am of opinion the boldest measures are the safest; and our Country demands a most vigorous exertion of her force, directed with judgment. In supporting you, my dear Sir Hyde, through the arduous and important task you have undertaken, no exertion of head or heart shall be wanting from your most obedient and faithful servant,

Nelson and Brontë.

Nelson himself had not sailed in the Baltic since he had commanded *Albemarle* but apart from the Russian experts, there were a number of captains in the fleet who had considerable experience of the dangers and difficulties of these waters. Also on board the principal ships were pilots culled from the Baltic trade, but they, in Nelson's view, suffered from the defect of being ignorant of warfare and therefore liable to be over-influenced by the careful considerations of peacetime navigation.

Plainly he favoured the direct, and the quickest, approach, through the Sound, and this was the basic message of his letter; what he had to destroy was the idea—and it was prevalent and not unacceptable to Sir Hyde—that the British fleet might wait in the Kattegat until the Danish, Swedish and Russian fleets emerged from the Baltic. Absurd as it seems, even when numerical superiority alone was considered, it was a course which could appeal to an irresolute commander.

The letter, to be taken by boat from *St George* to *Lion*, was meant to put backbone into Sir Hyde Parker. But before it was sent Parker decided to move, but not in the direction favoured by Nelson. Entry to the Baltic was to be made by the circuitous and dangerous Belt route, and the fleet was ordered to weigh anchor and make course for the westerly channel. Then Sir Hyde had doubts, which most likely arose out of conversations with Domett, and Otway, his flag captain, and sent for Nelson and Captain Murray of *Edgar*, who was much experienced in the Baltic, to come aboard *London*.

On board, Nelson read the rough draft of his letter to the Commander-in-Chief. Only later, after the battle, did Nelson actually send a final copy to Parker, in a chivalrous attempt to shield his senior from criticism, 'as it brings forward all which passed on that occasion'. Sir Hyde did in fact agree to take the fleet past Kronborg, but not to Nelson's suggestion of detaching a squadron of ships to attack the Russians at Reval. He did however accept Nelson's other suggestion, that the Danes should be taken from the south, a course of action which would involve ships in sailing first south and then north, a not uncomplicated manoeuvre, and one which depended upon the vagaries of wind and weather. This is what 'pass *up* the deepest and the straightest Channel above the Middle Grounds; and coming *down* the Garbar or King's Channel' meant. Thus on the morning of March 30, after Parker had engaged in a fruitless parley with the Governor of Kronborg Castle, who declared he would fire on a fleet in strength if within range, the ships finally set sail, with a favourable wind, direct for Copenhagen.

It should be remembered that Sir Hyde Parker was ultimately responsible for success or failure. He was armed with very general orders, by now out of date, so that discretion was his. Nelson had persuaded him to action, by the Sound, but both Domett, his right-hand man, and Otway, his flag captain, agreed with Nelson. The other admiral, Graves, seems to have been less sanguine. The dangers were of two types, from enemy action and from navigational and weather hazards. Enemy action would make itself felt at two stages, during the passage of the Sound and when the fleet engaged the defences off Copenhagen. The navigational and wind hazards went together, so could the fleet be taken south and then again north in waterways known to be bedevilled by shoals and sandbanks?

Among Nelson biographers it was Mahan, with sea experience of his own under both sail and steam, who first comprehended the extent to which Nelson behaved as if for him winds did not exist, an extraordinary thing in a commander in the age of sail. Perhaps he believed, as Ball declared, that he was a 'heaven born admiral', but certainly a great part of his genius lay in the fact that 'he himself never trifled with a fair wind, nor with time'. The risks at Copenhagen were therefore more considerable than at the Nile or Trafalgar, but Nelson knew, and accepted, which was another thing, that war could not be made without risk.

From the evening of March 26 the fleet had been at anchor six miles from Kronborg detained by head winds and calms and during this time Nelson shifted his flag from *St George* to the lighter *Elephant*, a 74, and thus acquired Foley as his flag captain. He had commanded *Goliath* at the Nile and had been the unsuccessful suitor for the hand of the lady who was now Mrs Fremantle, wife of the captain of *Ganges*. Just before sunrise at 5.36 on Monday March 30 the signal to weigh anchor flew from the signal halyards of *London*, followed by 'Form Line of Battle'. *Monarch* and her captain, J. R. Mosse, led the fleet; it was to be his last battle, 'At about 6 being abreast the Castle [Kronborg]' recorded Midshipman Millard, 'the Captain ordered the Colours to be hoisted . . . before the ensign was halfway to the peak, a shot was fired from the Castle, and with such precision as to drive water into the lower deck ports, though it fell short of the ship. We immediately commenced firing . . .'.

The passage of the rest of the fleet was a considerable anti-climax. Not a gun was fired from the Swedish shore, and all the shots from the Danes fell short as the British ships hauled towards the Swedish shore, once it was realised that there was no danger from that side, thus putting themselves out of range. Some captains, like Mosse, fired at the Danish fortress, others did not even bother. Bomb vessels, placing them in position had been Nelson's idea, did reply to the batteries, both with little discernible effect. The only casualties in the whole British fleet were two seamen on board *Monarch*, slightly injured by a recoiling gun.

The one person quite definitely not surprised by this turn of events was Nelson, commanding the van division. During the fleet's passage of the Sound he was in his cabin writing letters. 'More powder and shot, I believe, never was thrown away' was his comment. 'The *Elephant* did not return a single shot, I hope to reserve them for a better occasion.' Mere bravado? Probably much more likely a nice calculation of risks. He could not know that the Swedish batteries would not fire, but he may have suspected it of the most inactive and lukewarm partners in the Tsar's alliance.

Even assuming that the Swedish guns, lighter than those of the Danes, had been used the risk to moving ships would not have been great. The width of the Sound at this point was two and a half miles, and the maximum effective range of a 32-pounder gun was one and a half miles. The Danish guns were in fact 36-pounders, but their range was no more.

Denmark had been at peace for years and their artillerymen were extremely unlikely to be up to the standard that only constant practice can give. A hit at a range of over a mile would be by luck, and wooden ships could take a lot of shot. At the very worst, if both Swedes and Danes were firing, the range, if ships kept to the middle of the channel, was one and three quarters of a mile, and for ships sailing at the minimum of six knots the time spent under fire would be only about quarter of an hour. In one of his letters Nelson wrote that he 'received directions from Sir Hyde Parker to take under my directions ten sail of the line, four frigates, four sloops, seven bombs, two fireships and twelve gun brigs which have to be employed on a particular service'. He had already prepared a memorandum for his captains, for though Parker retained overall command the real battle was to be his. The myth that Kronborg Castle was the 'guardian of the Sound', had been punctured, but ahead lay the defences of Copenhagen which were real and formidable.

At about 10 o'clock on the morning of March 30 the fleet was safely anchored in two lines between the islands of Ven and Amager and Sir Hyde decided upon a reconnaissance. Captain Riou, a young man of whom Nelson speedily formed a high opinion, was told off with his frigate *Amazon* to take on board Parker, Nelson, Graves, Domett and Colonel Stewart, so that they could survey and consider the problem before them. It all seems rather leisurely, but the Danes had chosen to rely upon static defence rather than a moving fleet, partly so that their small fleet could be reinforced by floating batteries. Consequently they had given themselves no alternative but to surrender or fight. They had also, like the French in Aboukir Bay, boxed themselves in, and so once more Nelson was able to profit from the dispositions of his enemy.

Even more forcibly, now that the fleet was safely past Kronborg, one can see even better the wisdom of Nelson's suggestion, rejected by Parker, that the main body should go on to the Russian ports, leaving a holding force to watch the Danes. It is one of the ironies of history that if that course had been adopted there would have been no battle of Copenhagen at all. For unknown to both the Danes and to the British, what Nelson called the 'trunk' of the Armed Neutrality had been sawn through. At the same time as Nelson was drafting his letter to Parker in the Mikhailovsky Palace the Tsar of all the Russias had been strangled with an officer's sash. Insanity and oppressions, excessive even by Russian standards, had driven a band of conspirators, Counts Rostopchin, Panin and Pahlen, the latter the commander of the St Petersburg garrison, and Generals Ouvaroff and Bennigsen, to desperate means. The Grand Duke Alexander, the Tsarevitch, had certainly been privy to a plot to dethrone his father, but had perhaps stopped short at patricide. Paul had been forced to sign an instrument of abdication before his death, which was announced officially as being due to an apoplectic fit.

Russia now had a new Tsar, and in consequence there was a shift in foreign policy. Though later Alexander I was to be in turn neutral, enemy and ally in Britain's struggle with France, with his accession the Armed Neutrality fell apart. News travelled slowly in 1801, so a group of British officers continued their task of considering how to reduce the capital of a country with which their own was not at war.

In the considerable time given to them by the dilatory methods of British diplomacy, combined with Parker's remarkable lack of vigour, the Danes had prepared a formidable array of armaments. They could also place some confidence in the natural difficulties of any approach to their capital, which they had increased by removing all the navigational buoys. The Sound, opposite the citadel and harbour of Copenhagen, was divided into two channels, the Outer Deep to the east, and the King's Channel to the west, by an extensive shoal, the Middle Ground. From Kronborg the British fleet had sailed southwards down the Outer Deep and now to approach inshore and attack Copenhagen from the south it would be necessary to take ships northwards up the King's Channel.

The defences of the city were stronger to the north than the south, no doubt because it was assumed any attacker would move from north to south. The northern approach was guarded by the Trekroner batteries which were two forts mounted on piles in the water, armed with thirty 24-pounder guns and thirty-eight 36-pounders. The Trekroner, the three crowns of the once-united kingdoms of Sweden, Denmark and Norway, guarded the approach to the inner harbour, and in the actual entrance were two two-decked hulks, *Elephanten* and *Mars*, and in the fairway were two 74's, a frigate and two eighteen-gun brigs. Stretching to the south the Danes had placed a line, more than a mile long, of eighteen warships, armed hulks and floating batteries, covering the east front of the city, their 600 guns pointing in the direction of the danger-ous sands of the Middle Ground. These vessels were moored in the King's Channel. On the shoals and the actual shore behind them were also a number of supporting batteries.

This was the opposition which had to be considered at the Council of

War which assembled on board *London*. After inspecting the Danish defences, Nelson was probably the only optimistic senior officer. The armament looked formidable enough to 'those who are children at war' yet 'with ten sail of the line I think I can annihilate them; at all events, I hope to be allowed to try'. Then the discussion ranged further afield than the immediate problem of Copenhagen and once again, as Stewart recorded, it was Nelson who had the task of carrying his colleagues with him by his own enthusiasm:

> During this Council the energy of Lord Nelson's character was remarked: certain difficulties had been started by some of the members, relative to each of the three Powers we should either have to engage, in succession or united, in those seas. The number of Russians was, in particular, represented as formidable. Lord Nelson kept pacing the cabin, mortified at everything which savoured either of alarm or irresolution. When the above remark was applied to the Swedes, he sharply observed, 'The more numerous the better'; and when to the Russians he repeatedly said, 'So much the better, I wish they were twice as many; the easier the victory, depend on it'. He alluded, as he afterwards explained in private, to the total want of tactique among the Northern Fleets; and to his intention, whenever he should bring either the Swedes or Russians to action, of attacking the head of their Line, and confusing their movements as much as possible. He used to say, 'Close with a Frenchman, but out-manoeuvre a Russian'.

Perhaps Nelson exaggerated his confidence, but no doubt he felt he had to, for apart from Sir Hyde's caution the doubts of other senior officers had also to be overcome, Graves feeling that they would be 'playing a losing game, attacking stone walls' and Fremantle that the fleet had arrived too late.

It was not until the afternoon of March 31 that Nelson knew that he was at last to be allowed to put his plan into practice. Generously, Sir Hyde had assigned him two more ships of the line than he had requested. From then on all was bustle and activity, much of it at night as senior officers, Hardy included, took soundings of the depth of the channel, and as small boat parties replaced, as best they could, the buoys and markers removed by the Danes.

On April 1 Nelson made a final examination in *Amazon*. At 1 p.m. the signal for Nelson's squadron to weigh anchor was given, there were cheers from all ships and Captain Riou led the detachment down the Outer Channel to moor at the southern end of the Middle Ground. All that was now needed was a favourable wind to take Nelson's force of *Elephant, Edgar, Bellona, Russell, Ganges, Monarch* and *Defiance*, all 74's, and *Polyphemus, Agamemnon, Glatton* and *Isis*, plus six frigates and the sloops and bomb vessels, northwards through the King's Channel and also to take Sir Hyde's remaining eight ships through the Outer Deep. The requirements for the two admirals were not, of course, the same. Current, depth of water, and the ill-defined presence of shoals had also to be considered, and a fair wind for Nelson's squadron would require a considerable amount of tacking and manoeuvring by Parker's. Even in distance the courses for the two squadrons were not comparable, Parker's ships had to get beyond the northernmost tip of the Middle Ground shoal before they could perform any useful function, and Nelson's ships would be in action against the lower reaches of the Danish line long before Parker's heavier ships could exercise any influence over the battle. In any event the function of Parker's squadron was largely psychological. It might be used in an emergency but it was there as a reserve, and its presence might help to overawe the Danes, although the actual battle was going to be won or lost by Nelson.

The events of the night before action were intensely dramatic, and, centred around the arrival of Hardy on board *Elephant*, fresh from a daring feat of reconnaissance. In an open boat, with muffled oars, equipped with a long pole, he had been sounding the depth of water right up to the sides of the moored Danish vessels. Contrary to what might have been expected, close inshore the depth was considerable, certainly some of the enemy could have been 'doubled' as at the Nile. However, perhaps that would have been too much of a risk even for Nelson, to put some of his ships between the Danish fleet and the shoal on the Copenhagen side of the Channel.

In the great cabin of *Elephant* there was now assembled something akin to the first band of brothers. Before Hardy's arrival they had sat down to dinner, late, by the standards of the day; Rear-Admiral Graves, Nelson's second-in-command, Foley his flag captain, Captain Riou the new acquisition, and Fremantle the old friend, Colonel Stewart and Lieutenant-Colonel Hutchinson, who commanded the detachment of the 49th Foot. Hardy's coming on board signalised that all had been done to investigate the enemy's strength and the hazards of shoals and depths. Nelson was in high spirits and drank to a fair wind the next day, at the moment there was but a late evening breeze from the south-west, but the conviviality of the gathering, often represented in pictures and prints, gives something of a false impression of the occasion. Certainly Nelson sought to inspire his captains, but that other side of genius, hard work and preparation, was also demonstrated that night.

It is likely that Nelson, and even more so his brother officers, over-estimated the strength of the Danish position. The Nile had shown the disadvantages of moored ships opposed to a moving enemy. Yet here at Copenhagen was what seemed a solid wall of ships and guns, and they were to be fought from one side only. On the other hand, the Danish power to resist was under-estimated. They had little recent experience of war, but they had their capital at their back to provide both incentive and reinforcements. For Brueys in Aboukir Bay a ship destroyed meant the irrevocable loss of men and guns. For the Danish Crown Prince and his two principal officers, Commodore Johan Fischer and Captain Steen Bille, a battery knocked out could be repaired while the places of gunners killed or wounded could be filled from men on shore. The principal disadvantage in their position was their confined arc of fire, as opposed to that of Nelson's ships, moored by the stern, and therefore moveable by means of another rope, a 'spring', secured to the anchor cable.

Nelson had found out as much as he could about the enemy, and from the conclusion of his dinner until the early hours he was busy, with the aid of six clerks, in drafting his orders. They were headed 'General Orders H.M.S. *Elephant*, Copenhagen Roads, 2 April 6 a.m.' and set out precisely the task of each ship under his command. The enemy were numbered in order and described with an estimate of each vessel's gun power:

No.	Rate	Supposed number of guns mounted on one side	Station of the line as they are to anchor and engage
I	74 (in fact *Proevesteen*)	28	*Agamemnon*. The *Desirée* is to follow *Agamemnon* and rake No. I

and so through the list to number 20, 'a small float supposed a bomb'. The British ships were to concentrate on the southern part of the line and then Numbers 1, 2, 3 and 4 being subdued, 'which is expected to happen at an early period', cut their cables and move on.

There were separate detailed orders for the British bomb vessels to attack the arsenal and flat-bottom boats were to be ready to land and disembark the soldiers under Stewart and Hutchinson. Riou was given virtually independent command of the frigates.

Nelson took cat naps in his cot throughout the night, despite the remonstrances of his servant, Tom Allen, and repeatedly enquired of the wind and what progress the clerks, scratching away with their quills, were making. By 5.30 a.m. the task was still not completed, but Nelson was determined that each captain should have his separate orders, and they were each issued with individual instructions written on cards. This was, in the Navy of the time, planning of an unprecedented order and it is noteworthy that Nelson, a planner before action, made few signals once action was joined. There were three excellent reasons which favoured this course. First, that if captains were well-briefed beforehand signals were unnecessary. Second, that flags were frequently obscured by smoke in action. Third, that the signalling system, though much improved by the use of Admiral Popham's Signalling Code, was still cumbersome and slow. A limited number of orders before battle to captains, allowed to use their own initiative, was worth hundreds of signal flags during action, which might fail to convey the commander's intention.

Once the captains had their orders, and a wind, which had been east-by-south, was freshening and veering to south-by-east, there remained only one obstacle, the opinions of the sailing masters and pilots. Nelson was all impatience but the caution still shown by the technical experts was significant in two respects. First, it showed that Sir Hyde's caution was not totally misplaced, and second, as an indication supported by later events, of the very real risks that Nelson did run. The masters and pilots were summoned by flag on board *Elephant* between 8 and 9 o'clock in the morning, and as Nelson wrote afterwards, 'I experienced the misery of having the honour of our country entrusted to a set of pilots who had no other thought than to keep the ships clear of danger, and their own silly heads clear of shot.'

In that one sentence he put succinctly the difference between his own attitude and theirs. Of course the attitude of pilots from the merchant service was different to that of a resolute fighting admiral. The *raison d'être* of their profession was to preserve ships, and lives, and cargoes;

his task was the fighting and winning of battles. That was his duty, and that of every officer and man in the Navy, and in the process risks had to be taken and, at the worst, ships and men lost. Frederick the Great had in the previous century put the military imperative in classic form to his Guard, when they had hesitated in battle, 'dogs, do you want to live forever?'

The pilots displayed what Colonel Stewart thought 'a most unpleasant degree of hesitation', but Nelson's urging had its effect. Alexander Briarly, sailing master of *Bellona*, who had been master of *Audacious* at the Nile was a navy man, not a civilian, and he 'declared himself prepared to lead the Fleet'. His example was catching, or shaming, and the other masters and the pilots returned to their own ships while Briarly went on board *Edgar*. The orders to prepare for action had already been given and obeyed on board every ship. Nelson's journal bears the entry, 'at half-past nine made the signal to weigh and engage the Danish line'. *Edgar* led the van under Briarly's direction and almost as soon as she was under way there was smoke and flame from the guns on the Danish shore. The rest of the squadron followed, astern of *Edgar*, in a slow stately fashion. A midshipman on board *Monarch*, from a point of vantage at the rear of the line, described the scene, 'a more beautiful and solemn spectacle I never witnessed'.

CHAPTER TWENTY-SEVEN

The Baltic

ALMOST AS soon as Nelson's squadron began to move up the King's Channel and along the length of the Danish guns many of the pilots' fears were confirmed. The first move against the southernmost enemy ships and batteries was a sort of leap-frog. Thus *Edgar* was to fire as she passed the Danish line, but was to come to anchor abreast of Number 5, the two-decked *Jylland*, *Ardent* was to pass *Edgar*'s starboard and disengaged side, and anchor abreast of the Danish Numbers 6 and 7, the frigate *Kronborg* and a floating battery. The task of *Glatton* with her heavy guns was to take on Commodore Fischer's flagship, *Dannebrog*. *Isis* and *Agamemnon* were to come up and anchor parallel with the Danish Number 2 and Number 1.

However, *Agamemnon* failed to negotiate the southern tip of the Middle Ground. Nelson, seeing what she was about to do, warned Captain Fancourt by signal flag of his danger. Fancourt anchored, but it was too late, for the powerful current drove him on to the shoal. His situation was similar to that of Troubridge at the Nile for despite continuous efforts to warp the ship off the shoal to windward *Agamemnon* was stuck fast, unable to use her guns at that range, and she took no further part in the battle. *Isis* took *Agamemnon*'s place, and Nelson ordered *Polyphemus*, last in line and destined for the northernmost position, to place herself astern of *Isis* and engage *Proevesteen*. Captain Langford succeeded in doing this, aided by the frigate *Desirée* which managed at considerable risk to place herself across the bows of the Danish ship and rake the three-decker, as instructed in her original orders.

Though a 64 had been lost to the battle, quick thinking had almost compensated. Next in order were *Bellona*, *Elephant*, *Ganges*, *Monarch*, *Defiance* and *Russell*; *Polyphemus* having moved out of station. Almost immediately worse was to follow, for *Bellona*, kept too much to starboard by her master and an over-apprehensive pilot, also ran aground.

Nelson's agitation, the stump of his right arm jerking spasmodically, has been testified to, and his thoughts can be imagined as he put *Elephant* into the position which should have been taken by *Bellona*. Admittedly her guns could be used, unlike those of *Agamemnon*, but the advantage she possessed over her adversaries, of movement, had been lost. Astern of Nelson's flagship was Fremantle in *Ganges*, conning the ship himself as the master had been killed, and the pilot had lost his arm. Astern of *Ganges* was *Monarch* and Admiral Graves's flagship, *Defiance*, with *Russell* astern of her. However, planned order was now fast disappearing, as, less than an hour after its commencement, the battle became general. The British ships inevitably began to crowd each other. About two hundred yards separated them from their designated targets, but still masters and pilots insisted upon starboard courses. Not from fear of gunfire but of running aground to port, though it might have been guessed, what Hardy had in part proved, that where there was depth enough to take a Danish ship of the line or a frigate, there was also enough water for a British ship as well. Nevertheless even Nelson was compelled to defer to his own sailing master, and *Elephant* was anchored further from *Dannebrog* than he wished.

There was soon yet another set-back, as in the smoke and confusion Captain Cuming's *Russell* went aground almost immediately astern of *Bellona*. She too was unable to free herself and, though her guns could be fired with effect, in little more than an hour Nelson had lost the full effectiveness of three out of his total of eleven capital ships. In the circumstances the captains behaved with admirable independence. Mosse in *Monarch* took his ship close along the whole length of the Danish line, firing broadside after broadside, until he dropped anchor opposite *Sjaelland*, a two-decker, unrigged, which was thirteenth in order from the south. *Monarch* in that position was also within range of the Trekroner fort and immediately took terrific punishment, one of the first fatal casualties being the captain himself, killed on the quarter-deck, his speaking trumpet in his right hand and Nelson's 'card of instructions' in his left. His body was placed in the stern walk and a flag thrown over it.

The last first rate to take up her position was Admiral Graves's *Defiance*, covering *Holsteen* and also within range of the guns of the Trekroner. Between the heaviest gunned British ships and the stationery Danes in Nelson's words, 'Here was no manoeuvring; it was downright fighting'. There now only remained, unplaced, Riou's frigates and the bomb vessels and minor craft. The frigates, *Amazon*, *Blanche*, *Alcmene*, *Dart* and *Arrow*, rather surprisingly considering their lighter armament, took up positions even further ahead than *Defiance* and in that order were ranged almost directly opposite the Trekroner batteries.

Thus the British ships, from *Arrow*, almost at the northern tip of the Middle Ground shoal, now stretched on an inward curving line back to *Polyphemus* and the grounded *Bellona* and *Russell*, the frigate *Desirée* and the *Harpy* sloop, at the southern tip of the shoal, and opposite the first Danish ship, the seventy-four-gun *Proevesteen*.

The time was now just about mid-day, though the logs of the various ships, as was common at the time, recorded wide disparities for actions which can be proved to have been simultaneous. In fact it was something of a miracle that logs were kept at all, as the British and the Danes at short range set down to a pounding match. Casualties mounted on both sides. On board *Bellona* Captain Sir Thomas Thompson had lost a leg. On board *Indfodstretten*, Captain Thura was dead and very soon only one lieutenant and a marine officer were alive and unwounded. The flagship *Dannebrog*, pounded by *Glatton's* carronades, burst into flames and Commodore Fischer transferred his pendant to *Holsteen*. The Danish Prince Royal, on shore by the batteries, received constant requests to replace dead or wounded captains, officers and men. There was no lack of volunteers, not only sailors but soldiers and even civilians leaving the safety of the shore to work the guns.

Plainly the will and ability of the Danes had been underestimated and the floating batteries, low in the water and therefore a difficult target for a tall-sided sail of the line, were proving much more effective than the British would have supposed. There can be no doubt that Nelson's nerves were on edge, a lieutenant on board *Elephant* who reported to Foley the grounding of *Bellona* and *Russell* was sharply reprimanded not only by his captain, but the admiral as well, for 'a desponding opinion'. The ships at the southern end of the Danish line, *Proevesteen* and *Valkyrien*, which Nelson had confidently expected to knock out early on, continued to fire their broadsides so that *Isis* and *Polyphemus* could not be transferred to help their sister ships to the north. Broadsides delivered by British vessels sailing northwards which could have crippled an enemy also sailing, had little effect on moored ships and batteries which had no sails or rigging to bring down, which functioned even if dismasted, and which could scarcely be bombarded until they sank, a rare enough occurrence even in a sailing fleet.

Nelson, though rattled, never lost his zest for a battle which he knew he could win, though it was obvious that his own ships were taking terrific punishment. All around, British warships were suffering damage to masts, spars, sails and rigging. Captain Bligh's concern, in *Glatton*, though he was a perfectionist, epitomised the danger; the British force was mobile but in this battle was fast losing its mobility. On board *Bellona*, Captain Thompson was below, in great pain, one leg a stump, reflecting that he was 'now totally disabled and my career is run through, only at the age of thirty-five', there was suddenly a deafening explosion from the forward end of the lower deck. A great hole had appeared in the main deck, the gangway and timbers had been torn away, and the wooden carriages of guns had been smashed. The smoke cleared to reveal dead and dying men, and the fact that one of the 32-pounder guns had been blown apart. An hour later the same thing happened again, and eighty-three men were killed or wounded, whether by faulty guns or inattention by the guns' crews it is impossible to say. Among the wounded was Lieutenant Thomas Southey, brother of Nelson's biographer.

Every hazard that could be visited upon a sailing fleet, grounding, enemy action and accident, seemed to be happening in Copenhagen Roads. The British logs recorded comparable damage to the Danes but so often also the last phrase was, 'but continued firing'. Many a British officer and seaman, with experience of other fights behind them, must have reflected that these peaceful Northerners were very different from Spaniards or Frenchmen, whom they were always confident of beating, being men with as much skill and endurance as themselves.

While Nelson's force had taken the westernmost channel Sir Hyde Parker in *London*, with *Defence, Ramillies, Veteran, Saturn, Warrior, St George* and *Raissonable* had beaten more slowly, roughly north-north-east, up the Outer Deep, to take up their final position off the northern tip of the Middle Ground. In the light of subsequent events it is important to realise that *London*'s position, and therefore the Commander-in-Chief's point of observation, was about four miles to leeward of Nelson's squadron, and that the nearest engaged vessels were Riou's five lightly-armed frigates, suffering considerably from the powerful guns of the Trekroner Battery.

Leaving aside the very different temperaments of the two admirals, Parker's view of the action was of necessity less hopeful than Nelson's. By 1.30 p.m. when Nelson's division had been fighting for the best part of four hours, it had suffered considerably and had apparently achieved no advantage. It was not difficult therefore to understand why Parker began to have doubts about the whole action. Not that a bold or resolute commander would have necessarily felt the same way, but Parker was neither bold nor resolute.

Nelson himself was 'agitated', according to Stewart, but 'It was not, however, the agitation of indecision but of ardent, animated patriotism panting for glory, which had appeared within his reach and was vanishing from his grasp'. Nelson had the adrenalin of action pumping into his veins and was also better placed than Parker to feel that, with a little more endurance and time, victory could be within his grasp. Four miles off, out of action, Parker took a different view. He discussed his apprehensions with both Domett and Otway and the latter opposed what was now in Parker's mind, to order Nelson to break off action. Otway's opinion was of course highly significant, for he was in the same situation as his admiral, tacking towards the scene of action at something like one mile an hour, yet he took the opposite view. The discussion between the three men was somewhat confused, but eventually it was decided that Domett should go on board *Elephant* to take Nelson's opinion. Domett went below to prepare himself for a boat journey, but while he was absent Otway persuaded Parker to allow him to go in his place. It is not difficult to surmise why; especially as, permission granted, Otway immediately hailed a passing boat, and, despite the fact that it was loaded with a rope hawser, commanded it to take him to *Elephant*. While Otway's boat was still carrying him to Nelson's flagship one of the most controversial signals in naval history was hoisted on board *London*. Parker, left with Domett, less resolute than Otway, had allowed his fears to overcome him.

The argument about Signal 39, 'to discontinue action', has raged ever since, though it is a little difficult to see quite why. It was not a permissive signal, and Otway had no orders for Nelson to ignore it when he saw it, or to use his discretion whether to obey or disobey. Such an idea may have occurred to Parker, but to those on the receiving end, Nelson, his captains and Rear-Admiral Graves, there was no doubt as to what the Commander-in-Chief's signal meant. It was made 'General with 2 guns' and therefore certainly not directed to Nelson alone, but to every unit of the fleet. Every flag officer and captain, from Nelson and Foley on *Elephant* down to the most junior lieutenant in command of a sloop, who saw that signal, was bound to acknowledge it, repeat it and, most important of all, obey it.

Colonel Stewart's description of how the signal was received on board *Elephant* has passed into legend:

> Lord Nelson was at this time, as he had been during the whole action, walking the starboard side of the quarter deck; sometimes much animated, and at others heroically fine in his observations. A shot through the mainmast knocked a few splinters about us. He observed to me, with a smile, 'It is warm work, and this day may be the last to any of us at any moment', and then stopping short at the gangway, he used an expression never to be erased from my memory, and said with emotion, 'but mark you, I would not be elsewhere for thousands'.
>
> When signal Number 39 was made, the signal lieutenant reported it to him. He continued his walk, and did not appear to take notice of it. The lieutenant meeting his Lordship at the next turn asked 'whether he should repeat it?'
>
> Lord Nelson answered, 'No, acknowledge it'. On the officer returning to the poop his Lordship called after him, 'Is No 16 (Engage the enemy more closely) still hoisted?' The lieutenant answering in the affirmative, Lord Nelson said, 'Mind you keep it so'. [Nelson] now walked the deck considerably agitated, which was always known by his moving the stump of his right arm.
>
> After a turn or two he said to me, in a quick manner, 'Do you know what's shown on board of the Commander-in-Chief, No 39?'
>
> On asking him what that meant, he answered, 'Why, to leave off action. Leave off action!' he repeated, and then added with a shrug, 'Now damn me if I do!'

It was a few minutes later, Parker's signal still flying, that Nelson, half as a joke, half out of irritation, turned to his flag captain and said, 'You know, Foley, I have only one eye—and I have a right to be blind sometimes', and then, putting his small telescope to his blind eye for a moment, exclaimed, 'I really do not see the signal'.

What followed on board the other ships of Nelson's squadron is as interesting as that famous incident. Captains were now faced with a dilemma. Their own immediate superior still commanded close action with signal Number 16 flying, and did not repeat Parker's signal. Yet for those who could see the flags on *London*'s halyards, or the repeat hoisted by their own sister ships, there was a plain order from the Commander-in-Chief to break off action.

Rear-Admiral Graves rose to the occasion with a splendid piece of compromise. He delayed answering Parker's signal for a quarter of an hour, and when he repeated it he hoisted his own signal at the starboard main topsail yardarm where it could not be seen from *Elephant*. At the same time he kept Nelson's Number 16 flying at the mainmast head, and *Defiance* stayed in action. In the master's log there is no mention of even receiving Parker's signal.

For others less senior than Graves, and perhaps unable to see Nelson's negative reaction, the results were disastrous, and confirmatory of Nelson's judgment as opposed to Parker's. For Captain Riou the difficulty was at its most acute, he could see *London*'s signal, then followed by that of *Defiance*. Nelson's flagship and the other sail of the line were still in action and showed no sign of obeying the signal. His own frigates were in difficulties, he himself had already been wounded by a shell splinter, but it was very reluctantly that he gave the order to cut the cable and let fall the topsails to make way out of action. That, however, was a hazardous operation, for *Amazon*, her guns no longer firing, had to turn away from the Trekroner fortress to bear up to join Parker's division. 'What will Nelson think of us?' muttered Riou. As *Amazon* swung round her stern, unprotected, and the whole ship was no longer shrouded in her own gun smoke, she was raked from stern to stem, the captain's clerk went down, and a whole file of marines hauling on the mainbrace. 'Come then, my boys, let us all die together,' shouted Riou, astride a gun. The words were hardly out of his mouth when another shot literally cut him in two. Lieutenant Quilliam, who was later signals lieutenant in *Victory* at Trafalgar, took over *Amazon* and with her consorts of the frigate squadron, she left action.

The frigates, and a few minor craft, were the only vessels to obey Parker's signal. The sail of the line continued to obey Nelson and stayed put. Half an hour after Parker's signal, despite confusion caused by the fact that the Danish unrigged ships and floating batteries had no obvious method of indicating surrender, and some without ensigns continued to fight, it was obvious that the tide of battle had turned in favour of the British. Five of the eight Danish blockships had surrendered, or were out of action, only two remained with but a handful of guns still firing. Three of the four floating batteries were knocked out. The sixty-gun *Dannebrog* was on fire and *Saelland*, a 74, with her cable cut had drifted, badly damaged, out of the line. *Holsteen* was so badly damaged that Commodore Fischer had now left her and transferred his flag to the Trekroner battery. All three auxiliary transports had been driven out of the line and the three frigates and eleven gunboats were out of action. On every Danish vessel there were large numbers of dead and wounded; nearly a fifth of the total effective strength were casualties and already there were 370 men dead and 665 wounded, of whom 106 were to die later.

By contrast, though, three British ships were aground and *Monarch*, especially, had suffered heavy damage and many casualties, not one of the nine sail of the line but was out of action and incapable of sustaining the fight. *Bellona* and *Russell*, though aground, still had their guns firing. To add to the Danes' misfortunes, shot from their own land batteries aimed at British ships was falling short and killing their own men on vessels and floating batteries which had already surrendered.

'It was a sight', Nelson wrote later, 'which no real man could have enjoyed.' It was to him a 'massacre' and therefore 'the moment of a complete victory was surely the proper time to make an opening with the Nation we had been fighting with'.

The 'opening' was for a truce, for he realised that if he did not make some move the pointless and confused slaughter would continue. So standing with his purser, Thomas Wallis, by the casing of *Elephant*'s rudder head, he wrote one of his most famous letters, Wallis taking a copy:

> Lord Nelson has directions to spare Denmark when no longer resisting but if the firing is continued on the part of Denmark Lord Nelson will be obliged to set on fire all the floating batteries he has taken, without having the power of saving the brave Danes who defended them.
> Dated on board His
> Brittanick Majesty's Ship *Elephant*
> Copenhagen Roads, April 2nd, 1801.
> Nelson and Bronte. Vice admiral under the Command
> of admiral Sir Hyde Parker.
> To the brothers of Englishmen,
> the Danes.

The address was a typical Nelson touch, as was his insistence that the letter had to be properly sealed, not stuck together with a gummed wafer, which would indicate undue haste. Though the first man sent below for the Nelson seal—silver, ivory-mounted and bearing his coart-of-arms—was killed on the way, eventually the wax was brought and heated with a candle and the seal affixed, all in the midst of battle.

Then Captain Thesiger was sent on shore under a flag of truce with orders to deliver it to the Danish Prince Royal.

The Crown Prince, in some doubt as to what Nelson proposed, sent his naval aide-de-camp Captain Lindholm on board *Elephant* to elucidate matters and there Nelson wrote another letter direct to the Prince. Soon after its receipt the Danish batteries ceased firing, and Sir Hyde Parker, still three miles from the Trekroner battery, was able to enter in his journal at 3.15 p.m. 'observed the *Elephant* to hoist a flag of truce'.

The battle of Copenhagen was over, but the situation between the Danish government and a British fleet, which now dominated the capital, was by no means resolved. The truce, concluded on April 2, was prolonged until April 9 and during that time neither the Danes nor the British relaxed, both still acting as if prepared to renew hostilities if necessary.

That night, after considerable to-ing and fro-ing in his gig to see Hyde Parker and to consult with captains and Danish representatives, Nelson slept on board *St George* but not before he had endorsed a sheet, '*St George*, April 2nd 1801, at 9 o'clock at night very tired after a hard fought battle', and written to Emma Hamilton telling her of the fate of the Danish ships: 'of eighteen sail, large and small, some are taken, some sunk, some burnt, in the good old way'. He also wrote her a short love poem entitled *Lord Nelson to his Guardian Angel*.

The morning after the battle it was difficult to see what either side was to do next. The Danish navy was wrecked and quite incapable of taking offensive action against the British fleet which, despite a number of ships considerably damaged, was still sea- and battle-worthy and Parker's squadron was untouched. The only course of action remaining open would have been to bombard Copenhagen itself. This, Parker, in his original orders, had been expressly told to avoid save in the most dire circumstances. In any event what did the British wish to extract from the Danes by threat of bombardment of their capital city? It was a problem which would have occupied a suite of professional diplomats some months at least. In the event, negotiations were begun the next day, not by the British Commander-in-Chief, but by his battle-weary second-in-command. Nature had not intended Nelson to be a diplomat, and it was a task he took to only for the sake of speed, so that, the Danes settled, he could be ready to deal with the Swedes and then the Russians. However, no ambassador nor home government could complain of the results he achieved. But before he could come to grips with the Danish authorities there were three tasks Nelson wanted to perform: reassure himself about the wounded, the state of his ships and finally to ascertain Parker's attitude to what had been, without doubt, a clear breach of his orders.

The casualties at Copenhagen had been high, from victors as well as vanquished; of Nelson's battles only Trafalgar exceeded the figure of 253 killed and 688 wounded. Nelson visited as many ships as was feasible within his squadron. It was the sort of gesture that was never forgotten and a diminutive one-armed admiral, though clad on this occasion in a voluminous green loden weatherproof coat, had his distinctive appearance on his side. Wounded sailors'and marines, and captured and wounded Danes for that matter, had no doubt afterwards who it was who concerned himself with their welfare, not just some senior officer but Nelson himself.

The reputation of Britain's most intrepid admiral certainly had its effect upon the Danes and perhaps this was just as well, for in the aftermath of battle, ships flying his Blue Ensign hardly made an impressive showing. *Monarch*, attempting to weigh anchor, got stuck on a shoal, but only for a brief space of time as Fremantle's *Ganges* accidentally took her amidships thus pushing her out of her difficulties. *Glatton* was also in trouble but managed to get clear, not so *Defiance* and Nelson's own *Elephant*, both going firmly aground. Only by the next day was the squadron free of shoals and sandbanks, yet another demonstration of the risks that Nelson had run with his manoeuvres.

Nelson's meeting with Sir Hyde Parker produced no scene or record, as when Jervis had warmly congratulated Commodore Nelson on a breach of orders. Parker was a very different man from Jervis; the disobeyed signal was ignored, but the work-load of the forthcoming negotiations was pushed onto the shoulders of his energetic junior. At noon on April 5 Nelson went on shore to meet Frederick, the Danish Prince Royal. A carriage and a cavalry escort had been provided, the latter as much to protect him from the danger of hostile crowds as to do him honour. In fact he was received, according to the Danish account, 'neither with acclamation or with murmurs; the people did not degrade themselves with the former, nor disgrace themselves with the latter'. Nelson declined the carriage and walked to the palace surrounded and followed by a large crowd, anxious to catch a glimpse of their famous enemy, thus setting a problem for his mounted escort.

Fremantle, writing to the Duke of Buckingham, not as an eye-witness

but as someone who had taken breakfast with Nelson the next morning
and presumably heard his account, said that 'he was hailed with cheers by
the multitudes' and also mentioned shouts of 'Viva Nelson', somewhat
improbable on Danish tongues. The Court's pro-Russian policy was
certainly not popular, especially with the merchant community, but it
seems inherently unlikely that the crowd would cheer the man who,
twenty-four hours ago, had caused the death and wounding of so many
of their fellow countrymen.

Fremantle's account is a good example of the exaggerated adulation
which afflicted 'Nelsonites'—the word was first coined by Hoste—and
which when reported and repeated tends to do their hero a disservice by
tacking onto his reputation a number of heroic improbabilities. The
careful Colonel Stewart, and he too admired Nelson, was about right in
his description, 'the populace showed a mixture of admiration, curiosity
and displeasure', not an unreasonable combination, and some preparation
for the two-hour session with the Crown Prince which was polite, to the
point, and not unfriendly.

Fortunately the Prince spoke English as did the only other person
present, Captain Lindholm, the Royal Adjutant General, or principal
aide-de-camp. Nelson's account was set down at length for the eyes of
the Prime Minister, and perhaps the crucial exchange was the question
by the Prince: 'for what is the British fleet come into the Baltic?' My
answer—'to crush a most formidable and unprovoked Coalition against
Great Britain'. The Prince declared that his ships should never join any
power against England, 'but it required not much argument to satisfy
him that he could not help it'.

The conversation had opened with compliments on both sides,
Frederick had commended Nelson's humanity in bringing the battle to
a close when lives were being expended to no purpose, and Nelson had
said that the French could not have withstood punishment for one hour
which the 'Danes had supported for four'. Then there had been a general
discussion of the Armed Neutrality from which Nelson had extracted a
feeling that the Danes were well-disposed towards Britain, but that fear
of Russia was 'the preponderating consideration'. Perhaps this was so, but
it was not quite as simple an equation as Nelson thought. However, the
Prince's question brought the discussion down to brass tacks: What did
Britain now want from Denmark and what was Nelson prepared to do
if his demands were not granted?

His reply was that Parker would suspend his orders to attack the

Danish capital in exchange for the Danes abrogating their treaty with Russia. The Prince assented, saying 'that you shall have with pleasure' to Nelson's request for the fleet to enter Copenhagen and 'the free use of everything we may want from it'. It is difficult to see that he had much alternative, but the sticking-point was reached with two of Nelson's suggestions, first, to join their fleet with the British, or else disarm, and second, the demand that in exchange for British naval protection the Danes would sever their connection with the Armed Neutrality in general and Russia in particular.

From the Danes' point of view they had to choose between two threats, the British fleet present and visible, its power demonstrated, and the Russian fleet, not with a high reputation for efficiency plus whatever other action a mad Tsar might take. There was another element which the British Government had failed to take into account; what was called Danish 'intransigence'. It was a natural enough reluctance to submit to dictation from Britain and concern for their own position as neutrals, their reason for joining the Armed Neutrality in the first place.

Nelson's task, with no assistance from his Commander-in-Chief, nor from London, too far distant for communication, was to steer a course between these diplomatic shoals. This he managed by something like the same sort of boldness with which he had approached the naval battle. It was not a brutal, tactless approach, and there were further meetings with the Crown Prince and his advisers, Nelson being at pains to stress the British desire for friendship. At his first meeting he had admittedly been curt with Count Bernstorff, the Foreign Minister, whom he regarded as the principal pro-Russian at the Danish Court, but with that one exception his manner was uniformly courteous. There can be no doubt that he went out of his way to exercise his charm, and that his personality and manner played a considerable part in the negotiations. His superscription 'to the brothers of Englishmen, the Danes' had been no mere flourish. At the same time, though the Danes were intrigued and perhaps almost complimented to find themselves dealing with the most famous sailor of the age, they were never allowed to forget that the 'little one-eyed man in a fine long navy blue uniform coat, the sleeve flapping where his arm should have been and a turn up hat' was an admiral accustomed to victory.

At one stage in argument with the 'Commissioners' appointed to negotiate the truce, Lindholm and General Waltersdorff, one of their staff, appreciating that Scott, acting as interpreter, spoke Danish, muttered something in an aside in French which seemed to suggest he doubted if the British would renew hostilities. To his surprise Nelson picked up the phrase and rounded on him. 'Renew hostilities!' he said, and turning to Scott, said with some force, 'Tell him that we are ready at a moment, ready to bombard this very night!' It was obvious that it could be done for the citadel and the inner harbour of Copenhagen were threatened by the bomb vessels ranged at anchor, their mortars, like the guns of the fleet, ready to fire at Nelson's order. Later the same day there was a demonstration to his own subordinate officers of his firmness of purpose. It was at the reception before a formal dinner in the stateroom of the Amalienborg Royal Palace. As he ascended the staircase on Colonel Stewart's arm in the wake of the Crown Prince, Nelson, noticing that furniture and paintings had been removed, whispered 'Though I have only one eye, I see all this will burn very well'. It is possible that it was a stage whisper and was intended to carry further than the ears of the colonel who noted, 'He was even then thinking more about the bombardment than the dinner'.

Stewart observed that 'much cordiality prevailed' at the meal, at which fifty distinguished guests sat down, with Nelson on the Crown Prince's right, but there was one noticeable absentee, Count Bernstorff.

Both Sir Hyde Parker, as a cypher, and Bernstorff, an opponent of the present policy, had been removed to the sidelines. The question of an agreement and a truce was very much between two men, the Prince Royal and Nelson. It was after dinner that the Danes learnt of Tsar Paul's death and the news was conveyed to the Prince who, cautiously, kept it to himself and did not tell Nelson. Probably without that news there would have been an agreement anyway, but with the shadow of Paul removed there was no obstacle in the way of a truce. The Prince argued successfully for fourteen weeks for its duration as opposed to Nelson's sixteen, but accepted that his country was no longer part of the Armed Neutrality. However, he was not quite prepared to yield to Nelson when he said, 'Now, Sir, that is settled, suppose we write Peace instead of Armistice'. The Prince's response was admirably cautious and far-sighted, even with the advantage of his secret information. He said he 'should be happy to have a peace, but he must bring it about slowly, so as not to make new wars'. The next day, April 9, the formal Armistice was signed by Nelson, Colonel Stewart, the two commissioners, Waltersdorff and Lindholm, and ratified by Sir Hyde Parker and finally, in the late afternoon, by the Prince Royal of Denmark.

13 'Paradise Merton'

14a Nelson's favourite portrait of Emma by Schmidt

14b Nelson in full dress by Füger

15a Nelson's ships. From left to right:
Agamemnon, Captain, Vanguard, Elephant and *Victory*

15b *Trafalgar* by Turner

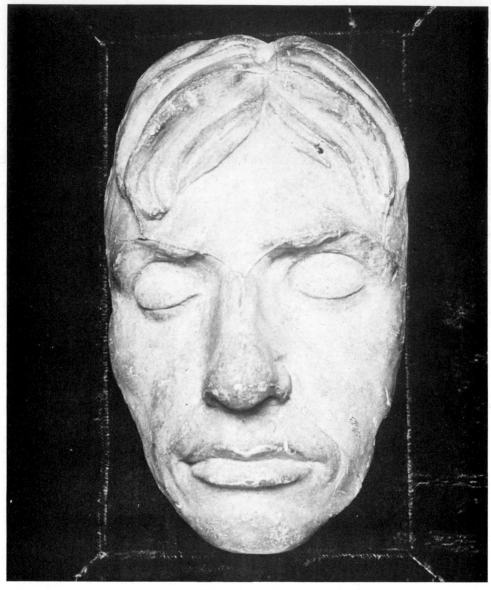

16 Nelson's death mask

Nelson took the copy ashore for the royal signature and his pleasure was obvious. As he wrote to Lady Hamilton, 'I am sure, could you have seen the adoration and respect, you would have cried for joy; there are no honours that can be conferred equal to this'.

Nevertheless the aftermath of the battle and the successful negotiation was to be irritation and frustration. There were four matters which concerned him immediately, and three of them were the responsibility of Sir Hyde Parker. The fourth would not have bothered a man less touchy of his reputation and arose from a statement by Commodore Fischer suggesting that the British had won their victory because of their numerical superiority and also that with his truce offer Nelson had deceived or tricked his opponents. The excuses of a beaten enemy for domestic consumption were hardly worth bothering about, but Nelson did bother, joining in the argument with a strongly-worded letter to Lindholm.

Nelson's disputes with Parker were more important, though two were 'domestic' in the sense that they only concerned the British fleet. Nevertheless they gave an idea of the sort of man Parker was, petty and selfish, despite a battle and the possibility of further action. Some at least of the Danish ships captured could have been repaired and taken to England as prizes, thus producing a welcome financial bonus to officers and seamen. Instead Parker, himself a rich man, gave the order for all save one, *Holsteen*, to be burnt. In another internal matter, promotion, he also offended many whom he commanded. Vacancies by death or wounds had to be filled, and the obvious choice for many ships would have been the second-in-command, but instead Parker promoted his own favourite lieutenants to posts of command, many from his own flagship and his squadron, which had seen no action. The feelings of those passed over who had borne the brunt of the battle can be imagined. The final and most important conflict between the two admirals was on the question of the next move. Nelson, from the start, had seen very clearly that he was engaged in a Baltic campaign. The coercion of Denmark was but one part of it, and there was still Sweden and Russia to be considered. Parker had been indecisive and dilatory before the actual battle, but now, after a victory which he might well have aborted, he revealed the same qualities again.

Nelson was all for pressing on to Reval. Instead, by Parker's order he was left off Copenhagen with the task of dealing with the captured prizes, while Parker's own squadron dawdled in Kioge Bay south of

Copenhagen. It was there, on April 14, that Parker received news, from
Captain Sutton in *Amazon* returning from the Swedish naval base at
Carlskrona, that the Swedish fleet was at sea. Swedish foreign policy
was difficult to define for the young Gustavus IV had swung much
further towards Russia, the age-old enemy, than many of his advisers
and most of his subjects wished. The silent guns on the eastern shore had
been symptomatic of Swedish indecision.

Parker's reaction to the news was, for a man of his sluggish temperament, very quick indeed. He ordered the squadron to the northern tip
of the island of Bornholm to intercept the Swedes, and sent for Nelson
to come immediately to hoist his flag in Foley's *Elephant*. Nelson was
then in *St George* with some of her guns on board a merchantman,
preparatory to negotiating the channel and complaining about his
health, but the effect of possible action electrified him and Mr Briarly
described what happened next:

> he ordered a Boat to be manned, and without even waiting for a boat-
> cloak (though you must suppose the weather pretty sharp here at this
> season of the year), and having to row about twenty-four miles with
> the wind and current against him, jumped into her, and ordered me
> to go with him, I having been on board the *St George* till she had got
> over the Grounds.
> All I had ever seen or heard of him could not half so clearly prove to
> me the singular and unbounded zeal of this truly great man. His
> anxiety in the Boat for nearly six hours (lest the Fleet should have
> settled before he got on board one of them, and lest we should not
> catch the Swedish squadron) is beyond all conception, I will quote
> some expressions in his own words.
> It was extremely cold, and I wished him to put on a great-coat of mine
> which was in the boat: 'No, I am not cold; my anxiety for my
> country will keep me warm. Do you think the Fleet has sailed?' 'I
> should suppose not, my lord.' 'If they are, we shall follow them to
> Karlscrona, by God!'
> The idea of going in a small boat, rowing six oars, without a single
> morsel of anything to eat or drink the distance of about fifty
> leagues, must convince the world, that every other earthly considera-
> tion than that of serving his country was totally banished from his
> thoughts.
> We reached our Fleet by midnight, and went on board the *Elephant*,

Captain Foley, where I left his Lordship in the morning, and returned to my ship.

The Swedes in fact retired behind the defences of Carlskrona where they were informed of the Danish Armistice. Sir Hyde returned to Kioge Bay and it was there that he and Nelson received news and orders from London dated April 17.

The news was of the Government's approval of the Armistice, though in cautious words which irritated Nelson, and congratulations to both admirals. A reference to 'the late Emperor' of Russia was the first intimation that they received that there was a new ruler in St Petersburg, the Danes having kept their secret. The orders therefore suspended any direct hostile action against Russia and Parker and Nelson were now to enquire what Tsar Alexander's intentions were with regard to the embargo on British ships and the imprisonment of their crews. It was expected that they would meet with a more friendly attitude but in case this were not so they were given power to commence hostilities after the expiry of a twelve-hour written notice.

A more active man than Parker would immediately have sailed for Reval, but he delayed in Kioge Bay. Nelson wrote impatiently to St Vincent, and at the same time applied for his return to England on grounds of ill health. Apart from his usual complaints, his eye, his stomach, his heart flutters, his dislike of cold weather and his seasickness, he had experienced a bout of what he diagnosed as influenza, probably a chill caught in the trip in the open boat described by Briarly.

When the Admiralty did take its next step with regard to the Baltic Fleet it could well have found that its newly designated Commander-in-Chief had left the ships he was ordered to command. For Sir Hyde finally and reluctantly allowed Nelson to sail home, on grounds of ill health, in the frigate *Blanche* at dawn on May 5.

However, that same day Colonel Stewart who had been to London with the Copenhagen dispatch returned on board *London* with further dispatches from the Admiralty. Sir Hyde noted in his journal:

I received the King's and their Lordships' approval of the Armistice with the Danes, but what was my astonishment and surprise at reading the next paragraph of the letter, which was an order to resign the command of the Fleet to Lord Nelson and shift my flag on board a frigate or a two-decker and return to Yarmouth Roads.

So Parker, not Nelson, transferred to *Blanche* at 3 p.m., and at 4.30 p.m. sailed for England. Next morning at daylight the signal flags broke out from *St George*, with the new Commander-in-Chief's first order, 'The Fleet to hoist in all boats and prepare to weigh'.

Colonel Stewart, now as confirmed a Nelsonite as Hoste, had this to say:

> This at once showed how different a system was about to be pursued— Lord Nelson, who foresaw every bad consequence from the inactive mode of proceeding owed his bad health more to chagrin than to any other cause. The joy with which the signal was received not only manifested what are the customary feelings on those occasions, but was intended as peculiarly complimentary to the Admiral.

CHAPTER TWENTY-EIGHT

Off-Shore Squadron, Boulogne

THE REST of Nelson's time in the Baltic is shortly told for his work had been done at Copenhagen. To talk of a commander's name being enough to strike terror into his enemies' hearts has become such a figure of speech that it is difficult to think of it being literally true. Yet it was so in Nelson's case and he joined that rare band of military leaders whose name has personified to the enemy his country and the service he led. It was not 'the British' or 'the British Navy', but just 'Nelson'. Before him there had been 'Drake' for the Spaniards on the seas, then 'Monsieur Malbrouk' as the French called Marlborough, and soon to overshadow them all, 'Nap' or 'Boney' to the British, and Napoleon to the rest of his opponents.

The Swedes stayed behind their harbour defences at Carlskrona. What the Russian attitude would have been had Paul been alive it is difficult to tell, but under their new ruler their reactions were cautious and conciliatory.

Nelson's own attitude had also changed, 'I shall now go there as a friend,' he said, 'but the two fleets [at Reval and Cronstadt] shall not form a junction, if not already accomplished, unless my orders permit it'.

He arrived on May 12 in the outer bay of Reval, but with only twelve ships of the line, the bomb vessels and fireships remaining anchored off Bornholm island. A complimentary letter was sent on shore as if this was some courtesy visit by the ships of a friendly power. The Russian fleet had in fact already left Reval for Cronstadt, which did not stop Nelson considering how he would deal with the harbour, if forced to, and the next day he went on shore to pay a call upon the Governor. He found, not without pleasure, that his reputation had preceded him. As Mrs St George had noticed in Dresden, spectators were struck by his similarity to a famous contemporary who had died the previous year. Nelson confided to Emma, 'All the Russians have taken it into their heads that I am like Suwaroff, le jeune Suwaroff'. Hardly a compliment,

for though the Russian marshal and Nelson shared a smallness of frame
and thin intensity of features, the young Suvorov had been promoted
out of the Imperial Guard because a former Tsar had objected to his
ugliness.

A letter arrived on May 16 from St Petersburg from Count Pahlen,
former conspirator and now principal minister, which according to
Stewart caused Nelson a good deal of agitation. The tone was brusque
and as Nelson wrote to St Vincent 'it is doubtful if he [Pahlen] would
have written such a letter if the Russian fleet had been at Reval'.

'The Emperor, my Master,' wrote Pahlen, 'does not consider this step
compatible with the lively desire manifested by His Britannic Majesty,
to re-establish the good intelligence so long existing between the two
Monarchies. The only guarantee of the loyalty of your intentions that
His Majesty can accept, is the prompt withdrawal of the fleet under your
command, and no negotiation with your Court can take place, so long
as a naval force is in sight of his ports.'

Nelson ordered the fleet to weigh that very night, and the next
morning his twelve capital ships made sail for Bornholm and anchored
on the 24th in the harbour of Rostock, the Prussian port on the Baltic.
Physically he had departed, but he did not give up the diplomatic battle,
for before leaving Reval he had replied to Pahlen pointing out that he
had brought, 'not one seventh of his fleet in point of numbers', an
exaggeration, no doubt, but making the point that his visit was friendly,
and leaving it to the Russians to imagine an unfriendly one. In fact for
an admiral who confessed to having no diplomatic skills, it was a very
diplomatic letter. Certainly it achieved its object, for while at Rostock
Nelson had Pahlen's reply, full of apologies, distinguished sentiments,
and an invitation to St Petersburg, but more important, 'His Imperial
Majesty has ordered the immediate raising of the embargo upon the
English merchant ships'.

In reporting events to St Vincent Nelson, who felt that 'our diplomatic
men are so slow', was in no doubt as to the superiority of admirals to
ambassadors, and with justice on his side. Now there was nothing to keep
him in Northern seas and he waited none too patiently until Vice-
Admiral Pole relieved him on June 19. The same day he left the fleet in
the brig *Kite* and landed at Yarmouth on July 1.

England, home and beauty now awaited him, but as at every other
stage of his life no pleasure was to be unalloyed. So far as England was
concerned, both with officialdom and the man and woman in the street,

there was no doubt of his status. St Vincent had written a handsome letter which suggested a change of opinion by one who had previously taken the view that Nelson was a superlative fighting admiral, but not much more. The judgment and diplomacy displayed in the Baltic had obviously persuaded him that Nelson was capable of the highest command, certainly at sea, if not necessarily in the Admiralty. Lord Spencer, semi-retired and taking the cures of Bath, added his congratulations, 'the Battle of Copenhagen will be as much coupled with the name of Nelson as that of the Nile'. That was true and Nelson's abilities had been recognised in the most obvious manner by the sacking of Sir Hyde Parker, who had, incidentally, sailed out of history when he had left the fleet. Some of the early ballads written hastily on the news of Copenhagen coupled his name with Nelson's, but his dismissal raised little sympathy. Only Lord Minto even bothered to comment, 'I feel sorry for Sir Hyde', but added 'no wise man would ever have gone with Nelson or over him, as he was sure to be in the background in every case'. That was a trifle uncharitable, as Parker had possessed no choice in the matter, but had been ordered to the Baltic. The fault lay much more with those such as St Vincent who had picked him in the first place.

It was Nelson who showed most consideration for his dismissed chief, by sending him his draft letter written on the eve of battle, and by refraining from saying anything in public about the disobeyed signal. Parker at one stage had thought of making an issue of his removal from command, but it was Nelson who, with the utmost tact, persuaded Sir Hyde that his reputation would not be improved, but would only suffer by a public airing of his grievances. Officially, the former Commander-in-Chief of the Baltic Fleet might never have existed, save that his name had appeared in the Motion of Thanks approved by both Houses of Parliament on April 16. Admiral Graves received a Knighthood of the Bath, bestowed by Nelson, acting for the King, as almost his last official act on the quarter-deck of St George before quitting the Baltic. Nelson himself on May 22 was raised one step in the peerage to Viscount but Parker got nothing.

Once again, as after the Nile barony, Nelson's closest admirers, the Hamiltons and Davison in particular, thought that an earldom, a marquisate or perhaps even a dukedom, would have been more appropriate. But Nelson had not been a Commander-in-Chief for at the time of the battle that had been Parker's post. There was however, another reason for official restraint, Britain had not actually been at war with

Denmark, an awkward fact which also inhibited the Lord Mayor of London from recognising the victory save by setting up a fund for the wounded and the wives and children of the dead. In consequence, and this was unfair, there were no medals for the captains, officers, seamen and marines who had taken part in what had been an extremely arduous and bloody battle. Nelson protested and argued, and also sent an acrimonious letter to the Lord Mayor who was hardly the principal offender, but to no avail.

He could have declined his Viscountcy but it had been awarded early, although if he had done so Sir William Hamilton would not have been treated to what he rightly regarded as an incredible spectacle, the Reverend William Nelson dancing a jig on receipt of the news, overjoyed with the thought of what might come to him, eventually, in the way of honours.

Emma also danced, on hearing of the victory, but she performed a spirited and lengthy tarantella wearing out a succession of partners including her husband and Fatima, the Coptic maid. Still, Emma was Nelson's Guardian Angel and there had been a flow of absurd letters from the Baltic to 'Mrs Thompson', 'but my dear friend you are so good, so virtuous, there is certainly more of the angel than the human being about you, I know you prayed for me both at the Nile and here, and if the prayers of the Good, as we are taught to believe, are of avail at the Throne of God, why may not yours have saved my life'. There had also been a dinner on board Nelson's flagship on 'Saint Emma's Day', April 26, Lady Hamilton's birthday, to which a number of captains and Sir Hyde Parker had all been invited. Twenty-four senior officers had raised their glasses and drunk 'the toast of 'Santa Emma', proposed by her lover.

Emma now represented what Nelson regarded as home. At sea before the fleet had proceeded to Copenhagen he had written what was intended to be a final dismissal to Fanny. He had done all he could for Josiah, and he had provided for her in his will, 'therefore my only wish is to be left to myself; and wishing you every happiness, believe me that I am Your affectionate Nelson and Brontë.'

Overall it had been a melancholy letter, whether genuine or to fob Fanny off, it is difficult to say, perhaps he did feel miserable writing to her. Anyhow, the tone so surprised her that she sent it to Maurice Nelson, Horatio's favourite brother, who maybe out of kindness, 'desires me not to take the least notice of it, as his brother seemed to have forgot himself'.

However, that link between the two had now been broken, for while negotiating with Count Pahlen Nelson had been informed of the death of his brother, 'of inflammation of the brain'. Maurice had never reached his ambition, a place on the Navy Board, though it was promised at the time of his death, for he had got himself into financial difficulties and, though a bachelor, left behind a 'Mrs Nelson', in law Mrs Ford. When Nelson returned to England he assumed financial responsibility for 'Mrs Nelson' or 'Old Blindy', for Mrs Ford was blind as well as poor. Of Catherine Nelson's eight sons, three had died in infancy, Edmund had died in 1789 and Suckling ten years later and now Maurice had gone. As Horatio observed, it was not a good record, now there was only William and himself, and he had never been really fond of William. Only Maurice had been close, and neither of his two brothers-in-law, Thomas Bolton, Susannah's husband, and George Matcham, married to Catherine, engaged much of his regard. There were a considerable number of nephews and nieces though only William's son Horatio and his daughter Charlotte bore the name of Nelson. Horatio was said to resemble his distinguished uncle and namesake, but now that Fanny and Josiah had been dismissed, the only real family that Nelson possessed were the two people he could not acknowledge as such, Emma his 'wife in the eyes of Heaven' and Horatia, whom neither could acknowledge.

So Copenhagen passed; certainly Nelson's most difficult and hard fought battle, and the one in which he came nearest to defeat. Its effect, on the Armed Neutrality, and on Bonaparte, who had hoped for much from that combination, was considerable. Within the Navy it advanced Nelson's reputation, and with the public at large, but its aftermath left him dissatisfied. Fanny had put her pride in her pocket and had written to congratulate him on his victory and safe deliverance, but the Press had been critical of a battle against a neutral which since the death of Tsar Paul had been unnecessary. The eccentric old King, George III, had received him affably enough at a levée, but had never mentioned Copenhagen.

Dissatisfaction was with a man of Nelson's temperament endemic and his attitude was as always too personalised and somewhat short-sighted. Aged forty-two, Horatio Nelson, Viscount and Vice-Admiral of the Blue, was probably no more content with his lot than he had been nearly thirty years ago, as an ambitious midshipman with few prospects. Age and experience had taught him nothing; the successful admiral was no

more capable of taking a philosophical or detached view of his own
situation than had been the callow twelve-year-old walking the deck of
Raisonnable. True, he had his Saint, whom he continually told he really
believed to be such, though she had to be constantly assured that he was
not thinking of setting up house with his 'aunt', now Viscountess Nelson,
again. There can be no doubt of his own absolute devotion, and though,
as Mahan put it, 'the sincerity of which checks the ready smile, but elicits
no tenderness for a delusion too gross for sympathy', Nelson knew that
many of his contemporaries also smiled, and sneered, behind his back.
Formerly to Fanny, his letters had revealed a minor delusion that the
world was against him, now it was against both him and Emma. 'Curse
them that treat you unkindly' was a typical encouragement to his
mistress to bear her burdens.

He had written from the Baltic, 'I am fixed to live a country life and
to have many (I hope) years of comfort which God knows I never yet
had—only moments of happiness'. Returning to England he hoped that
happiness and comfort were to be combined immediately, but he was
to be disappointed. On the heels of Copenhagen had come the news of
General Sir Ralph Abercromby's land victory over the remaining
French at Aboukir, and also of the death of that sturdy old Scot mortally
wounded on the field. As a result, Addington's Government, never very
strong or pugnacious, but faithfully representing the British people,
heartily tired of war, was putting out peace feelers. Although there was
not to be a formal peace treaty between France and Britain until March
1802 the war, and the war effort in Britain, was running down, Lord
Keith, in command of the fleet off Egypt, was still active as was Sir
Sidney Smith, Blackwood, Louis and Hallowell. On land Major-General
Sir John Moore and Hely-Hutchinson, Abercrombie's successor, were
moving from Aboukir on both Cairo and Alexandria, but Bonaparte
was not prepared to let Egypt go without a fight. In June 1801, following
the Treaty of St Petersburg, which Denmark signed in October and
Sweden in March 1802, an agreement which in effect accepted Britain's
right of search of neutral vessels, Britain and Russia were formally
reconciled. From then until the peace treaty of Amiens in the next year
both Britain and France jockeyed for positions which would be of
advantage when the peace negotiations actually began. There was no
land war on the Continent since the Treaty of Lunéville, but one of
Bonaparte's devices to over-awe the stubborn inhabitants of the British
Isles was the preparation of an invasion force on the French coast. There

was no intention on his part of committing his armies to an actual invasion attempt, but though the mammoth bluff was suspected for what it was, nevertheless in London, in the Cabinet and at the Admiralty, no one could be quite sure. St Vincent had said, trenchantly, that 'I do not say that the French cannot come, I only say that they cannot come by sea'. Still, there was always just the possibility which could not quite be ignored, and public opinion, less convinced than naval, had to be reassured.

It was in these circumstances that Nelson found himself, soon after his arrival at Yarmouth, still actively employed, though against his will and inclinations. While the volunteer regiments paraded in Hyde Park, all leave for regular soldiers was stopped and committees were formed in south-eastern coastal towns to raise corps of local 'sea fencibles', he was permitted three weeks' respite and then appointed to command 'a squadron on a particular service'. It was a curious command for the ships, thirty of them, were mostly frigates and gunboats, and with them Nelson was expected to cover the defence of the coast from Beachy Head to Orfordness. For an admiral who had made his name in three big ship actions, it was an odd sort of task. Defending Britain's shores against the armada of flat-bottomed boats that, it was supposed, would deliver the veterans of the French army onto her beaches. He hoisted his flag in *Amazon*, but the task of what he called 'this boat business', was not one that appealed to him. Anything remotely resembling 'the band of brothers' was also markedly absent. Hardy had the frigate *Isis* in the Downs and Berry the 64, *Ruby*, on the North Sea Station, but that was all. Samuel Sutton, his flag captain in *Amazon*, had been in *Alcmene* at Copenhagen, but probably Nelson's closest confidant was the young, devoted, and penniless Edward Parker, now a captain, whom he had first noticed in the Baltic. Josiah had gone, not caring whether his step-father was 'dead or damned' and the place in Nelson's affections for a son-cum-protégé was filled by young Parker, keen, attentive and courageous.

Though the Prime Minister put it more sonorously, St Vincent told Nelson quite plainly why he was there, 'to keep the old women, inside and out, quiet'. Nelson complained and wrote to the First Lord, 'the services on this coast are not necessary for the personal exertions of a Vice-Admiral'. St Vincent agreed, but he replied officially in much the same vein as the Prime Minister. 'The public mind is so much tranquilized by your being at your post that it is extremely desirable that you should continue there: in this opinion all His Majesty's servants, with Sir Thomas Troubridge, agree.'

St Vincent's tactful mention of Troubridge, the old friend and former messmate, had the worst effect imaginable. Nelson was convinced that Troubridge, from his position of power in the Admiralty, had purposely consigned him to this command to prevent his seeing Lady Hamilton. He had now become an object of the gravest suspicion, to have him as 'one of my lords and masters' was bad, he was known not to favour Emma, therefore 'I believe it is all the plan of Troubridge', Nelson wrote to her as an explanation for not seeing her in London. When Troubridge wrote, kindly enough, suggesting exercise by walking on the shore and advising the wearing of flannel next to the skin as protection in bad weather, Nelson, suspicious and hypersensitive, reacted badly, 'He is, I suppose, laughing at me'.

It would be wrong though to think of Nelson neglecting an unpleasant duty. Soon after taking up his command he prepared, on July 25, a memorandum 'on the defence of the Thames etcetera', for the Admiralty. It is not a document which could be put forward to enhance Nelson's reputation as a strategist. Admittedly it was done in haste and was confined within the limits set by the Admiralty, that if there were an attack it would be some sort of gigantic raid on London rather than full-blown invasion. However, that is no excuse for Nelson's curious assumption that the body of men, assumed to be 40,000, would be divided by Bonaparte into two, making separate landing-points and taking different routes to the capital for 'they are too knowing to let us have but one point of alarm of London'. Nelson had himself always practised concentration, it was of the essence of his attack at the Nile and Copenhagen, and therefore it is difficult to see why he should have assumed that the French would sacrifice that advantage for the sake of a temporary ruse. There was, in the general tenor of his memorandum no lack of fighting spirit, but putting himself in the mind of others, especially soldiers, was not Nelson's forte. He was on much safer ground when he wrote, 'Whatever plans may be adopted, the moment the enemy touch our coast, be it where it may, they are to be attacked by every man afloat and on shore: this must be perfectly understood. Never fear the event.' Perhaps the most interesting aspect of the document is that he did take an invasion threat seriously, some of his superiors never did, though he was to discover after some hard-bought investigation that it was an unlikely possibility in the summer of 1801.

On July 30 the British public heard of an episode with a Nelsonic air about it, but not performed by the Vice-Admiral who was still bored and frustrated protecting the coast line with his flotillas of small ships and boats. After the British success at Aboukir in June, one of the few successful conjoint operations so far—even Nelson had said 'the very finest act that even a British army could achieve'—Bonaparte had one last throw at attempting to save Egypt for France. It consisted of a rather complicated combination of French and Spanish ships, Rear-Admiral Linois from Toulon and Rear-Admiral de Moreno from Cadiz coming together to produce a force of three French and six Spanish capital ships, plus three frigates. On July 6, however, Linois was intercepted off Algeciras by Sir James Saumarez in command of six British sail of the line. At first, the action went badly, the British *Hannibal* being captured, but Saumarez, a sort of reverse image of Nelson, could be just as resolute in battle and finally the French *St Antoine* struck, and incredibly, in the confusion, the Spanish *Real Carlos* and *Hermenegildo* fired on each other, caught alight and both exploded and sank.

Thus Bonaparte's final attempt to hold Egypt ended on a note which would have been farcical, had it not been for over 2000 Spanish dead. Saumarez became the hero of the hour and received the Knighthood of the Bath and the thanks of both Houses of Parliament. In the Lords Nelson spoke warmly of one of his former captains, though his speech was too long for the patience of his fellow peers; however, Saumarez, just as difficult a character as his former chief, was aggrieved as he had expected a peerage, an honour he only achieved much later in life.

Two days after the rejoicing at the Battle of Algeciras, Nelson, provoked by a combination of curiosity, professional zeal and perhaps boredom, was stung into action. It was August 1, the anniversary of the Nile, and he was determined to find out what was actually happening at Boulogne. At the cost of a few wounded and a lot of mortar ammunition fired without great effect into the town and the harbour he discovered that Boulogne was well-defended but hardly a springboard for invasion. It is difficult, therefore, to understand what prompted him to make a second more serious attack in the middle of the month. Everything was against such a venture, no great purpose would be served by it in any event, and the French had been forewarned not only by the first attack, but by accurate speculation in the British Press. It was a repetition of his mistake at Teneriffe and, as on the first occasion, Nelson concerned himself with all the details of pre-operational planning, but he simply failed to appreciate, just as on that previous occasion, that the whole concept was dead before it was put into practice.

The attack was made on the night of August 15 with seventy boats divided into four divisions, all under the direction of Nelson from the frigate *Medusa*. In his plan of attack he had set down all the disadvantages, that 'the enemy may naturally be supposed to be alarmed', the problem of winds, tides and the uncertainties on a dark night. The fates of the divisions can easily be summarised, only three of them reached their objective, the fourth becoming a victim to the tide and never entering the harbour proper at all. Of those that did so, only two made contact with the enemy's ships, as one was totally repulsed by heavy gun fire. The first division did capture a brig but was unable to tow it away as it had been chained in position, and eventually musket and grape shot forced the British to retreat. The third division, commanded by Parker, Nelson's favourite, attempted to board the enemy commander's brig but was prevented by protective nets and again heavy fire from on board and ashore. Parker lost two-thirds of his men killed or wounded and was himself severely wounded in the thigh. All told, casualties were forty-four dead and 128 wounded and it is difficult to resist the judgment that they had been thrown away by Nelson for no purpose.

The French were cock-a-hoop and enquired if the famous Lord Nelson would now be created Baron of Boulogne and Chevalier of the Channel, the latter title in French making him sound like Don Quixote who had tilted at windmills. The British Press had not been particularly complimentary about Copenhagen, and it was positively rude about Boulogne though Nelson was praised for his attention to the wounded after the action. St Vincent on receiving the dispatch used exactly the same expression in writing to Nelson as after Teneriffe, hardly a coincidence. Especially as previously he had said it twice over, 'it is not given to us to command success'; the trouble was that Nelson thought that he could.

True, he suffered remorse but as after Teneriffe, his form of regret was typically Nelsonic. 'I own', he wrote to St Vincent, 'I shall never bring myself again to allow any attack to go forward, where I am not personally concerned. My mind suffers much more than if I had a leg shot off in this late business.' Doubtless he had in mind the fate of poor Parker whose thigh bone was fractured in three places and Langford, his first lieutenant, also now in lodgings at Deal, who had a leg filled with grapeshot.

A Mr Hill who had lost a relative and now threatened to expose the

Admiral as incompetent, or even worse, unless he received £100 to be left at a London Post Office could perhaps be dismissed from mind, but posters set up in Deal and Margate were a different matter. They called on seamen not to be butchered again by Nelson. When Nepean at the Admiralty suggested that Flushing, another potential invasion port, should be subjected to a 'boat expedition' Nelson refused and asked, vainly, to be relieved of his command, referring to the criticism he knew to be about in wardrooms and midshipmen's berths. Mrs Nelson, the rector's wife, the old Reverend Edmund, Sir William and Emma, all came to Deal and it was with Lady Hamilton in company that the Admiral visited Captain Parker. It was now obvious that that gallant little Nelsonite was in grave danger, the doctors had suggested amputation as the only remote possibility, of saving his life. The operation was performed on September 18 and Parker lingered until the 27th, and Nelson's misery during this period was genuine, for he had looked on the young man as a son. 'He is my child', he said, 'for I found him in distress.' There was a real father who turned up for the funeral, performed the next day with full naval honours. Nevertheless, it was Nelson who settled Parker's debts and paid for his sick lodgings and the funeral. Parker senior turned out to be disreputable and, having borrowed money from Nelson and other officers, decamped. The other wounded Nelson protégé, Lieutenant Langford, made a slow and painful recovery.

Lady Hamilton had shared her lover's grief with the air of one who accepted such things as part of the role of a hero's mistress. Peace was coming very near. Unknown in Britain as yet, the last French troops had evacuated Egypt the day after Parker's funeral, and on October 4 the news reached London of peace preliminaries signed in Paris three days before. Nelson welcomed peace but was still suspicious of the French and described the London crowd as mad which had cheered General Lauriston, Bonaparte's envoy. Emma welcomed peace with less reservation, because she had plans.

While Nelson had been on shore at Deal or off-shore in *Medusa*, she had been pursuing a campaign of her own. Its object was to get Nelson to herself and the methods and the stages were various. If she believed Nelson's protestations and denials, written almost day by day while engaged at Copenhagen and in the Baltic, there was no possibility of his ever returning to Fanny. Nevertheless she was jealous and possessive and hardly a lady with a subtle touch. Therefore by letter and presumably in conversation, she waged a denigratory war on the lady who was now

Viscountess Nelson and her son, Captain Nisbet. Emma called them Tom Tit and the Cub. At the same time she agreed with and flattered Nelson, thus demonstrating the difference between herself, a sort of Britannia among women, and the quiet reserved Fanny.

The next move was to bring Nelson's relations into her camp, his brother and his two sisters Mrs Bolton and Mrs Matcham and his old father. Much of the energy she spent in this direction was probably wasted as Nelson had a very clear idea of the sort of man his brother was, and does not seem to have been particularly fond of his sisters. In fact it was a double waste of time and energy because, after some reluctance on the part of his sisters, and none by his brother, all three transferred their allegiance from Fanny to Emma once they were convinced that their famous and influential brother had made his choice. The only one of Nelson's family who fought any sort of rearguard action for Fanny was the Admiral's seventy-one-year-old father and so he should have done, as she had been his companion, nurse and friend for many years. Still he was an old man, who had never possessed much in the way of character, and so eventually, probably very much for the sake of peace and quiet, he too came round to accepting his son's re-orientation of his domestic life.

Emma Hamilton does not come out of the whole episode very well, but neither do any members of the Nelson family, including Nelson himself who allowed his infatuation for his mistress to overcome his judgment of his wife. Emma Hamilton's final move was to set up the nearest approach possible, within the conventions of the time, to a marital home. Nelson had always had a vision of some peaceful retreat from the sea, now it was to materialise, but he was to share it with his mistress and her husband.

The house that Emma had found was at Merton, then a country village, about ten miles out of London. There were fifty-two acres of land, and a medium-sized house in a not very good state of repair. Mr Hazlewood, Nelson's solicitor, procured a surveyor's report which was unfavourable, so for that matter was Mr Haslewood, nevertheless Nelson bought the property for £9000 without seeing it. It was no bargain, and Nelson's disposable capital at the time was very little over £10,000, but the thought of living again under the same roof, and his roof this time, with Emma was obviously irresistible.

Merton could be described, with a little stretch of the imagination, as a gentleman's residence, the house was about a hundred years old, but it was by no means a landed property appropriate to a peer of the realm.

Its purchase, as well as marking his desire to do anything to please Emma, also underlined the fact that Nelson, unlike less distinguished naval colleagues who had made fortunes out of prize money, was never a rich man. Hyde Parker, for instance, would never have considered such a house, but both Emma and Nelson were content, and for them, despite its deficiencies, it became what they called it, 'Paradise Merton'.

The negotiations had been going on while Nelson had been engaged at Boulogne and were only completed in time to allow Nelson, with his flag still flying, but released from active duty on the coast, to move into occupation when peace was only a matter of weeks away. Sir William and Emma moved in first and sent him glowing reports of his property, including the fact that Lady Hamilton and her mother were taking enthusiastically, and with their customary energy, to the keeping of ducks and hens. Nelson himself first saw Merton on October 22, 1801; four years of his life remained to him, and he was to have one and a half of them at Merton, a year and a half of peace, the first long period away from war since his five years of frustration on half-pay.

It was probably the first and last time during his forty-seven years that he experienced happiness. For Emma it was not the first time, there had been a time in London with Greville and then with Sir William in their first years of marriage in Naples, but the period at Merton with Nelson was also her last.

CHAPTER TWENTY-NINE

Temporary Peace

NELSON'S SUSPICION of the peace agreement was to be justified by events though it would be over-flattering to credit him with too much prescience; his wariness with regard to the faith and intentions of the French state was attributable more to a sort of instinct than any process of reasoning. The majority of the nation seemed delighted that at last an end had come to a flagging war, but there were others, besides Nelson, who were either unenthusiastic about the actual peace terms or pessimistic about the future.

By the Treaty of Amiens, finalised in the next year, Britain returned to France, Spain and Holland, all her conquests of the war with the exception of Ceylon, and Trinidad. For a nation dependent upon an overseas empire and sea power she thereby demonstrated a lack of self-interest quite exceptional in the circumstances. The principal territories she gave up were, in the Mediterranean, the islands of Elba, Malta and Minorca; in the West Indies Tobago, St Lucia and Martinique, and the Dutch possessions in Guiana, and in India various military and commercial stations both Dutch and French.

France, in her turn, guaranteed Portugal all her possessions and agreed to evacuate her troops from Naples and the Papal States and also to acknowledge the independence of the so-called Republic of the Seven Islands; Corfu and others, which had been Venetian, then became French by the Treaty of Campo Formio, and were then captured jointly by Turkey and Russia. France also undertook to return Egypt to Turkey and agreed, as did Britain, to restore Malta to the Knights of St John, guaranteed by a third power.

In the light of future events the last two items in the treaty were the most significant as their implementation, though in different ways, became highly relevant to the whole question of good faith between France and Britain. Critics of the treaty were able to take as their starting-point the fact that Bonaparte knew that his troops had left Egypt, before the preliminaries were signed, something which was kept from the British negotiators, and therefore conceded nothing and began the whole process of peace-making with a piece of deception. This atmosphere of bad faith and lack of trust, as will be seen, persisted throughout the eighteen months of uneasy peace and the status of Malta was to provide the final *casus belli*.

The period, which seems in retrospect but a pause in what was almost exactly a quarter of a century of war between Britain and France, was marked by a series of unpleasant surprises for the British Government. The Ministry itself at first thought that it had ensured the foundation of a lasting peace. Its critics, in Parliament, but not in Government, were allowed to be sceptical, but that is the function of 'His Majesty's Loyal Opposition'. However at its lowest, and Pitt was at first inclined to accept the analysis, it was thought that the fires of Revolutionary France had burnt themselves out and now, Britain and France having set limits to their ambitions and their spheres of influence, the two countries could settle down to peaceful co-existence.

'We have the satisfaction,' said Pitt, 'of knowing that we have survived the violence of the revolutionary fever, and we have seen the extent of its principles abated.'

Now everything depended upon the man who ruled France, with more power in his hands than Bourbon kings had ever possessed. Napoleon Bonaparte was now at the height of his popularity and was soon to be elected Consul for life, and as an indication of his near-regal status, adopted his Christian name as his official signature.

This time of peace was also to be Nelson's domestic period and its beginning can really be signalised by the arrival, and return, of one letter. It was delivered to Merton in the Christmas week of 1801:

16 Somerset Street.

My dear Husband,

It is some time since I have written to you; the silence you have imposed is more than My affection will allow me and in this instance I hope you will forgive me in not obeying you. One thing I omitted in My letter of July, which I now have to offer for your accommodation a comfortable warm House. Do, my Dear Husband, let us live together, I can never be happy until such an event takes place. I assure you again I have but one wish in the world. To please you. Let everything be buried in oblivion; it will pass away like a dream. I can only now intreat you to believe I am, most sincerely and affectionately,

Your wife,
Frances H. Nelson.

The letter was sent back to Fanny, the cruellest gesture of Nelson's life, endorsed, 'Opened by mistake by Lord Nelson, but not read' and it was signed, 'A. Davison'.

There was now to be no turning back. Nelson's second attempt at domestic felicity was begun, and it was to be ended by two almost simultaneous events, the death of the husband of his mistress and the re-opening of the French war. After those two happenings Horatio and Emma were to spend only twenty-five more days together. Inevitably the time that they did spend together at Merton, or at least based on Merton, provokes speculation as to the sort of life they might have led together if Nelson had survived Trafalgar.

The portents were not encouraging, if one accepts the view of Lord Minto. Admittedly he did not approve of the liaison, he disliked Lady Hamilton though fond of Nelson. However, he was honest enough to admit his prejudices. He stayed at Merton just before the treaty was signed at Amiens, and sent a report to his wife in Scotland:

> The whole establishment and way of life is such as to make me angry, as well as melancholy; but I cannot alter it, and I do not think myself obliged or at liberty to quarrel with him for his weakness, though nothing shall ever induce me to give the smallest countenance to Lady Hamilton. She looks ultimately to the chance of marriage, as Sir W. will not be long in her way, and she probably indulges a hope that she may survive Lady Nelson; in the meanwhile she and Sir William and the whole set of them are living with him at his expense. She is in high looks; but more immense than ever. She goes on cramming Nelson with trowelfuls of flattery, which he goes on taking as quietly as a child does pap. The love she makes to him is not only ridiculous, but disgusting; not only the rooms, but the whole house, staircase and all, are covered with nothing but pictures of her and him, of all sizes and sorts, and representative of his naval actions, coats of arms, pieces of plate in his honour, the flagstaff of L'Orient, etcetera.—an excess of vanity which counteracts its own purpose. If it was Lady H's house there might be a pretence for it; to make his own a mere looking-glass to view himself all day is bad taste. Braham, the celebrated Jew singer, performed with Lady H. She is horrid, but he entertained me in spite of her. Lord Nelson explained to me a little the sort of blame which has been imputed to Sir Hyde Parker for Copenhagen.

There were many less flattering and more malicious descriptions of the 'tria juncta in uno' and they appeared in the gossipy columns of the London newspapers. Nelson and the Hamiltons were news but they made little attempt to avoid publicity, in fact by their actions they positively courted it. Nelson, like many public figures, was much in demand for ceremonies and functions, and he must have enjoyed them. His oft-professed desire for the quiet life in some rural retreat hardly accords with the programme he accepted in the next eighteen months. Something must be allowed for Emma's influence, and her perpetual desire for the lime-light, but the only complaint came from Sir William, not from the man who now really influenced her life.

Much of the time at Merton was not spent there at all, but travelling about the country from engagement to engagement rather like a domestic Grand Tour. The three of them, Nelson, Emma and Sir William, almost always travelled and appeared together, but they were on most occasions accompanied by a circus of relations, friends and hangers-on. The tour was planned for six weeks and encompassed Oxford, Gloucester, Worcester, Monmouth, Milford, Swansea and Birmingham. The entertainments, and the purposes of the visits differed in detail, but of one thing there could be no doubt, the warmth of the reception by the ordinary British public.

At Oxford, the starting-place, Honorary D.C.L.s were conferred upon Nelson and Sir William Hamilton, and the Reverend William Nelson, already a Doctor of Divinity at Cambridge, received the equivalent from the other university, as an undeserved distinction by association. The Matchams with their son, George, and Mrs William Nelson with her son Horatio, were also present.

The two ladies, Mrs Matcham and Mrs Nelson, were in deep mourning for on April 26 the Rev. Edmund Nelson, had died in Bath. Warned by a letter from George Matcham of his father's approaching end, his famous son had sent a discouraging reply, 'Had my father expressed a wish to see me, unwell as I am, I should have flown to Bath, but I believe it would be too late, however should it be otherwise, and he wishes to see me, no consideration shall detain me for a moment.' Nevertheless some consideration must have detained him. He was suffering from some form of stomach or bowel disorder, but there was also St Emma's birthday to celebrate, and the christening of Fatima, her black maid, now aged twenty, at Merton Church as 'Fatima Emma Charlotte Nelson Hamilton'. So 'our Father' was comforted on his death bed only by Fanny, Viscountess Nelson, and it was she too who was the only close relation, though by marriage, present at his funeral. Perhaps Nelson feared to meet Fanny.

In contrast to the sombre black of the two ladies, Sir William and Nelson were positive peacocks, decked out with their stars and ribbons. Sir William with the crimson ribbon of the Bath, and the blue with red border of St Ferdinand, and Nelson outshining him with two more, one pink and the other green. It is a sad comment upon Nelson's delight in medals, chains and ribbons that, despite George III's permission to wear them, the two latter were both dubious in origin. The pink ribbon attached itself to the star of the Ottoman Order of the Crescent, but only because the Sultan, or his advisers, had discovered that Nelson referred to himself as a Knight of the Crescent. The Ottoman Empire's recognition of the Admiral's prowess at the Nile had been the customary pelisse and the chelengk. The Order of the Crescent had been created for him; if that was how Europeans rewarded their heroes, very well, the East would follow suit; the ribbon had followed as a sort of afterthought, a fact which has led some biographers to think that Nelson was decorated twice by the Sultan.

The green ribbon which accompanied a large ornamental Maltese cross was Nelson's latest and last acquisition, but was bogus. It was the insignia of a Knight Grand Commander of the Most Illustrious Order Equestrian Secular and Capitular of St Joachim, and perhaps even Nelson had been a bit suspicious, as its Chancellor, the Baron d'Eiker and Ekoffen had been forced to write to him twice in order to gain his acceptance. The Baron had been, apparently, Chamberlain to the late King of Poland, as well as now being some sort of ceremonial functionary to a couple of reigning German princes. The moving spirit though in making the offer to Nelson was most likely an Englishman, 'Sir' Levett Hanson, his knighthood also being by courtesy of the Order of St Joachim. He was in the service of the Duke of Modena and had the rank of Brigadier General, but had been associated with other Orders in his time, for instance, two which were sold by the Duke of Linburgh-Styrum to pay for his oriental mistress. Apparently the Order of St Joachim could also be purchased. Perhaps the acquisition of a real hero in the shape of Nelson made the distinction more desirable by others, it may even have put the price up. There were admittedly to be other English wearers of the Order besides Nelson, four in number, but the only one of any note was Philip d'Auvergne, Rear-Admiral of the Blue, last heard of as a midshipman in the Arctic expedition. In 1807, perhaps a little more was known about it than in 1802, for the King refused permission to Mr Robert Kerr Porter to wear the Order.

After Oxford what the newspapers called 'Lord Nelson's tourists' decided, without invitation or acquaintance with its owner, to visit Blenheim Palace. Not all doors however opened at the magic of the name of Nelson, and certainly not when he was accompanied by his mistress. His Grace of Marlborough was therefore not at home, but sent out refreshments to the park. These were refused and the tourists departed, defeated and in a quite unjustifiable fury.

Gloucester was more in Nelson's style with welcoming crowds and a visit to the cathedral with the bells ringing overhead. At Oxford Nelson had left a sum of money for the prisoners in the gaol, in Gloucester he visited the prison. Early nineteenth-century prisons were hardly show-places, but perhaps he remembered that many of his 'people' came from them, or chose the sea in preference. Ross was next on the list and from there by boat on the River Wye to Monmouth. Here there was some-thing entirely appropriate for a sea officer, a Naval Temple on Kymin Hill, erected by Admiral Boscawen's daughter. There were plaques celebrating Rodney and Hawke, and Nelson's name was added. The town band turned out to lead the procession.

At Brecon the local farmers gave the hero a cheer; he had been making notes, which eventually reached the Prime Minister, on the oaks of the Forest of Dean, the raw material of ships of the line. The Matchams had gone off to Bath after Gloucester, but at Milford, where there was con-siderable Hamilton property, Charles Greville, once Emma's lover and protector, was waiting to greet her husband, his uncle, and the new lover. August 1 to 9 were spent at Milford, enabling the Nile anniversary to be celebrated in style. There was a fair and a cattle show and Nelson praised the harbour at a grand banquet in the New Hotel. The Hamiltons had a financial interest in the development of the port. Captain Foley, for it was his part of the country, turned up, and Nelson laid the foundation stone of a new church.

Then on to Haverfordwest where the Admiral's carriage was drawn through the streets to another Freedom. At Swansea sailors, cheering as was their wont, took over the task of traction. By August 19 the party, minus Greville, who was feeling unwell, were back in Monmouth. The Kymin Temple was visited again, there were bands and cannon and this time dinner was taken at the Beaufort Arms and Lady Hamilton sang.

Then Ross, Rudhall, Hereford, the Freedom in an apple wood box, then Ludlow, and by August 30 Worcester, with the Freedom in a china vase. Then Birmingham where Nelson attended, and by his presence interrupted, a performance of *The Merry Wives of Windsor*. The next day Emma sang at the celebration dinner. Finally, Warwick and Coventry, with similar scenes, a call on Lord Spencer at Althorp, and home to Merton on September 5.

'Oh, how our Hero has been receved,' wrote Emma to Mrs Matcham. *The Times* took the view that the country had repaid its debt for Lord Nelson's services in an ample degree, the *Post* pointed out that more acclaim had attended the Admiral's progress than those of George III. Other journals had provided tit-bits for their readers so that there could hardly be anyone in Britain who could read who would have been in the least doubt as to the relationship between Nelson and Emma Hamilton, except those who puzzled over the part played by Sir William Hamilton.

Back at Merton the two lovers engaged in a number of subterfuges, to enable them both, and especially Nelson, to see Horatia who was still in the care of Mrs Gibson in London. It is difficult to follow the movements exactly from the letters which have survived, but it seems that on one occasion Horatia was brought to Margate where Nelson arranged to see her. At another level of existence the peace was not going well, and the British and the French newspapers were already engaged in a slanging match. If hostilities were to break out again Nelson was most likely to have the command of the Mediterranean fleet. It was a post that St Vincent had said should only go to 'an officer of splendour' and that was exactly what Nelson was.

The year 1802 brought together many strands of his existence. Merton Place, as it now began to be called, provided a home and a base, something that he had never possessed before. He was now the undoubted head of the family, and because of his pre-eminence and also, because of Emma's deliberate planning, his family was gathered round him, with three exceptions, his estranged wife, his stepson, and his daughter Horatia. Fanny and Josiah were now completely excluded, the only link the quarterly allowance. The Nelsons, the Matchams, and the Boltons were however almost constant guests and visitors. With them Lady Hamilton's plan of getting herself accepted as Nelson's hostess at Merton had succeeded. To be fair, to Mrs Bolton, and, to a lesser extent, Mrs Matcham, both continued to write to Lady Nelson and their acceptance of Lady Hamilton had only been with several backward glances in the direction of their brother's wife. The Reverend Doctor (Nelson found the title faintly ridiculous) on the other hand, and his wife, 'your Jewell', Emma called her, would have visited and courted their influential brother had he been living with Lucretia Borgia, provided that there had been a chance of a Deanery, or a prebend's stall, in it for William. Though to be absolutely fair to William he probably preferred the company of the brash, vulgar Lady Hamilton to that of the unassuming, genteel Viscountess Nelson.

What they all thought of the relationship between Horatio and Emma it is difficult to tell. Outward respectability was imposed by the presence of Sir William as a sort of male chaperon so presumably they were all entitled to see only what they wanted to see. George Matcham, however, did confide his thoughts to paper and came to the conclusion that his brother-in-law's marriage had been a cold, loveless affair, and would have been unsatisfactory even if Lady Hamilton had never existed. There was an element of truth in this, but there was also a considerable element of comforting self-deception as well.

It would be wrong though to assume that Nelson's brother and his two sisters gained a great deal in the material sense from Horatio. William certainly owed his doctorate of divinity at Cambridge, and at Oxford, and his minor advancement in the Church to his relationship to a national hero. There were also gifts of money to various relations, and help with Horace's education at Eton, but on the other hand George Matcham lent Nelson money to buy some of the adjoining fields round Merton. Nelson's principal legacy to his relations, appropriately for one who put decorations and honours before money, came about, after his death, by the terms of his patent of peerage, which was gazetted anew in 1802.

Considerable latitude was, unusually, allowed to his own wishes in the matter, and he based his representations upon the fact that he was, officially, childless. In the event of his death without issue, which now seemed likely, his peerage descended to his brother William and thence to his son Horace. The unusual provision, though, was the number of cross remainders so that if William or Horace pre-deceased him, or Horace pre-deceased William, instead of dying out, the Viscountcy and the Barony, 'of the Nile and Hilborough' then passed to the male descendants of Nelson's two sisters with the stipulation that they should change their name from Bolton or Matcham to Nelson. Typically, William, supported by his new friend and ally Emma, felt that the title should descend through his daughter as well as by way of his son.

One Nelson relation, his nephew William, a naval captain for whom Nelson had fiddled time to obtain quick promotion, did actually find himself the recipient of an unexpected dignity in May 1803. It was in that month that Nelson should at last have been formally installed as a Knight of the Bath in Westminster Abbey, and two of his young nephews had been chosen as esquires. However, by then Nelson was absent from the Kingdom so a proxy had to be found. Captain Bolton was in London for his wedding to his first cousin Kitty Bolton, the reception to be in Lady Hamilton's house in Clarges Street. So the Captain stood proxy for the Admiral, but in order to do so he had to be knighted himself, which ceremony was carried out a day before the investiture.

The fact that, by the time Captain Sir William had by his marriage transformed his bride into Lady Bolton, his distinguished uncle was at sea, and Lady Hamilton was back in London, necessitates a return to the events of the previous year.

While Nelson, after his return from his progress, had occupied himself with what passed for domesticity at Merton Place, interspersed with trips to London on official business and to see Horatia, war clouds had been gathering in Europe. When opening Parliament the King's speech had obliquely referred to the deterioration of Anglo-French relations. It was his drive to Westminster that on this occasion provided the opportunity for Colonel Despard's hare-brained assassination attempt which was in its turn to necessitate Nelson's giving evidence soon after at his trial, in defence of an old comrade. In February 1803 Mrs Bolton wrote to Lady Hamilton, 'What is the rumour of war that our papers are full of? I hope the storm will blow over. God forbid my Lord should be called for again'. She also hoped in the letter that Sir William's health would be improving. Very quickly in all three respects she was to be disappointed.

Even before the signing of the Treaty of Amiens the British Government had grounds for being suspicious of Bonaparte. His signature of the preliminaries of peace, knowing of the French defeat in Egypt, might have been regarded as only sharp diplomacy but the takeover of a piece of Brazilian territory, thereby giving control to French Guiana of the northern outlet of the Amazon, hardly agreed with his guarantee of Portuguese territory. Spain's cession of Louisiana was known to the Ministry, and to the public by January 1802, but it added to the accumulation of concerns as to French intentions. In December 1801 a French fleet of twenty ships of the line and a force of 20,000 troops had been despatched to quell the rebellion in Haiti, and incidentally to fail to do so, but Britain thought it expedient to reinforce the Jamaican station. On January 26, 1802 Bonaparte had accepted the presidency of the Cisalpine Republic, soon to be re-named Italian, another ominous indication of future ambitions. It was a wonder in these circumstances that the formal treaty was signed, though Britain obtained the concession that the Guiana border should be pushed back to safer limits.

If British ministers were still hopeful their hopes were soon to be dashed. Elba was made over, by its joint owners, Tuscany and Naples, to France. Then Bonaparte appeared as mediator in the settlement of the boundaries of the small German states, throwing his weight on the side of Prussia and against Britain's former ally, Austria, the settlement being, in his own words, 'entirely to the advantage of France'.

On September 11 Piedmont and Elba were both formally incorporated as French territories and a sizeable bite was taken out of Genoese territory as well. In August internal dissensions in Switzerland provided an excuse for French interference. Soon General Ney and 30,000 soldiers were within the territory of an independent state, ostensibly to assist the cause of republicanism.

In October the British Government, stung into retaliation, sent dispatches to the West Indies, Dutch Guiana and the Cape of Good Hope to prevent the return of former French and Dutch colonies. It was an earnest of British good intentions that these dispatches were countermanded but too late, for by the time the second set of orders arrived war had broken out. While one set of dispatches chased another, it was becoming obvious that France and Britain were at loggerheads. M. Otto, the French Minister in London, more tactfully than Bonaparte in Paris, demanded, 'the whole Treaty of Amiens; nothing but the Treaty of Amiens' to which the response of Lord Whitworth, the Ambassador in Paris, was 'the state of the Continent when the Treaty of Amiens was signed, and nothing but that state'. Admittedly there were still British troops in Egypt and Malta but then there were still French troops in Holland and Bonaparte was talking of 'the Empire of the Gauls'.

In January 1803 the *Moniteur* published Colonel Sebastiani's notorious report on his mission to the Levant. It was deliberately well publicised and it renewed Bonaparte's old project of a French Eastern Empire; the re-occupation of Egypt, the necessary first step, was talked of as a practical possibility. On March 8 Parliament was informed by the Government that in consequence of military preparations going on in the ports of France and Holland His Majesty had judged it expedient to adopt

additional measures of precaution for the security of his dominions. This
was preparative to counteract any French move when it was learnt in
Paris that the Cape of Good Hope, due to the initiative of the British
commander on the spot, had not been given up.

In April Lord Whitworth was instructed to propose a settlement which
recognised what was now the status quo; this involved of course Britain's
retention of Malta, to which proposal the First Consul returned his
celebrated remark to the effect that he would as soon see the British on
the heights of Montmarte as in possession of that island. The basic
difference was that Bonaparte wanted the right of unfettered interference
in the affairs of Continental Europe and this Britain was not prepared to
concede. There was no compromise possible and on May 12 Whitworth
—Bonaparte had 'shouted at him like a coachman' he said—left Paris and
on the 16th Great Britain declared war on France.

On the afternoon of the 18th Nelson hoisted his flag in *Victory* at Portsmouth and two days later sailed for the Mediterranean to take up the post
of Commander-in-Chief. Almost his last act before returning to service
had been to arrange for the baptism of his daughter at the parish church
of St Marylebone, the parish in which Mrs Gibson lived with her charge.
Most of the other infants christened on that day were aged a few months,
'Horatia Nelson Thompson' was two and a half, though her date of birth
was given as October 29, 1800, a time when Lady Hamilton was out of
England. It was another of the subterfuges engaged in by Nelson and
Emma but as usual they were not very clever in their attempts to give
Horatia another identity, for though neither of them was present, a
sensible precaution, instead of the mythical Thompsons being entered as
parents, Horatia was credited with no parents at all. The new anonymity
revealed Emma's next plan.

By enticing the Nelsons, Boltons and Matchams to Merton Place she
had been playing an obvious game to alienate them from Fanny. Now
there was a sub-plot, for with Nelson's brother and sisters came a host of
his nephews and nieces, this providing a camouflage for the appearance of
'the orphan', Horatia.

Paradoxically, precautions had to be intensified after April 6, 1803, for
on that day Sir William Hamilton had died, but not at Merton for,
sensing that his end was soon to come, the old diplomat, with an excess
of propriety and consideration, had had himself taken to his London
home, with Emma and Nelson keeping vigil for his last six days. There
can be no doubt of the genuine sorrow of them both. As well as an

affection for the man, it was a piece of their past, of so much shared experience, the aftermath of the Nile, Naples and Sicily, which had gone forever.

He was buried, as he had wished, on his Pembrokeshire estate, by the side of his first wife, but in the codicil to his will he made his first and last comment on his later life, 'The copy of Madame de Brun's picture of Emma, in enamel, by Bone, I give to my dearest friend, Lord Nelson, Duke of Brontë; a very small token of the great regard I have for his Lordship, the most virtuous, loyal and truly brave character I ever met with. God bless him, and shame fall on those who do not say "Amen".'

Two days later Nelson wrote to his sister, Mrs Bolton, saying 'Lady Hamilton suffers very much' and in her confused emotional way no doubt that was true. It obviously did not seem inappropriate or excessive to her to issue instructions to Mrs Gibson that Horatia, as a sign of respect, was to stay confined to the house until after the funeral. Other proprieties, perhaps more understandable, were also observed. Mrs William Nelson travelled up to London to chaperone the widowed Lady Hamilton, and Vice-Admiral Lord Nelson moved out from the late Sir William's house to take lodgings at 19 Piccadilly. However, the strangeness of a curious relationship persisted, for at that address Nelson shared expenses with Charles Greville, his mistress's former lover, who had virtually sold her some years back to his recently-deceased uncle.

Lady Hamilton was now very much alone, without the comfort and security which Sir William had always provided, and of course the cloak of respectability that his presence had always thrown over her relationship with Nelson. Her lover was now at sea, and she had the task of coping with 'the orphan' and yet another problem which also necessitated secrecy and diplomacy, for she was again pregnant. When Nelson had sailed off with the Baltic Fleet Gillray had published a cruel cartoon depicting a monstrously fat Emma, as Dido, swooning and weeping as her Aeneas and his ships disappeared over the horizon. She was now, as then, again 'embonpoint', as the gossips put it, but much more thrown back upon her own devices.

So far as practical problems were concerned, money was the obvious necessity and bearing in mind her ultimately penurious state after Nelson's death it is an appropriate time to examine Lady Hamilton's financial circumstances in the early months of 1803.

The Hamiltons had always appeared chronically short of money since their return from Naples. Sir William often complained and Emma, extravagant and careless, perhaps hardly noticed or at least never seemed to worry. Sir William had sold many of his pictures and antiquities and had tried to obtain a pension. Nelson on shore had reverted to half-pay, and had spent most of his capital on the purchase of Merton Place. He still provided Fanny with an allowance, and had also disposed of some of his possessions, mostly presentations, for cash.

His total income on shore, from half-pay and pensions, was £3418 per year, made up of £2000 Exchequer pension for the Nile, £923 Navy pension for the loss of an eye and an arm, and £465 Vice-Admiral's half-pay, and £30 interest on £1,000 invested at three per cent. The allowance to Fanny, the assistance to Old Blindy, and nephew Horace's fees at Eton, made up the sum of £2650 a year. Also included in that sum was the interest he had to pay on money he had borrowed to buy Merton, and the adjoining Axe estate, the mortgages totalling around £6000 plus £4000 borrowed to fit out for his Baltic and Channel commands. Thus he had £768 a year to live on. Back at sea his pay and allowances increased by about £500, but he had arranged to allow Emma £100 a month. Therefore his spending money must have been calculated in tens of pounds rather than hundreds and, as he was paying for Merton and the improvements that were taking place there, he was still in debt.

As for the estate of Sir William, Greville was the executor and this involved him in some rather unsavoury wrangles with his uncle's widow exacerbated by the fact that he was mean and she generous. All sorts of sums, both during and after Sir William's lifetime, went to her relations, principally the Connors who had turned up from nowhere as soon as she settled at Merton. However, Emma received £800 immediately from her husband's estate, and an allowance of £800 a year. The furniture in Piccadilly also went to her, which was only right as she had bought it from the sale of her jewellery, when Sir William had been in one of his economising phases soon after they had returned to Britain. Greville took his uncle's other possessions, and wanted to sell the lease of the house as soon as possible to settle Sir William's debts which amounted to almost £5500.

Thus Emma was by no means rich, nor was she poor. Horatia had to be kept, and Mrs Gibson paid, but with reasonable care no one should have starved. Unfortunately the words 'reasonable care' applied to Emma Hamilton only raise a laugh of desperation, and she had no intention of starving. She found herself temporarily the guest in a parsonage, her host the Reverend William, now a prebend of Canterbury Cathedral. She was accepted at last as one of the family, but that status depended upon the life of Horatio Nelson.

Both Nelson and Emma thought that they ought to have had more money. He argued that both St Vincent and Duncan had been more generously rewarded for their lesser victories and she because Sir William had been unsuccessful in obtaining for her the reversion of his own pension of £1200, for her services in Naples.

This double grievance was the genesis of claims by Emma for governmental assistance after Nelson's death. He wrote to her 'I have known the pinch and shall endeavour never to know it again', and tried to economise and, literally with his dying breath, to gain more for Emma and Horatia. Unfortunately, though, he was not financially activated, like his brother William or Sir Hyde Parker; glory and Emma were his twin passions and neither were profitable. The Dukedom of Brontë was almost symbolic of the financial pattern of Nelson's life, and was one of the outward dignities which contributed to the general belief that Lord Nelson was 'amazingly rich'. In fact the estates brought in nothing, the only person who had gained anything from them was Graeffer the steward, recently deceased, and he had only made a living.

However, Nelson had a destiny and on March 9, during a debate in Parliament on the country's defences, he had put it succinctly in a note passed hurriedly to Addington, 'Whenever it is necessary, I am your Admiral'.

CHAPTER THIRTY

War Resumed

IN PORTSMOUTH Harbour, two days after the declaration of war, on May 20, 1803, at about 3.30 p.m., the ensign of a Vice-Admiral of the Blue climbed to the foremast of *Victory* and a gun salute boomed out thirteen times. Nelson was saluting the flag of the Commander-in-Chief of the Channel Fleet, his old friend 'Billy' Cornwallis, who had himself already departed to his duties somewhere off Brest.

Partly because *Victory* was undermanned, despite the 'hottest' press ever remembered in the sea ports and the boarding of merchantmen to take off seamen who did not even know that war had been declared, and partly because there was some doubt as to whether she should go to Cornwallis's command, Nelson arrived at Gibraltar in the frigate *Amphion*. He returned to *Victory* in August and remained on board her in the Mediterranean, with only short intervals, for the next twenty-eight months. His haste to join his command was understandable, his arrival in Gibraltar bringing the first news that Britain was at war.

It was to be a long campaign because of the nature of the enemy forces. They took longer to assemble than Nelson's ships, but they were, in their own way, just as formidable. They consisted of 190,000 French soldiers; seven army corps, six divisions of cavalry and a division of the Consular Guard which, with the self-elevation of its master, was soon to become known to the world as the Imperial Guard. The seven corps were deployed at Hanover, Utrecht, between Flushing and Dunkirk, at Boulogne, outside Boulogne, at Montreuil and Brest. They were commanded respectively by Generals Bernadotte, Marmont, Davout, Soult, Lannes, Ney and Augereau. The Guard was commanded by General Bessières and the cavalry by General Murat. Everyone of these young but experienced soldiers would become a Napoleonic Marshal and Europe would resound with their exploits and victories for ten years after Nelson's death. This force, 'the Army of the Coasts of the Ocean', was the nucleus of the Grand Army which was eventually to stretch its outposts from Malaga to Moscow and it was the very epitome of the power of France.

Mahan encapsulated, in a famous passage, the nature of the struggle which was to occupy the next two years:

Far away, Cornwallis off Brest, Collingwood off Rochefort, Pellew off Ferol, were battling the wild gales of the Bay of Biscay, in that tremendous and sustained vigilance which reached its utmost tension in the years preceding Trafalgar, concerning which Collingwood wrote that admirals need to be made of iron, but which was forced upon them by the unquestionable and imminent danger of the country. Further distant still, severed apparently from all connection with the busy scene at Boulogne, Nelson before Toulon was wearing away the last two years of his glorious but suffering life, fighting the fierce north-westers of the Gulf of Lyon and questioning, questioning continually with feverish anxiety, whether Napoleon's object was Egypt again or Great Britain really. They were dull, weary, eventless months, those months of watching and waiting of the big ships before the French arsenals. Purposeless they surely seemed to many, but they saved England. The world has never seen a more impressive demonstration of the influence of sea power upon its history. Those far distant, storm-beaten ships, upon which the Grand Army never looked, stood between it and the dominion of the world.

This was the task and the duty that Nelson was now taking up, in *Victory*, whose flag captain was his favourite Thomas Masterman Hardy.

Mahan was right to stress a number of elements, the fact that other commands and other ships than Nelson's were involved, the tedium and the very real threat of invasion. For there was still an air of doubt about it all. In Britain volunteer regiments were raised and drilled and paraded, and bathing ladies in Kent and Sussex got into a panic lest Bonaparte's soldiers should suddenly appear and ravish them as it was said had happened in George III's Electorate of Hanover. There was also a very real hatred of Bonaparte, 'the Corsican ogre', who was credited with every vice, including incest with his sisters, and was also used, rather illogically, as a threat to quieten fractious infants. Yet in the inner recesses of the Admiralty in Whitehall it was not believed, as St Vincent had not believed it, that the French would come by sea, but what then was the purpose of the soldiers assembled on the French coast and the flat-bottomed boats?

For Nelson there must have been a considerable sense of *déjà vu* as he cruised the Mediterranean, writing to Emma and Davison, enquiring about Horatia and Merton, and revisiting Naples where Hugh Elliot was now the British Minister, the King had gone into a decline and the Queen had taken a lover called St Clair, an officer of mixed Irish-French nationality. There were rumours of the Spaniards coming into the war on the side of the French which should provide a flag officer, hard pressed financially, with a chance of rich prizes. Writing to Emma he described it as an odd war without a battle. Meanwhile Captain Sir William Bolton was to be brought out and advanced if possible as some compensation to Nelson's sister, mother of William's bride Catherine, whose own son George had been taken on as a midshipman but had died of 'the flux' in 1799, on his way to the Mediterranean.

The overriding question in Nelson's mind was what were Bonaparte's intentions? Where and how would he make the first move? The situation in 1803 was not unlike the first year of the Second World War, which became known as the phoney war. Indeed some historians have doubted, especially in view of later events in 1805, if Bonaparte ever really intended to invade Britain.

To sustain the argument that he did so intend, and that the invasion army and the flotillas of boats were not all part of some gigantic bluff, it is necessary for a moment to look at the military state of the antagonists, Britain and France, when they entered into their renewed war in 1803.

At sea Britain was much better prepared than France, her superiority in ships being almost two to one. It was she who had declared war, and there can be little doubt that Bonaparte would have preferred to stave off hostilities. Nevertheless he realised that Britain was his most implacable foe and in order to concentrate upon that one enemy he had made certain preparations. He had sold the recently acquired Louisiana to the United States in order better to concentrate upon Europe. The Haiti expedition against Toussaint L'Ouverture, the black slave leader, was abandoned, although the fleet had not yet returned to European waters. Efforts were also made to improve the French navy and a ship-building programme was put into operation under the painstaking but uninspiring Minister of Marine, Admiral Decrés, although trained sailors were still in short supply.

Still, by the time of the British declaration of war there was still one other brake upon his plans for a showdown with the 'stubborn islanders', the internal state of France, for although the Treaty of Amiens had enormously enhanced his prestige, Citizen First Consul Bonaparte was by no means universally popular. The conspiracy in early 1804 of General Pichégru, its purpose the kidnapping and overthrow of Bonaparte, though foiled, led on to the capture of the Duc d'Enghien, and his execution on March 21. Bonaparte's retaliatory severity had as its object, in which it succeeded, the stamping out of Royalist plots and paved the way for his own proclamation as Emperor of the French on May 18. His coronation as Napoleon I followed seven months later. All these moves to consolidate his régime took time, energy and attention away from invasion plans.

After Trafalgar Napoleon, who was an accomplished and unprincipled liar, denied that the plans had been real but he can hardly be believed in the face of the military and naval preparations sustained for almost two years. Further, none of his Marshals, Marmont, his oldest friend, Davout, his most loyal disciple, Ney his most intrepid leader, and Berthier, his faithful Chief of Staff, ever suggested that the invasion preparations were anything but in deadly earnest.

Nevertheless, though the soldiers practised embarking and disembarking, took courses in rowing, and the Guard was taught to swim, while 1200 landing craft were built and prepared, and though Bonaparte was heard to muse, by his gigantic telescope, 'Yes—a favourable wind, and thirty-six hours', and in Paris a medal was struck with the inscription 'Invasion of England. Struck in London 1804', the British could still be excused for being sceptical and singing to the tune of 'The Bluebells of Scotland':

> When and Oh when does this little Boney come?
> Perhaps he'll come in August, perhaps he'll stay at home.

So Nelson sailed and watched and waited. Like all the other admirals, Cornwallis, Keith and Collingwood, he complained of the state of his ships. However, men could also be worn out and Nelson's two concerns were health and the alleviation of boredom. Before he had embarked he had seen his old friend Dr Moseley at Chelsea Hospital, as his good eye was giving him trouble. The diagnosis had not been encouraging and there had been talk of an operation, and the Admiral had been forced to remind the doctor that he had but one eye. However on March 11, 1804 Nelson wrote to Moseley, more concerned with the health and morale of others than his own. It was a full letter and it touched upon almost all of Nelson's problems, for as he said 'as I rise in rank, so do my exertions'.

The great thing in all Military Service is health; and you will agree with me, that it is easier for an Officer to keep his men healthy, than for a Physician to cure them. Situated as this Fleet has been, without a friendly Port, where we could get all the things so necessary for us, yet I have, by changing the cruising ground, not allowed the sameness of prospect to satiate the mind—sometimes by looking at Toulon, Ville Franche, Barcelona, and Rosas; then running round Minorca, Majorca, Sardinia and Corsica; and two or three times anchoring for a few days, and sending a Ship to the last place for onions, which I find the best thing that can be given to Seamen; having always good mutton for the sick, cattle when we can get them, and plenty of fresh water. In the winter it is the best plan to give half the allowance of grog, instead of all wine. These things are for the Commander-in-Chief to look to; but shut very nearly out from Spain, and only getting refreshments by stealth from other places, my Command has been an arduous one.

Cornwallis has great merit for his persevering cruise, but he has everything sent him; we have nothing. We seem forgotten by the great folks at home. Our men's minds, however, are always kept up with the daily hopes of meeting the Enemy. I send you, as a curiosity, an account of our deaths, and sent to the Hospital, out of six thousand men. The Fleet put to sea on the 18th of May, 1803, and is still at sea; not a Ship has been refitted, or recruited, excepting what has been done at sea. You will readily believe that all this must have shaken me. My sight is getting very bad; but I must not be sick until after the French Fleet is taken. Then I shall hope to take you by the hand, and have further recourse to your skill for my eye.

I am always glad to hear good accounts of our dear Lady Hamilton. That she is beloved wherever she is known, does not surprise me; the contrary would, very much. I am sure she feels most sincerely all your kindness. Believe me for ever, my dear Doctor, your much obliged friend,

Nelson and Brontë.

It was a period during which Nelson wrote many letters, but few concerned the great strategic design, and there was little in the way of action to describe. Many of the letters are short and concerned with administrative matters within the fleet. However, they give as good a picture of life at sea, the tasks of a Commander-in-Chief and the sort of man Nelson was, as any written in the more exciting times in his life.

Few details in his command seem to have escaped his notice and an innate concern for individuals shines through and it is not difficult to see why those who served under him realised that there was something special about Nelson. Perhaps when he wrote on August 25 1803 off Toulon to Mr Benjamin Baynton he remembered another midshipman going aboard *Raisonnable*, somewhat confused in the world in which he found himself:

Sir,
Your son I was sorry to find, had been in very great distress for his chest, but Captain Sutton has been so good as to order some clothes for him at Gibraltar; and as our numbers are so great in the *Victory*, he has taken him with him into the *Amphion*. There is, I assure you, only one voice about him,—that he is one of the very best lads ever met with; everybody seemed to love him. His chest is arrived, and will be forwarded to him the first opportunity, with your letter. I am, dear Sir, your most obedient servant,

Nelson and Brontë.

It is sad, but instructive of the hazards of navy life, to discover that the subject of the letter was promoted lieutenant, was severely wounded in 1810, but was only promoted commander in 1841, when he was older than his admiral had been in 1803.

Baynton, though, was an officer, and there have been commanders who have succeeded in being very popular with their commissioned brethren, but without sparing much thought for the lower deck, regarding them as a race apart. In the Georgian navy 'the people' in a warship were a race apart, the division reflecting the social stratification of the time. Their dress, their pay, their rewards, their food and drink, their habits and speech and the privileges they were not allowed marked them off from the officers who commanded them. Of course Nelson was a man of his time, a sea officer who had to maintain discipline and not a social reformer, but he did have a kind heart and never forgot that the men under his command, who won his victories for him, were also human beings.

An unknown admiral who wrote to him in January 1804, interceding for a young officer who had disobeyed his captain, seeking to avoid a court martial for his protégé, received an illuminating, and disappointing answer:

The young man has pushed himself forward to notice, and he must take the consequences. We must recollect, my dear Admiral, it was upon the Quarter-deck, in the face of the Ship's Company, that he treated his Captain with contempt; and I am in duty bound to support the authority and consequences of every Officer under my command. A poor Seaman is for ever punished for contempt to *his* superior.

I am, &c,

Nelson and Brontë.

Perhaps Nelson's Christianity helped and the only time he forgot his principles was in his dealings with Fanny, and his relationship with Emma. In the latter case of course he managed to get himself into some absurd mental and spiritual contortions which reached their height when he reminded his mistress that their taking the Sacrament together in Merton church bore witness to the essential purity of their relationship.

There was also another aspect of Nelson's character which singled him out from many of his brother flag officers. In an age of snobs, Nelson was no snob. He may have been an 'upwards' snob, in the sense that he glorified in his own elevation and was obviously taken with the notion of hobnobbing with Royalty at the Court of Naples. A 'downwards' snob, though, he was not. A real snob would never have tolerated Emma Hamilton as an acquaintance, let alone as a mistress, and if God, as he imagined He might, removed the 'impediment' (Fanny) as a wife. Time and time again, he mentions in his letters his anger and contempt for those of the aristocracy who despised Emma for her origins. The fact that some of them may have quite genuinely regarded her as thoroughly unlikeable on other grounds was quite beyond his imagining.

He even tolerated the presence of Emma's plebeian relations at Merton, something which even the long-suffering Sir William could not take, and for whom Mrs Cadogan was the limit. In Nelson's view Berry was not only an officer but a gentleman while Sir Hyde Parker, for instance, might have demurred as Berry senior was a shopkeeper. Perhaps the Cambridge bakers in Nelson's family were remembered. Running alongside Nelson's anti-snobbery was also a strong sense of family obligation; he may not have been particularly fond of his relations, with the exception of Maurice, but he did do all in his power to help them. Certainly, unlike some rising and risen men, he never attempted to disown or disregard them. Though he made fun of William, the arch-snob and opportunist, he still assisted him in his inappropriate ambitions. It was a characteristic, curiously enough, which he shared with another risen man, the Emperor of the French.

That particular gentleman did not occupy much of Nelson's correspondence in those dull days in the Mediterranean, 'Our days pass so much alike that having described one, you have them all'. Some speculation certainly, but letters coming to Nelson even from the Government could tell him little, if the French fleet came out he knew what he had to do, while letters from Nelson could not contain much of interest until the French fleet did come out.

A not unfamiliar situation during war were the bundles of private letters Nelson received dealing with domestic problems and situations far removed from his own existence, and over which he attempted to exercise some control. This was usually, because of the time-lag, virtually impossible. Emma was his constant correspondent, and her concerns have mostly to be conjectured from his replies as he destroyed her letters. The Commander-in-Chief in the Mediterranean was bombarded with details of the improvements going ahead under her direction at Merton, and the doings of Mr Chawner, builder and architect, and Mr Cribb, gardener.

Obviously Emma also wrote on less mundane matters and for those who care to speculate on those letters received by Nelson, a sample of her style, and sentiments, but addressed to Alexander Davison, may be offered. She wrote to him on July 24, 1804, by which time he was temporarily in prison for alleged corrupt practices in a Parliamentary election. The subject is a contrast between herself and Fanny, who may not at first be recognised even as the widow of Escalopes (Aesculapius), otherwise Dr Nisbet:

> The apoticary's widdow, the Creole with Her Heart Black as Her feind-like looking face, was never destined for a Nelson, for so noble-minded a Creature. She never loved Him for Himself. She loved Her poor dirty Escalopes if she had love, and the 2 dirty negatives made that dirty affirmative that is a disgrace to the Human Species. She then starving took in an evil hour our Hero. She made him unhappy. She disunited Him from His family. She wanted to *raise up* Her own vile spue at the expence and total abolation of the family which shall be immortalized for having given birth to the Saviour of His Country. When He came home, *maimed, lame,* and covered with Glory. She put in derision His Honnerable wounds. She raised a clamour against Him, because He had seen a more lovely, a more virtuous woman, who had

served with him in a foreign country and who had her heart and senses
open to His Glory, to His greatness, and His virtues. If He had lived
with this daemon, the blaster of His fame and reputation, He must have
fallen under it, and His Country would have lost their greatest
ornament.

Nelson had gained another family correspondent, Miss Horatia Nelson
Thomson, and he wrote his first letter to her on October 21, 1803,

My dear Child,
Receive this first letter from your most affectionate Father. If I live, it
will be my pride to see you virtuously brought up; but if it pleases God
to call me, I trust to Himself: in that case, I have left Lady H. your
guardian. I therefore charge you, my Child, on the value of a Father's
blessing, to be obedient and attentive to all her kind admonitions and
instructions. At this moment I have left you, in a Codicil dated the 6th
of September, the sum of four thousand pounds sterling, the interest of
which is to be paid to your guardian for your maintenance and education. I shall only say, my dear Child, may God Almighty bless you and
make you an ornament to your sex, which I am sure you will be if you
attend to all Lady H's kind instructions; and be assured that I am, my
dear Horatia, your most affectionate Father,
                                                    Nelson and Brontë.

Codicils and wills were one of Nelson's occupations on board ship, and
an attempt to regulate matters on shore. The particular one referred to in
this letter was remarkable in two respects. First, because Nelson was
presuming on the existence of £4000 from his estate, and second because
he states that he hopes that his daughter will make 'a fit wife for my dear
nephew Horatio Nelson who I wish to marry her, if he should prove
worthy, in Lady Hamilton's estimate, of such a treasure as I am sure she
shall be'.

The latter, an attempt to regulate matters beyond the grave, lived on
in the recollection of Horatia's family, though soon rendered impossible
by Horatio's premature death, as Viscount Trafalgar, three years after the
battle.

Nelson's letters during this time reveal a kind of double life, the contrast between the two heightened by the slowness and uncertainty of communications and the leisurely pace of sailing ships. On one hand he
learned of events and personalities at home, on the other he cruised the

blank face of the Mediterranean day in day out watching for the sight of French sails. Nelson was on board *Victory* with Rear-Admiral George Murray as his Captain of the Fleet, the only time he ever had such a subordinate, and Hardy as his flag captain with one 80, *Gibraltar*, six 74's, *Belleisle, Donegal, Kent, Renown, Superb* and *Triumph* and two 64's, *Agincourt* and *Monmouth*. This was the end of a long chain of ships which stretched from the Morea to the Texel. This was all as the result of Napoleon's initiative; although with a man of his mental complexity and breadth of interests, it is difficult to be categoric as regards intentions. As far back as November of 1803 he had written to Cambacères, then a fellow Consul, saying of the Channel, 'It is a ditch which one can jump whenever one is bold enough to try it'. Nevertheless the difficulty is to identify the occasions when he thought and acted positively towards an invasion project. The troops and the barges were ready, but it was only he who could give the order for them to embark, and only he who could give the orders to the units of his fleet in French harbours to co-ordinate their actions to command the Channel so that the troops might have a chance of reaching British shores. It was this second order which he shied away from, almost as though he didn't realise the necessity for it. In fairness to Napoleon, though, his admirals, because of the constant vigilance of the Royal Navy—its ships, as a Secretary to the Admiralty put it, working 'like post horses in an election'—never thought that they had much of a chance.

On October 9, 1803, Napoleon, by an alliance with Spain which was dressed up in the guise of a declaration of neutrality, added thirty-two Spanish ships of the line to his potential, and imposed upon the British the task of watching not only Brest, Toulon, Rochefort and the Dutch ports, but Cartagena, Cadiz and Ferrol as well. After this reinforcement there appeared for the first time the plan of decoying British ships to the West Indies. Admiral Latouche-Tréville, who had repulsed the Boulogne expedition, was to evade Nelson with his ten ships, slip through the Straits of Gibraltar, pick up six more ships at Rochefort and sail to the West Indies. The plan assumed that Nelson, or possibly some other admiral, would follow Latouche-Tréville across the Atlantic, anxious for the safety of the British colonial islands. However, the French fleet would merely reinforce the French islands of Martinique and Guadeloupe with troops and stores, and then return to Brest and Ferrol and there combine with the French and Spanish squadrons and then proceed up the Channel to cover the invasion fleet.

As a refinement upon the decoy theory Napoleon thought that Nelson might miss the French completely and search for them towards Sicily or even Egypt. The projected date for this attempt was to be September 1804. However, in the interim no French admiral was able to give any hope to the Emperor of being able to break the British blockade and he became very impatient with his senior naval officers. He therefore decided to dismiss them, but in the event this was not necessary. Admiral Truquet at Brest resigned and Latouche-Tréville died. Their replacements were Vice-Admiral Ganteaume at Brest, who had brought General Bonaparte back from Egypt, and at Toulon Vice-Admiral Villeneuve, who had escaped Nelson in 1798 at Aboukir.

The blockade continued and the September date disappeared as a possibility. By then Napoleon was writing to Ganteaume about an invasion of Ireland. A few days later and he was writing to Vice-Admiral Decrés, his perplexed Minister of Marine, with a new plan which involved three separate expeditions from Rochefort, Toulon and Brest, capturing Dominica, St Lucia, Surinam, and the other Dutch colonies, and St Helena. None of this came to pass in 1804, and it was only in 1805 that any positive moves to break or avoid the British blockade were made, and by then Napoleon had reverted to the West Indian decoy plan with variations.

Overall one is forced to the conclusion that Napoleon either could not, or would not, understand the basic facts of naval warfare, and so took refuge in schemes and subterfuges which his admirals knew were virtually impossible in practice. He committed the opposite mistake to Nelson. On land the Admiral, bored with the complicated problems of soldiers, went for short cuts. At sea the Emperor, impatient with the simple difficulties of admirals, provided them with plans which were too clever by half.

None of this, or very little, was apparent to Nelson who received his news ten weeks late, and then often only from captured French newspapers which were severely censored. His base was now Madalena on neutral Sardinia, and it was there that he heard of the death of Latouche-Tréville. It was rumoured that the fifty-nine-year-old admiral had worn himself out by climbing the signal tower at Sepet to look at the British fleet. At the same time there was news of the death of an old enemy of Neapolitan days, Charles Lock, who had died of fever in Malta en route for Egypt. 'The World' said the Commander-in-Chief in the Mediterranean, 'will go on very well without either of them.'

Since Malta in June of 1803 he had not been on shore, and since that

July had not been out of *Victory*. The daily routine on board that ship was described by Dr Gillespie who, having recently joined her as medical officer, was still taken by the romance, and not yet worn down by the boredom:

At 6 o'clock my servant brings a light and informs me of the hour, wind, weather and course of the ship, when I immediately dress and generally repair to the deck, the dawn of day at this season and latitude being apparent at about half or three-quarters past six. Breakfast is announced in the Admiral's cabin, where Lord Nelson, Rear-Admiral Murray, the Captain of the Fleet, Captain Hardy, commander of the *Victory*, the chaplain, secretary, one or two officers of the ship, and your humble servant assemble and breakfast on tea, hot rolls, toast, cold tongue, etc., which when finished we repair upon deck to enjoy the majestic sight of the rising sun scarcely ever obscured by clouds in this fine climate surmounting the smooth and placid waves of the Mediterranean, which supports the lofty and tremendous bulwarks of Britain, following in regular train their admiral in the *Victory*. Between the hours of 7 and 2 there is plenty of time for business, study, writing and exercise, which different occupations I endeavour to vary in such a manner as to afford me sufficient employment. At 2 o'clock a band of music plays till within a quarter of 3, when the drum beats the tune called, 'The Roast Beef of Old England', to announce the Admiral's dinner, which is served up at exactly 3 o'clock, and which generally consists of three courses and a dessert of the choicest fruit a fact which bespeaks the frequency of communications with the land together with three or four of the best wines, champagne and claret not excepted. If a person does not feel himself perfectly at his ease it must be his own fault, such is the urbanity and hospitality which reign here, notwithstanding the numerous titles, the four orders of Knighthood, worn by Lord Nelson, and the well earned laurels which he has acquired. Coffee and liqueurs close the dinner about half past 4 or 5 o'clock, after which the company generally walk the deck, where the band of music plays for nearly an hour. At 6 o'clock tea is announced, when the company again assemble in the Admiral's cabin, where tea is served up before 7 o'clock, and, as we are inclined, the party continue to converse with his lordship who at this time generally unbends himself, though he is at all times as free from stiffness and pomp as a regard to proper dignity will admit, and is very communicative. At 8 o'clock a rummer of punch with cake or biscuit is served up, soon after which we wish the Admiral a good night who is generally in bed before 9 o'clock. Such is the journal of a day at sea in fine or at least moderate weather, in which this floating castle goes through the water with the greatest imaginable steadiness.

Another doctor, Doctor Beatty, who was to be present at Nelson's death, joined *Victory* after Gillespie and concentrated more on Nelson's physical attributes and character:

An opinion had been very generally entertained, that Lord Nelson's state of health, and supposed infirmities arising from his former wounds and hard services, precluded the probability of his long surviving the battle of Trafalgar, had he fortunately escaped the Enemy's shot: but the writer of this can assert that his Lordship's health was uniformly good, with the exception of some slight attacks of indisposition arising from accidental causes; and which never continued above two or three days, nor confined him in any degree with respect to either exercise or regimen: and during the last twelve months of his life, he complained only three times in this way. It is true, that his Lordship, about the meridian of his life, had been subject to frequent fits of the gout; which disease, however, as well as his constitutional tendency to it, he totally overcame by abstaining for the space of nearly two years from animal food, and wine, and all other fermented drink; confining his diet to vegetables, and commonly milk and water. And it is also a fact, that early in life, when he first went to sea, he left off the use of salt, which he then believed to be the sole cause of scurvy, and never took it afterwards with his food.

His Lordship used a great deal of exercise, generally walking on deck six or seven hours in the day. He always rose early, for the most part shortly after daybreak. He breakfasted in summer about six, and at seven in winter; and if not occupied in reading or writing despatches, or examining into the details of the Fleet, he walked on the quarter-deck the greater part of the forenoon; going down to his cabin occasionally to commit to paper such incidents or reflections as occurred to him during that time, and as might be hereafter useful to the service of his country. He dined generally about half-past two o'clock. At his table there were seldom less than eight or nine persons, consisting of the different Officers of the Ship: and when the weather and the Service permitted, he very often had several of the Admirals

and Captains in the Fleet to dine with him; who were mostly invited
by signal, the rotation of seniority being commonly observed by his
Lordship in these invitations. At dinner he was alike affable and attentive to every one: he ate very sparingly himself; the liver and wing of
a fowl, and a small plate of macaroni, in general composing his meal,
during which he occasionally took a glass of champagne. He never
exceeded four glasses of wine after dinner, and seldom drank three:
and even those were diluted with either Bristol or common water.

Few men subject to the vicissitudes of a Naval life, equalled his Lordship in a habitual systematic mode of living. He possessed such a
wonderful activity of mind, as even prevented him from taking
ordinary repose, seldom enjoying two hours of uninterrupted sleep;
and on several occasions he did not quit the deck during the whole
night. At these times he took no pains to protect himself from the
effects of wet, or the night air; wearing only a thin great coat: and he
has frequently, after having his clothes wet through with rain, refused
to have them changed, saying that the leather waistcoat which he wore
over his flannel one would secure him from complaint. He seldom
wore boots, and was consequently very liable to have his feet wet.
When this occurred he has often been known to go down to his cabin,
throw off his shoes, and walk on the carpet in his stockings for the
purpose of drying the feet of them. He chose rather to adopt this uncomfortable expedient, than to give his servants the trouble of assisting
him to put on fresh stockings; which, from his having only one hand,
he could not himself conveniently effect.

From these circumstances it may be inferred, that though Lord
Nelson's constitution was not of that kind which is generally denom-
inated strong, yet it was not very susceptible of complaint from the
common occasional causes of disease necessarily attending a Naval life.
The only bodily pain which his Lordship felt in consequence of his
many wounds, was a slight rheumatic affection of the stump of his
amputated arm on any sudden variation in the state of the weather;
which is generally experienced by those who have the misfortune to
lose a limb after the middle age. His Lordship usually predicted an
alteration in the weather with as much certainty from feeling transient
pains in his stump, as he could by his marine barometer; from the
indications of which latter he kept a diary of the atmospheric changes,
which was written with his own hand.

His Lordship had lost his right eye by a contusion which he received

at the siege of Calvi, in the island of Corsica. The vision of the other
was likewise considerably impaired: he always therefore wore a green
shade over his forehead, to defend this eye from the effect of strong
light; but as he was in the habit of looking much through a glass while
on deck, there is little doubt that had he lived a few years longer, and
continued at sea, he would have lost his sight totally.

News from outside filtered slowly and fitfully into this floating,
separate and self-contained world. Early in 1804 Nelson learnt that his
second child by Emma had been born, another girl, and had died. Considering the fuss both parents made over Horatia this infant mortality did
not seem to cause either of them much grief. Later he learnt that Addington had resigned, in fact in April, and that Pitt was again Prime Minister.
As a consequence St Vincent was no longer First Lord and Troubridge
was out of the Admiralty and his new political master was Pitt's old crony
Dundas, now Lord Melville. Soon after, Nelson himself, as part of a
general promotion, reached the highest rank he was ever to hold, Vice-
Admiral of the White, so the ensign over *Victory*'s stern changed from
blue to white, a colour that Nelson always favoured, as being more easily
distinguishable than either red or blue. Nepean had retired from the
Admiralty through ill health, had been given a baronetcy and been
replaced by Mr William Marsden. He also learnt that his long delayed
legal action against St Vincent had been at last, on appeal, successful.
Ironically, as will be seen, though he had gained one sum of money, the
principle established with regard to prize money was to lose him the
possibility of much more. He wrote to Emma describing his double
existence, 'I have not a thought except on you and the French fleet, all
my thoughts, plans and toils tend to those two objects.' His officers came
and went; some of his old band of brothers such as Berry appeared
briefly; Bolton proved to be not really up to standard and, though a
temporary captain, could not be made post; Rear-Admiral Campbell had
to be sent home as he had broken down mentally. In the circumstances,
as no French fleet had appeared, Nelson began to think of his own health
and the possibility of return to Merton and Emma and asked the
Admiralty if he might be relieved. However, before that could happen
Britain by her own making acquired a new enemy in the Mediterranean,
by means of actions of which Nelson totally disapproved.

The position of Spain was ambiguous, technically neutral, but in
reality completely under the influence of France. Pitt, at the head of a

government presumed to be more active and aggressive than Addington's, decided that here was a suitable and profitable target. Accordingly,
orders went out from the Admiralty on September 18 to Cornwallis to
detain some Spanish frigates en route from Rio de la Plata carrying a
million pounds in gold and silver. Curiously, as he was further away,
Nelson was sent his orders to detain all Spanish ships carrying bullion or
military stores, a week later. The result was a muddle. Nelson, if he had
received his orders in time, would have sent *Gibraltar* as the principal ship
in a force which would almost without doubt have persuaded the
Spaniards to surrender without a fight. But he did not receive any orders
but learnt of the proposed action in a roundabout way. Cornwallis sent
Captain Moore, General Sir John's brother, in command of the frigates
Indefatigable and *Lively* off Cadiz, to intercept. There, he met with two of
Nelson's frigates, *Medusa* and *Amphion*, which he took under command.
Not without protest, for Captain Gore of *Medusa* wrote immediately to
Nelson complaining. This was the first news Nelson had of what seemed
inexplicable and inexcusable action by Cornwallis, interfering in the
command of another admiral, and acting in a warlike manner without
war declared.

On October 5 four Spanish frigates, the equal of Moore's command,
were sighted. They were pursued and called upon to surrender, but
refused. Action followed, three of the Spaniards did eventually surrender,
but only after the fourth had exploded and sunk, carrying its whole crew
and a number of civilians, including women and children, to the bottom.
War with Spain was now inevitable, brought about in the worst possible
manner and it was declared by the Spaniards on December 12. Nelson did
finally receive his orders from the Admiralty but he ordered Gore to leave
Spanish ships alone until war was declared. Almost unbelievably, though,
there was another shock on its way for Nelson. He had indicated his wish
to come home and, presumably because of that, Sir John Orde, Nelson's
rival of many years ago, was given a new and separate command in
October, Commander-in-Chief of the Cadiz station. Bearing in mind
the brewing situation with Spain the profitability of such a post was
not lost on Sir John. Mr Marsden wrote to Nelson to tell him that
Amphion and *Medusa* were no longer his, but were now under Orde's
command.

As a result about £10,000 from the captured Spanish frigates which
would have been Nelson's share, went to Sir John Orde on the principle,
enunciated in the St Vincent prize case, that Nelson was absent, and

coming home. The only flaw in the argument was that Nelson was not absent, nor, because of the Spanish war, coming home at all.

This blatant piece of unfairness, made worse by the fact that Orde continued to take prizes and make money, while Nelson did not, needless to say provoked a reaction from the victim, who said that two Boards of Admiralty had treated him badly for, quoting Shakespeare, he argued that he had 'done the State some service'.

The appeal fell on deaf ears. St Vincent, despite a defeat in the Law Courts, might have taken some notice. Melville, soon to be removed from office for corrupt mishandling of Admiralty funds, was not the man to worry because one admiral was making money, and the other not. He was, however, prepared to listen to Davison on the subject of a pension for Lady Hamilton; after all, what was one pension more or less? Davison, appearing to know more about these matters than a mere sailor, was always more optimistic than Nelson who in March 1803 had told him, 'I much doubt whether the Pension will ever be given—more shame for them.'

When the Committee of Naval Enquiry, which had been working away for over two years, published its report revealing Melville's mishandling of funds as Treasurer of the Navy, and when the House of Commons accepted that report, and therefore Melville's guilt, by a majority of one vote, Emma's chances of receiving a pension for her alleged services before the battle of the Nile virtually disappeared. The new First Lord of the Admiralty, an elderly admiral, Sir Charles Middleton, ennobled as Lord Barham, was not the man to concern himself with such a matter. This was so during Nelson's life and after his death the argument for a pension was based on grounds which were even less acceptable.

Orde's 'Spanish squadron' was an irritant to Nelson on more than financial grounds. Dispatches to Nelson and from him to the Admiralty had to pass through the Straits and there were disputes and arguments between junior officers answerable to the one or the other of the admirals, and worse still, Sir John, crippled with gout and of a cautious disposition, was not the man to co-operate with Nelson.

That is not to say that Orde's approach to his duties was entirely wrong, and Nelson's totally right. All British squadrons watched a number of different ports for the French, Spanish or Dutch to emerge. When Nelson had been opposed to Latouche-Tréville, he had likened his task to that of a cat waiting by a mouse hole. Overall, the British Navy was blockading the enemy ports, but there were different methods of carrying out that process.

An admiral like Orde did his duty if, by his constant presence, he kept the French or Spanish ships in. If, and it was an important proviso, they did not succeed in leaving harbour, then there could be no invasion attempt. If, however, fleets at Brest, Toulon, Ferrol or Rochefort did get out, the danger was that two or more of these squadrons would continue to give the British the slip and combine in the Channel. Therefore if enemy fleets did get out, and were not intercepted, then those British admirals who could do so were expected to close on the approaches to the British Isles.

It was in this respect that Nelson's approach differed from that of his colleagues. When the Lord Mayor of London wrote congratulating him on the blockade of Toulon, rather unfairly as he was no naval expert, he received a sharp reminder that the Commander-in-Chief in the Mediterranean was not trying to keep the French in, but hoping to delude them into coming out. Nelson's intention was to destroy the French and Spanish fleets, an ambition which if fulfilled would of course dispose of any invasion threat much more effectively than any policy of mere defensive containment. If a French or Spanish fleet appeared, its suspicions lulled by Nelson's only visible watch of a mere frigate, then it was to be pursued wherever it went and brought to battle. There were, of course, more risks involved in Nelson's tactics and it must be remembered that all the admirals could not have followed his example, for there had to be some squadrons left on station, since there had to be longstops.

It was not until January 1805 that the French made a determined sortie, so the old year of 1804 died quietly. Nelson finally received permission from the Admiralty on Christmas Day to come home, and he thought he might be at Merton in February or March. In November Mrs Gibson had rendered what was to be her last account for Horatia's care, and Lady Hamilton would soon transfer her daughter to Merton, the two eldest Bolton girls were there before school, and the Reverend Doctor and his jewel were visiting. Emma railed against Sir John Orde to Davison, and wrote love poems to her absent Nelson. Mrs Bolton and Mrs Matcham had both, separately, met with Lady Nelson, but her manner had either been too friendly or too aloof, it was difficult to say which, but certainly it had failed to please. Neither of the two women seemed to realise that the part of a wronged wife was a very difficult one to play, especially if she were married to a national hero, and her audience was the hero's sisters.

CHAPTER THIRTY-ONE

Threat of Invasion

EIGHTEEN-HUNDRED-AND-FIVE WAS the last year in which Napoleon seriously contemplated the invasion of Britain, and even then only for its first seven months, for on August 24 he began dictating to Marshal Berthier, his Chief of Staff, the orders which broke up the invasion force with its headquarters at Boulogne and sent the Grand Army marching eastwards across Europe to the Danube.

Napoleon had considered the project on a number of occasions but it is difficult to pinpoint when it was really at the forefront of his mind. Certainly there was hardly a time when it occupied his attention to the exclusion of all other military projects, and, taking as evidence his orders to his generals and admirals, there were a bewildering number of occasions when he blew alternately hot and cold.

There was a time, though not of long duration, when he actually thought of invasion by means of flotillas of barges without the command of the Channel being secured beforehand. However, the fact that only a limited proportion of his force could leave with each tide and would be at the mercy of a British fleet in the Channel was somehow brought home to Napoleon, so that his eventual plan envisaged a combined operation.

There was no problem with the soldiers for the French army was superbly trained and organised as was to be shown by its performance at the end of 1805, profiting from the preparation it had received in two years on the Channel coast. This then was the period, from January to the autumn of 1805, that can be identified as the time when if there were to be an invasion at all it would have been then. Further, the serious attempts towards obtaining mastery of the Channel were all concentrated within these months, if for no other reason than that Spain's entry into the war in December 1804 had swelled the size of the available battle fleet.

Nelson's last year of life was spent in frustrating attempts by the French and Spanish navies to obtain that mastery of the Straits which as Napoleon said, if obtained for six hours, 'we shall be masters of the world'. To judge Nelson and Trafalgar therefore it is necessary to evaluate the French threat and the means he took to combat it. The overall principle which the Royal Navy observed under the control of Lord Barham at the Admiralty was concentration, and most vitally in the Channel. No diversionary tactics by Frenchmen or Spaniards could be permitted to take the eyes of the First Lord away from that essential. Nelson's own techniques were an addition, and in this respect he had become a sort of freelance among admirals with his own priorities and plans evolved from experience. Far more than anyone else he was determined to bring the enemy to battle, and a battle in which the opposing fleet could be as near as possible annihilated. In order to do this he had moved further away from the concept of the old action in line than any of his contemporaries.

At the same time, his potential opponents were far removed in their battle tactics from his thinking. Indeed the French admiral who was to oppose him at Trafalgar is on record as saying, shortly before the battle, 'We have obsolete naval tactics; we only know how to manoeuvre in line, which is what the enemy wants'. The fact that Villeneuve realised this in advance brings one onto the next consideration; Nelson, in his officers and seamen, had a superb instrument with which to practise his art whereas the French did not.

Napoleon complained, in exile on St Helena, 'there is a specialisation in this profession [seamanship] which blocked all my ideas. They always returned to the point that one could not be a good seaman unless one was brought up to it from the cradle.' At the time however this was something that the Emperor could or would not realise. It was known well enough to his admirals but they never succeeded in persuading him. Worse, he evolved a master plan for invasion which took little or no notice of the disparity between the two navies and his admirals were forced to put his theories into practice, with a few variations of their own, dictated by caution or compelled by desperation.

The result was that French naval plans in 1805 were based upon the idea that by some disposition, some stratagem, some deception, the British could be tricked into leaving the Channel free or poorly protected, ideally without the French being drawn into fighting at all. Napoleon was quite prepared that his fleet should fight a battle, in which it could be given the advantage by previous dispositions, but his admirals, realising that such manoeuvres were of doubtful value, were reluctant to fight a battle at all, because in their own sound professional judgment they were pessimistic as to its outcome.

Sir Julian Corbett, considering Napoleon's plan said, 'Englishmen with judgment unoppressed by the Napoleonic legend, will see in it the work of a self-confident amateur in naval warfare, the blindness of a great soldier to the essential differences between land and sea strategy'. This is a sweeping comment, but it catches the essence of the months at sea leading up to Trafalgar.

Napoleon's plan had, at least at first, the virtue of simplicity. The central concept was that the squadrons in French and Spanish ports, evading the British, should sail westwards to the West Indies, and there unite and then return eastwards, overcome the British at their concentration area off Ushant and, having done so, would then, by dominating the Channel, be able to secure a safe passage for the invasion flotillas. It supports Corbett's judgment when one realises that Napoleon who on land always tried to assess the enemy's strength—a card index of every regiment in the Austrian army was prepared before his soldiers marched eastwards—had made little effort to assess British strength and capability. Worse, no allowance was made in his master plan for any counter-moves by the enemy. All French naval initiatives, while the invasion force stood ready to embark, were variations on this one Napoleonic theme.

The first move was made by Admiral Missiessy who managed to get out of Rochefort with a small squadron on New Year's Day, 1805. On January 17 Villeneuve with eleven of the line and nine frigates escaped from Toulon and sailed to join Missiessy, already on his way to the West Indies.

It was not until January 19 that Nelson, off the southern tip of Sardinia, finally learnt that, aided by fog, Villeneuve was at sea. Where he was and in which direction he was sailing he had no idea. Nelson's assumption, and it was not unreasonable, was that Villeneuve's object was Sardinia, so he stayed put. In fact, he had little alternative, as a westerly gale held him there until January 26. That abated, he sailed for Greece and then for Alexandria, but nothing was stirring at that end of the Mediterranean so by February 19 the British fleet of twelve line-of-battle ships and two frigates was at Malta where Nelson learnt that the westerly gale which had held him in check had forced Villeneuve in confusion back to Toulon.

There were two lessons to be learnt. The first was that Nelson had relied on his own judgment and had been wrong, 'I have consulted no man', he wrote to the Admiralty, 'therefore the whole blame of ignorance in forming my judgment must rest with me'. The second was that the French fleet's general standard of seamanship was poor. On that Nelson had this to say, to Collingwood, 'Bonaparte has often made his boast that our fleet would be worn out by keeping the sea, and that his was kept in order and increasing by staying in port; but now he finds, I fancy, if Emperors hear truth, that his fleet suffered more in a night than ours in a year.' Nelson had put his finger on the French dilemma in that one phrase 'if Emperors hear truth'. Napoleon did not hear truth for his admirals and his Minister of Marine were all terrified of him. On a battlefield he could control his generals and he could see, or be told, what they were doing. At sea once his admirals were out of port they were beyond his control and subject to hazards of wind and weather beyond either his influence or his imagining. He heard of their failures, but he did not comprehend their explanations which he dismissed as mere excuses.

The only result of the January sortie was that Missiessy was still in West Indian waters, off Martinique, and on February 27 he was ordered to stay there to await the arrival of other French naval forces. Another variation on the theme was about to be played. As before, Nelson would have to make a decision and act upon it. This time the plan was more grandiose and complicated, and, although it had the disadvantage of more than one object, it did have more luck on its side.

All French admirals were to make the attempt to reach a rendezvous in the West Indies, the well-fortified French island of Martinique. Thus Admirals Gourdon at Ferrol, Ganteaume at Brest and Villeneuve at Toulon were all to break out, collect and take with them Spanish ships where they could. Only Villeneuve was successful on March 30 with his flagship, the eighty-gun *Bucentaure*, three other 80's, seven 74's and eight frigates. There were 3000 soldiers on board his ships under the command of General Lauriston, an artillery general and Imperial aide-de-camp of Scots descent last encountered as Bonaparte's peace envoy in London. Originally there had been a complicated joining plan and time-table for the various French detachments, but now that was all abandoned, the only fleet at large being Villeneuve's and, as was learned later, a Spanish squadron of eight of the line from Cadiz under Gravina.

The problem for Nelson was again, what was Villeneuve's destination? He was at Palmas when he heard of the French admiral's escape. Rumours of the loading of muskets and saddlery for Lauriston's soldiers had made him think again of an Egyptian expedition, but this time Nelson was more cautious than in 1798. Finally, on April 18, he learnt that Villeneuve had passed through the Straits of Gibraltar. The nearest British admiral to the juncture of Villeneuve's and Gravina's squadrons was Sir John Orde with his station off Cadiz. His force was only four sail of the line and when he discovered that he was faced with overwhelming numbers he took the path of extreme caution, although it was the correct one. Sir John Orde's logic was impeccable, a combined French and Spanish fleet sailing westwards could only mean one thing, ultimately at least, an attempt upon the British Isles. In coming to his conclusion and deciding on his course of action Orde demonstrated two things: first, that he was no Nelson, and second, the flimsiness of all Napoleon's grand plans to deceive the British as to his final objective. Orde's four ships set sail to join the main British fleet off Ushant in order to help augment the defensive build-up in the western approaches of the English Channel.

Nelson found himself demonstrating, to his fury, yet another limitation upon Napoleonic plans for fleets. Sailing ships depended on wind and for Nelson, anxious to be off to the Scilly Isles, there was none. It could just as well have happened to Villeneuve or Gravina. Anyhow, Nelson was becalmed in the Mediterranean, but because of the delay imposed upon his plans—'I am locked up in the Mediterranean', was how he described his situation—he heard on May 6 from a British commodore, serving with the Portuguese navy, that the French and Spanish ships had definitely headed for the West Indies. Portugal's position being equivocal, and being much pressurised by France through Spain, the British officer, Donald Campbell, was dismissed the service for imparting the information, while Nelson was pushed towards his decision which led to what his biographers have customarily called 'the Long Chase'. It is a perfectly accurate description of the events which stretched into August, but somewhat misleading because it is so often regarded as an automatic precursor to Trafalgar, which it was not.

Nelson chose to follow Villeneuve to the West Indies, but he need not have done so. When Lord Barham at the Admiralty heard of Villeneuve's destination he ordered Collingwood and a squadron of twelve ships of the line to follow him, a sufficient force to bring the French admiral to battle or to prevent depredation of the British sugar islands. For a time the Admiralty didn't know where Nelson was. Collingwood only discovered by chance from Rear-Admiral Bickerton, Nelson's second-in-command, left in the Mediterranean, and so did not sail westwards but took up station off Cadiz.

The departure of Nelson's squadron to the West Indies, 3,500 miles from Europe, still regarded as the principal and most important scene of likely action, aroused considerable adverse comment in the British Press.

Reacting to the clamour, Mr Marsden at the Admiralty ordered Sir John Orde, who had behaved correctly, but had not bothered to send even a frigate to shadow Villeneuve, to strike his flag and come on shore.

With Nelson on his way to the West Indies, nothing could be done, no doubt it was thought it was better to wait upon results. Once again Nelson had acted against orders, or rather without orders, and it is right to examine his motives in so doing.

First of course as a man of his time he gave more importance to Britain's West Indian possessions than today one would think they deserved. Perhaps it should not be forgotten that Villeneuve's destination was the scene of his own early service as a young officer. As he put it himself, 'I was bred, as you know, in the good old school, and taught to appreciate the value of our West India possessions, and neither in the Field or the Senate, shall their just rights be infringed whilst I have an arm to fight in their defence or a tongue to launch my voice.' Grand sounding stuff, but what was there for him to do that Collingwood could not? The answer must be to fight a French fleet, wherever it might be found. Immodestly, but accurately, Nelson was convinced that he could do that task better than any admiral afloat.

However, two questions remain, from Barham's point of view, at the Admiralty, directing overall strategy. What would have happened if a number of admirals, all convinced of their own tactical skills, had taken it into their heads to behave in this way? Also what chances did Nelson actually possess of bringing the French to battle in the West Indies?

The chances when he set sail were poor. Villeneuve had a considerable start, and Nelson was following with a squadron of what he called 'crazy' ships, which had been at sea constantly for an average of two years or more, and were desperately in need of refit and repair. There was of course one quality upon which Nelson could rely, the high standard of British seamanship, and it was employed to the utmost by an impatient admiral; nevertheless, it was the imponderable elements which came to his aid. Once again he was lucky. Villeneuve's squadron took thirty-four days to cross the Atlantic, Nelson's took twenty-four, arriving off Barbados in the early morning of June 4.

From Carlisle Bay he wrote to Emma, 'I find myself within six days of the Enemy, and I have every reason to hope that the 6th June will immortalize your own Nelson, your fond Nelson'. According to his information the French were 'supposed' to have attacked Tobago and Trinidad and were landing troops. In fact the supposition was wrong,

Nelson's information had come, via Admiral Cochrane on board
Northumberland and Sir William Myers, Governor of the Leeward Isles,
from General Brereton who was in command of the garrison on St Lucia.
Brereton, who had been a companion-in-arms at the sieges of Bastia and
Calvi, had reported the French and Spanish sailing south, in the direction
of either Barbados or Trinidad. Nelson was doubtful, but on all sides he
was assured that Brereton could be relied upon. What mistake the
general did commit has never come to light, but soon Nelson was to
damn him and his intelligence, because it was totally inaccurate. Villeneuve was at Martinique. By his diversion to Trinidad, carrying some of
Sir William Myers's troops, Nelson had given the French admiral another
head start. Villeneuve had learnt of the presence of Nelson's ships and had
no intention of meeting them and providing another Aboukir Bay in the
Caribbean. His original instruction to rendez-vous with other French,
and possibly Spanish, ships was obviously now a dead letter for there were
none to come. The second part of his instructions from Paris, what
Nelson contemptuously called 'orders from the banks of the Seine',
which took little account of naval reality, had been to harry British
possessions unhampered by the presence of a British force able to match
his own. That force was now on his tail, and commanded by an admiral
whose skill with a fleet he had witnessed at the Nile. Nelson's fear had
been a French attempt on Jamaica, hence his doubts about Brereton's
information, but all that Villeneuve had been able to accomplish had been
the recapture of H.M.S. *Diamond Rock*, not a ship of war, but a pinnacle
of rock in the entrance to Fort Royal, so called because of its capture by
British sailors in February 1804. They had held out for more than a year,
a blot on the honour and prestige of France, but had been forced to yield
to the Combined Fleet. It was hardly a great victory, but now Villeneuve
prepared to re-cross the Atlantic. After a further comedy of errors of
identification and information among the islands, where the British relief
force was mistaken for French invaders, a thwarted Nelson prepared to
follow twenty ships with his own eleven.

   This time Villeneuve had only five days start, and there was still a hope
that the British squadron might catch up. By a mixed process of intuition
and piecing together available facts Nelson had come to the conclusion
that Villeneuve had been ordered to return, which was not quite what
had happened, because the French admiral's orders had in fact petered
out, or become irrelevant, but 'so far from being infallible, like the Pope,
I believe my opinions to be very fallible, and therefore I may be mistaken

that the Enemy's fleet is gone to Europe, but I cannot bring myself to think otherwise'. For once, Nelson, perhaps because he was depressed at his failure to fight a battle, had underestimated himself, or rather his own reputation. For Villeneuve was fleeing across the Atlantic away from Nelson. On June 13, the British squadron set sail from Antigua northwards for the first leg of the journey home, Villeneuve being then five days ahead.

It is an appropriate time to consider what Nelson had achieved by his dash to the West Indies in the wake of the Combined Fleet, 'I flew to the West Indies', he said, 'without any orders, but I think the Ministry cannot be displeased'. As will be seen the Ministry had to be satisfied. It has become customary to say that Nelson had saved the West Indies, or at least had prevented Villeneuve from taking something like 200 sugar ships. First of all there is the debatable question as to just how important, in the long run, they were, save to a number of London merchants, but the whole West Indian argument is disposable on the basis that Collingwood would have gone if Nelson had not. But with one proviso, would Collingwood have had the same effect upon Villeneuve as Nelson? Undoubtedly he would have imposed a check upon the French plans to harass the colonies, eleven capital ships under a courageous and capable commander could not have been wished away. Paradoxically, might the French admiral have risked a battle with Collingwood though not with the dreaded Nelson? From what one can judge of Villeneuve and his fleet, which had landed 1,000 sick sailors, soldiers and marines on Martinique and buried many others, the answer is probably not.

The speed with which Nelson had arrived in the West Indies, but with which Collingwood would also have arrived, had once again demonstrated the long and powerful arm of the Royal Navy, its essential activity and ever ready pugnacity, but it is difficult to isolate and identify what precisely Nelson contributed to a situation which could not have been rendered by any other reasonably comparable admiral and Collingwood was very soon to prove in battle that though he may have lacked the fire and dash, the charisma of his chief, he was perfectly capable of leading a body of ships successfully and courageously.

So much for Nelson's presence in the West Indies; Villeneuve's return was to provide an opportunity of considering the possible effect of Nelson's consequent absence from home waters. As far as what Nelson called the 'run back' was concerned, there was perhaps little chance of his catching up with Villeneuve, even if the two fleets had been following identical courses. In fact they did not. Nelson's guess was that Villeneuve would head for the Straits of Gibraltar, and the Mediterranean, and he steered his own course accordingly. The guess was wrong, Villeneuve was steering for Ferrol on the northern Iberian coast. Thus as their ships sailed further and further eastwards the courses of the two fleets increasingly diverged, Villeneuve moving broadly east-north-east and Nelson east-south-east.

Meantime, Barham, sitting like a spider at the centre of its web, received information on the French from an occasional sighting frigate, and attempted his counter-moves with the squadron he had nearest to his hand. Nelson's own movements were also reported in advance by his own frigates dispatched ahead of the fleet, which communicated with the Admiralty either directly to Portsmouth and thence by semaphore to London, or else by relay to other frigates or smaller fast craft.

Now the issue was the possible interception of Villeneuve on his return, and in that operation Nelson could play no part. Collingwood, off Cadiz, guessed rightly that Villeneuve's course would be set for Ferrol, Rochefort or Ushant, though he still thought that the enemy had designs upon Ireland. Nelson, however, thought in terms of a French fleet re-entering the Mediterranean and not taking refuge in a friendly port, but proceeding upon some mission eastwards. Seemingly he had not yet perceived that the West Indies had not been a primary objective but merely an assembly point for Villeneuve and fleets which had not arrived, something which Collingwood had realised, a feint as he put it, 'to take off the naval force'.

By July 18 Nelson was off Cape Spartel, North Africa, 'but no French fleet, nor any information about them'. As on his previous pursuit of almost seven years ago he was plunged in gloom. On July 20 he was at Gibraltar and entered in his diary 'went on shore for the first time since June 16th 1803, and from my foot out of the *Victory*, two years wanting ten days'.

It had been an incredible performance of seamanship and endurance by any standards, and witnessed the determination and zest for battle of one man, who had undoubtedly sustained the morale of the whole fleet. It is sad therefore to record that on July 22, only two days later, Villeneuve's fleet was intercepted off Finistere by a no means comparable admiral, Sir Robert Calder, who had been critical of Nelson's break with conformism at St Vincent. The action took place at long range in misty weather, Villeneuve's fleet was twenty strong, Calder's numbered fifteen. The odds were therefore against the British, but they were by no means unacceptable. The result was disappointing, Calder still stuck to the standards of the old style of naval warfare. He succeeded in capturing two Spanish ships and then, after four days, losing the enemy. Content with his prizes he broke off action without further pursuit or shadowing. Duty done, as he saw it, Sir Robert then retired back upon Cornwallis's main force. Villeneuve's fleet sailed south and then, hugging the shore, slipped into Vigo where three ships remained and thence to Ferrol, which happy haven was reached by August 1.

Meanwhile, delayed by contrary winds, Nelson had been trying to join the Channel Fleet from Gibraltar. Under Cornwallis, flying his flag in *Ville de Paris*, it was twenty-five miles off Ushant, and *Victory* fired her salute to the senior admiral a day after Calder had done the same.

It was now August 12. On July 9 Barham at the Admiralty had learnt of Villeneuve's position and conjectured course from the frigate *Curieux*. The First Lord was in his eightieth year, but moved quickly enough to satisfy younger men, and had made his dispositions for Villeneuve's reception. But he made those dispositions with the admirals he had under his control, and Nelson was not among them though Sir Robert Calder was. If Nelson had not followed Villeneuve to the West Indies and back, and that task had been performed by Collingwood, Nelson in nearly three weeks could have been brought up from the Mediterranean to take on the returning Combined Fleet.

The British public and press felt that Nelson would have done better than Calder, and demanded his court martial, his cautious conduct being criticised in the light of the new standards set at Aboukir and Copenhagen. Nelson himself read the comments in newspapers given him by Cornwallis, but showed commendable restraint in not criticising. To William he wrote, 'We must not talk of Sir Robert Calder's battle; I might not have done so much with my small force.' Dog does not eat dog, so perhaps Nelson chose not to remember that Barham's aim was to deploy a reinforced fleet against Villeneuve. Fremantle had also provided Nelson with newspapers and Nelson used a slightly different argument to a brother officer than to his clerical brother, 'I should have fought the enemy; so did my friend Calder; but who can say that he will be more successful than another?' It was not that Nelson had suddenly become modest, or even decided to assume modesty. While chasing Villeneuve he had stated quite plainly his intention to 'put it out of his power to do further mischief', even at the cost of 'great sacrifices'. Years ago *Agamemnon* had been 'built to be risked', and so now was a large part of Nelson's, or any other, squadron if in the process enemy ships were also destroyed. Britain had a considerable numerical superiority in warships, and she could afford to lose some in order, as Nelson put it, to stop Admiral Villeneuve's career.

Later, thinking forward to Trafalgar with Captain Keats, who had nursed the decrepit *Superb* all the way to the West Indies and back, Nelson, perhaps inadvertently, let fall his reply to a question he must have been asked either by Pitt himself or one of his Ministers:

> But this I ventured without any fear—that if Calder got fairly alongside their twenty-seven or twenty-eight sail, that by the time the Enemy had beat our Fleet soundly, they would do us no harm this year.

There can be no doubt that Nelson would have tried his hardest to 'get fairly alongside' Villeneuve's ships but by the time that opportunity had occurred, Nelson, because of a wild goose chase, was elsewhere.

He had joined Cornwallis, but Villeneuve was in port, so he was now allowed to proceed home, and *Victory* with *Superb* in company anchored at Spithead at nine in the morning on August 18. The pleasure of home-coming could not entirely obscure the natural sense of frustration and, more significantly, a feeling that he would not be well received at the Admiralty, this latter foreboding being confirmed by an order to produce his journal and logs for the inspection of Lord Barham. It was an order he pretended to resent, but it was hardly surprising since he had taken himself and his fleet off to the West Indies on his own initiative.

A smashing victory over the French would have been complete justification but, 'I have brought home no honour for my Country, only a most faithful servant', as he told Emma. It has always been assumed that having examined Nelson's day-to-day account of the Long Chase Lord Barham was completely satisfied. However, there is no proof, it is more likely that the First Lord took the view that Nelson had obviously harried the French and made their secondary objective, causing damage to the English sugar trade, impossible to achieve. He had also flushed Villeneuve out of the Caribbean back to home waters, and the fact that he would have been better employed waiting for him in ambush was now in the past. There was also the force of public opinion to be considered, for who would dare rebuke Nelson publicly?

After some delay, imposed by the Port Admiral because yellow fever was rife in Spain, and as Nelson had called in at Gibraltar, he was in danger of being kept in quarantine; he came on shore with Murray, Captain of the Fleet, at 7 p.m. on the evening of August 19. The reception from the townspeople of Portsmouth took even Nelson aback. Despite heavy rain the whole of the harbour area was packed with a cheering waving crowd; men, women and children jostling for a view of the easily recognised little admiral as he arrived in his barge, as he disembarked, as he paid his courtesy calls on the Commander-in-Chief and the Commissioner, and as he went to drink tea and wait at The George for the post chaise that would take him that night to Merton.

There could be no doubt in the mind of any of His Majesty's Ministers that John Bull had decided that Nelson should be praised and not blamed for his chase to the West Indies. He had shown the true fighting spirit, and the fact that luck had been against him was just one of those things. The West Indian merchants were happy and grateful, and were soon to express their feelings publicly, and the City was relieved that its financial and trading interests had been preserved. Nelson's friends, such as Minto, congratulated him on his endurance and persistence, of which there could be no doubt. The fact that the French fleet had escaped was seen as Calder's fault and he would probably have to face a court of inquiry. Fremantle was right in his estimate of public opinion, 'at no period, according to my judgment, did you ever stand higher in the estimation of the public'. Even in the eighteenth century this was something that Cabinet Ministers could not ignore. Of course they knew, they had seen it proved twice, that as a tactical handler of a fleet Nelson had no equal. If they privately wondered about his regard for strategy when his own conviction that he alone could not only defeat, but destroy, the French fleet was involved, they kept it to themselves.

They must have realised that in Nelson they had a superb instrument to their hands with which to win naval victories. Certainly they lost no opportunity of using it as quickly as possible in the most appropriate and advantageous circumstances.

The object of the public's regard and Ministerial interest reached Merton at 6 a.m. on the morning of August 20 after a quick drive through a very wet night. He could not know it, though he may have had some idea that his sojourn might well be short, as *Victory* was kept ready for him, but he had only twenty-five days to spend in England.

CHAPTER THIRTY-TWO

Paradise Merton

WITH THE burden of hindsight it is very difficult not to over-play the drama of Horatio Nelson's last days at 'Paradise Merton' with the woman he loved, and their child. And it is difficult to remember that they could not appreciate that this was their last time together. Admittedly, there were words, expressions and incidents which made those twenty-five days intensely dramatic, but it must not be forgotten that both Nelson and Emma Hamilton were larger than life, both played their roles for all they were worth, and both had a considerable element of the histrionic in their make-up. At the end of the period, Nelson was summoned away to risk his life in battle, to command yet again a fleet in action. Even if either of them had been reticent, undemonstrative characters, their passions, hopes and fears kept under firm control, some elements of the drama, the great events with which they were involved, might well have crept into their behaviour. Given the characters they did both possess, a sense of the inevitability of fate, a consciousness of the approaching drum beats of an unavoidable destiny was almost impossible to avoid.

The obvious antidote to the danger of over-dramatisation is to relate the events from August 20 as factually as possible, but there is another. It is to look away from Nelson and his mistress and their personal drama and consider the chain of events which led up to the battle of Trafalgar. For so long as the action in which Nelson met his death is considered to be inevitable, or as an automatic outcome of French military and naval policy in October 1805, then the end of the Merton idyll must seem also in consequence predestined.

The myth is that Nelson spent twenty-five days in loving tranquillity with Emma and Horatia, until apprised of the sudden and dangerous excursion of Villeneuve with the French and Spanish fleets which had to be fought to save Britain from Napoleon's attempt at invasion.

In a number of respects the myth is false. Nelson arrived at Merton on August 20. Six days later at Boulogne Napoleon began dictating, with the aid of Menéval, his secretary, and a corps of clerks, his orders to Marshal Berthier, his Chief of Staff. The orders were extensive and detailed and they were issued from the Imperial headquarters on August 29. Their purpose was, as Napoleon put it, to 'pirouette' the Grand Army and march it towards Vienna.

The landing craft which had been assembled at various Atlantic ports for the English invasion were now all to be concentrated at Boulogne. To counteract any British attempt to take advantage of the disappearance of French troops from the Channel ports, Marshal Brune, with the 3rd battalion of each regiment of line infantry, was left on the coast to give the impression that the invasion force was still in being. When on September 4 Napoleon left Boulogne for Paris and Malmaison, his army was already marching at a planned and regulated fifteen miles a day eastwards.

The enemy was the Austrians and the Russians, and the first objective was the defeat of the Austrian army before it could be joined by the Russians coming from Cracow. British diplomacy, backed up as usual by British subsidies, had brought into being a Third Coalition against France and the threat from the east posed by a combined Austrian and Russian onslaught could no longer be ignored.

Napoleon learnt on September 13 in Paris that an Austrian army had, three days before, crossed the river Inn and invaded Bavaria, the Elector was a French ally and a satellite. A week later it was known that the Austrians had assembled their army near Ulm, and were taking up positions along the line of the river Iller. On September 24 Napoleon left Paris en route for Strasbourg to take command of his armies in the field.

During the Long Chase Nelson had been right in one of his assumptions, that Villeneuve was sailing eastwards in response to orders. This was so, Ganteaume had not joined him in the West Indies within the forty days allowed so Villeneuve had been ordered to steer for Ferrol. After his clash with Calder he took refuge, as has been seen, on the north-western Iberian coast. On July 16 Villeneuve had been ordered to join Ganteaume at Brest, but he had been given permission to take refuge at Cadiz. On August 14 Villeneuve and his squadron were at sea again, but he sighted five sail from the Rochefort squadron, now commanded by a new admiral, Allemand. These he mistakenly took to be British so he scuttled south again to Cadiz. Almost up until the last moment before August 26 Napoleon had still thought an invasion possible. Faced with the danger of the Third Coalition and the cautionary advice of Decrés, his Minister of Marine, and Villeneuve's failure to appear in the Channel,

Napoleon gave up his navy and began preparing orders which were operative in a field which he understood.

This does not mean that Napoleon had forgotten entirely about his admirals and his fleets, for in his view they had failed him, and he had given them, and especially Villeneuve, their chance with his superb strategic plan, and their response had been disappointing. They were consigned therefore to a secondary level of his own mental activity. Obviously they still received orders but often they were not very good orders. For instance on September 17 Napoleon ordered Decrés to send out small naval harrying forces to St Helena, Martinique, Barbados, San Domingo, Jamaica, Cayenne, Senegal and Mauritius in order to make life difficult for the British and to direct the attention of the Third Coalition away from his principal move on land. In fact, because every French and Spanish port was blockaded fast, none of the ships ever moved out of harbour. Villeneuve's position was slightly different for he had broken out to the West Indies, had under command a considerable number of capital ships, and appeared to be Napoleon's best bet. So both when at sea and in port he was the recipient of more ambitious orders, though once the Grand Army was committed to an eastward advance Villeneuve was demoted to commanding a sort of southernmost but seaborne wing of that army. Unfortunately, to operate as such the French admiral would have been better placed if he had been at Toulon, but, chased by Nelson and driven by the rest of the Royal Navy, he was now bottled up at Cadiz.

One other factor is necessary to appreciate the genesis of Trafalgar—the viewpoint of the British. Villeneuve's Combined Fleet was a powerful collection of ships of the line, and it had broken out to the West Indies. Napoleon's intentions were by no means immediately obvious in London, certainly his complete military volte-face was not at once appreciated. Villeneuve was at Cadiz, not Toulon, therefore his intentions appeared to be more westwards than eastwards inclined. If not invasion, then perhaps the depredation of British shipping. Once Villeneuve was at sea, who could tell in which direction he would seek to strike? Therefore, paradoxically, it so happened that coincident upon Napoleon's decision to abandon an invasion attempt and strike at Austria before she could be supported by Russia, there was a perfectly natural revival of invasion fear in Britain. Once it was learned that Villeneuve and the Combined Fleet were 'out', there was an immediate reaction in the Admiralty in London that a British fleet under a rigorous admiral should be sent to defeat and destroy him. There really was only one man who could be given that task, and he was at Merton attempting to play host to a gathering of family and friends who had hastened to invite themselves once the news of his return was known.

Considering what was to follow, no doubt it all seemed idyllic. Merton Place was now much improved in its decoration and amenities, and the grounds were in good order, although all this had not been done without expense. Nelson was at last united with his mistress, and Horatia was now, as he put it, 'fixed' as a permanent member of the household, and had been provided, in a letter from him to Emma, with a bogus biography as an adopted daughter to whom Lady Hamilton acted as guardian.

Nevertheless, it would give the wrong impression if it were to be suggested that the days spent at Merton were either peaceful, quiet, or unoccupied. Perhaps if he had returned from Trafalgar and Emma Hamilton had become less of a bustling, noisy, sociable creature it would have been so. However, because of the near certainty of Nelson's being called away to deal with the Combined Fleet, a lot of the Admiral's time was spent in visits to London for which Merton served as a convenient base, but the haven of rest itself was invaded on occasions by professional acquaintances as well as friends. On one side there was the company of Emma, still as loving and flattering as ever, Horatia, his brother William, his two sisters, Mrs Bolton and Mrs Matcham, and a shifting population of nephews and nieces. On the other side there were professional conversations with Ministers, from Pitt downwards, and sea officers, either in London or less frequently, at Merton.

Only for a very brief time was Nelson out of the public eye, and even the approximation to the 'cottage' idyll he had so often referred to in the past could only be sustained until the early morning of September 2. At five o'clock in the morning of that day a carriage with a blue-coated sea officer drove up to Merton Place. Captain Henry Blackwood, of the frigate *Euryalus*, was on his way from Portsmouth to the Admiralty, but felt himself justified even at that hour in the morning in breaking his journey to impart the news he carried to a senior officer who was bound to be concerned.

Nelson, who was an early riser, guessed the purpose of Blackwood's visit as soon as he saw him, 'I am sure you bring me news of the French and Spanish fleets, and I think I shall yet have to beat them.' The news was that Villeneuve, having touched in at Vigo Bay, then Ferrol and

Corunna, was now with thirty-four ships at Cadiz, watched by three British admirals, Collingwood, Calder, and Bickerton commanding a force of twenty-five sail of the line.

Lady Hamilton was later to tell Harrison of a scene (Emma's life was as full of scenes as a stage drama) in which she played a considerable part in persuading Nelson to travel to London to offer his services. 'Nelson', so she addressed him apparently, she did not call him Horatio though Henry had been used as a pet name and something of a pseudonym, 'however we may lament your absence, offer your services immediately . . .'. Nelson's reply, with tears in his eyes, began with the famous, 'Brave Emma! Good Emma! if there were more Emmas, there would be more Nelson'.

It does of course all sound like a bad play, but that alone does not mean that the exchange did not take place, or something very like it. Nelson did travel directly to London, but it was hardly necessary for him to offer his services, for they were in demand. Lord Barham said that he could pick his own officers, and there was a long meeting with the Prime Minister, who listened attentively to the Admiral's exposition of strategy and tactics. At the end of their conversation Pitt handed Nelson to his carriage, a courtesy which its recipient felt would not have been accorded to a Prince of the Blood.

In the short time that remained before Nelson's departure to resume his command, on September 13, there was a jumble of encounters, official and unofficial. George Matcham, his sixteen-year-old nephew, kept a diary from the 4th to 11th, having arrived at Merton late one night as yet another guest 'to see Lord N, my uncle, before his departure'. He was a sharp lad, and noted for instance with what pleasure his distinguished uncle related the story of Mr Pitt's escorting him to his carriage. In London Lord Minto had found his old friend walking in Piccadilly surrounded by an admiring crowd, but had joined him only to be 'mobbed' himself. The popular admiration for Nelson, he told his wife, 'is beyond anything represented in a play or a poem of fame'. The gentle, pacific author of the *Essays of Elia* also saw the Admiral in the street; Charles Lamb had not previously been an admirer of Nelson, but seeing him in Pall Mall, 'looking just as a Hero should look' stirred his fancy.

Nelson, on his visits to London, had to sandwich together appointments with officialdom and administrative tasks on his own behalf. One such was a call upon Mr John Salter at his shop at 33, The Strand. Salter's trade was jeweller and swordsmith, and he had in safe-keeping a number of the Admiral's presentation swords and boxes. Only recently, the design of flag officers' swords having been changed by Admiralty decree, the Commander-in-Chief designate had taken delivery of a special order. A new fighting sword in the standard length scabbard for appearance's sake, but short enough for an admiral with only a left arm to draw with ease. Even at forty-seven Nelson did not think that hand-to-hand fighting should 'be left to captains'. By September 6 the Press was aware of Nelson's appointment and his new responsibilities, the whole of the Mediterranean and the watch on Cadiz. The Press was pleased and recorded that his Lordship had the selection of his favourite officers. An honour no doubt, but as Nelson had made plain to Barham and Pitt, not something of great account, as all the available captains were of quality, though he had written to Collingwood asking him to be second-in-command.

Nelson's heavy baggage for *Victory* had already been dispatched by waggon for Portsmouth. There was a visit from Mr Beckford whom George Matcham did not take to, and from the Duke of Clarence, a companion of West Indian days eighteen years ago. Lord Castlereagh, Secretary for War and the Colonies, had to be seen, and Mr George Canning, Treasurer of the Navy, and Mr Rose, and there was just time to drive over to Richmond to see Lord Sidmouth, formerly Mr Addington, and sketch out on a small study table, which his Lordship preserved, his tactical plan for dealing with the Combined Fleet at sea. There were the Perrys, neighbours at Merton (the husband was editor of the *Morning Chronicle*) and old companions like Sir Thomas Thompson, who had lost a leg at Copenhagen, met by chance. The Prince of Wales inconveniently insisted on saying his farewells to a national hero, and Nelson met Sir Sidney Smith at the Admiralty. However, in these short days there were three encounters which stand out as giving a last significant view of Nelson privately, and as a public man. An old friend, a sea officer, and another commander all recorded their impressions.

Lord Minto, second to none in his regard for Nelson, and jealous of Lady Hamilton's influence, went down to Merton and 'found Nelson just sitting down to dinner, surrounded by a family party, of his brother the Dean, Mrs Nelson, their children, and the children of a sister. Lady Hamilton at the head of the table and Mother Cadogan at the bottom. I had a hearty welcome. He looks remarkably well and full of spirits. His conversation is a cordial in these low times. Lady Hamilton has improved and added to the house and the place extremely well without his knowing she was about it. He found it all ready done. She is a clever being after all; the passion is as hot as ever.'

To Lord Sidmouth Nelson had explained 'Rodney broke the line in one point, I will break it in two' but to a fellow professional, Captain Keats, late of *Superb*, at Merton he expanded further:

No day can be long enough to arrange a couple of Fleets, and fight a decisive Battle, according to the old system. When we meet them, for meet them we shall, I'll tell you how I shall fight them. I shall form the Fleet into three Divisions in three Lines. One Division shall be composed of twelve or fourteen of the fastest two-decked Ships, which I shall always keep to windward, or in a situation of advantage; and I shall put them under an Officer who, I am sure, will employ them in the manner I wish, if possible. I consider it will always be in my power to throw them into Battle in any part I may choose; but if circumstances prevent their being carried against the Enemy where I desire, I shall feel certain he will employ them effectually, and, perhaps, in a more advantageous manner than if he could have followed my orders. With the remaining part of the Fleet formed in two Lines, I shall go at them at once, if I can, about one-third of their Line from their leading Ship.

He paused and then asked, 'What do you think of it?'
[Keats had little time to reply.]

I'll tell you what I think of it. I think it will surprise and confound the Enemy. They won't know what I am about. It will bring forward a pell-mell Battle, and that is what I want.

The third meeting was in Castlereagh's anteroom and within days of Nelson's departure. Perhaps Castlereagh intended his two visitors to meet, in which case he rendered a service to posterity, perhaps it was just the result of a typical bureaucratic delay. The two men had never met before though the General in his bold direct hand had written to the Admiral from India two years ago. Nelson found himself alone with an unknown hawk-nosed sun-tanned officer in a scarlet coat, the Hon. Arthur Wellesley, who had won the Battle of Assaye in September 1803, as he put it himself, by the exercise of 'a very ordinary degree of common sense'.

Many years later Field-Marshal the Duke of Wellington recalled the scene for the benefit of John Croker, who had himself been Secretary to the Admiralty:

> Lord Nelson was, in different circumstances, two quite different men. I only saw him once in my life and for, perhaps, an hour. It was soon after I returned from India. I went to the Colonial Office in Downing Street, and there I was shown the little waiting room on the right hand, where I found, also waiting to see the Secretary of State, a gentleman whom from his likeness to his pictures and the loss of an arm I immediately recognized as Lord Nelson. He could not know who I was, but he entered at once into conversation with me, if I can call it conversation, for it was almost all on his side, and in, really a style so vain and silly as to surprise and almost disgust me.
>
> I suppose that something I happened to say may have made him guess that I was somebody, and he went out of the room for a moment, I have no doubt to ask the office-keeper who I was; for when he came back he was altogether a different man, both in manner and in matter. All that I had thought a charlatan style had vanished, and he talked of the state of the country, and of the aspect and probabilities of affairs on the Continent with a good sense, and a knowledge of subjects both at home and abroad that surprised me equally, and more agreeably, than the first part of our interview had done. In fact he talked like an officer and a statesman.
>
> The Secretary of State kept us long waiting, and certainly for the last half or three quarters of an hour I don't know that I ever had a conversation that interested me more. Now, if the Secretary of State had been punctual, and admitted Lord Nelson in the first quarter of an hour, I should have had the same impression of a light and trivial character that other people have had. But luckily I saw enough to be satisfied that he was really a very superior man. Certainly, a more sudden and complete a metamorphosis I never saw.

On September 13 Nelson wrote in his diary,

> Friday night at half past Ten drove from dear, dear Merton where I left all which I hold dear in this World, to go to serve my King and Country. May the Great God whom I adore enable me to fulfil the expectations of my Country, and if it is His good pleasure that I should return, my thanks will never cease being offered up to the Throne of His Mercy. If it is His good providence to cut short my days upon

Earth, I bow with the greatest submission, relying that He will protect those so dear to me that I leave behind.

His Will be done. Amen. Amen. Amen.

He had returned four times to bid farewell and to pray over a sleeping child and the entry in his diary was typically Nelson, love for Emma and Horatia and concern for their future, echoes of phrases from his upbringing in the Parsonage House at Burnham Thorpe, but no more than a realistic assessment of the chances of life or death for an admiral hoping to fight a pell-mell battle.

At Portmouth he tried, unsuccessfully, to avoid a cheering, weeping, praying crowd which finally had to be kept back by soldiers so that he could embark in his barge for his flagship. Mr Rose and Mr Canning had dinner on board.

By the 17th *Victory* was off Plymouth from whence more ships were to come out to augment the fleet. Nelson wrote to Emma, 'I entreat you my Dear Emma that you will cheer up and we will look forward to many many happy years and be surrounded by our Children's Children. God Almighty can when he pleases remove the impediment. My heart's soul is with you and Horatia.'

A tearful Emma had been a feature of many visitors' recollections of Merton in the last few days. The impediment was of course Fanny who, charitable rumour maintains, was visited by the decent, kind-hearted Captain Hardy before he embarked. On September 28 *Victory* joined the fleet which already consisted of the two squadrons commanded by Collingwood and Calder. By order Nelson's flag was not given the customary thirteen-gun salute so that the news of his arrival should not reach the enemy, it being hoped that Villeneuve's fleet would be drawn off, not confined in, Cadiz. The next day the Commander-in-Chief reached his forty-seventh birthday.

On the way out Nelson had taken time to write a quick note, taken home by a passing frigate, to the Duke of Clarence, 'If your Royal Highness has any weight with our fellow governments, let not General Mack be employed, for I knew him at Naples to be a rascal, a scoundrel and a coward.' It might have been better to write to Mr Pitt, but it was a waste of time in any event, the Austrians were not going to change their commander at the behest of the British, and anyhow it was too late. On Nelson's birthday the Austrian army, technically commanded by the young Archduke Ferdinand, but in reality by Mack, had taken up its position at the juncture of the Danube and the Iller at Ulm, there to await Napoleon and his marshals. Napoleon himself with his Imperial Guard was somewhere between Strasbourg and Stuttgart. More than a fortnight before he had sent his last orders to Villeneuve at Cadiz. They were to break out of that port with the thirty-two French and Spanish ships at his disposal, and make for Cartagena, there to pick up any more Spanish ships available and then sail to Naples landing French reinforcements there, and then to proceed to Toulon for refit. Enemy convoys were to be intercepted and this meant not only British but Austrian and Russian as well. As an order it was very much the afterthought of a man whose mind was concentrated on other things, and once again it assumed that the British navy would either be absent or remain static throughout. If the Emperor did give a thought to opposition it can only be assumed that he hoped Villeneuve, who had been lucky so far in avoiding the enemy, would continue to be so fortunate. A couple of days later the Emperor had other thoughts about his admiral. General Lauriston, in charge of troops, had used his position as an Imperial A.D.C. to intrigue against and criticise Villeneuve direct to the Emperor. It was enough. Decrés, the Minister of Marine, was ordered to send Admiral Rosily south into Spain to recall Villeneuve and himself take over command.

Naturally unconscious of all this Nelson could now view the enemy, thirty-five capital ships all told, stationary in Cadiz harbour. His own arrival in command, taking over from the painstaking but not over-popular Collingwood, had been welcomed by his captains. 'For Charity's sake send us Lord Nelson, ye men of power!' had been the wish of Codrington, *Orion*'s captain, and no doubt the sentiment had been shared by others.

Now Codrington's wish had been granted and action could be expected, but it did depend upon a decision by the man who commanded the forest of bare masts discernible in Cadiz harbour. There was no method of drawing the French and the Spaniards out, even though there were rumours that Cadiz, because of the blockade of merchant ships, was very short of food. However, this was akin to wishful thinking in the British fleet, it is doubtful if any sea officer really thought that even a starving population could drive a fleet out to battle.

Obviously Villeneuve would only come out in response to orders and then only if he thought he would not sail straight into the arms of the enemy. Therefore Nelson made his dispositions in the hope that the French and Spanish could be lured out into the open sea. Napoleon in giving his last orders to Villeneuve had perhaps believed that the British force off Cadiz was not in any great strength, and this was precisely the impression that Nelson tried to give.

He had at his disposal by the time of the battle twenty-seven capital ships, four frigates, a schooner and a cutter. Under his own command in what was designated the Weather Column were *Victory* and *Britannia* flying the flag of Rear-Admiral the Earl of Northesk, both of one hundred guns, two 98s, *Neptune* and *Temeraire*, six 74's, *Conqueror*, *Leviathan*, *Ajax*, *Orion*, *Minotaur* and *Spartiate* and two 64's, *Africa* and the old familiar *Agamemnon* commanded by Sir Edward Berry. The Lee Column, under Collingwood in *Royal Sovereign*, of 100 guns, consisted of *Prince* and *Dreadnought* 98s, *Tonnant* 80, and ten 74's, *Mars*, *Belleisle*, *Bellerophon*, *Colossus*, *Achille*, *Revenge*, *Swiftsure*, *Defence*, *Thunderer* and *Defiance*, plus one 64, *Polyphemus*. This was the roll of ships actually in battle on October 21, before that date there were additions to and subtractions from the fleet, but in round numbers Nelson had a slightly smaller number of ships under command than were in the Combined Fleet.

Nelson gave a dinner party on his birthday in *Victory* for fifteen of his captains and almost the same number came the next day. There was a slight air of celebration about it as Nelson re-met old friends, and as they met each other, for the stern Collingwood had not encouraged such intercourse between his subordinates. But these were 'working dinners' for Nelson began to expound the ideas he had put to Keats in the garden at Merton and which he had sketched with his finger on Lord Sidmouth's study table. A tactical memorandum was issued from the flagship on October 10 and a rough sketch has also survived. The plan for a battle in the open sea was not, could not, be as precise as his exact dispositions before Copenhagen, nor could it be as controlled a conflict as at Aboukir where the enemy was stationary. The basic concept was that three columns of ships should drive at the enemy's line as nearly at right-angles as possible. Wind and current and therefore speed could not be predicted nor of course the dispositions and actions of the enemy, and a great deal had to depend, as always in a Nelson battle, on the initiative of individual captains. The purpose of the three-pronged attack, though on the day it was only two-pronged because of a shortage of ships, was to bring the enemy virtually to a halt, and then proceed with the pell-mell battle, ship against ship, to destruction.

Nelson called it the 'Nelson touch', which may have, as an expression, had its origin in a pun on his old rival Latouche-Tréville, and was something of a joke between him and Lady Hamilton. He described for her its reception by his officers, 'I believe my arrival was most welcome, not only to the Commanders of the Fleet, but to almost every individual in it; and when I came to explain to them the Nelson touch it was like an electric shock. Some shed tears, all approved, "It was new—it was singular—it was simple!" and from admirals downwards it was repeated, —"It must succeed if ever they will allow us to get at them. You are, my Lord, surrounded by friends, whom you inspire with confidence." '

As well as explaining his tactics, Nelson was also engaged in something just as important, the creation of a new band of brothers. The Press, when he had been appointed to his new command, had talked of his choosing his officers but, with one or two exceptions, he had to take what was available, as no doubt he had realised. Only eight of the captains on board *Victory* on those two days had served under Nelson before. Hardy, Fremantle, and Berry were old friends, Collingwood even older, but only Hardy, and he had been a volunteer at Copenhagen not in command, was present at all three of Nelson's battles. Only five of the captains present at Trafalgar had previously commanded a capital ship in battle so there was still room, but little time, to bring the fleet towards efficiency and cohesion. In fact on October 2 Nelson was forced to say farewell to two of the original band of brothers. Benjamin Hallowell in *Tigre* who had commanded *Swiftsure* at the Nile, and Thomas Louis, now a rear-admiral, in *Canopus*, who had commanded *Minotaur*. Plus three other ships, *Spencer*, *Queen* and *Zealous*, they had to be ordered away to Gibraltar and Tetuan for water and provisions and thence to convoy a British military force destined for Naples and Sicily. Curiously, both Britain and France, independently, had decided on a combined operation with the same objective that autumn. Nelson said to Louis that he hoped to have him back for the battle, but both Louis and Hallowell rightly suspected that they would miss the battle of their lives.

It was only by October 14 that Nelson had under command all the ships that he would actually use in the battle, as some of his reinforcements came in late, the last to arrive being Berry's *Agamemnon*, occasioning the comment from the Admiral, 'Here comes Berry! Now we shall have a battle'. As well as last-minute additions there were two unusual absentees. Murray, his former Captain of the Fleet, had been unable to join him because of family commitments so he had, before what was obviously to be a momentous fleet action, no chief of staff. That task fell upon the broad shoulders of Hardy who also had to double as flag captain. No doubt Nelson could have obtained a suitable officer if he had bothered, and somewhat unfairly he later became irritable because Hardy could not do two jobs at once. The other absence, and for a more curious reason, was that of Sir Robert Calder.

Originally he and Collingwood had been seen as Nelson's two seconds, both being senior to Northesk. However, Calder was required at home to attend the Court of Inquiry into his conduct off Finistere. He was no friend of Nelson's and it is a wonder that Nelson allowed him to sail home, as he requested, in his flagship *Prince of Wales*. He could perfectly well have gone in *Dreadnought* as the Admiralty suggested—she was the slowest sailer in the fleet and due for refit—or for that matter in a frigate. However, Nelson decided not to humiliate Calder by turning him out of his ship, and wrote to the Admiralty explaining why, and accepting responsibility, and so deprived himself of a ninety-gun ship on the eve of battle. Lest it be thought that Nelson was pleased to see the back of Calder at any price it must be noted that just as the battle did commence Nelson turned to Hardy and said, 'What would poor Calder give to be with us now!' This goes a long way to explain a remark of Captain Malcolm of *Donegal*, 'Nelson was the man to love'.

With Calder went the captains of *Ajax* and *Thunderer*, also to give evidence at the inquiry, leaving their ships to their first lieutenants, Pilford and Stockham, to command. Captain Durham of *Defiance* refused to go home, preferring the prospect of battle to giving evidence for Calder. Durham had not been happy under Sir Robert's command, and had no cause to love him, but he had a better sense of priorities than his two fellow captains and Calder himself, who could have stayed if he had wished.

Nelson's dispositions, once the main body of his fleet was joined, were simple. Collingwood, a sound cautious commander, had blockaded Cadiz close, Nelson now reversed the process. Blackwood in command of his squadron of frigates was sent close inshore within visual distance of the masts in the harbour. The main body of the fleet was stationed fifty miles west-south-west of the Spanish port so that if Villeneuve headed for the Channel or for the Straits of Gibraltar and the Mediterranean there was an almost equal chance of interception. At the same time the distance away from Cadiz meant that even if Villeneuve suspected that there was a British fleet somewhere in the offing there still remained a temptation for him to make a dash either to the west or the south. From Blackwood to Nelson there was a line of frigates and then capital ships at the very limits of telescope vision, whose task was to relay signals.

Five ships at a time were detached to Gibraltar for water and other necessities, and to Tetuan for beef.

It was as near an ambush as could be devised at sea; there was a considerable risk that Villeneuve might get clean away, but all that was really needed, and hoped for, in the British fleet was that the French and Spaniards would try.

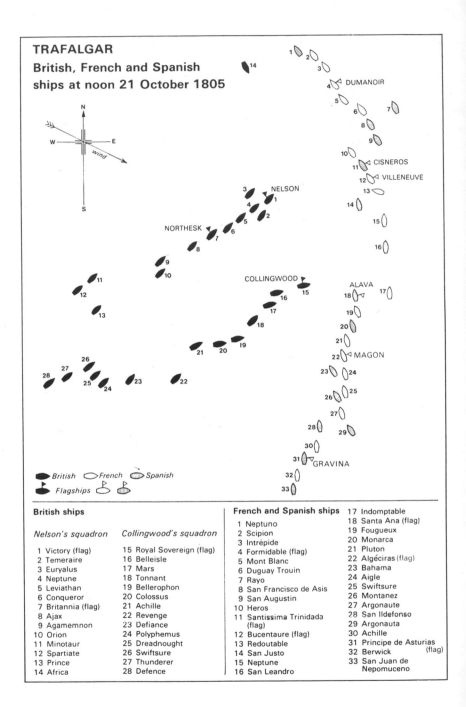

TRAFALGAR

British, French and Spanish ships at noon 21 October 1805

British ships

Nelson's squadron

1 Victory (flag)
2 Temeraire
3 Euryalus
4 Neptune
5 Leviathan
6 Conqueror
7 Britannia (flag)
8 Ajax
9 Agamemnon
10 Orion
11 Minotaur
12 Spartiate
13 Prince
14 Africa

Collingwood's squadron

15 Royal Sovereign (flag)
16 Belleisle
17 Mars
18 Tonnant
19 Bellerophon
20 Colossus
21 Achille
22 Revenge
23 Defiance
24 Polyphemus
25 Dreadnought
26 Swiftsure
27 Thunderer
28 Defence

French and Spanish ships

1 Neptuno
2 Scipion
3 Intrépide
4 Formidable (flag)
5 Mont Blanc
6 Duguay Trouin
7 Rayo
8 San Francisco de Asis
9 San Augustin
10 Heros
11 Santissima Trinidada (flag)
12 Bucentaure (flag)
13 Redoutable
14 San Justo
15 Neptune
16 San Leandro
17 Indomptable
18 Santa Ana (flag)
19 Fougueux
20 Monarca
21 Pluton
22 Algéciras (flag)
23 Bahama
24 Aigle
25 Swiftsure
26 Montanez
27 Argonaute
28 San Ildefonso
29 Argonauta
30 Achille
31 Principe de Asturias (flag)
32 Berwick
33 San Juan de Nepomuceno

CHAPTER THIRTY-THREE

Trafalgar

RIGHT UP until the moment when the French did come out, rumours were rife in the British fleet. Some were accurate, that the French and the Spaniards were at loggerheads; some were not, such as the belief held by Nelson, that Decrés, not Villeneuve, commanded at Cadiz. Right up until that moment too, Nelson had been complaining in his letters home to the Admiralty of his lack of frigates, 'the last Fleet was lost to me for want of Frigates: God forbid this should'.

When the moment did come the surveillance system worked perfectly, though Blackwood's frigates were much aided in their task by poor winds and bad seamanship. Because of a combination of the two it took from dawn on October 19 to dawn the following day for Villeneuve to get his whole fleet clear of harbour. The British frigates, *Euryalus* and *Sirius*, and the tiny sloop *Weazle* raced off with the news hoisting the signal flags with the figure combination 370 to their mastheads. It is doubtful if any signal midshipman, as the signal was acknowledged and repeated along a fifty-mile line of ships, had to refer to his code book to decipher, for 370 meant what all had been expecting, 'Enemy ships are coming out of port'.

Early on the morning of the 20th Nelson was in the process of asking Collingwood and the captain of the nearby *Bellerophon*, among others, to dinner, but William Cumby, first lieutenant of *Bellerophon*, who had abnormally keen sight, was watching the distant *Mars* which was signalling. Cumby said it was 370 but Captain Cooke, his superior, could not make out the flags or the colours, just visible over the horizon. Then, as Cumby predicted she would, *Mars* hoisted the 'distant' signal, a flag, a pendant and a ball at the three different mastheads. Before *Bellerophon*'s signalmen could hoist their signal *Victory* was acknowledging to *Mars*. At 9.30 *Victory* cancelled the dinner invitation by flags, hoisted 'general chase', and ordered a course to be steered south-east towards the Straits of Gibraltar.

No one in the fleet from vice-admiral to powder monkey cared a damn as to why the enemy were coming out of Cadiz, only in which direction would they go and could they be caught. Nevertheless, the reason why Villeneuve had made his decision provides one of the ironies of history. Having determined to rid himself of Villeneuve, Napoleon had sent Rosily to replace him, carrying both the order of dismissal, and his own new orders which allowed him considerable discretion, something denied to Villeneuve by his last orders. Rumours of Rosily's imminent arrival, and his purpose, reached Villeneuve, by a leak from the Ministry of Marine, perhaps from Decrés himself, but Admiral Rosily, delayed by a broken carriage spring in Madrid, still did not arrive. Driven on by a combination of motives, hurt pride and a determination to prove himself among them, Villeneuve decided to sail before he was sacked, and so gave his order, despite the objections of his Spanish colleagues, to sail on the 18th. The Spanish objections were on the grounds of present and approaching weather and they were sensible. Two days to get out of harbour should have been a warning, and there was worse to come, but Villeneuve persisted, and so sailed out to an unnecessary battle. Rosily did eventually arrive in Cadiz, but only in time to learn of the virtual destruction of the Combined Fleet.

Nelson had been right to ask for more frigates and to tell Blackwood, the commander of those he had, of his utmost reliance upon him. For without their aid in the twenty-four hours that remained before the battle even Nelson could have lost the enemy. Not, it must be said, due to their supreme cunning, and certainly not because of their handling of their ships, which was markedly inferior to that of their opponents, but due to the sheer chances of wind and weather which imposed a confusing number of chops and changes upon the movements of a collection of badly-handled and poorly-manned ships.

Against Nelson's twenty-seven of the line, four frigates, a schooner and a cutter, Villeneuve deployed thirty-three of the line, eighteen French and fifteen Spanish, five frigates and two brigs. It is pertinent therefore to attempt, before battle is joined, a comparison of the two fleets. In sailing performance and gun power there was little to choose between them, though of course Villeneuve had in fact six more capital ships and one more frigate. The Spanish admirals, Admiral Gravina, Vice-Admiral Alava and Rear-Admiral Don Hidalgo Cisneros were flying their flags in the largest warships afloat, respectively *Principe d'Asturias* and *Santa Ana*, both of 112 guns, and *Santissima Trinidada* of 130. Villeneuve's *Bucentaure* was an eighty-gun ship as was the flagship of his second-in-command,

Rear-Admiral Drumanoir, *Formidable*. The French third-in-command, Rear-Admiral Magon, flew his flag in *Algeciras*, a 74, the standard ship of the line for all three navies.

It was not, however, ships or guns which distinguished the fleets, but seamanship, gunnery and the quality of captains and of crews. In the twenty-four hours manoeuvring before a gun was fired the British demonstrated their superiority in such a way that when the battle was commenced the enemy was already suffering from a sense of inferiority.

Trafalgar as a battle has been examined and analysed almost out of existence in the search for some formula for success, some pattern of universal application. The quest has always been for exactitude, as by the Commission set up by Admiralty in 1913 which examined individual ships' logs, minutely considered signals and times, and, taking into account enemy records as well, attempted to reach a definite conclusion. Yet when even a few causes of inaccuracy and uncertainty are considered, times kept by unsynchronised pocket watches, records filled in later by anonymous hands, signals unseen or unacknowledged, visibility blocked by drifting gunsmoke, and overall the sheer chaos of battle, it becomes increasingly apparent that a mathematical evaluation of why Nelson won and Villeneuve lost, is an impossibility.

Both commanders had a plan, certainly; Nelson's better defined than Villeneuve's, but when it came to execution, for different but pressing and immediate reasons, neither was put very closely into effect. Further, Nelson took risks on the day of the actual battle which he could not have taken had he been opposed to a fleet of comparable quality to his own. Curiously, perhaps, this combat superiority was best demonstrated before the battle rather than during it. However, that superiority was vital, for it was by its exercise that Nelson brought Villeneuve to battle at all. The French admiral's purpose was to clear Cadiz and then take his fleet on a semi-circular course westwards and then eastwards in the open sea through the Straits of Gibraltar into the Mediterranean. Nelson's purpose was first to ascertain Villeneuve's proposed objective, lure him far enough away from Cadiz so that he could not double back, and then attack his line from windward with his two columns.

If one cause can be isolated as to why Nelson was able to do just that, it lay in his employment before battle of Blackwood and his four frigates, *Euryalus*, *Naiad*, *Phoebe* and *Sirius*. When Nelson had worried about his paucity of frigates, his instinct, as usual, had been right. Villeneuve in fact had one more than he had, and though undoubtedly, so far as the main

body of his fleet was concerned, Franco-Spanish jealousies and disagreements affected the chain of command there was no such excuse available
for his misuse of his frigates, as they were all French. As frigates, the 'eyes
and ears' of a fleet, they were useless. They stayed with the main body of
slow-moving capital ships as if they were passengers which is what they
became, as of course their guns were no match for those of a capital ship.
The advantages they did possess, speed, manoeuvrability and sometimes,
because of those attributes and their smaller size, near-invisibility, they
never used.

Blackwood's command, on the other hand, was used superbly, and to
the full, as soon as the Combined Fleet prepared to leave Cadiz. For a day
and a night they shadowed, harried and reported on the French and the
Spaniards, signalling by flag by day, by flares and guns by night, and,
when all other methods of communication failed, by actually sailing at
top speed the thirty miles of sea which separated the fleets. Nelson later on
October 21 said to Blackwood that he would 'bleed his frigates' but he
had already done just that, and as a result at almost all times Nelson knew
where Villeneuve was, and what he was doing; at no time, until too late,
did Villeneuve know where Nelson was.

The thirty-five-year-old Blackwood, who had been at sea for twenty-
four years, was a master of his craft, essentially a small ship man. His
entries in his log on board *Euryalus* were essays in the laconic, and tersely-
accepted hours of endurance and effort by the whole ship's company;
what they did not quite do, however, was to disguise his pleasure in his
duty. On the night of the 20th he wrote:

> Up mainsail and kept on the enemy's weather beam, about two or
> three miles. Made and shortened sail occasionally. Fired guns and
> burned false fires as necessary.

He was between the two fleets, in squally weather, and even 'the false
fires' had a double purpose, sometimes they were signals, but sometimes
they worried and misled the enemy. By that time Villeneuve's course
during the night was south-south-east, and Nelson's was parallel to him,
fifteen miles ahead, hoping still to have been undetected so as not to scare
the enemy back to Cadiz. Briefly, on leaving Cadiz, Villeneuve had stood
to the westward and his ships had been formed into three columns with
Admiral Gravina commanding the windward station, that is, furthest to
the west. With a change in the wind to the west, Villeneuve ordered a
change of course to south-south-west and the ships under his command

were executing that manoeuvre when the light failed. Almost at that moment, a sighting of a part of the British fleet was reported to Villeneuve. Accordingly, he gave his order to form line of battle, to change from three columns, which could not receive an attack without danger of firing upon each other, to one long line of ships.

Thus Villeneuve, on being threatened by attack, though Nelson had no intention of springing his trap so early or in darkness, automatically reverted to the old classical patterns for war at sea. Perhaps though, as well as being old-fashioned he was being careful, sensibly unambitious, and, overall, realistic. The fleet movements of the previous day had been clumsy and incompetent, some of the Spaniards had split their sails in reefing and had fallen off to leeward, and when the wind had changed any formation there had been had dissolved into disorder. Now, throughout the night, the Combined Fleet struggled to take up positions in line ahead, but when morning broke there was little cohesion, the French and Spanish ships were more or less in line, but unevenly bunched and grouped.

Throughout this time the British fleet, by a series of more co-ordinated and sophisticated evolutions, had conformed, but at a distance, to Villeneuve's movements. Nelson's final change of course being at 4.30 in the morning, wearing his ships to north-north-west so that with daylight he would be sailing to intercept Villeneuve. By half-past five on the morning of October 21 it was possible on board the British ships to see the Combined fleet about nine miles to leeward, its towering topsails discernible against the dawn. As the morning cleared Collingwood could describe the enemy disposition as being 'a crescent, convexing to leeward', sailing north to south, that is, away from Cadiz, roughly in the direction of the Straits.

Because of the position of the rising October sun Villeneuve had to wait longer than Nelson to see his enemy; when he could, the British fleet seemed to be in no obvious order. This however was to prove something of an illusion. French admirals regarded Nelson as being impetuous, daring and foolhardy; if Villeneuve drew any consolation from his enemy's dispositions he was forgetting the Nile and still judging his opponent by outdated standards.

On board his flagship, Nelson, with more leisure and facilities than most, had made his personal preparations for battle. More lowly beings had, if they could write, written last letters home, and had made disposition of their belongings after death, in most cases simply to shipmates who had agreed to reciprocate if positions were reversed. On October 19 at noon Nelson had written to Emma:

My Dearest beloved Emma, the dear friend of my bosom, The signal has been made the Enemy's Combined Fleet are coming out of Port. We have very little Wind, so that I have no hopes of seeing them before to-morrow. May the God of Battles crown my endeavours with success, in all events I will take care that my name shall ever be most dear to you and Horatia, both of whom I love as much as my own life, and as my last writing before the Battle will be to you, so I hope in God that I shall live to finish my letter after the Battle. May Heaven bless you prays your

Nelson and Brontë.

The next day he added a paragraph:

October 20th—in the morning we were close to the Mouth of the Streights, but the wind had not come far enough to the Westward to allow the Combined Fleets to weather the Shoals off Trafalgar; but they were counted as far as forty Sail of Ships of War, which I suppose to be 34 of the Line and six Frigates. A group of them was seen off the Lighthouse of Cadiz this morning, but it blows so very fresh and thick weather, that I rather believe they will be into the Harbour before night. May God Almighty give us success over those fellows and enable us to get a Peace . . .

He also wrote a short note to Horatia:

The Combined Fleets of the enemy are now reported to be coming out of Cadiz, and therefore I answer your letter, my dearest Horatia, to mark to you that you are ever uppermost in my thoughts. I shall be sure of your prayers for my safety, conquest, and speedy return to dear Merton, and our dearest good Lady Hamilton. Be a good girl, mind what Miss Connor says to you. Receive, my dearest Horatia, the affectionate parental blessing of your father,

Nelson and Brontë.

On October 21 when the enemy fleet was actually in sight there was one other task to be done. As the document he had in mind was a sort of will, though without any legal validity, Nelson decided to have two

witnesses to it, Hardy and Blackwood, who were on board the flagship
for last-minute instructions.

The document read as follows:

October the twenty-first, one thousand eight hundred and five, then in
sight of the Combined Fleets of France and Spain, distant about ten
miles.

Whereas the eminent services of Emma Hamilton, widow of the
Right Honourable Sir William Hamilton, have been of the very
greatest service to our King and Country, to my knowledge, without
her receiving any reward from either our King or Country;—first,
that she obtained the King of Spain's letter, in 1796, to his brother, the
King of Naples, acquainting him of his intention to declare war against
England; from which letter the Ministry sent out orders to then Sir
John Jervis, to strike a stroke, if opportunity offered, against either the
Arsenals of Spain, or her Fleets. That neither of these was done is not
the fault of Lady Hamilton. The opportunity might have been offered.
Secondly, the British Fleet under my command, could never have
returned the second time to Egypt, had not Lady Hamilton's influence
with the Queen of Naples caused letters to be wrote to the Governor of
Syracuse, that he was to encourage the Fleet to be supplied with everything, should they put into any Port in Sicily. We put into Syracuse,
and received every supply, went to Egypt and destroyed the French
Fleet. Could I have rewarded these services, I would not now call upon
my Country; but as that has not been in my power, I leave Emma
Lady Hamilton, therefore, a Legacy to my King and Country, that
they will give her an ample provision to maintain her rank in life. I also
leave to the beneficence of my Country my adopted daughter, Horatia
Nelson Thompson; and I desire she will in future use the name of
Nelson only.

These are the only favours I ask of my King and Country at this
moment when I am going to fight their Battle. May God bless my
King and Country and all those who I hold dear. My relations it is
needless to mention; they will of course be amply provided for,

Nelson and Brontë.

The fact that a commander-in-chief on the morning of battle could
have the time to write a will, however important he might think it to be,
illustrates as well as anything the curious atmosphere of this, the last great
battle under sail. For it was at a speed of about two knots that the two

great fleets came together, ample time for ships to be cleared for action, for Nelson's portrait of Emma in his cabin to be taken down, and stowed safely, for meals to be eaten, for ships' bands to play and for unoccupied sailors to dance a hornpipe to the scrapings of a shipmate's fiddle. Officers in their best uniforms went round the decks seeing all was well, and sailors chalked patriotic slogans on their guns. There was little wind but a heavy swell, a sign of bad weather to come, but there was little that either Villeneuve or Nelson could do.

There was an air of inevitability about it all as both commanders had a very good idea what the other would do. Nelson's plan had been for an attack in three columns but now he chose two, Collingwood in *Royal Sovereign* leading the lee division. At first the two fleets had been steering roughly parallel courses, Nelson to the north, Villeneuve to the south, that is away from Cadiz. The wind being south-west Nelson ordered his fleet to wear in succession so as to head to the east directly towards the French and Spanish line, aiming for the centre and rear of a line of ships which stretched for about four miles. Villeneuve retaliated by a man-oeuvre which has been a matter of controversy ever since; he ordered his ships to wear together, and form line of battle in reverse order. So that they were required to turn away from the enemy, with the wind, and then form themselves in a line sailing in the opposite direction, towards Cadiz.

The comment of Commodore Churruca, commanding *San Juan Nepomucino*, 'this fleet is doomed. The French admiral does not know his business. He has compromised us all', has often been quoted to demon-strate Villeneuve's incompetence. What is often forgotten is that Churruca's ship had been leading the fleet south, with the reversal of direction she now became the rearmost heading north. Doubtless his compatriot commanding *Neptuno*, now the leading ship heading for Cadiz, felt somewhat differently.

So far as the safety of the whole fleet was concerned it is difficult to argue that Villeneuve's decision was a wrong one. To continue to press southwards was to take ships which might be damaged further and further away from refuge and safety after the battle. The disadvantage which did attend upon Villeneuve's order was that by imposing a further manoeuvre upon a badly trained and co-ordinated fleet he made the formation of a close-knit, well-spaced line of battle even more unlikely.

Meanwhile, as the French and Spanish ships endeavoured to take their positions astern of each other, the two British divisions moved steadily towards them. For someone of Nelson's temperament, and not only for him, the pace was not fast enough, studding sails not normally used in battle, as they impeded gunnery and boarding, were crowded on, and every inch of canvas aloft, but both fleets were now almost entirely in the control of a slight but steady south-west breeze and a rolling swell.

Nelson had appeared early on the quarter-deck, leaving his sword behind in his cabin, for the first time in any action. October 21, he told his officers, was a date of good omen, though he left them mystified, as he did not explain why. None of them knew it was the old Nelson family celebration of Captain Suckling's little victory in 1757 that he had in mind. He had said, 'the 21st of October will be our day' previously to both Hardy and Dr Scott the Chaplain, but again without explanation. Perhaps it was a little family thing that he decided to hug to himself, because he did tell those around him that it was pleasant to think that this day was also the date of the annual fair at Burnham Thorpe. Just as in his last days at Merton, so with his last hours in *Victory*, the incidents and remarks come clustering thick and fast to suggest an inexorable fate, but the temptation should be resisted. His sword did not matter. His dress was his usual uniform, not full dress but his old undress coat, with epaulettes and a minimum of gold braid; the replicas of his orders stitched on in gold and silver wire, for he was not wearing the full stars in silver and gilt and enamel as some paintings suggest. Of course he was still a discernible target as so was any admiral, British, French or Spanish, unless he chose to disguise himself and skulk somewhere off the quarter-deck. There was certainly talk among his officers about his decorations, Dr Beatty the Surgeon being particularly worried, but he was dissuaded by Dr Scott from mentioning them, and the other Scott, Nelson's secretary, said, 'I would not be the man to mention such a matter to him'.

It seems, however, that someone did, probably Hardy, but received the brusque reply that it was no time to be shifting a coat. Blackwood was also concerned about his admiral's safety, and suggested he should transfer to *Euryalus*, as frigates stayed out of the way when battleships closed. Reasonably enough Nelson refused, though he seemed to lend a receptive ear to Blackwood's second suggestion, that some ship other than *Victory* should lead the van. Indeed he eventually gave the order to Captain Harvey of *Temeraire* to take the lead. Though when Harvey did succeed in ranging his ship up to *Victory*'s quarter, with difficulty as she continued under full sail, a proud and determined admiral hailed him with the words:

I'll thank you Captain Harvey, to keep in your proper station, which is astern of the *Victory*.

Perhaps it should be remembered that Collingwood in *Royal Sovereign* was behaving in exactly the same way, taking advantage of his own ship's superior sailing capabilities to allow him to lead his division by a number of ships' lengths. Of course the van ships were bound to take tremendous punishments in broadsides at a time when they could not reply, but that much was implicit in Nelson's plan of attack. All British ships, though to a lesser degree than the leaders, bows on to enemy broadsides, would have a period when they would be at the mercy of Villeneuve's line. It was a risk that obviously Nelson thought he could take, his captains would move in as quickly as possible to come alongside, and use their guns, and he had no high opinion of French or Spanish gunnery. Ultimately in war risks have to be taken, and the reaction of Captain Hargood of the *Belleisle* in Collingwood's division, when his first lieutenant suggested a deflection to fire a broadside, was the right one, 'No,' he said, 'we are ordered to go through the line, and go through she shall, by God!'

At about eleven o'clock Nelson went down to his cabin for the last time, and added to the already written entry in his private diary his famous payer,

> May the Great God, whom I worship, grant to my Country, and for the benefit of Europe in general, a great and glorious Victory; and may no misconduct in anyone tarnish it; and may humanity after Victory be the predominant feature in the British Fleet. For myself, individually, I commit my life to Him who made me, and may His blessing light upon my endeavours for serving my Country faithfully. To Him I resign myself, and the just cause which is entrusted to me to defend. Amen. Amen. Amen.

As he was kneeling at his desk, praying or writing, John Pasco, the signals lieutenant, entered, meaning to ask to resume the place his seniority entitled him to on board *Victory*, that is first lieutenant, 'but he could not at such a moment disturb his mind with any grievance of mine'. Pasco's forbearance cost him the chance of promotion to post rank after the battle.

About half-an-hour or so later he and Blackwood were witnesses and participants in an incident which has gone down to legend. Captain Blackwood speaks first:

I was walking with Nelson on the poop when he said, 'I'll now amuse the fleet with a signal'; and he asked me if I did not think there was one thing yet wanting. I answered that I thought the whole of the fleet seemed very clearly to understand what they were about, and to vie with each other who should first go nearest the *Victory* or *Royal Sovereign.*

Nelson then turned to Pasco, who takes up the narration:

His Lordship came to me on the poop, and about a quarter to noon said, 'Mr Pasco, I want to say to the fleet, ENGLAND CONFIDES THAT EVERY MAN WILL DO HIS DUTY. You must be quick, for I have one more to add, which is for close action'. I replied, 'If your Lordship will permit me to substitute EXPECTS for CONFIDES, the signal will sooner be completed, because the word EXPECTS is in the Signal Book, and CONFIDES must be spelt.' His Lordship replied in haste, and in seeming satisfaction, 'That will do, Pasco; make it directly.'

The thirty-two coloured flags from Admiral Popham's Code Book climbed up *Victory*'s halyards, bearing the most famous signal in naval history. Reactions were, however, not quite as might have been expected, nor were they immediate, as the signal had to be translated by officers and then communicated to the lower deck. Some sailors were a trifle mystified, some saying they had always done their duty; anyhow they cheered, probably not the sentiment, but the admiral, dutifully enough.

Dour old 'Coll's' reaction, leading his own division—he was called 'Old Cuddie' by his subordinates—was utterly typical of the man, and almost as noteworthy as the signal itself:

What is Nelson signalling about? We all know what we have to do.

The thirty-two bits of bunting came down and were replaced by two at the top gallant masthead, a white flag with a blue cross, and a red, white and blue lateral tricolour. This was Number 16 and needed less deciphering, it was 'Close Action', and it stayed aloft until it was shot away.

Nelson's determination to cut through Villeneuve's line was obvious, and almost at the last minute Villeneuve signalled to Dumanoir to reinforce the centre of the line, an idea that had occurred to Churruca as well, in anger and frustration at his superiors; however, the signal was ignored. In the British fleet all three admirals had hoisted their respective flags to the masthead and every ship, as ordered, the white St George's Ensign at the stern.

It was Collingwood's *Royal Sovereign* that was the first to hit the enemy line, slightly astern of Alava's flagship *Santa Ana*. There were now shots being fired at *Victory* and Nelson sent the frigate captains to their ships with orders for every captain to get into action as quickly as possible. As he left the poop Blackwood offered his hand:

I trust, my Lord, that on my return to the *Victory*, which will be as soon as possible, I shall find your lordship well and in possession of twenty Prizes.' 'God bless you, Blackwood', replied Nelson, 'I shall never speak to you again.'

Within minutes the van of the two British divisions was enveloped in smoke and flame and the roar of gunfire. One of the first casualties in *Victory* was Nelson's secretary. A cannon ball almost cut him in two as he stood on the quarter-deck talking to Hardy. Captain Adair of the Marines immediately ordered up a sailor to remove the bloody corpse. 'Is that poor Scott?' asked Nelson as the body went overboard.

Soon the battle resolved itself into individual actions as ship after ship of the two divisions cut, blundered or crashed into French and Spanish opponents. Speed was of the essence, and all nice plans were thrown to the winds as captains, as one put it, 'scrambled into action' to hasten the moment when they could bring their own broadsides to bear. Individual actions, but Trafalgar divided itself as the day wore on into three separate battles with the French van, centre and rear, and those battles subdivided into conflicts between groups of ships. To this extent *Victory*'s own part was typical, though she suffered more dead than any other British ship.

By chance her first broadside and her carronades were fired into the stern of Villeneuve's *Bucentaure*. The next nearest enemy ships were the gigantic four-decked *Santissima Trinidada*, and the French 74, *Redoutable*, commanded by Captain Lucas, probably the most efficient and pugnacious of all the French captains, who had made a point of training boarding parties and sharp shooters for close combat. Captain Harvey's *Temeraire* had, despite Nelson's admonition, followed *Victory* so closely into action as almost to collide with her. The distance involved and the destruction inflicted can be gauged from the fact that both *Victory* and

Temeraire fired broadsides into Lucas's ship when they were almost touching, killing nearly 500 men and wounding over eighty.

Before close action was joined, walking the quarter-deck together, for there was not much else for commander-in-chief and flag captain to do at that stage, Nelson and Hardy, as shot whistled and ricochetted around them, had both thought the other wounded. They had paused and looked anxiously at each other, but the only damage was Hardy's shoe buckle whisked away by a splinter.

'This is too warm work to last long', said Nelson as they resumed their steady pacing.

After less than an hour of close action *Redoutable* had been so pulverised with round shot that she sank next day, and *Victory*'s decks had been almost cleared of sailors and marines, Captain Adair among them, by a combination of fire from attempted boarding parties, and from the fighting tops of the French ship.

At about a quarter-past one Hardy turned on his heel and then realised that a familiar smaller figure was no longer beside him. The Admiral was on his knees on the deck supporting his weight for a moment with the fingers of his left hand. Then his arm buckled and he fell on his side, his frock coat being soiled with blood still on the deck from Scott's fatal wound. Sergeant Secker of the Marines and two of his men rushed across to lift him up.

'They have done for me at last, Hardy', gasped Nelson.

'I hope not.'

'Yes,' said Nelson, 'my backbone is shot through.'

The three marines carried the Admiral below to the cockpit. On the middle deck Nelson told the midshipman on duty to ask Hardy to order the tiller ropes to be re-rove, *Victory* was being steered by a team of men pulling these ropes as the wheel on deck had been smashed to bits by gun fire. He then covered his face with his handkerchief in the hope that his men would not see he had been wounded.

In the cockpit Nelson was undressed and laid on a bed and covered with a sheet. A gold framed miniature of Emma as a Bacchante was removed from around his neck. Mr Burke, the Purser, had taken over from the marines and supported the Admiral's shoulders so that he sat almost half upright, the position which seemed to give him least pain. There were forty others, officers and men, dying and wounded, also in the cockpit, among them Lieutenant Pasco, who was to survive. Beatty, the Chief Surgeon, with his assistants was trying in a confined space to deal with many cases which he knew to be hopeless, and Scott the chaplain, doing his best to overcome his nausea and horror, was present to minister to the dying.

There was obviously a moment or two when Nelson thought he was going to die there and then, and in near panic he insisted to Scott 'I am gone'. 'Remember me to Lady Hamilton. Remember me to Horatia.' The distracted chaplain was also told to remind Mr Rose that the Admiral had left a will and 'left Lady Hamilton and Horatia to my country'.

It was Dr Beatty who left the most complete record of Nelson's last hours compiled with the careful attention of a man of science but of course he was also a man with other duties, and a simple examination, and Nelson's own unemotional description of his symptoms, soon convinced him that there was no hope for operation or recovery, as Nelson himself well knew, despite assurances of Scott and Burke to the contrary.

All around were the sounds of battle, the roar and convulsions of *Victory*'s broadside, and the occasional cheer as another French ship struck her colours. Nelson, in conditions nearly intolerable for a dying man, afflicted by pain and plagued with thirst and still conscious of his responsibilities, wished that he had remained on deck. At least there he would have known what was going on. Pasco attempted to be his informant but he wanted to see Hardy who, he became convinced, had suffered some misfortune which was being kept from him. A midshipman, Mr Bulkeley, reported that the flag captain's presence was still required on deck, but that he would come below as soon as possible.

At about half-past two Hardy at last arrived and Nelson rallied his strength. In Beatty's words:

They shook hands affectionately, and Lord Nelson said, 'Well, Hardy, how goes the battle? How goes the day with us?' 'Very well, my Lord', replied Captain Hardy, 'we have got twelve or fourteen of the Enemy's ships in our possession: but five of their van have tacked, and shew an intention of bearing down upon the *Victory*. I have therefore called two or three of our fresh ships round us, and have no doubt of giving them a drubbing.' 'I hope', said His Lordship, 'none of *our* ships have struck, Hardy.' 'No, my Lord,' replied Captain Hardy; 'there is no fear of that.' Lord Nelson then said, 'I am a dead man, Hardy. I am going fast: it will be all over with me soon. Come nearer to me. Pray let my dear Lady Hamilton have my hair, and all other things belonging to me.'

Mr Burke was about to withdraw at the commencement of this conversation; but His Lordship, perceiving his intention, desired he would remain. Captain Hardy observed, that 'he hoped Mr Beatty would yet hold out some prospect of life. 'Oh! no,' answered His Lordship; 'it is impossible. My back is shot through. Beatty will tell you so.' Captain Hardy then returned on deck, and at parting shook hands again with his revered friend and commander. His Lordship now requested the Surgeon, who had been previously absent for a time attending Mr Rivers, to return to the wounded, and give his assistance to such of them as he could be useful to; 'for' said he, 'you can do nothing for me.'

Later Nelson told Beatty that he had no feeling now in his limbs.

'You know I am gone.'
'My Lord, unhappily for our Country, nothing can be done for you.'

Then Beatty turned away, overcome by his emotions. Scott gave the Admiral drinks of lemonade and Burke fanned him with a paper fan he had made. Much that Nelson now said was repetitive, often saying, 'God be praised I have done my duty', and mentioning Lady Hamilton and Horatia. About fifty minutes later Hardy re-appeared and Beatty again described the scene:

Lord Nelson and Captain Hardy shook hands again: and while the Captain retained His Lordship's hand, he congratulated him even in the arms of Death on his brilliant victory; 'which,' he said, 'was complete; though he did not know how many of the enemy were captured, as it was impossible to perceive every ship distinctly. He was certain however of fourteen or fifteen having surrendered.'

His Lordship answered, 'That is well, but I bargained for twenty:' and then emphatically exclaimed, 'Anchor, Hardy, anchor!'

To this the Captain replied, 'I suppose, my Lord, Admiral Collingwood will now take upon himself the direction of affairs.'

'Not while I live, I hope, Hardy!' cried the dying Chief; and at that moment endeavoured to raise himself from the bed. 'No,' added he; 'do you anchor, Hardy.'

Captain Hardy then said, 'Shall we make the signal, Sir?'

'Yes,' answered His Lordship: 'for if I live, I'll anchor.'

He then told Captain Hardy, 'he felt that in a few minutes he should be no more'; adding in a low tone, 'Don't throw me overboard, Hardy.'

The Captain answered, 'Oh no, certainly not!'

'Then,' replied His Lordship, 'you know what to do: and,' continued he, 'take care of my dear Lady Hamilton, Hardy; take care of poor Lady Hamilton. Kiss me, Hardy.'

The Captain now knelt down, and kissed his cheek; when His Lordship said, 'Now I am satisfied. Thank God, I have done my duty.'

Captain Hardy stood for a minute or two in silent contemplation: he then knelt down again, and kissed His Lordship's forehead.

His Lordship said: 'Who is that?'

The Captain answered: 'It is Hardy;' to which His Lordship replied, 'God bless you, Hardy!'

The flag captain withdrew and after about a quarter of an hour Nelson could no longer speak. His last whispers were to Scott, 'Doctor, I have not been a great sinner. Remember that I leave Lady Hamilton and my daughter Horatia as a legacy to my country', then requests for a drink, the fan and for Scott to continue rubbing his chest which gave some relief, and finally, very distinctly, 'Thank God, I have done my duty.'

The midshipman of the watch later entered up in pencil the log of *Victory*, 'Partial firing continued until 4.30, when a victory having been reported to the Right Hon. Lord Viscount Nelson K.B., and Commander in Chief, he died of his wound.'

From *Belleisle* the view was not untypical, 'Just under the setting rays of the sun were five or six dismantled prizes; on the one hand lay the *Victory* with part of our fleet and prizes, and on the left hand the *Royal Sovereign* and a similar cluster of ships. To the northward, the remnant of the combined fleets was making for Cadiz. *Achille*, with the tricoloured ensign still displayed, had burnt to the water's edge about a mile from us . . .'

Only when darkness fell upon a scene of unexampled devastation and defeat did the exultant but weary victors, on looking towards the flagship, notice with foreboding that there were no admiral's lights shining on board *Victory*.

CHAPTER THIRTY-FOUR

Aftermath

'THERE NEVER was so complete an annihilation of a fleet', wrote
Collingwood. Of the thirty-three French and Spanish ships
engaged, eighteen had been captured on the day, four ships which
had been taken to the north under Dumanoir, who was criticised henceforth by his compatriots for what looked like avoidance of the battle,
were all captured two weeks later by Sir Richard Strachan off Cape
Ortegal. Of the eleven survivors which reached Cadiz, none ever put to
sea again as fighting ships. Rosily's command was surrendered to the
Spaniards, by then enemies of the French, in 1808. No British ship,
despite heavy damage to many, was lost.

Nelson's dying injunction to Hardy to anchor, which was disregarded,
had not been misplaced. For four days after Trafalgar a storm raged which
to those who survived it, the British complement in their own ships,
British prize crews and captured Frenchmen and Spaniards, was an ordeal
far worse than the actual battle. As a result only four of the prizes captured ever reached England as sorely damaged ships sank, or were
abandoned, and in one case was regained by its original crew.

Because of the storm which drove ships dismasted and battered on to
the lee shore of Cape Trafalgar, it was not until October 26 that Collingwood, now in command of the fleet, could send Lieutenant Lapenotière
in the schooner *Pickle*, home with his dispatches. In the mouth of the
Tagus, *Pickle* fell in with a lugger, *Nautilus*, commanded by Captain Sykes
and Lapenotière imparted the news of the victory to him. From then on
the news travelled to London by way of the two officers, Sykes landing at
Plymouth and Lapenotière at Falmouth. In fact Lapenotière won the race
by minutes and with nineteen changes of post horses, and was able to
inform Mr Marsden of the great news at 1 o'clock in the morning of
November 6. Lord Barham and Mr Pitt were both aroused from their
beds. Admiralty clerks worked all night, and the next day there was an
Edition Extraordinary of the *London Gazette* and a special edition of *The
Times*. The Nelson sisters and their brother, and Lady Hamilton were

written to by Admiralty clerks: only to the widowed Viscountess Nelson did Lord Barham write in his own hand, informing her of the personal tragedy involved in the victory.

The dichotomy of Lapenotière's opening words, 'we have won a great victory but we have lost Lord Nelson' was echoed in every report and announcement, every comment, and, when they began to arrive, every letter home from every officer in the fleet. A few hours before London heard of Trafalgar there had been news of, on October 20, the defeat of the Austrian army at Ulm by Napoleon, and the surrender of General Mack with 30,000 men and sixty guns. Without the death of Nelson the news of a victory would have been a welcome antidote. As it was, the normal illuminations, decorations and celebrations to mark the victory in the capital were muted and half-hearted because of the death of the man the *Morning Post* called 'Britain's Darling Son'.

Nelson's two previous victories had been commemorated with special set pieces in the theatres, and Trafalgar was no exception, but with a difference. At Covent Garden, after the performance of *She Would and She Would Not* the curtain rose again to show a painted backdrop of the British fleet riding at anchor. On stage there stood a group of sea officers and seamen standing in attitudes of admiration. 'Suddenly a medallion descended, representing a half length of the Hero of the Nile, surrounded by rays of glory, and with these words at the bottom, "Horatio Nelson". The effect was electrical and the house resounded with the loudest plaudits and acclamations.' Soon the audience was on its feet singing 'Rule Britannia', and then the orchestra played the Dead March from Handel's *Saul*.

Lady Bessborough realised that there were some who had a direct personal concern with the details of the victory, who wanted to know more than they could ascertain from Collingwood's first incomplete list of killed and wounded. 'The scene at the Admiralty' she reported, 'was quite affecting—crowds of people, chiefly women, enquiring for husbands, brothers, children – – –'

It was not until November 27 that the *London Gazette* published a list, without names, of numbers of killed and wounded in each ship by rank. The total killed being 21 officers, 16 petty officers, 299 seamen and 113 marines; and wounded, 43 officers, 59 petty officers, 900 seamen and 212 marines. On December 3 the *Gazette* identified the officers and petty officers, but no one below that rank was mentioned by name.

In fact British casualties, both in dead and wounded, were surprisingly

small for such a close-joined battle. There was no French dispatch published, and the official newspaper, the *Moniteur*, never mentioned the
battle. There were official Spanish reports, but they were not specific
about Spanish or French casualties, though one account mentioned
10,000 men as having been killed and wounded in the Combined Fleet.
Lady Bessborough also commented on the victory and the death of
Nelson in writing to Lord Granville Leveson-Gower:

'Good heavens! What news!' she wrote, 'How glorious if it was not so
cruelly damped by Nelson's death. How truly he has accomplished his
prediction that when they met it must be to extermination. To a man
like him he could not have pick'd a finer close to such a life. But what
an irreparable loss to England! . . . Do you know, G, it makes me feel
almost as much envy as compassion; I think I should like to die so. Think
of being mourned by a whole nation, and having my name carried down
with gratitude and praise to the latest generations.'

There was no doubt of the feeling of personal loss in the fleet which
Nelson had commanded. Collingwood had guessed from the demeanour
of the officer sent to tell him that Nelson was wounded that the wound
was mortal, and when the death of his old friend was confirmed tears
were seen on the cheeks of a stoical senior officer renowned for never
showing emotions of any kind. From the lower deck of his flagship,
Royal Sovereign, came the comment of a seaman who only knew his
admiral by reputation, 'Our dear Admiral Nelson is killed! so we have
paid pretty sharply for licking them. I never set eyes on him, for which I
am both sorry and glad; for, to be sure, I should like to have seen him—
but then, all the men in our ship who have seen him are such soft toads,
they have done nothing but Blast their Eyes, and cry, ever since he was
killed. God bless you! chaps that fought like the Devil sit down and cry
like a wench.'

Nelson had many admirers known and unknown, and his effect upon
a sophisticated subordinate, though a man of the cloth and not the sword,
Victory's chaplain encapsulated the attractive side of his personality,
'What an affectionate, fascinating, little fellow he was', said Dr Scott.
But Scott, and many others like him, were mere acquaintances.

It is difficult to think of anyone who filled the bill of close personal
friend: Troubridge he had quarrelled with, Hardy was very much the
dutiful junior, even Collingwood, despite their many years' service
together, in the latter years could never overcome the bounds of their
difference in rank. Davison had been a keen friend and a useful adviser,

but Nelson had overstepped him in the race for power and position, and he had declined into the status of trusted agent.

Perhaps Lord Minto, distinguished in his own right, and in a different field, never an uncritical admirer, came closest to the category. On Nelson's private life he had been outspoken, 'the shocking injury done to Lady Nelson is not made less or greater by anything that may—or may not—have occurred between him and Lady Hamilton', and he had seen the Admiral in success and failure. Later than most he heard of Trafalgar, and wrote to his sister,

> I received this morning, at Forfar, the account of Lord Nelson's victory and death, and my sense of his irreparable loss, as well as my sincere and deep regret for so kind a friend, have hardly left room for other feelings, which belong, however, hardly less naturally to this event.
>
> —One knows, on reflection, that such a death is the finest close, and the crown, as it were, of such a life; and possibly if his friends were angels, not men, they would acknowledge it as the last favour Providence could bestow and a seal of security for all the rest. His glory is certainly at its summit, and could be raised no higher by any length of life; but he might have lived at least to enjoy it.
>
> There was a sort of heroic cast about Nelson that I never saw in any other man, and which seems wanting to the achievement of impossible things, and which became easy to him, and on which the maintenance of our superiority at sea seems to depend against the growing army of the enemy . . . However, his example will do a great deal I have no doubt.

On December 5 at ten in the morning *Victory*, with her Vice-Admiral's flag and the White Ensign at half-mast, anchored at Spithead with Nelson's body on board preserved in a cask of wine. The weather was poor and squally, and it was with considerable difficulty that the damaged and jury-masted ship was brought to the Nore where the body was conveyed by the Commissioner's yacht to Greenwich. It was there in the Painted Hall that Nelson lay in state, paid his last respects by an estimated 30,000 people, until the time for his funeral on January 9 at St Paul's Cathedral.

Nelson had often considered death, and thinking that he might 'be interred at the public expense' had expressed a preference for St Paul's as opposed to Westminster Abbey which he had heard had been built 'on a spot where once existed a deep morass'. The Abbey he feared might subside and eventually disappear 'without leaving a trace'. His other post-mortem wish was also observed, and so his body was enclosed in the coffin made from the mast of *Orient* and presented to him by Hallowell after the Nile, though an unknown official discovered an unused sarco-phagus, originally designed for Cardinal Wolsey, which was thought to be suitable for the reception of the plain wooden coffin.

The English have long been experts in grand State Funerals and, with Nelson's, officialdom almost exceeded itself, especially when one con-siders the fate of the remains of nearly everyone else killed at Trafalgar, with the exception of two of his captains, life-long friends, Duff of *Mars* and Cooke of *Bellerophon*, who were also buried in St Paul's. The immense black wooden funeral car, representing the stern of *Victory* and pulled by six black horses from the Royal Mews, stood on Horse Guards Parade to receive the coffin from the Admiralty and the procession was so long that the detachment of Light Dragoons at its head had reached the Cathedral before the tail-end of senior officers had properly moved off from the parade ground. The Chief Mourner was Admiral Sir Peter Parker, the senior Admiral in the Navy, and all flag officers had been invited. The only one of note to refuse, on grounds of ill health, was Lord St Vincent. All the Royal Dukes, the sons of George III, attended, and the Duke of Clarence was seen to enter the Cathedral in tears.

Among the thirty-one admirals and a hundred captains were a number whose paths had crossed Nelson's, Lord Hood, Sir Samuel Hood, Bligh, Domett, Orde and Calder. Hardy and Blackwood were present, but Collingwood and most of the other Trafalgar captains were still at sea. In the procession amidst the military bands playing Handel's Dead March, the statesmen, admirals and peers of the realm and heralds, the Nelson family in their coaches, and artillery 'with eleven pieces of cannon', there marched forty-eight seamen from *Victory*, wearing blue jackets, white trousers and black scarves round their arms and round their hats, and with their specially issued gold Trafalgar medals round their necks.

Lady Elizabeth Harvey said, 'the show altogether was magnificent, but the common people, when the crew of the *Victory* passed, said, "We had rather see them than all the show." '

George Matcham, Nelson's nephew, the youngest member of the family present, continuing his diary, gave his description of the funeral service which lasted from 2 p.m. until nearly 6 o'clock.

'At St Paul's we got out, and walked in procession up the Passage. It was the most aweful sight I ever saw. All the Bands played. The Colours were all carried by the Sailors and a Canopy was held over the Coffin, supported by Admirals.'

As was customary with a State Funeral, as the coffin was about to be lowered into the crypt Sir Isaac Heard, Garter King of Arms, recited in a loud voice the titles of the deceased, but, inserted a sentence of his own, 'the Hero who in the moment of Victory fell, covered with Immortal glory—' The final incident, also unrehearsed by the Heralds' Office, was the most affecting and remained in the memory of all those who witnessed it. The sailors of *Victory* had borne in the procession and into the cathedral the three shot-torn ensigns of the flagship, Union Standard, Vice-Admiral's flag and the White Ensign, these being meant to be interred with the coffin. But as it was lowered out of sight they seized the largest of the three, the White Ensign, and tore it into strips which they pushed into their jackets as their memento.

'That was Nelson,' said Mrs Codrington, wife of *Orion*'s captain, 'the rest was so much the Herald's Office.'

An unofficial spectator of the funeral was Admiral Villeneuve, up on parole from Winchester; the two most notable absentees were Viscountess Nelson and Lady Hamilton.

The atmosphere of excessive funeral pomp reflected much of the official Government attitude to anything or anybody connected with Nelson, after his death. Collingwood received a barony, Hardy a baronetcy and Lord Northesk, though rather tardily, a Knighthood of the Bath, and many officers present at Trafalgar, especially those in *Victory*, were given a step-up in rank. This was very much common form for a victory, but the most incredible recognition of a successful sea battle was the raising of the Reverend William from the Viscountcy, which he inherited automatically from his deceased brother, to the dignity of an Earldom; Nelson of Trafalgar and of Merton. In one or two letters, written in the past to his brother, Horatio had wryly referred to the possibility of meeting the French again in battle, and if unlucky, raising William to the peerage, and now it had come about.

The 'Trafalgar honours' were announced unusually close upon the receipt of the news of the victory, on November 9. William's full style was now Earl Nelson of Trafalgar, and of Merton in the County of Surrey, with the subsidiary title of Viscount Merton. Collingwood's barony, though he was also promoted from Vice-Admiral of the Blue to Vice-Admiral of the Red, had no connection with the battle, 'of Caldbourne and Hethpoole in the County of Northumberland', which had a very civilian ring about it, and could only descend, in the normal way of peerages, through male heirs, and Collingwood, disappointingly, had only daughters. The far greater honour bestowed upon William, who had risked nothing, descended to his male heirs, but, most unusually failing, these would then continue through the male heirs successively of Susannah Bolton and Catherine Matcham, Nelson's sisters.

The granting of peerages was the prerogative of the Sovereign, though presumably George III had received Ministerial advice. There were how-ever further rewards in store for the Nelson family, and as these involved public money, had to receive the assent of Parliament. Accordingly, it was in February of the next year that a pension of £2000 per annum was approved for Fanny. That was fair and reasonable, what however was surprising was the proposal in May that Parliament should approve a pension of £5000 per annum to whomsoever should be Earl Nelson, and £120,000 to enable him to buy an estate and to give lump sums to Susannah and Catherine.

Parliament did approve, but not without debate in Committee on July 15, but it is somewhat surprising that in the Commons there was not more objection to beneficence bestowed, not upon a distinguished living commander, that had happened, for instance, with Marlborough, but upon his collateral relations. Two speakers in the Commons, Colonel Thomas Wood of Brecon and Mr Phillip Francis of Appleby both felt that public money was being used on far too lavish a scale, Colonel Wood on grounds of general economy, and Mr Francis more particularly because 'Lord Nelson's collateral relations, personally, are unknown to the public, and can have no claim, but what they derive from the acci-dental honour of bearing his name, and from services in which they had no share'. Mr John Fuller, a Sussex M.P., was the only Member to make any suggestion that the Commons should consider 'the wish expressed by the illustrious founder of the family in his last moments', this oblique reference to Emma and Horatia was made when the original Resolution came before the House in May, and Mr Fuller's hope was that the Nelson family would 'show some degree of generosity'.

When however in Committee in July the House discussed details, Lord Henry Petty, the junior Minister proposing the actual Bill, referred to Lord Nelson's sisters 'in limited circumstances'—'both of whom he bequeathed to His Country for that provision which it was not in his power to give them'. Whether this was a genuine mistake or a straight piece of Ministerial licence it is impossible to tell.

The Bill was passed without a division and received the Royal Assent on July 22, 1806, the final provision being £15,000 to each Nelson sister, leaving £90,000 for the purchase of an Estate. This proved to be not enough for an estate 'which seemed desirable' to the Trustees so in May 1815 another £9,000 was granted to Earl Nelson to complete the purchase of the Standlynch estate near Downton Wells in Wiltshire, the house on the property coming to be called Trafalgar House. Oddly enough there was a strong local tradition that the property had once belonged to the Herbert family, Fanny's forebears. So far as this last gift of public money was concerned, perhaps not surprisingly, although 111 M.Ps. voted for the proposal, sixty-six voted against.

This ludicrous over-provision for William, Susannah and Catherine, none of whom were actually in dire need, contrasts badly, so every writer on Nelson has always observed, with the official indifference displayed towards Lady Hamilton and Horatia. The fact that King, Government and Parliament over-reacted to the death of Nelson does not, however, of necessity, form the basis of a good argument in favour of a grant of public money for an admiral's mistress and his illegitimate daughter. Lady Hamilton's old argument about her so called 'services' as Ambassa-dress was a fairly transparent excuse for the actualities, and Nelson's original assessment that that pension would never be paid was realistic. No one who has urged that some official provision should have been made for Emma and Horatia seems to have considered sufficiently how such a grant might have been made. Should Emma have received the same sum as Fanny? Or more? Or less? Should Horatia have been declared the child of Nelson and Emma, particularly as Lady Hamilton and Nelson's solicitor, Hazlewood, steadfastly maintained that Horatia's mother was some mysterious lady whose name they could not reveal? Indeed this belief was imparted so strongly to Horatia that throughout her life she also maintained, even in written argument with Sir Nicholas Harris Nicolas, editor of *Nelson's Dispatches and Letters*, that Lady Hamilton was not her mother, largely on the prin-ciple that her father could not have deceived his old friend Sir William Hamilton.

Finally, perhaps those who argue that Emma and Horatia should have been provided for in the terms of Nelson's so-called 'codicil' might think of the wording of the Bill which Parliament would have had to approve and, further, the debate which would have attended its passage and the vote at the end of the inevitable argument.

The fact that after Nelson's death Emma Hamilton, though not without some means, fell rapidly into debt, was principally her own fault. She had always been an extravagant woman, careless of money; she also became a woman with a grievance, almost a fixation, that in some way the Country, or the Government, or the anonymous 'they' of bureaucracy and officialdom, the establishment, should have somehow implemented her lover's last wishes. After Trafalgar her life presented a picture of sad decline relieved only by the loving care she lavished on Horatia. Eventually she took to drinking to drown her sorrows and her health deteriorated, a number of friends and acquaintances helped her and gave her assistance with her mounting debts, but there can be no doubt that in her last years of her life she had become a burden even to her sympathisers and an embarrassment to her daughter. Eventually, with Horatia, she took herself to Calais, once the first peace between Britain and France had been declared, and it was in Calais on January 15, 1815 that she died. There is now no trace of her pauper's grave, she was possibly converted to Catholicism in her last days, certainly she was buried according to the rites of the Catholic Church.

Horatia was then fourteen, and remembering those last sad days of a woman whom she had been taught to regard as merely a guardian and not her mother, she said, 'for some time before she died she was not kind to me, but she had much to try her, alas, to excite her . . .'

Emma's incredible silence with her daughter as to their true relationship, maintained even on her deathbed, was the last service, misplaced, generous and heart-breaking, that she rendered to the memory of her Hero. Horatia was rescued by William, Earl Nelson, brought back to England and henceforth brought up by the Matchams. If blame, outside herself, attaches to anyone for Lady Hamilton's condition in her last years, it must be levelled at the Reverend William, well provided for and selfish, who had once fawned upon his brother's mistress, but who was only recalled to any sense of Christian charity or obligation ten years later when she was conveniently out of the way.

Horatia, who had a distinct physical resemblance to her father, a similarity which grew with the years, and none, unfortunately, to her once beautiful mother, married the Reverend Philip Ward in 1822 and thus returned to a Nelson family tradition of close connection with the Church. She lived until 1881, taking as her married name Nelson-Ward, and she bore nine children, thus demonstrating two other Nelson family characteristics.

During her lifetime there was considerable public speculation and controversy which grew as more and more became known of her father's life, as to her real parentage; speculation and controversy which she sternly resisted to such an extent that her descendants remember it as a banned subject within the family circle. She was buried in Paine's Lane Cemetery, Pinner, and the original description on her gravestone as the 'Adopted Daughter of Vice-Admiral Lord Nelson' was later changed by an anonymous kindly hand to read 'the Beloved Daughter'.

Nelson left two sorrowing women behind him, both with grievances. Fanny, first and last Viscountess Nelson, perhaps it is needless to say, bore hers stoically, only on one or two occasions ever referring to her 'broken heart'. Josiah, having left the Navy, married in 1819 and took up a financial and investment business at which he prospered. He died of pleurisy in Paris on July 9, 1830, in the middle of a second French Revolution and was buried at Littleham near Exmouth. He left a widow and three daughters, one of whom married a naval officer eventually to become a vice-admiral. His mother, who had been befriended after Trafalgar by the Duke of Clarence, Lord Bridport and Admiral Lord Vernon, died in London a year after her son and was buried beside him at Littleham.

The subsequent history of the Nelson peerage, and those who bore its title, has been complicated and provides material for criticism of the original, unusual, and unjustified grant. The Reverend William, 1st Earl Nelson and 2nd Duke of Bronté, died in 1835. He was predeceased by his first wife, and married for a second time. He was also, however, predeceased by his son Horatio, Viscount Trafalgar, who died at the age of twenty. Consequently the Dukedom of Bronté descended by Sicilian law through his, Horatio's, sister Charlotte, who married in 1810 Samuel Hood, 2nd Baron Bridport. The Sicilian dukedom has thereafter stayed with the Hood-Bridport family to this day.

As a result of young Horatio's early death the Earldom of Nelson descended to Susannah's son, Thomas Bolton, who changed his name as he was required to do to Nelson, but survived his uncle by only eight months. The subsequent history of the family has been of no particular public interest, an occasional naval officer appearing in the collateral branches and by marriage, and perhaps the most remarkable feature being a return to Nelson longevity, the 3rd, 4th and 5th Earls all living into their nineties.

In 1948 the public pension to the Nelson family was discontinued, as it had been begun, by Act of Parliament, the payments ceasing with the life of Edward Agar Horatio, 5th Earl Nelson, who died in 1951.

There never had been a battle quite like Trafalgar, and there was never to be another like it again. Napoleon, who had won his victory the day before, dismissed it in one sentence, the only comment upon it he ever made, 'les tempêtes nous ont fait perdre quelques vaisseaux après un combat imprudemment engagé'.

On November 14 his victorious army entered Vienna and on December 2 he routed both Austrians and Russians at Austerlitz. William Pitt, on hearing the news in London said, 'roll up the map of Europe' and by January the Prime Minister was a dead man, worn out, it was said, by his exertions and his disappointments. The next year, at Jena, Napoleon defeated the Prussian army, the last remaining military force in Europe that could be opposed to his own, though the Third Coalition had been wrecked in the previous year, the year of Britain's most spectacular victory at sea.

What then did Trafalgar achieve? The war against Napoleon's empire continued for another ten years, until Waterloo. The worst setbacks that Napoleon suffered were in the Peninsula, where his armies were drained away by what he called 'the Spanish ulcer', and in the disastrous 1812 campaign in Russia. The complaint of Britain's allies, subsidised, but unco-operative, was that, apart from money, Britain's contribution to the war was to assert her power at sea, defend her own island, maintain her own colonies and take over those of others, but not to commit herself wholeheartedly to the mainland of Europe where the ultimate battle had to be fought.

There was a great deal to the assertion, especially if the contest was seen from Berlin, Vienna or St Petersburg. However, it was no minor advantage that London was preserved from the invader, because it was there that coalitions were made, often with the aid of monies made in India or the West Indies; it was there, as Napoleon recognised, that his most determined opponents were still to be found, unconquered. After Trafalgar Britain could not be defeated at sea, the threat of invasion had lifted before October 21, but after that date there was no possibility that Napoleon, however successful on the continent of Europe, would revive the project. It might, at its lowest, only mean that Britain's navy could not be challenged by a battle fleet, but that did mean that Austrians, Prussians, Russians, and, later, Spaniards and Portuguese, were assured of one ally. The centuries old concept, popular in Paris and sometimes in Madrid, of Franco-Spanish control of the sea approaches to Britain was smashed. If the idea lingered on at all it was only as one of the contributory factors to Napoleon's attempt to control Spain and Portugal which when it occurred produced a war in the Peninsula. Admittedly in that campaign Sir John Moore and even more so, Wellington, were immensely aided by the native populations, but a British army could not have been put into Spain to win victories and ultimately march into France if it had not been for virtual inviolability at sea. As Wellington put it to Rear-Admiral Markham, sent by the Admiralty to confer with him in Spain in September 1813:

> If anyone wishes to know the history of this war, I will tell them it is our maritime superiority gives me the power of maintaining my army while the enemy are unable to do so.

Ultimately Napoleon had to be beaten on land, but Britain by her victories at sea had confined him to a continental strategy. To get at Britain after Trafalgar he had to resort to a war against her trade which led him to his Continental System, the Berlin Decrees and attempts to enforce his wishes upon European nations, allies, satellites and neutrals. That policy led to a deterioration of his relations with Russia and thence to the catastrophic campaign of 1812.

Thus, though Trafalgar, following the Nile, did not, indeed could not, win the war for Britain, it made it virtually certain that Britain could not be defeated by France. No doubt Waterloo had to be won, but what, however, if Britain had lost Trafalgar? Obviously such a result would not have precipitated an immediate invasion attempt with Marshal Brune's skeleton forces. If Nelson had survived there would have been another battle, if he had not there were other admirals and other fleets. However, as soon as one begins to consider such possibilities, one becomes aware of the fighting skill and will possessed by one man over and above his contemporaries. Alive or dead he did inspire by his example a fighting service, already formidable, to consider and prove itself invincible. Nevertheless, if Villeneuve had destroyed a number of British ships or managed to return to Cadiz in triumph with enemy prizes in tow who can doubt that Napoleon's interest in naval operations would have been revived. There would have followed a period, perhaps of many years, during which Britain would have been thrown back again on the defensive. If Trafalgar had been lost Britain could have been again excluded from the Mediterranean and the Atlantic coast of the Iberian peninsula. Napoleon's occupation of Spain would have been opposed by a guerilla resistance, but not by a British army.

Ultimately, though Austrians, Prussians and Russians affected contempt for Britain's efforts on land, what if Britain's reputation at sea had suffered from a considerable reverse? Would Napoleon then have not appeared invincible, what point would there then have been in considering resistance in the next ten years? What purpose in joining an alliance against him? Could one have ruled out a steadily growing demand in Britain for a compromise peace, another more permanent Treaty of Amiens? Morale could have declined to such an extent that it would have been unnecessary for Napoleon to have invaded Britain.

War is a question of imponderables only answered by putting events to the test, and in none more so than the long struggle with Napoleon, a conflict in which an accumulation of inter-related factors slowly wore down a military genius, master of a state almost entirely adapted to war. Trafalgar removed a whole series of possible moves from the board. To change the metaphor, by the actions of one afternoon Napoleon was permanently disabled, henceforth he fought with one arm tied behind his back.

Nelson's reputation as an admiral rests upon three battles, but in different degrees. The Nile and Trafalgar were cumulative in their effect, directed against the principal enemy. Copenhagen dealt with a special problem in a particular theatre though the result was a reverse for French policy. Essentially though its effect was short-term. Later Britain had again to assert herself by naval action in the Baltic under Saumarez, and Alexander I, hailed as friendly on his accession, was to conclude at Tilsit an agreement with Napoleon, though later, after Russia had been invaded, he again became an ally. What Copenhagen did do was to increase the reputation of the Royal Navy, and of Nelson in particular, thus contributing to the morale and experience of the Service in 1805. By then neither the French nor the Spanish had any confidence left in their abilities at sea, and expected to lose in a fleet action. Trafalgar only confirmed the pessimism of Villeneuve and Gravina and demonstrated the futility of challenging the British at sea.

Nelson in his dying hour had the consolation of knowing of a victory won but the three wounded Spanish admirals, Gravina, Alava and Cisneros, had no such comfort. Commodore Churruca, who had criticised Villeneuve's final dispositions, died of his wounds on board ship; the

French rear-admiral, Magon, knew in his dying moments that the Combined Fleet was defeated; Gravina's arm was shattered by grape shot, and because he refused amputation blood poisoning set in and he lingered on for four months after the battle; dying, he said that he hoped he was going to join the heroic Nelson.

Villeneuve's fate was perhaps the saddest. He returned to France from his captivity in Britain, which had not been arduous, to find himself disgraced and Napoleon's scapegoat for a defeat which was much more the fault of the emperor than the admiral. On April 22, 1806 he died of stab wounds in the bedroom of a Rennes hotel; whether he committed suicide out of remorse, or was removed by Imperial agents, it is impossible to say. The official version of his death, once referred to publicly and contemptuously by Napoleon, was that he had taken his own life.

All of Nelson's friends and brother officers continued to serve in a navy which was still engaged in a war, but nothing in their lives was ever to approach the excitements and triumphs of the period from the Nile to Trafalgar. Three of them died early. Louis contracted a fever in Alexandria and died there in 1807 and was buried in Malta. In the same year Troubridge, always an unlucky man, died at sea. He had been with the Indian Squadron but with changes in the command structure he was given the new command of the Cape of Good Hope. Leaving in *Blenheim* from Madras on December 1 he was off Madagascar on February 1 when he sailed into a cyclone; *Blenheim*, her whole complement, and Troubridge, were never seen again. Two years later Alexander Ball died on Malta. He was buried there, the tributes of all sections of society on the island bearing witness to his efforts and exertions on behalf of a people he genuinely loved and who returned his feelings.

Collingwood succeeded Nelson as Commander-in-Chief in the Mediterranean and it was in that post that he died in 1811, completing a pattern begun when the two friends had been young officers in the West Indies. He often requested the Admiralty to be relieved and to return home, but continued, typically, to perform his duty, unspectacularly and conscientiously, until the end.

Samuel Hood became a vice-admiral and died in 1816. Three years later Fremantle, rewarded for his services by a baronetcy, died suddenly in Naples, the scene of his early adventures, and where his married life to his Betsy had begun. The war had been over for four years, and though it was now a peacetime navy, senior officers, often on half-pay, continued to be promoted up the Flag List. Cornwallis died in 1820 and Lord St

Vincent in 1823, at the ripe age of ninety, outliving his protégé by eighteen years.

Berry became a rear-admiral, but never served as such and died in 1831. Blackwood whose last rank was vice-admiral, and whose last appointment was commander-in-chief at the Nore from 1827–1830, followed him a year later. Foley, a vice-admiral, died at Portsmouth in 1833. Hallowell became a full admiral and changed his name to Carew to inherit a fortune from a distant relative, his complaint being that it came too late in life for him to really enjoy it for he died in 1834.

Saumarez became a vice-admiral and was finally in 1831 rewarded for his considerable services by a peerage. He died in 1836. The last survivor of all that gallant company was, perhaps appropriately, Thomas Masterman Hardy. He had received his baronetcy in 1806. In 1830 he was a rear-admiral, and First Sea Lord, and seven years later he was promoted vice-admiral. In 1839 he died at Greenwich as a Governor of the Navy Hospital.

By then the age of Nelson was becoming a distant memory, but British naval primacy continued into the era of steam, armour plate and long-range guns, until the end of the century with scarcely a serious challenge from any other power. The sheer force of Nelson's reputation also continued, incredibly, until the eve of Jutland, a battle before which the German High Seas Fleet felt genuine trepidation at the thought of pitting itself against Nelson's navy. However, Nelson cannot be judged by traditions which continued long beyond the age of sail. The only true comparison lies within his own time and against his contemporaries, whether in his own service or among his enemies.

Enough has perhaps already been seen of the man, as distinct from the commander, to realise that he was an incredibly mixed human being. Wellington discerned in the course of one meeting the two contrasting aspects of the public man; virtues and vices, sense and foolishness, were similarly opposed in his private life. However it is not unusual in men of outstanding character that their faults and deficiencies are commensurate with their abilities.

Nelson's infatuation with Lady Hamilton of course increased his private foolishness, but it is as a commander that he has his place in history. No commander exists who has not made mistakes and that Nelson's were confined to land operations is not perhaps a crippling defect in an admiral who had St Vincent, the Nile, Copenhagen and Trafalgar to his credit.

As a commander he had the qualities of physical courage, speed of decision, tactical flair and, what is sometimes forgotten, the habit of detailed preparation before action. Of course he took risks but they were taken with a superb instrument, the British fleet with its well trained men and intrepid officers. Villeneuve who was an enforced spectator, as a prisoner, of the conduct of the Royal Navy in the storm after Trafalgar, remarked that the captains were 'all Nelsons'; they were certainly of outstanding quality, but it was his example which set the standard and put him at the head of his contemporaries. Strategically, as opposed to tactically, he had defects, largely of temperament. It is difficult to visualise him aged forty-seven, or even eighty carrying out Lord Barham's task of central planning. He was essentially a man of action, a commander of battle fleets. To that task he brought a special quality, the ability to inspire, to raise morale, to convince captains, officers and men that they were invincible under his command.

Coleridge may perhaps at first sight be regarded as a curious choice as a commentator upon Nelson, but he was a man of perception and sensitivity, who from his close association with Alexander Ball had an excellent opportunity of seeing the admiral through the eyes of an able subordinate. By chance Coleridge was in Naples, a city which had seen so much of Nelson's contrasting character, when the news of Trafalgar and Nelson's death was announced:

> The tidings arrived at Naples on the day that I returned to that city from Calabria; and never can I forget the sorrow and consternation that lay on every countenance. Even to this day there are times when I seem to see, as in a vision, separate groups and individual faces of the picture. Numbers stopped and shook hands with me, because they had seen the tears upon my cheek, and conjectured, that I was an Englishman, and several, as they held my hand, burst, themselves, into tears. And though it may awake a smile, yet it pleased and affected me, as a proof of the goodness of the human heart struggling to exercise its kindness in spite of prejudices the most obstinate, and eager to carry on its love and honor into the life beyond life, that it was whispered about Naples, that Lord Nelson had become a good Catholic before his death. The absurdity of the fiction is a sort of measurement of the fond and affectionate esteem which had ripened the pious wish of some kind individual through all the gradations of possibility and probability into a confident assertion believed and affirmed by hundreds.

Perhaps something however may be allowed to literary licence, and even to the demonstrative Neapolitan temperament, but on Nelson's internal effect, upon the fleets he commanded, Coleridge, deriving his information from Ball, was precise:

> Lord Nelson was an Admiral, every inch of him. He looked at every thing, not merely in its possible relations to the Naval Service in general, but in its Immediate Bearings on his own Squadron; to his officers, his men, to the particular Ships themselves his affections were as strong and ardent as those of a Lover. Hence, though his temper was constitutionally irritable and uneven, yet never was a Commander so enthusiastically beloved by men of all ranks, from the Captain of the Fleet to the youngest Ship-boy.

Robert Graves in his poem, *1805*, imagines a conversation at Nelson's funeral between a general and an admiral. The general has heard from one of the admiral's colleagues that perhaps, in the view of some of the more conservative admirals, 'Nelson's exit though to be lamented, falls not inopportunely, in its way'. The admiral agrees and goes on to list Nelson's faults and deficiencies, ultimately provoking the general to ask, what then was the secret of his victories? To receive the reply, 'By his unservice-like, familiar ways, Sir, he made the whole Fleet love him, damn his eyes'.

The final comment though must go, not to a poet, but to a brother sea officer who knew Nelson as well as any man, and who had a wealth of experience to draw upon. After Copenhagen, St Vincent wrote to his former protégé, congratulating him on another victory, and concluded with the words, 'it does not become me to make comparisons; all agree there is but one Nelson'.

Sources and Bibliography

HORATIO NELSON has suffered much from authors and it is impossible not to agree with Sir John Laughton who, having completed the Nelson entry in the *Dictionary of National Biography*, observed that though the bibliography was enormous, 'comparatively little of it has any real value'.

Accordingly, and because a complete list of books, memoirs and articles on and around the subject would be insufferably long, I have indicated my principal sources, and at the same time attempted to do something towards compiling a selective list for the reader wishing to learn more about the admiral, his contemporaries, and the period.

In my text I have endeavoured to explain each substantial quotation by author and circumstance, for instance Cornelia Knight's descriptions of Nelson and the Hamiltons in Naples and Sicily, and of their journey through Europe, appear in her *Autobiography*. This I have done deliberately so as to avoid a plethora of footnotes, or distracting numbers of asterisks.

Direct contemporary observations therefore appear in the memoirs, diaries, autobiographies and biographies of what a lawyer would call the witnesses. The difficulty of listing such witnesses in any manageable form lies in the fact that almost everyone who ever encountered Nelson in the flesh tended to mention the occurrence, although the rest of their recollections may have had very little to do with him, or the Navy, or any closely related subject. When one moves away from direct observation or reported speech, into the realm of criticism and comment, the unanswerable question is, where does one stop? It would be easy to include valuable observations by S. W. Roskill or A. J. Marder. Neither wrote directly on Nelson but they would be 'in', as surely as two films and Künnecke's operetta *Lady Hamilton* and Lennox Berkeley's opera *Nelson* would be 'out'. What however about the references to Nelson in the literary works of such people as Charles Lamb, Samuel Taylor Coleridge, Jane Austen, Thomas Hardy, Joseph Conrad, and Bernard Shaw? For that matter, both Goethe and Casanova mention the

Hamiltons, but then they, like the contemporaries Lamb, Coleridge and Jane Austen, rank as 'witnesses'.

The starting-point must therefore be the seven volumes of *Letters and Despatches* edited by Sir Nicholas Harris Nicolas, and published between 1844 and 1846. These should be supplemented by other collections of letters which are in chronological order, the *Letters of Lord Nelson to Lady Hamilton*, an anonymous work published in two volumes in 1814, the *Collection of Autograph Letters and Historical Documents* formed by Alfred Morrison, the *Hamilton and Nelson Papers*, privately printed and circulated in 1893, and a superb modern production, edited by George P. B. Naish for the Navy Records Society in 1958, *Nelson's Letters to his Wife and other documents 1785–1831*.

Katherine Lindsay-MacDougall, who, as custodian of Manuscripts at the National Maritime Museum, aided the editor of that work, has also assisted all subsequent Nelson researchers with her article in the *Mariners' Mirror* of 1955, 'Nelson's Manuscripts at the National Maritime Museum'. This sets out the history and provenance of the various collections of letters, documents and papers which have come to rest at Greenwich. These are now catalogued as the Bridport, Stewart, Jervis, Berry, Elliot, Hood, Keith and Cornwallis Papers and the Nelson-Ward, Phillips, Trafalgar, Walter, Girdlestone and Autograph Collections.

The history of all this material, a great deal of it originally in the possession of William, 1st Earl Nelson, Lady Hamilton, and Mrs Bolton, is a story in itself. Originals appearing, disappearing and re-appearing and being made eventually accessible to the public by inheritance, acquisition and donation. The title of Katherine Lindsay-MacDougall's article in fact errs on the side of modesty as she also traces the history of those documents originally in the hands of Viscountess Nelson, William Hazlewood, Nelson's solicitor, and Lady Hamilton at Merton, which were finally acquired by Lady Llangattock, and presented by her to the Nelson Museum at Monmouth, and also those now in the British Museum catalogued as Additional MSS 34,902–34,992.

The story of the Monmouth MSS is not untypical of a great deal of original Nelson material. Some letters and documents were used early on by Clarke and M'Arthur, but they were not seen in the 1840s by Nicolas, and the first modern biographer able to make use of the material, then still almost entirely unpublished, was Carola Oman in 1948, with her *Nelson*, the most detailed description of Horatio Nelson, the man, to date.

As manuscript material has only gradually come to light over a considerable period of years, it will be realised that it is only comparatively recently that the whole has been available. In consequence, although some biographers, Clarke and M'Arthur, Harrison and Pettigrew among them, have had access to part of the material, many early works on Nelson are of necessity partially invalidated by the non-availability of important sources.

Bearing this in mind any Nelson biographer owes a particular debt of gratitude to Oliver Warner for producing in 1955 his *Lord Nelson, A Guide to Reading* which lists, with helpful comments, all the significant works on the admiral from 1798 until 1952. It would be presumptuous for someone who follows after to seek to add or subtract from Oliver Warner's work in a field he has made so very much his own, save to commend his authoritative and readable *Portrait of Lord Nelson*, published in 1958.

Since 1952, however, a number of writers have made use of the three main manuscript sources, the Nelson Papers at the British Museum, at Greenwich and at Monmouth, and material in the Public Record Office, and elsewhere, to produce works which have increased our knowledge of Nelson. In the field of straight biography Tom Pocock's *Nelson and his World* appeared in 1968, Sir Arthur Bryant's *Nelson* in 1970, and Geoffrey Bennett's *Nelson the Commander* in 1972. Horatia Nelson is the subject of an attractive biography, so entitled, by Winifred Gérin, published in 1970. In 1963 Hugh Tours produced his *Life and Letters of Emma Hamilton* and Oliver Warner's *Lady Hamilton and Sir William* had appeared in 1960. Probably the most perceptive and entertaining study of the 'tria juncta in uno' appears in Jack Russell's *Nelson and the Hamiltons*, published in 1969 when Sir William had a biography in his own right with Brian Fothergill's *Sir William Hamilton, Envoy Extraordinary*.

With regard to Nelson's contemporaries, Ludovic Kennedy's excellent *Nelson's Band of Brothers* first appeared in 1951, but was revised last year with the title, *Nelson and his Captains*. There is no modern biography of Lord Howe, Sir John Barrow's *Life of Earl Howe* appeared in 1883, and Lady Bourchier's *Memoir of Sir Edward Codrington* was published in 1873 which, as well as dealing with her father, includes much about his mentor and patron. Oliver Warner's *Glorious First of June*, 1961, provides an up-to-date assessment of Howe as commander. The *Life and Correspondence of John, Earl of St Vincent* was edited by Captain E. P. Brenton in

1838, and David Bonner Smith edited *The St Vincent Papers*, published in two volumes in 1921 and 1927. J. S. Tucker's *Memoirs of the Earl of St Vincent* appeared in 1844, and there were two biographies, by O. A. Sherrard in 1933 and Sir W. M. James in 1950. *Nelson's Dear Lord* by Evelyn Berckman, published in 1962, is the most modern study.

A Selection from the Public and Private Correspondence of Vice-Admiral *Lord Collingwood* was edited by G. L. Newnham Collingwood in 1829, and *The Private Correspondence of Admiral Lord Collingwood* by Edward Hughes for the Navy Records Society in 1957. Two biographies, by G. Murray and D. F. Stephenson, were published in 1936 and 1948, and in 1965 Oliver Warner produced *The Life and Letters of Vice-Admiral Lord Collingwood. Nelson's Hardy* by A. M. Broadley and R. G. Barlot was published in 1909, and Nelson's distinguished fellow captain is the subject of Philip Ziegler's sympathetic and attractive *King William IV*, published in 1971. *The Keith Papers* were edited by Christopher Lloyd in 1950, and the *Life and Letters of Admiral Cornwallis* by F. M. Cornwallis-West in 1927. *The Letters and Papers of Charles, Lord Barham* were edited by J. K. Laughton in 1911 for the Navy Records Society.

Nelson's political masters may be studied in *Pitt and the Great War*, by J. Holland Rose, published in 1911; the same author produced his *Life of Napoleon I* in 1934, although to see Bonaparte as Nelson's land rival, General Marshal-Cornwall's *Napoleon as Military Commander*, published in 1967, cannot be bettered for its clarity and scholarship.

Pitt's wartime speeches have been introduced and edited by R. Coupland, the third edition being published in 1940. The Hon. G. Pellew is the author of *The Life and Correspondence of the Rt. Hon. Henry Addington, 1st Viscount Sidmouth. The Private Papers of the 2nd Earl Spencer* have been edited for the Navy Records Society by Rear-Admiral R. W. Richmond, and the *Diaries and Correspondence of the Rt. Hon. George Rose* were edited by L. V. Harcourt in 1860. Nelson's friend may be studied in the *Life and Letters of Sir Gilbert Elliot, 1st Earl of Minto*, edited by the Countess of Minto in 1874, and a less friendly observer in *The Diary of Sir John Moore*, edited by F. Maurice in 1904. The general is also the subject of an excellent biography by Carola Oman.

Sir Arthur Bryant's *The Years of Endurance*, 1943, and *The Years of Victory*, 1944, should be read by anyone who wishes to absorb the atmosphere of Britain's struggle with France. My former tutor, Steven Watson, has written the standard history of *The Reign of George III*, published in 1960. The atmosphere of Britain under the threat of invasion is captured by Carola Oman in her *Britain against Napoleon*, published in 1942.

Sir J. S. Corbett in 1911 dealt with *Some Principles of Maritime Strategy* and Mahan's *Influence of Sea Power upon the French Revolution and Empire*, published in 1892, is a valuable supplement to his biography of Nelson published five years later. Corbett again dealt with *Fighting Instructions 1530–1816* in 1905, and *Signals and Instructions* in 1908, but John Cresswell's *Naval Warfare*, 1942, and his *British Admirals in the 18th Century: Tactics in Battle*, 1972, and *A History of Naval Tactics* by S. and M. Robinson, published in 1942, should be read as giving a more balanced and practical view of the vexed question of the latitude allowed captains in battle.

For the actual sea battles R. A. Sturges Jackson's *Logs of the Great Sea Fights*, published for the Navy Records Society, is invaluable, though comparison is necessary with individual ships' logs in the custody of the Public Records Office. Oliver Warner has covered the Nile, Copenhagen and Trafalgar in his *Nelson's Battles*, published in one volume in 1965. Christopher Lloyd in 1963 dealt with St Vincent and Camperdown in one volume. Dudley Pope's *England Expects*, 1960, is a re-examinatino of Trafalgar, as is David Howarth's superbly readable *Trafalgar, the Nelson Touch*, published in 1969. Perhaps the fullest treatment of one individual battle, and the commanders involved, is Dudley Pope's *The Great Gamble, Nelson at Copenhagen*, published in 1972. It is also the first work on the subject to consider fully the Danish point of view and make use of the Danish documents and authorities. *The War in the Mediterranean 1803–1810* is covered by Piers Mackesy's work, with that title, published in 1957, which skilfully blends economic and political factors as well as military. *The Campaign of Trafalgar*, by J. S. Corbett, was published in 1910. *The Trafalgar Campaign* by C. Eastwicks, published in 1933, is a translation of a work first published in 1907, E. Desbrières's *La Campagne Maritime de 1805* which of course gives the enemy point of view, as does Jurien de la Gravières's *Guerres Maritime de la France sous la République et l'Empire* published in 1883, and the eighth volume of C. F. Duro's *Armada Espanola*, published in 1902. Edward Fraser's *The Enemy at Trafalgar* examines the vanquished in that one battle.

The naval mutinies are covered by three works, *The Naval Mutinies of 1797* by Conrad Gill, published in 1913, *The Floating Republic* by G. Manwaring and B. Dobreé, published in 1935, and, most recently, in 1966, *The Great Mutiny* by James Dugan.

Finally, on the Navy of the time more generally, Volume II of the *Naval History of England* by C. J. Marcus, published in 1971, cannot be bettered. *The British Seaman* by Christopher Lloyd, published in 1968, gives a more precise view of the lower deck than John Masefield's well-known *Sea Life in Nelson's Time*, but like Peter Kemp's *The British Sailor*, published in 1970, covers a much wider period than the age of Nelson. For the reader anxious to learn more about that unique social organism there can be only two recommendations, Michael Lewis's *England's Sea Officers*, published in 1939, and his *A Social History of the Navy, 1793–1815*, published in 1960.

On the technical side of Nelson's craft there are a number of modern works of varying quality. The history of H.M.S. *Victory* is well covered in two full-length works, and a number of pamphlets and illustrated articles. Naval gunnery is perhaps the most easily understood of the tasks of the eighteenth-century sailor, and there is no better guide to the subject than Dudley Pope. Admiral William Smyth's *A Sailor's Word Book*, published in 1878, is useful for technical terms, as is *Falconer's Marine Dictionary*, though perhaps the best appreciation of the sea officer's skills can be gained by a glance through what must have been for many of Nelson's contemporaries their Bible, the anonymous, two-volume *The Elements and Practice of Rigging, Seamanship and Naval Tactics*, first published in 1800. In his preface to the second edition, published in 1807, the editor criticises previous works on the subject as being 'too abstruse for general use'. The modern reader can at least make use of an excellent *Explanation of the Terms used in Seamanship* and realise something of the complications of no longer practised arts.

Index

All names in italics are those of ships